OXFORD MONOGRAPHS IN
INTERNATIONAL LAW

General Editor: Professor Ian Brownlie QC, DCL, FBA
*Chichele Professor of Public International Law in the University of
Oxford and Fellow of All Souls College, Oxford.*

THE HUMAN RIGHTS COMMITTEE:
ITS ROLE IN THE DEVELOPMENT
OF THE INTERNATIONAL COVENANT
ON CIVIL AND POLITICAL RIGHTS

OXFORD MONOGRAPHS IN
INTERNATIONAL LAW

The aim of this series of monographs is to publish important
and original pieces of research on all aspects of public international law. Topics which are given particular prominence
are those which, while of interest to the academic lawyer,
also have important bearing on issues which touch the actual
conduct of international relations. None the less the series is
wide in scope and includes monographs on the history and
philosophical foundations of international law.

ALSO IN THIS SERIES

The Juridical Bay
GAYL WESTERMAN

The Exclusive Economic Zone in International Law
DAVID ATTARD

Judicial Remedies in International Law
CHRISTINE GRAY

Occupation, Resistance and Law
ADAM ROBERTS

The Legality of Non-Forcible Counter-Measures in
International Law
OMER ELAGAB

State Responsibility and the Marine Environment
BRIAN D. SMITH

The Shatt-al-Arab Boundary Question: A Legal
Reappraisal
KAIYAN HOMI KAIKOBAD

Relevant Circumstances and Maritime Delimitation
MALCOLM D. EVANS

Land-Locked and Geographically Disadvantaged
States in the International Law of the Sea
S. C. VASCIANNIE

Surrender, Occupation, and Private
Property in International Law
NISUKE ANDO

THE HUMAN RIGHTS COMMITTEE

Its Role in the Development of the International Covenant on Civil and Political Rights

DOMINIC McGOLDRICK

CLARENDON PRESS · OXFORD

*This book has been printed digitally and produced in a standard design
in order to ensure its continuing availability*

OXFORD
UNIVERSITY PRESS

Great Clarendon Street, Oxford OX2 6DP

Oxford University Press is a department of the University of Oxford.
It furthers the University's objective of excellence in research, scholarship,
and education by publishing worldwide in

Oxford New York

Athens Auckland Bangkok Bogotá Buenos Aires Cape Town
Chennai Dar es Salaam Delhi Florence Hong Kong Istanbul Karachi
Kolkata Kuala Lumpur Madrid Melbourne Mexico City Mumbai Nairobi
Paris São Paulo Shanghai Singapore Taipei Tokyo Toronto Warsaw

with associated companies in Berlin Ibadan

Oxford is a registered trade mark of Oxford University Press
in the UK and in certain other countries

Published in the United States
by Oxford University Press Inc., New York

!SBN 0-19-825894-1

Editor's Preface

By 1 May 1990 fifty States of the ninety-one States which had ratified or acceded to the International Covenant on Civil and Political Rights had also accepted the competence of the Human Rights Committee in respect of individual communications to the Committee. The machinery of the Committee has its limitations, and a substantial part of these derive from its modest funding. Nevertheless, in an institutional setting, it is the universalist counterpart to regional organs such as the European Commission and European Court of Human Rights, and the Inter-American organs. Thus the Committee forms a significant part of the system of accountability in human rights matters, that is to say, the zone in which objective assessment overrides assertion and propaganda.

The literature of human rights is extensive indeed but there is room for a substantial and reasonably definitive study of the Human Rights Committee and its work. Dr. McGoldrick has produced such a study and has taken considerable care to place his subject within the general context of the development of human rights since 1945.

All Souls College,
Oxford
25th October 1990

IAN BROWNLIE

Acknowledgements

This book is a revised and updated version of a doctoral thesis submitted to the University of Nottingham in October 1988. I acknowledge an enormous debt of gratitude to Professor David Harris for his expert supervision, and to Professor Stephen Bailey for his advice and encouragement. I would also like to thank the two United Kingdom experts who have served on the Human Rights Committee with such distinction, Sir Vincent-Evans and Professor Rosalyn Higgins, for their assistance and advice.

I would like to thank the Secretariat in the Human Rights Centre in Geneva, in particular Markus Schmidt and Helga Klein, and the library staff of the University of Nottingham, Nottingham Polytechnic, and the University of Liverpool. I am most grateful to Richard Hart and Jane Williams of the Oxford University Press for their unfailing assistance.

It would not have been possible to finish this book without the continued encouragement of the McGoldrick and Owen families, and many friends. In particular I acknowledge the support of my wife, April, and the assistance of my brother, John.

This book is dedicated to my mother and father. *Carpe Diem*.

D.M.

Faculty of Law,
Liverpool University,
August, 1990

Contents

Table of Cases

Where a case appears in the main text of the work, the paragraph number is given. Where a case appears in the notes at the end of each chapter, the paragraph number is given with the relevant note number in brackets. For example:

4.68 (n. 476) means that the case can be found in the notes of paragraph 4.68 at note 476.

4.69 means that the case can be found in the main text of paragraph 4.69.

Table of Agreements, Charters, Committees, Conventions, Declarations, Resolutions, Treaties

Where an item appears in the main text of the work, the paragraph number is given. Where an item appears in the notes at the end of each chapter, the paragraph number is given with the relevant note number in brackets. For example:

4.68 (n. 476) means that the item can be found in the notes of paragraph 4.68 at note 476.

4.69 means that the item can be found in the main text of paragraph 4.69.

Table of Statutes

Where a Statute appears in the main text of the work, the paragraph number is given. Where a Statute appears in the notes at the end of each chapter, the paragraph number is given with the relevant note number in brackets. For example:

4.68 (n. 476) means that the Statute can be found in the notes of paragraph 4.68 at note 476.

4.69 means that the Statute can be found in the main text of paragraph 4.69.

Abbreviations

AI	Amnesty International
AJIL	American Journal of International Law
AFDI	Annuaire français de droit international
AFR	African Charter of Human and People's Rights
ADRD	American Declaration of the Rights and Duties of Man
Akron LR	Akron Law Review
Am. J. Comp. L.	American Journal of Comparative Law
AMR	American Convention on Human Rights
Am. ULR	American University Law Review
ASIL Proc.	Proceedings of the American Society of International Law
Australian YIL	Australian Yearbook of International Law
Bossuyt, *Guide*	Bossuyt, *Guide to the Travaux Préparatoires of the International Covenant on Civil and Political Rights*
Boston Coll. ICLR	Boston College International and Comparative Law Review
Bracton LJ	Bracton Law Journal
Brit. JIS	British Journal of International Studies
Brownlie	Principles of Public International Law (4th edn.)
Buff. LR	Buffalo Law Review
Bull. GDR Committee	Bulletin of the German Democratic Republic Committee for Human Rights
BYIL	British Yearbook of International Law
Cal. West ILJ	California Western International Law Journal
Can. Bar. Rev.	Canadian Bar Review
Can. YIL	Canadian Yearbook of International Law
CD	Collection of Decisions of the European Commission on Human Rights
CEDAW	Committee on the Elimination of Discrimination against Women
CERD	Committee on the Elimination of Racial Discrimination
CHRYB	Canadian Human Rights Yearbook
CLR	Criminal Law Review
CLP	Current Legal Problems
Cmd.	UK Command Papers
Col. HRLR	Colombia Human Rights Law Review
Col. J. Trans. L.	Colombia Journal of Transnational Law
Col. LR	Colombia Law Review
Comm. LB	Commonwealth Law Bulletin
Corn. ILJ	Cornell International Law Journal

D. &. R.	Decisions and Reports of the European Commission of Human Rights
Denver JILP	Denver Journal of International Law and Politics
Doc.	Document
ECHR	European Convention on Human Rights
ECOSOC	Economic and Social Council
ESC	European Social Charter
ETS	European Treaty Series
EUCM	European Commission of Human Rights
EUCT	European Court of Human Rights
Fawcett	*The Application of the European Convention on Human Rights* (2nd edn.)
GA	General Assembly
GAOR	General Assembly Official Records
GC	General Comments of the Human Rights Committee
GYIL	German Yearbook of International Law
Handbook	Handbook of existing rules pertaining to human rights in the interamerican system (1983)
Harv. ILJ	Harvard International Law Journal
Harv. HRY	Harvard Human Rights Yearbook
Hofstra LR	Hofstra Law Review
Hous. JIL	Houston Journal of International Law
HRC	Human Rights Committee
HRCion	Human Rights Commission
HRLJ	Human Rights Law Journal
HRQ	Human Rights Quarterly
HR Rev.	Human Rights Review
IACM	Inter-American Commission on Human Rights
IACT	Inter-American Court of Human Rights
ICCPR/CCPR	International Covenant on Civil and Political Rights
ICERD	International Convention on the Elimination of all Forms of Racial Discrimination
ICESCR	International Covenant on Economic, Social, and Cultural Rights
ICJ	International Court of Justice
ICLQ	International and Comparative Law Quarterly
ILA Report	International Law Association Report
ILM	International Legal Materials
ILO	International Labour Organization
ILR	International Law Reports
Iowa LR	Iowa Law Review
Ind. JIL	Indian Journal of International Law
Ind. YWA	Indian Yearbook of World Affairs
Int. Affairs	International Affairs
Int. Conc.	International Conciliation
Int. Org.	International Organization

Int. Prob.	International Problems
Int. SQ	International Studies Quarterly
Isr. HRY	Israeli Human Rights Yearbook
Jap. Annual IL	Japanese Annual International Law
J. Int. L. & Econ.	Journal of International Law and Economics
LQR	Law Quarterly Review
Merrills	*The Development of International Law by the European Court of Human Rights*
Minn. LR	Minnesota Law Review
MLR	Modern Law Review
NGO	Non-governmental Organization
NIEO	New International Economic Order
NILR	Netherlands International Law Review
NWICO	New World Information and Communication Order
NYLSLR	New York Law School Law Review
NYUJILP	New York University Journal of International Law and Politics
OP	Optional Protocol to the International Covenant on Civil and Political Rights
OP2	Second Optional Protocol to the International Covenant on Civil and Political Rights
PL	Public Law
PSQ	Political Science Quarterly
RDH/HRJ	Revue des droits de l'homme/Human Rights Journal
Rec. des cours	Recueil des cours de l'Académie de droit International
Rev. ICJ	Review of the International Commission of Jurists
Rev. Int. Stud.	Review of International Studies
RIAA	United Nations Reports of International Arbitral Awards
RIDP	Revue de l'Institut de Droit Pénal
Santa Clara LR	Santa Clara Law Review
SD	Human Rights Committee: Selected Decisions Under the Optional Protocol (Vol. I)
SD2	Human Rights Committee: Selected Decisions Under the Optional Protocol (Vol. II)
South African YIL	South African Yearbook of International Law
SR	Summary Record
Temple LQ	Temple Law Quarterly
Tex. ILJ	Texas International Law Journal
UDHR	Universal Declaration of Human Rights
UKTS	UK Treaty Series
UNESCO	United Nations Educational, Scientific, and Cultural Organization
UNCAT	United Nations Committee Against Torture
UNCIO	United Nations Conference on International Organization
Univ. Ill. LF	University of Illinois Law Forum
Univ. NSWLJ	University of New South Wales Law Review

Univ. Tor. LJ	University of Toronto Law Journal
UNTS	United Nations Treaty Series
U. Pa. LR	University of Pennsylvania Law Review
Va. JIL	Virginia Journal of International Law
Van Dijk and Van Hoof	Van Dijk and Van Hoof, *Theory and Practice of the European Convention on Human Rights* (2nd edn.)
Vand. J. Trans. L.	Vanderbilt Journal of Transnational Law
VCLT	Vienna Convention on the Law of Treaties 1969
Vill. LR	Villanova Law Review
Wayne LR	Wayne Law Review
WG	Working Group of the Human Rights Committee
WHO	World Health Organization
Will. & Mary LR	William and Mary Law Review
Wisc. LR	Wisconsin Law Review
Yale JWPO	Yale Journal of World Public Order
YBWA	Yearbook of World Affairs
YEL	Yearbook of European Law
ZaoRV	Zeitschrift Für auslandisches öffentliches Recht und Volkerrecht

Annual Reports of the
Human Rights Committee

States Parties to the International Covenant on Civil and Political Rights

122 States Parties (as of 1 September 1993)

Afghanistan, Albania, Algeria, Angola, Argentina, Armenia, Australia, Austria, Azerbaijan, Barbados, Belarus, Belgium, Benin, Bolivia, Bulgaria, Brazil, Burundi, Cambodia, Cameroon, Canada, Central African Republic, Chile, Colombia, Congo, Costa Rica, Cote d'Ivoire, Croatia, Cyprus, Czech Republic, Democratic People's Republic of Korea, Democratic Yemen, Denmark, Dominica, Dominican Republic, Ecuador, Egypt, El Salvador, Equatorial Guinea, Estonia, Ethiopia, Federal Republic of Germany, Finland, France, Gabon, Gambia, Grenada, Guatemala, Guinea, Guyana, Haiti, Hungary, Iceland, India, Iran, Ireland, Israel, Italy, Jamaica, Japan, Jordan, Kenya, Latvia, Lebanon, Lesotho, Libyan Arab Jamahiraya, Lithuania, Luxembourg, Madagascar, Mali, Malta, Mauritius, Mexico, Moldova, Mongolia, Morocco, Mozambique, Nepal, Netherlands, New Zealand, Nicaragua, Niger, Nigeria, Norway, Panama, Paraguay, Peru, Philippines, Poland, Portugal, Republic of Korea, Romania, Russian Federation, Rwanda, Saint Vincent and the Grenadines, San Marino, Senegal, Seychelles, Slovak Republic, Slovenia, Somalia, Spain, Sri Lanka, Sudan, Suriname, Sweden, Syrian Arab Republic, Togo, Trinidad and Tobago, Tunisia, Ukraine, United Kingdom, United Republic of Tanzania, United States of America, Uruguay, Venezuela, Vietnam, Yugoslavia, Zaïre, Zambia, Zimbabwe.

Entry into force: 23 March 1976.

Introduction to Paperback Edition

The publication of the paperback edition of this work affords the opportunity to highlight the principal developments concerning the Committee since 1990.[1]

CHAPTER 1

There has been a healthy growth towards universality in the number of States parties to the Covenant and its First Optional Protocol. As of 1 September 1993 there were 122 States parties to the Covenant. The most notable addition is the United States.[2] A number of ex-Soviet and ex-Yugoslavian republics have also become parties.[3] The number of States parties to the First Optional Protocol has increased to seventy-four. The most notable addition here is the Russian Federation.[4] German ratification of the Optional Protocol was accompanied by a controversial reservation relating to article 26. The English translation of the reservation is as follows: 'The Federal Republic of Germany formulates a reservation concerning article 5 paragraph 2 (a) to the effect that the competence of the Committee shall not apply to communication ... (c) by means of which a violation of the Covenant on Civil and Political Rights is reprimanded, if and insofar as the reprimanded violation refers to rights other than those guaranteed under the aforementioned Covenant.' The wording of the reservation is ambiguous. The Human Rights Committee never makes a finding of violation of a right other than those guaranteed under the Covenant.[5] The reservation seems to be directed at precluding a finding of violation of article 26 in relation to substantive rights which are not covered by the Covenant, for example social security rights. If this is correct it is the first reservation to the First Optional Protocol which purports to limit the ability of the Committee to find violations of a substantive Covenant right. While the number of reservations that have been made to the First Optional Protocol is strong evidence of their acceptability in principle, I have grave doubts about the validity of the German reservation. It could gravely damage the integrity of the Human Rights Committee's jurisprudence under the Covenant. That should be viewed as being contrary to the object and purpose of the First Optional Protocol.

The United Kingdom continues to remain aloof from the First Optional Protocol. Its position is becoming increasingly isolated and indefensible. The number of States parties to the Second Optional Protocol has risen to nineteen.

The use of the Covenant in domestic law systems steadily increases both numerically and in influence.[6] Particularly notable are developments in Japan,[7] Australia,[8] and, to a more limited extent, the United Kingdom.[9] Non-governmental[10] and academic interest in the Committee and the Covenant continues to grow apace.[11] Important additions to the literature are the English edition of Manfred Nowak's *Commentary on the U.N. Covenant on Civil and Political Rights*, published in 1993,[12] and the excellent volume *The United Nations and Human Rights—A Critical Appraisal*, edited by Phillip Alston.[13]

CHAPTER 2

There has been little change in the membership of the Human Rights Committee.[14] At the end of 1990 Mr Mommersteg and Mr Cooray departed. They were replaced by Mr Herndl and Mr Sadi. At the end of 1992 Mr Mullerson, Mr Serrano Caldero, and Mr Wako departed to be replaced by Mrs Evatt (Australia),[15] Mr Francis (Jamaica) and Mr Bruni Celli (Venezuela). In 1993 Mr Ando was elected Chairman for a period of two years. During the Committee's forty-ninth session (autumn 1993), Mr Fodor (Hungary) passed away.

Secretariat resources remain inadequate. The Committee's view is that a 'substantial increase' is required.[16]

CHAPTER 3

The Committee has continued to develop and consolidate its practices and procedures under the reporting system.[17] Delayed submission of reports remains a major problem.[18] The essential structure for the consideration of initial and periodic reports has remained the same. Efforts continue to refine the procedures and improve their efficiency. The Committee has adopted revised guidelines for the preparation of States party reports.[19] The text of the revised guidelines is as follows:

A. CONSOLIDATED GUIDELINES FOR THE INITIAL PART OF REPORTS OF STATES PARTIES

Land and People

1. This section should contain information about the main ethnic and demographic characteristics of the country and its population, as well as such socio-economic and cultural indicators as per capita income, gross national product, rate of inflation, external debt, rate of unemployment, literacy rate and religion. It should also include information on the population by mother tongue, life expectancy, infant mortality, maternal mortality, fertility rate, percentage of population under 15 and over 65 years

of age, percentage of population in rural areas and in urban areas and percentage of households headed by women. As far as possible, States should make efforts to provide all data disaggregated by sex.

General Political Structure

2. This section should describe briefly the political history and framework, the type of government and the organization of the executive, legislative and judicial organs.

General Legal Framework within which Human Rights are Protected

3. This section should contain information on:

(*a*) Which judicial, administrative or other competent authorities have jurisdiction affecting human rights;

(*b*) What remedies are available to an individual who claims that any of his rights have been violated and what systems of compensation and rehabilitation exist for victims;

(*c*) Whether any of the rights referred to in the various human rights instruments are protected either in the constitution or by a separate bill or rights and, if so, what provisions are made in the constitution of bill or rights for derogations and in what circumstances;

(*d*) How human rights instruments are made part of the national legal system;

(*e*) Whether the provisions of the various human rights instruments can be invoked before, or directly enforced by, the courts, other tribunals or administrative authorities or whether they must be transformed into internal laws or administrative regulations in order to be enforced by the authorities concerned;

(*f*) Whether there exist any institutions or national machinery with responsibility for overseeing the implementation of human rights.

Information and Publicity

4. This section should indicate whether any special efforts have been made to promote awareness among the public and the relevant authorities of the rights contained in the various human rights instruments. The topics to be addressed should include the manner and extent to which the texts of the various human rights instruments have been disseminated, whether such texts have been translated into the local language or languages, what government agencies have responsibility for preparing reports and whether they normally receive information or other inputs from external sources, and whether the contents of the reports are the subject of public debate.

B. GUIDELINES REGARDING THE FORM AND CONTENTS OF INITIAL REPORTS FROM STATES PARTIES

1. Under article 40 of the International Covenant on Civil and Political Rights, each State party has undertaken to submit, within one year of the entry into force of the Covenant in regard to it and thereafter whenever the Human Rights Committee established under the Covenant so requests, reports on the meaures which it has adopted to

give effect to rights recognized in the Covenant and on the progress made in the enjoyment of those rights. Article 40 also provides that the reports shall indicate the factors and difficulties, if any, affecting the implementation of the Covenant.

2. In order to assist it in fulfilling the tasks entrusted to it pursuant to article 40 of the Covenant, the Committee has decided that it would be useful to inform States parties of its wishes regarding the form and contents of reports. Compliance with the following guidelines will help to ensure that reports are presented in a uniform manner and enable the Committee and States parties to obtain a complete picture of the situation in each State as regards the implementation of the rights referred to in the Covenant. This will also reduce the need for the Committee to request additional information under its rules of procedure.

3. *The general part of the report* should be prepared in accordance with the consolidated guidelines for the initial part of the reports of States parties to be submitted under the various international human rights instruments, including the covenant, as contained in document HRI/1991/1.

4. *The part of the report relating specifically to parts I, II and III of the Covenant* should describe in relation to the provisions of each article:

    (*a*) The legislative, administrative or other measures in force in regard to each right;

    (*b*) Any restrictions or limitations, even of a temporary nature, imposed by law or practice or any other manner on the enjoyment of the right;

    (*c*) Any other factors or difficulties affecting the enjoyment of the right by persons within the jurisdiction of the State;

    (*d*) Any other information on the progress made in the enjoyment of the right.

5. When a State party to the Covenant is also a party to the Optional Protocol, and if in the period under review the Committee has issued views finding that the State party has violated provisions of the Covenant, the report should include a section explaining what action has been taken relating to the communication concerned. In particular, the State party should indicate what remedy it has afforded the author of the communication whose rights the Committee found to have been violated.

6. The report should be accompanied by copies of the principal legislative and other texts referred to in the report. These will be made available to members of the Committee. It should be noted, however, that, for reasons of expense, they will not normally be reproduced for general distribution with the report except to the extent that the reporting State specifically so requests. It is desirable therefore that when a text is not actually quoted in or annexed to the report itself, the report should contain sufficient information to be understood without reference to it.

7. The Committee will welcome at any time information on any significant new development in regard to the rights referred to in the Covenant, but in any event it intends, after the completion of its study of each State's initial report and of any additional information submitted, to call for subsequent reports under article 40(1)(b) of the Covenant. The aim of such further reports will be to bring the situation up to date in respect of each State.

8. On the basis of reports prepared according to the above guidelines, the Committee is confident that it will be enabled to develop a constructive dialogue with each State

party in regard to the implementation of the Covenant and thereby contribute to mutual understanding and peaceful and friendly relations among nations in accordance with the Charter of the United Nations.

C. GUIDELINES REGARDING THE FORM AND CONTENTS OF PERIODIC REPORTS FROM STATES PARTIES

1. Under paragraph 1 of article 40 of the Covenant every State party has undertaken to submit reports to the Human Rights Committee on the implementation of the Covenant

(*a*) Within one year of the entry into force of the Covenant for the State party concerned,

(*b*) Thereafter whenever the Committee so requests.

2. At its second session, in August 1977, the Committee adopted general guidelines for the submission of reports by States parties under article 40. In drawing up these guidelines, the Committee had in mind in particular the initial reports to be submitted by States parties under paragraph 1(*a*) of article 40. These guidelines have been followed by the great majority of States parties that have submitted reports subsequent to their issuance, and they have proved helpful both to the reporting States and to the Committee.

3. In paragraph 5 of those guidelines, the Committee indicated that it intended, after the completion of its study of each State's initial report and of any subsequent information submitted, to call for subsequent reports under article 40, paragraph 1(b), of the Covenant.

4. At its eleventh session, in October 1980, the Committee adopted by consensus a statement concerning the subsequent stages of its future work under article 40. It confirmed its aim of engaging in a constructive dialogue with each reporting State and determined that the dialogue should be conducted on the basis of periodic reports from States parties to the Covenant (para. (d)). It also decided that in the light of its experience in the consideration of initial reports, it should develop guidelines for the purpose of subsequent reports. Pursuant to this decision and to the decision taken by the Committee at its thirteenth session to request States parties to submit reports under article 40, paragraph 1(b), on a periodic basis, the Committee has drawn up the following guidelines regarding the form and contents of such reports, which are designed to complete and to bring up to date the information required by the Committee under the Covenant.

5. *General information* should be prepared in accordance with the consolidated guidelines for the initial part of reports of States parties to be submitted under the various international human rights instruments including the Covenant (HRI/1991/1).

6. *Information relating to each of the articles in parts I, II and III of the Covenant* should concentrate especially on:

(*a*) The completion of the information before the Committee as to the measures adopted to give effect to rights recognized in the Covenant, taking account of questions raised in the Committee on the examination of any previous report and including in particular additional information as to questions not previously answered or not fully answered;

(*b*) Information taking into account general comments which the Committee may have made under article 40, paragraph 4, of the Covenant;

(*c*) Changes made or proposed in the laws and practices relevant to the Covenant;

(*d*) Action taken as a result of experience gained in co-operation with the Committee;

(*e*) Factors affecting and difficulties experienced in the implementation of the Covenant;

(*f*) The progress made since the last report in the enjoyment of rights recognized in the Covenant.

7. When a State party to the Covenant is also a party to the Optional Protocol and if, in the period under review, the Committee has issued views finding that the State party has violated provisions of the Covenant, the report should include a section explaining what action has been taken relating to the communication concerned. In particular, the State party should indicate what remedy it has afforded the author of the communication whose rights the Committee found to have been violated.

8. It should be noted that the reporting obligation extends not only to the relevant laws and other norms, but also to the practices of the courts and administrative organs of the State party and other relevant facts likely to show the degree of actual enjoyment of rights recognized by the Covenant.

9. The report should be accompanied by copies of the principal legislative and other texts referred to in it.

10. It is the desire of the Committee to assist States parties in promoting the enjoyment of rights under the Covenant. To this end, the Committee wishes to continue the dialogue which it has begun with reporting States in the most constructive manner possible and reiterates its confidence that it will thereby contribute to mutual understanding and peaceful and friendly relations among nations in accordance with the Charter of the United Nations.

In March 1992 the Committee decided that, at the end of the consideration of each State party's report, comments would be adopted reflecting the views of the Committee as a whole. The comments are additional to, and do not replace, the comments made by individual members. The comments are dispatched to the States parties concerned and are included in the Committee's reports to the General Assembly. The Comments of the Committee provide a general evaluation of a State party's report and of the dialogue with the delegation and make note of positive developments that may have occurred during the period under review, factors and difficulties affecting the implementation of the Covenant, and of specific issues of concern relating to the application of the provisions of the Covenant. They include suggestions and recommendations to the State party concerned. These short but *specific* reports on each State remedy what had been an important deficiency in the reporting procedures.[20]

At its forty-ninth session (autumn 1993) the Committee took a number of decisions related to its methods of work under the reporting procedure. Taking into account the experience gained in adopting comments at the end of the consideration of States parties' reports, it formalized this practice by revising Rule 70 of the Committee's Rules of Procedure. The Committee further decided that States parties would be requested, on a systematic basis, to report in their next periodic report on the measures they have adopted to follow up on the Committee's comments. The State party representatives are to be informed, at the conclusion of the consideration of the country's report, that the Committee's comments will be made available to them at the last meeting of the Committee's session and made public afterwards. The Committee formally affirmed the practice of having documents submitted by non-governmental organizations officially distributed to all members of the Committee in the language(s) received. The Committee also agreed that, where consideration of a State report submitted under Article 40 of the Covenant revealed a grave human rights situation, it would request the Secretary-General to inform the competent organs of the United Nations, such as the Security Council, as appropriate.

The Committee has made some specific requests for reports under article 40(1)(b).[21] In 1991 the Committee took a decision under article 40(1)(b) requesting Iraq to 'submit its third periodic report without delay for discussion by the Committee at its forty-second session in July 1991 and, in any event to submit by 15 June 1991 a report, in summary form if necessary, relating in particular to the application at the present time of Articles 6, 7, 9 and 27 of the Covenant'.[22] An article 40(1)(b) request was also made to Peru in 1992. Also of major importance was the decision of the Chairman of the Committee in September 1992, discussed in the Human Rights Committee in October 1992, concerning the situation in the former Yugoslavia.[23] The text of the decision was as follows:

The Human Rights Committee, through its Chairman acting on behalf of and in consultation with the members of the Committee,

— *Deeply concerned* by recent and current events in the territory of the former Yugoslavia that have affected human rights protected under the International Covenant on Civil and Political Rights;
— *Noting* that all the peoples within the territory of the former Yugoslavia are entitled to the guarantees of the Covenant;
— *Acting* under Article 40, paragraph 1(b) of the Covenant;

1. *Requests* the Government of the [Republic of Croatia] [Federal Republic of Yugoslavia (Serbia and Montenegro)] [Republic of Bosnia-Herzegovina] to submit a short report, as soon as possible and not later than 30 October 1992, on the following issues in respect of persons and events now coming under its jurisdiction:

(*a*) Measures taken to prevent and combat the policy of 'ethnic cleansing' pursued, according to several reports, on the territory of certain parts of the former Yugoslavia, in relation to Articles 6 and 12 of the International Covenant on Civil and Political Rights;

(*b*) Measures taken to prevent arbitrary arrests and killings of persons, as well as disappearances, in relation to Articles 6 and 9 of the International Covenant on Civil and Political Rights;

(*c*) Measures taken to prevent arbitrary executions, torture and other inhuman treatment in detention camps, in relation to Articles 6, 7, and 10 of the International Covenant on Civil and Political Rights;

(*d*) Measures taken to combat advocacy of national, racial or religious hatred constituting incitement to discrimination, hostility or violence, in relation to Article 20 of the International Covenant on Civil and Political rights.

2. *Invites* the Government of the [Republic of Croatia] [Federal Republic of Yugoslavia (Serbia and Montenegro)] [Republic of Bosnia-Herzegovina] to appear, through their representatives, before the Human Rights Committee during the third week of its forthcoming session (2–4 November 1992);

3. *Requests* the Secretary-General to bring this decision to the attention of the Government of the [Republic of Croatia] [Federal Republic of Yugoslavia (Serbia and Montenegro)] [Republic of Bosnia-Herzegovina].

Reports from Croatia, Yugoslavia (Serbia and Montenegro), and the Republic of Bosnia-Herzegovina were submitted and were considered by the Committee in November 1992.[24] The Committee adopted Comments in relation to each State.[25] The decision of the Committee set an important precedent in terms of the succession of obligations under International Human Rights Treaties.[26] After the decision on Yugoslavia the Committee adopted an amendment to its rules of procedure to cover the submission of special reports.[27]

At its forty-ninth session (autumn 1993) the Committee restated that all the peoples within the territory of a former State party to the Covenant remain entitled to the guarantees of the Covenant. On that basis it considered that Armenia, Georgia, Kazakhstan, Kyrgyzstan, Macedonia, Tajikistan, Turkmenistan and Uzbekistan were bound by the obligations flowing from the Covenant as from the date of their independence. Reports under Article 40 therefore became due one year after that date. The Committee requested that such reports be submitted.

The Committee has adopted three further general comments.[28] General Comment 20 on article 7 *replaces* General Comment 7, reflecting and further developing it.[29] General Comment 21 on article 10 *replaces* General Comment 9, reflecting and further developing it.[30] General Comment 23 on article 18 (Freedom of Religion) was adopted in July 1993.[31] There has still been no General Comment on article 27 of the Covenant.[32] A draft General Comment on Article 27 was discussed at the Committee's forty-ninth session (autumn 1993). As well as explaining the content of Article 27, the General

Comment is likely to explain its relationship to other rights in the Covenant, and in particular to self-determination (Article 1), equality and non-discrimination (Article 2, 26).

The texts of the three General Comments adopted are as follows:

GENERAL COMMENT 20

Article 7 (Forty-fourth Session, 1992)

1. This general comment replaces general comment 7 (the sixteenth session, 1982) reflecting and further developing it.

2. The aim of the provisions of article 7 of the International Covenant on Civil and Political Rights is to protect both the dignity and the physical and mental integrity of the individual. It is the duty of the State party to afford everyone protection through legislative and other measures as may be necessary against the acts prohibited by article 7, whether inflicted by people acting in their official capacity, outside their official capacity or in a private capacity. The prohibition in article 7 is complemented by the positive requirements of article 10, paragraph 1, of the Covenant, which stipulates that 'All persons deprived of their liberty shall be treated with humanity and with respect for the inherent dignity of the human person'.

3. The text of article 7 allows of no limitation. The Committee also reaffirms that, even in situations of public emergency such as those referred to in article 4 of the Covenant, no derogation from the provision of article 7 is allowed and its provisions must remain in force. The Committee likewise observes that no justification or extenuating circumstances may be invoked to excuse a violation of article 7 for any reasons, including those based on an order from a superior officer or public authority.

4. The Covenant does not contain any definition of the concepts covered by article 7, nor does the Committee consider it necessary to draw up a list of prohibited acts or to establish sharp distinctions between the different kinds of punishment or treament; the distinctions depend on the nature, purpose and severity of the treatment applied.

5. The prohibition in article 7 relates not only to acts that cause physical pain but also to acts that cause mental suffering to the victim. In the Committee's view, moreover, the prohibition must extend to corporal punishment, including excessive chastisement ordered as punishment for a crime or as an educative or disciplinary measure. It is appropriate to emphasize in this regard that article 7 protects, in particular, children, pupils and patients in teaching and medical institutions.

6. The Committee notes that prolonged solitary confinement of the detained or imprisoned person may amount to acts prohibited by article 7. As the Committee has stated in its general comment No. 6(16), article 6 of the Covenant refers generally to abolition of the death penalty in terms that strongly suggest that abolition is desirable. Moreover, when the death penalty is applied by a State party for the most serious crimes, it must not only be strictly limited in accordance with article 6 but it must be carried out in such a way as to cause the least possible physical and mental suffering.

7. Article 7 expressly prohibits medical or scientific experimentation without the free consent of the person concerned. The Committee notes that the reports of States

parties generally contain little information on this point. More attention should be given to the need and means to ensure observance of this provision. The Committee also observes that special protection in regard to such experiments is necessary in the case of persons not capable of giving valid consent, and in particular those under any form of detention or imprisonment. Such persons should not be subjected to any medical or scientific experimentation that may be detrimental to their health.

8. The Committee notes that it is not sufficient for the implementation of article 7 to prohibit such treatment or punishment or to make it a crime, States parties should inform the Committee of the legislative, administrative, judicial and other measures they take to prevent and punish acts of torture and cruel, inhuman and degrading treatment in any territory under their jurisdiction.

9. In the view of the Committee, States parties must not expose individuals to the danger of torture or cruel, inhuman or degrading treatment or punishment upon return to another country by way of their extradition, expulsion or refoulement. States parties should indicate in their reports what measures they have adopted to that end.

10. The Committee should be informed how States parties disseminate, to the population at large, relevant information concerning the ban on torture and the treatment prohibited by article 7. Enforcement personnel, medical personnel, police officers and any other persons involved in the custody or treatment of any individual subjected to any form of arrest, detention or imprisonment must receive appropriate instruction and training. States parties should inform the Committee of the instruction and training given and the way in which the prohibition of article 7 forms an integral part of the operational rules and ethical standards to be followed by such persons.

11. In addition to describing steps to provide the general protection against acts prohibited under article 7 to which anyone is entitled, the State party should provide detailed information on safeguards for the special protection of particularly vulnerable persons. It should be noted that keeping under systematic review interrogation rules, instructions, methods and practices as well as arrangements for the custody and treatment of persons subjected to any form of arrest, detention or imprisonment is an effective means of preventing cases of torture and ill-treatment. To guarantee the effective protection of detained persons, provisions should be made for detainees to be held in places officially recognized as places of detention and for their names and places of detention, as well as for the names of persons responsible for their detention, to be kept in registers readily available and accessible to those concerned, including relatives and friends. To the same effect, the time and place of all interrogations should be recorded, together with the names of all those present and this information should also be available for purposes of judicial or administrative proceedings. Provisions should also be made against incommunicado detention. In that connection, States parties should ensure that any places of detention be free from any equipment liable to be used for inflicting torture or ill-treatment. The protection of the detainee also requires that prompt and regular access be given to doctors and lawyers and, under appropriate supervision when the investigation so requires, to family members.

12. It is important for the discouragement of violations under article 7 that the law must prohibit the use of admissibility in judicial proceedings of statements or confessions obtained through torture or other prohibited treatment.

13. States parties should indicate when presenting their reports the provisions of their criminal law which penalize torture and cruel, inhuman and degrading treatment or punishment, specifying the penalties applicable to such acts, whether committed by public officials or other persons acting on behalf of the State, or by private persons. Those who violate article 7, whether by encouraging, ordering, tolerating or perpetrating prohibited acts, must be held responsible. Consequently, those who have refused to obey orders must not be punished or subjected to any adverse treatment.

14. Article 7 should be read in conjunction with article 2, paragraph 3, of the Covenant. In their reports, States parties should indicate how their legal system effectively guarantees the immediate termination of all the acts prohibited by article 7 as well as appropriate redress. The right to lodge complaints against maltreatment prohibited by article 7 must be recognized in the domestic law. Complaints must be investigated promptly and impartially by competent authorities so as to make the remedy effective. The reports of States parties should provide specific information on the remedies available to victims of maltreatment and the procedure that complainants must follow, and statistics on the number of complaints and how they have been dealt with.

15. The Committee has noted that some States have granted amnesty in respect of acts of torture. Amnesties are generally incompatible with the duty of States to investigate such acts; to guarantee freedom from such acts within their jurisdiction; and to ensure that they do not occur in the future. States may not deprive individuals of the right to an effective remedy, including compensation and such full rehabilitation as may be possible.

GENERAL COMMENT 21

Article 10 (*Forty-fourth session, 1992*)

1. This general comment replaces general comment 9 (the sixteenth session, 1982) reflecting and further developing it.

2. Article 10, paragraph 1, of the International Covenant on Civil and Political Rights applies to any one deprived of liberty under the laws and authority of the State who is held in prisons, hospitals—particularly psychiatric hospitals—detention camps or correctional instututions or elsewhere. States parties should ensure that the principle stipulated therein is observed in all institutions and establishments within their jurisdiction where persons are being held.

3. Article 10, paragraph 1, imposes on States parties a positive obligation towards persons who are particularly vulnerable because of their status as persons deprived of liberty, and complements for them the ban on torture or other cruel, inhuman or degrading treatment or punishment contained in article 7 of the Covenant. Thus, not only may persons deprived of their liberty not be subjected to treatment that is contrary to article 7, including medical or scientific experimentation, but neither may they be subjected to any hardship or constraint other than that resulting from the deprivation of liberty; respect for the dignity of such persons must be guaranteed under the same conditions as for that of free persons. Persons deprived of their liberty

enjoy all the rights set forth in the Covenant, subject to the restrictions that are unavoidable in a closed environment.

4. Treating all persons deprived of their liberty with humanity and with respect for their dignity is a fundamental and universally applicable rule. Consequently, the application of this rule, as a minimum, cannot be dependent on the material resources available in the State party. This rule must be applied without distinction of any kind, such as race, colour, sex, language, religion, political or other opinion, national or social origin, property, birth or other status.

5. States parties are invited to indicate in their reports to what extent they are applying the relevant United Nations standards applicable to the treatment of prisoners: the Standard Minimum Rules for the Treatment of Prisoners (1957), the Body of Principles for the Protection of All Persons under Any Form of Detention or Imprisonment (1988), the Code of Conduct for Law Enforcement Officials (1978) and the Principles of Medical Ethics relevant to the Role of Health Personnel, particularly Physicians, in the Protection of Prisoners and Detainees against Torture and Other Cruel, Inhuman or Degrading Treatment or Punishment (1982).

6. The Committee recalls that reports should provide detailed information on national legislative and administrative provisions that have a bearing on the right provided for in article 10, paragraph 1. The Committee also considers that it is necessary for reports to specify what concrete measures have been taken by the competent authorities to monitor the effective application of the rules regarding the treatment of persons deprived of their liberty. States parties should include in their reports information concerning the system for supervising penitentiary establishments, the specific measures to prevent torture and cruel, inhuman or degrading treatment, and how impartial supervision is ensured.

7. Furthermore, the Committee recalls that reports should indicate whether the various applicable provisions form an integral part of the instruction and training of the personnel who have authority over persons deprived of their liberty and whether they are strictly adhered to by such personnel in the discharge of their duties. It would also be appropriate to specify whether arrested or detained persons have access to such information and have effective legal means enabling them to ensure that those rules are respected, to complain if the rules are ignored and to obtain adequate compensation in the event of a violation.

8. The Committee recalls that the principle set forth in article 10, paragraph 1, constitutes the basis for the more specific obligations of States parties in respect of criminal justice, which are set forth in article 10, paragraphs 2 and 3.

9. Article 10, paragraph 2(a), provides for the segregation, save in exceptional circumstances, of accused persons from convicted ones. Such segregation is required in order to emphasize their status as unconvincted persons who at the same time enjoy the right to be presumed innocent as stated in article 14, paragraph 2. The reports of States parties should indicate how the separation of accused persons from convicted persons is effected and explain how the treatment of accused persons differs from that of convicted persons.

10. As to article 10, paragraph 3, which concerns convicted persons, the Committee wishes to have detailed information on the operation of the penitentiary system of the State party. No penitentiary system should be only retributory; it should essentially seek the reformation and social rehabilitation of the prisoner. States parties are invited to specify whether they have a system to provide assistance after release and to give information as to its success.

11. In a number of cases, the information furnished by the State party contains no specific reference either to legislative or administrative provisions or to practical measures to ensure the re-education of convicted persons. The Committee requests specific information concerning the measures taken to provide teaching, education and re-education, vocational guidance and training and also concerning work programmes for prisoners inside the penitentiary establishment as well as outside.

12. In order to determine whether the principle set forth in article 10, paragraph 3, is being fully respected, the Committee also requests information on the specific measures applied during detention, e.g., how convicted persons are dealt with individually and how they are categorized, the disciplinary system, solitary confinement and high-security detention and the conditions under which contacts are ensured with the outside world (family, lawyer, social and medical services, non-governmental organizations).

13. Moreover, the Committee notes that in the reports of some States parties no information has been provided concerning the treatment accorded to accused juvenile persons and juvenile offenders. Article 10, paragraph 2(b), provides that accused juvenile persons shall be separated from adults. The information given in reports shows that some States parties are not paying the necessary attention to the fact that this is a mandatory provision of the Covenant. The text also provides that cases involving juveniles must be considered as speedily as possible. Reports should specify the measures taken by States parties to give effect to that provision. Lastly, under article 10, paragraph 3, juvenile offenders shall be segregated from adults and be accorded treatment appropriate to their age and legal status in so far as conditions of detention are concerned, such as shorter working hours and contact with relatives, with the aim of furthering their reformation and rehabilitation. Article 10 does not indicate any limits of juvenile age. While this is to be determined by each State party in the light of relevant social, cultural and other conditions, the Committee is of the opinion that article 6, paragraph 5, suggests that all persons under the age of 18 should be treated as juveniles, at least in matters relating to criminal justice. States should give relevant information about the age groups of persons treated as juveniles. In that regard, States parties are invited to indicate whether they are applying the United Nations Standard Minimum Rules for the Administration of Juvenile Justice, known as the Beijing Rules (1987).

GENERAL COMMENT 22

Article 18 (Forty-eighth Session, 1993)

1. The right to freedom of thought, conscience and religion (which includes the freedom to hold beliefs) in article 18(1) is far-reaching and profound; it encompasses

freedom of thought on all matters, personal conviction and the commitment to religion or belief, whether manifested individually or in community with others. The Committee draws the attention of States parties to the fact that the freedom of thought and the freedom of conscience are protected equally with the freedom of religion and belief. The fundamental character of these freedoms is also reflected in the fact that this provision cannot be derogated from, even in time of public emergency, as stated in article 4(2) of the Covenant.

2. Article 18 protects theistic, non-theistic and atheistic beliefs, as well as the right not to profess any religion or belief. The terms belief and religion are to be broadly construed. Article 18 is not limited in its application to traditional religions or to religions and beliefs with institutional characteristics or practices analogous to those of traditional religions. The Committee therefore views with concern any tendency to discriminate against any religion or belief for any reasons, including the fact that they are newly established, or represent religious minorities that may be the subject of hostility by a predominant religious community.

3. Article 18 distinguishes the freedom of thought, conscience, religion or belief from the freedom to manifest religion or belief. It does not permit any limitations whatsoever on the freedom of thought and conscience or on the freedom to have or adopt a religion or belief of one's choice. These freedoms are protected unconditionally, as is the right of everyone to hold opinions without interference in article 19(1). In accordance with articles 18(2) and 17, no one can be compelled to reveal his thoughts or adherence to a religion or belief.

4. The freedom to manifest religion or belief may be exercised 'either individually or in community with others and in public or private'. The freedom to manifest religion or belief in worship, observance, practice and teaching encompasses a broad range of acts. The concept of worship extends to ritual and ceremonial acts giving direct expression to belief, as well as various practices integral to such acts, including the building of places of worship, the use of ritual formulae and objects, the display of symbols, and the observance of holidays and days of rest. The observance and practice of religion or belief may include not only ceremonial acts but also such customs as the observance of dietary regulations, the wearing of distinctive clothing or headcoverings, participation in rituals associated with certain stages of life, and the use of a particular language customarily spoken by a group. In addition, the practice and teaching of religion or belief includes acts integral to the conduct by religious groups of their basic affairs, such as, *inter alia*, the freedom to choose their religious leaders, priests and teachers, the freedom to choose their religious leaders, priests and teachers, the freedom to establish seminaries or religious schools and the freedom to prepare and distribute religious texts or publications.

5. The Committee observes that the freedom to 'have or to adopt' a religion or belief necessarily entails the freedom to choose a religion or belief, including, *inter alia*, the right to replace one's current religion or belief with another or to adopt atheistic views, as well as the right to retain one's religion or belief. Article 18(2) bars coercions that would impair the right to have or adopt a religion or belief, including the use of threat of physical force or penal sanctions to compel believers or non-believers to adhere to their religious beliefs and congregations, to recant their religion or belief or to convert.

Policies or practices having the same intention or effect, such as for example those restricting access to education, medical care, employment or the rights guaranteed by article 25 and other provisions of the Covenant are similarly inconsistent with article 18(2). The same protection is enjoyed by holders of all beliefs of a non-religious nature.

6. The Committee is of the view that article 18(4) permits public school instruction in subjects such as the general history of religions and ethics if it is given in a neutral and objective way. The liberty of parents or legal guardians to ensure that their children receive a religious and moral education in conformity with their own convictions, set forth in article 18(4), is related to the guarantees of the freedom to teach a religion or belief stated in article 18(1). The Committee notes that public education that includes instruction in a particular religion or belief is inconsistent with article 18(4) unless provision is made for non-discriminatory exemptions or alternatives that would accommodate the wishes of parents and guardians.

7. According to article 20, no manifestation of religions or beliefs may amount to propaganda for war or advocacy of national, racial or religious hatred that constitutes incitement to discrimination, hostility or violence. As stated by the Committee in its General Comment 11[19], States parties are under the obligation to enact laws to prohibit such acts.

8. Article 18(3) permits restrictions on the freedom to manifest religion or belief only if limitations are prescribed by law and are necessary to protect public safety, order, health or morals, or the fundamental rights and freedoms of others. The freedom from coercion to have or to adopt a religion or belief and the liberty of the parents and guardians to ensure religious and moral education cannot be restricted. In interpreting the scope of permissible limitation clauses, States parties should proceed from the need to protect the rights guaranteed under the Covenant, including the right to equality and non-discrimination on all grounds specified in articles 2, 3 and 26. Limitations imposed must be established by law and must not be applied in a manner that would vitiate the rights guaranteed in article 18. The Committee observes that paragraph 3 of article 18 is to be strictly interpreted: restrictions are not allowed on grounds not specified there, even if they would be allowed as restrictions to other rights protected in the Covenant, such as national security. Limitations may be applied only for those purposes for which they were prescribed and must be directly related and proportionate to the specific need on which they are predicated. Restrictions may not be imposed for discriminatory purposes or applied in a discriminatory manner. The Committee observes that the concept of morals derives from many social, philosophical and religious traditions; consequently, limitations on the freedom to manifest a religion or belief for the purpose of protecting morals must be based on principles not deriving exclusively from a single tradition. Persons already subject to certain legitimate constraints, such as prisoners, continue to enjoy their rights to manifest their religion or belief to the fullest extent compatible with the specific nature of the constraint. States parties' reports should provide information on the full scope and effects of limitations under article 18(3), both as a matter of law and of their application in specific circumstances.

9. The fact that a religion is recognized as a State religion or that it is established as

official or traditional or that its followers comprise the majority of the population, shall not result in any impairment of the enjoyment of any of the rights under the Covenant, including articles 18 and 27, nor in any discrimination against adherents of other religions or non-believers. In particular, certain measures discriminating against the latter, such as measures restricting eligibility for government service to members of the predominant religion or giving economic privileges to them or imposing special restrictions on the practice of other faiths, are not in accordance with the prohibition of discrimination based on religion or belief and the guarantee of equal protection under article 26. The measures contemplated by article 20, paragraph 2, of the Covenant constitute important safeguards against infringements of the rights of religious minorities and of other religious groups to exercise the rights guaranteed by articles 18 and 27, and against acts of violence or persecution directed toward those groups. The Committee wishes to be informed of measures taken by States parties concerned to protect the practice of all religions or beliefs from infringement and to protect their followers from discrimination. Similarly, information as to respect for the rights of religious minorities under article 27 is necessary for the Committee to assess the extent to which the freedom of thought, conscience, religion and belief has been implemented by States parties. States parties concerned should also include in their reports information relating to practices considered by their laws and jurisprudence to be punishable as blasphemous.

10. If a set of beliefs is treated as official ideology in constitutions, statutes, proclamations of the ruling parties, etc., or in actual practice, this shall not result in any impairment of the freedoms under article 18 or any other rights recognized under the Covenant nor in any discrimination against persons who do not accept the official ideology or who oppose it.

11. Many individuals have claimed the right to refuse to perform military service (conscientious objection) on the basis that such right derives from their freedoms under article 18. In response to such claims, a growing number of States have in their laws exempted from compulsory military service citizens who genuinely hold religious or other beliefs that forbid the performance of military service and replaced it with alternative national service. The Covenant does not explicitly refer to a right of conscientious objection, but the Committee believes that such a right can be derived from article 18, inasmuch as the obligation to use lethal force may seriously conflict with the freedom of conscience and the right to manifest one's religion or belief. When this right is recognized by law or practice, there shall be no differentiation among conscientious objectors on the basis of the nature of their particular beliefs; likewise, there shall be no discrimination against conscientious objectors because they have failed to perform military service. The Committee invites States parties to report on the conditions under which persons can be exempted from military service on the basis of their rights under article 18 and on the nature and length of alternative national service.

CHAPTER 4

The number of communications submitted to the Committee rises inexorably. The status of the 556 communications registered as of 25 October 1993 is as follows:

(*a*) concluded by views under article 5, paragraph 4, of the Optional Protocol: 161;

(*b*) declared inadmissible: 171;

(*c*) discontinued or withdrawn: 87;

(*d*) declared admissible, but not yet concluded: 39;

(*e*) pending at the pre-admissibility stage: 98.

A substantial number of communications are also on file pending further information required before they can be considered for registration. The terms of reference of the Special Rapporteur on New Communications have been published in the Committee's Annual Report.[33]

The proportion of views in which violations are found remains high; violations were found in 121 cases. The Special Rapporteur for the Follow-Up has continued in existence. In the summer and autumn of 1993 the Committee discussed ways and means of improving the follow-up procedure.[34]

CHAPTERS 4–11

The jurisprudence on the provisions of the Covenant and the First Protocol continues to expand. In particular, the deficiencies of the criminal justice system in Jamaica have provided the opportunity for the jurisprudence on articles 7 and 14 to become highly developed and refined.[35] It now appears part of the established jurisprudence of the Committee that prolonged periods of detention under a severe custodial regime on death row cannot *generally* be considered to constitute cruel, inhuman, or degrading treatment if the convicted person is merely availing himself of appellate remedies.[36] In April 1993 an important decision on articles 19 and 27 was adopted concerning the use of the English language in Quebec, Canada.[37] The jurisprudence of the Committee on article 26 has been maintained,[38] but its application has been very cautious.[39] In the summer and autumn of 1993 two important and controversial decisions on extradition were adopted (both concerned Canada). Any reference to the doctrine of 'margin of appreciation' in the Committee's jurisprudence remains conspicuous by its absence.[40] This appears to be a deliberate policy decision. The search for consensus obviously slows down the decision-making on individual communications, but the number of individual opinions remains relatively small.

I hope in time to prepare a second edition of this work which covers all of the rights in the Covenant. I remain grateful for the constructive comments of reviewers and readers.

Faculty of Law, University of Liverpool   D.M.

November 1993

NOTES

1 For an excellent overview of United Nations human rights instruments see the 'Interim Report on the updated study by Philip Alston', which was made available to the World Conference on Human Rights in 1993, UN Doc. A/CONF. 157/PC/ 62/Add. 11/Rev. 1, 22 Apr. 1993.

2 See ch. 1 pr. 1.25 below; 'Senate Committee on Foreign Relations Report on the International Covenant on Civil and Political Rights', 31 ILM (1992), pp. 645–61; D. P. Stewart, 'U.S. Ratification of the Covenant on Civil and Political Rights: The Significance of the Reservations, Understandings and Declarations', 14 HRLJ (1993), pp. 77–83. The relevant texts appear, ibid., pp. 123–4, with critical comments by the Lawyers Committee for Human Rights, pp. 125–9. The United States also made the declaration under article 41 of the Covenant in relation to the inter-State procedure. This procedure has still never been invoked.

3 See also text to nn. 21–5 below.

4 See ch. 1, pr. 1.26 below.

5 See ch. 4, prs. 4.53–4.58 below.

6 See '1992 High Level Judicial Colloquium, Balliol College—Selected Papers', 18 Comm.L.Bull. (1992), pp. 1205–403. On the situation in Finland see M. Scheinin, *Human Rights in Finnish Law* (with an English summary) (Akateem Inen Kirjakauppa, Jyvaskyla, 1991).

7 See Y. Iwasawa, 'International Human Rights Adjudication in Japan', in *The Role of Domestic Courts in the Enforcement of International Human Rights*, proceedings of a conference in Siena, June 1993, to be published in 1994.

8 See *Mabo v. Queensland* (1992), 66 ALJR 408; M. Kirby, 'The Australian Use of International Human Rights Norms from Bangalore to Balliol—A View from the Antipodes', 18 Comm. LB (1992), pp. 1306–25.

9 See the decision of the Court of Appeal in *Derbyshire County Council v. Bookbinder* [1992] 3 All ER 65. The House of Lords did not make any reference to the Covenant, see [1993] 1 All ER 1011.

10 In the UK, for example, Liberty is publishing a series of reports on specific aspects of the implementation of the Covenant before the consideration of the UK's next periodic report, due in 1994. The first two reports have concerned mental health and criminal justice. See also *Broken Covenants—Violations of International Law in Northern Ireland*, Report of the Northern Ireland Human Rights Assembly (London: Liberty, 1993). See also *Democratic Audit* (Essex University, 1993).

11 In 1994 a collection of essays is being published under the auspices of the Human Rights Centre, Nottingham University, on the Covenant and United Kingdom law. See also W. A. Schabas, *The Abolition of the Death Penalty in International Law* (Cambridge: Grotius, 1993).

12 N. P. Engel, Kehl Am Rhein/Strasburg/Arlington. See also M. Nowak, 'The Activities of the UN Human Rights Committee: Developments from 1 August 1989 through 31 July 1992', 14 HRLJ (1993), pp. 9–19.

13 Oxford: Oxford University Press, 1992. This includes an essay on the Human Rights Committee by the late Torkel Opsahl, pp. 369–443.

14 See ch. 2 pr. 2.5 below.

15 Mrs Evatt was formerly a member and Chairperson of the Committee on the Elimination of Discrimination Against Women.

16 Doc. A/46/40, pr. 667.

17 For a valuable assessment of the practical effect of the Covenant see C. A. Cohn, 'The Early Harvest: Domestic Legal Changes Related to the Human Rights Committee and the Covenant on Civil and Political Rights', 13 HRQ (1991), p. 295.

18 Acceptance of a single combined periodic report on the Covenant from a State with a number of overdue reports would seem to be the most sensible way to proceed.

19 See Doc. A/46/40, Ax. VII. See also the *United Nations Manual on Human Rights Reporting Under Six Major International Human Rights Instruments* (New York: UN, 1991).

20 The absence of these is noted in ch. 3, prs. 3.45–3.46 below. The Comments are three or four pages long.

21 See ch. 3, prs. 3.8–3.81, 3.47 below.

22 See Doc. A/46/40, Ax. VI and prs. 618–56. See generally P. Rowe (ed.), *The Gulf War in International and English Law* (London: Routledge, 1993).

23 See UN Doc. CCPR/C/SR/1178/Add. 1; repr. in *15 European Human Rights Reports* (1992), 233. The requests were sent on 7 Oct. 1992. See also *Case Concerning Application of the Convention on the Prevention and Punishment of the Crime of Genocide*, Provisional Measures Orders of April and September 1993, *ICJ Reports 1993*.

24 See Doc. A/48/40.

25 See text to n. 20 above.

26 See generally R. Mullerson 'The Continuity and Succession of States, by Reference to the Former USSR and Yugoslavia', 42 ICLQ (1993), pp. 473–93.

27 The new rule 66(2) provides: 'Requests for submission of a report under article 40(1)(b) of the Covenant may be made in accordance with the periodicity decided by the Committee or at any other time the Committee may deem appropriate. In the case of an exceptional situation when the Committee is not in session, a request may be made through the Chairman acting in consultation with the members of the Committee.' See SR 1205/Add. 1.

28 See ch. 3, prs. 3.34–3.38 below.

29 General Comment 20 was adopted in 1992.

30 General Comment 21 was also adopted in 1992.

31 See Doc. A/48/40, Ax.

32 See ch. 3, pr. 3.38 below.

33 See Doc. A/46/40, Ax. X.

34 See Nowak, 'Activities of the UN Human Rights Committee', pp. 710–12. In March 1993 Mr Mavrommatis succeeded Mr Fodor as Special Rapporteur for the Follow-Up on Views. See also M. Schmidt, 'Individual Human Rights Complaint Procedures Based on United Nations Treaties and the Need For Reform', 41 ICLQ (1992), p. 645; A. De Zayas, 'The Follow-Up Procedures of the UN Human Rights Committee', 47 ICJ Review (1991), p. 28.

35 See generally R. M. B. Antoine, 'The Judicial Committee of the Privy Council—An Inadequate Remedy for Death Row Prisoners', 41 ICLQ (1992), pp. 179–90.

36 See e.g. *Barrett and Sutcliffe* v. *Jamaica*, Communication Nos. 270/1988 and 271/
1988, Doc. A/47/40, Ax.; *Campbell* v. *Jamaica*, Communication No. 307/1988,
Doc. A/48/40, Ax. Cf. *Pratt and Another* v. *Attorney-General for Jamaica and
Another*, [1993] 4 All ER 769, in which the Privy Council advised that if execution
takes place more than five years after sentence then there would be strong grounds
for believing that the delay was such as to constitute inhuman or degrading treatment or punishment or other treatment. A State that wished to retain capital
punishment had to accept the responsibility of ensuring that execution followed as
swiftly as practicable after sentence, allowing a reasonable time for appeal and
consideration of reprieve. It is an interesting phenomenon for the Privy Council to
have a more humanitarian jurisprudence than the HRC.

37 *Ballantyne, Davidson and McIntyre* v. *Canada*, Communications Nos. 359/1989
and 385/1989, Doc. A/48/40, Ax.; also published in 14 HRLJ (1993), pp. 171–8.

38 See ch. 4, prs. 4.55–4.58 below.

39 See A. Lester and S. Joseph, 'ICCPR Obligations of Non-Discrimination, and UK
Compliance', one of the collection of essays to be published in 1994 by the Human
Rights Centre, Nottingham University, see n. 11 above.

40 Reference to the doctrine has only ever been made once: see ch. 11, prs. 11.19–
11.19.2 below.

Introduction

According to Louis Henkin, 'Human rights is the idea of our time'. In concrete terms the 'idea' of human rights is given expression through a myriad of regional and global international instruments. The most general of those instruments, the Universal Declaration of Human Rights (1948), the International Covenant on Civil and Political Rights (1966), the Optional Protocol thereto (1966), and the International Covenant on Economic, Social, and Cultural Rights (1966), collectively form the 'International Bill of Rights'. The two Covenants and the Optional Protocol entered into force in 1976.

Under the terms of the International Covenant on Civil and Political Rights a 'Human Rights Committee' was established in 1977 with certain functions in respect of the Covenant and the Optional Protocol. This book examines the work of the Human Rights Committee. Through that examination it is possible to determine and evaluate the nature of the Human Rights Committee and assess its contribution to the development of the 'idea of our time'.

Chapter 1 and the opening section of Chapter 4 provide brief accounts of the origins, drafting, and significance in international law of the Covenant and the Optional Protocol. A knowledge of these matters is a necessary precondition to a proper evaluation of the work of the Human Rights Committee. Chapter 2 analyses the institutional nature of the Human Rights Committee. The aim is to determine what kind of a body the Human Rights Committee is. Chapters 3 and 4 provide a full examination of the practices and procedures under the two systems operated by the Human Rights Committee to date. These are the reporting system provided for in article 40 of the Covenant and the individual communications system provided for in the Optional Protocol. Each chapter offers an appraisal of the development of the respective system to date.

To obtain a more specific insight into the work of the Human Rights Committee the book proceeds with the examination of its work under the two implementation systems in respect of selected rights in the Covenant. Initially it was hoped to consider each of the articles on which the Human Rights Committee had seen fit to express a General Comment under article 40(4) of the Covenant. In the event that proved to be impossible. However, each of the articles examined has been the subject of a General Comment by the Human Rights Committee and this may perhaps be taken as some reflection of their relative importance in the view of the Human Rights Committee. In any event it is submitted that the articles chosen are self evidently important.

Chapter 5 considers article 1 (self-determination). Chapter 6 considers article 2 (general obligations to respect and ensure the rights in the Covenant, to give effect to it, and to provide a remedy in the event of violation). Chapter 7 considers article 4 (derogation provision). Chapter 8 considers article 6 (right to life). Chapter 9 considers article 7 (torture and other prohibited treatment and punishment), and, in part, article 10 (treatment of persons deprived of their liberty). Chapter 10 considers article 14 (Fair Trial). Chapter 11 considers article 19 (freedom of opinion and expression). Chapter 12 considers article 20 (war propaganda and advocacy of national, racial, or religious hatred). Each of Chapters 5 to 12 concludes with a general appraisal which links the consideration of the respective articles to the general themes of the nature of the Human Rights Committee and the development of the Covenant and the Protocol.

Chapter 13 provides a general appraisal of the work of the Human Rights Committee in giving life to the structures and mechanisms of the Covenant and the Protocol and meaning to its language.

In December 1989 the General Assembly adopted a second optional protocol (OP2) to the ICCPR. As of July 1990 OP2 had not entered into force. The provisions of OP2 are included in Apx. IV below. Its effects on the work of the HRC when in operation are noted in the relevant chapters of this book.

This book takes account of the work of the Human Rights Committee up to 27 July 1990, the closing date of its thirty-ninth session. More generally, I have taken account of information available to me up to 18 October 1990.

The Origins, Drafting and Significance of the International Covenant on Civil and Political Rights[1]

A. ORIGINS

1.1 The traditional rule of international law[2] was that, apart from the treatment of aliens,[3] and possibly humanitarian intervention,[4] the rights of individuals were not matters regulated by international law.[5] Some of the earliest examples of international law concerning itself with individual rights can be observed in the attempts in the nineteenth century to abolish slavery and the slave trade.[6] The revolutionary development of the twentieth century (though some would argue it is more properly viewed as an evolutionary development)[7] has been the internationalization of the concept of human rights.[8] Among the most significant milestones in this development were the Covenant of the League of Nations (1919),[9] the Mandates System,[10] the establishment of the International Labour Organization (1919),[11] the Minorities Treaties and Declarations,[12] President Roosevelt's 'Four-Freedoms' address in his message to Congress on 6 January 1941,[13] the Declaration of the 'United Nations' of 1 January 1942,[14] and the Charter of the United Nations (1945).[15]

1.2 The rise of totalitarianism and the horrors and excesses of the Second World War had shaken the moral, legal, and political foundations of the world community. The defence and re-establishment of human rights came to be seen, in a sense, as one of the 'war aims'.[16] By the early 1940s a widespread human rights movement had developed that was to exercise a critical influence on the injection of human rights provisions into the institutional framework of the new post-war world order.[17]

1.3 Some of the early American drafts of the United Nations Charter included a Bill of Rights or a Declaration of Human Rights.[18] However, in the Dumbarton Oaks Proposals (1944) for the United Nations Charter there was only one general reference to the promotion of respect for human rights and fundamental freedoms as one of the functions of the proposed General Assembly, and under its authority the Economic and Social Council (ECOSOC).[19] The United Nations Conference on International Organization

(1945) considered a large number of amendments to the proposed United Nations Charter that would have made more detailed and specific reference to human rights and fundamental freedoms. Support for these amendments came not only from various states but also from numerous non-governmental interest and pressure groups.[20] Only in the final stages were the sponsoring powers persuaded to accept the proposed amendments but with their support success was assured.[21] The result was that the highest constitutional document of the new world order,[22] the United Nations Charter (1945), specifically refers to human rights in its Preamble and in six of its articles.[23] The nature of the human rights obligations imposed on States by the UN Charter has been extensively debated but there is no doubt that their inclusion in the Charter was of fundamental importance to the internationalization of human rights.[24]

Among the proposals not adopted at the Conference were those that would have incorporated within the UN Charter some form of an 'International Bill of Rights'.[25] The Conference did not adopt these proposals because the time available did not permit the detailed consideration thought necessary. One proposal which was adopted was the inclusion in article 68 of the Charter of a specific reference to the establishment by the ECOSOC of a Commission for the promotion of human rights. The United States Secretary of State commented in his Report to the President on the Conference that, 'The unanimous acceptance of this proposal may well prove one of the most important and most significant achievements of the San Francisco Conference'.[26] It was clearly envisaged therefore that one of the first tasks of the new Human Rights Commission (HRCion) would be to draft an International Bill of Rights.[27] The ECOSOC established the HRCion and instructed it to submit proposals, recommendations, and reports regarding an International Bill of Rights and suggestions regarding ways and means for the effective implementation of human rights and fundamental freedoms.[28]

B. DRAFTING[29]

1.4 The HRCion held its first session in early 1947.[30] Mrs F. D. Roosevelt was elected Chairman. She held that office until 1951 and remained a member of the HRCion for a further year. She exerted an immensely important influence in the HRCion in its formative years when the first steps towards an International Bill of Rights were taken.[31] The HRCion's discussions began with a general debate on the form and content of an International Bill of Rights. The possible forms included a Declaration,[32] a Resolution of the General Assembly, a multilateral Convention binding on all States ratifying it, or an amendment to the Charter of the UN. The initial consensus was that the Bill would be a Declaration to be adopted by

Resolution of the General Assembly. A Drafting Committee of eight members was ultimately established to prepare a preliminary draft International Bill of Rights.[33] The drafting Committee initially based its work on a draft Declaration prepared by the Secretariat.[34]

1.5 In the drafting Committee the different views as to the form the International Bill should take were further developed.[35] The major division was between those who favoured a Declaration or Manifesto and those who favoured a Convention. The divisions proved not to be fundamental. Those who favoured a Declaration agreed that it should be accompanied or followed by a Convention or a series of Conventions on specific groups of rights. Similarly those who favoured a Convention agreed that the General Assembly, in recommending a Convention to member States, might make a Declaration which was wider in content and more general in expression. Accordingly, it was decided to draft two documents. The Draft Declaration was to set forth general principles or standards of human rights. The Draft Convention was to define specific rights and the limitations or restrictions on their enjoyment. The Drafting Committee also considered the question of implementation and transmitted a memorandum on this matter prepared by the Secretariat.[36]

At its second session in late 1947 the HRCion decided that it would prepare a Declaration and a Convention (to be called a Covenant) as well as measures of implementation. The term 'International Bill of Rights' was to apply to all three documents in preparation.[37] Three working groups were established to consider each of these matters. A draft Declaration and a draft Covenant were produced and, along with the report of the working group on implementation, were transmitted to Governments for observations, suggestions, and proposals.[38]

The third session of the HRCion in 1948 concentrated on the draft Declaration.[39] The revised draft was submitted to the ECOSOC which after brief consideration transmitted the draft Declaration to the General Assembly for adoption.[40] The 'Universal Declaration of Human Rights' (UDHR) was finally adopted by the General Assembly on 10 December 1948.[41] The first stage of the International Bill of Rights was complete.

1.6 Attention then focused on the draft Covenant and measures of implementation.[42] At its fifth session (1949) the HRCion conducted a detailed article-by-article examination of the draft Covenant.[43] Increasing attention was being focused on the question of implementation. A variety of proposals were made for the establishment of an International Court or Committee of Human Rights with different powers and functions. The HRCion requested the Secretary-General to prepare a methodical questionnaire for governments on the basis of the proposals put forward.[44] One of the most significant matters considered by the HRCion was whether a right of petition to an international conciliation body would extend to individuals and groups of individuals. The HRCion was equally divided on this issue, there being eight votes for and eight against. Under the HRCion's rules of procedure this meant that the proposal was not adopted.[45] Although similar proposals were consistently made at subsequent sessions none was ever adopted.[46]

At its sixth session (1950)[47]the HRCion gave further consideration to the question of implementation. By a narrow vote the HRCion approved the principle of the establishment of a permanent body in the measures of implementation in the draft Covenant. That body was to be known as the *Human Rights Committee* (HRC). The HRC would consider inter-State complaints but not complaints from individuals or non-governmental organizations.[48] The HRC was to offer its good offices to the States concerned with a view to the friendly solution of the matter on the basis of respect for human rights as defined in the Covenant. A proposal that the HRC should have as one of its functions the general supervision of the observance of the provisions of the Covenant was rejected.[49]

On the question of economic, social, and cultural rights it was decided that they should not be included in the first Covenant but that the HRCion would proceed at its next session to consider 'additional covenants and measures dealing with economic, social, cultural, political and other categories of human rights'.[50] It was also decided to secure the co-operation of the Specialized Agencies in the drafting of articles on economic, social, and cultural rights.[51]

1.7 The ECOSOC considered the draft Covenants at its eleventh session (1950).[52] In one of its most important decisions concerning the Covenants it requested the General Assembly to take four policy decisions.[53] The first policy decision concerned the general adequacy of the first eighteen draft articles. The General Assembly expressed the opinion that the draft should be revised to include additional rights and to define the rights and the permissible limitations with the greatest possible precision.

The second policy decision concerned the desirability of including special articles on the application of the Covenant to federal States and non-self-governing and trust territories. The General Assembly requested the HRCion to study a federal State article and prepare recommendations which would, 'have as their purpose the securing of the maximum extension of the Covenant to the constituent units of federal states and the meeting of the constitutional problems of federal States'.[54] Notwithstanding the clear recognition of the constitutional problems of federal States by the GA the HRCion interpreted this decision as a direction to exclude any provision for a federal State article. This is the position adopted in the final text of the Covenant.[55] Regarding the territorial application (or colonial clause) the GA was more direct. It instructed the HRCion to insert a specified text into the Covenant.[56] That text, however, was subsequently deleted in the Third

Committee of the GA.[57] The GA also requested the HRCion, 'to study ways and means which would ensure the right of all peoples to self-determination and to prepare recommendations' thereon.[58] Professor Humphrey has commented that, 'these decisions marked the beginning of the politicization of the Covenants. The developing countries were in revolt and new voices were beginning to be heard'.[59]

The third policy decision concerned the desirability of including articles on economic, social, and cultural rights. The GA decided that these rights should be included in the Covenant on human rights together with an explicit recognition of the equality of men and women in related rights as set forth in the UN Charter. The HRCion was requested to include in the draft Covenant, 'a clear expression of economic, social, and cultural rights in a manner which relates them to the civil and political freedoms proclaimed in the draft Covenant'.[60]

The final policy decision related to the adequacy of the articles relating to implementation. The GA requested the HRCion, 'to proceed with the consideration of provisions, to be inserted in the draft Covenant or in separate Protocols, for the receipt and examination of petitions from individuals and organizations with respect to alleged violations of the Covenant', and to take into consideration a number of proposals on measures of implementation.[61] However, as we have noted, the HRCion never adopted measures to give individuals or organizations a right of petition.[62]

1.8 At its seventh session (1951)[63] the HRCion drafted fourteen articles on economic, social, and cultural rights and ten articles on measures of implementation under which States parties would submit periodic reports to the ECOSOC concerning the progress made in achieving the observance of economic, social, and cultural rights.[64] The HRCion did not decide whether the reporting system would be applied to civil and political rights. The provisions concerning the proposed Human Rights Committee were also further revised.

The policy decision of the GA to have a single Covenant had not ended the disagreements between States over this issue. The matter was again considered by the ECOSOC at its thirteenth session (1951). After a protracted debate it decided to invite the GA to reconsider its decision on the matter.[65] The GA took up this invitation and after a bitter debate it requested the ECOSOC to ask the HRCion,

To draft two Covenants on human rights . . . , one to contain civil and political rights and the other to contain economic, social and cultural rights, in order that the General Assembly may approve the two Covenants simultaneously and open them at the same time for signature, the two Covenants to contain, in order to emphasise the unity of the aim in view and to ensure respect for and observance of human rights, as many similar provisions as possible.[66]

The GA also decided to include in the Covenants an article stipulating that, 'All peoples shall have the right to self-determination', and that, 'all States, including those having responsibility for the administration of Non-Self-Governing Territories, should promote the realization of that right, in conformity with the purposes and principles of the United Nations, and that States having responsibility for the administration of Non-Self-Governing Territories should promote the realization of that right in relation to the peoples of such territories'.[67]

In response to the GA's decision most of the HRCion's eighth session (1952)[68] was taken up with the drafting of a provision on self-determination which it was decided would be included as article 1 of each of the Covenants. Further revision took place of both draft Covenants. A proposal to request the GA to reconsider the decision to prepare two Covenants was not adopted.

1.9 At its ninth session (1953)[69] the HRCion adopted additional articles dealing with civil and political rights and revised the provisions concerning the establishment, composition, and jurisdiction of the proposed Human Rights Committee.[70] Again a proposal to request the GA to reconsider its decision to have two Covenants was not adopted. However, a special implementation procedure for the right of self-determination was adopted.[71]

The HRCion concluded its work on the draft Covenants at its tenth session (1954).[72] The articles relating to the system of periodic reports for the implementation of economic, social, and cultural rights were redrafted. A new article was adopted on a reporting procedure for the Civil and Political Rights Covenant. The State reports were to cover, 'The legislative or other measures, including judicial remedies, which they have adopted and which give effect to the rights recognized herein'. The reports were also to indicate the factors and difficulties, if any, affecting the progressive implementation of draft article 22(4) of the Covenant which concerned the equality of rights and responsibilities of spouses as to marriage, during marriage, and at its dissolution and special measures for the protection of children.[73] The reports were to be transmitted, 'for the ECOSOC which may transmit them to the Commission on Human Rights for information, study and, if necessary, *general recommendations*'.[74] The HRCion also did not adopt any provisions concerning the applicability of the inter-State complaint procedure under the draft ICCPR to the Economic, Social, and Cultural Rights Covenant.[75] There was further discussion of extending the right of petition but no provision was adopted. Finally, the provision extending the civil and political Covenant to all parts of federal states was adopted.[76] The HRCion's final drafts were then submitted through the ECOSOC to the GA.[77]

1.10 The GA reviewed the draft Covenants at its ninth session (1954)[78] and recommended that its Third Committee (Social, Humanitarian, and

Cultural Questions) begin an article-by-article discussion at its tenth session. So began over a decade of detailed scrutiny. A series of amendments were made to the substantive rights adopted by the HRCion. A new article on the rights of the child was adopted but proposals for a right to asylum and a right to property failed. To assist the Third Committee in its consideration of measures of implementation the Secretary-General had prepared, at the request of the GA, a detailed explanatory paper which examined all of the possibilities in the light of contemporary developments in international implementation procedures. That paper clearly indicated the feasibility of reporting and petition systems as international implementation measures.[79]

I.II The result of the Third Committee's deliberations were some fundamental changes in the measures of implementation.[80] The final text of the ICCPR provided for three measures of international implementation.

First, a compulsory reporting procedure covering all of the rights set forth in the Covenant (Article 40).[81] The reports were to indicate, 'the progress made in the enjoyment of those rights', and to indicate the factors and difficulties, if any, affecting the implementation of the Covenant. The particular implementation provision dealing with the rights and responsibilities of spouses and protection for children was deleted[82] as was the special implementation procedure for the right of self-determination.[83] The State reports were to be considered by the new Human Rights Committee rather than by the ECOSOC and the HRCion.[84] The HRC was to 'study' the reports and 'transmit its reports, and such general comments as it may consider appropriate, to the States parties'.[85] The role envisaged for the Specialized Agencies was minimal.[86]

Secondly, the inter-State Good Offices, Fact-Finding, and Conciliation procedure was made optional rather than mandatory as it had been under the HRCion's draft.[87] The provisions themselves were spelt out in much greater detail and became a more distinct two-stage procedure. During the first stage the HRC would exercise its Good Offices (article 41). The second stage would be conducted by a Conciliation Commission appointed by the HRC with the consent of the States parties (article 42). It is also noteworthy that all references in the HRCion's draft to the International Court of Justice were deleted, even its election of members of the HRC. This has been seen as an adverse reaction to the judgment of the ICJ in the *South West Africa Cases* (1966).[88]

Thirdly, the Third Committee introduced an optional provision for the receipt and consideration by the HRC of communications from individuals, but not non-governmental organizations, claiming to be victims of violations of rights recognized in the Covenant. The HRC would then express 'its views' on the communication. This provision ultimately emerged as the Optional Protocol to the ICCPR.[89]

1.12 The HRC had clearly survived then to become the central international implementation organ in the ICCPR and the OP.[90] It was to study the reports submitted by States parties and make such 'general comments' as it considered appropriate (article 40); exercise its good offices concerning inter-State complaints (article 41); appoint a Conciliation Commission if its good offices failed to resolve the matter (article 42); and consider and express its views on communications submitted by individuals under the OP. In addition to altering its functions the Third Committee increased the size of the HRC from nine to eighteen members and provided for it to be elected at meetings of States parties to the Covenant.[91]

1.13 In Resolution 2200 (XI) of 16 December 1966 the GA adopted and opened for signature the International Covenant on Economic, Social, and Cultural Rights, the International Covenant on Civil and Political Rights and the OP.[92] Thus the International Bill of Rights was complete.[93] The Bill was the product of almost two decades of detailed consideration by the HRCion, the ECOSOC, the Third Committee of the GA, and to a lesser extent the plenary GA. At each stage of preparation governments were afforded the opportunity of close consultation through the submission of their observations, recommendations, and proposals. The HRC has thus been left with a wealth of *travaux préparatoires* at their disposal which could be of enormous value when faced with problems of interpretation and application.[94]

1.14 No account of the drafting of the International Bill of Rights would be complete without drawing attention to two highly significant influences on its development. First, the Secretariat of the then UN Human Rights Division played a fundamental role.[95] It continually acted in a positive and constructive manner introducing new ideas and initiatives either of its own motion or through the State representatives in the HRCion and in the Third Committee.

1.15 Secondly, throughout the drafting process a large number of non-governmental organizations made a very positive contribution.[96] Their representatives served to keep the pressure on governmental representatives to produce the most comprehensive provisions to protect rights and the most effective international measures of implementation possible. Non-governmental organizations have played a very significant role in the development of a consciousness of human rights at both national and international levels. We have already noted that it was partly their efforts that led to the inclusion of the human rights provisions in the UN Charter.[97] Their activities have continued and expanded ever since and their work represents a very important part of the machinery for the international protection of human rights.[98]

We now examine some of the principal issues that arose during the drafting.

C. ONE COVENANT OR TWO[99]

1.16 We have already noted how this question was finally resolved during the drafting by the decision of the General Assembly in 1951–2 to have two separate Covenants.[100] The question bitterly divided both the HRCion and the Third Committee of the GA. Those who favoured two Covenants argued that civil and political rights were 'enforceable', or 'justiciable' and of an 'absolute character' and that this was not the case with economic, social, and cultural rights. Civil and political rights were said to be immediately applicable and obliged States to protect individuals against unlawful action by the State. Moreover, economic, social, and cultural rights were to be progressively implemented, called for positive action by the State to promote them and depended on domestic and international economic and social conditions.[101] Against this view it was argued that human rights could not be so neatly divided into different categories and should not be so classified in a hierarchical manner. All human rights should be protected and promoted at the same time.[102]

The question of whether there should be one or two Covenants was inextricably linked to that of the appropriate systems of implementation. It was strongly argued that whatever the merits of the preceding arguments the two groups of rights called for different implementation machinery. To incorporate two systems of implementation within one Covenant would have resulted in a Covenant within a Covenant.[103] In the HRCion it was originally argued that while an inter-State complaint machinery was appropriate to civil and political rights which were to be given immediate effect the progressive nature of economic, social, and cultural rights rendered some form of reporting machinery more appropriate.[104]

Debate continues as to the relationship between the two sets of rights and the most appropriate implementation machinery for them.[105] In retrospect it is submitted that the separation of the two sets of rights has proved beneficial from the point of view of the ICCPR. The HRC's brief of twenty-seven substantive articles (Articles 1–27 ICCPR) is still very wide and onerous. However, the subsequent chapters of this book will relate how the HRC has built up a constructive practice on the framework of the article 40 reporting procedure and the OP individual petition procedure.[106] By contrast the record of the implementation procedures and practices established under the ICESCR has been somewhat disappointing to date.[107] Indeed, the contrasting fortunes of the two sets of implementation machinery are vividly illustrated by the fact that a new Committee on Economic, Social, and Cultural Rights, largely modelled on the HRC, has now been established to replace the machinery established under the ICESCR.[108] The fears of those who argued that the separation of human rights into two Covenants with different implementation machinery would relegate the importance of, and hinder the effective implementation of, economic, social, and cultural rights have in practice been realized.[109]

D. PROGRESSIVE OR IMMEDIATE OBLIGATIONS[110]

1.17 There were marked differences of opinion during the drafting on the matter of the obligations that would be incurred by a State party to the ICCPR. Some representatives argued that the obligations under the ICCPR were absolute and immediate and that, therefore, a State could only become a party to the ICCPR after, or simultaneously with, its taking the necessary measures to secure those rights. If there were disparities between the Covenant and national law they could best be met by reservations. These representatives criticized the draft article 2(2) of the ICCPR whereby States would undertake 'to adopt such legislative or other measures as may be necessary to give effect to the rights recognized in this Covenant', where they were not already provided for, because it introduced the notion of progressiveness.[111] Similar criticism was also directed to the draft reporting procedure.[112]

Against this view it was argued that the prior adoption of the necessary measures in domestic law was not required by international law.[113] Moreover,

At the same time the need for paragraph two arose because it was essential to permit a certain degree of elasticity to the obligations imposed by the Covenant, since all States would not be in a position immediately to take the necessary legislative or other measures for the implementation of its provisions. The Covenant, it was pointed out, unlike ordinary Conventions, concerned a vast field so that no State could claim its legislation to be in complete harmony with all its provisions. Paragraph two would also take into account the constitutional processes of various countries which differed as regards the implications of an act of ratification of an international instrument.[114]

It was further suggested that the draft article 2(2), unlike a system of reservations, would not perpetuate the law of any State that did not conform to the Covenant.

Proposals to provide that the necessary measures be taken within a specified time limit or within a reasonable time were rejected as was a suggestion that each State fix its own time limit in its instrument of ratification. The only clear intentions of the HRCion that emerged were those of avoiding excessive delays in the full implementation of the Covenant and of not introducing the general notion of progressiveness that was a feature of the obligations under the then draft ICESCR.[115]

The objections to the draft article 2(2) were again voiced in the Third

Committee but the provision remained unchanged. The Committee's report stated that,

It represented the minimum compromise formula, the need for which, particularly in new States building up their body of legislation, was manifest. The notion of implementation at the earliest possible moment was implicit in article 2 as a whole. Moreover, the reporting requirement in article 49 (later article 40) would indeed serve as an effective curb on undue delay.[116]

The approach of the HRC to article 2 of the ICCPR is dealt with below.[117]

E. INTERNATIONAL MEASURES OF IMPLEMENTATION[118]

1.18 There was general agreement during the drafting that the primary obligation under the ICCPR would be implementation at the national level by States.[119] There was continuing disagreement, however, on the question whether there should also be international measures of implementation. A minority of States, principally the Soviet bloc, insisted that there should be provisions to ensure implementation but that there should be no international measures of implementation.[120] It was argued that such measures were a system of international pressure intended to force States to take particular steps connected with the execution of obligations under the Covenant. They were, therefore, contrary to the principle of domestic jurisdiction in article 2(7) of the United Nations Charter,[121] would undermine the sovereignty and independence of States[122] and would upset the balance of powers established by the UN Charter. Moreover, the establishment of petitions systems would transform complaints into international disputes with consequent effects upon peaceful international relations.

1.19 Against these views it was argued that the undertaking of international measures of implementation was an exercise of domestic jurisdiction and not an interference with it. International measures were essential to the effective observance of human rights, which were matters of international concern. However, even within those States that agreed that international measures were essential, there were significant differences of opinion as to the appropriate types of measures.[123] The proposals included an International Court of Human Rights empowered to settle disputes concerning the Covenant;[124] settlement by diplomatic negotiation and, in default, by *ad hoc* fact-finding Committees; the establishment of an Office of High Commissioner (or Attorney-General) for Human Rights;[125] the establishment of reporting procedures covering some or all of the provisions in the Covenant; empowering the proposed Human Rights Committee to collect information on all matters relevant to the observance and enforcement of human rights and to initiate an inquiry if it thought one necessary.[126]

1.20 There was further division of opinion as to whether, if an international right of petition were included, it would be limited to States or whether it would be extended to individuals, groups of individuals, or to all or selected non-governmental organizations.[127] As noted, the HRCion rejected the latter possibilities in 1949 and never reversed that position.[128] Only during its final session did the Third Committee adopt the Optional Protocol to the ICCPR which provides an international right of petition for individuals but not for non-governmental organizations.[129]

1.21 The lengthy drafting process of the ICCPR largely coincided with the depths of cold war confrontation, the explosive development of notions of self-determination[130] and independence, the accompanying political tensions of large scale decolonization, and the consequential effects of a rapidly altering balance of diplomatic power within the United Nations.[131] In retrospect then it must be acknowledged than it was much more difficult to agree on the text of a Covenant containing binding legal obligations and limited measures of international implementation that it had been to agree upon the statement of political principles in the Universal Declaration in 1948.[132] It is submitted, therefore, that the completion of the ICCPR and the OP should be viewed as an achievement of considerable significance. The presence of at least some limited international implementation procedures offered some hope that the Human Rights Committee, the body of independent experts to be established to operate them, could fashion something constructive and influential from them. The subsequent chapters of this work essentially seek to determine whether that hope has been fulfilled.[133]

F. SELF-DETERMINATION[134]

1.22 Perhaps the most controversial provision included in the ICCPR was the provision on self-determination. As we have noted it was considered and included at the request of the GA in 1950.[135] However, its inclusion was strenuously opposed on various grounds particularly by the Western powers. It was argued that it was a vague and undefined concept, that it was a political principle rather than a legal right, that it was a collective rather than an individual right, that the implementation systems in the Covenant could not be applied to it and that its inclusion would disturb the system of functions and powers allocated to the United Nations organs in the Charter. The opponents of its inclusion in the Covenant suggested that it could be included in a separate covenant or protocol. In the event, however, the tide of political opinion in favour of including a right of self-determination proved irresistible.[136] Its proponents argued that it was a fundamental collective human right and a precondition to the enjoyment of all the rights and freedoms of the individual.

A minority of States argued that the right should be limited to the colonial situation. The majority, however, including those States that opposed inclusion, took the view that if the right was to appear in the Covenant it should not be limited to colonial territories but should apply to the people of any territory whether independent, trust, or non-self-governing. A particular fear expressed with respect to self-determination was its invocation by minorities and the consequential destruction of the sovereignty and territorial integrity of States.[137] It is, therefore, important to note that the drafting history clearly indicates that the Covenant does not accord to minorities, as such, the right of self-determination generally.[138] The problems of minorities were conceived of as different matters. Thus limited provision dealing with ethnic, religious, or linguistic minorities was included as article 27 ICCPR. This provides that such minorities shall not be deprived of the right 'to enjoy their own culture, to profess and practice their own religion, or to use their own language'.[139]

1.23 In the HRCion an important addition to the proposed right of self-determination was that it would include a right to permanent sovereignty over natural wealth and resources.[140] Those opposed to this addition argued that the concept of permanent sovereignty had little meaning and was untenable because any State could voluntarily limit its own sovereignty. Moreover, concern was expressed that the article could sanction unwarranted expropriation or confiscation of foreign property and would permit the unilateral denunciation of international agreements. Against this view it was argued that the right to permanent sovereignty over natural wealth and resources was an essential part of self-determination. The purpose of the article was not to threaten foreign investment as suggested but to prevent such foreign exploitation as would deprive the local population of its means of subsistence. To meet some of the objections, however, the Third Committee deleted the reference to permanent sovereignty and inserted a reference to 'obligations arising out of international economic co-operation, based upon the principle of mutual benefit, and international law' (article 1(2)).[141]

It has been argued, however, that the subsequent adoption of article 47 of the ICCPR has substantially altered the compromise reached on the content of article 1. Article 47 provides that, 'Nothing in the present Covenant shall be interpreted as impairing the inherent right of all peoples to enjoy and utilize fully and freely their natural wealth and resources'.[142] Article 47 attracted great opposition from the Western States who argued that it was designed to modify the effect of the substance of article 1.[143] Some commentators have accepted that the purpose of article 47 was indeed to override the contents of article 1.[144]

In the final event then an identical text on self-determination appears in article 1 of each of the Covenants. From the perspective of the ICCPR this raises the question of whether this right is subject to the same implementation procedures as the other rights and freedoms in the ICCPR.[145] In terms of the practice of the HRC the answer has been in the affirmative. The right to self-determination has been considered under the reporting procedure in article 40,[146] has been the subject of a general comment by the HRC under article 40(4),[147] and has been the subject of a number of important decisions under the Optional Protocol.[148]

The practice of the HRC concerning the right to self-determination is considered below.[149]

G. THE TERRITORIAL (COLONIAL) CLAUSE, THE FEDERAL CLAUSE, RESERVATIONS

1.24 We have already noted the outcome concerning the territorial and federal State clauses.[150] It only remains to note that both provisions were the subject of considerable controversy. Questions concerning the territorial application of the ICCPR and its application in federal States have arisen and the approach of the States parties and the HRC are noted below.[151]

The matter of reservations was also subject to extensive consideration.[152] In the event no provision dealing with reservations appears in the ICCPR or in the OP.[153] Their admissibility and validity are thus matters regulated by general international law.[154] In fact a considerable number of reservations and interpretative declarations have been made to the ICCPR and to the OP.[155] A number of objections have been made to these.[156] Many of those reservations raise interesting questions as to their validity and indicate in some cases how States parties interpret their obligations under the ICCPR and the OP. Their presence also raises the question as to whether the HRC has jurisdiction to pronounce on the validity of a reservation during the consideration of reports or under the OP process.[157] The approach of the HRC to these questions is noted at various points in this thesis.[158]

H. THE POSITIONS OF THE SUPERPOWERS

1.25 It is interesting to note briefly the positions of the two superpowers concerning the Covenants. In the early post-World War II years the United States assumed the position of leadership of the international human rights movement with Mrs Roosevelt as a major force and inspiration.[159] However, from 1948 onwards there were signs that the US Senate would reject any human rights treaty.[160] Concerted domestic opposition and concern over the constitutional implications of ratification of international human rights treaties culminated in the introduction of the celebrated 'Bricker Amendments' (1952–3) which would have restricted the treaty making powers under the Constitution.[161] Although the amendments were defeated they substantially contributed to the adoption of a new policy by the administration concerning human rights treaties. Essentially this new policy rejected the treaty approach as the proper and most effective way to promote human rights. With respect to the International Covenants the policy meant that henceforth the US would not actively participate in the drafting of binding human rights Covenants and would not, in any event, ratify any Covenant approved by the United Nations.[162] The alternative approach advocated by the US was the so-called 'Action Programme' which in time made an important contribution to the United Nations human rights programme.[163]

The US did continue to take part in the drafting of the Covenants but with decidedly less vigour. On specific issues the initial US position as regards the proposed international measures of implementation was that it favoured inter-State procedures rather than petition procedures for individuals or non-governmental organizations.[164] This position was later modified to support the latter procedures.[165] The US supported the reporting procedures, favoured two Covenants, opposed the inclusion of the article on self-determination (although it supported the principle of self-determination), and fought vigorously for the inclusion of a provision that would take account of the constitutional problems of federal states.[166]

More recently the Carter presidency gave a new momentum to the international human rights movement by his efforts to integrate human rights considerations as priority aspects of US foreign policy.[167] A number of human rights treaties, including the ICCPR, but not the OP, were submitted to the Senate for advice and consent to ratification but unfortunately such consent was not forthcoming.[168] There seems little prospect of the present US administration supporting the ratification of the ICCPR or the OP.[169]

As for the USSR, and indeed the rest of the Soviet bloc, with the partial exception of Yugoslavia,[170] we have already noted their different understanding of implementation and their opposition to all international measures of implementation.[171] They favoured provisions on economic, social, and cultural rights, opposed the separation of human rights into two Covenants, and opposed what they considered to be special exceptions clauses in favour of federal States and colonial powers.[172]

1.26 Considering the position of most of the Soviet bloc as regards international measures of implementation it was perhaps surprising when the USSR and the other members of the bloc ratified the two international Covenants.[173] They are, therefore, subject to the respective reporting procedures of the two Covenants although they may take a limited view of the nature and purpose of those reporting procedures.[174] In 1988 Hungary became the first East European State to ratify the Optional Protocol and in 1989 the USSR indicated before the HRCion that it would also become a party to the Optional Protocol.[175] Accession by the USSR would make the US position appear even more embarassing.[176]

1.27 The adoption of a new human rights policy of the US in the early 1950s allowed the USSR to assume, at least formally, the mantle of human rights leadership at the United Nations.[177] The absence of the US from the International Covenants, and indeed from most of the UN human rights treaty network, is greatly to be regretted.[178] Apart from depriving the American people of international protection of their basic human rights, and setting a poor precedent for other States,[179] it more particularly deprives the ICCPR and the OP of the world wide publicity attendant upon any American international involvement. Ironically, however, it may have allowed the HRC to escape the overt 'politicization' of most other UN human rights institutions.[180] The consequences of such 'politicization', real or imagined, have led most recently to US withdrawal from UNESCO,[181] and to repeated threats of USSR withdrawal from the ILO.[182] The absence of politicization and conflict has allowed the HRC to develop a remarkable consensus practice.[183] To date no decision taken by the HRC has been forced to a vote. This consensus has allowed the development of a surprisingly constructive and critical practice under the reporting procedure (article 40)[184] and the emergence of a potentially effective system of individual petition under the OP.[185]

I. AN OUTLINE OF THE ICCPR

1.28 The ICCPR consists of a Preamble and fifty-three articles divided into six parts. The Preamble recognizes the inherent dignity of the human person as a source of equal and inalienable rights and proclaims that the 'ideal of free human beings enjoying freedom from fear and want can only be achieved if conditions are created whereby everyone may enjoy his civil and political rights, as well as his economic, social and cultural rights'. The Preamble also notes the obligations on States under the United Nations Charter to promote human rights,[186] and the duties and responsibilities of the individual.[187] In accordance with General Assembly Resolution 543 (VI) the preambles in the two Covenants are identical, *mutatis mutandis*. The aim was to underline the unity of the two Covenants.[188]

1.29 Part I (article 1) concerns the right of all peoples to self-determination.[189] Part II (articles 2–5) contains certain general provisions relevant to all of the rights set out in the ICCPR. Article 2 contains the basic undertakings to respect and ensure the rights in the Covenant, to adopt the necessary measures to give effect to all those rights, and to ensure that an effective remedy exists and is enforced in the event of violation of those rights.[190] Under article 3 States parties undertake to ensure the equal rights of men and women to the enjoyment of the rights in the ICCPR. Article 4 is the derogation provision. Derogation is permitted, 'in time of public emergency which threatens the life of the nation'. However, it is only permitted to the extent strictly required by the exigencies of the situation and no derogation is permitted from certain specified articles. There is also a requirement of notification of derogation.[191] Article 5(1) is a provision designed to avoid abuse of the ICCPR by preventing the use of the ICCPR as a justification for the destruction of the rights in the ICCPR or at their limitation to a greater extent than is provided for in the ICCPR.[192] Article 5(2) is a saving provision which prevents the use of the ICCPR to restrict or derogate from human rights that are recognized or exist in a State party.

1.30 Part III (articles 6–27) contains a catalogue of civil and political rights. Each article begins with a general statement of the right concerned. This is then followed by a more detailed formulation of aspects of that right and any applicable limitations or restriction.[193] In general terms the rights and freedoms in Part III cover the right to life (article 6),[194] the prohibition of torture and cruel, inhuman, or degrading treatment or punishment (article 7),[195] the prohibition of slavery, servitude, and forced or compulsory labour (article 8), the liberty and security of the person (article 9), the humane treatment of persons deprived of their liberty (article 10),[196] non-imprisonment for failure to fulfil a contractual obligation (article 11), freedom of movement and residence (article 12), the expulsion of aliens lawfully in the territory of a State party (article 13), the right to a fair trial (article 14),[197] the prohibition of the retroactive application of criminal law (article 15), equal recognition of persons before the law (article 16), the right to privacy (article 17), freedom of thought, conscience, and religion (article 18), freedom of opinion and expression (article 19),[198] the prohibition of propaganda for war or advocacy of national, racial, or religious hatred (article 20),[199] the right to peaceful assembly (article 21), the right to freedom of association (article 22), rights relating to marriage and to the family (article 23), certain rights relating to children (article 24), certain political rights of citizens (article 25), equality before the law and equal protection of the law (article 26), and rights of ethnic, religious and linguistic minorities (article 27).[200]

1.31 Part IV (articles 28–45) contains provisions for the establishment and operation of an independent Human Rights Committee and provisions concerning two international measures of implementation. First, a reporting procedure under which each State party submits periodic reports for examination by the HRC (article 40).[201] Secondly, an inter-State complaint procedure (articles 41 and 42).[202] Note should also be made of article 45 which provides that the HRC shall submit an annual report on its activities to the General Assembly through the ECOSOC.[203]

1.32 Part V (articles 46–7) deals with two matters of interpretation of the ICCPR. First, the ICCPR shall not be interpreted as impairing the provisions of the UN Charter and the constitutions of the specialized agencies which define the respective responsibilities of the various organs of the UN and of the specialized agencies in regard to matters dealt with by the ICCPR (article 46).[204] Secondly, nothing in the ICCPR is to be interpreted as impairing the inherent right of all peoples to enjoy and utilize fully and freely their natural wealth and resources (article 47).[205]

1.33 Part VI (articles 48–53) contains the final clauses dealing with signature, ratification, or accession (article 48),[206] entry into force (article 49), the extension of the ICCPR to all parts of federal States without any limitations or exceptions (article 50),[207] amendments to the ICCPR (article 51),[208] and the authentic texts (article 53).[209] There are no provisions dealing with denunciations[210] or reservations.[211]

For convenience the provisions of the OP are outlined in the chapter on the OP.[212]

J. THE SIGNIFICANCE OF THE ICCPR IN INTERNATIONAL LAW[213]

1.34 The most signally important feature of the ICCPR is that it is a universal instrument which contains binding legal obligations for the States parties to it.[214] The rights enshrined within it represent the basic minimum set of civil and political rights recognized by the world community. The fact that the ICCPR was adopted by more than one hundred States in 1966 and has been ratified by 92 States (as of 27 July 1990) from all of the geo-political regions of the world renders it less susceptible to criticism as being founded on a Western, individualistic, or alien philosophy.[215] Moreover, whatever the disagreement over the nature of the human rights obligations in the United Nations Charter[216] and in the Universal Declaration of Human Rights,[217] there is no doubt that the obligations in article 2 of the ICCPR to 'respect and ensure' the rights in the ICCPR are legally binding.[218] The debate over the precise effect of those obligations and the fact that there is no coercive mechanism to enforce those obligations does not alter this conclusion.[219]

1.35 The ICCPR is also of significance with respect to the standards required of States in the treatment of aliens.[220] It is a controversial question of international law as to whether an alien is entitled to the protection of an 'international minimum standard' of treatment or only to equality of treatment with the nationals of the State concerned, that is, 'national treatment'.[221] However, most of the rights in the ICCPR are stated to be applicable to 'everyone', or to 'all persons', or 'every human being'. As Professor Lillich has commented, 'The inescapable conclusion is that aliens are generally covered'.[222] Further support for this conclusion can be adduced from the non-discrimination and equality provisions of articles 2(1) and 26 of the

ICCPR and the provision in article 16 ICCPR that, 'Everyone shall have the right to recognition as a person before the law'. Articles 12 and 13 concerning freedom of movement and the expulsion of aliens lawfully within the State's territory are clearly of specific concern to aliens. Conversely, the article 25 guarantee of certain political rights is extended only to 'every citizen'. Clearly then an alien may be entitled to a greater measure of protection under the ICCPR than under general international law and the ICCPR may itself contribute to the further development of customary international law concerning aliens.[223] Finally in this respect attention should be drawn to the fact that communications under the OP may be submitted by 'individuals subject to [the] jurisdiction [of the] State party' (article 1 OP). This clearly includes aliens, and indeed, communications from aliens have been considered by the HRC.[224]

1.36 The ICCPR may well be of some significance even for States which are not party to it. This argument is based on the view that at least some of the provisions in the ICCPR reflect norms of customary international law and are therefore binding on States on that basis.[225] It could also be argued that the provisions of the ICCPR are declaratory of the law laid down in the United Nations Charter and therefore bind the members of the UN on that basis.[226] Although there is a clear historical link between the UN Charter and the International Bill of Rights[227] it is difficult to sustain this declaratory theory particularly as the complex of rights and limitations in the ICCPR have only been accepted by just over half of the members of the UN. It is submitted that the link between the ICCPR and the UN Charter is not sufficiently strong to justify recourse to the latter to impose the obligations of the ICCPR on non-States parties. A further argument on which the applicability of the ICCPR to non-States parties could be based is that certain of its provisions may reflect 'the general principles of law recognized by civilized nations'.[228] This argument may be more acceptable with respect to particular provisions of the ICCPR than the declaratory theory noted above.[229]

1.37 The status of the ICCPR in international law is also important from the perspective of domestic law.[230] According to the particular constitutional system of a State it may be open to an individual to invoke the ICCPR as directly applicable superior law or as persuasive authority as regards the interpretation of constitutional, legislative, and administrative provisions.[231] The provisions of the ICCPR are increasingly being invoked in this manner in, for example, Australia,[232] Canada,[233] Federal Republic of Germany,[234] France,[235] India,[236] The Netherlands,[237] New Zealand,[238] the United Kingdom,[239] the United States,[240] Norway,[241] and Yugoslavia.[242] Similarly national commentators have attempted to compare domestic provisions with standards established in the ICCPR in, for example, Canada,[243] Australia,[244] India and Finland,[245] Japan,[246] New Zealand,[247] the USSR,[248] the US,[249] and the UK.[250]

1.38 As a basic universal standard the ICCPR is frequently invoked in resolutions of the General Assembly of the United Nations,[251] the reports[252] and resolutions[253] of the United Nations human rights bodies, regional institutions,[254] and national Parliaments.[255] It is also interesting to note the reference to the ICCPR in the Final Act of the Conference on Security and Co-operation in Europe (the Helsinki Final Act)[256] and in the Treaty between the United Kingdom and China concerning Hong Kong.[257] The ICCPR is often used as the standard by which to measure and assess the human rights performance of States[258] and as the starting point for the development of new international human rights instruments.[259]

1.39 Finally, it is useful to set the ICCPR in its international perspective both in terms of the rights established by it and its implementation procedures. As to the rights established we have already noted that the Covenants were intended to be a further development of the Universal Declaration of Human Rights (1948).[260] We have also drawn attention to the division of human rights into a set of civil and political rights and a set of economic, social, and cultural rights.[261] The two international covenants coexist with a myriad of international human rights instruments.[262] The official UN compilation contains sixty such instruments which detail human rights and provide for various implementation procedures.[263] Many of these instruments are of relevance to particular rights established in the ICCPR and reference has been made to them in the procedures established by the ICCPR.[264] However, the principal overlap in terms of rights covered lies at the regional level in the form of the American Declaration of the Rights and Duties of Man (1948),[265] the American Convention on Human Rights (1969),[266] the European Convention for the Protection of Human Rights and Fundamental Freedoms (1950),[267] and most recently, the African Charter on Human and Peoples' Rights (1981).[268]

As regards implementation procedures there now exists a sophisticated range of organs and procedures with jurisdiction to implement the human rights provisions established in the international and regional instruments noted above.[269] For the purposes of this thesis the most instructive comparisons to be drawn are those concerning the work of the Inter-American Commission on Human Rights (IACM) and Court (IACT),[270] the European Commission of Human Rights (EUCM) and Court (EUCT),[271] and the Committee on the Elimination of Racial Discrimination (CERD) under the International Convention on the Elimination of Racial Discrimination.[272]

We begin our examination of the practices and procedures developed under the ICCPR by considering the permanent body established by the ICCPR: the *Human Rights Committee.*

NOTES

1 This account is mainly drawn from the following United Nations records. The Reports of the Human Rights Commission, 1947–54: 1st session, UN Doc. E/259, ECOSOC OR, fourth session, Supp. 3, (1947); 2nd session, UN Doc. E/600, ECOSOC OR, sixth session, Supp. 1, (1948); 3rd session, UN Doc. E/800, ECOSOC OR, seventh session, Supp. 2, (1948); 5th session, UN Doc. E/1371, ECOSOC OR, ninth session, Supp. 10, (1949); 6th session, UN Doc. E/1681, ECOSOC OR, eleventh session, Supp. 5, (1950); 7th session, UN Doc. E/1992, ECOSOC OR, thirteenth session, Supp. 9 (1951); 8th session, UN Doc. E/2256, ECOSOC OR, fourteenth session, Supp. 4 (1952); 9th session, UN Doc. E/2447, ECOSOC OR, sixteenth session, Supp. 8, (1953); 10th session, UN Doc. E/2573, ECOSOC OR, eighteenth session, Supp. 7 (1954). An excellent annotation of the work of the HRCion can be found at UN Doc. A/2929, 10 GAOR, Annexes, Agenda Item 28, Part II (1955).

From 1954 to 1966 the draft Covenants were considered by the Third Committee of the General Assembly. For its Reports see the following UN Documents: A/2808 and Corr. 1, 9 GAOR, Annexes, Ag. Item 58, part I, (1954); A/2907, 10 GAOR, Annexes, Ag. Item 28, part I (1955); A/3077, 10 GAOR, Annexes, Ag. Item 28, part I (1955); A/3525, 11 GAOR, Annexes, Ag. Item 31 (1956); A/3764, and Corr. 1, 12 GAOR, Annexes, Ag. Item 33 (1957); A/4045, 13 GAOR, Annexes, Ag. Item 32 (1958); A/4299, 14 GAOR, Annexes, Ag. Item 34 (1959); A/4625, 15 GAOR, Annexes, Ag. Item 34 (1960–1); A/5000, 16 GAOR, Annexes, Ag. Item 35 (1961–2); A/5365, 17 GAOR, Annexes, Ag. Item 43 (1962); A/5655, 18 GAOR, Annexes, Ag. Item 48 (1963), which is accompanied by A/5411, a Report of the Secretary-General updating A/2929 above; A/6173, 20 GAOR, Annexes, Ag. Item 65 (1966); A/6546, 21 GAOR, Annexes, Ag. Item 62 (1966).

There is an extensive literature dealing with the matters dealt with in this chapter. See H. O. Agarwal *Implementation of Human Rights Covenants with Special Reference to India* (1983); A. Cassese, *International Law in a Divided World*, ch. 11 (1986); R. Chakravarti, *Human Rights and the United Nations* (1958); R. Cohen, 'International Covenant on Civil and Political Rights', 6 International Problems (1968) pp. 38–49; A. L. Del Russo, *International Protection of Human Rights*, chs. 1–3 (1971); P. N. Drost, *Human Rights as Legal Rights—The Realization of Human Rights in Positive International Law* (1951, 1965); G. Ezejiofor, *Protection of Human Rights under the Law*, chs. 2–3 (1964); T. J. Farer, 'The United Nations and Human Rights: More Than a Whimper Less Than a Roar', 9 HRQ (1987) pp. 550–85; D. P. Forsythe, 'The United Nations and Human Rights', 100 Pol. SQ (1985) pp. 249–69; M. Ganji, *International Protection of Human Rights* (1962); J. F. Green, *The United Nations and Human Rights*, chs. 1–3 (1956); W. P. Gormley, 'The Implementation of United Nations Human Rights Covenants: Contemporary Legal Precedent and Future Procedural Remedies', 3 vols., (Ph.D. thesis, Manchester, 1972); W. Korey, 'The Key to Human Rights—Implementation', 570 International Conciliation (Nov. 1968) pp. 5–70; L. Henkin, 'Introduction', to L. Henkin (ed.), *The International Bill of Rights—The Covenant on Civil and Political Rights*, pp. 1–31 (1981); J. P. Humphrey, *Human Rights and the United Nations—A Great Adventure* (1984); Fareed Nabiel Jamiel, *The United Nations Commission on Human Rights and its Work for Human Rights and Fundamental Freedoms* chs. 1 and 3 (1979); F. Jhabvala, 'The Practice of the Covenants' Human Rights Committee 1976–82: Review of State Party Reports', 6 HRQ (1984) p. 81 at pp. 81–95; H. Lauterpacht, *International Law and Human Rights*, Part II (1950); H. Lauterpacht, 'The International Protection of the Individual', in E. Lauterpacht (ed.), H. Lauterpacht, *International Law-Collected Papers*, Vol. iii, *The Law of Peace*, pp. 407–30 (1977); M. Lippman, 'Human Rights Revisited—the Protection of Human Rights under the ICCPR', 26 NILR (1979) pp. 221–77; E. Luard (ed.), *The International Protection of Human Rights*, chs. 1–4 (1967); M. S. McDougal and G. Bebr, 'Human Rights in the United Nations', 58 AJIL (1964) pp. 603–41; M. Moscowitz, *Human Rights and World Order—The Struggle for Human Rights* (1958); M. Moscowitz, *The Politics and Dynamics of Human Rights* (1968); M. Moscowitz, *International Concern with Human Rights*, ch. 1 (1974); M. Neal, 'The United Nations and Human Rights', 489 International Conciliation (Mar. 1953) pp. 111–74; V. Pechota, 'The Development of the Covenant on Civil and Political Rights', in Henkin (ed.), *The International Bill of Rights—The ICCPR*, above, ch. 2 (1981); A. H. Robertson and J. G. Merrills, *Human Rights in the World*, ch. 2 (3rd, 1989); P. Sieghart, *The International Law of Human Rights*, chs. 1 and 2 (1983); J. Simarsian, periodic notes on the drafting at 42 AJIL (1948) pp. 879–83, 43 AJIL (1949) pp. 779–86; 45 AJIL (1951) pp. 170–7; 46 AJIL (1952) pp. 710–18; L. B. Sohn, 'A Short History of United Nations Documents on Human Rights', in *The United Nations and Human Rights*, Eighteenth Report of the Commission to Study the Organization of Peace, pp. 39–186 (1968); E. Schwelb, 'Notes on the Early Legislative History of the Measures of Implementation of the Human Rights Covenants', in *Mélanges offerts à Polys Modinos*, pp. 270–89 (1968); E. Schwelb, 'Civil and Political Rights: The International Measures of Implementation', 62 AJIL (1968) pp. 827–68 (revised in 12 Tex. ILJ (1977) pp. 141–86); E. Schwelb, 'Some Aspects of the International Covenants on Civil and Political Rights 1966', in A. Eide and A. Schou (eds.), *The International Protection of Human Rights*, pp. 103–29 (1968); L. Sohn and T. Buergenthal, *International Protection of Human Rights*, pp. 505–56 (1973); I. Szabo, 'Historical Foundations of Human Rights and Subsequent Developments', in K. Vasak (ed.), P. Alston (English Edition, ed.), *The International Dimensions of Human Rights*, Vol. i, ch. 2, (1982); H. Tolley, Jr., *The U.N. Commission on Human Rights*, chs. 1–3 (1987); United Nations Action in the Field of Human Rights, UN Doc. ST/HR/2/Rev. 2, chs. 1 and 2 (1983); J. H. W. Verzijl, *International Law in Historical Perspective*, Vol. v, ch 4 (1972); Ton. J. M. Zuidjwick, *Petitioning the United Nations—A Study in Human Rights*, ch. 1, A, sections 7–10 (1982).

2 Traditional international law is taken as all international law (both customary and conventional) predating the UN Charter in 1945.

3 See in particular Chakravarti, n. 1 above, ch. 1; R. B. Lillich, *The Human Rights of Aliens in Contemporary International Law*, pp. 1–40 (1984); M. McDougal,

H. Lasswell, and L. C. Chen, *Human Rights and World Public Order*, pp. 473–508 (1980). For some examples of seventeenth- and eighteenth-century treaties providing for human rights protection see Verzijl, n. 1 above.

4 See in particular Sohn and Buergenthal, n. 1 above, ch. 3; Ganji, n. 1 above, ch. 1; R. Lillich, 'Forcible Self-Help to Protect Human Rights', 53 Iowa LR (1967) pp. 325–51; M. Akehurst, 'Humanitarian Intervention', in H. Bull (ed.), *Intervention in World Politics*, pp. 93–118 (1984); I. Pogany, 'Humanitarian Intervention in International Law: The French Intervention in Syria Re-examined', 35 ICLQ (1986) pp. 182–90; N. Ronzitti, *Rescuing Nationals Abroad Through Military Coercion and Intervention on Grounds of Humanity* (1985); F. R. Teson, *Humanitarian Intervention* (1988).

5 See Sohn and Buergenthal, n. 1 above, ch. 1; L. Oppenheim, *International Law*, H. Lauterpacht (ed.), pp. 636–42 (8th, 1955). A State could, however, assume legal obligations towards individuals by virtue of an international agreement. See the *Case Concerning the Jurisdiction of the Courts of Danzig*, PCIJ Series B, No. 15 (1928). For a recent view see R. Higgins, 'Conceptual Thinking about the Individual in International Law', 4 Brit JIS (1978) pp. 1–19, reprinted in R. Falk *et al.* (eds.), *International Law—A Contemporary Perspective*, pp. 476–94 (1985).

6 See Ganji, n. 1 above, ch. 3; Robertson and Merrills, n. 1 above, pp. 14–16. For more recent developments see *UN Action in the Field of Human Rights*, UN Doc. ST/HR/2/Rev. 3, ch. 8, B (1988); 'Slavery', UN Doc. E/CN. 4/Sub. 2/1982/20/Rev. 1 (1984), updating report by B. Whittaker; K. Zoglin, 'U.N. Action against Slavery: A Critical Evaluation', 8 HRQ (1986) pp. 306–39.

7 See F. Capotorti, 'Human Rights: The Hard Road Towards Universality', in R. St. J. MacDonald and D. M. Johnstone (eds.), *The Structure and Process of International Law*, pp. 977–1000 at p. 978 (1984).

8 See Humphrey, n. 1 above, p. 46 (1984); Humphrey, 'The World Revolution and Human Rights', in A. Gotlieb (ed.), *Human Rights, Federalism and Minorities*, pp. 147–79 (1970); L. B. Sohn, 'The New International Law: Protection of the Rights of Individuals Rather Than States', 32 Am. ULR (1982) pp. 1–64.

9 The League of Nations Covenant does not specifically mention human rights but some important international developments did take place concerning limited areas of human rights matters, see Green n. 1 above, pp. 8–13.

10 See Sohn and Buergenthal, n. 1 above, ch. 5.

11 See. E. A. Landy, *The Effectiveness of International Supervision—Thirty Years of I.L.O. Experience* (1966); N. Valticos, 'The I.L.O.', in Vasak Alston (eds.), n. 1 above, pp. 363–99; F. Wolf, 'Human Rights and the I.L.O.', in T. Meron (ed.), *Human Rights in International Law—Legal and Policy Issues*, pp. 273–304 (1984).

12 See P. De Azcarate, *League of Nations and National Minorities—An Experiment* (1945); Sohn and Buergenthal, n. 1 above, ch. 4; Ganji, n. 1 above, ch. 2; J. F. Green, 'Protection of Minorities in the League of Nations and the United Nations', in Gotlieb (ed.), n. 8 above, pp. 180–210; W. McKean, *Equality and Discrimination under International Law*, chs. 1 and 2 (1983).

13 87 Congressional Record, Pt. I, pp. 46–7 (77th Congress, 1st session).

14 For the text see 36 AJIL Supplement (1942) pp. 191–2. 27 other countries later

adhered to the Declaration, see UN Yearbook (1946–7), p. 1. Mention should also be made of the influential 'Declaration of The Rights of Man' adopted by the Institute of International Law in 1929, see 35 AJIL (1941), pp. 662–5; and Professor Lauterpacht's work, *International Bill of Rights*, (1945).

15 Text in Brownlie, *Basic Documents in International Law*, pp. 1–34 (3d, 1983).

16 See Green, n. 1 above, p. 13. See also the Atlantic Charter (1941), 35 AJIL (1941), Supp. p. 191, and the second preambular paragraph of the UN Charter.

17 See Humphrey, n. 1 above (1984), pp. 12–13.

18 See Huston, n. 25 below.

19 See ch. 9, sect. A (I) of the Dumbarton Oaks Proposals, UNCIO iv, 13. Text in L. M. Goodrich, E. Hambro, and A. P. Simons, *Charter of the United Nations*, p. 664 at p. 672 (3d, 1969).

20 See Green, n. 1 above, p. 16 and n. 17 above.

21 See Green, n. 1 above, pp. 15–23.

22 Cf. R. St. J. MacDonald, 'The United Nations Charter: Constitution or Contract', in R. St. J. MacDonald and D. M. Johnstone (eds.), n. 7 above, pp. 889–912.

23 Articles 1(3), 13(1)(*b*), 55(*c*) (and see article 56), 62, 68, and 76.

24 Many of the works cited in n. 1 above deal with this question. See also E. Schwelb, 'The International Court of Justice and the Human Rights Clauses of the Charter', 66 AJIL (1972) pp. 337–51; N. Singh, *Enforcement of Human Rights in Peace and War and the Future of Humanity*, pp. 20–36 (1986); L. Sohn, 'The Human Rights Law of the Charter', 12 Tex. ILJ (1977) pp. 129–40; R. Lillich and F. Newman, *International Human Rights—Problems of Law and Policy*, problems 1 and 2 (1979); *Case Concerning United States Diplomatic and Consular Staff in Tehran*, ICJ Reports (1980), p. 3.

25 See e.g. UNCIO, Vol. i, p. 425 (proposal of South Africa); UNCIO, Vol. iii, pp. 266–9 (Panama); UNCIO, Vol. iii, pp. 64, 70, 91 (Mexico). See J. Huston, 'Human Rights Enforcement Issues at the United Nations Conference on International Organization', 53 Iowa LR (1967), pp. 272–90.

26 *Charter of the United Nations—Report to the President*, p. 118 (1945, reprint 1969). See also UNCIO, Vol. i, p. 683 (President Truman).

27 The establishment and work of the Human Rights Commission is dealt with in a number of works in n. 1 above. In particular see those by Lauterpacht, Jamiel, Tolley, and Zuidjwick. A Panamanian proposal that the first General Assembly adopt a Declaration on Human Rights was not adopted, see GA Resn. 43 (I), 11 Dec. 1946.

28 See ECOSOC Resns. 5(I) and 9(II), ECOSOC OR, 1st year, 2nd session, pp. 400–2 (1946).

29 See n. 1 above.

30 Doc. E/259, n. 1 above. See Humphrey, n. 1 above, pp. 23–8.

31 See A. J. Glen Mower, Jr., *The U.S., the U.N. and Human Rights—The Eleanor Roosevelt and Jimmy Carter Eras*, Part I (1979); M. G. Johnson, 'The Contributions of Eleanor and Franklin Roosevelt to the Development of International Protection of Human Rights', 9 HRQ (1987) pp. 19–48.

32 On the legal status of a Declaration see *UN Action*, n. 1 above, p. 318.

33 For details see Humphrey, n. 1 above.

34 See UN Human Rights Yearbook, 1947, p. 484.

35 See Doc. E/CN.4/56; E/CN.4/AC.3/SR.1–9 (1947).

36 See Doc. E/CN.4/21, Ax. H, pp. 68–74, Report of the Drafting Committee (1947).

37 Doc. E/600, n. 1 above, pr. 18.

38 Ibid., annexes (A–C). The representative of the Ukrainian SSR withdrew from the working group on implementation on the basis that the question of implementation demanded previous knowledge of the rules to be implemented. It is interesting to note the measures of implementation proposed at this stage in annex III. It was agreed that the primary responsibility for the enforcement should be at the State level and that each state should be under an obligation to incorporate (in the sense of giving effect through national laws and practices) the provisions of the Covenant. This basic principle survived to become article 2 of the ICCPR. See ch. 6 below. Disputes concerning alleged violations were to be referred to a Standing Mediation and Conciliation Committee, appointed by the ECOSOC, which would provide a remedy if possible. Disputes not settled by this Committee would be sent to the HRCion, which would decide whether the dispute should be referred to an international tribunal to be created. The decisions of that tribunal were to be binding on the States parties and were to be implemented by the General Assembly.

39 Doc. E/800, n. 1 above.

40 UN ECOSOC OR, 7th session, Vol. i (1948), pp. 642–60, 694–702.

41 GA Resn, 217(A), GAOR, 3rd session, Part I, Resolutions, p. 71. See Green, n. 1 above, pp. 24–37; Tolley, n. 1 above, pp. 19–24; P. Alston, 'The Universal Declaration at 35', 31 Rev. ICJ (Dec. 1983) pp. 60–70; H. Lauterpacht (1950), n. 1 above, pp. 394–428; B. G. Ramcharan (ed.), *Thirty Years after the Universal Declaration* (1979); id., *The Concept and Present Status of the International Protection of Human Rights—Forty Years After The Universal Declaration* (1989); The Proclamation of Tehran (1968), *Human Rights—A Compilation of International Instruments*, pp. 43–6 (1988).

42 GA Resns. 217B and E (III) (1948).

43 See Doc. E/1371, n. 1 above. New articles were proposed concerning economic and social rights. See also the survey prepared by the UN Secretary-General of the activities of UN organs and Specialized Agencies falling within the scope of articles 22–7 UDHR which cover economic and social rights, Doc. E/CN.4/364.

44 That questionnaire itself constitutes an interesting document, see Doc. E/1371, n. 1 above, Ax. III, pt. II.

45 See UN Docs. E/1371, n. 1 above and E/CN.4/SR 118. It is interesting to note the voting pattern at this stage. The following States voted for a resolution laying down that a right of petition by individuals, groups, and organizations should be recognized forthwith in the Covenant: Australia, Denmark, France, Guatemala, India, Lebanon, the Philippines, and Uruguay. The following States voted against: China, Egypt, Iran, the Ukraine, the USSR, the UK, the US, and Yugoslavia.

46 Note also the negative position taken by the HRCion itself that it had no jurisdiction to take any action with regard to complaints concerning human rights. That

position was maintained until the late 1960s. See Zuidjwick, n. 1 above; Tolley, n. 1 above, pp. 16–19 and ch. 4.

47 Doc. E/1681, n. 1 above.

48 Ibid., prs. 34–50. Humphrey, n. 1 above, comments that, 'It was clear from the voting patterns that opposition to an effective right of petition was hardening', p. 108.

49 'To this end it should collect information, including legislation and judicial decisions, regarding the observance within States parties to the Covenant, of human rights as defined in the Covenant, and initiate an inquiry if it thought it necessary', Doc. E/1681, pr. 43.

50 Doc. E/1681, n. 1 above, prs. 34–46 and Ax. I.

51 Ibid., prs. 29–33.

52 See ECOSOC OR, 11th session, SR 377–9 and E/CN.4/AC.7/SR.139–57 and 159.

53 ECOSOC Resn. 303I (XI). See Humphrey, n. 1 above, pp. 119–33. A bitter debate ensued at ECOSOC's 12th session on receipt of the GA's policy decisions, ECOSOC OR, 12th session (1951), SR. 438–42.

54 GA Resn. 421C (V) (1950). For some contemporary views see Y. L. Laing, 'Colonial and Federal Clauses in U.N. Multilateral Instruments', 45 AJIL (1951) pp. 108–28; Lauterpacht (1950), n. 1 above, pp. 359–65; M. Sorensen, 'Federal States and the International Protection of Human Rights', 46 AJIL (1952) pp. 195–218. See also Johnson, n. 31 above, pp. 41–4.

55 See article 50 ICCPR and article 10 OP. Similarly in article 9 of OP2.

56 GA Resn. 422 (V), (1950). See Doc. A/2929, n. 1 above, ch. 1, pr. 21.

57 See Doc. A/6546, n. 1 above, prs. 131–8.

58 GA Resn. 421D (V), (1950).

59 Humphrey, n. 1 above, p. 129.

60 GA Resn. 421E (V), (1950). Humphrey, n. 1 above, notes that, 'After the British defeat in the United Nations (when it was decided to include economic and social rights in the Covenant), the Government was considering not only abandoning the Covenant but withdrawing from the Commission', p. 145.

61 GA Resn. 421F (V), (1950).

62 See n. 45 above and ch. 4 below.

63 Doc. E/1992, n. 1 above.

64 A State party could, however, refer to a report which it had submitted to a Specialized Agency.

65 ECOSOC Resn. 384 (XIII), ECOSOC OR, 13th session.

66 GA Resn. 543 (VI), (1952), GAOR, 6th session, Supp. 20 (A/2199), p. 36. See Humphrey, n. 1 above who comments that, 'The largely ideological controversy and decision split the United Nations down the middle', pp. 129, 160.

67 GA Resn. 545 (VI). See Humphrey, n. 1 above, p. 163.

68 Doc. E/2256, n. 1 above. Humphrey, ibid., pp. 167–8.

69 Doc. E/2447, n. 1 above.

70 The proposed nine-member Human Rights Committee was to be chosen for five-year terms by the International Court of Justice from nominations made by States parties to the Covenant.

71 Draft article 48, Doc. E/2447, n. 1 above, p. 48. The GA at its eighth session (1953) discussed the questions of a federal State article and a right of petition but made no policy decision on either question.

72 See Doc. E/2573, n. 1 above.

73 This draft provision became article 23(4) ICCPR.

74 Doc. E/2573, n. 1 above, draft article 49 (my emphasis). It was argued that the HRCion was a more appropriate body to receive reports as the proposed Human Rights Committee would be a 'quasi-judicial' organ concerned with inter-State complaints, ibid., pr. 178. It was explained that the words 'general recommendations' had been taken from the system of periodic reports adopted for inclusion in the draft Covenant on economic, social, and cultural rights, ibid., prs. 124, 128, 132, and 181.

75 Ibid., prs. 215–25. Proposals to that effect were withdrawn.

76 See text to note 55 above.

77 For the text of the HRCions final draft see Doc. E/2573, n. 1 above.

78 GAOR, 9th session, Third Committee, SR. 557–86; Plenary Meetings, SR. 504. See GA Resn. 833 (IX), Doc. A/2929, n. 1 above, ch. 1, pr. 50.

79 GA Resn. 1843B (XVII) of 19 Dec. (1962). For the Secretary-General's paper see Doc. E/5411, n. 1 above.

80 See in particular Jhabvala, n. 1 above, and ch. 3 below. The changes made by the Third Committee were accepted by the General Assembly in 1966.

81 This procedure is examined in detail in ch. 3 below.

82 See n. 73 above.

83 Doc. E/6546, n. 1 above, prs. 541–3. See n. 71 above, and Green, n. 1 above, p. 53.

84 See n. 74 above.

85 Ibid.

86 On the HRC and Specialized Agencies see ch. 3, prs. 3.13–3.16 below.

87 See Doc. A/2929, n. 1 above, ch. 7, prs. 59–98; Doc. E/6546, n. 1 above, prs. 398–436; n. 48 above.

88 ICJ Rep. 1966, p. 6. See n. 70 above; n. 91 below; Pechota, n. 1 above, p. 62; Korey, ibid., p. 56; Cf. article 22 ICERD (1965).

89 This procedure is examined in detail in ch. 4 below.

90 On the HRC see ch. 2 below.

91 See Doc. A/6546, n. 1 above, prs. 188–303.

92 The ICESCR was adopted by 105 votes to none; the ICCPR by 106 votes to none. The OP to the ICCPR was adopted by 66 votes to 2 with 38 abstentions. See UN Yearbook, 1966, p. 418; UN Juridical Yearbook, 1966, pp. 69–70, 170–95. The ICCPR and the OP both entered into force on 23 March 1976.

93 See F. Newman, 'The International Bill of Rights: Does it Exist?', in A. Cassese (ed.), *Current Problems of International Law*, pp. 107–16 (1975); C. W. Jenks, 'The United Nations Covenants on Human Rights Come to Life', in *Recueil d'études en hommage à Paul Guggenheim*, pp. 805–13 (1968); E. Schwelb, 'Entry into Force of the International Covenants on Human Rights and the Optional Protocol', 70 AJIL (1976) pp. 511–19.

94 See M. Bossuyt, *A Guide to the Travaux Préparatoires to the ICCPR and OP*

(1987). The HRC have had recourse to the *travaux préparatoires* on a number of occasions.

95 See in particular Humphrey, n. 1 above and ch. 2 prs. 2.16–2.17 below. A number of Specialized Agencies also contributed to the drafting of the Covenants. These included the ILO, UNESCO, WHO. The Commission on the Status of Women, and the Sub-Commission on the Prevention of Discrimination and the Protection of Minorities also had an input. On the HRC and Specialized Agencies see ch. 3, prs. 3.13–3.16 below.

96 The representatives attending each session of the HRCion are recorded in the reports of the HRCion, n. 1 above.

97 See n. 17 above.

98 For some of the roles played by NGOs see P. Archer, 'Action by Unofficial Organizations on Human Rights', in E. Luard (ed.), n. 1 above, pp. 160–82; J. D. Armstrong, 'Non-Governmental Organizations', in R. J. Vincent (ed.), *Foreign Policy and Human Rights*, pp. 243–60 (1986); C. Desmond, *Persecution East and West: Human Rights, Political Prisoners and Amnesty* (1983); M. Kamminga and N. S. Rodley, 'Direct Intervention at the U.N.: NGO Participation in the Commission on Human Rights and its Sub-Commission', in H. Hannum (ed.), *Guide to International Human Rights Practice*, ch. 11 (1984); V. Leary, 'A New Role for NGO's in Human Rights: A Case Study of NGO Participation in the Development of International Norms of Torture', in A. Cassese (ed.), *U.N. Law/ Fundamental Rights—Two Topics in International Law*, pp. 197–210 (1979); J. Shestack, 'Sisyphus Endures: The International Human Rights NGO', 24 NYSLR (1978) pp. 89–123; H. Thoolen and B. Verstappen, *Human Rights Missions* (1986); D. Weissbrodt, 'The Contribution of International NGO's to the Protection of Human Rights', in T. Meron (ed.), *Human Rights in International Law—Legal and Policy Issues*, ch. 11 (1984); id., 'The Role of International NGO's in the Implementation of Human Rights', 12 Tex. ILJ (1977) pp. 293–320; id., 'Fact-Finding by NGOs', in B. Ramcharan (ed.), *International Law and Fact-Finding in the Field of Human Rights*, ch. 9 (1982). On the HRC and NGOs see ch. 3, prs. 3.17–3.18 below.

99 See Doc. A/2929, n. 1 above, ch. 2, prs. 4–12; Pechota, ibid., pp. 41–3; Green, ibid., pp. 39–42; Neal, ibid., pp. 126–9; Th. C. Van Boven, 'Distinguishing Criteria of Human Rights', in Vasak, Alston (eds.), ibid., pp. 43–59.

100 See prs. 1.7–1.8 above.

101 Cf. the comments of the EUCT in *Airey* v. *Ireland*, Vol. 32, EUCT, Series A, pr. 26 (1979).

102 Generally see M. Bossuyt, 'La distinction juridique entre les droits civils et politiques et les droits économiques, sociaux et culturels', 8 RDH/HRJ (1975), pp. 783–820.

103 See Humphrey, n. 1 above, pp. 144 and 162. See e.g. E/CN.4/SR.273 p. 13.

104 At this time the HRCion proposal was for a compulsory inter-State complaints procedure for the ICCPR and a reporting procedure for the ICESCR. Note that the compulsory individual applications procedure and the optional inter-State complaint procedure under the American Convention on Human Rights (1970) (AMR) do apply to the economic, social, and cultural rights in Article 26 though

that Article is clearly in terms of progressive development, see T. Buergenthal, R. Norris, and D. Shelton, *Protecting Human Rights in the Americas* (2d, 1986). See now Article 19 of the 'Additional Protocol to the AMR in the Area of Economic, Social and Cultural Rights' which distinguishes two categories of protection, 28 ILM (1989) p. 156.

105 See e.g. D. Harris, *The European Social Charter*, pp. 268–72 (1984); A. Berenstein, 'Economic and Social Rights: Their Inclusion in the ECHR—Problems of Formulation and Interpretation', 2 HRLJ (1981), pp. 257–80; L. J. MacFarlane, *The Theory and Practice of Human Rights*, ch. 7 (1985); P. Sieghart, *The Lawful Rights of Mankind*, pp. 81–4 (1985). See the important GA Resn. 32/130 (16 Dec. 1977) discussed by B. Ramcharan, 'A Critique of Third World Responses to Violations of Human Rights', in A. Cassese (ed.), (1979), n. 98 above, pp. 249–58; Principle 6 of the Draft Principles on Responsibility, n. 187 below. Note that the African Charter of Human and Peoples Rights draws no distinction between categories of rights, see n. 268 below.

106 See chs. 3–12 below.

107 See Report of the Sessional Working Group on the Implementation of the ICESCR, Doc. E/CN.4/1981/64 (1981). See 27 Rev. ICJ (1981) pp. 26–39; Alston, n. 108 below.

108 See P. Alston, 'Out of the Abyss: The Challenge Confronting the New U.N. Committee on Economic, Social and Cultural Rights', 9 HRQ (1987) pp. 332–81; P. Alston and B. Simma, 'First Session of the UN Committee on Economic, Social and Cultural Rights', 81 AJIL (1987) pp. 747–56; id., 'Second Session of the UN CESCR', 82 AJIL (1988) pp. 603–15. Anon., 'UN Committee on Economic, Social and Cultural Rights', 42 Rev. ICJ (1989) pp. 33–9.

109 See prs. 1.7–1.8 above. Note that almost every State that has ratified the ICCPR has also ratified the ICESCR.

110 See the Report of the Working Group on Implementation, Doc. E/600, n. 1 above, prs. 26–7; Doc. A/2929, ibid., ch. 7, prs. 162, 165; UN Doc. A/5655, ibid., pr. 21. See also the literature cited in ch. 6, n. 1 below.

111 See Doc. A/2929, n. 1 above, ch. 5, pr. 10; Doc. A/5655, ibid., pr. 21.

112 See Doc. E/2573, n. 1 above, prs. 171–205.

113 This view was supported by a Legal Opinion submitted by the Secretary-General at the request of a drafting Committee of the HRCion, see UN Doc. E/CN.4/116 (1948).

114 UN Doc. A/2929, n. 1 above, ch. 5, pr. 8.

115 See E. W. Vierdag, 'The Legal Nature of the Rights Granted in the ICESCR', 9 NYIL (1979) pp. 69–105; G. J. H. Van Hoof, 'The Legal Nature of Economic, Social and Cultural Rights: A Rebuttal of some Traditional Views', in P. Alston and K. Tomasevski (eds.), *The Right to Food*, pp. 97–110 (1984).

116 See UN Doc. A/5655, n. 1 above, pr. 23. See also O. Schacter, 'The Obligation to Implement the Covenant in Domestic Law', in Henkin (ed.), n. 1 above, p. 311 and p. 325.

117 See ch. 6 below.

118 This matter is dealt with in many of the works cited in n. 1 above. See e.g. Green, pp. 50–3; P. Sieghart, *The Lawful Rights of Mankind*, ch. 10 (1985).

119 See n. 38 above. P. Sieghart, n. 118 above, ch. 9. It was frequently proposed during the drafting that States parties be obliged to establish national human rights commissions to review the national provisions for the protection of the rights in the Covenant and report to the Head of State and to the Government. The proposals were not adopted and the question was submitted for further study to the HRCion, see UN Doc. A/6546, prs. 557–61, 613–26. For subsequent developments see *UN Action in the Field of Human Rights*, n. 6 above, pp. 347–9; Report of the Secretary-General, 'National Institutions for the Promotion and Protection of Human Rights', Doc. E/CN.4/1987/37.

120 With the exception of Yugoslavia. See e.g. the USSR statement with regard to the drafts and proposals on implementation of 18 May 1948, in Doc. E/1371, n. 1 above, pp. 47–8. See Ganji, n. 1 above, pp. 186–9; F. Jhabvala, 'The Soviet Bloc's View of the Implementation of Human Rights Accords', 7 HRQ (1985) pp. 461–91; V. Kartashkin, 'The Socialist Countries and Human Rights', in K. Vasak, P. Alston (eds.), n. 1 above, pp. 631–50. The soviet bloc was, however, willing to accept an international system of implementation for the right of peoples to self-determination, see UN Doc. E/CN.4/SR.476, and notes 71 and 83 above.

121 On this fundamental question see R. Bernhardt, 'Domestic Jurisdiction of States and International Human Rights Organs', 7 HRLJ (1987) pp. 205–16: F. Ermacora, 'Human Rights and Domestic Jurisdiction', 124 Receuil de cours, 1968–I, pp. 371–415; J. Fawcett, 'Human Rights and Domestic Jurisdiction', in E. Luard (ed.), n. 1 above, pp. 286–303; G. J. Jones, *The United Nations and the Domestic Jurisdiction of States*, ch. 3 (1979); R. Higgins, *The Development of International Law through the Political Organs of the United Nations*, Part II, particularly at pp. 118–39 (1963); L. Henkin, 'Human Rights and Domestic Jurisdiction', in T. Buergenthal (ed.), *Human Rights, International Law and the Helsinki Accords*, pp. 21–40 (1970); H. Lauterpacht, *International Law and Human Rights*, ch. 12 (1950); H. Kelsen, *The Law of the United Nations*, pp. 27–50 (1950); M. Markovic, 'Implementation of Human Rights and the Domestic Jurisdiction of States', in Eide and Schou (eds.), n. 1 above, pp. 47–68; J. S. Watson, 'Autointerpretation, Competence and the Continuing Validity of Article 2(7) of the U.N. Charter', 71 AJIL (1977) pp. 60–83; M. Bossuyt, 'Human Rights and Non-Intervention in Domestic Matters', 35 Rev. ICJ (1985) pp. 45–52; See also Principle 42 of the Draft Principles on Responsibility, n. 187 below.

122 See R. Falk, *Human Rights and State Sovereignty* (1981); H. Lauterpacht, 'State Sovereignty and Human Rights', in H. Lauterpacht, *International Law*, E. Lauterpacht (ed.), Vol. iii, pp. 416–30 (1977).

123 See Doc. E/600, n. 1 above, pp. 43–44; Humphrey, ibid., pp. 37–49.

124 Australia was the leading proponent of this view. See, e.g. Doc. E/1371, n. 1 above, pp. 36–49 (1949); Doc. E/2573, Ax. III.

125 See Korey, n. 1 above, pp. 59–64; Humphrey, ibid., p. 130. See R. S. Clark, *A United Nations Commissioner for Human Rights* (1972).

126 Doc. A/2929, n. 1 above, prs. 87–9 (India).

127 The respective arguments are briefly rehearsed in ch. 4, prs. 4.2–4.3 below.

128 See pr. 1.6 above.

129 See n. 127 above.

130 See pr. 1.22 below and ch. 6 below.

131 See Pechota, n. 1 above, pp. 63–4. For a political history of part of the period see E. Luard, *A History of the United Nations, Vol. 1: The Years of Western Domination* (1982). See also J. F. Green, 'Changing Approaches to Human Rights: The U.N. 1954 and 1974', 12 Tex. ILJ (1977) pp. 223–38.

132 See Green, n. 1 above, pp. 65–7, and n. 41 above.

133 Note that the ICERD (1965) contains a mandatory reporting procedure (art 9), a mandatory inter-state complaint procedure (arts 11–13), and an optional provision on individual communications (art. 14). Humphrey, n. 1 above, suggests that their inclusion without substantial objection can be explained in terms of the UN's preoccupation with discrimination, pp. 331–4. A petition system relating to the implementation of the 1960 Declaration on the Granting of Independence to Colonial Countries and Peoples had also been established, see Zuidjwick, n. 1 above ch. 6.

134 See UN Doc. A/2929, n. 1 above, ch. 4; Doc. E/2256, ibid., prs. 27–77; Doc. E/CN.4/SR. 252–66; UN Doc. A/3077, n. 1 above prs. 27–77; see A/C.3/SR.562–73, 575, 578, 580–2 (9th session), SR 641–55, 667–76 (10th session); Ganji, ibid., pp. 192–203; Green, ibid., pp. 48–50; Humphrey, ibid., pp. 165–9; Chakravarti, ibid., ch. 4. See also ch. 5 below.

135 See pr. 1.7 above.

136 The important 'Declaration on the Granting of Independence to Colonial Countries and Peoples', GA Resn. 1514 (XV) had been adopted in 1960.

137 The central problem of GA Resn. 1514 is the conflict between self-determination of the people and the maintenance of the sovereignty and territorial integrity of the State. For a recent view see K. W. Blay, 'Self-Determination Versus Territorial Integrity in Decolonization Revisited', 25 Ind. JIL (1985) pp. 386–410.

138 See e.g. A. Cassese, 'The Self-Determination of Peoples', in Henkin (ed.) (1981), n. 1 above, p. 92 at 96; n. 134 above. This does not necessarily mean that a minority cannot have a right to self-determination. That depends on whether or not they constitute a 'people' and that in itself is a most difficult question.

139 On art. 27 see L. Sohn, 'The Rights of Minorities', in Henkin (ed.) (1981), n. 1 above, pp. 270–89; F. Capotorti, 'Study on the Rights of Persons Belonging to Ethnic, Religious and Linguistic Minorities', Doc. E/CN.4/Sub. 2/384/Rev. 1. (1979).

140 See Doc. E/2556, n. 1 above, pr. 67 (proposal of Chile), Doc. E/2573, ibid., prs. 62, 65–6. See Humphrey, n. 1 above, p. 167. In 1962 the General Assembly had adopted an important resolution on 'Permanent Sovereignty over Natural Resources', GA Resn. 1803 (XVII), A/5217, GAOR, 17th session, Supp. 17. See also GA Resn. 2158 (XXI) of 25 Nov. 1966; 'The Declaration on the Establishment of a New International Economic Order', GA Resn. 3201 (S–VI), 1 May 1974; and the 'Charter of Economic Rights and Duties of States', GA Resn. 3281 (XXIX), 1974. For recent works on this subject see G. Elian, *The Principle of Sovereignty over Natural Resources* (1979), K. Hossain and S. R. Chowdhury, *Permanent Sovereignty over Natural Resources in International Law—Principle and Practice* (1984).

141 See Doc. A/3077, n. 1 above.

142 An identical text appears in article 25 ICESCR.

143 See Doc. A/6546, n. 1 above, prs. 95–101.

144 See K. P. Saskena, 'International Covenants on Human Rights', 15–16 Ind. YIA (1970) pp. 596–613 at p. 602; Y. Dinstein, 'Collective Rights of Peoples and Minorities', 25 ICLQ (1976) pp. 102–20 at p. 110–11; E. Schwelb in Eide and Schou (eds.), n. 1 above, p. 112; D. Halperin, 'Human Rights and Natural Resources', 9 William and Mary Law Review (1968) pp. 770–87.

145 For comment see e.g. Ganji, n. 1 above, pp. 192–203. We have already noted that a different implementation mechanism was proposed at one time in the HRCion for the right of peoples to self-determination, see notes 71 and 83 above.

146 See ch. 5 below.

147 Ibid.

148 See ch. 5, prs. 5.20–5.23 below. However, the effect of the view of the HRC in *Lubicon Lake Band v. Canada* (1990) is to take the right of self-determination out of the OP system, see ch. 5, pr. 5.22 below.

149 See ch. 5 below.

150 See pr. 1.7 above; Doc. A/2929, n. 1 above, ch. 10, prs. 8–12, 13–20; Green, n. 1 above, pp. 53–9.

151 See ch. 6 below.

152 See Doc. A/2929, n. 1 above, ch. 10, prs. 25–39; Doc. E/2573, ibid., prs. 28–33, 274–301.

153 See article 2 of OP2. Cf. D. Shelton, 'State Practice on Reservations to Human Rights Treaties', 1983 CHRYB pp. 205–34.

154 See articles 19–23 VCLT (1969) on which see I. Sinclair, *The Vienna Convention on the Law of Treaties*, ch. 3 (2nd, 1984). Generally see the *Reservations to the Convention on Genocide Case*, ICJ Rep. (1951), p. 15; R. Higgins, 'Human Rights: Some Questions of Integrity', 52 MLR (1989) pp. 1–21 at pp. 11–17; P. H. Imbert, 'Reservations and Human Rights Conventions', 3 HR Rev. (1981) pp. 28–60; P. H. Imbert, 'Reservations to the European Convention on Human Rights before the Strasbourg Commission: The Temeltasch Case', 33 ICLQ (1984) pp. 558–95; D. Shelton, n. 153 above; S. Marks, 'Reservations unhinged: the *Belilos* Case before the EUCT', 39 ICLQ (1990) pp. 300–27.

155 See 'Reservations, Declarations, Notifications and Objections Relating to the International Covenant on Civil and Political Rights and the Optional Protocol Thereto', Note by the Secretary-General, Doc. CCPR/C/2/Rev. 2 (12 May 1989). *Human Rights—Status of International Instruments*, pp. 25–94 (1987).

156 Ibid.

157 This question has been raised within the HRC but no formal decision has been taken, see ch. 6, pr. 6.3 below. Cf. T. Meron, *Human Rights Law-Making in the United Nations*, pp. 49–50, 52 (1986).

158 See e.g. ch. 4, prs. 4.92–4.96 below.

159 See n. 31 above; Simarsian, n. 1 above; N. K. Hevener, 'Drafting the Human Rights Covenants—An Exploration of the Relationship between U.S. Participation and Non-Ratification', 148 World Affairs (1986) pp. 233–44.

160 See Green, n. 131 above.

161 See W. Bishop, *Cases and Materials on International Law*, pp. 110–12 (3rd, 1971);

V. Van Dyke, *Human Rights, the United States and the World Community*, ch. 7 (1970); S. Garrett, 'Foreign Policy and the American Constitution: The Bricker Amendment in Contemporary Perspective', 16 Int. SQ (1972) pp. 187–220; N. H. Kaufman and D. Whiteman, 'Opposition to Human Rights Treaties in the United States Senate: The Legacy of the Bricker Amendment', 10 HRQ (1988) pp. 309–337; Johnson, n. 31 above, who comments that, 'it was designed in part as a unilateral federal state clause, denying effect to any treaty which would have been unconstitutional as a simple act of Congress', p. 45.

162 For the US announcement see UN Doc. E/CN.4/SR.340, pp. 8–12 (1953); US Dept. of State Bulletin, Vol. 28, p. 592 (20 Apr. 1953). See Green, n. 1 above, pp. 59–64; Ganji, n. 1 above, pp. 221–4; Humphrey, n. 1 above, pp. 176–7; Johnson, n. 31 above, pp. 44–7. See the Dulles Memorandum of 20 Feb. 1953, 'United States Policy Regarding Draft International Covenants on Human Rights', in *Foreign Relations of the United States, 1952–54*, Vol. iii, pp. 550–5 (1979), cited in Johnson, n. 31 above, p. 46 n. 90.

163 On the Action Programme see Green, n. 1 above, ch. 3; UN Action in the Field of Human Rights, n. 6 above, pp. 341–7; Humphrey, n. 1 above, pp. 174–81; Tolley, n. 1 above, ch. 3.

164 See n. 41 above. As early as 1947, however, the US had submitted a draft proposal supporting individual and group petitions, see Doc. E/CN.4/21, p. 95 (1 July 1947). For its view in 1948 see Doc. E/800, n. 1 above, p. 41 n. 1.

165 See e.g. the draft US proposal for a protocol on petitions from individuals and non-governmental organizations in Doc. E/1992, n. 1 above, Ax. V (1951), later withdrawn.

166 See Ganji, n. 1 above, pp. 168–72; Green, n. 1 above, pp. 53–5; see pr. 1.7 above.

167 Johnson, n. 31 above, points out that the Carter presidency picked up on increased Congressional activity on human rights from 1970 to 1975. See generally Brown and Maclean (eds.), *Human Rights and U.S. Foreign Policy* (1979); 'Symposium: Human Rights and U.S. Foreign Policy', 14 Virg. JIL (1973–4) pp. 591–701; N. K. Hevener, *The Dynamics of Human Rights in U.S. Foreign Policy* (1981); R. Lillich and F. Newman, *International Human Rights: Problems of Law and Policy*, Problem xii (1979); J. Mayall, 'The United States', in R. J. Vincent (ed.), *Foreign Policy and Human Rights*, pp. 165–87 (1986); A. G. Mower, n. 31 above; J. C. Tuttle (ed.), *International Human Rights Law and Practice* (1978). For some specific analyses and criticisms of US human rights foreign policy see N. Chomsky and E. S. Herman, *The Washington Connection and Third World Fascism—The Political Economy of Human Rights*, Vol. i (1979); H. Shue, *Basic Rights, Subsistence, Affluence and US Foreign Policy* (1980).

168 See S. Exec. C, D, E and F, 95th congress, 2d Sess, iii–iv (1978). M. L. Nash, 'Contemporary Practice of the U.S. Relating to International Law', 72 AJIL (1978) pp. 620–31; M. D. Craig, 'The ICCPR and U.S. Law: Department of State Proposals for Preserving the Status Quo', 19 Harv. ILJ (1978) pp. 845–86; D. Weissbrodt, 'U.S. Ratification of the Human Rights Covenants', 63 Minn. LR (1978) pp. 35–78; B. MacChesney, 'Should the U.S. Ratify the Covenants? A Question of Merits, Not of Constitutional Law', 62 AJIL (1968) pp. 912–17; R. Lillich (ed.), *U.S. Ratification of Human Rights Treaties: With or Without*

Reservations (1981); U. Haksar, 'The International Human Rights Treaties: Some Problems of Policy and Interpretation', 126 U. Pa. LR (1978) pp. 886–929; J. Skelton, Jr., 'The U.S. Approach to Ratification of the International Covenants on Human Rights', 1 Hous. JIL (1979) pp. 103–25; P. Alston, 'US Ratification of the Covenant on Economic, Social and Cultural Rights: The Need for an Entirely New Strategy', 84 AJIL (1990) pp. 365–93.

169 Note though that the US ratified the Genocide Convention in 1988, see 80 AJIL (1986) pp. 612–22; 28 ILM (1989) pp. 754–85. See also L. Sohn, 'Improving the Image of the U.S. in International Human Rights', 82 AJIL (1988) pp. 319–20.

170 Yugoslavia does not consistently vote with any political caucus at the UN.

171 See pr. 1.18 above; Jhabvala, n. 120 above; H. O. Bergeson, 'Human Rights—The Property of the Nation State or a Concern for the International Community?—A Study of Soviet Positions Concerning U.N. Protection of Civil and Political Rights Since 1975', 14 Cooperation and Conflict (1979) pp. 239–54.

172 Note that the USSR is itself a federal State. See generally A. P. Movchan, 'The Human Rights Problem in Present Day International Law', in G. Tunkin (ed.), *Contemporary International Law* (1969); id., *Human Rights and International Relations* (1988); J. Carey, 'Human Rights—The Soviet View', 53 Kentucky LJ (1964) pp. 115–34; A. Rees, 'The Soviet Union', in R. J. Vincent (ed.), n. 167 above, pp. 61–83; V. Kartashkin, 'Human Rights and Peaceful Co-Existence', 9 RDH/HRJ (1976) pp. 5–19; V. Kartashkin, n. 120 above.

173 For comment see K. Tudin, 'The Development of Soviet Attitudes Towards Implementing Human Rights under the United Nations Charter', 5 RDH/HRJ (1972) pp. 399–418; Jhabvala, n. 120 above. 'In 1953 Mrs. Roosevelt expressed the view that, "Many of us are fairly sure that it (the Soviet Union) will not ratify"', cited in Johnson, n. 31 above, p. 46.

174 By 1963, however, the USSR and the other eastern bloc States had declared that the reporting provisions of both draft Covenants were acceptable in principle, see A/C.3/SR.1273, p. 13, (2 Dec. 1963); Tudin, n. 173 above.

175 UN Doc. E/CN.4/1989/SR.55 pr. 22, and before the HRC in SR 929 pr. 14. Such developments may have very significant long-term implications for the status of the individual in international law as the traditional view of Eastern European States has been that individuals have no standing in international law.

176 The USSR has also recently accepted the jurisdiction of the International Court of Justice in respect of six international human rights treaties, see 83 AJIL (1989) p. 457. On the traditional approach of Eastern European States see G. Tunkin, *Theory of International Law*, pp. 83–6 (1974). See also R. Szawlowski, 'The International Protection of Human Rights—A Polish and a Soviet View', 28 ICLQ (1979) pp. 775–81.

177 See pr. 1.25 above; Humphrey, n. 1 above, p. 180.

178 The US have ratified only seven out of the twenty-two principal international human rights instruments listed in the UN's *Status of International Instruments*, n. 155 above (as updated to 1 Sept. 1989). Cf. D. Dhelton, 'The Baby Boy Case', 2 HRLJ (1981) pp. 309–18.

179 A number of other non-states parties might then follow the US in ratifying the ICCPR.

180 Particularly the HRCion, see Tolley, n. 1 above.

181 See 23 ILM (1984), p. 218 and 24 ILM (1985), p. 489. The UK and Japan have also left.

182 For a comment see *The Economist*, Vol. 296, No. 7403, pp. 50–1 (20 July 1985). The US withdrew from the ILO from 1977–8.

183 See ch. 2, pr. 2.7.

184 See ch. 3 below.

185 See ch. 4 below.

186 See n. 24 above.

187 See the 'Draft Body of Principles and Guidelines on the Right and Responsibility of Individuals, Groups and Organs of Society to Promote and Protect Human Rights and Fundamental Freedoms', of the Sub-Commission on the Prevention of Discrimination and the Protection of Minorities', Doc. E/CN.4/Sub.2/1985/30. The draft is now being considered by a working group of the HRCion. For its latest report see Doc. E/CN.4/1990/47. See also art. 29 UDHR; arts. 27–9 AFR; art. 32 AMR.

188 See text to n. 66 above.

189 See prs. 1.22–1.23 above and ch. 5.

190 See ch. 6 below.

191 See ch. 7 below.

192 See e.g. ch. 4, prs. 4.84–4.85 below for an interpretation of the Covenant and the Protocol based in part on article 5 of the Covenant.

193 See generally E. I. A. Daes, *The Individual's Duties to the Community and the Limitations on Human Rights and Freedoms under Article 29 of the UDHR*, UN Doc. E/CN.4/Sub. 2/432/Rev. 2 (1983, reprinted 1990); E. Orucu, 'The Core of Rights and Freedoms: The Limits of Limits', in T. Campbell *et al.* (eds.), *Human Rights: From Rhetoric to Reality*, pp. 37–59 (1986); A. Kiss, 'Permissible Limitations on Human Rights', in Henkin (ed.), n. 1 above, pp. 290–310. For an example of the HRC's approach to limitation clauses see the consideration of art. 19 in ch. 11 below.

194 See ch. 8 below.

195 See ch. 9 below.

196 Ibid.

197 See ch. 10 below.

198 See ch. 11 below.

199 See ch. 12 below.

200 See Capotorti, n. 139 above; Sohn, ibid.; C. Tomuschat, 'Protection of Minorities under Article 27 of the ICCPR', in R. Bernhardt, W. K. Geck, G. Jaenicke, and H. Steinberg (eds.), *Volkerrecht als Rechtsordnung, Internationale Gerichtsbarkeit. Mensrechten: Festschrift für Hermann Mosler*, pp. 949–79 (1983); F. Ermacora, 'The Protection of Minorities before the United Nations', 182 Recueil des cours (1983–IV) pp. 247–370. The most notable omissions from the ICCPR are the right of asylum, to a nationality (except for children, article 23(4)), and a right to property.

201 See ch. 3 below.

202 This procedure has not yet been used and is not considered in this work. See

Rules 72–7E of HRC's Rules of Procedure; Doc. A/34/40, prs. 28–53; SR 156 and 169. See Tyagi, ch. 4.

203 See ch. 3, pr. 3.40 below.

204 See Bossuyt, *Guide*, pp. 731–4.

205 Ibid., pp. 735–6. See pr. 1.23 above; J. N. Hyde, 'Permanent Sovereignty over Natural Wealth and Resources', 50 AJIL (1956) pp. 854–67.

206 Bossuyt, *Guide*, pp. 737–52. Objections have been made to this article by most of the Eastern European states on the basis that it is of a discriminatory nature and that the Covenants should be open to all States concerned. See e.g. *Human Rights—Status of International Instruments*, p. 46 (USSR) (1987). The General Assembly has repeatedly called for all States that had not done so to become parties to the Covenant, see e.g. GA Resn. 42/103 (7 Dec. 1987).

207 See pr. 1.7 above.

208 See Bossuyt, *Guide*, pp. 769–79. Cf. article 11 OP.

209 The HRC have discovered at least one difference in the authentic texts of the OP concerning article 5(2)(*a*) OP, see ch. 4, notes to pr. 4.87 below.

210 There is no denunciation clause in the ICCPR although there is one in article 12 of the OP. Schwelb has argued, correctly it is submitted, that in the light of article 56 VCLT (1969) it is not possible to denounce the ICCPR. See E. Schwelb, 'The Law of Treaties and Human Rights', in W. M. Reisman and B. H. Weston (eds.), *Towards World Order and Human Dignity*, pp. 262–90 (1976); P. Sieghart, *The International Law of Human Rights*, pp. 199–21 (1983). See generally P. Weis, 'The Denunciation of Human Rights Treaties', 8 RDH/HRJ (1975) pp. 3–7.

211 See pr. 1.24 above.

212 See ch. 4, prs. 4.4–4.5 below. For OP2 see Apx. IV below.

213 The significance of the OP to the ICCPR is dealt with in ch. 4, prs. 4.2–4.3, 4.19 below.

214 See F. Jhabvala, 'The ICCPR as a Vehicle for the Global Promotion and Protection of Human Rights', 15 Isr. YHR (1985) pp. 184–203; C. Tomuschat, 'Human Rights in a World Wide Framework', 45 ZaoRV (1985) pp. 547–84; C. Tomuschat, 'Is Universality of Human Rights an Outdated Concept', in *Das Europa der zweiten Generation—Gedachtnisschrift Für Christophe Sasse*, pp. 585–609 (Vol. ii, 1981); R. Bystricky, 'The Universality of Human Rights in a World of Conflicting Ideologies', in A. Eide and A. Schou (eds.), n. 1 above, pp. 83–93; F. Capotorti, n. 7 above. The strongest challenge to the 'universality' of the ICCPR has come in the form of arguments based on cultural relativism. See J. Donnelly, 'Cultural Relativism and the Consequences for Human Rights', 6 HRQ (1984) pp. 400–19; R. Howard, 'Is There an African Concept of Human Rights?', in R. J. Vincent (ed.), n. 167 above, pp. 11–32 (1986); A. D. Renteln, 'The Unanswered Challenge of Relativism and the Consequences for Human Rights', 7 HRQ (1985) pp. 514–40; F. R. Teson, 'International Human Rights and Cultural Relativism', 25 Virg. JIL (1985) pp. 869–98. The only State reported to have expressly rejected the philosophy of the UDHR is Iran, see *Sunday Times*, 20 Jan. 1985, 8ᵃ, and Tomuschat, this note, p. 553, n. 21. However, Iran has remained a party to the ICCPR. See generally, International Commission of Jurists, *Human Rights in Islam* (1982); M. I. Malik, 'The

Concept of Human Rights in Islamic Jurisprudence', 3 HRQ (1981) pp. 56–67 Artz, ch. 6 n. 84 below.

215 See P. Alston, 'The U.D.H.R. at 35: Western and Passé or Alive and Universal', 31 Rev. ICJ (1983) pp. 60–70; O. M. Garibaldi, 'On the Ideological Content of Human Rights Instruments: The Clause: "In A Democratic Society"', In T. Buergenthal (ed.), *Contemporary Issues in International Law*, pp. 23–68 (1984); H. M. Scoble and L. S. Wiseberg, *Access to Justice—The Struggle for Human Rights in South East Asia* (1985); R. P. Claude, 'The Western Tradition of Human Rights in Comparative Perspective', 14 Comparative Judicial Review (1977) pp. 3–66.

216 See n. 24 above.

217 See n. 41 above.

218 On article 2 of the ICCPR see ch. 6 below.

219 The disparity between human rights standards and the human rights practices of States raises important questions concerning the validity of human rights law. For some contributions to the debate see J. S. Watson, 'Autointerpretation, Competence and the Continuing Validity of Article 2(7) of the Charter', 71 AJIL (1977) pp. 60–83; J. S. Watson, 'Legal Theory, Efficacy and Validity in the Development of Human Rights Norms in International Law', Univ. Illinois Law Forum (1979) pp. 609–41; E. Lane, 'Demanding Human Rights: A Change in the World Legal Order', 6 Hofstra LR (1978) pp. 269–95; E. Lane, 'Mass Killings by Governments: Lawful in the World Legal Order?', 12 NYUJILP (1979) pp. 239–80; L. Sohn, 'The International Law of Human Rights', 9 Hofstra LR (1981) pp. 347–56; R. Higgins, 'Reality and Hope in International Human Rights', 9 Hofstra LR (1981) pp. 1485–99; L. F. Schechter, 'The Views of "Charterists" and "Skeptics" on Human Rights in the World Legal Order: Two Wrongs Don't Make a Right', 9 Hofstra LR (1981) pp. 357–98; A. D'Amato, 'The Concept of Human Rights in International Law', 82 Col. LR (1982) pp. 1110–59.

220 See R. B. Lillich, n. 3 above (1984), ch. 3; P. S. Chandra, *Civil and Political Rights of Aliens* (1982).

221 A third possibility is that there is no international standard at all and that a State may treat aliens at its complete discretion and not necessarily as favourably as it treats its own nationals. This view can possibly be seen in the Charter of Economic Rights and Duties of States, GA Resn. 3281 (XXIX). See generally I. Brownlie, *Principles of Public International Law*, ch. 23 (4th, 1990); D. J. Harris, *Cases and Materials on International Law*, ch. 8 (3rd, 1983).

222 Lillich n. 3 above, p. 145. See also the important general comment by the HRC on the position of aliens, GC 15/27, in Doc. A/41/40, p. 117.

223 Lillich, n. 3 above.

224 See ch. 4, pr. 4.67 below.

225 Torture might be an obvious example in this respect, see *Filartiga* v. *Pena-Irala*, 630 F. 2d. p. 876 (1980), 19 ILM (1980), p. 966, US Circuit Court of Appeals, 2nd Circuit; N. Rodley, *The Treatment of Prisoners in International Law*, ch. 2 and pp. 104–6 (1987); Lillich, n. 3 above, pp. 44–7. See also T. Meron, *Human Rights and Humanitarian Norms as Customary International Law* (1989).

226 E. Schwelb has advanced a similar argument as regards the ICERD, see n. 24

above (1972), p. 337 at p. 351; D'Amato, n. 219 above, pp. 1128–49. See also Singh, n. 24 above.

227 See ch. 1, prs. 1.1–1.3 above. See also the preamble to the ICCPR, Apx. I below.

228 Article 38(1)(c) of the Statute of the ICJ. See N. K. Hevener and S. A. Mosher, 'General Principles of Law and the U.N. Covenant on Civil and Political Rights', 27 ICLQ (1978) pp. 596–613.

229 See n. 226 above.

230 In addition to the references below see the bibliography in Bossuyt, *Guide*, pp. 826–36, and the bibliography compiled by the Secretary of the Human Rights Committee in Geneva. On the domestic implementation of the ICCPR see ch. 6 below on article 2 ICCPR. Cf. A. Drzemczewski, *European Human Rights Convention in Domestic Law* (1983). As of July 1990 the ECHR was directly applicable in 16 out of the 23 member States of the Council of Europe.

231 See R. Lillich, 'The Role of Domestic Courts in Enforcing International Human Rights Law', in H. Hannum (ed.), *Guide to International Human Rights Practice*, ch. 13 (1984); id., 'The Enforcement of International Human Rights Norms in Domestic Courts', in J. C. Tuttle (ed.), n. 167 above, pp. 105–31; id., 'Invoking International Human Rights Law in Domestic Courts', 54 Univ. Cin. LR (1985) pp. 367–415; *Developing Human Rights Jurisprudence—The Domestic Application of International Human Rights Norms*, 2 volumes (Commonwealth Secretariat, 1988, 1990).

232 See *Lebanese Muslim Association* v. *Minister for Immigration and Ethnic Affairs*, 67 ALR 195 (1986). *Kioa* v. *Minister for Immigration and Ethnic Affairs*, 62 ALR 321 (1985), *Daemar* v. *Industrial Commission of NSW*, 79 ALR 591 (1988). See also the Australian Bill of Rights Bill (1985), and Explanatory Memorandum.

233 See e.g. *Re Mitchell and the Queen* (1983) 42 OR (2d) p. 481 (article 15); *Re Vincent and Minister of Employment and Immigration* (1983) 148 DLR (3d) p. 385 (article 13). Both cited in 22 Can. YIL 1984 (1985) pp. 405–7. Before the HRC in 1984 the Canadian representative stated that the Covenant was influencing the interpretation of the Charter. There were at least twenty decisions to date in which judges referred to the Covenant and other human rights instruments to interpret provisions of the Charter (SR 559 pr. 26). W. Tarnopolsky, 'The Canadian Experience with the ICCPR as seen from the Perspective of a Former Member of the HRC', 20 Akron LR (1987) pp. 611–28.

234 See Tomuschat, ch. 6 n. 1 below (1984), p. 38 who cites a decision of the Federal Administrative Court in 1982 which cited the decision of the HRC in the *Mauritian Women Case* which is dealt with in ch. 4, pr. 4.75 below.

235 Before the HRC in 1983 the French representative stated that the Covenant had been invoked in one case concerning a doctor who had invoked freedom of opinion in refusing to pay his contribution to a professional association, SR 439 pr. 10. The Nicaraguan representative stated that the Covenant was frequently invoked in courts, SR 428 pr. 11.

236 See H. O. Agarwal, n. 1 above, chs. 4–6 (1983); Justice Bhagwati, 'Human Rights as Evolved by the Jurisprudence of the Supreme Court of India', 13 Comm. LB. (1987) pp. 236–45; statement of the Indian representative before the HRC, Doc. A/39/40, pr. 268.

237 See SR 321 pr. 3 (48 reported cases in which Covenant mentioned in the courts opinion). See e.g. notes in NYIL (1984), pp. 424–5, 445–7, 641–4, 451, n. 101, 448–50.

238 See *R.v. Wjee* [1981] 1 NZLR 561; *Broadcasting Corporation of New Zealand* v. *Attorney-General* [1982] 1 NZLR 120; *Department of Labour* v. *Latailakepa* [1982] 1 NZLR 632. See also Tay, NZLJ (1979) pp. 365–70.

239 See *Ministry of Home Affairs and Another* v. *Fisher and Another* [1980] AC 319; *R.* v. *Secretary of State for the Home Office, ex. p. Chubb* (Queens Bench Divisional Court, 1 July 1986, unreported); *The Bank of Tokyo Ltd.* v. *Karoon* (QBD, 1 May 1986, unreported).

240 See e.g. the celebrated decision in *Filartiga* v. *Pena-Irala*, n. 225 above; *Thompson* v. *Oklahoma* 101 L. Ed. 702 (1988) (Stevens J.); *Stanford* v. *Kentucky*, 109 S.Ct. 2696. See also Lillich, n. 231 above and R. B. Lillich, *International Human Rights Instruments* (1983).

241 D. Sanders, 'The Re-Emergence of Indigenous Questions in International Law', Can HRY (1984–5), at pp. 24–5 cites a Norwegian case in which article 27 ICCPR was cited although the decision of the Supreme Court was not based on it.

242 See the decision of the Constitutional Court of Yugoslavia in the ICJ Study, ch. 7, n. 1 below, p. 84, nn. 121–2. It is understood that the provisions of the ICCPR played an important part in the consideration within Yugoslavia of the appropriate interpretation of a certain law concerning discrimination on political grounds in the context of employment.

243 See H. Fischer, 'The Human Rights Covenants and Canadian Law', 15 Can. YIL (1977) pp. 42–83; A. Bayefsky, 'The Human Rights Committee and the Case of Sandra Lovelace', 20 Can. YIL (1982) pp. 244–66; A. Brudner, 'The Domestic Enforcement of International Covenants on Human Rights: A Theoretical Framework', 35 Univ. Tor. LJ (1985) pp. 219–54; W. S. Tarnopolsky, 'A Comparison between the Canadian Charter of Rights and Freedoms and the International Covenant on Civil and Political Rights', 8 Queens LJ (1982–3) pp. 211–31.

244 See G. Triggs, 'Australia's Ratification of the ICCPR: Endorsement or Repudiation?', 31 ICLQ (1982) pp. 278–306; id., 'Australia's Ratification of the ICCPR: its Domestic Application to Prisoners Rights', 3 HRLJ (1982) pp. 65–102; S. K. N. Blay, 'The ICCPR and the Recognition of Customary Law Practices of Indigenous Peoples: The Case of Australian Aborigines', 19 CILSA (1986) pp. 199–219.

245 See Agarwal, n. 1 above; G. H. Guttal, 'Human Rights: The Indian Law', 26 Ind. JIL (1986) pp. 53–71; K. Tornudd, *Finland and the International Norms of Human Rights* (1986).

246 See S. Yasuhiko, 'Japan and Human Rights Covenant', 2 HRLJ (1981) pp. 79–107; Y. Iwasawa, 'Legal Treatment of Koreans in Japan: The Impact of International Human Rights Law on Japanese Law', 8 HRQ (1986) pp. 131–79; Y. Kawashima, 'The International Covenants on Human Rights and the Japanese Legal System', 22 Japanese Annual of International Law (1978) pp. 54–74; C. I. Chee, 'Alien Registration Law of Japan and the International Covenant for Civil and Political Rights', 10 Korea and World Affairs (1986) pp. 649–86.

247 J. B. Elkind, 'Application of the International Covenant on Civil and Political Rights in New Zealand', 75 AJIL (1981) pp. 169–72; J. B. Elkind and A. Shaw, *A Standard for Justice* (1986).

248 V. Kartashkin, 'Covenants on Human Rights and Soviet Legislation', 10 RDH/ HRJ (1977) pp. 97–115.

249 A. Noble, 'The Covenant on Civil and Political Rights as the Law of the Land', 25 Vill. LR (1979) pp. 119–40. See n. 168 above.

250 See e.g. the JUSTICE Report, *Compensation for Wrongful Imprisonment* (1982).

251 See e.g. GA Resn. 40/144, Declaration on the Human Rights of Individuals who are not Nationals of the Country in which they live (13 Dec. 1985) and the resolutions cited by Weissbrodt in 80 AJIL (1986) pp. 685–99; Zuidjwick, n. 1 above, p. 380 *et seq*.

252 For example, the reports of UN Human Rights Working Groups and Special Rapporteurs consistently make reference to the Covenant. See e.g. the reports on summary and arbitrary executions in ch. 8, n. 1 below.

253 See e.g. Commission on Human Rights, Report of 45th session, 1989, ECOSOC OR 1989, Supp. 2; UN Doc. E/CN.4/1989/86.

254 See e.g. Resolutions of the European Parliament, 4 HRLJ (1983) pp. 1–17. The ICCPR has also been referred to in a number of cases under the ECHR.

255 See e.g. G. Marston, 'UK Materials in International Law', 56 BYIL 1985 pp. 426–31 (1986); id., 59 BYIL 1988 pp. 457–71 (1989).

256 14 ILM (1975) p. 1292. See J. Frowein, 'The Interrelationship between the Helsinki Final Act, the International Covenants on Human Rights and the European Convention on Human Rights', in T. Buergenthal (ed.), *Human Rights, International Law and the Helsinki Accords* (1977), pp. 71–82. The language of the ICCPR is heavily drawn on in the CSCE Concluding Documents of Vienna (1989) and Copenhagen (1990).

257 Joint Declaration of the Governments of the UK and the Peoples' Republic of China on the Question of Hong Kong, 26 UKTS (1985); Cmnd. 9543. How the application of the Covenant is to be secured after 1997 if China does not become a party to the Covenant is somewhat problematic. See the 'Commentary on the draft Hong Kong Bill of Rights Ordinance 1990', (March 1990).

258 See e.g. E. R. Cohen, *Human Rights in the Israeli-Occupied Territories 1967–1982* (1985).

259 See e.g. H. Hannum, *The Right to Leave and Return in International Law and Practice* (1987); W. H. Bennett, Jr., 'A Critique of the Emerging Convention on the Rights of the Child', 20 Corn. ILJ (1987) pp. 1–64; R. Higgins, 'Some Recent Developments in Respect of the Right to Leave in International Law', in B. Cheng and E. D. Brown (eds.), *Contemporary Problems of International Law: Essays in Honour of George Schwarzenberger*, pp. 138–56 (1988); UN Convention on the Rights of the Child, 28 ILM (1989) pp. 1448–1476.

260 See ch. 1, prs. 1.4–1.5 above.

261 Ibid., and pr. 1.16 above.

262 See T. Meron, *Human Rights Law-Making in the United Nations: A Critique of Instruments and Process* (1986); J. Donnelly, 'International Human Rights: A Regime Analysis', 40 Int. Org. (1986) pp. 599–642; A. A. Cancado Trindade,

'Co-Existence and Co-Ordination of Mechanisms of International Protection of Human Rights', 202 Recueil des cours (1987–II) pp. 9–435.

263 *Human Rights: A Compilation of International Instruments*, UN Doc. ST/HR/1/Rev. 3 (1988).

264 See chs. 3–12 below.

265 OAS Resn. XXX, adopted by the Ninth International Conference of American States, Bogota, Colombia (1948). Reprinted in *Handbook of Existing Rules Pertaining to Human Rights in the Inter-American System*, OEA, Series L/V/II.60, doc. 28 (1983). See P. Sieghart, *The International Law of Human Rights*, pp. 28, 55 (1983).

266 OASTS No. 36, p. 1. Reprinted in *Handbook*, n. 265 above, pp. 31–63; P. Sieghart, ibid., pp. 28–9. See T. Buergenthal, 'The Inter-American System for the Protection of Human Rights', in T. Meron (ed.), n. 11 above, ch. 12; T. Buergenthal *et al.*, n. 104 above; R. Piza, 'Coordination of the Mechanisms for the Protection of Human Rights in the American Convention with Those Established by the United Nations', 30 Am. ULR (1981) pp. 167–87; C. M. Quiroga, *The Battle of Human Rights: Gross, Systematic Violations and the Inter-American System* (1988).

267 UKTS p. 70 (1950); Cmnd. 8969. See P. Van Dijk and G. J. H. Van Hoof, *The Theory and Practice of the European Convention on Human Rights* (2nd, 1990); J. Fawcett, *The Application of the European Convention on Human Rights* (2nd, 1987); R. Higgins, 'The European Convention on Human Rights', in T. Meron (ed.), n. 11 above, ch. 13; R. Beddard, *Human Rights in Europe* (2nd, 1980).

268 21 ILM (1982) pp. 58–68; 7 Comm. Law. Bull (1982) pp. 1057–68. See R. Gittleman, 'The African Charter on Human and Peoples' Rights: A Legal Analysis', 22 Virg. JIL (1982) pp. 667–714; E. G. Bello, 'The African Charter on Human and Peoples' Rights—A Legal Analysis', 194 Recueil des cours (1985-V) pp. 21–268 (1987); B. O. Okere, 'The Protection of Human Rights in Africa and the African Charter on Human and Peoples Rights: A Comparative Analysis with the European and American Systems', 6 HRQ (1984) pp. 141–59; U. O. Umozurike, 'The African Charter on Human and Peoples' Rights', 77 AJIL (1983) pp. 902–12; N. S. Rembe, *Africa and Regional Protection of Human Rights* (1985); 'Documentation on the African Commission on Human Rights', 9 HRLJ (1988) pp. 326–62.

269 Arguably too many. See L. Sohn, 'Human Rights: Their Implementation by the United Nations', in T. Meron (ed.), n. 11 above, pp. 369–401; A. P. Vijapur, 'The UN Mechanisms for the Promotion and Protection of Human Rights', 25 Ind JIL (1985) pp. 576–611; A. A. C. Trindade, n. 262 above; B. H. Weston, R. A. Lukes, and K. M. Hnatt, 'Regional Human Rights Regimes: A Comparison and Appraisal', 20 Vanderbilt J. Transnational Law (1987) pp. 585–637.

270 See n. 265 above.

271 See n. 266 above.

272 UKTS 77 (1969) Cmnd. 4108; 660 UNTS p. 195; 60 AJIL (1966) p. 690. See N. Lerner, *The United Nations Convention on the Elimination of Racial Discrimination* (2nd, 1980); T. Meron, n. 262 above, pp. 7–52; Tolley, n. 1 above, pp. 45–50.

2

The Human Rights Committee[1]

INTRODUCTION

2.1 As we noted in chapter 1 the principle of establishing a Human Rights Committee (HRC), a permanent human rights body to implement the Covenant, only just survived the drafting process.[2] The HRC emerged as the only organ with express functions with respect to the Covenant and the Protocol. However, key changes had been made in the Third Committee concerning the composition and functions of the proposed Committee.[3] This chapter examines the composition, organization, functions, nature, and status of the HRC.

A. MEMBERSHIP

2.2 Article 28(1) of the Covenant provides for the establishment of a 'Human Rights Committee' to consist of eighteen members and to carry out the functions provided for in the Covenant and the Protocol. The members of the HRC shall both 'be elected and shall serve' in their personal capacity (article 28(3)).[4] Article 28(2) provides that members 'shall be of high moral character and recognized competence in the field of human rights, consideration being given to the usefulness of participation of some persons having legal experience'. In the election of the Committee, 'consideration shall be given to equitable geographical distribution of membership and to the representation of the different forms of civilization and of the principal legal systems' (article 31(2)).[5]

The experience of international human rights organs would suggest that the independence of the HRC members from governmental or other institutional influences is fundamental to its nature and at least gives it the potential to be effective.[6] However, the Covenant does not stipulate that a member must be personally independent of his government.[7] In practice membership of the HRC has included former cabinet and government ministers, members of Parliament,[8] former ambassadors, and senior governmental representatives.[9] Membership of the HRC is part-time. Although members of the HRC receive emoluments from the United Nations rather than their respective national governments the level of emoluments has been very low.[10] The effect in practice has been that membership of the HRC has been limited to persons receiving a regular salary, for example, in academic or government posts.[11] As the work of the HRC is very demanding both in terms of difficulty and the time involved there is an obvious case to be made for making membership of the HRC a full-time salaried occupation.[12] However, the continuous contact of members with high level political and legal activity within their respective national systems brings critically important practical knowledge and expertise to the HRC's considerations. It is submitted that the HRC should remain a part-time body but that its members should be properly remunerated 'having regard to the importance of the Committee's responsibilities' (article 35).[13]

2.3 Nominees for the HRC have been of a very high quality.[14] To some extent this suggests that States parties regard the HRC and the Covenant as important. Moreover, the fact that highly qualified individuals are willing to devote a substantial part of their time over a period of years bears testimony to the importance they see in the role of the HRC.[15] However, the reference to 'legal expertise' in article 28 has perhaps been too literally applied. Members of the HRC to date have all been legal experts of some kind. Although many of the members have had various periods of their careers as, for example, journalists or politicians,[16] the expertise of the HRC could usefully be broadened by experts from other disciplines such as social sciences or economics. No woman served on the HRC until one was elected in 1983 to replace the expert from Canada who resigned to take up a judicial appointment.[17] As of 27 July 1990 two women are serving on the HRC.[18]

2.4 Whatever the governing provisions of a treaty or of a resolution establishing an independent human rights organ the proof, of course, lies in the practice. Since its inception members of the HRC have continually stressed their independence from governments, the Secretariat, and other United Nations bodies.[19] Whilst there is no denying that there have been marked differences between members as to the HRC's functions and powers and different approaches to the implementation of particular rights, these differences appear to stem from the various ideological and legal approaches mandated in the HRC's membership (article 31(2)) rather than from political pressures from governments or other forces.[20] The line between the two is a thin and difficult one but in practice HRC members do appear to operate as independent experts.[21] The fundamental precondition to the HRC's continued development is that they should continue to do so.[22]

B. ELECTION

2.5 The members of the HRC are elected by secret ballot by States parties to the Covenant at meetings convened by the Secretary-General of the United

Nations.[23] The Secretary-General convened the first meeting of the States parties on 20 September 1976.[24] Subsequent elections take place every two years.[25] A list of nominees is submitted by the Secretary-General to the States parties no later than one month before the date of each election.[26] Each state party to the Covenant is entitled to nominate not more than two persons who shall be nationals of the nominating State.[27] The HRC may not include more than one national from the same State.[28] The persons elected are those nominees who obtain the largest majority of the votes and an absolute majority of the votes of the representatives of States parties present and voting.[29]

Each member of the HRC is elected for a term of four years.[30] The States parties decided that the term of office of the initial members of the HRC should begin on 1 January 1977.[31] The terms of nine of the initial members, chosen by lot by the Chairman of the initial meeting of the States parties, expired at the end of two years.[32] Consequently the States parties meet every two years to replace the nine members whose terms are to expire. This ensures some continuity of membership as does the provision in article 29(3) permitting the renomination of HRC members. The HRC has been fortunate in having both a good record of attendance by members and a strong degree of continuity of membership in its first decade, although there have been a number of significant changes recently.[33] As of 27 July 1990 only two of the original members remain.[34] A member elected to fill a vacancy holds the office for the remainder of the term of the member who vacated the seat.[35] As of 27 July 1990 the composition of the HRC was as follows:[36] (* Term expires on 31 December 1990; ** Term expires on 31 December 1992).

Name of member	*Country of Nationality*
Mr AGUILAR URBINA**	Costa Rica
Mr ANDO*	Japan
Ms CHANET*	France
Mr COORAY**	Sri Lanka
Mr DIMITRIJEVIC*	Yugoslavia
Mr EL-SHAFEI*	Egypt
Mr FODOR**	Hungary
Mrs HIGGINS**	United Kingdom of Great Britain and Northern Ireland
Mr LALLAH**	Mauritius
Mr MAVROMMATIS**	Cyprus
Mr MOMMERSTEEG*	Netherlands
Mr MYULLERSON**	Union of Soviet Socialist Republics
Mr NDIAYE*	Senegal
Mr POCAR**	Italy

Mr PRADO VALLEJO*	Ecuador
Mr SERRANO CALDERO**	Nicaragua
Mr WAKO**	Kenya
Mr WENNERGREN*	Sweden

As regards geographical representation there is no precise rule in the Covenant beyond that in article 31(2)[37] but in practice the States parties have considered the geographical spread of States parties at the time of each election and sought to balance the membership of the HRC accordingly.[38] Each of the six elections to date has produced a broadly balanced Committee in geographical terms though imbalances inevitably arise if the balance of membership changes between elections.[39]

In accordance with article 43 the members of the HRC 'shall be entitled to the facilities, privileges and immunities of experts on mission for the United Nations as laid down in the relevant sections of the Convention on the Privileges and Immunities of the United Nations'.[40]

C. ORGANIZATION OF WORK

2.6 In accordance with article 37(1) the initial meeting of the HRC was convened at the headquarters of the United Nations in New York. Subsequent meetings were to be held in accordance with the Rules of Procedure drawn up by the HRC under article 39(2) and were normally to be held in New York or Geneva.[41] In its Rules the HRC provided that it would hold such sessions as were required for the satisfactory performance of its functions.[42] Initially the HRC decided to hold two sessions a year but as the volume of its work increased the practice of the HRC since 1978 has been to hold three sessions a year of three weeks' duration.[43] Normally one session has been held in New York in the spring and two sessions in Geneva in the summer and the autumn. However, in its early years, economic constraints seemed to be forcing the HRC into a situation of holding almost all of its sessions in Geneva. The normal pattern has been resumed in recent years but in 1989 the matter was again raised by the representative of the Secretary-General and although the proposal attracted severe opposition from the HRC it appears increasingly likely to be adopted.[44] Each session is normally preceded by one or two working groups of up to five days.[45] Financial constraints within the United Nations system forced the cancellation of the HRC's proposed session in the autumn of 1986 and only permitted the establishment of one pre-sessional working group at HRC's spring and summer sessions in 1987, instead of the customary two.[46] The HRC has pressed strongly to retain its three sessions per year.[47] Only one session has been held outside of New York or Geneva.[48] In accordance with the Rules the HRC established the offices of Chairman, three Vice-Chairmen, and a Rapporteur.

The officers are elected for two years and may be re-elected. However, the understanding of the HRC expressed in March 1989 is that the officers of the HRC will only serve for two-year terms.[49]

2.7 The Rules provide that, 'the meetings of the Committee and its subsidiary bodies shall be held in public unless the Committee decides otherwise or it appears from the relevant provisions of the Covenant or the Protocol that the meetings shall be held in private'.[50] The relevant provisions are article 41(1)(*d*) of the Covenant and article 5(3) of the Protocol which provide that the Committee shall hold closed meetings when considering inter-State and individual communications respectively. In practice almost all of the HRC's meetings are held in public except when they are considering communications under the Optional Protocol.[51] A small number of representatives of non-governmental organizations attend HRC meetings but members of the public have rarely been present.[52] The Covenant contains only two mandatory rules of procedure. Article 39(2) provides that (*a*) twelve members shall constitute a quorum and that (*b*) decisions of the Committee shall be made by a majority vote of the members present. Notwithstanding this clear rule the appropriate method of decision making was the subject of intensive discussion within the HRC. From its inception the HRC had taken decisions on the basis of consensus.[53] When it came to adopting its Rules of Procedure the question arose as to whether the principle of decision making by consensus should be formally expressed within the corpus of the Rules.[54] In particular the independent experts from Eastern Europe were strongly in favour of its being formally expressed.[55] They referred to the increasing use of consensus decision making in international organizations.[56] However, a strong majority emerged against formal incorporation.[57] In the event the HRC adopted the draft rule referring to majority voting but with the following footnote in its Rules,

1. The members of the Committee generally expressed the view that its methods of work should normally allow for attempts to reach decisions by consensus before voting, provided that the Covenant and the Rules of Procedure were observed and that such attempts do not unduly delay the work of the Committee.

2. Bearing in mind paragraph 1 above, the Chairman at any meeting may, and at the request of any member shall, put the proposal to a vote.[58]

In retrospect the adoption of consensus decision making has proved to be one of the most significant decisions made by the HRC. Despite the inevitable differences that have arisen between members on many issues the HRC has shown a remarkable ability to reach decisions by consensus. As of 27 July 1990 no decision of the HRC has been taken by vote.[59] More than a decade of constructive development on the basis of consensus has made it something of a psychological barrier which members are loath to see destroyed. In theory there are obvious merits and demerits in consensus decision making.[60] A more realistic assessment of its worth can only be made on the basis of the HRC's actual practice in specific areas. Hence an assessment is offered in the concluding chapter of this work after the practices and procedures of the HRC have been examined in some detail.[61] More generally, however, it can be noted that the working relationships between members have been very good and references are consistently made to the 'conciliatory and co-operative spirit prevailing within the Committee based on mutual respect'.[62] The most striking aspect of this has, of course, been the practice of consensus decision making itself. As Sir Vincent-Evans pointed out, this internal co-operation also assists in establishing relationships with the States parties, 'States have consistently co-operated well and it appeared that the characteristic restraint and lack of polemics in the Committee's proceedings had helped it to gain the confidence of States parties'.[63] The good relationships between members are evident to any observer of the proceedings of the HRC.

2.8 The official languages of the HRC are Chinese, English, French, Spanish, Russian and, since 1984, Arabic. Its working languages are English, French, Spanish, Russian and, since 1984, Arabic.[64] The Rules provide that, 'Any speaker addressing the Committee and using a language other than one of the official languages shall normally provide for interpretation into one of the working languages'.[65] The HRC's Rules provide that the summary records of public meetings of the Committee shall be documents of general distribution unless, in exceptional circumstances, the Committee decides otherwise.[66] The summary records of private meetings are subject to restricted distribution.[67] The reports and other official documents of the HRC are of general distribution unless the HRC decides otherwise. Official documentation related to articles 41 and 42 of the Covenant (the inter-State procedure) and to the Optional Protocol are subject to restricted distribution.[68] Recently, temporary financial restrictions had meant that summary records were only provided for two weeks per session.[69]

2.9 The HRC has consistently recognized the importance of publicity for its work.[70] Press releases are prepared on its consideration of State reports and announcing the publication of its views under the Optional Protocol.[71] Press conferences are held to try and publicize its work.[72] The HRC's consistent pressure for broader publication of its records has had some success. Six volumes of a *Yearbook of the Human Rights Committee* have been published but they only cover its first six years.[73] Further volumes are planned but financial constraints seem certain to hinder publication and in any event they are increasingly dated. More helpful has been a publication of a volume of Selected Decisions under the Optional Protocol.[74] A second volume was published in 1990.[75] Publicity for the work of the HRC is also given by the United Nations *Human Rights Bulletin* and the *United Nations Yearbook on Human Rights*.[76] On a number of occasions members of the

HRC have publicized the work of the HRC by representing it at international human rights meetings, training courses, and workshops in various locations.[77] Similarly a number of HRC members have published articles explaining and commenting on the work of the HRC and the provisions in the Covenant.[78] The obvious problem faced by the HRC in attracting national and international publicity is that because it has conducted its work in a serious, de-politicized manner it is less 'newsworthy' than, for example, the Human Rights Commission. Moreover, its sessions take place in countries which are not parties to the Covenant. Therefore, the publicizing roles of the Secretariat, national and international non-governmental organizations, and academics assume critical importance.[79]

D. FUNCTIONS

2.10 The functions of the HRC are those provided for in the Covenant and the Protocol.[80] These lay down three substantive procedures directed toward the effective observance of the rights in the Covenant.

2.11 First, there is a mandatory reporting procedure. Article 40 of the Covenant provides for the 'consideration' and 'study' by the HRC of the national reports submitted by States parties on the measures they have adopted to give effect to the rights recognized in the Covenant and on the progress made in the enjoyment of those rights. The HRC must transmit 'its reports' and such 'general comments' as it may consider appropriate to the States parties. The HRC may also transmit to the Economic and Social Council (ECOSOC) these comments along with copies of the reports it has received from States parties to the Covenant. This reporting procedure is examined in detail in chapter 3.

2.12 Secondly, there is an optional inter-State procedure. Articles 41 and 42 of the Covenant provide for a system of inter-State complaints that another State party is not fulfilling its obligations under the Covenant. The HRC's competence only arises if both States parties have made a declaration under article 41 recognizing the HRC's competence to receive and consider such communications. Under article 41 the HRC 'shall make available its good offices to the States parties concerned with a view to the friendly solution of the matter'. If the matter is not resolved within the framework of article 41 further functions may, with the prior consent of the States parties, be exercised with respect to such allegations but by an *ad hoc* Conciliation Commission appointed under article 42 of the Covenant rather than by the HRC.[81] However, as of 27 July 1990 the inter-State procedure has not been invoked and it is not, therefore, examined in this thesis.[82]

2.13 Thirdly, there is an optional individual communications procedure under the Optional Protocol to the Covenant. Under the Protocol the HRC is competent to receive and consider communications from individuals subject to the jurisdiction of a State party to the Protocol who claim to be victims of a violation of any of the rights set forth in the Covenant. On completing its examination the HRC 'shall forward its views to the State party concerned and to the individual'.[83] The Optional Protocol entered into force on 23 March 1976.[84] The procedure under the Optional Protocol is examined in detail in chapter 4.

2.14 In addition to these substantive tasks the HRC is required to submit to the General Assembly, through the ECOSOC, an Annual Report on its activities under the Covenant containing a summary of its activities under the Protocol.[85] The contents and function of these reports are considered in the appropriate parts of chapters 3 and 4 below.

2.15 Finally, in April 1987 the HRC adopted a 'Statement on the Second Decade to Combat Racism and Racial Discrimination'.[86] The HRC has no express jurisdiction to issue such statements.

E. RELATIONS WITH THE SECRETARIAT

2.16 Article 36 of the Covenant provides that, 'The Secretary-General of the United Nations shall provide the necessary staff and facilities for the effective performance of the functions of the Committee under the present Covenant'. The Secretariat for the HRC is provided by the UN Centre for Human Rights in Geneva. Different Secretariat staff service the HRC under the reporting and petition procedures.[87] From as early as the HRC's fifth meeting it was apparent that adequate provision for secretariat resources had not been made although some improvement has taken place since.[88] The HRC has recommended in its Annual Reports that the Secretariat be granted the necessary personnel and resources.[89] As will be noted below,[90] the HRC has a peculiar status in that its Secretariat is provided by the UN but it is not a UN organ. As Sir Vincent-Evans commented, 'The Committee was a unique body and might frequently find itself asking the Secretariat to perform unusual tasks. Rather than straitjacket the Secretariat, it might be better to define the Secretariat's rights and duties empirically. The Committee and the Secretariat should act as a team with a common purpose of promoting human rights'.[91]

Generally, the working relationship between the HRC members and the Secretariat has been very good. Members of the HRC have consistently commended the work of the Secretariat. There have been some problems but they appear to be ones of communication difficulties rather than of substance.[92] However, during discussion of the HRC's rules of procedure it was evident that the HRC members did not wish to delegate any substantive decision making power to the Secretariat.[93]

2.17 The role of the Secretariat was acutely raised in the reaction of the HRC to a speech delivered by Mr Van Boven (then Director of the then Division of Human Rights) at the opening of the HRC's seventh session in which he commented on the HRC's work and pointed to some of the fundamental questions before it.[94] A number of HRC members expressed misgivings about the speech and concern about the role the Secretariat was assuming while others expressed their appreciation of the support given by the Secretariat.[95] Mr Van Boven himself commented forcefully,

He recognized that the Secretariat should be impartial and objective, but did that mean that the Secretariat was neutral? He did not think that the Secretariat should be a neutral and amorphous organ. In his opinion, that would not be in keeping with the provisions of the Charter. He cared greatly for the independent responsibility of the Secretariat as laid down in article 100 of the Charter. It was in the spirit of the Charter that all organs established in pursuance of the Charter should promote human rights and fundamental freedoms, and it was against that background and in that spirit that he raised those issues . . .[96]

In practice the Secretariat has had an increasing influence on the practices of the HRC under both the Covenant and the Optional Protocol. The Secretariat plays a major role in the preparatory work for the consideration of State reports under article 40,[97] the drafting of decisions on admissibility and final views under the Optional Protocol,[98] and the Annual Report of the HRC.[99] Other important aspects of its work include giving publicity to the work of the HRC,[100] keeping HRC members informed of world wide developments concerning human rights,[101] developing technical assistance and training schemes to assist States parties in complying with their reporting obligations under the Covenant.[102]

The HRC has always struggled to cope effectively with its workload. Increases in that workload appear to be inevitable. Notwithstanding the slowdown in ratifications of the Covenant there has been a substantial increase in individual communications in recent years. With increased publicity for its work and an increasing awareness of the Covenant and the Optional Protocol the HRC will almost certainly find it necessary to delegate more substantive tasks to the Secretariat. If so the role of the Secretariat and its relationship with the HRC will be of increasing significance. The good relationship to date augurs well for such a development to take place constructively.[103]

F. THE STATUS OF THE HUMAN RIGHTS COMMITTEE

2.18 The fundamental point to note here is that the Human Rights Committee is not, strictly speaking, a United Nations organ. It is a treaty based organ created by the States parties to the Covenant.[104] Having recognized this independent status the HRC has sought to exert a degree of autonomous decision making on the basis of it. This has manifested itself in a number of decisions concerning, for example, the holding of and venue of sessions,[105] rules of procedure,[106] distribution of documents,[107] and the role of the Secretariat under the Covenant and the Optional Protocol.[108] It is also interesting to note that the HRC's request that its Chairman be invited to present its first Annual Report to the General Assembly was refused on the ground that it might give the impression that the HRC was accountable to the General Assembly.

2.19 Realistically, however, it must be recognized that in practice the HRC is, in effect, in the position of a United Nations organ.[109] With one exception the HRC's sessions have been held at the two main seats of the United Nations and are likely to continue to do so.[110] They are totally financed from the United Nations budget and are therefore subject to the same general and particular fiscal constraints as are imposed on all United Nations organs. The members of the HRC receive emoluments from the United Nations.[111] The administrative functioning and servicing of the HRC depends totally on the assistance of the Secretariat within the United Nations Centre For Human Rights in Geneva. This extreme financial dependence on the United Nations was particularly evident when the HRC was equally, if not disproportionately, affected by the across-the-board financial cuts implemented by the United Nations Secretary-General because of the financial crisis at the United Nations. In the final event this led, *inter alia*, to the cancellation of the HRC's proposed session in autumn 1986.[112]

Various other provisions of the Covenant and the Protocol underline the link between the HRC and the UN. The UN Secretary-General has an important role in the conduct of elections to the HRC by the States parties and those elections take place at the UN.[113] The Secretary-General is the depository for ratifications and accessions to the Covenant and the Protocol and circulates the information relating to them.[114] Amendments to the Covenant and the Protocol must be submitted to the General Assembly for approval.[115] Finally, as we have already noted, the Annual Report of the HRC is submitted to the General Assembly, through ECOSOC.[116] In practice the Annual Report is considered in some detail by the Third Committee of the General Assembly.[117] By contrast the meetings of the States parties have played no substantive role in the implementation of the Covenant or the Protocol.[118]

G. THE NATURE OF THE HUMAN RIGHTS COMMITTEE

2.20 We noted in chapter 1 the major changes made by the Third Committee to the functions of the HRC in the Human Rights Commission's draft.[119] We have also referred to the key elements in the composition of the HRC, namely, the independent status of HRC members, their geographical distribution, and the representation of the different forms of civilization and of the principal legal systems.[120] One of the major purposes of the subsequent chapters of this work is to indicate the nature of the HRC through its practices and procedures. However, on a number of occasions members of the HRC have indicated their perceptions of the institutional character and nature of the HRC and it is instructive to note some of these.[121]

2.21 Mr Uribe-Vargas described it as a body whose work was of a 'judicial nature'.[122] Mr Mora-Rojas said that 'The Committee was quite different in nature from other bodies and, even though it was not a court or a tribunal, it did hear testimony and had evidence presented to it'.[123] Mr Tomuschat has commented that, 'The Committee was . . . ruled by the Covenant and while it was true that members were not judges they had the task of applying the provisions laid down in the Covenant and therefore had to exercise judgement. It was the duty of the Committee to ensure that States parties fulfilled their obligations under the Covenant.'[124] Mr Tomuschat has also said that 'The Committee was not an international court but was similar to one in certain respects, particularly in regard to its obligation to be guarded by exclusively legal criteria—which rightly distinguished it from a political body'.[125] Mr Ermacora was concerned that the Committee should avoid giving the impression that it was 'a sort of advisory service, or had technical, assistance functions, whereas in fact its activities were based on legally binding instruments, with all the attendant consequences that that entailed'.[126] Mr Aguilar commented that the Committee 'was not a judicial body' and 'its role was not to find fault'.[127] Mr Bouziri commented that the 'Committee was not a court of law'.[128] Mr Pocar commented that the Committee's function 'was not to judge and then either to condemn or congratulate States parties'.[129] Mr Graefrath 'did not share the view that the work of the Committee could be compared to that of a court . . . Unlike a court the Committee was not required to make judgements, but simply to consider and comment on reports and to act as a conciliatory body in dealing with complaints and communications'.[130] Mr Opsahl has described the HRC as the 'executive organ' of the Covenant.[131] Emphasis is often put on the HRC's role as a promoter, monitor, or supervisory body with respect to improved human rights performances.[132] However, some members have expressed doubts as to whether the HRC can properly be called a 'supervisory body' or a 'parent organ'.[133] Finally, Mr Suy (UN Legal Advisor) believed the HRC to be 'neither a legislative nor a judicial body but that every expert body was sui generis',[134] and Mr Herndl, former Under Secretary-General of the United Nations, recently described the HRC as 'the guardian of the Covenant'.[135]

2.22 Clearly then, there are some differences within the HRC as to its nature and its purposes. However, many of these comments broadly accord with the shift from the largely judicial nature of the HRC envisaged in the Human Rights Commission's draft to an HRC with a more amorphous nature. That nature includes elements of judicial, quasi-judicial, administrative, investigative, inquisitorial, supervisory, and conciliatory functions. It is submitted that to understand the true nature of the HRC it must be recognized that its nature may alter in accordance with its exercise of the various functions and roles it performs or could perform.[136]

We now examine in turn the principal functions of the HRC to date under the systems of periodic reporting (ch. 3) and of individual communications under the Optional Protocol (ch. 4).

NOTES

1 See M. J. Bossuyt, 'Le Règlement intérieur du Comité des Droits de L'homme', 14 Revue belge de droit international (1978–9) pp. 104–56; G. Cote-Harper, 'Le Comité de Droits de L'homme des Nations Unies', 28 Cahiers des droits (1987) pp. 533–46; E. Decaux, 'La Mise en vigueur du Pacte International Relatifs aux Droits Civils et Politiques', 84 Revue générale de droit international public (1980) pp. 487–534; F. Capotorti, 'The International Measures of Implementation Included in the Covenants on Human Rights', in *Eide and Schou*, ch. 1 n. 1 above, pp. 131–48; M. Lippman, ibid., pp. 250–1; A. H. Robertson, 'The Implementation System: International Measures', in Henkin (ed.), ibid., pp. 337–41; F. Jhabvala, ibid, pp. 81–95; E. Schwelb, ibid. (1968) pp. 835–8; M. Nowak, ch. 3 n. 1 below, pp. 143–6; A. J. G. Mower, 'Organizing to Implement the UN Civil/Political Rights Covenant: First Steps by the Committee', 3 HR Rev. (1978) pp. 122–31; A. J. G. Mower, 'The Implementation of the UN Covenant on Civil and Political Rights', 10 RDH/HRJ (1977) pp. 271–95; E. Mose and T. Opsahl, ch. 4 n. 1 below; P. S. Brar, ch. 3 n. 1 below, ch. 1; V. Dimitrijevic, *The Roles of the Human Rights Committee* (1986); Tyagi, ch. 2.

2 See ch. 1, prs. 1.6–1.12 above.

3 Ibid. See in particular, Jhabvala, n. 1 above.

4 Under article 38 every member of the Human Rights Committee must make a solemn declaration that he will perform his functions impartially and conscientiously.

5 Article 8 ICERD follows article 31(2) ICCPR. The presence of experts from different legal systems can assist the HRC in its consideration of reports under article 40. For example, during consideration of the report of Morocco it was useful to have members of the HRC who were conversant with Islamic laws. The provision in article 31(2) can give States parties the confidence that their approach will at least be understood even if disagreed with and avoids the necessity of having provision for an '*ad hoc*' representative nominated by the particular State party concerned which could only detract from the independent status of the HRC. *Ad hoc* representation was proposed during the drafting

stages but was deleted by the HRCion in 1951, see Doc. E/1992, ch. 1 n. 1 above, pr. 78. See SR 299 pr. 11 (Movchan).

6 Independent international human rights bodies include the EUCM, EUCT, CEDAW, CERD, IACM, IACT, Committee Against Torture, Sub-Commission on the Prevention of Discrimination and the Protection of Minorities, the Committee of Independent Experts under the ESC, the Committee of Experts on the Application of Conventions and Recommendations of the ILO; and the new UN Committee on Economic, Social and Cultural Rights. The Committee on the Rights of the Child under the UN Children's Convention (1989) will also be composed of independent experts.

7 Cf. Rule 4 of Rules of the EUCT, see *ECHR—Collected Texts* (1986) p. 147.

8 e.g. Mr Ermacora is a member of the Austrian Parliament.

9 e.g. Mr Graefrath has represented the GDR in the Third Committee of the General Assembly.

10 The Chairman receives $5,000. The members receive $3,000 per year. See SR 263. There have been consistent complaints from HRC members concerning the level of emoluments and problems with other facilities, e.g. lack of medical insurance. Under article 8(6) ICERD members of the CERD receive their expenses from the national governments. There have been problems in members receiving their expenses. It has been argued that the ICCPR represents an advance in this respect.

11 See the comments of Mr Van Boven, SR 150 pr. 71.

12 'There is a strong case for making membership on the Committee a salaried occupation to which members could devote all their time', Robertson, n. 1 above, p. 339.

13 This submission is also based on the view that the UN Secretariat will need to play an increasing role in the work of the HRC, see prs. 2.16–2.17 below.

14 See the bibliographies published for the meeting of States parties to elect members of the HRC, documents prefixed CCPR/SP. By contrast the regional groupings consistently failed to nominate enough candidates for the Sessional Working Group of Experts under the ICESCR. See Alston, n. 38 below, p. 346 n. 97. On the CEDAW see Byrnes, ch. 3 n. 1 below, pp. 8–12.

15 The sessions of the HRC cover approximately three months of the year in total.

16 e.g. the ex-Chairman, Mr. Prado-Vallejo, was formerly a journalist.

17 Docs. A/38/40 pr. 8; A/39/40 pr. 6.

18 Mrs Higgins, independent expert from the UK, is Professor of international law at the University of London, London School of Economics. Ms Chanet, independent expert from France, is a judge.

19 'The Committee operated on a contractual basis, namely, the Covenant', SR 572 pr. 11 (Movchan). See B. Graefrath, 'Trends Emerging in the Practice of the Human Rights Committee', 3 Bull. GDR Committee for Human Rights (1980) pp. 3–32.

20 See ch. 3, prs. 3.29–3.38 below.

21 Occasionally members of the HRC have strayed into more overtly political questioning. See SR 364, 365, 366, and 368 on Iran.

22 See SR 729; Doc. A/42/40, pr. 7.

23 Article 30(1), (4).

24 See Doc. CCPR/SP/7 (1976): decisions of the first meeting of the States parties to the ICCPR.

25 Hence elections have taken place in 1978, 1980, 1982, 1984, 1986, 1988, and 1990. See the series of documents prefixed CCPR/SP.

26 See article 30 for details.

27 Article 29. Cf. article 8(2) ICERD; article 36(2) AMR.

28 Article 32.

29 Article 30(4).

30 Article 32.

31 Doc. CCPR/SP/SR 2.

32 Article 32.

33 In particular the following influential members have left: Sir Vincent Evans (UK), Tomuschat (FRG), Graefrath (GDR), and Opsahl (Norway).

34 Mr Mavrommatis, and Mr Prado-Vallejo.

35 Article 34(3). Article 33 of the Covenant deals with members ceasing to carry out functions, and with deaths and resignations.

36 Doc. A/44/40, Annex II, p. 157. The previous members of the HRC are shown in the HRC's annual reports.

37 See pr. 2.2 above.

38 Cf. the 'relatively inflexible formula' of five geographical groupings in the rules for the CESCR, see P. Alston, 'Out of the Abyss: The Challenges Confronting the New U.N. Committee on Economic, Social and Cultural Rights', 9 HRQ (1987) pp. 332–81 at p. 349. See also Committee on Economic, Social and Cultural Rights, Report of First Session, ECOSOC OR, 1987, Supp. 17 (1987); P. Alston and B. Simma, 'First Session of the New UN Committee on Economic, Social and Cultural Rights', 81 AJIL (1987) pp. 747–56; P. Alston and B. Simma, 'Second Session of the UN Committee on Economic, Social and Cultural Rights', 82 AJIL (1988) pp. 603–15.

39 See Mower, n. 1 above (1978); Decaux, ibid.

40 Convention on the Privileges and Immunities of the United Nations, 1 UNTS 15. See *Applicability of Article VI, Section 22 of the Convention on the Privileges and Immunities of the United Nations*, ICJ Reps. (1989), p. 177.

41 Article 37(2), (3). The HRC adopted 'Provisional Rules of Procedure' at its first and second sessions (hereinafter 'Rules'). Subsequent amendments were made at its third, seventh, and thirty-sixth sessions. See Doc. CCPR/C/3/Rev. 1 (1979), and Rev. 2 (December 1989) Doc. A/44/40, pp. 179–82. The Rules were made definitive in July 1989, see SR 918. On the Rules see in particular, Bossuyt, n. 1 above; Mower (1978), ibid.; Robertson, ibid. The CERD has recently upgraded its provisional rules, see Doc. CERD/C/35/Rev. 3 (1986).

42 Rules 1 and 2.

43 The General Assembly accepted the arguments of the HRC on the need for a third session.

44 See the discussion in SR 880. Some rescheduling of the HRC's sessions was experienced in the HRC's early years. HRC members have stressed the importance of holding at least one session a year in New York on the basis that it

is the major headquarters of the UN, the information media there is more developed, and it is a more suitable venue for a number of States parties, particularly developing countries most of which have permanent missions in New York which is not the case in Geneva. A number of States have requested that their reports are considered in New York rather than Geneva. See SR 44 prs. 20–2; SR 177 prs. 6–17; Doc. A/35/40, pp. 96–7; Doc. A/44/40, pr. 27; SR 880.

45 The use of pre-sessional working groups has been an almost constant feature of the HRC's work subject to occasional resource problems. The working groups continue to meet during the sessions of the HRC.

46 Docs. A/41/40, prs. 425–34; A/42/40, prs. 4, 12–14. The single working group found it impossible to deal with its workload, SR 758 prs. 22–35.

47 Support has been expressed in the Third Committee for maintaining the normal pattern of the Committee's meetings, Doc. A/42/40, pr. 27.

48 The fourteenth session was held in Bonn. See Docs. A/36/40, prs. 28–32; A/37/40, pr. 4; SR 290. Particularly in its early years many members of the HRC indicated the desirability of the HRC holding sessions outside of New York or Geneva. The possibility was examined by the Secretary-General at the request of the General Assembly (GA Resn. 38/145). The Secretary-General drew attention to GA Resn. 31/140 which provides in part that, 'UN bodies may hold sessions away from their established headquarters when a Government issuing a request for a session to be held within its territory has agreed to defer ... the actual additional costs directly and indirectly involved'. The financial crisis at the UN makes any change in the governing rules extremely unlikely. It is submitted that the developed States should give serious consideration to hosting a session of the HRC.

49 See SR 868 prs. 13–14. The HRC has paid tribute to the expert chairmanship of Mr Mavrommatis during its first ten years, Doc. A/42/40, pr. 11.

50 R. 33. The understanding was that the HRC would meet in private only in exceptional cases, see SR 5 and 6.

51 The working of the Optional Protocol has sometimes been discussed in public session.

52 It would be helpful if the annual reports of the HRC listed the non-governmental representatives who have attended its sessions even though they have no formal role in the HRC's proceedings. Cf. Report of CESCR, n. 38 above, prs. 6–7. Private individuals rarely attend HRC meetings and have often faced difficulties in gaining access. See the comments at SR 91 pr. 43; SR 263 pr. 32; SR 282 pr. 53.

53 See Fischer, Ch. 3 n. 1 below, pp. 149–51. K. Zemanek, 'Majority Rule and Consensus Technique in Law-Making Diplomacy', in R. St. J. MacDonald and D. Johnstone (eds.), ch. 1 n. 7 above, pp. 857–87; B. F. Selassie, *Consensus and Peace* (UNESCO, 1980).

54 For the HRC's discussion of consensus see SR 4, 5, 6, 7, 13, 14, and 15; Doc. A/32/44, prs. 27–34. SR 14 pr. 2 contains a summary of the various suggestions.

55 See e.g. the comments at SR 7 prs. 5 (Hanga), 9 (Koulishev), 10 (Graefrath), 22 (Movchan).

56 e.g. by the Conference on the Law of the Sea, the International Law Commission and the Conference on Security and Co-operation in Europe.

57 They argued, *inter alia*, that the consensus principle might be interpreted in a sense incompatible with the independence of members, that it might in practice operate as a veto and create working difficulties.

58 Rule 10.

59 The consensus was nearly broken over the drafting of a general comment on article 20, see ch. 12 below.

60 See n. 53 above. For some comments see SR 357 p. 60 (Vincent-Evans); SR 34 pr. 39 (Opsahl).

61 See ch. 13 below.

62 SR 6 pr. 9. See Anon., 'The New Human Rights Committee', 19 Rev. ICJ (1977) pp. 19–22. The first meetings of the new CESCR were not so harmonious although the situation has improved since, see E/CN.12/1987/SR. 1–28, and 1990/SR. 1–26.

63 SR 232 pr. 24. See also SR 260 pr. 17 (Graefrath).

64 Rule 28. See Doc. A/39/40, pr. 24.

65 R. 30. So, for example, Iran provided its own translators when it appeared before the HRC under the reporting process. R. 30 was adopted on the understanding that, 'the Committee had taken note of the fact that it might have to assist petitioners in providing for interpretation', SR 14 prs. 12–27.

66 R. 36(1). See SR 6 prs. 29–44; SR 14 prs. 1–17. The summary records are drafted in English and French and then translated into the other languages. Some long translation delays have occurred, see Doc. A/42/40, pr. 24; ECOSOC Resn. 1987/4 pr. 14.

67 R. 36(2). See SR 6 prs. 48–53. So documents relating to the Optional Protocol are confidential. Inadmissibility decisions and the views of the HRC under article 5(4) are made public.

68 R. 64.

69 Doc. A/41/40, pr. 432.

70 See Docs. A/34/40 prs. 21–3; A/35/40 prs. 13–19; A/36/40 prs. 19–27; A/37/40 prs. 17–20; A/38/40 prs. 19–25; A/39/40 prs. 26–35.

71 See R. 75.

72 See Doc. A/41/40, pr. 10.

73 *Yearbooks of the Human Rights Committee*: 1977–8, vol. i, Doc. CCPR/1 (1986); vol. ii, Doc. CCPR/C/Add. 1 (1986); 1979–80, vol. i, Doc. CCPR/2 (1988); vol. ii, Doc. CCPR/2/Add. 1 (1989); 1981–2, vol. i, Doc. CCPR/3 (1989); vol. ii, Doc. CCPR/C/3/Add. 3 (1989). Future volumes will be entitled *Official Records of the Human Rights Committee*, Doc. A/43/40, pr. 15.

74 Selected Decisions, vol. i, ch. 4 n. 1 below.

75 Selected Decisions, vol. ii, ch. 4 n. 1 below.

76 See e.g. the Special UN Human Rights Bulletin (Geneva, 1986).

77 See Doc. A/38/40, prs. 35–9; Doc. A/43/40, pr. 19.

78 Members who have published include Tomuschat, Graefrath, Tarnopolsky, Dimitrijevic, Cote-Harper, Lallah, Higgins, and Movchan.

79 See prs. 2.16–2.17 below.

80 Article 28. See also OP2 in Apx. IV below. See ch. 1 pr. 1.18–1.21 on inter-national implementation measures.

81 See rules 72–7E; Doc. A/34/40, prs. 28–53.

82 See article 4 of OP2. On the inter-State procedure see Robertson, n. 1 above, pp. 351–6; Tyagi, ch. 4. Cf. the compulsory inter-State procedure under article 11 ICERD. See generally S. Leckie, 'The Inter-State Complaint Procedure in International Law: Hopeful Prospects or Wishful Thinking?', 10 HRQ (1988) pp. 249–303.

83 Article 5(4) OP.

84 See ch. 4, prs. 4.37–4.43.

85 Article 45 Covenant; article 6 OP. The Annual Report will presumably also cover OP2 once it enters into force as the provisions of OP2 apply as additional provisions of the Covenant, see article 6 of OP2.

86 See SR 725; Doc. A/42/40, pr. 18 and Apx. VI.

87 The International Instruments Unit and the Communications Unit respectively. The Secretary-General informed the General Assembly that he accepted the responsibilities under article 36. See also GA Resn. 31/86.

88 See SR 5 pr. 11 (Schreiber, Director of the then Human Rights Division); SR 42 prs. 44, 45; SR 74 pr. 38.

89 See Doc. A/32/44, prs. 178–80. The Human Rights Centre faces continuing difficulties in securing the necessary resources. Less than 1% of the regular budget of the United Nations is allocated to the human rights sector. The effect is that apart from the routine servicing of meetings there is minimal secretariat assistance available to members of the HRC who, for example, might be trying to secure information on the human rights situation in a particular State party. For the HRC's most recent comments on lack of secretariat services see Doc. A/44/40, prs. 34, 618.

90 See prs. 2.18–2.19 below.

91 SR 153 pr. 7.

92 See the comments at SR 572 prs. 14–17; SR 727 pr. 3.

93 See the discussion in SR 5 on the information to be provided to the HRC by the Secretariat.

94 See SR 152 prs. 2–16.

95 SR 153 prs. 4–12; SR 179 prs. 22 *et seq*.

96 SR 153 pr. 11. Subsequently Mr Van Boven's contract with the UN was not renewed.

97 See ch. 3 below.

98 See ch. 4 below.

99 See ch. 3, pr. 3.40 below.

100 See pr. 2.9 above.

101 See ch. 3 below.

102 Ibid.

103 Mose and Opsahl, ch. 4 n. 1 below, suggest that the HRC needs the assistance of a permanent Secretariat, p. 330. Secretariats often play a very influential role in the development of international human rights law and practice.

104 See pr. 2.4 above; Doc. A/32/44, pr. 19. Mose and Opsahl, ch. 4 n. 1 below comment, 'Nor is the activity of the Committee under the Protocol subject to any

kind of control or review by other bodies, or backed by any machinery of enforcement. We have noted its independent status in not being a United Nations' organ. Depending on the Committee's approach, this position may be seen as a source of considerable weakness as well as a source of strength in some respects', p. 326.

105 See SR 3 prs. 37–46.

106 See e.g. SR 6 pr. 59 (Vincent-Evans); SR 8 pr. 27 (Movchan).

107 See e.g. SR 8 pr. 44 (Opsahl); Doc. A/32/44, prs. 35–7.

108 See prs. 2.16–2.17 above.

109 See Farer, ch. 1 n. 1 above, p. 567.

110 See pr. 2.6 above.

111 Article 35. See pr. 2.2 above.

112 See Docs. A/41/40 prs. 425–34; A/42/40 pr. 4.

113 See pr. 2.5 above.

114 See articles 48–9, 51–3 Covenant; articles 8–9, 13–14 OP.

115 See article 51 Covenant; article 11 OP.

116 See pr. 2.14 above.

117 See ch. 3, pr. 3.40 below.

118 See ch. 3, pr. 3.39 below. Mose and Opsahl, ch. 4 n. 1 below, comment, 'Whether the meeting (of States parties) may exercise additional or inherent powers in its electoral capacity or assume other functions has not yet been explored. It does not seem to be intended that such a meeting should act as a representative of the collectivity of States in matters of substance, for example, by issuing binding instructions to the Committee', p. 284. Cf. the views of Mr Scott, Office of Legal Affairs, UN Secretariat, on the CERD. Doc. A/C.3/40/SR.46, p. 8, noted in UKMIL 1985 in 1985 BYIL pp. 408–9.

119 See ch. 1, prs. 1.6–1.12 above.

120 See prs. 2.2–2.5 above.

121 See also ch. 3, prs. 3.29–3.38 below.

122 SR 6 pr. 73.

123 SR 7 pr. 17.

124 SR 7 pr. 19.

125 SR 117 pr. 35.

126 SR 306 pr. 20.

127 SR 743 pr. 12 and SR 719 pr. 32 respectively.

128 SR 231 pr. 29.

129 SR 719 pr. 29.

130 SR 7 pr. 1.

131 SR 342 pr. 68. 'In effect the meetings of States parties was the legislative organ for the Covenant', ibid. Cf. the comment of Mose and Opsahl in n. 118 above.

132 SR 50 pr. 7 (Opsahl); SR 232 pr. 44 (Tarnopolsky); SR 117 pr. 35 (Tomuschat), and the discussion in SR 231.

133 See SR 174 Add. 1 pr. 28 (Graefrath), 45 (Hanga), 47 (Koulishev).

134 SR 13 pr. 6 (Mr Suy, Under-Secretary-General, Legal Counsel).

135 SR 702 pr. 4.

136 See V. Dimitrijevic, n. 1 above.

3

The System of Periodic Reporting[1]

INTRODUCTION

3.1 Periodic reporting is the most widespread and established implementation technique for the international implementation of human rights.[2] The obligation to submit reports is the only obligation which States parties to the ICCPR assume, *ipso facto*, on ratification or accession. The national reports submitted are considered and examined by the Human Rights Committee (HRC), the independent body of experts established under article 28 of the ICCPR.[3] This chapter analyses the reporting procedure as it has developed in the practice of the HRC.

The reporting obligation is contained in article 40 of the ICCPR which provides that,

1. The States parties to the present Covenant undertake to submit reports on the measures they have adopted which give effect to the rights recognized herein and on the progress made in the enjoyment of those rights:

(a) Within one year of the entry into force of the present Covenant for the States Parties concerned;

(b) Thereafter whenever the Committee so requests.

2. All reports shall be submitted to the Secretary-General of the United Nations, who shall transmit them to the Committee for consideration. Reports shall indicate the factors and difficulties, if any, affecting the implementation of the present Covenant.

3. The Secretary-General of the United Nations may, after consultation with the Committee, transmit to the specialized agencies concerned copies of such parts of the reports as may fall within their field of competence.

4. The Committee shall study the reports submitted by the States Parties to the present Covenant. It shall transmit its reports, and such general comments as it may consider appropriate, to the States Parties. The Committee may also transmit to the Economic and Social Council these comments along with copies of reports it has received from States Parties to the present Covenant.

5. The States Parties to the present Covenant may submit to the Committee observations on any comments that may be made in accordance with paragraph 4 of this article.

A. THE NATIONAL REPORTS

3.2 In practice three types of reports have emerged: initial, supplementary, and periodic.[4] It is necessary to explain these to understand the HRC's decisions on periodicity.

1. The initial reports

3.3 These are the reports submitted by the States parties in accordance with the basic obligation under article 40(1)(*a*) ICCPR. The HRC has emphasized that, 'the submission of such reports was an international legal obligation under article 40, paragraph 1(a), of the Covenant'.[5] States parties are required to report on the 'measures they have adopted which give effect to the rights recognized herein and on progress made in the enjoyment of those rights'. The general term 'measures' was preferred in the Third Committee of the General Assembly to more specific formulations as it was argued that it would afford States parties greater freedom to report on the entire range of laws and practices ensuring compliance with the Covenant.[6] The 'rights recognized' are the rights contained in articles 1–27 of the Covenant[7] although other articles may also be relevant.[8] It is not open to States parties to accept only certain of the rights established in the ICCPR.[9] In accordance with article 40(1)(*a*), the first initial reports were due to be submitted on 23 March 1977, one year after the entry into force of the ICCPR for the original States parties.[10]

The Covenant itself gives no further indication of the required form and contents of State reports. The extreme qualitative and quantitative diversity of the early reports submitted clearly demonstrated the need for guidelines indicating the wishes of the HRC in this regard. Having gained some initial experience in the consideration of reports, the HRC had no hesitation in producing general guidelines for the assistance of States parties in complying with their reporting obligations.[11] The HRC stated that compliance with the guidelines 'will help to ensure that reports are presented in a uniform manner and enable the HRC and States Parties to obtain a complete picture of the situation in each State as regards the implementation of the rights referred to in the Covenant', and, 'reduce the need for the Committee to request additional information under its rules of procedure'.[12] In accordance with the general guidelines the initial reports of States were to be in two parts as follows.[13]

Part I: General. This part should briefly describe the general legal framework within which civil and political rights are protected in the reporting State. In particular it should indicate:

    (a) Whether any of the rights referred to in the Covenant are protected either in the Constitution or by a separate 'Bill of Rights', and, if so, what provisions are made in the Constitution or in the 'Bill of Rights' for derogations and in what circumstances.

(b) Whether the provisions of the Covenant can be invoked before and directly enforced by the courts, other tribunals or administrative authorities or whether they have to be transformed into internal laws or administrative regulations to be enforced by the authorities concerned.

(c) What judicial, administrative or other competent authorities have jurisdiction affecting human rights.

(d) What remedies are available to an individual who claims that any of his rights have been violated.

(e) What other measures have been taken to ensure the implementation of the provisions of the Covenant.

Part II: Information relating to each of the articles in parts I, II and III of the Covenant. This part should describe in relation to the provisions of each article:

(a) The legislative, administrative, or other measures in force in regard to each right;

(b) Any restrictions or limitations even of a temporary nature imposed by law or practice or any other manner on the enjoyment of the right;

(c) Any other factors or difficulties affecting the enjoyment of the right by persons within the jurisdiction of the State;

(d) Any other information on the progress made in the enjoyment of the right.

The general guidelines also state that the State report should be accompanied by copies of the principal legislative and other texts referred to in the report and that the HRC will welcome at any time information on any significant new development in regard to the rights referred to in the Covenant. On the basis of the reports the HRC hoped to 'develop a *constructive dialogue* with each State Party in regard to the implementation of the Covenant'.[14] This emphasis on 'constructive dialogue' has been the keynote of the HRC's practice under article 40.

2. Supplementary (or Additional) reports[15]

3.4 Notwithstanding the general guidelines established by the HRC the problem of incomplete reports has bedevilled its work under article 40 of the ICCPR. Many reports have been characterized by their brevity and inadequacy, containing little more than generalities and unsubstantiated references to national legislative and administrative provisions. Abstract legalism has been accompanied by proclamations of wholesale compliance with the Covenant.[16] Few reports have made any serious attempt to identify the 'factors and difficulties' affecting the implementation of the Covenant (Article 40(4)).[17] States are perhaps naturally reluctant to identify their own difficulties and shortcomings although when State representatives appear before the HRC they are more forthcoming in identifying obstacles to the implementation of the Covenant.[18]

Faced with inadequate and incomplete reports and the fact that in the course of its consideration of State's reports Committee members have often been prompted to raise questions which State representatives have left unanswered, the Committee have in the case of all reports to date requested additional information in the oral hearings.[19] Similarly in many cases State representatives have promised additional information. This information is submitted in Supplementary (or Additional) reports. Whether States parties are under a legal obligation to submit such information has occasionally been questioned within the HRC. The majority of members, however, appear to take the view that a legal basis for such requests exists either in the obligation on States parties to comply fully with the basic reporting obligation under article $40(1)(a)$ or in the HRC's power to request a subsequent report whenever it chooses to do so (art. $40(1)(b)$) on the basis that this implies a lesser power to request additional information.[20] It is submitted that the majority view is correct on either basis. It should not sensibly be open to a State to submit an inadequate report and then refuse to supply any further information. On a number of occasions the HRC have made it clear that they did not regard the consideration of a State's report as complete until it had received and considered further information.[21] In an important recent development the HRC reached a consensus that it had the power under article $40(1)(b)$ to request additional information from a State in response to particular events.[22]

No guidelines have been established for Supplementary reports. Their content has varied from State to State. They have contained information omitted from initial reports, additional information to bring matters up to date or thought by the State party to be relevant, and answers and replies to questions put by members of the HRC during the consideration of the initial report.[23]

As of 27 July 1990 the Committee has considered 84 initial reports and a small number of supplementary reports most of which were prepared after publication of the general guidelines.[24] Although the Committee has noted that the guidelines have been followed by the majority of reporting States and proved useful both to those States and to the Committee, it has indicated that it would review them in due time to see whether they could be improved.[25] It has not yet chosen to do so. This might suggest that the Committee is reasonably satisfied with the guidelines as they stand. It can be argued, however, that part of the need which the Committee members have felt to ask a large number of questions requesting further information, explanations, and detailed clarifications, stem from the very generality in which the guidelines are framed. There is no indication of the specific aspects of each article on which the HRC wishes to have information. The guidelines of the ILO Committee of Experts and the Committee of Independent Experts under the European Social Charter are much more detailed and have produced fuller information.[26] Similarly, the Committee on the Elimination of Racial Discrimination has issued revised general guidelines on the form and content of State reports under article 9 of the ICERD which specify the information required in respect of each article of the ICERD.[27] Those revised guidelines have included some of the Recommendations of the CERD adopted under article 9(2) of the ICERD. It could be argued that the very generality of the HRC's guidelines has been fruitful in that it has resulted in an extensive, substantial, and informative dialogue between the HRC and the States parties, through their State representatives. However, it is submitted that the HRC should revise and expand its general guidelines into more specific guidelines taking account of the General Comments adopted by it under article 40(4) and its established repertoire of questions under the article 40 reporting procedure.[28] More specific guidelines would make for a more efficient and productive consideration of future reports and allow more time for substantive comments by members rather than an extended series of questions and requests for further information. However, it must be recognized that the practical effect of new guidelines would not be very great as it is periodic reports which have now assumed more importance.

3. Periodic reports

3.5 In an important '*Consensus Statement*'[29] on its duties under article 40 of the Covenant the HRC reaffirmed its aim to be that of engaging in a 'constructive dialogue' with States parties on the basis of periodic reports submitted under article 40(1)(*b*) of the ICCPR.[30] The aim of the periodic reports is to complete the information required by the HRC and to bring to the HRC's attention any development with respect to the implementation of the ICCPR since the consideration of the previous State report. At its thirteenth session (July 1981) the HRC adopted the following guidelines as regards the form and content of periodic reports under article 40(1)(*b*).[31] Again the reports were to be in two parts.

Part I: General

This part should contain information concerning the general framework within which the civil and political rights recognized by the Covenant are protected in the reporting State.

Part II: Information in relation to each of the articles in Parts I, II and III of the Covenant.

This part should contain information in relation to each of the provisions of individual articles.

Under these two main headings the contents of reports should concentrate especially on:

(a) the completion of the information before the Committee as to the measures adopted to give effect to rights recognized in the Covenant, taking account of the questions raised in the Committee on the examination of any previous report and including in particular additional information as to questions not previously answered or not fully answered;

(b) information taking into account general comments which the Committee may have made under Article 40, paragraph 4, of the Covenant;

(c) Action taken as a result of experience gained in co-operation with the Committee;

(d) changes made or proposed to be made in the laws and practices relevant to the Covenant;

(e) factors affecting and difficulties experienced in the implementation of the Covenant;

(f) the progress made since the last report in the enjoyment of rights recognized in the Covenant.

It should be noted that the reporting obligation extends not only to the relevant laws and other norms, but also to the practices of the courts and administrative organs of the State party and other relevant facts likely to show the degree of actual enjoyment of rights recognized in the Covenant.

The report should be accompanied by copies of the principle legislative and other texts referred to in it.

3.5.1 In July 1989 the HRC adopted a recommendation by one of its working group on consolidated guidelines for initial and periodic reports submitted under United Nations human rights instruments. The guidelines cover land and people, general political structures, general legal framework within which human rights are protected, and information and publicity (see pr. 3.53 below).

4. The periodicity of reports

3.6 Having confirmed that the dialogue with States parties was to be conducted on the basis of the regular periodic reports to be submitted under article 40(1)(*b*) the HRC then considered the question of the appropriate reporting period.[32] The Covenant is silent on the periodicity of reports other than the initial ones. The operative part of the HRC's periodicity decision, adopted at its thirteenth session (1981), provides that,

In accordance with article 40, paragraph 1(b), the Human Rights Committee requests:

(a) State parties which have submitted their initial reports or additional information relating to their initial reports before the end of the thirteenth session to submit subsequent reports every five years from the consideration of their initial report or their additional information;

(b) Other States parties to submit subsequent reports to the Committee every five years from the date when their initial report was due.

This is without prejudice to the power of the Committee, under article 40, paragraph 1(b), of the Covenant, to request a subsequent report whenever it deems appropriate.[33]

The five-year periodicity was established without prejudice to moving to a three- or four-year periodicity at a later stage as soon as this appeared feasible in terms of the HRC's workload.[34] It has not yet proved feasible and seems unlikely to do so. Bearing in mind the detailed consideration of reports by the HRC, the wide scope of the rights covered by the Covenant, and the large number of international reporting obligations imposed on States parties, it is submitted that five years is a sensible and practicable period and should not be reduced unless the various international reporting procedures are rationalized.[35]

The apparent simplicity of the periodicity decision belies the complexity of the issues involved. In the event members clearly acknowledged that the decision did not cover all aspects of a State's reporting obligations and that a number of issues awaited resolution.[36] One of those issues concerned the effect on periodicity, if any, of the submission by States of Supplementary reports. The HRC had recognized that it might have to take account of the submission and consideration of such reports in setting submission dates for periodic reports. In its Consensus Statement it had indicated that, 'As far as the States parties whose additional information or supplementary reports have already been considered by the Committee are concerned, these reports may be considered to be their second periodic reports'.[37] In fact the HRC has not generally considered Supplementary reports as second periodic reports.

Amendment to the periodicity decision

3.7 In practice there have been substantial difficulties and delays in obtaining the Supplementary reports promised by State parties. Members of the HRC perceived the source of these difficulties to be its own periodicity decision which had given States parties the impression that the HRC would not take any action subsequent to the consideration of the initial report for a period of five years.[38] The failure of States to submit reports meant that the 'dialogue' between the HRC and States parties was breaking down for very long periods. In an effort to induce States to submit supplementary reports and continue their dialogue with the HRC, the HRC adopted an amendment to its periodicity decision. The amendment provides that,

3. In such cases where a State Party submits additional information within one year or such other period as the Committee may decide, following the examination of its initial report or of any subsequent periodic report and the additional information is examined at a meeting with representatives of the reporting State, the Committee will, if appropriate, defer the date for the submission of the State party's next periodic report.[39]

The amendment was a useful one in that it offered some encouragement to States parties to submit supplementary reports punctually while clearly retaining the discretion to defer the date of submission of the State party's next periodic report. The discretion has already been exercised in a number of cases, for example, that of Canada.[40] It is important to note that the amendment was trying to be realistic regarding periodic reports rather than trying to get States to submit supplementary reports by deferring the submission dates for reports. As for the future it appears from recent decisions noted below that the consideration of a supplementary report by the HRC is likely to be the exception rather than the rule. If so the amendment to the periodicity decision is likely to be rarely invoked. This is unfortunate in that it may again lead to States defaulting on the submission of Supplementary reports. It does though clearly stress that the focus is going to be on the five-year periodic review.

The scope of article 40(1)(b) of the ICCPR

3.8 A second matter left open in the original periodicity decision was the scope of the HRC's authority to 'request' a report under article 40(1)(*b*) of the ICCPR. Does this provision authorize the Committee to request *ad hoc* reports or only regular periodic reports in accordance with the general application of its periodicity decision? This issue has been variously mooted by members in respect of the troubled and emergency situations prevailing in Iran, Uruguay, Chile, and elsewhere. An excellent summary of the views expressed in the HRC appears in its Annual Report:

Members of the Committee exchanged views on what some of them called the general problem of derogation and notification under article 4 of the Covenant and its relation to the reporting system and the obligations of both the States parties and the Committee under the Covenant, particularly article 40 (see CCPR/C/SR.334, 349 and 351). Reference was made to paragraph 3 of general comment 5/13 which, it was noted, implied that the procedures of notification and reporting were equally important but which did not explain how those two procedures should interact.

Maintaining that the Committee could not discharge its responsibilities under the Covenant if it did not consider major changes in a country's constitution or law, or suspension thereof, which had a bearing on the protection of human rights, and that States parties under article 40(1)(b) had undertaken to submit reports whenever the Committee so requested, some members were of the opinion that whenever a notification under article 4(3) of the Covenant had been made, it should be transmitted forthwith to the members of the Committee, that the Committee had the power to request a special report on how [the] public emergency affected human rights; that the Committee should avail itself of all information available, at least in the United Nations system, in this regard; that such situation or report should be considered, if need be, at an extraordinary session of the Committee or by an intersessional working group, and that the procedure for requesting such reports must be formalised and be applied to all States parties without exception and should reflect a quick response to emergency situations and prevent possible cases of *excès de pouvoir* by States parties.

The position of some members who favoured the establishment of a procedure for requesting reports on emergency situations was contested on various grounds. It was pointed out by other members that article 4 of the Covenant specifically provided for the possibility of a State party's derogating from obligations under the Covenant in time of national emergency, that measures taken in such situations in accordance with article 4 could not be characterised as wrongful nor considered violations of the Covenant because the effect of such a derogation is that certain obligations are temporarily suspended and that the proclamation of a state of emergency might well be the last resort to protect human rights and that was precisely what was envisaged in article 4. It was also maintained that there was nothing in article 4 to indicate or justify the assumption that States parties had conferred on the Committee any competence to determine whether a situation threatening the life of a nation existed; that information from a State derogating from the Covenant was to be transmitted to other States parties or the Committee for approval or that States parties had accepted any third party scrutiny in regard to whether derogations were limited to the extent strictly required by the exigencies of the situation. It was recalled that, under article 4, a State party availing itself of the right of derogation was required to inform not the Committee but the other States parties and that only a notification, and not a report, was required. The Committee's role under article 4 was described as being limited to ascertaining whether other States parties had been immediately informed, what rights were affected by the emergency measures and whether there had been derogations from the provisions mentioned in article 4(2) and determining what were the reasons by which the State had been actuated and when the derogations had been terminated. Citing cases of public emergencies declared in several States parties, some of them dating back to the time when the Covenant came into force, and in connection with which no special report had been requested from any one of them, one member wondered what changes had occurred, prompting some members to urge the establishment of such a procedure now. He warned that if the proposal was adopted the Committee might lay itself open to criticism that it was biased and be faced with suspicion and reluctance to co-operate on the part of States parties.

Other members, while asserting that the motives of Committee members were beyond question, stressed that it was important that the Committee should be seen to be acting with impartiality. Referring to article 1 of the Covenant, one member stated that the situation with regard to self-determination in southern Africa was even graver than a state of emergency, since it represented the institutionalization of the negation of humanity by law. Although South Africa was not a party to the Covenant, it was the duty of the Committee to bring the situation in that country to the attention of States parties. The Committee might wish to try to understand those people who thought that sanctions were desirable where the victims were white but not where they were non-white and that it should be seen to act, not because it contained members from third world countries or because it wished to politicize matters or react selectively, but because its deliberations reflected the provisions of the Covenant. It was pointed out that, in considering situations under article 4 of the Covenant, the Committee, for the time being, could only consider that article in terms of its functions under article 40, that the role of the Committee, however, was not limited to taking note of reports which had been submitted because if that had been the case there would have been no need for its independence to be safeguarded by the Covenant; that if the Committee requested a report on the emergency situation it would merely receive some indication of the legal framework; that the Committee should do everything possible to make States aware of their obligations under the Covenant, perhaps by altering the rules for the submission of reports or by making general comments. It was also suggested that the Committee could consider emergency situations in terms of their relevance to the implementation by the reporting State of its obligations under the Covenant in the course of the Committee's exercise of its functions under article 40.

Members of the Committee agreed to defer for further consideration the question of derogations and notifications under article 4 of the Covenant and other questions raised during the discussion in relation to the reporting system and the obligations of States parties under article 40 (see CCPR/C/SR.379).[41]

3.8.1. It is submitted that the majority opinion is the better one and certainly this approach would seem to be more in line with the general purpose of the ICCPR and especially the need to ensure non-derogation of the rights in article 4(2) in such emergency situations. Moreover, the Committee's decision on periodicity was expressly adopted without prejudice to the power of the Committee to 'request a subsequent report whenever it deems it appropriate'.[42] However, the objections of some members had prevented any further progress being made on the issue of *ad hoc* reports. No developments seemed likely on this matter and this seemed to illustrate again the limitations of consensus decision making.[43] However, in what could have proven to be an important precedent the HRC has recently acted under article 40(1)(*b*) in response to the assassination of the Chairman of the Human Rights Commission of El Salvador. Under article 40(1)(*b*) the HRC requested the government of El Salvador, 'to provide it with information on measures it has taken relative to this case in its supplementary report due before the end of 1988'.[44] However, the El Salvador precedent now appears wholly exceptional. In practical terms the HRC has clearly recognized that it cannot cope with more than the regular periodic reports.

B. THE SUBMISSION OF REPORTS[45]

3.9 Before proceeding to consider the nature of the examination to which State reports are subjected some attention must be directed to the matters of compliance by States parties with their reporting obligations both quantitatively and qualitatively. As noted, initial reports are due from States parties within one year of the entry into force of the ICCPR for that State.[46] Four were overdue as of 27 July 1990.[47] However, very few of them have been submitted on time.[48] The length of delayed submission has varied from a matter of months to several years. The worst case is that of Zaïre whose report was submitted nine years late.[49] The excuses advanced by States have been various and diffuse, including unforeseen preparatory difficulties, pending constitutional or governmental reforms, co-ordination between the various domestic ministries, consultations required under federal systems, status as a developing country, and concurrent obligations to other international forums. These may well be valid reasons in some cases and the Committee must respond flexibly if convinced that the difficulties are genuine rather than evidence of bad faith.[50] More reprehensible was the failure of Belgium to submit its initial report due in 1983 until December 1987.[51] There is no doubt that the reporting obligation under the ICCPR is a demanding one. In its first series of general comments under article 40(4) the HRC drew the immediate attention of States in the process of ratifying the ICCPR to their reporting obligations and stressed that, 'The proper presentation of a report which covers so many civil and political rights necessarily does require time'.[52]

Although the record on the ultimate submission of reports is perhaps surprisingly good the persistent delays in submission has represented a continuing problem to the HRC. In practice a fairly uniform set of procedures have emerged in dealing with defaulting States. The first steps are for the HRC to send a series of reminders to the State concerned couched in increasingly firmer language.[53] If these reminders seem to produce no effect the HRC has attempted to establish direct personal contacts with the State concerned. These have taken the form of personal approaches from either the Chairman of the HRC, a member of the HRC from the same geographical region as the State concerned, or the Director of the United Nations Centre for Human Rights (formerly the Human Rights Division).[54] The approaches are usually made to the Mission concerned in Geneva or New York, accompanied by an extremely firmly worded *aide-mémoire*.

On a number of occasions representatives from the permanent missions have been invited to an informal discussion with the HRC or the Bureau of the HRC concerning its reporting obligations.[55] The most advanced form of direct contact established by the HRC was for a personal visit by a member of the HRC, Mr Ndiaye, to Guinea with the consent of the State party to discuss its reporting obligations and the work of the HRC.[56] The visit was apparently a success and the report of Guinea was submitted shortly thereafter, some years late. Unfortunately, however, no representative from Guinea appeared before the HRC when its report was being considered. A representative finally appeared before the HRC in March 1988.[57]

If the above steps do not succeed three further sanctions have been developed. First, HRC has had resort to the sending of a letter to the meeting of the States parties to the ICCPR informing the meeting of the non-compliance with their reporting obligations of the States concerned.[58] Secondly, expressly citing those States which have failed to submit reports in its Annual Report to the General Assembly under article 45 of the ICCPR.[59] Thirdly, a Special 'Chairman's letter' is sent, on behalf of the HRC, directly to the Minister for Foreign Affairs of the States concerned. These letters have produced very positive results particularly with regard to initial reports.[60]

As regards Supplementary reports we have already noted that there have been substantial difficulties and delays in the submission of these.[61] As noted, these problems eventually resulted in an amendment to the HRC's decision on periodicity.[62] That decision as regards the consideration of Supplementary reports does not appear to have been very successful.[63]

3.10 The record of submission of second and third periodic reports from States parties has also been disappointing. Thirty-three periodic reports due in the period 1983 to November 1989 had not been submitted and a number of them were due from States parties whose third periodic reports were due in 1988.[64] As of 27 July 1990 thirty second periodic and twenty third periodic reports were overdue. Seventeen third periodic reports are due in 1990.

The responses of the HRC have mirrored its approach to the submission of initial and periodic reports.[65] However, the HRC has also given some consideration to the question of technical assistance to States parties.[66] It was decided to make an informal request to the Secretary-General of the United Nations as to how technical assistance could be provided to States parties which requested it, for example, with regard to the preparation of their national reports.[67] A number of initiatives have been taken in this context, for example, training schemes on the preparation and submission of reports by States parties to the various international human rights Conventions, and others are actively being developed.[68] Similarly, the meetings of the Chairmen of the international human rights bodies may result in some moves towards the rationalization of, and co-ordination between, States' reporting obligations.[69]

In its considerations the HRC has expressed continuing concern over the matter of the delayed submission of reports. That concern and the flexible approaches developed by the HRC have served clearly to indicate to States parties the seriousness which the HRC attaches to the reporting obligation in the Covenant. In perspective, however, the record of submission is reasonably good and stands comparison with the records of submission under ILO Conventions,[70] the European Social Charter,[71] and under the International Covenant on Economic, Social, and Cultural Rights.[72]

Among the State reports which have been seriously delayed have been those of Iran, Libya and Madagascar,[73] Saint Vincent and the Grenadines, and Vietnam[74] Guinea,[75] Zaïre,[76] and Belgium.[77] However, it must be recognized that at no stage has the HRC been without reports to consider and, indeed, some reports have not been considered until some considerable time after submission.[78]

3.11 Even more serious has been the deficient quality of a number of reports.[79] The reporting obligation under the Covenant is a very extensive and demanding one. Preparation of an adequate report clearly demands time and expertise.[80] The HRC's inquiry as to assistance to States parties in respect of their reporting obligations has resulted in some useful developments.[81] Moreover, on many occasions the initial consideration of a report by the HRC has indicated to the State representatives the breadth of information required by the HRC and has produced substantial additional information from the State representative and in the Supplementary report of the State party. Similarly as the HRC adopts more and more General Comments these will provide further assistance to States parties. It has also been submitted that the HRC could much improve its 'General Guidelines' on the form and content of initial periodic reports. It must be acknowledged, however, that in the light of the slow pace of new accessions to the Covenant it is the periodic reports which are going to assume paramount importance rather than initial reports.

To date the HRC has tended to attempt to exhaust all possible use of reminders, *aide-mémoires*, and personal contacts, even if the processes have taken years, and it has been rather reluctant to publicize defaulting States. Such an approach may have been apposite as the HRC gained experience in the consideration of reports and developed its procedures for their consideration. In the final analysis, however, the HRC must have properly compiled reports and additional information if it is to perform its functions of consideration and study under article 40. If States parties do not comply with their reporting obligations by submitting adequate and timely national reports, then the HRC must give effective publicity to the breaches by the States concerned of their international legal obligations under the ICCPR. More trenchant and public criticism by the HRC as a body rather than just from individual members would clearly convey to States parties the seriousness which the HRC attaches to the reporting obligations under the ICCPR. The Conference of States parties, ECOSOC, and the Third Committee of the General Assembly are all bodies in which the HRC's criticisms should be considered and direct political pressure brought on States parties to comply fully with their reporting obligations.[82]

C. SOURCES OF INFORMATION[83]

3.12 One aspect which necessarily plays some part in determining the very nature of the Committee's examination of States reports is the source and nature of the information that comes before it. The national reports submitted by the States parties inevitably present the official version of the situation regarding the implementation of the rights in the ICCPR. Despite the provision in article 40(2) requiring States 'to indicate the factors and difficulties if any, affecting the implementation of the Covenant', one could hardly expect States to do anything less than present their information in a subjective and most favourable light.[84]

The question of the availability or otherwise of other sources of information outside the State reports and the ability of the Committee to verify and complete the information transmitted to it thus assumes major proportions in any assessment of the effectiveness of its role as an implementation organ.[85]

The specialized agencies

3.13 The natural or obvious source of some potentially valuable information might well be thought to be the specialized agencies to which, in accordance with article 40(3) of the ICCPR, the Secretary-General may, after consultation with the Committee, transmit such parts of the State reports as may fall within their fields of competence.[86] In fact the character of the relationship between the Committee and the specialized agencies has proved to be both complex and elliptical and a brief look at the evolution of that relationship is useful.

The specialized agencies upon which most attention has been concentrated are the International Labour Organization (ILO) and the United Nations Educational, Scientific, and Cultural Organization (UNESCO) both of which have repeatedly expressed the desire to establish strong and fruitful co-operation with the Committee.[87] The general approach of the Committee was not to take any decision in haste but rather to wait until it had acquired the practical experience to enable it to give the question of co-operation fuller and more mature consideration.

The necessity for co-operation at both the procedural and normative levels was appreciated by the Committee on a number of counts. Among these were the need to avoid conflicting standards and definitions of rights common to other international instruments, the advantages of considering those studies already completed in order to avoid conflicting decisions at the international level and any obligations incumbent on States parties to both the ICCPR and to ILO and UNESCO Conventions, the petitions procedures for violations of human rights under the Optional Protocol and those established by UNESCO. Further advantages of co-operation pointed to by members of the Committee were that the information and decisions which the specialized agencies could supply would facilitate a useful intermediate stage in the procedure since they would enable members to put more pertinent and meaningful questions to the State representatives concerning their obligations under the ICCPR.

3.14 Quite clearly then the Committee recognized the value of co-operation and evinced a strong desire to establish close and effective co-operation. To formalize that recognition however proved a difficult task. The first problem concerned the determination of 'such parts of the reports as may fall within their fields of competence'. Some members considered that to transmit the whole of States' reports would be *ultra vires* article 40(3). Such an interpretation raised practical difficulties since references to articles were often scattered throughout and could only be understood in the context of the rest of a national report. In practice the complete reports are sent with an accompanying note to indicate those parts considered to fall within their field of competence.

More difficult and substantive problems for the Committee concerned the question of whether article 40(3) might be thought to accord any more positive role to the specialized agencies on their receipt of the parts of the national reports referred to them by the Committee and the legal value to be placed on any material supplied by the specialized agencies. At its simplest the fundamental question before the Committee was whether the role envisaged for the specialized agencies included the submission of comments on the reports transmitted to them under article 40(3). In adopting its procedural Rules in 1977 the Committee had included a provision that, 'The Committee may invite the specialized agencies to which the Secretary-General has transmitted parts of the reports to submit comments on those parts within such time limits as it may specify'.[88] A minority of the members indicated that they would find such comments valuable in the consideration of States reports but the majority of the members were clearly against such a role and suggested that on further reflection they considered rule 67(2) to be *ultra vires* the Covenant. Among the most influential arguments was that to give the specialized agencies power to make specific comments and judgments would be to usurp and surpass the Committee's own role in commenting on possible violations of human rights and effectively place the specialized agencies in a position to claim that a State party was not fulfilling its obligations under the Covenant, something for which article 41 of the ICCPR had laid down a special procedure. It was argued that such an approach was undesirable not only because it would enable States parties to the specialized agencies but not to the ICCPR to comment on the performance of the States who were. Moreover, it was likely to dissuade States from acceding to the ICCPR and co-operating with the Committee if they conceived of article 40 as a procedure of inquiry whereby they might effectively be accused of transgressions by an agency not privy to the 'intimate dialogue' to which States believed they were committing themselves. It was further suggested that the authors of the Covenant were unaware that the Committee's documents would be documents of general distribution and thus the purport of article 40(3) as drafted was rather for the Committee to help the specialized agencies than vice-versa.

3.15 The provisional decision taken by the Committee was to the effect that,

The specialized agencies could not submit comments, it being understood that the Committee could revert to the matter at a later stage and in the light of the experience it had gained, seek ways to further strengthen its co-operation with the specialized agencies.[89]

As to the nature of the information to be received it was agreed that information, mainly on the specialized agencies interpretation of, and practice in relation to, the corresponding provisions of their instruments should be made available to members of the Committee on a regular basis, and that information of any other kind may be made available to them on request during meetings of the Committee which were attended by representatives of the specialized agencies concerned. This decision was adopted on the understanding that members were free to use the information in any manner they deemed fit.[90]

3.16 In practice only one specialized agency, the ILO, has responded to the HRC's desire for information. All members of the HRC receive the notes supplied by the ILO.[91] Although the ILO has consistently supplied information to the HRC, its representatives are rarely present at HRC meetings.[92] The reluctance of other specialized agencies to supply the HRC with information is perhaps a result of the rather negative approach of the HRC to the question of co-operation with the specialized agencies. The impression given is that the HRC will allow the specialized agencies an almost negligible role in the implementation of the ICCPR. Symptomatic of this negative attitude of the HRC was the reaction of certain members to the proposed inclusion in the HRC's Annual Report in 1984 of a section entitled, 'Co-operation with the Specialized Agencies'.[93] The section would have stated that the HRC 'Took note with appreciation the information'[94] supplied by the ILO. Objection was taken to this section by Mr Movchan and Mr Graefrath on the grounds that the matter had not been formally included on the HRC's agenda at any of the sessions concerned, the HRC had not devised a formula for its relations with specialized agencies, and although its previous decisions had indicated that the HRC might request information from specialized agencies it had never in fact done so.[95] The eventual result was that the section in question was deleted from the Annual Report on the understanding that it would be taken up again at some future date.[96]

This attitude of the HRC, dictated by the opposition of the two members, is most unfortunate. The breadth and quality of the work done by the major specialized agencies, particularly the ILO, could be of significant assistance to the HRC, bearing in mind its wide approach to some of the rights in the ICCPR.[97] However, it should not be overestimated.[98] It is submitted that the HRC could at least take a much more positive attitude to the role of the specialized agencies even if it maintains the view that they cannot submit comments to the HRC on the reports of the States Parties. The HRC has certainly now acquired the experience and maturity on the basis of which it could seek to further develop and strengthen its co-operation with the specialized agencies.[99]

Non-governmental organizations

3.17 Apart from article 40(3) of the ICCPR dealing with specialized agencies there is no other provision in the ICCPR dealing with the question of sources of information open to members of the HRC. In particular there is no provision according to non-governmental organizations (NGOs) any role or function in the implementation procedures.[100] A minority of members, notably Mr Graefrath and Mr Movchan, have argued that the absence of any further provision means that the HRC is not entitled to base its consideration of reports on anything other than the official report of the State party or other United Nations documentation.[101] The majority of members of the HRC, however, have rejected this view and accepted that the ICCPR places no restriction on the sources of information that the Committee is entitled to use.[102] Many of the questions and comments of members, including Mr Graefrath and Mr Movchan[103] are clearly based on outside information.[104] The general, though not invariable, practice of members though has been not to refer directly to the source of their information. So members often simply say that, 'I understand', 'I have reason to believe', 'It had been reported.',[105] 'He had information',[106] or refer only to 'other sources'[107] or 'reliable sources'.[108] This general practice makes it difficult to determine the sources and the extent of the use made of outside information. However, those occasions when members have indicated their sources reveal the following examples:

1. Information derived from the HRCion Resolution 1503 procedure;[109]
2. The Reports of the *Ad Hoc* Working Group and the Special Rapporteur on Chile;[110]
3. The reports of the Special Rapporteurs of the HRCion on El Salvador,[111] Afghanistan;[112]
4. The Reports of the HRCion Working Group on Enforced and Involuntary Disappearances;[113]
5. The Reports of the IACM;[114]
6. The ILO;[115]
7. The International Commission of The Red Cross and National Red Cross Commissions;[116]
8. Cases decided in the EUCT;[117]
9. The national reports submitted to the CERD and the Committee on the Elimination of Discrimination against Women;[118]
10. The considerations of the CERD;[119]
11. National human rights institutions;[120]
12. Parliamentary debates and Parliamentary Committee reports;[121]
13. The Bar Association of New York;[122] the Lima Lawyers Association;[123]
14. Non-governmental Organizations,[124] like Amnesty International,[125] the International Commission of Jurists,[126] and the International League for Human Rights;[127]
15. Church organizations;[128]

16. The Press,[129] the British Press,[130] and the European Press;[131]
17. Information derived from the consideration of cases under the OP.[132]

3.18 It is submitted that in the light of the fact that the HRC has no independent fact-finding machinery under the ICCPR and that National Reports under Article 40 will almost always be self-serving it is completely unrealistic for any members of the HRC to suggest that members should limit themselves to the State report and other official UN information. Many State reports have been abstract, legalistic, insubstantial, and have totally ignored the existence of human rights problems and difficulties. Official UN documents are not sufficient to present a comprehensive perspective on the human rights situations in all the States parties. Therefore, recourse to a whole range of outside information is both inevitable and essential. Indeed, the broader the range of material consulted the more likely that a reliable picture of the prevailing human rights situation will be obtained.[133] The general practice of refraining from direct reference to the source of material should be maintained and should be sufficient to avoid the reporting procedure being perceived as an adversarial trial for the State concerned, an image which the HRC has been at pains to avoid. On occasions State representatives have asked for the source of or access to the information used by HRC members. Such requests should be complied with so long as to do so would not endanger the sources. Among the national and international bodies who should engage in the important task of supplying the HRC members with information are, for example, trade unions, civil rights bodies, human rights commissions, parliamentary associations, pressure groups, and NGOs.[134]

3.18.1 The situation above has changed significantly since 1986. The effects of *glasnost* have reached the HRC and many members specifically cite sources, have good relations with non-governmental organizations, and receive a wide range of material. For example, during consideration of the second periodic report of Japan members of the HRC received materials from medical groups, political parties, lawyers, and individuals. The question of the use of such sources by HRC members is no longer an issue in the HRC.

D. THE PROCESS OF CONSIDERATION: INITIAL AND SUPPLEMENTARY (OR ADDITIONAL) REPORTS

3.19 The general rule is that the National Reports submitted by States parties are considered in chronological order as they are received. Exceptionally, however, the HRC may accord priority to a report because of the critical human rights situation in the State concerned.[135] In scheduling the consideration of reports the HRC used to attempt to maintain a geographical balance between the reports considered at each session but this often proved impossible and the HRC now deals with reports as they are due and States are willing to make themselves available. Experience has shown that the HRC had found it difficult to consider more than four initial reports per session, each report taking two or three days to consider. The consideration of Supplementary reports usually takes a shorter period. The consideration of periodic reports has generally taken as long, if not longer, than the consideration of initial reports but the HRC hopes to reduce this time by further rationalization of the procedure for the consideration of such reports.

After an exchange of views within the HRC the following provisional practice was adopted in respect of the examination of initial reports.[136] In accordance with Rule 68 of the HRC's Rules of Procedure the HRC invites the State concerned to have a representative attend the meetings at which its report is to be discussed and make an oral introduction to that report.[137] Many States have made full use of this opportunity to deliver a comprehensive oral supplement to the written report, setting that report in its relevant socio-economic context and adding significant new information in the light of political or legal changes.[138]

1. The first round

3.20 In what became known as the 'first round' of the consideration of the report members of the HRC were accorded the opportunity of addressing comments and putting questions to the State representatives. It became customary that the first speaker was a member from the same geographical region as the State party concerned. Similarly, it is customary practice that members do not address questions and comments to the representatives of the State of which they are a national.[139] This is a sensible approach because it avoids a member being put in the position of criticizing the State of which he is a national. There is no reason, however, for the HRC to be deprived of the particular member's familiarity with the human rights problems of the State concerned. There is no difficulty in the members concerned informally making other members aware of the human rights problems and difficulties on which, in his or her opinion, attention can best be focused.

The State representatives are allowed the time necessary to prepare replies to the matters raised and they may then give comprehensive oral replies or refer such questions as they choose back to their respective governments along with requests from HRC members for additional information. The additional information is supplied in Supplementary reports.[140] After the State representative has replied members of the HRC occasionally address them again to draw attention to important questions and comments which have received unsatisfactory or incomplete replies. Finally, the State representative is often asked to indicate when the HRC will receive the Supplementary report from the State party. The whole process normally lasts between two and three full days. There is no formal determination by the HRC of whether a report is satisfactory or not or whether the replies of State representatives have been adequate.[141]

2. The second round

3.21 The consideration of the Supplementary report follows the practice of the so-called 'second round'.[142] The questions and comments tend to be more specific and detailed and they are presented together according to the particular parts or provisions of the Covenant. The questions are again directed to the State representative to be answered *ad hoc*, if possible, as they are put. The 'dialogue' nature of the examination is much more in evidence during this second round.[143] In the early years of HRC practice a critical problem arose which threatened to destroy the atmosphere of co-operation and consensus within the Committee. This concerned the function of the 'second round' examination.[144] Committee members were agreed that the general purport was to deepen and strengthen the 'dialogue' initially established but the tendency of certain members to put questions in the manner of a cross-examination led to a withdrawal of Eastern European members from active participation in the 'second round' examination for a period of time.[145] The different conceptions of the 'second round' relate closely to the general and more important question of the very extent of the Committee's jurisdictional power under the ICCPR, which will be discussed below.[146] It is sufficient to note at this point that after extensive discussion the Committee adopted the 'Consensus Statement' on its future work on State reports and since the twelfth session all members have contributed to the second round process.

3.21.1 In 1984 the HRC took some important decisions with respect to the consideration of Supplementary reports. The HRC's Working Group on article 40 suggested that before Supplementary reports were placed on the agenda the working group or a member of the HRC would go through them and determine whether they were comprehensive enough to form a topic for special consideration. If so they would be placed on the agenda for consideration in the normal way and, in accordance with its amendment to the decision on periodicity, the HRC would then have to decide whether it was appropriate to defer the date for the submission of the State party's next periodic report. Normally, however, it was expected that the HRC would just take note of the Supplementary reports and discuss them together with the next periodic report.[147]

This approach was formalized at the HRC's twenty-sixth session (1985) when the HRC agreed to the following procedure for the handling of any additional information submitted by States parties and for dealing with cases where additional information had been promised but not submitted: (*a*) whenever additional information is received at the same time as the next periodic report or shortly before the next periodic report is due, to consider the additional information together with the periodic report; (*b*) when additional information is received at other times, to decide on a case to case basis, whether it should be considered, and to notify the State party concerned of any eventual decision to examine the additional information; (*c*) where promised additional information has not been received, the Bureau of the Committee will consider sending appropriate reminders to the States parties. The Secretariat, in corresponding with States parties concerning the date for submission of their next periodic report, is also to remind them of their promise, during consideration of their previous reports, that additional information would be supplied to the Committee.[148]

It is submitted that these decisions were sensible ones. The HRC maintains its flexibility to consider a Supplementary report if it regards it as sufficiently important to do so but it retains the option of postponing consideration of the Supplementary report until the next periodic report is considered.[149] In practice this is what happens and Supplementary reports are now very exceptionally considered. The result thus combines flexibility with practicality and should save the HRC some time which it can then devote to matters of more pressing importance.

3.22 There can be no doubt that the HRC has largely been successful in achieving its stated aim of establishing and developing a 'constructive dialogue' with each State party in regard to the implementation of the Covenant.[150] The work of the HRC under article 40 on selected articles of the Covenant is analysed in chapters 5–12 below. States parties have generally co-operated with the HRC as regards the submission of reports although, as we have noted, there have been problems of inadequacy and delay. Similarly, all States parties, including Guinea,[151] have sent a representative or group of representatives to appear before the HRC. This is a remarkably good record and compares favourably with the experience of the CERD.[152] Some States have sent large top-level delegations while others have sent low-level representatives usually from the Permanent Missions in New York or Geneva.[153] The existing practices of the HRC for the consideration of reports subject State representatives to intensive time pressure and experience has shown that a single representative will not normally be in a position to deal adequately with all the questions and comments made by members.[154] The HRC has clearly recognized the vital role that State representatives have in establishing the dialogue which it regards as so important.[155] In its very first General Comment under article 40(4) the HRC commended States for their co-operation and noted that, 'the level, experience and the number of representatives has varied. The Committee wishes to state that if it is to be able to perform its functions under article 40 as effectively as possible and if the reporting State is to obtain the maximum benefit from the dialogue, it is desirable that the State representatives should have such status and experience (and preferably be in such number) as to respond to questions put, and comments made, in the Committee over the whole range of matters covered by the Covenant.'[156]

3.23 However, the procedures adopted by the HRC to consider initial and Supplementary reports have been criticized by some members of the HRC. Mr Dieye criticized the existing procedures as too time-consuming and proposed that the introductory statements by State representatives should be briefer and that the 'second round' practice alone should be used in the consideration of State reports. These suggestions, however, met with strong opposition, for example, on the ground that the dialogue method used for the second round would not be useful in the initial consideration of a State's report because members' questions often raised very technical questions which could not be answered immediately.[157]

The first round practice was seen to facilitate the duplication of questions by members and to place intensive pressures on State representatives and on Committee members. The problem noticeably lessened as the Committee gained experience and members refrained from repetition unless they wanted to further develop a previous question, but the need to systematize the procedure into a more progressive and constructive process has been recognized.[158] One possibility that warrants further investigation and has been mooted on a number of occasions is that of decentralizing the consideration of initial reports to special rapporteurs.[159] A variation on this theme would be to assign small groups of members particular articles for them to look at in depth. The groups could rotate if that was thought desirable and the right of each member to make comments and ask questions on any matter he wished would obviously be preserved. Not all members seem to favour decentralization, however, and prefer instead to try to improve the Committee's existing working methods. The essential organizational problem is that there is no discussion by the HRC as to how to consider a particular State report as there is before the consideration of periodic reports.[160]

3.24 As each member of the HRC addresses questions and comments individually to the State representatives the questions put tend to reflect the particular interests of each member. It should also be noted that members rarely reply specifically to the comments of other members.[161] For example, Mr Bouziri has repeatedly made clear his view that it should be open to women to secure abortions if they wish to do so.[162] Normally, the other members of the HRC make no direct reply to his comments. This could be taken to mean that they agree with him, that they had no particular view on the matter, or perhaps that they consider that the matter is not within the scope of the Covenant at all. However, the consequence of the procedures used by the HRC is that a common position does tend to emerge on the view of the HRC of the human rights performance of the State party concerned in general and on the key human rights issues affecting that State.[163] This is particularly evident in the practice of members of making 'final observations' at the end of the consideration of a State's periodic report. Those observations have often included an evaluation of the human rights performance of the States concerned.[164]

It is submitted that many of the criticisms of the HRC's practices for the consideration of reports relate back to the inadequate general guidelines on the form and contents of reports adopted by the HRC.[165] Their inadequacy has been a factor in producing inadequate reports. Such reports have attracted hundreds of questions as members have attempted to obtain the basic information on the implementation of the Covenant. The time spent asking questions has subjected State representatives to unreasonable burdens. They are left trying desperately to fill in the huge gaps in the reports submitted by their respective governments. Many State representatives have been surprised by the range and depth of information desired by members of the HRC and many matters have had to be referred back to the government concerned. Moreover, time spent asking questions reduces the time available for critical and constructive comments from HRC members. These deficiencies have been accentuated by the individually orientated and unstructured procedure for the consideration of reports. The only particularly positive aspect of the procedure is that it manages to avoid the cross-examination format while achieving the cross-examination effect. It is submitted then that the HRC could do much to improve its general guidelines and to rationalize and structure the consideration of reports, for example through more decentralized procedures. The HRC's procedures for the consideration of periodic reports are of a more rational and structured nature as we will see below.[166] Another suggestion which might then be taken up is that of creating a working group to consider the adequacy of a State report before its consideration by the plenary Committee or that a similar function be performed by the Secretariat.[167] With the co-operation of the State party this might then ensure that when the report is considered by the HRC it is substantive enough for the HRC to be able to build up a constructive dialogue with the State party on the basis of it. Another suggestion with the same aim of obtaining more adequate reports is the drawing up by the Secretariat of a list or digest of the questions most frequently asked by members relating to various subjects under the ICCPR. Such documents, up-dated from time to time, were to be circulated to the States parties for their information.[168] In fact only one such document has been produced but it is very brief, has never been formally adopted by the HRC, and has never been up-dated.[169]

E. THE PROCESS OF CONSIDERATION: PERIODIC REPORTS

1. Second periodic reports

3.25 In the 'Consensus Statement' on its duties under article 40 the HRC looked forward to the consideration of second periodic reports.[170] It decided that two procedures would be adopted. First, before the consideration of the report with the State representatives a working group of three members of the HRC would meet to review the information so far received by the Committee in order to identify those matters which it would seem most helpful to discuss with the representative of the reporting State.[171] This procedure was expressly adopted without prejudice to any member of the Committee raising any other matter which appeared to him to be important. Secondly, the HRC would request the Secretariat to prepare an analysis of the examination of each report. The analysis would set out systematically both the questions asked and the responses given with precise references to the domestic legal sources, quoting the main ones.[172]

3.26 The first of the 'second periodic reports' scheduled for consideration was that of Yugoslavia in October 1983.[173] The HRC's Working Group on General Comments (now known as the Working Group on article 40) submitted a Conference Room Paper to the HRC entitled, 'Proposed Approach and Procedure for the Consideration of Second Periodic Reports'.[174] The working group suggested that the HRC should focus on the progress made in each State party and on the points stressed in pr. (*g*) of the 'Consensus Statement' of Duties[175] and elaborated in pr. I(*b*) of the guidelines for periodic reports.[176] As to the procedure to be followed it was submitted that the method for considering second periodic reports need not in principle differ significantly from that followed by the Committee in considering initial reports, although a different method whereby replies to questions posed could be expected during the same meeting may be desirable provided that the States parties representative would be willing to do that, and that the State party could be approached in advance to secure its acceptance to the conduct of the dialogue in this way.

3.27 After some discussion[177] the HRC agreed to the setting up of the working group envisaged in the Consensus Statement and the Secretariat prepared an analysis of the examination of the initial report of Yugoslavia.[178] The analysis was not intended to pass any value judgments on the initial report but simply to facilitate the task of the members. The list of issues and questions prepared by the working group was quite brief containing four general questions, for example, on progress made and responses to the proceedings of the HRC, and questions on ten articles of the Covenant.[179] Though some members expressed misgivings it was decided to transmit the informal, unofficial list, with some supplementary questions, to the Mission of Yugoslavia with a note indicating, however, that the questions were not exhaustive and that members of the HRC retained the right to put additional questions. It was also decided that the list of questions would be put by the members of the working group on the points that they had selected. It was accepted by members that the procedure satisfied most members of the HRC and made for a frank and informative dialogue in which the co-operation of the Yugoslavian representative was a major factor.[180]

The working group was asked to repeat a similar process with respect to the consideration of the reports of Chile and the GDR. The lists prepared by the working group are considered, discussed, and amended by the HRC.[181] The lists attempt to be as country specific and exhaustive as possible so that the HRC can expect immediate replies from the State representatives who would have had the list for some period in advance of consideration by the HRC. It was again stressed that members reserved the right to put any additional questions and comments to State representatives, though these were expected to be reduced to a minimum, and the State representatives would be accorded time to prepare their replies to further questions if necessary. The list of issues is accompanied by an explanation of the procedure to be followed. When they appear before the HRC the representatives of the States parties are asked to comment on the issues listed, section by section, and to reply to any additional questions raised by members. Finally the Chairman of the HRC invites members to make '*final observations*' and may request an indication of when any additional information that may have been promised will be submitted.[182]

In discussing the HRC's procedures on periodic reports members have stressed a number of matters including the need for rational and structured consideration of periodic reports, with the lists serving as 'a frame of reference for organizing the discussion';[183] the importance of obtaining precise information on the actual human rights situation in States; the key role played by the State representatives who appeared before the HRC;[184] the necessity of focusing on a smaller number of particularly important human rights issues; and the need for members to exercise self-discipline in order not to frustrate the very purpose of the new procedures, which was to allow the most efficient and effective consideration of reports as possible.[185]

3.28 As of 27 July 1990 the HRC has completed the consideration of 41 second periodic reports on the basis of the procedures indicated above.[186] A number of members have expressed concern about and even opposition to the new procedures. It was observed that the lists were too long, too many questions were asked and aspects discussed that were not of any real interest, and that the consideration had gone on too long and, therefore, had not solved the problem of the time constraints on the HRC.[187] It was noted that the drawing up of lists created problems because it required a subjective judgment[188] and because care had to be taken to ensure that the wording used did not appear to label the reporting States.[189] Some members though saw some merit in the procedure, which they considered to be balanced,[190] time well-spent,[191] and a marked improvement over the procedure for the consideration of initial reports, which had, in their view, become almost impossible because of the countless questions asked.

Ultimately it was decided to set up a 'Working Group on Article 40' to, *inter alia*, prepare further lists of issues and to review the HRC's methodology in the light of its experience of consideration of second periodic reports and the comments expressed by members.[192]

The working group submitted that there should be no radical departure from the experimental procedure for the consideration of periodic reports, that the lists had to be more concise and be forwarded to the State party concerned as far in advance as possible and that the HRC should inform the State representatives of how it intended to proceed.[193] Opinion was divided, however, on the question of whether the procedure should be flexible, depending on the quality of the State representatives, or applied to all States without distinction. The procedures adopted for periodic reports are still in operation as of 27 July 1990 and it appears likely that they will be continued though there may be further attempts to refine them as the procedure for the consideration of third periodic reports develops.[194]

The general opinion of Committee members seemed to be that the procedures it had established to consider reports had been substantially effective in establishing the desired dialogue with States parties, many of whom had remarked on the value of the questions, comments and observations of individual members. The procedure is very good at getting at detail. The practice of making *final observations* has also emerged as a more distinct part of the procedure and is very useful in conveying the general sense of the HRC's view of the human rights situation in a particular country and highlighting particular themes or concerns of the HRC. The main problem with the procedure is that it can be wrecked by State representatives that make a lengthy introduction or that answer questions or comments at enormous length, as has happened in a number of cases, for example, Afghanistan, Czechoslovakia, Iraq, and Ecuador. As already noted a number of suggestions have been made to improve yet further the effectiveness of those initial stages, but it was generally recognized that the Committee had not yet fulfilled its full potential of collective 'study' prescribed in article 40(4) and that steps should be taken to complete the process, though differences soon emerged as to the mode and purpose of that follow-up process.

It is evident from the summary records of the HRC that many State representatives have found the detailed questions, comments, and criticisms of the HRC somewhat disconcerting if not intimidating. It has often been necessary to assure State representatives that the approach of the HRC is consistent from State to State.[195] Many State representatives have ultimately replied with detailed information, sometimes accepting difficulties of implementation and providing lengthy explanations. Many State representatives have thanked the HRC in their final comments for its serious considerations, offered their continued co-operation, and expressed the hope that the process had contributed to the universal implementation of the Covenant.

2. Third periodic reports

3.28.1 In March 1989 the HRC adopted the following decision on the methodology for the consideration of third periodic reports:

1. The method to be applied by the Committee in considering third periodic reports, or subsequent periodic reports, should be *generally similar to that used for considering second periodic reports*, the main objective being to maintain and strengthen the *dialogue* between the Committee and the States parties and to promote the effective implementation of human rights.

2. A revision of the existing guidelines should only be made on the basis of the Committee's experience in the consideration of periodic reports.

3. The lists of issues prepared in advance of the examination of third periodic reports for transmission to States parties should be *more concise and more precise* than is presently the case in respect of second periodic reports. In principle, these lists should *concentrate on developments* after the submission of the second periodic report and should not include issues extensively dealt with during the consideration of previous reports except for those identified as giving rise to concern.

4. Henceforth, States parties should be informed in writing, by an explanatory note attached to the list of issues, of factors relating to the consideration of reports by the Committee such as the need for brevity in introducing reports, the fact that the lists of issues are only indicative and are usually supplemented by oral questions from members and that members customarily make *general observations* at the conclusion of the dialogue. (Such explanatory notes should also be attached to the lists of issues prepared in advance of the consideration of second periodic reports).

5. The analytical study of the State party reports prepared by the Secretariat should clearly reflect the salient questions raised and responses provided during the consideration of each prior report as well as the relevant information supplied in the report that is to be considered by the Committee.

6. Unless the Committee decides otherwise, *the consideration of third periodic reports will be completed in no more than three meetings.*[196]

The decision on methodology is a clear response from the HRC to the need to rationalize its procedures, concentrate on the key problems and issues raised, and preserve the 'constructive dialogue' that it regards as fundamental to its work. The new procedure was applied to the third periodic reports of the USSR and Chile in October–November 1989 and appears to have worked well: see SR 928–31 (on USSR) and SR 942–5 (on Chile).

F. THE COMMITTEE'S JURISDICTION UNDER ARTICLE 40[197]

3.29 Under article 40(2) and (4) of the ICCPR the Committee's mandate is to engage in the 'consideration' and 'study' of the reports submitted to it in accordance with article 40(1). The vague and rather ill-defined nature of these terms was commented upon in the course of the article's drafting history but no further clarification was inserted.[198] In practice, terms such as appraisal, analysis, comparison, and evaluation could be applied to the tasks positively undertaken by Committee members as they have subjected States reports to very close, critical, and specific analysis.[199]

3.30 The 'study' of reports is to be followed by the Committee's transmission of 'its reports, and such general comments as it may consider appropriate, to the States Parties'. Two central but related jurisdictional difficulties have arisen within the Committee in the interpretation of this vital sentence. The first concerns the reports to which 'its reports' refers, the second to the scope and meaning of the phrase 'general comments'. The difficulties can only be understood in the light of the differing approaches that have emerged regarding the very nature of the reporting procedure under article 40 and, as Jhabvala has noted, much of the discussion reflects a 'manifestation of the various views expressed during the drafting stages of the Covenant in the Commission on Human Rights and the Third Committee of the General Assembly'.[200]

The first school of thought

3.31 Broadly speaking there emerged two distinct schools of thought. The first school of thought was shared by the majority of the members at the time.[201] They took what might be described as a liberal, purposive approach to the scope of its powers under article 40 bearing in mind the object of the Covenant to promote and ensure the observance of the civil and political rights recognized therein. The limitations of an abstract, theoretical approach to the consideration of reports was stressed as was the ineffectiveness of bland general comments. Reference was made to the independent nature of the Committee and the attributes specified for its members and the adoption of rule 70(3),[202] which it was suggested reflected the purpose of the study called for in article 40(4).

According to this school the purpose of the studies to be undertaken by the Committee was to ascertain whether or not a State party had implemented the rights in the Covenant. The nature of this exercise was neither to be inquisitorial nor accusative and its end was to be neither condemnation nor approbation. Rather the dialogue was to be constructive and instructive, pointing to situations in which a State's domestic provisions were at variance with the Covenant or made insufficient provision for the rights protected under the Covenant, with suggestions being made as to how States could overcome the factors and difficulties that hindered the full implementation of the Covenant.

This approach was given textual justification by reference to the phrase 'its reports' in article 40(4) which it was argued could refer to separate reports drawn up by the Committee in respect of each of the reporting States, for example, commenting article by article on how well each State was fulfilling its obligations under the Covenant. Only such specific comments, it was argued, would allow the Committee effectively to supervise the implementation of the Covenant. Any other approach, such as that restricting the Committee to general comments addressed to all States, was dismissed as implicitly condoning violations of human rights in certain countries and a procedure that 'risked being nothing more than a stylistic exercise' whereby 'human rights would suffer by an excess of diplomacy' and whereby the Committee would be abdicating its duties under the Covenant. Further the Annual Reports sent through ECOSOC to the General Assembly under article 45 were not 'reports' in the sense of article 40(4) because they contained neither positive nor negative results and were essentially only descriptive accounts. Mr Lallah argued that if separate reports were adopted the Annual Report to the General Assembly under article 45 should continue to give only 'general indications of the Committee's work since it was essential to preserve the dialogue established between States parties and the Committee and to protect that dialogue from the disadvantages which might arise from discussion of those matters by the General Assembly'.[203]

While advocating such a liberal interpretation of article 40(4) the majority view recognized that the preparation of separate reports would be a complex and time-consuming activity which would almost certainly call for a restructuring of the consideration of reports through working groups, more efficient Committee practices, additional resources from the Secretariat, and perhaps even extended or additional sessional time. The subject of comments might need precise definition and the substance of such reports would have to be flexible enough to allow them to indicate whether there had been a consensus or a majority or a divergence of views. These separate reports would be transmitted to the State party concerned which, in accordance with article 40(5), would be entitled to submit to the Committee any observations on the comments contained therein.

More generally it was argued that the adoption of separate reports would in no way preclude the Committee from adopting general comments based on an overall analysis of the major trends and difficulties which emerged from its experience in considering State reports, for example, possible amendments to the ICCPR, the general aspects of the reporting obligations, general and specific implementation difficulties, the status of the ICCPR in the national law of States parties, the general and particular nature of the rights in the ICCPR.

The second school of thought

3.32 The second school of thought conceived of the nature of the Committee's mandate in a much more restrictive way. The only duty on States was to report and the 'dialogue' between the HRC and the States parties was purely voluntary in nature. Mr Graefrath commented that, 'The purpose of the State reports and their study by the Committee was ... to exchange information, to promote co-operation among States, to maintain a steady dialogue and to assist States to overcome difficulties ... The Committee was not called upon to make an appraisal or to indicate whether or not a given State had failed to fulfil its obligations. Nor could it say that a State had failed to fulfil its obligations or that certain national actions were contrary to the Covenant. To do so would be to go beyond its mandate'.[204] It logically followed then that the Committee had no jurisdiction to prepare separate reports for each State concerned and no Rule of procedure adopted by it (Rule 70(3)) could give the Committee jurisdiction beyond that in the ICCPR.[205] The 'reports' which the Committee was required to submit under article 40(4) were, it was argued, the Annual Reports submitted to the General Assembly under Article 45.[206] Otherwise, it was argued, the Covenant would have specified the content of the reports and the States parties for whom they were intended, as it did in articles 41 and 42. General comments were what they literally indicated, that is, comments of a general character relating to matters of common interest to the States parties, for example, matters of general importance affecting the implementation of the Covenant or of the specific rights in the Covenant, but not in the form of suggestions or recommendations to particular States. It was for the States parties to draw their own conclusions from the Committee's Annual Report and any General Comments the Committee chose to prepare. Through these mediums the Committee could promote the observance of human rights in a constructive way with the voluntary assistance of States. Any other approach would be an unjustified interference in the internal affairs of States.[207]

The consensus statement

3.33 Recognizing the vital role that their consideration of reports was likely to play in their efforts to secure the implementation of the ICCPR all members of the Committee, despite the differing opinions which existed, were anxious to make at least some progress. To that end a working group was set up to meet before the Committee's eleventh session to consider the formulation of such general comments 'as would be likely to gather the support of the Committee as a whole, and to examine what further work, if any, the Committee should undertake at this stage to give effect to its duties under article 40 of the Covenant'. After extensive informal consultations and intensive work within the group a 'Consensus Statement' was adopted on 'The Duties of the Human Rights Committee under article 40 of the Covenant'.[208] Committee members stressed that the consensus was no more than a first, though useful compromise step, that the procedure agreed upon was without prejudice to further consideration of the Committee's duties under article 40(4), on which members retained their previous positions, and that the Committee recognized that it had to keep its procedures for the examination of reports under constant review in the light of its experience.[209]

With respect to the issue of General Comments the consensus stated that:

(b) In formulating general comments the Committee will be guided by the following principles:

They should be addressed to the States Parties in conformity with Article 40, paragraph 4 of the Covenant;
They should promote co-operation between States Parties in the implementation of the Covenant;
They should summarize experience the Committee has gained in considering States reports;
They should draw the attention of States Parties to matters relating to the improvement of the reporting procedure and the implementation of the Covenant;
They should stimulate activities of State Parties and international organizations in the promotion and protection of human rights.

(c) The general comments could be related, inter alia, to the following subjects;

The implementation of the obligation to submit reports under article 40 of the Covenant;
The implementation of the obligation to guarantee the rights set forth in the Covenant;
Questions related to the application and the content of individual articles of the Covenant;
Suggestions concerning co-operation between States Parties and international obligations in applying and developing the provisions of the Covenant.

(d) The Committee confirms its aim of engaging in a constructive dialogue with each reporting State. This dialogue will be conducted on the basis of periodical reports from States Parties to the Covenant.[210]

General Comments

3.34 The two schools of thought again appeared when the Committee reconsidered the consensus statement with a view to taking certain decisions based upon it.[211] The particular difficulties arose because some of the members argued that paragraph (*b*) of the 'Consensus Statement' was ambiguous as it would permit of an interpretation allowing country specific comments as well as general comments addressed to all States parties. The view which prevailed, even amongst those who advocated separate reports containing specific comments addressed to individual States, was that for the time being the Committee should proceed initially with the preparation of comments relating to States generally bearing in mind the principles outlined in the consensus statement. This approach allowed the Committee to make further progress in performing its functions under article 40 while preserving its right to proceed further on individual reports at a later date. In accordance with this decision a working group of five met before the Committee's thirteenth session to draft general comments which after discussion and amendment were adopted.

According to the Committee the purpose of those general comments was to make the Committee's cumulative experience 'available for the benefit of all States in order to promote their further implementation of the Covenant; to draw their attention to insufficiencies disclosed by a large number of reports; to suggest improvements in the reporting procedure and to stimulate the activities of these States and international organizations in the promotion and protection of human rights. These comments should also be of interest to other States, especially those preparing to become parties to the Covenant ...'.[212] Certainly the comments adopted to date have been very much concerned with reporting obligations rather than specific, concrete instances of non-implementation of the ICCPR. There is no doubt however that their adoption does little or nothing to resolve the divergent interpretations of article 40(4).[213] However, short of adopting country specific reports, in practice it appears that it is the liberal view of the HRC's role which is now accepted and applied by all members of the HRC including the Eastern European members.

The initial drafts are prepared by the Working Group on article 40 (formerly known as the Working Group on General Comments) of the HRC. After consideration by its members and taking account of the views and written proposals submitted by other members, the working group then attempts to submit a consensus text to the HRC. That draft is then considered in the HRC, sometimes in public sessions. Members may comment on the draft text, seek explanations or clarifications, and propose additions or amendments. Normally the draft is referred back to the working group for further consideration in the light of the views expressed by members of the HRC. If a consensus text is finally reached by the HRC it is adopted, sometimes initially in a single- or two-language version.[214] The comments are transmitted to all States parties by *notes verbales*, and are included in the Annual Report of the HRC[215] and given publicity in a number of other ways.[216]

3.35 As of 27 July 1990 the HRC has adopted nineteen general comments.[217] The first set of general comments dealt with certain aspects of the reporting obligations and procedures,[218] the obligation on States parties under article 2 to take specific activities to enable individuals to enjoy their rights, the importance of individuals knowing their rights under the Covenant, and of all administrative and judicial authorities being aware of their obligations under the Covenant.[219]

Subsequent general comments have dealt with elements of the implementation of article 3,[220] article 4,[221] article 6,[222] article 7,[223] article 9,[224] article 10,[225] article 19,[226], article 20,[227] article 1,[228] article 14,[229] the position of aliens under the Covenant,[230] article 17,[231] article 24, non-discrimination and article 23.[232] All of the general comments to date have been addressed to all States parties and not to individual States.[233] Some of these general comments have been of a high quality and represent valuable indications of the content of the respective rights and the steps that States parties could or should undertake to ensure the implementation of those rights. Other general comments have been much less helpful. The terms of most of the general comments are dealt with elsewhere in this work in their relevant contexts. The HRC has stressed the importance of the use of the general comments primarily within the context of the reporting system but also in other areas, for example, the adoption of views under the Optional Protocol.[234] The guidelines adopted by the HRC for periodic reports specifically refers to the need to take account of the general comments adopted by the HRC in the preparation of such reports.[235] A copy of the HRC's general comments is sent to State representatives with the list of issues prior to the consideration of periodic reports. The HRC has recently agreed that it should be more specific in soliciting information from States parties concerning its general comments. The HRC has decided to include, on a systematic basis, in the lists of issues prepared for States parties prior to consideration of their periodic reports, appropriate questions relating to the degree to which the standards contained in the general comments were being observed.[236] As the number of general comments adopted has increased members have increasingly referred to them during the examination of State reports and referred to general comments to support proposed amendments to the HRC's procedures.[237] Similarly, some State reports have expressly referred to the general comments adopted but not in sufficient numbers to satisfy the HRC.[238] In 1985 the Congo and Madagascar were the first States to make formal use of the opportunity in article 40(5) of the ICCPR to submit observations to the HRC on general comments adopted by the HRC on articles 1 and 14 of the ICCPR.[239] The observations submitted by the two States were not observations on the general comment adopted by the HRC but an account of how their respective domestic systems implemented the provisions of the article concerned. The HRC made no formal response to the observations submitted but requested the Secretariat to convey its gratitude to the States concerned and indicate to them that the information submitted might have more appropriately been included in the information submitted by those

States to the HRC for consideration under the reporting procedure. Subsequently comments under article 40(5) have been received from a small number of States.[240] Mr Graefrath has suggested that it 'might be useful to give Governments some guidance on the form and content of the observations expected of them'.[241] This suggestion should be acted upon as it would be a useful way of continuing the 'dialogue' between the HRC and the States parties between the consideration of State reports. It would be important, however, that this be done in a way which did not appear to damage the standing or authority of the general comments.

3.36 The only substantive comment and observations on the general comments adopted by the HRC has come from the Third Committee of the GA.[242] Those comments, sometimes critical, are noted in the respective context of each general comment.[243] Further publicity to the general comments is given by the Centre for Human Rights in Geneva, which regularly draws attention to them in the various organs it serves. Similarly, academic commentators and interest organizations are increasingly referring to the general comments in their respective publications.[244]

3.37 Some criticism has been expressed within the HRC of its procedures for the preparation of general comments.[245] It has been suggested that their preparation was too dependent on the isolated initiatives of members of the HRC and that despite repeated appeals members had been slow to make suggestions and proposals for general comments. The working group on article 40 is now spending most of its time on the lists of issues for periodic reports. The preparation of general comments is one area where the Secretariat could play a greater role by initiating proposals and undertaking research on the articles concerned including relevant work undertaken by other human rights bodies. The Secretariat has offered more assistance in this direction and this is now being more fully realized.

3.38 The general comments serve rapidly to develop the jurisprudence of the HRC under the Covenant. They are potentially very important as an expression of the accumulated and unparalleled experience of an independent expert human rights body of a universal character in its consideration of the implementation of the ICCPR. Whether this potential has been realized is considered in the relevant parts of subsequent chapters. It is appropriate at this point, however, to note that it is necessarily a most difficult task to obtain a consensus agreement from eighteen experts from different geographical regions and legal schools. The application of the technique of consensus decision making in this context inevitably results in general comments that to some extent represent the highest common denominator between members. The chairman of the HRC acknowledged this point recently when, in the light of substantial difficulties among members regarding a draft general comment concerning article 27 of the ICCPR (minority rights), he suggested to members that they would have to try to be less maximalistic in their approach if there was to be any hope of reaching a consensus.[246] Ultimately, the draft general comment on article 27 was dropped because, it was argued, there was not enough information available to form a sound basis for decision.[247] As Professor Higgins pointed out, the lack of information available might have been taken to indicate the desirability of making a general comment that would indicate to States parties the information the HRC required.[248] However, at least the HRC emerged from the debate on article 27 with established criteria to guide its work in respect of general comments. The applicable considerations are: 'the relevance of the proposed subjects to the problems encountered by States parties in implementing the Covenant; the topicality of the proposed subject; and the prospects for reaching consensus within the Committee on the eventual draft general comments'.[249]

G. THE ROLE OF THE ECOSOC

3.39 In accordance with article 40(4) of the ICCPR the HRC shall transmit 'its reports' and 'may' also transmit copies of any general comments it considers appropriate to adopt to the States parties. The HRC 'may' also transmit these comments to the ECOSOC along with the copies of the reports it has received from the States parties.[250] There is no express indication in the ICCPR of the role, if any, of ECOSOC on receipt of any general comments transmitted to it by the HRC and the reports of States parties. Presumably then it is open to the ECOSOC to exercise whatever powers it assumes under its general jurisdiction to consider human rights matters. Arguably this could include making specific, formal recommendations directly to particular States on the basis of the general comments adopted by the HRC and the State reports. There is a precedent for this in a similar function performed by ECOSOC under the periodic reporting system established in ECOSOC Resolution 624B (XXII) and operated by the Human Rights Commission.[251] In practice, however, ECOSOC has not taken any action with respect to the general comments of the HRC or the reports of States parties.

Under article 45 of the ICCPR the HRC is obliged to submit an Annual Report on its activities to the General Assembly through the ECOSOC.[252] There is no indication in the ICCPR of whether the ECOSOC is to conduct any consideration of the Annual Report. Again any such powers can only be deduced from ECOSOC's general jurisdiction. It was apparent at the first occasion on which the HRC's Report was transmitted to ECOSOC that ECOSOC was unclear as to what its role should be.[253] It is clear that at least some delegations envisaged that ECOSOC would play an active role in considering reports.[254] In practice, however, the ECOSOC has authorized the Secretary-General to transmit the Annual Report of the HRC directly to the General Assembly unless the ECOSOC is invited at the request of either a member or the Secretary-General to consider it.[255] To date no such request has ever been made. The non-consideration of the report by ECOSOC ensures that there is no danger of the report not being considered by the General Assembly in the same year as its adoption.[256] It is difficult to see what useful function the ECOSOC could perform with its composition and political nature bearing in mind the consideration of the HRC's Annual Report by the Third Committee of the General Assembly.

H. THE ANNUAL REPORT OF THE HRC TO THE GENERAL ASSEMBLY

3.40 Article 40(5) of the ICCPR provides that, 'The Committee shall submit to the General Assembly of the United Nations, through the Economic And Social Council (ECOSOC), an annual report on its activities'.[257] The Annual Report serves as a vital link between the HRC, the States parties, and the General Assembly.[258] The Annual Reports have in practice been substantial documents containing thorough accounts of the consideration of reports and of communications under the OP together with basic information on the practices and procedures of the HRC. As noted, to date the ECOSOC has not exhibited any serious interest in the work of the HRC.[259]

Within the GA the Annual Report is considered by the Third Committee of the GA (Social, Humanitarian, and Cultural Questions) in the autumn of the same year of its publication.[260] The role of the Third Committee is not spelt out in the ICCPR. In fact since 1978 the Third Committee has spent an increasing amount of its time discussing the HRC's Annual Report. Indeed, it is an interesting question as to the relationship between the HRC and the Third Committee.[261] We have already noted that the HRC is not a United Nations body but an independent body established by the States parties to the Covenant, although the HRC is dependent on the UN for finance and administration.[262] A number of members have suggested that the HRC is not bound by the opinion of the Third Committee.[263] In recent discussions, 'It was understood that the members of the Committee, notwithstanding their capacity as independent experts, would bear in mind, in the exercise of their functions, the observations made by delegations'.[264]

During its spring session (normally in New York) the HRC discusses the considerations of the Third Committee.[265] HRC members have recognized the importance of establishing an effective dialogue with the Third Committee and giving serious consideration to the views expressed by it. Generally the Third Committee has commended the work done by the HRC. The Annual Report has been subjected to searching consideration and various views have been expressed, for example, on the procedures adopted by the HRC, the functions of the HRC under the reporting procedure, the comments, proposals, and amendments considered by the HRC, the comments expressed with regard to particular countries, views expressed under the OP, publicity for the Covenant, the Optional Protocol, and the work of the HRC. Very occasionally, however, certain representatives in the Third Committee have seen fit to attack certain aspects of the HRC's work, for example, an alleged political cover up by certain members of the systematic genocide of the Palestinian Peoples.[266] Similarly, Uruguay raised some objections to the HRC's practices under the Optional Protocol,[267] and a number of States criticized parts of the HRC's second General Comment on article 6.[268] More generally the Third Committee has drawn the attention of the HRC to the standard-setting work of some of the other human rights organs, called for it to deepen the reporting process and the follow-up action, requested the HRC to give specific content to the rights recognized in the Covenant and indicate any weak points that might need to be improved, asked the HRC to consider the role of people in the processes engaged in by their governments under the ICCPR, called upon all States to become parties to the Covenant,[269] and recognized the need to co-ordinate the reporting obligations of States parties under the various international reporting procedures and organize the flow of information among the relevant bodies.[270]

I. APPRAISAL

3.41 This chapter has reviewed the institutional aspects of the reporting system established by the ICCPR and the practices and procedures adopted by the HRC in implementing that system. The system must be subject to critical appraisal in the light of the increasing criticism of international reporting procedures. It has been argued that the systems are inherently defective and that the increasing number of them has led to an apparent decline in the willingness of States parties to submit reports and to financial and logistical problems.[271] As we noted in chapter 2 the HRC has established itself as a respected body of independent, highly qualified members who have attracted consistent praise for the serious and constructive nature of their deliberations both from State representatives that have appeared before them and in the Third Committee. We also noted that in its consideration of reports under article 40 it has established a remarkable consensus practice and although there are clear political differences between members the HRC has avoided the overt politicization evident in many human rights institutions.[272] It is perhaps a measure of the HRC's success that the new Committee on Economic, Social, and Cultural Rights has been modelled to some degree on the HRC and its practices under article 40.[273] The groundwork for the success of the HRC has been established by the commitment displayed by the members who have served on the HRC in its formative years. Its continued success will to a large part depend on the continuing integrity of its present and future members.[274]

3.42 With respect to the submission of reports the HRC has displayed great patience and flexibility. Although the eventual record of submission has been commendable the delays involved have often been considerable. Having established itself as a serious and important human rights body the HRC would do well to take a firmer line regarding the delayed submission of reports. The HRC's very success gives it greater potential to exert pressure on States parties to submit reports on time and, if that fails, to give effective publicity to that default. However, it must be recognized that the problem is a very difficult one to resolve. The co-operation of States parties is critically important and the HRC must retain sufficient flexibility to be able to respond to situations on a case-by-case basis as they arise. Some delays, however, for example that of Belgium in submitting an initial report, must be open to severe criticism.

3.43 It has been submitted that the guidelines for the preparation of initial reports could be expanded and improved. Despite suggestions to this effect within the HRC no action has been taken.[275] Similarly the procedure for the consideration of initial reports is capable of rationalization. Such rationalization might even allow the consideration of initial reports, provided they are substantial enough, to be conducted in accordance with the 'second round' procedure developed by the HRC. This is important because the second round procedure is generally much more productive than the 'first round' and the use of the second round procedure may be greatly reduced in the light of the HRC's decision that henceforth whether the HRC will conduct a consideration of a Supplementary Report will be decided on a case-to-case basis depending in part on the timing of the submission of reports.[276] The procedures for the consideration of periodic reports are now well established and although there may be some refinement, subtantial changes seem unlikely. Those procedures appear to work very well and the comments by both HRC members and State representatives suggest that consideration of periodic reports to date has been very useful and informative in obtaining a better understanding of the implementation of civil and political rights in the States concerned and of the factors and difficulties encountered. This is critically important as it is the consideration of periodic reports that will come to play the major role in the future work of the HRC.

3.44 The great majority of States have exhibited an attitude of co-operation with the HRC and appear to have taken their reporting obligations very seriously. Many of the second periodic reports of States parties have been substantially better than their initial reports. That all States have eventually sent a representative or a group of representatives to appear before the HRC bears testimony to that seriousness and to respect for the HRC. The even higher quality of State representatives who have attended for the consideration of periodic reports confirms this view. In retrospect the decision of the HRC to invite State representatives to appear before it constitutes one of its most important procedural decisions to date. The presence of State representatives has been fundamental to the establishment of the 'constructive dialogue' sought by the HRC. The development of this dialogue has enabled members of the HRC to indicate clearly whether they are of the view that violations of the Covenant have occurred or that domestic legislation or provisions are inconsistent with the Covenant. It can be argued that this dialogue with the State party, through its representatives, has pre-empted any necessity for the HRC to adopt formal determinations of non-compliance. Such a course could ultimately be adopted by the HRC if its deliberations are seen to produce no effective results but there has been no consensus to date in favour of such a development. Indeed, as we have noted, considerable disagreement exists within the HRC concerning its jurisdictional powers under article 40, including the permissible scope of its 'General Comments'.[277] At present it seems unlikely that there will be any development towards the adoption of country specific reports or of general comments addressed to one particular State party. This may encourage members to try and make the established reporting procedures as specific and penetrating as possible, to make the general comments as specific as possible in respect of each right in the ICCPR and further develop the *general observations* and evaluations of the performance of a State in their concluding statements.[278]

However, it appears from the consideration of reports that members of the HRC have legitimate differences on the question of implementation in particular States.[279] It would seem then that it would in any event be difficult, if not impossible, to reach a consensus agreement on specific reports on each State party or on general comments addressed to particular States. The alternative of majority voting has not commended itself to the HRC and has, indeed, become something of a psychological barrier.[280]

3.45 Only time will reveal whether the HRC's failure to draw up specific reports on each State party and general comments addressed to particular State parties are fundamental defects in the reporting procedure. Part of the relative success of the reporting systems of the ILO and under the European Social Charter has stemmed from the publicity and political support given to the observations, reports, and conclusions reached by the relevant examining bodies.[281] Under the ICCPR it is uncertain as to which body, if any, is charged with taking any further action subsequent to the work of the HRC. The absence of any State specific reports or State specific general comments makes the task of any superior political body very difficult because it has no agreed basis from which to work. For example, the considerations of the Third Committee of the General Assembly are based on the Annual Reports of the HRC. The Annual Reports are drafted in a neutral manner and merely summarize the considerations of the HRC. It does not form an adequate basis for the adoption of specific recommendations addressed to particular States concerning the implementation of their obligations under the ICCPR. In the absence of State specific reports and State specific general comments the inevitable tendency will be for the considerations of the HRC to lie largely hidden within the mass of general United Nations documentation. Without effective publicity and specific political back-up the effectiveness of the HRC's considerations is likely to be marginal in all but the most exceptional of cases.[282] Therefore, national and international non-governmental organizations have an important role to play in following up the consideration of State reports. Similarly national Parliaments or Assemblies, where they exist, could play a role.

3.46 The establishment of a periodicity of five years would appear realistic considering the range of rights covered by the ICCPR and the existence of several other international reporting procedures that are time consuming for States. However, as the rate of new ratifications or accessions has declined consideration should be given to reducing the period to three or four years as envisaged in the HRC's original periodicity decision but it has been submitted that the issue is not crucial.[283] The establishment of any shorter period than this might prejudice the quality of reports and the practice of only considering the reports in the presence of State representatives.

It was unfortunate that the original periodicity decision had the unintended effect of reducing the incentive for States parties promptly to submit Supplementary Reports containing additional information. The subsequent amendment to correct this defect may yet prove to be effective but seems to date to have produced little result. The approach now developed by the HRC as regards Supplementary Reports is both sensible and flexible.[284] It is submitted that it is important for the HRC to keep open the possibility of the consideration of Supplementary Reports because the second round procedure used has often proved very useful and has done much to remedy the inadequate first round consideration of reports.

3.47 We noted that no general decision was adopted concerning the HRC's powers to request a report 'whenever it deems it necessary' other than in accordance with its general periodicity decision.[285] It is submitted that the proposals made should have been adopted as they were sufficiently flexible to leave the decision to the HRC on a case-by-case basis but would have removed the appearance of them being selective, *ad hoc*, and political requests. The absence of a general, formal decision on this matter is to be regretted. However, the decision to request a report from El Salvador under article 40(1)(*b*) after the killing of a member of their national human rights commission may have set an important precedent.[286]

3.48 A disappointing aspect of the reporting procedures is the minimal role played by the specialized agencies and the non-governmental organizations.[287] Of the specialized agencies only the ILO regularly submits notes to the HRC members and it rarely sends a representative to the meetings of the HRC at which State reports are being considered. As for non-governmental organizations, they have no formal role at all and are limited to submitting information to HRC members in their individual capacities.[288] However, though this was a contentious issue in the early years of the HRC, all members now receive and accept such information on a reguar basis. Indeed many actively seek out such information. None the less, it seems doubtful that the HRC will adopt any formal decision recognizing a legitimate role for the non-governmental organizations. It is vital, therefore, that HRC members make NGOs aware that they are willing and ready to receive appropriate information and that NGOs continue to take an active interest in the work of the HRC notwithstanding the absence of a formal decision recognizing their role. Similarly, it has been submitted that the HRC could exhibit a much more positive attitude to the specialized agencies even if the HRC does not change its present formal decision that they are not competent to submit comments on the reports submitted by States.

3.49 Having regard to the absence of any judicial determination, binding decisions or recommendations, and enforcement powers it is apparent that the key to the effectiveness of the reporting procedure established by the ICCPR will be the HRC's powers to persuade. The HRC's weight lies in its moral and legal authority as a respected and independent human rights body. Further pressure and persuasion can be derived from effective publicity and the political support of superior bodies.[289] Unfortunately, the former has been sadly lacking. Consideration of the United Kingdom's reports, for example, attracted little national publicity. Ironically, the serious and depoliticized nature of the HRC's considerations have made it less newsworthy. Academic attention to the actual practices of the HRC has also been infrequent although it is now increasing.

3.50 The political support for the HRC could have come from various bodies. However, the Conference of States parties and ECOSOC have taken no substantive roles concerning the HRC's work. The only serious attention to the HRC's work has come from the Third Committee of the GA during its discussion of the HRC's Annual Report. We have noted the development of extensive consideration of the HRC's work in the Third Committee with various views and opinions being expressed. The actual relationship between the HRC and the Third Committee is not spelt out in the ICCPR but in practice the HRC has given very serious consideration to the views expressed in the Third Committee. The Third Committee is an important forum where at least a limited amount of political pressure can be brought to bear on State parties who default on their obligations to submit reports and on their obligations to implement the provisions of the Covenant.

3.51 The substantive deliberations of the HRC under the article 40 process are extensively illustrated in chapters 5–12 with respect to selected rights in the ICCPR. The foregoing account would appear to suggest that the HRC has established a workable reporting procedure. An oral dialogue has been established with all States. That dialogue has been conducted in a searching, critical manner by members of the HRC. Acrimonious exchanges with State representatives and the introduction of inter-State disputes have generally been avoided though a number of exchanges have been marked by a degree of tension.[290] There is also some limited evidence that the HRC's considerations have had some direct effect on the protection of human rights in some States parties. This evidence is considered in chapter 13. However, it is much less systematic than the record of formal changes in laws and practices that can be given under the system of ILO Conventions[291] or under the European Social Charter.[292]

3.52 On balance, despite some of the deficiencies noted in this chapter, the reporting procedure has been developed into a much more useful procedure of international implementation (in the broad sense) than might confidently have been predicted when the Covenant was adopted in 1966.[293] Moreover, as Professor Tomuschat has noted, there is a broader dimension to the HRC's work which must not be overlooked:

The meetings being held by the Committee marked a turning point in the history of human rights: for the first time, a procedure had been established which applied to the States of all regions in the world, irrespective of the ideological and political differences separating them, and which was designed to exercise, through a friendly and constructive dialogue, a kind of international control.[294]

However, there remains little doubt that some fundamental jurisdictional questions remain unresolved and the system is open to further improvement, rationalization, and development along the lines suggested in this chapter. The HRC is actively considering improvements. In July 1990 the HRC instructed the Working Group under article 40 to look into a number of issues including Special Rapporteurs on individual State reports, emergency cases, and periodicity after the consideration of third periodic reports (see SR 1003, 1024).

3.53 Within the context of the general reporting system developments in the HRC's system may well be affected by proposals to improve the functioning of the various reporting systems. A number of proposals were made in the report of the meeting of Chairpersons of the human rights treaty bodies in October 1988.[295] These include consolidating the respective guidelines of the treaty bodies concerning the initial part of each State party's report,[296] improving technical assistance and advisory services, increased computerization, an expert study on possible long-term approaches to the consideration of supervision of human rights instruments,[297] more adequate staffing,[298] greater use of accessible annual statistical information, preparation of a detailed reporting manual for States parties,[299] revision of decisions on periodicity, greater use of individual rapporteurs or co-ordinators and working groups to expedite the consideration of periodic reports, consideration of general time limits on speakers, facilitating regular meetings with special rapporteurs of the HRCion and Sub-Cion, ensuring a more specific and direct dialogue with specialized agencies, and increasing publicity for treaty bodies at national and international levels.

NOTES

1 See Bossuyt, *Guide*, pp. 615–33. There have been a number of studies dealing with the provisions of the Covenant on reporting. There is a small but growing literature on the actual practices of the HRC under those provisions. See P. S. Brar, 'International Law and the Protection of Civil and Political Rights: A Critique of the United Nations' Human Rights Committee's Nature, Legal Status, Practices, Procedures and Prospects', (MALD Thesis, The Fletcher School of Law and Diplomacy, USA, 1984); M. Bossuyt, ch. 2 n. 1 above (1978–9); F. Capotorti, ch. 2 n. 1 above (1967); K. Das, 'United Nations Institutions and Procedures Founded on Conventions on Human Rights and Fundamental Freedoms', in K. Vasak/P. Alston (eds.), *The International Dimensions of Human Rights*, Vol. i, p. 303 and pp. 336–8 (1982); E. Decaux, ch. 2 n. 1 above (1980) p. 487 at pp. 512–19; H. M. Empell, *Die Kompetenzen des UN-Menschenrechtsausschusses im Staatenberichtsverfahren* (1987); J. L. Gomez Del Prado, 'United Nations Conventions on Human Rights: The Practice of the Human Rights Committee and the Committee on the Elimination of Racial Discrimination in Dealing with the Reporting Obligations of States Parties', 7 HRQ (1985) pp. 492–513; B. Graefrath, 'Trends Emerging in the Practice of the HRC', GDR Committee for Human Rights Bulletin, No. 1/80 (1980) pp. 3–32; B. Graefrath, ch. 6 n. 1 below; D. Fischer, 'Reporting under the Covenant on Civil and Political Rights: The First Five Years of the HRC', 76 AJIL (1982) pp. 142–53; D. Fischer, 'International Reporting Procedures', in H. Hannum (ed.), *Guide to International Human Rights Practice*, p. 165 at pp. 168–73 (1984); M. Lippman, ch. 2 n. 1 above (1979); F. Jhabvala, 'The Practice of the Covenant's HRC, 1976–82: Review of State Party Reports', 6 HRQ (1984) pp. 81–106; P. Gormley, ch. 1 n. 1 above (1972); M. Nowak, 'The Effectiveness of the ICCPR—Stocktaking after the First Eleven Sessions of the U.N. Human Rights Committee', 1 HRLJ (1980) p. 136 at pp. 146–51 and 163–70; id., 3 HRLJ (1982) p. 207 at pp. 207–10; id., 5 HRLJ (1984) p. 199 at pp. 199–203; T. Opsahl, 'Human Rights Today: International Obligations and National Implementation', 23 Scandinavian Studies in Law (1979) p. 156; A. G. Mower, ch. 2 n. 1 above (1977); id., ch. 2 n. 1 above (1978); B. Ramcharan, 'The Emerging Jurisprudence of the HRC', 6 Dalhousie LJ (1980) pp. 7–40; id., 'Implementing the International

Covenants on Human Rights', in B. Ramcharan (ed.), *Human Rights—Thirty Years after the Universal Declaration*, p. 159 at pp. 174–87 and 190–5 (1979); Robertson, ch. 2 n. 1 above, pp. 341–51 (1984); E. Schwelb, 'The International Measures of Implementation of the International Covenant on Civil and Political Rights and of the Optional Protocol', 12 Tex. ILJ (1977) pp. 141 at 154–60;

For purposes of comparison to other international reporting procedures reference is made in this chapter to the following works: P. Alston, ch. 2 n. 38 above (1987); T. Buergenthal, 'Implementing the Racial Convention', 12 Tex. ILJ (1977) pp. 187–221; M. Galey, 'International Enforcement of Women's Rights', 6 HRQ (1984) pp. 463–90; D. Harris, *The European Social Charter* (1984); E. A. Landy, *The Effectivenes of International Supervision—Thirty Years of ILO Experience* (1966); F. Wolf, 'Human Rights and the I.L.O.', in T. Meron (ed.), *Human Rights in International Law—Legal and Policy Issues*, vol. ii., ch. 7 (1984); T. Meron, *Human Rights Law-Making in the United Nations* (1986); N. Valticos, *The International Labour Organization* (1979); N. Lerner, *The United Nations Convention on the Elimination of Racial Discrimination* (2d, 1980); A. Byrnes, 'The "Other" Treaty Body: The Work of the Committee on the Elimination of Discrimination Against Women', 14 Yale JIL (1989) pp. 1–67.

2 See article 22 of the Covenant of the League of Nations; articles 19 and 22 of the Constitution of the ILO; articles 73*e*, 87*a*, and 88 of the UN Charter; article VIII of the Constitution of UNESCO; articles 21 and 22 of the European Social Charter; article 57 ECHR; articles 16–22 of ICESCR (see now Alston, n. 1 above); articles 9 ICERD. In 1956 the ECOSOC established a system of periodic reporting by States on development and progress on human rights, ECOSOC Resn. 624B (XXII). The system was terminated by the General Assembly in 1980, apparently on the initiative of the UN Secretariat, GA Resn. 35/209. On that system and criticisms of its termination see *UN Action in the Field of Human Rights*, p. 313 (1988); J. P. Humphrey, ch. 1 n. 1 above, p. 178; id., 'The Implementation of International Human Rights Law', 24 NYSLR (1978) pp. 31–62; L. Sohn, ch. 1 n. 1 above, p. 39 at pp. 74–9.

3 See ch. 2 above.

4 The national reports are published as official UN documents. The reports for the years 1977–1978 appear in Yb. HRC (1977–8) vol. ii; 1979–80 in Yb. HRC (1979–80) vol. ii; 1981–2 in Yb. HRC (1982–2) vol. ii. The reports form an extremely valuable account of the implementation by States parties of the provisions of the Covenant and provide important material for human rights researchers. The United Kingdom reports are compiled by the Foreign and Commonwealth Office from information provided by more than half a dozen departments and the administration of the Dependent Territories.

5 SR 756 pr. 77; Doc. A/42/40, pr. 40.

6 Doc. A/6546, ch. 1 n. 1 above, pr. 384.

7 See the questions raised by Mr Errera in a decision under the OP concerning self-determination, ch. 5, pr. 5.20–5.21 below. States parties to OP2 are to include in their reports information on measures adopted to give effect to OP2, see article 3 of OP2.

8 For example, article 47 may be relevant to article 1, see ch. 1, pr. 1.23 above and ch. 5, pr. 5.12 below.

9. Cf. article 20 European Social Charter, as to which see Harris, n. 1 above, pp. 14–21.

10 Initial Reports of States Parties due in 1977, Note by the Secretary-General, Doc. CCPR/C/1; Yb. HRC (1977–8) Vol. ii, p. 15.

11 'General Guidelines Regarding the Form and Content of Reports from States Parties under Article 40 of the Covenant', Doc. CCPR/C/5; Doc. A/32/44, Apx. IV. Adopted by HRC at its 44th meeting (2nd session), 29 August 1977. The guidelines are not legally binding but HRC members have strongly encouraged their use.

12 'General Guidelines', pr. 2.

13 Ibid., pr. 3. Many national reports have been accompanied by substantial documentary appendices. The UK's second periodic report was accompanied by 42 reference documents, Doc. CCPR/C/32/Add. 5, p. 21 (1984). The two reports submitted by Nicaragua were accompanied by 77 appendices.

14 'General Guidelines', prs. 4–6 (my emphasis). Similarly in CEDAW, see Byrnes, n. 1 above, pp. 19–28.

15 The terminology applied by the HRC has varied from time to time. This account uses the term 'supplementary'.

16 See Jhabvala, n. 1 above, pp. 102–4. During consideration of the report of the Lebanon Mr Graefrath commented that, 'The report appeared, however, to deal at greater length with, for example, legislation on prostitution than with the real situation of human rights and the Government's difficulties', SR 442 pr. 37. 'It might be useful . . . to read the report of the Democratic Republic of Korea (Docs. CCPR/C/22/Add. 3 (1983) and Add. 5 (1985) and the summary records covering the consideration of that report (SR 509, 510, and 516) in order to understand how difficult it is to come to grips with facts and not remain in a mollifying nirvana of sheer verbalism', Tomuschat, ch. 1 n. 214 above, p. 577 (1985).

17 For an example of one that did see the report of Cyprus, Doc. CCPR/C/1/Add. 28, pp. 18–22.

18 See e.g. SR 764 pr. 57 (State representative, Trinidad and Tobago). See also ch. 6 below.

19. Note Rule 70 of the HRC's rules which provides that, 'If a report of a State party to the Covenant, in the opinion of the Committee, does not contain sufficient information, the Committee may request that State to furnish additional information which is required, indicating by what date the said information should be submitted'.

20 See e.g. the discussion in SR 630.

21 e.g. Uruguay, El Salvador.

22 See pr. 3.8.1 below.

23 For example the UK Supplementary Report, Doc. CCPR/C/1/Add. 35 (1978).

24 Figures calculated from the Annual Reports of the HRC and information supplied by the UN Secretariat.

25 See GC 2/13; Doc. A/36/40, Ax. VII. Also issued in Doc. CCPR/C/21.

26 See Landy, n. 1 above, pp. 15–16, 23–5; Valticos, n. 1 above, prs. 591–2; Harris, n. 1 above, pp. 201–2.

27 See Doc. CERD/C/70/Rev. 1, (6 Dec. 1983); Doc. A/35/18. See Gomez Del Prado, n. 1 above.

28 Some members of the HRC have made similar suggestions, see SR 306 pr. 30 (Tomuschat), SR 414 pr. 20 (Hanga); Doc. A/41/40, pr. 26. CEDAW's guidelines have also been criticised for being too general, see Byrnes, n. 1 above, pp. 13–16.

29 'Statement on the Duties of the Committee under Article 40 of the Covenant', Doc. A/36/40, Ax. IV. Also issued in Doc. CCPR/C/18. See generally prs. 3.29–3.38 below.

30 Ibid., pr. (*d*).

31 'Guidelines Regarding the Form and Contents of Reports from States Parties under Article 40, Paragraph 1(b) of the Covenant', Doc. A/36/40, pp. 105–6, adopted by the HRC at its 308th meeting, thirteenth session, on 27 July 1981. Also issued in Doc. CCPR/C/20.

32 For the HRC's discussion see SR 295, 296, 299, 303, 306, and 308. See also pr. (*f*) of the HRC's 'Consensus Statement' on its Duties, pr. 3.5 above.

33 'Decision on Periodicity', Doc. A/36/40, Ax. V. Adopted by the HRC at its 303rd meeting (22 July 1981). Also issued in Doc. CCPR/C/19.

34 Doc. A/36/40, pr. 388. On the periodicity under the ICESCR see Alston, ch. 2 n. 2 above, pp. 361–2.

35 See Alston, ch. 2 n. 38 above, pp. 332–3. Essentially States are complaining of too many and unduly onerous obligations and questioning their effectiveness. The General Assembly has recognized the problem and called for meetings of the Chairpersons of the supervisory bodies entrusted with the consideration of reports submitted under United Nations conventions on human rights, GA Resn. 42/405. See Doc. A/40/600 (1985). The first meeting was held in October 1988, see Doc. A/44/98, 'Reporting Obligations of States Parties to the United Nations Instruments on Human Rights, Note by the Secretary-General'.

36 See n. 33 above. See also SR 312 pr. 65, 318 pr. 68.

37 See pr. (*f*) of the 'Consensus Statement', pr. 3.5 above.

38 See SR 349, 357, and 359.

39 Doc. A/37/40, Ax. IV. Adopted by the HRC at its 380th meeting on 28 July 1982. Also issued in Doc. CCPR/C/19/Rev. 1.

40 See SR 569 prs. 77–80.

41 Doc. A/37/40, prs. 340–4. See also SR 334, 349, and 351 on the general problem of derogation and notification under article 4 of the Covenant and the obligations of both the States parties and the HRC under article 40.

42 See pr. 3.6 above.

43 See ch. 2, pr. 2.7 above.

44 SR 747 pr. 1. For the HRC's discussion see SR 762.

45 At each session the HRC is informed of and considers the status of the submission of reports. Details of the submission of reports in the period under review are given in each of the Annual Reports adopted by the HRC, see pr. 3.40 below. See also Note by the Secretary-General, 'Reporting Obligations of States Parties to the International Covenants on Human Rights and the International Convention on the Elimination of Racial Discrimination', Doc. A/39/484 (1984); 'Report of the Secretary-General Concerning the Obligations of States Parties to the UN Conventions on Human Rights', Doc. A/40/600 and Add. 1 (1985).

46 Article 40(1)(*a*).

47 For details see Doc. A/45/40, Ax. IV.

1985, was submitted in 1987 and was considered as an initial report in March 1988.

76 Initial report due 1978, submitted 1987.

77 Initial report due 1984, submitted December 1987.

78 For example the reports of Iceland and Austria were submitted to the HRC in March and April 1981 respectively but were not considered by the HRC until October 1982 and March 1983 respectively.

79 See e.g. the initial report of Zambia, Doc. CCPR/C/36/Add. 1 (1987) (8 pp.).

80 See GC 1/13, Doc. A/36/40, pp. 107–8.

81 See also SR 758 (Martenson).

82 See SR 760 and 872 for the HRC's recent discussions. The HRC have accepted the need to deal with problems on a case-by-case basis, SR 760 pr. 61 (Chairman). For a recent discussion see SR 901, prs. 1–29.

83 See Fischer, n. 1 above (1982), pp. 146–7; Y. K. Tyagi, 'Co-operation between the HRC and Non-Governmental Organizations', 18 Tex. ILJ (1983) pp. 273–90. There are many sources the HRC could consult. See Amnesty International Reports on individual countries and its Annual Report (latest Report 1989); The annual 'Freedom House Comparative Survey—Freedom in the World: Political and Civil Liberties', edited by G. Gill; The Annual Reports of the United States Department to Congress on Human Rights, 'Country Reports on Human Rights and Practices' (latest Report 1989); *World Human Rights Guide* (revised and updated, 1986 and 1987) compiled by Charles Humana; J. Carey, *U.N. Protection of Civil and Political Rights*, ch. 11 (1970). There have been calls within the United Nations for 'An Annual Worldwide Report on the Progress Made in the Implementation of Human Rights in Each and Every Country', (Ecuador, 39th session General Assembly, 1984). For some of the problems involved in obtaining and assessing human rights information see D. L. Cingranelli (ed.), *Human Rights: Measurement and Theory* (1988); J. I. Dominguez, 'Assessing Human Rights Conditions', in J. I. Dominguez *et al.*, *Enhancing Global Human Rights*, pp. 21–116 (1979); N. S. Rodley, 'Monitoring Human Rights Violations in the 1980s', ibid., pp. 117–51; J. Salzberg, 'Monitoring Human Rights Violations—How Good is the Information?', in P. G. Brown and D. Maclean (eds.), *Human Rights and U.S. Foreign Policy*, pp. 173–82 (1979); Symposium 'Statistical Issues in the Field of Human Rights', 8 HRQ (1987) pp. 551–699. See also the UN Legal Opinion on 'The use of information by the CERD from sources other than States parties to the ICERD, and the conditions under which co-operation could be established between the CERD and ILO and UNESCO bodies dealing with discrimination', 1972 UN Juridical Yearbook pp. 163–7. The opinion concluded, *inter alia*, that, 'especially in respect of article 9 (the reporting procedure) it is not clear that CERD is precluded from using extraneous information for ancillary purposes, i.e., in evaluating the completeness of the reports submitted to it and in formulating requests for supplementary data, and the early practice of the Committee indicates that it does indeed rely on such information. Thus there would not seem to be any legal bar to the utilization, within the indicated limits, of information obtained from ILO or UNESCO', pr. 8.

84 See Jhabvala, n. 1 above, p. 102.

85 See Capotorti, ch. 2 n. 1 above, p. 137. On the practice of CEDAW see Byrnes, n. 1 above, pp. 35–42.

86 In the Third Committee of the General Assembly it was understood that the Secretary-General would not transmit the report of a State that was not a member of the Specialized Agency concerned, Doc. A/6546, ch. 1 n. 1 above, pr. 385. See also article 46 ICCPR, Ax. I below. There were some difficulties in determining which articles actually fell within the fields of competence of the specialized agencies. The HRC agreed to draw the attention of the UNESCO to the relevant parts of the States' parties reports concerning articles 18, 19, and 27. The UNESCO Board intimated that it further wished to study articles 6, 7, 8, 13, 22, 23, and 24. UNESCO also submitted a document to the Committee detailing its contribution to the implementation of the ICCPR (108/EX/CR/SS.1). There was no similar difficulty with the ILO which indicated that the articles of interest to it were articles 8(3) and 22. See the comparative analysis of the International Covenants on Human Rights and International Labour Conventions and Recommendations, 52(2) ILO Bulletin (1969) pp. 181–216. The ICESCR contains much more specific provisions on the role of specialized agencies in the implementation of that Covenant, see P. Alston, 'The U.N. Specialized Agencies and the Implementation of the ICESCR', 18 Col. J. Trans. L. (1979) pp. 79–118; P. Alston, ch 2 n. 38 above, pp. 362–74. See also article 45 of the UN Convention on the Rights of the Child, ch. 1 n. 259 above.

87 See SR 180, 181, and Docs. CCPR/C/L.3 and Add. 1–3, in Yb. HRC (1977–8), Vol. ii, pp. 11–14.

88 R. 67(2).

89 See e.g. SR 99 prs. 39–46; Doc. A/34/40, pr. 605. A/35/40, pr. 414.

90 See SR 181; Doc. A/35/40, prs. 410–14. The practice of the CERD is similar, see Gomez Del Prado, n. 1 above, pp. 498–500; Yb. HRC (1977–8) vol. ii, p. 12; Lerner, n. 1 above, pp. 118–20.

91 Although apparently not all HRC members were aware of it. See also the discussion in SR 180.

92 It would be helpful if the HRC's Annual Report indicated which specialized agencies and non-governmental organizations had attended sessions of the HRC. The problem in doing this would be that it might suggest that the specialized agencies or the non-governmental organizations had some formal standing. Such information was included in the first report of the CESCR, ch. 2 n. 38 above.

93 See the discussion at SR 542 prs. 27–42.

94 This is the formula used by CERD.

95 See SR 542 pr. 36 (Movchan) and prs. 27, 38 (Graefrath).

96 The matter does not appear to have been dealt with since.

97 See e.g. the HRC's approach to article 6 ICCPR in ch. 8 below.

98 The obvious limitations on the jurisprudence of specialized agencies are that the precise terms of the relevant Conventions may be different and the reporting systems may be operating on different timetables.

99 In the General Assembly some representatives have expressed the hope that the exchange of information and experience would be extended under article 40.

100 See Tyagi, n. 83 above. Cf. As a subsidiary body of ECOSOC the CESCR has encouraged NGOs in consultative status to submit written communications on

issues of relevance to the work of the Committee. See also article 45 of the UN Convention on the Rights of the Child, ch. 1 n. 259 above.

101 See e.g. SR 65 pr. 30 and SR 345 pr. 36 (Graefrath), SR 366 pr. 30 and SR 473 prs. 45–6 (Movchan). Note the comment of Alston, ch. 2 n. 38 above, 'UN documentation is, at best, reticent about and, at worst, thoroughly averse to, reflecting information on the situation concerning civil and political rights', p. 374 n. 215.

102 See e.g. the comments in notes 103–4 below.

103 See e.g. SR 128 pr. 40 (Tomuschat), SR 346 pr. 10 (Tarnopolsky) and pr. 39 (Ermacora); SR 321 pr. 33 (Opsahl); SR 368 pr. 44 (Tarnopolsky); SR 483 pr. 40 (Dimitrijevic). SR 594 prs. 9–10 (Movchan), SR 595 pr. 39 (Movchan), SR 598 prs. 29–32 (Movchan).

104 Mr Movchan and Mr Graefrath have suggested that a 'gentleman's agreement' had been reached within the HRC that the Secretariat should not distribute insessional documents emanating from NGOs and that members should in no case refer to documents issued by an NGO or mention the name of an NGO during the exchange with delegations or in their presence. Mr Movchan complained that some members were violating this agreement and thereby damaging the HRC's prestige by not agreeing to the 'Rules of Play', SR 572 pr. 11. Mr Tomuschat replied that he wished to 'State specifically that, the Committee had no clearly defined rules that members had undertaken not to mention their sources. It seemed to him that there had never really been an agreement along those lines and that, consequently, there could be no question of violating established rules. He also considered that all members of the Committee had always been duly discreet in that regard', ibid., pr. 13.

105 e.g. SR 128 pr. 21 (Tomuschat on Chile).

106 e.g. SR 421 pr. 50 (Aguilar on El Salvador).

107 e.g. SR 271 pr. 7 (Opsahl on Kenya), SR 469 pr. 23 (Errera on El Salvador).

108 e.g. SR 365 pr. 17 (Dieye on Iran), SR 469 pr. 18 (Tomuschat on El Salvador).

109 e.g. SR 475 pr. 15 (Opsahl on Guinea).

110 Doc. E/CN.4/1310; E/CN.4/1984/7; A/38/385 and Add. 1.

111 E/CN.4/1983/20. It is interesting to note that the representative of El Salvador also relied on the official report to substantiate some of his replies to the HRC, SR 468 pr. 46.

112 Doc. E/CN.4/1985/21. The report is reproduced in 6 HRLJ (1985) pp. 29–76.

113 e.g. SR 421 pr. 16 (Ermacora on Nicaragua).

114 e.g. SR 421 pr. 40 (Aguilar on Nicaragua).

115 e.g. SR 281 pr. 37 (Tarnopolsky on Tanzania), SR 522 prs. 5–8 (Opsahl on Panama).

116 e.g. SR 422 pr. 28 (Prado-Vallejo on El Salvador).

117 e.g. SR 258 prs. 76–7 (Opsahl on Italy referring to the Guzzardi Case); SR 403 pr. 48 (Tomuschat referring to the *Sunday Times Case*, though as a standard rather than a source of information); SR 321 pr. 24 (Movchan on the Netherlands).

118 e.g. SR 522 prs. 19–21 (Cote-Harper on Panama). At its own request the HRC is now provided with reports submitted under the ICESCR, the ICERD, and the CEDAW, Doc. A/41/40, pr. 13.

119 SR 321 pr. 26 (Movchan on the Netherlands).

120 e.g. SR 421 pr. 26 (Tarnopolsky on Nicaragua), SR 403 pr. 24 (Graefrath on Australia).

121 e.g. SR 412 prs. 13–14 (Graefrath on Australia), SR 430 pr. 37 (Prado-Vallejo on Peru).

122 See SR 469 pr. 3 (Opsahl on El Salvador).

123 See SR 430 pr. 44 (Prado-Vallejo on Peru).

124 NGOs known to have supplied information to the HRC include the Minority Rights Group (London), the Americas Watch Group (on El Salvador), the Bahai International Association (on Iran), and the International League for Human Rights (on various States).

125 e.g. SR 282 pr. 36 (Tarnopolsky on Tanzania), SR 468 pr. 32 (Prado-Vallejo on El Salvador), SR 717 pr. 1 (Zielinski on El Salvador). Note that Zielinski is Polish.

126 e.g. SR 321 pr. 11 (referred to by the State representative from the Netherlands).

127 e.g. SR 436 pr. 10 (referred to by Tarnopolsky).

128 e.g. SR 430 pr. 37 (Prado-Vallejo on Peru), SR 522 pr. 10 (Opsahl on Panama), SR 421 pr. 51 (Errera on Nicaragua).

129 e.g. SR 364 pr. 36 (Sadi on Iran), SR 442 pr. 19 (Al Douri on Lebanon).

130 e.g. SR 248 pr. 21 (Vincent-Evans on Mali).

131 e.g. SR 547 pr. 40 (Cote-Harper on Chile).

132 See e.g. SR 373 pr. 12 (Vincent-Evans on Uruguay); SR 735 pr. 6 (Movchan on Zaïre).

133 As Mr Errera commented during consideration of the report of El Salvador, 'The coincidence and precision of the information received from a variety of sources could not but raise questions', SR 469 pr. 23.

134 See Tyagi, n. 83 above.

135 For example, the report of El Salvador was accorded priority on this basis, SR 462 Add. 1 prs. 1–24. Similarly, the second periodic report of Ecuador was not considered at the HRC's twenty-ninth session because of the recent earthquake in that country.

136 For the exchange of views see Doc. A/32/44, prs. 104–11; SR. 25. The practice has been maintained to date.

137 This practice copied that of the CERD where it had been introduced in 1972 after the General Assembly had suggested that it would facilitate the Committee's work, see Lerner, n. 1 above, p. 105. A similar practice has been adopted by the new CESCR.

138 See e.g. SR 108 prs. 2–26, SR 564 prs. 1–5 (USSR).

139 Cf. the practice of the HRC under the Optional Protocol to the ICCPR, see ch. 4, pr. 4.10 n. 124 below.

140 See pr. 3.4 above.

141 On the former practice of the CERD in this respect see Gomez Del Prado, n. 1 above, p. 507. Exceptionally, however, the HRC has stated that it had not finished consideration of a State's initial report until it had submitted further information, e.g. El Salvador.

142 For the discussion which preceded the adoption of this practice see SR 117 prs. 60–70. For the first example of the 'second round' in operation see the HRC's consideration of the report of Ecuador (Doc. CCPR/C/1/Add. 8 and 29) at SR 118, in 1978.

143 Fischer, n. 1 above (1982), comments that, 'This procedure is far from cross-examination, but it does result in a public record that exposes more clearly a country's efforts to evade or ignore uncomfortable issues', p. 170.

144 See Jhabvala, n. 1 above, pp. 84–95; Nowak (1980), ibid., pp. 150–1. See also Graefrath SR 275 pr. 12.

145 The reports concerned were those of Finland, Sweden, and Hungary, see SR 170–2, 188, 189, 225, and 228.

146 See prs. 3.29–3.38 below.

147 See SR 549 prs. 39–62.

148 Doc. A/41/40, pr. 45.

149 This has now been done on a number of occasions.

150 General Guidelines, pr. 3.3 above.

151 Guinea finally sent a representative in March 1988.

152 See Buergenthal, n. 1 above, p. 201.

153 Canada sent a top level delegation of a dozen members. India sent its Attorney-General to head its delegation. Some State representatives have been able to answer very few of the HRC's questions, for example, the representative of Barbados, SR 264, 265, and 267. It was very difficult for the United Kingdom to send an appropriate person before the HRC in respect of its Dependent Territories. The Soviet delegation in October 1989 included a People's Deputy from the elected Supreme Soviet.

154 300 questions were raised during consideration of the report of Yugoslavia. The French representative identified 153 separate questions put to him during the first round examination of the French report.

155 SR 351 pr. 12.

156 See GC 2/13 pr. 4; Doc. CCPR/C/21. Doc. A/36/40, pp. 108–9. See also the HRC's discussion of this comment at SR 308 pr. 44 *et seq.*

157 See SR 150 pr. 46 *et seq.* Mr Dieye criticized the HRC's procedures as irrelevant and academic as regards developing countries but he never complied with requests to submit concrete proposals for reform.

158 See e.g. SR 466 pr. 21 (Prado-Vallejo). The Iranian representative complained that at least five members of the HRC had put the same question concerning the treatment of the Bahais.

159 See e.g. SR 219 pr. 6.

160 Cf. the decentralized procedures for the consideration of State reports under the ILO system, see Landy, n. 1 above, pp. 28–31; and under European Social Charter, Harris, ibid., p. 223.

161 Although there has been an increasing tendency over the years to associate with the comments of another member.

162 On abortion see ch. 8, pr. 8.5 below.

163 The HRC has not adopted a practice of preparing specific reports on the implementation of the Covenant by each State party, see prs. 3.29–3.38 below.

164 See the discussion in SR 755 on the practice of making general observations.

165 See pr. 3.4 above.

166 See prs. 3.25–3.28 below.

167 See the discussion in SR 49 prs. 27–54. The representative of the then Division of Human Rights expressed doubts as to whether this could be done without

making substantive judgments on State reports and thereby usurping the role of the HRC.

168 Pr. (*h*) of the HRC's 'Consensus Statement', Doc. A/36/40, pp. 101–3.
169 See Doc. CCPR/C/XII/CRP.1.
170 Doc. A/36/40, pp. 101–3.
171 Ibid., pr. (*i*).
172 Ibid., pr. (*j*).
173 Doc. CCPR/C/28/Add. 1, considered at SR 483, 484, and 488.
174 Unpublished. Summarized in Doc. A/39/40, pr. 39.
175 See pr. 3.5 above.
176 See pr. 3.6 above.
177 SR 466 and 467; Doc. A/39/40, prs. 58–66.
178 Unpublished.
179 SR 480 pr. 1. Subsequent lists have tended to be longer and more detailed.
180 SR 488 prs. 38–49.
181 See e.g. consideration of the list of issues for the report of Chile, discussed in SR 519, 523, 524. The list of issues is now incorporated into the summary records of the HRC. See e.g. SR 934–7 (on Portugal). For the text of the letter which accompanies the list see SR 895 pr. 14.
182 Doc. A/41/40, pr. 44. In July 1989 the HRC decided that the explanatory notes that were to be attached to the lists of issues sent to States parties prior to the consideration of their third periodic reports should also be attached to the lists of issues prepared in advance of the consideration of second periodic reports. See pr. 3.28.1 below.
183 SR 523 pr. 22 (Serrano-Caldero).
184 See pr. 3.19 above.
185 See the comments at SR 540 prs. 28–41, SR 541 prs. 1–28, SR 542 pr. 75, SR 543 prs. 3, 9.
186 Figures calculated from the Annual Reports of the HRC and information supplied by the Secretariat.
187 The Iraqi representative spoke for so long before the HRC that only a few members were able to put comments and questions.
188 SR 541 pr. 7 (Tomuschat).
189 Ibid., pr. 3 (Cote-Harper).
190 SR 541 pr. 18 (Ermacora).
191 Ibid., pr. 6 (Tomuschat).
192 Ibid., pr. 27.
193 See SR 545 prs. 10–12; SR 598 pr. 20 (Graefrath).
194 See Doc. A/42/40, pr. 53. See n. 182 above and pr. 3.28.1 below.
195 See e.g. SR 364, 365, 366, and 368 (on Iran).
196 Doc. A/44/40, p. 176 (my emphasis). See SR 880. The explanatory note sent to governments states that, 'The introductory statements by the representatives of States parties are expected to be brief, lasting not more than 10 minutes', SR 895 pr. 15.
197 See Fischer, n. 1 above (1982), pp. 147–51; Jhabvala, ibid., pp. 91–5; Nowak, ibid., pp. 147–51. See also SR 48, 49, 50, 55, 73, 219 Add. 1 (Doc. A/34/40, prs.

15–20); SR 231, 232 (Doc. A/35/40, prs. 370–83); SR 275, 276, 295, 304, 306, 308, 309 (Doc. A/36/40, prs. 380–9).

198 See Jhabvala, n. 1 above, pp. 84–95.

199 See Schwelb, n. 1 above, p. 843.

200 Jhabvala, n. 1 above, p. 93. On the drafting of the Covenant see chapter 1 above.

201 Some of the key actors in the debate on jurisdiction have now left the HRC, notably Mr Graefrath, Mr Tomuschat, Sir Vincent-Evans, and Mr Opsahl. It is therefore uncertain whether the newer members take a different approach but there is no evidence of any significant pressure within the HRC to reopen or reconsider the issues involved. See, however, n. 277 below.

202 This rule provides that, 'If, on the basis of its examination of the reports and information supplied by a State party, the Committee determines that some of the obligations of that State party under the Covenant have not been discharged, it may, in accordance with article 40, paragraph 4, of the Covenant, make such general comments as it may consider appropriate'.

203 In practice the General Assembly has only considered the reports of the HRC in broad terms rather than in respect of specific States parties.

204 See SR 49 and 231

205 See n. 202 above.

206 See pr. 3.40 below.

207 See ch. 1, pr. 1.18 above.

208 Doc. A/36/30, pp. 101–3. Adopted by the HRC at its 260th meeting, 30th Oct. 1980. Also issued in Doc. CCPR/C/18. It is often referred to by members as the 'October Consensus'.

209 See SR 260. See also SR 525 prs. 16–18.

210 Doc. A/36/40, pp. 101–3.

211 See SR 275 and 276.

212 Introduction to the HRC's first general comments, Doc. A/36/40, p. 107.

213 Capotorti, ch. 2 n. 1 above, comments that the aim of the expression 'General Comment' is '. . . to exclude the possibility of specific recommendations, namely recommendations addressed to a single government and concerning its attitude in the field of human rights. But, evidently, only specific recommendations might be efficient instruments to promote respect of the Covenants'. He goes on to argue that whenever the examination of reports is superficial—as he suggests it is with the ICCPR because its verification machinery is ill-devised—'the only possible outcome consists in general recommendations: and these have the function of means for political pressure, rather than of true instruments for the observance of agreements', p. 138. Robertson, n. 1 above (1984) comments that, 'The term is not defined. It does not mean that these comments must be addressed to all States parties and not to particular States. As the drafting history makes clear, the Human Rights Committee may make recommendations to particular States parties. But they must in general terms and not relate to individual cases, and cannot therefore focus attention on specific violations and bring influence to bear to remedy them', pp. 350–1. The reference for this proposition, Doc. A/5411, pr. 22, does not, *per se*, support it.

214 This procedure has caused a number of problems when the HRC has attempted

to adopt the other language texts. See e.g. SR 537 on the General Comments on article 1.
215 See pr. 3.40 below.
216 See ch. 2, pr. 2.9 above.
217 The first seventeen general comments are collected in Doc. CCPR/C/21/Rev. 1 (19 May 1989). At its 894th meeting the HRC decided to start preparatory work on a general comment on article 23 of the Covenant as well as to update its general comments on articles 7, 9, and 10.
218 GC 1/13 and 2/13, Doc. A/36/40, pp. 107–8.
219 GC 3/13, ibid., p. 109.
220 GC 4/13, ibid., pp. 109–10.
221 GC 5/13, ibid., p. 110.
222 GC 6/16, Doc. A/37/40, pp. 93–4; GC 14/23, Doc. A/40/40, p. 162.
223 GC 7/16, Doc. A/37/40, pp. 94–5.
224 GC 8/16, ibid., pp. 95–6.
225 GC 9/16, ibid., pp. 96–7.
226 GC 10/19, Doc. A/38/40, p. 109.
227 GC 11/19, ibid., pp. 109–10.
228 GC 12/21, Doc. A/39/40, pp. 142–3.
229 GC 13/21, ibid., pp. 143–6.
230 GC 15/27, Doc. A/41/40, p. 117.
231 GC 16 (32), Doc. A/43/40, pp. 181–3, also issued in CCPR/C/21/Add. 6, adopted at the HRC's 791st meeting on 23 March 1988. See SR 749, 751, 752, and 770; Doc. A/42/40, pr. 392.
232 GC 17/35, Doc. A/44/40, p. 173 (article 24); GC 18/37, Doc. CCPR/C/21/Rev. 1/Add. 1 (9 November 1989) (on non-discrimination); GC 19/39, adopted on 19 July 1990, Doc. A/45/40, Apx.
233 'The Committee (CERD) has, thus far, adopted general recommendations and decisions aimed at obtaining more informative reports of States parties. The CERD has not yet formulated as a collective body formal suggestions (regarding a single State) or general recommendations (regarding a group of States or all States parties), concerning to what extent obligations under the Convention have been discharged at the national level', Gomez del Prado, n. 1 above, p. 507. The CERD has, however, adopted a number of country specific decisions concerning the problem of territories occupied or controlled *de facto* by another country. The cases have concerned the Golan Heights, the West Bank of the River Jordan, Cyprus, and the Panama Canal Zone. See ibid., pp. 502–3; Lerner, n. 1 above, ch. 4. On the interpretation and practice of CEDAW's power to make 'suggestions and general recommendations' see Byrnes, n. 1 above, pp. 42–51, who suggests that 'neglect of women's experiences pervades the general comments' of the HRC, p. 51.
234 For example, a specific reference was made to a General Comment by the HRC in *Hammel* v. *Madagascar*, Doc. A/42/40, p. 130, pr. 19.2.
235 See pr. 3.5 above.
236 SR 758 pr. 64; Doc. A/43/40, pr. 634.
237 See SR 595 prs. 39–40 (Movchan), pr. 34 (Mavrommatis on UK); reply at SR 596 prs. 3–5.

238 Members of the HRC have noted that that requirement has not been adequately met by many States parties, Doc. A/42/40, pr. 391; SR 744 pr. 30 (Movchan on Iraq).

239 Doc. CCPR/C/40 (18 July 1985). The feedback on general comments has been disappointing and compares unfavourably to the feedback to general re-commendations adopted by the CERD, see Gomez del Prado, n. 1 above, pp. 512–13.

240 See SR 729 pr. 3.

241 SR 633 pr. 14.

242 See pr. 3.40 below.

243 See e.g. in ch. 8 below on article 6.

244 See e.g. B. Ramcharan, ch. 8 n. 1 below; N. Rodley, *The Treatment of Prisoners in International Law*, ch. 9 n. 1 below.

245 See SR 525 prs. 14–23; 540 prs. 23–7; 545 prs. 15–17; 633. However, the consensus was that there should be no change in those procedures.

246 See SR 624 pr. 7.

247 SR 633 pr. 35 (Chairman).

248 SR 633 pr. 26.

249 Doc. A/41/40, pr. 411.

250 The reports are in fact transmitted, see SR 571 prs. 10–11.

251 See n. 2 above.

252 See pr. 3.40 below.

253 See Doc. E/SR 2087.

254 See A/C.3/SR 1435 pr. 13 (representative of Hungary).

255 See ECOSOC Resn. 1985/117.

256 The HRC has been very concerned to ensure that this remains the situation. See e.g. SR 571.

257 See also article 6 OP. Since 1979 the HRC's Annual Report has covered the Autumn, Spring, and Summer sessions. The draft annual report is prepared by the Rapporteur of the HRC with the substantial assistance of the Secretariat. The report is then considered, amended, and adopted by the HRC at the close of its summer session. There have occasionally been difficulties concerning its drafting, see e.g. SR 542, 543, and 544.

258 See ECOSOC OR, 16th session, Supp. 8, prs. 195–7.

259 See pr. 3.39 above.

260 The discussion of the HRC's reports is interspersed within the summary records of the Third Committee on the appropriate agenda item. See e.g. A/C.3/43/SR. 39, 41, 42, 43, 46, 51, 55, 57 (November 1988). For recent resolutions see GA Resns. 43/114 and 43/115 (1988), 44/129 (1989).

261 See Brar, n. 1 above, pp. 15–21.

262 See ch. 2 above.

263 See e.g. the discussion in SR 338.

264 See e.g. Doc. A/41/40, pr. 22.

265 At its fifteenth session (1982) the HRC decided to place on the agenda of its Spring session every year an item on, 'Action by the General Assembly on the annual report submitted by the Committee under article 45 of the Covenant', The views expressed in the HRC's debates are now reflected in its Annual Reports.

See e.g. SR 880 and 892, summarized in Doc. A/44/40, ch. 2, 'Action by the General-Assembly at its Forty-Third Session'.
266 Statement of the representative of the GDR, in the Third Committee.
267 See the comment at SR 318 pr. 7 (Tomuschat).
268 See ch. 8, prs. 8.12–8.13 below.
269 Cf. article 48 of the Covenant, Apx. I below. See ch. 1, pr. 1.33 above.
270 See e.g. the discussions of the Third Committee in the records cited in n. 260 above.
271 See Alston, ch. 2 n. 38 above; SR 760 pr. 38 (Mommersteeg). Cf. the problems of CEDAW, see Byrnes, n. 1 above, pp. 56–65, and of CERD, see UN Doc. A/44/18, pp. 91–2.
272 See ch. 2, pr. 2.7. See generally T. D. Gonzales, 'The Political Sources of Procedural Debates in the United Nations: Structural Impediments to the Implementation of Human Rights', 13 NYUJILP (1981) pp. 427–72.
273 See ch. 2 n. 38 above.
274 See the comments of Mr Herndl (Assistant Secretary-General for Human Rights), SR 702 pr. 3.
275 SR 633 pr. 7 (Aguilar), pr. 19 (Movchan); Doc. A/41/40, pr. 26.
276 See pr. 3.21.1 above.
277 See prs. 3.29–3.38 above. In July 1990 an informal meeting was held in Geneva on 'Making the ICCPR reporting procedure more effective'. It was attended by past and present members of the HRC and experts on the work of the HRC.
278 See pr. 3.24 above. See e.g. SR 743 pr. 4.
279 Compare the concluding comments of Tomuschat, SR 598 prs. 15–16, and Movchan, SR 598 prs. 29–32, on the UK.
280 See ch. 2, pr. 2.7 above.
281 See Landy, n. 1 above, ch. 3; Harris, ibid., ch. 5.
282 See Jhabvala, n. 1 above, pp. 104–6.
283 See pr. 3.6 above.
284 See pr. 3.21.1 above.
285 See prs. 3.8–3.8.1 above.
286 See pr. 3.8.1 above.
287 See prs. 3.13–3.16 above.
288 See prs. 3.17–3.18 above.
289 The HC has been concerned to see that its functions under article 40 have not been misrepresented or incorrectly reported by newspapers or academic commentators. For example, some members criticized the article by Professor Nowak, n. 1 above (1980), which pointed to alleged political differences within the HRC. See also SR 428 prs. 1–5 concerning a report in the *New York Times* on 31 Jan. 1987 on the HRC's consideration of the report of Nicaragua.
290 e.g. during the consideration of reports from Iran, Romania, Chile, El Salvador.
291 See Valticos, n. 1 above, prs. 618–19.
292 See Harris, n. 1 above, pp. 188–91 and appendices II and III.
293 See Capotorti, ch. 2 n. 1 above. Cf. 'The reporting system is essentially a means of providing information . . . the reporting system as articulated in article 40 is not a monitoring system', R. Wallace, *International Law*, p. 189 (1986).
294 SR 117 pr. 35.

295 Doc. A/44/98 (3 Feb. 1989), 'Reporting Obligations of States Parties to the U.N. Instruments on Human Rights'. In November 1988 there were some 500 reports overdue.

296 See 'Draft consolidated guidelines for the initial part of States parties' reports', Doc. A/44/40, p. 177. See now the draft consolidated format for reporting, UN Doc. A/44/539 (6 Oct. 1989).

297 An expert has already been appointed, see SR 892 pr. 5. For his report see UN Doc. A/44/668 (8 Nov. 1989). For the HRC's response see SR 997. See also Doc. E/CN.4/1990/39 on computerization of the work of human rights treaty bodies.

298 The long term future in terms of human rights staffing still appears rather bleak. The UN devotes less than 1% of its regular budget to human rights.

299 This manual is under preparation.

4

The Optional Protocol to the ICCPR[1]

INTRODUCTION

4.1 This chapter examines the work of the HRC in implementing the OP to the ICCPR. A right of petition (communication) to or against governments is of long historical standing both in national and international law.[2] Proposals to include such a right in the international bill of rights proved controversial. That controversy is briefly examined in section A. Section B concerns the structure and terms of the OP. Section C deals with the status of the OP and of communications submitted under it. Section D examines in detail how the practices and procedures of the HRC have developed the structure of the OP. These aspects are linked to section E which reviews how the HRC has approached and interpreted the terms of the OP, the ICCPR, and its own rules of procedure in the consideration of communications. The HRC's views on a series of substantive rights in the ICCPR are examined in the following chapters. Finally in this chapter, section F offers an appraisal of the work of the HRC under the OP.

It is important to be clear concerning the primary purpose of the chapter. That purpose is not to present a comprehensive analysis of the OP *per se*. Rather it is to examine how the practice of the HRC has developed the OP as an implementation technique. Through that examination it is possible to observe the role that the HRC perceives for itself under the OP. Is it to fulfil the role of a judicial body in proceedings of an adversarial or inquisitorial nature or a more dynamic role? How is it to be guided in matters concerning the burden and standard of proof, the admission and admissibility of evidence, and fact-finding generally? Will the practices and precedents of other international institutions, particularly human rights organs, be followed? How strictly will the conditions of admissibility be interpreted and applied? Are the powers of the HRC to be strictly construed from the express terms of the OP or will the HRC assume implied powers that it considers reasonably necessary for it to fulfil its functions effectively? On many of these matters the OP itself offers little or no guidance so the answers can only be sought in the practices and procedures of the HRC.

A. THE ORIGINS, DRAFTING, AND SIGNIFICANCE OF THE OPTIONAL PROTOCOL TO THE ICCPR

4.2 It is impossible to comprehend the significance in international law of the inclusion of a right of petition for individuals in the OP without at least an outline of its drafting history. As we noted in chapter 1, when the General Assembly approved the Universal Declaration of Human Rights in 1948 it instructed the Human Rights Commission (HRCion) to continue with the drafting of the international covenants and to consider measures of implementation including a right of individual petition. More specifically in 1950 the General Assembly called upon the ECOSOC to request the HRCion to proceed with the consideration of provisions, 'to be inserted into the draft covenant or in separate protocols, for the receipt and examination of petitions from individuals and organizations with respect to alleged violations of the Covenant'.³

Such proposals were almost necessarily going to be controversial as already some States had indicated that they considered the draft proposals for an inter-State procedure to be contrary to national sovereignty, international law, and article 2(7) of the United Nations Charter.⁴ Various proposals were made which would have extended the right of petition to individuals, groups of individuals, all or selected non-governmental organizations.⁵ Other proposals favoured empowering the Human Rights Committee to act of its own motion, merely granting the right to communicate but leaving the matter of any action thereafter to the initiative of the HRC or States parties.⁶ Yet another suggestion was to appoint a High Commissioner (Attorney-General) for Human Rights with jurisdiction to receive charges from any source and with authority to institute proceedings before the HRC.⁷

In the event proposals to extend the right of petition beyond States parties were seriously to divide the HRCion. Ultimately all such proposals were either rejected or withdrawn and the final HRCion draft contained no provisions for petitions by individuals or organizations.⁸

Opposition to these proposals on petitions were broadly based on three lines of argument. First, the traditional argument that only States were subjects of international law. The right of individuals and groups to complain of violations of their rights at the national level and the duty of States parties to ensure remedies for such violations had been recognized in the draft article 2 of the ICCPR;⁹ petitions in the case of Trust Territories and under the Minorities system of the League of Nations were said to be distinguishable;¹⁰ the State was the unit of international organization and only States were subjects of international law; no theory of supra-national authority had been generally accepted; the obligations of States under the United Nations

Charter to co-operate on human rights matters implied, apart from the Trusteeship system, no automatic recognition of the right of petition of individuals and non-governmental organizations; responsibility for observation of the Covenant should rest with States; extending the right of petition might violate the sovereignty of States and the sovereign equality of States.

Secondly, it was argued that the proposed system of inter-State complaints was sufficient to safeguard the provisions of the Covenant. There was no reason to doubt that States parties would fulfil their obligations; States parties would be free to take up cases of violations; most cases could be settled by direct diplomatic negotiations; charges brought before the Committee would be strictly confined to violations of the Covenant.

The third line of argument was that international responsibility for the promotion of human rights was a relatively recent development and so an extended petition system might be unacceptable to many countries. Some representatives accepted that, ideally, the right of individuals, or at least non-governmental organizations, ought to be recognized internationally as they were nationally. They argued, however, that the international community was not sufficiently developed for the right of petition to be granted immediately without fear of its being abused. The result might be a mass of irresponsible and mischievous allegations submitted for political and propaganda purposes. It was feared that the whole implementation machinery could thus be paralysed and it was doubted whether adequate safeguards could be introduced. Moreover, the inclusion of a right of petition might prevent States from ratifying the Covenant and thus delay or even prevent the Covenant from coming into force.

4.2.1 Those in favour of extending the right of petition beyond States parties argued that the question of effective implementation had to be examined from the point of view of the individuals concerned as well as States. The traditional theory that only States were subjects of international law was said to be under challenge. Various precedents were cited including the United Nations Charter, the Minorities System of the League of Nations, the International Labour Organization system, the Nuremburg trials, and the European Convention on Human Rights.[11] The views of several authors were cited as further support for this view.[12] Moreover, it was argued that under the very terms of the Covenant the individual was plainly a subject of international law and the purpose of the Covenant was to protect him against abuses of power by the State. The view was advanced that as each State was free to accept the Covenant or not, what was involved was not an invasion of sovereignty but rather a voluntary relinquishment of some national sovereignty.[13] Fears of abuse were countered with the view that adequate safeguards could be provided to protect States.

The advocates of an extended petition system argued strongly that an inter-State petition system alone was not sufficient to implement the

Covenant effectively. Violations by one State would cause moral rather than immediate and direct injury to other States parties so intervention would be unlikely. Past experience of the League of Nations and the ILO was cited to demonstrate that intervention by States to redress violations of human rights, even under treaty obligations, had been negligible and rarely fruitful. Political reality indicated that States would be unlikely to lay charges of violations against friendly States or States with which they had close political or economic ties. Conversely, allegations concerning a State with which the applicant State was not on friendly terms would be viewed as motivated by other than humanitarian purposes.[14]

It was argued that the Covenant had to give the individual human being a basic right to protest when his dignity was impaired. A particular plea was made to allow non-governmental organizations having consultative status with ECOSOC to have the right to petition. These organizations had played an important part in promoting human rights nationally and internationally, would act with great caution because of the potential fear of criticism from their own members and from ECOSOC, and had the advantage over private citizens of owing no allegiance to any particular State and would therefore be free to defend the interests of humanity as a whole.

4.3 The possibility of including an optional protocol on the right of petition was discussed in the HRCion as a potential solution to the objections of States opposed to the inclusion of this right in the text of the Covenant. However, this too was opposed. Some States maintained their objections in principle to the right of petition. Even the advocates of the right of petition did not favour this course because they considered that inclusion of the right of petition was indispensable for the proper implementation of the Covenant.[15] A draft protocol on petitions from individuals and non-governmental organizations was submitted by the United States but was subsequently withdrawn without there having been any detailed discussion.[16]

In the event then the final draft of the HRCion's text contained no provision for petitions from individuals or non-governmental organizations. During the consideration of the HRCion's draft in the Third Committee amendments were proposed to insert an article on the right of individual petition.[17] The debate on these proposals largely mirrored those in the HRCion. Those who supported a right of individual petition cited the precedents of the ECHR (1950) and the ICERD (1965) and argued that they had transformed the status of the individual in international law. In addition to pointing to the optional nature of the proposed right stress was laid on the safeguards within it that would prevent its being abused. As for the opponents of the right of petition particular concern was expressed in terms of the alleged infringement of State sovereignty involved, the dangers of abuse and undesirable publicity. Moreover, they argued that its inclusion might limit ratifications to the extent that the Covenant would not enter into force.

A key question raised in the debate was whether if a right of individual petition was to be included it should be embodied in the draft covenant or provided for in a separate protocol annexed to the draft protocol. Those in favour of the former stressed the 'organic unity' of the instrument; those in favour of the latter argued that the mere presence of such a provision in an instrument might of itself make it impossible, on grounds of principle, for many States to become parties. Eventually, the Third Committee narrowly adopted a proposal that the right of petition be included in a separate protocol annexed to the draft Covenant.[18] After further discussion and amendment the draft Protocol was approved by the Third Committee though with a substantial number of abstentions.[19] The Optional Protocol was finally adopted by the General Assembly by a vote of 66 to 2, with 2 abstentions.[20] After two decades of discussion and debate the 'International Bill of Rights' was complete.[21] Not until a decade later, however, were the two Covenants and the Optional Protocol to come into force. The rest of this chapter examines the first decade or so of practice under the OP. The final appraisal includes an examination of the significance of the Optional Protocol in international law.[22]

B. THE STRUCTURE AND TERMS OF THE OP TO THE ICCPR

4.4 According to the Preamble to the OP the HRC is given competence to consider communications from alleged victims, 'in order to further achieve the purposes of the ICCPR'.[23] Under article 1 of the OP a State party to the OP recognizes the competence of the HRC 'to receive and consider communications from individuals subject to its jurisdiction who claim to be victims of a violation by that State Party of any of the rights set forth in the Covenant'. The competent body then is the HRC[24] and only the HRC.[25] A suggestion in the Third Committee that the States parties to the OP should establish a separate Committee for the consideration of communications was not taken up.[26]

Communications are considered by all of the members of the HRC. Therefore, independent experts who are nationals of States which are not parties to the OP,[27] and which may in fact oppose recognition of the right of individual petition,[28] still participate fully in the consideration of communications. While there are obvious objections to this similar practices can be observed with respect to the ICJ,[29] the EUCM,[30] the EUCT,[31] the CERD,[32] the IACM,[33] and the IACT.[34] Hopefully, through the participation of their nationals in the development of the OP procedure States which are not parties can be encouraged and induced to ratify the OP. With the continuing involvement of their nationals in the OP procedures it may become increasingly difficult for the USSR and the Eastern European States to maintain their position in opposition to the right of individual petition. In 1988 Hungary became the first Eastern European State to become a party to the Optional Protocol. In 1989 the USSR suggested before the Human Rights Commission that it would also become a party. Such developments may be of radical significance for the position of the individual in international law.[35]

There is no provision in the OP for *ad hoc* members to join the HRC.[36] Consequently a State party may be a respondent before the HRC without one of its nationals or a person nominated by it being on the HRC.[37] We may also note here that the HRC does not possess any advisory jurisdiction.[38]

Early draft versions of what emerged as the OP used the term 'petition'.[39] This was changed to 'communication' but this does not seem to have been intended as a substantive change.[40] The OP only provides for communications to be submitted by 'individuals'.[41] As we have noted proposals to extend the right of petition to all or selected non-governmental organizations were not accepted.[42]

4.5 The communication submitted to the HRC must be in 'written' form (article 2 OP) and all available domestic remedies must have been exhausted (articles 2 and 5(2)(*b*) OP). There is no provision in the OP equivalent to that in article 14 ICERD which provides that a State party must establish or indicate a body within its national legal order which shall be competent to receive and consider petitions from individuals who claim to be victims of any of the rights in the ICERD and have exhausted all other available domestic remedies.[43] Presumably, however, a State party to the OP would not be precluded from establishing such a body and if it did so the individual would probably be required to have recourse to it in order to have exhausted all domestic remedies.

Article 3 of the OP provides that the HRC shall consider 'inadmissible' any communication which is anonymous,[44] or which it considers to be an abuse of the right of submission,[45] or incompatible with the provisions of the Covenant.[46] Subject to the provisions of article 3 OP communications are brought to the attention of the State party concerned (article 4(1)). The State party then has six months to submit to the HRC 'Written explanations or statements clarifying the matter and the remedy, if any, that may have been taken by that State' (article 4(2)).

Under article 5(2) OP the HRC shall not consider any communication from an individual unless it has ascertained that:

(a) The same matter is not being examined under another procedure of international investigation or settlement;[47]
(b) The individual has exhausted all available domestic remedies.[48]

This shall not be the rule when the application of the remedies is unreasonably prolonged.[49]

The examination of communications is to be conducted in closed meetings (article 5(3) OP). On completing its 'examination' the HRC 'shall forward its views to the State Party concerned and to the individual' (article 5(4) OP). There are no express provisions in the OP concerning a friendly settlement[50] or the exercise of good offices by the HRC.[51]

Article 6 OP instructs the HRC to include in its Annual Report under article 45 of the ICCPR a summary of its activities under the OP.[52] Article 7 OP provides that pending the achievement of the objectives of the General Assembly's 'Declaration on the Granting of Independence to Colonial Countries and Peoples' (1960),[53] the provisions of the OP, 'Shall in no way limit the right of petition granted to these people by the Charter of the United Nations and other international conventions and instruments under the United Nations and its specialized agencies'.[54]

Articles 8–10 OP are noted below.[55] Article 11 deals with amendments; article 12 concerns denunciations; article 13 provides for States parties to be informed of certain matters concerning the OP by the Secretary-General of the United Nations; article 14 provides that the Chinese, English, French, Russian, and Spanish texts of the OP are equally authentic.[56]

Like the provisions of the ECHR dealing with the right of individual petition the OP is notable for its brevity. This is partly accounted for by the haste in which the OP was drafted and adopted.[57] The consequence, however, is that the HRC was necessarily left with substantial scope and flexibility to establish the necessary procedural system to operate the OP. This system is given detailed attention after a brief consideration of the status of the OP and the status of communications placed before the HRC.

C. STATUS OF THE OP; STATUS OF COMMUNICATIONS UNDER THE OP

4.6 Although the ICCPR and the OP are substantially related, and the HRC is the implementation organ for both, they are separate international treaties.[58] The OP is open for signature by any State that has signed the ICCPR (article 8(1) OP). It can only be ratified or acceded to by a State which has ratified by or acceded to the ICCPR (article 8(2)(3) OP). The OP provides that it shall enter into force three months after the date of deposit of the tenth instrument of ratification or accession (article 9(1) OP). However, the entry into force of the OP was 'Subject to the entry into force of the ICCPR' (article 9(1) OP). In fact the OP entered into force on the same date as the ICCPR, 23 March 1976, because by that date there were already the necessary ten States parties to the OP.[59] For States subsequently ratifying or acceding to the OP, the OP enters into force three months after the date of the deposit of the instrument of ratification or accession (article 9(2) OP). As with the ICCPR the provisions of the OP, 'extend to all parts of federal States without any limitations or exceptions' (article 10 OP).[60]

There is no provision in the OP concerning its territorial scope.[61] The Netherlands has declared the OP applicable to the Netherlands Antilles.[62] There is also no provision concerning reservations to the OP.[63] In practice a number of states have made reservations to the OP some of which have been considered by the HRC.[64]

4.7 As of 27 July 1990 fifty of the ninety-two States which have ratified or acceded to the ICCPR have accepted the competence of the HRC to deal with individual communications by ratifying or acceding to the OP. These States are Algeria, Argentina, Austria, Barbados, Bolivia, Cameroon, Canada, Central African Republic, Colombia, Congo, Costa Rica, Denmark, Dominican Republic, Ecuador, Equatorial Guinea, Finland, France, Gambia, Hungary, Iceland, Ireland, Italy, Jamaica, Libyan Arab Jamahiriya, Luxembourg, Madagascar, Mauritius, Netherlands, New Zealand, Nicaragua, Niger, Norway, Panama, Peru, Philippines, Portugal, Republic of Korea, Saint Vincent and the Grenadines, San Marino, Senegal, Somalia, Spain, Suriname, Sweden, Togo, Trinidad and Tobago, Uruguay, Venezuela, Zaïre, Zambia.[65] A number of West European States are not parties.[66] The USSR and the East European bloc, with the exception of Hungary since 1988, are not parties.[67] A small number of African states are parties. The Philippines is the only Asian State party. As the United States has not ratified the ICCPR it is precluded from ratifying the OP.[68]

At its very first session (March–April 1977) the Secretary-General of the United Nations informed the HRC that some communications had been submitted for consideration by the HRC.[69] The HRC began its consideration of communications at its second session (August 1977).

4.8 As of 24 August 1990 418 communications have been placed before the HRC for consideration, concerning 32 States parties to the OP.[70] The status of the 418 communications is as follows:

(*a*) Concluded by views under article 5(4) OP: 110 (no violation in 18 cases);

(*b*) Concluded in another manner (inadmissible, discontinued, suspended or withdrawn):   172 (108 inadmissible; 64 discontinued);

(*c*) Declared admissible, not yet concluded: 34;

(*d*) Pending at pre-admissibility stage: 102.

D. THE PROCEDURAL FUNCTIONING OF THE OP

1. The receipt and transmission of communications[71]

4.9 Every year tens of thousands of communications concerning human rights matters are received by the United Nations. The task of channelling communications to the appropriate body is undertaken, on behalf of the Secretary-General of the UN, by the Communications Unit of the Centre for Human Rights in Geneva.[72] The nature and extent of the Secretary-General's powers are of immense importance in determining which communications are directed to the HRC for consideration under the OP.[73] There are no express provisions in the OP dealing with this matter. There was general agreement within the HRC that the function should be a 'purely administrative',[74] technical one rather than constituting a 'preliminary screening procedure'.[75] The exercise of any substantive discretion was to be reserved to the HRC.[76] Among the matters discussed were cases in which it was not clear whether a communication was intended as a formal complaint or not,[77] the need for clarifications to assist the HRC and the author,[78] and authors who had no knowledge of the provisions of the OP and no access to expert legal advice.[79]

Under the rule adopted, 'The Secretary-General shall bring to the attention of the Committee, in accordance with the present rules, communications which are or appear to be submitted for consideration by the Committee under article 1 of the Protocol'.[80]

Inevitably the selection and channelling of communications within the UN involves an element of discretion on the part of the Secretary-General notwithstanding the various guidelines indicated by bodies like the HRC.[81] The rule adopted by the HRC would appear to afford the Secretary-General sufficient latitude and flexibility to include borderline cases.[82]

Before taking a decision on transmission the Secretary-General may request clarification from the author as to his wish to have the communication submitted to the HRC for consideration under the OP.[83] If doubt as to the author's wish remains it is resolved in favour of the HRC being seized of the communication.[84]

The only situation explicitly provided for in the Rules is that of a communication against a State which is not a party to the OP. Such communications are not to be received by the HRC.[85] In practice the Secretary-General informs the author that the State concerned is not a party to the OP and that, therefore, the HRC has no jurisdiction.[86] The HRC considered it permissible for the Secretary-General to take such a decision because factually the matter would be clear.[87] There may, however, be difficult cases and these should in principle be decided by the HRC.[88]

During the discussion of the Rules concerning these matters various members made a number of comments on the general policy to be adopted. It was stressed that a restrictive transmittal policy should be avoided since the OP procedure was new and unknown. It was suggested that the Secretary-General should point out to the authors of communications the existence of the OP procedure whenever appropriate and indicate the possibility of them addressing their communications to the HRC. It was also suggested that the

Secretariat draw up a model communication and guidelines to assist communicants. A model communication has been prepared but communicants are not obliged to use it.[89]

No Rule was adopted by the HRC concerning the language in which authors could submit their communications. The view was expressed, however, that authors should be able to write in the language of their choice. It was also suggested that the initial acknowledgement sent to authors should be drafted in the language in which the communication was submitted, and dispatched not later than ten to twenty days after the receipt of their communication.[90]

As already noted there is no time limit in the OP concerning the submission of communications.[91] A draft Rule proposed by the Secretariat would have established a twenty-four month deadline.[92] This proposal raised an interesting discussion.[93] It was argued that the concept of a time limit was 'Customary',[94] 'A generally accepted principle and an important practical feature of domestic and international law',[95] and would protect the HRC from the consideration of claims relating to very old events.[96] The precedent set by the ECHR was cited.[97] However, the proposal met with strong opposition as being 'Neither legally nor morally defensible'[98] and as carrying the possibility of unfortunate consequences.[99] It was decided that there was no immediate need to adopt a Rule on the matter and that the HRC could revert to it if experience justified the consideration of such a provision.[100] No subsequent discussion on a time limit has been held in any public session and there remains no Rule on the point. In the course of the discussion a number of members pointed to the possibility that the HRC could treat an unreasonable delay in the submission of a communication as an abuse of the right of submission (article 3 OP) and accordingly declare the communication inadmissible.[101]

It should also be noted that no Rule deals with the matter of the withdrawal of a communication.[102] Again the point was discussed during the drafting of the Rules but the HRC decided to revert to the question if the need arose on the basis of its further experience.[103] No Rule has subsequently been adopted. In practice there have been withdrawals.[104]

The Secretary-General prepares and circulates to HRC members at regular intervals lists of communications submitted to the HRC with a brief summary of their contents.[105] This Rule is designed to avoid delay between the receipt of a communication by the Secretary-General and its submission to the HRC. It also ensures that members have a working document for each communication submitted for consideration. The full text of any communication is available to any member on his request.[106] A permanent register of every communication is maintained by the Secretary-General.[107] For each registered communication the Secretary-General prepares and circulates a summary of the relevant information.[108]

The HRC has given the Secretary-General authority to request clarification from the author concerning the applicability of the OP to his communication.[109] Such requests indicate a time limit with a view to avoiding undue delays.[110] Clarifications may be sought, in particular, regarding:

(*a*) The name, address, age and occupation of the author and the verification of his identity;

(*b*) The name of the State party against which the communication is directed;

(*c*) The object of the communication;

(*d*) The provision or provisions of the Covenant alleged to have been violated;

(*e*) The facts of the claim;

(*f*) Steps taken by the author to exhaust domestic remedies;

(*g*) The extent to which the same matter is being examined under another procedure of international investigation or settlement.[111]

A request for clarification does not preclude the inclusion of the communication in the list prepared by the Secretary-General for circulation to the HRC.[112]

2. General provisions regarding the consideration of communications[113]

4.10 Article 5(3) OP directs that the HRC hold closed meetings when examining communications under the OP. This is repeated in Rule 82 but with the important addition that, 'Meetings during which the Committee may consider general issues such as procedures for the application of the Protocol may be public if the Committee so decides'.[114] The HRC has exercised this discretion on a number of occasions and thus allowed some useful insights to be gained into the workings of the OP.[115]

All documents relating to the consideration of communications under the OP are confidential.[116] Thus while a communication is being considered no substantive information is made available to the public or the press. This applies to both the admissibility and merits stages.[117] A selection of decisions holding a communication inadmissible have been published in the HRC's Annual Reports and in two volumes of Selected Decisions.[118] The identity of the author or alleged victim is not normally revealed.[119] Decisions declaring a communication admissible are not published but their terms are sometimes revealed in the HRC's final views. The final views of the HRC under article 5(4) OP are made public. The text of these often includes the terms of earlier decisions on admissibility, requests for submissions, or other interim decisions. They are issued at the end of each session as press communiqués and are included in the HRC's Annual Reports. Two volumes of selected decisions have been prepared by the Secretariat under the guidance of the

HRC and have been published.[120] As the OP contains no express reference to the publication of HRC decisions and views the decision to publicize them is to be applauded as it may add greatly to their force.[121]

Members of the HRC considered that although the principle of confidentiality governed their consideration under the OP a minimum of information should be included in its Annual Reports. This was a reflection of the view that the general public had a legitimate interest in being informed of the approaches of the HRC. The Annual Reports now contain information on, for example, the status of communications, the issues considered, the rights concerned, and jurisdictional questions. The Annual Reports constitute valuable accounts of developments in the HRC's consideration of communications.

The Rules provide that a member shall not take part in the examination of a communication by the HRC if he has any personal interest in the case or has participated in any capacity in the making of any decision on the case covered by the communication.[122] If a question arises concerning these provisions it is dealt with by the HRC.[123] A second Rule is of wider scope providing for withdrawal if, 'For any reason a member considers that he should not take part or continue to take part in the examination of a communication'.[124] In practice resort has been had to both of these rules.[125]

A draft rule providing that the HRC or a Working Group 'may at any time request the State party concerned to take interim measures in order to avoid irreparable damage to the victim of the alleged violation', while a matter involving it was before the HRC evoked an interesting discussion.[126] Views differed on whether the HRC had such 'implied powers' as were necessary to enable it to perform its functions in a reasonable manner or whether the absence of any express provision in the OP denied the HRC competence to request such measures. The compromise which emerged omitted the stronger term 'request'. It stated that,

The Committee may, prior to forwarding its final views on the communication to the State party concerned, inform the State of its views whether interim measures may be desirable to avoid irreparable damage to the victim of the alleged violation. In doing so, the Committee shall inform the State party concerned that such expression of its views on interim measures does not imply a determination on the merits of the communication.[127]

The rule is clearly designed to deal with urgent, emergency situations. There can be no doubt that such views on interim measures are not binding on the State party.[128] The terms of the rule left open the question of whether views on interim measures could be forwarded before a decision on admissibility has been taken. The question was resolved in the affirmative in a number of cases concerning the imminent imposition of capital punishment in Jamaica.[129] It is submitted that in principle this approach is correct. It appears that in practice the rule on interim measures has been used on a number of occasions to useful effect.[130] The compromise on this rule set an important precedent in terms of the implied powers which the HRC considers necessary to enable it to function effectively. Subsequent debates on other suggested implied powers, for example, concerning follow up measures after the adoption of final views, have referred back to the decision on interim measures as a precedent.[131]

3. Access to the HRC

4.11 The HRC has strongly asserted the importance of individuals being allowed access to it under the OP. In *Antonaccio v. Uruguay*,[132] A's wife (V.S.) submitted the communication on behalf of A alleging, *inter alia*, that he had been arrested, tortured, denied medical attention, and denied the right to a fair trial. The author requested the HRC to take appropriate action to secure A's right to submit the communication himself.[133] After the communication had been held admissible the author further submitted that A had the right to be informed of that decision and afforded an opportunity to supplement her submissions.[134] In a subsequent Interim Decision the HRC decided,

That, as requested by Violeta Setelich, the State party should be requested to transmit all written material pertaining to the proceedings (submissions of the parties, decisions of the Human Rights Committee), to Raul Sendic Antonaccio, and that he should be given the opportunity to communicate directly with the Committee.[135]

The State party objected to this decision. It argued that the HRC's competence was limited by article 5(4) OP to the sending of its observations to the State party concerned.[136] The HRC had, therefore, 'arrogated to itself competence which exceeded its powers'.[137] Moreover,

The Committee on Human Rights is applying a rule which does not exist in the text of the Covenant and the Protocol, whereas the function of the Committee is to fulfil and apply the provisions of those international instruments. It is inadmissible for a body such as the Committee to create rules flagrantly deviating from the texts emanating from the will of the ratifying States. Those were the circumstances in which the decision in question was taken. Paragraph 3 requests, with absolutely no legal basis, that a detainee under the jurisdiction of a State party—Uruguay—be given the opportunity to communicate directly with the Committee. The Government of Uruguay rejects that decision, since to accept it would be to create the dangerous precedent of receiving a decision which violates international instruments such as the Covenant and its Protocol. Moreover, the Uruguayan Government considers that the provisions in those international instruments extend to States parties as subjects of international law. Thus these international norms, like any agreement of such a nature, are applicable to States and not directly to individuals. Consequently, the Committee can hardly claim that this decision extends to any particular individual. For the reasons given, the Government of Uruguay rejects the present decision of the Committee, which violates elementary norms and principles and thus indicates that the Committee is undermining its commitments in respect of the cause of promoting and defending human rights.[138]

This argument was emphatically rejected by the HRC:

The Human Rights Committee cannot accept the State party's contention that it exceeded its mandate when in its decision of 24 October 1980, it requested the State party to afford to Raul Sendic Antonaccio the opportunity to communicate directly with the Committee.

The Committee rejects the State party's argument that a victim's right to contact the Committee directly is invalid in the case of persons imprisoned in Uruguay. If governments had the right to erect obstacles to contacts between victims and the Committee, the procedure established by the Optional Protocol would, in many instances, be rendered meaningless. It is a prerequisite for the effective application of the Optional Protocol that detainees should be able to communicate directly with the Committee. The contention that the International Covenant and the Protocol apply only to States, as subjects of international law, and that, in consequence, these instruments are not directly applicable to individuals is devoid of legal foundation in cases where a state has recognized the competence of the Committee to receive and consider communications from individuals under the Optional Protocol. That being so, denying individuals who are victims of an alleged violation their rights to bring the matter before the Committee is tantamount to denying the mandatory nature of the Optional Protocol.[139]

It is submitted that this must be correct. Although there is no express provision in the ICCPR like the undertaking in article 25 of the ECHR 'not to hinder in any way the effective exercise', of the right of individual petition,[140] considerations of effectiveness demand that an alleged victim must be permitted to submit a communication to the HRC.[141] It is important to note the limits of the HRC's statement. It is not a general proposition concerning the status of individuals in international law.[142] The HRC only goes so far as to say that if a State has recognized the competence of the HRC under the OP it cannot then deny or obstruct an individual's exercise of the right to communicate with the HRC.

Similar considerations apply in the many cases when an alleged victim's communication to the HRC is assisted by having a legal representative. If States parties take action against or punish in any way those who represent alleged victims the effectiveness of the OP will be greatly reduced. The issue arose in *Hammel* v. *Madagascar*.[143] H had been expelled from Madagascar. He alleged, and the State party appeared to confirm, that this was due in part to his having represented alleged victims submitting communications to the HRC.[144] The HRC expressed the view that,

Were that to be the case, the Committee observes that it would be both untenable and incompatible with the spirit of the International Covenant on Civil and Political Rights and the Optional Protocol thereto, if States parties to these instruments were to take exception to anyone acting as legal counsel for persons placing their communications before the Committee for consideration under the Optional Protocol.[145]

When the HRC adopts final views its general practice is to inform the State party concerned that it is 'obliged' to transmit a copy of the views to the individual concerned. The authority for this is presumably the provision in article 5(4) OP that the HRC shall forward its views to the State party concerned and to the individual.

4. Legal representation and legal aid[146]

4.12 There is no express reference to legal representation in the OP.[147] Rule 90(1)(*b*) of the HRC's Rules states that the communication may be submitted by the individual himself or by his representative.[148] The HRC must have evidence that the representative has been duly authorized.[149] In practice alleged victims have been represented by lawyers, law professors, and non-governmental organizations.[150] Their role to date has been confined to drafting the original complaint, supplying further legal and factual information and observations, and responses to the submissions of the State party concerned. No oral hearings have been held to date.[151] If the HRC were to develop such a practice, with the consent of the State party, it is submitted that the alleged victim's legal representative, and the alleged victim, should be permitted to address the HRC on whatever terms the State party is heard.[152] This would seem to be demanded by the principle of 'equality of arms' which the HRC seeks to uphold.

There is also no provision in the OP or in the HRC's Rules concerning the provision of legal aid to a communicant. Thus whether a communicant receives aid will presumably depend on its availability under the domestic legal aid regulations of the State party concerned and in most cases this will be very unlikely. The present financial restrictions at the UN would suggest that it is also unlikely that any provision for legal aid will be made by the UN itself in the foreseeable future.[153] While the HRC's proceedings remain wholly written the absence of legal aid to communicants will be less significant a hurdle than if oral procedures are developed.[154] Assisting in the presentation of communications is an obvious avenue through which non-governmental organizations can contribute to the effective implementation of the OP.[155]

5. The determination of admissibility: procedures[156]

4.13 The HRC took the view that the order of the articles as they appeared in the OP did not reflect a chronological order of procedures to be followed in the consideration of communications. The OP established the conditions of admissibility but not the procedures for the determination of admissibility. Accordingly, the rules of procedure establish those detailed procedures. The discussion of those rules was premissed on the idea of making the procedures as flexible, practical, effective, and efficient as possible while maintaining the basic principle of equality of arms.[157]

The rules provide for the establishment of one or more working groups to examine communications and make recommendations concerning the fulfilment of the admissibility conditions in articles 1, 2, 3, and 5(2) OP.[158] In practice only one working group on communications has existed. The group consists of no more than five members and its composition is intended to reflect the geographical groupings of the HRC members. The normal practice has been for the Working Group to meet for one week before each of the HRC's three week sessions. The Working Group continues to meet during HRC sessions. It plays a fundamental role in the consideration of communications under the OP. Despite the use of the Working Group the HRC decided in 1989 that in order to expedite the consideration of communications it was necessary to appoint a Special Rapporteur on new communications who would also work intersessionally. The first Rapporteur was Mrs Higgins. In July 1989 the HRC adopted a new Rule of Procedure regularizing the position of the Special Rapporteur on new communications.[159]

4.14 The Special Rapporteur (formerly the Working Group) examines the initial communication together with the further material and information obtained by the Secretary-General.[160] *Rule 90* specifies a number of matters which shall be ascertained with a view to reaching a decision on admissibility:

1. (a) that the communication is not anonymous and that it emanates from an individual, or individuals, subject to the jurisdiction of a State party to the Protocol;

(b) that the individual claims to be a victim of a violation by that State party of any of the rights set forth in the Covenant. Normally, the communication should be submitted by the individual himself or by his representative; the Committee may, however, accept to consider a communication submitted on behalf of an alleged victim when it appears that he is unable to submit the communication himself;

(c) that the communication is not an abuse of the right to submit a communication under the Protocol;

(d) that the communication is not incompatible with the provisions of the Covenant;

(e) that the same matter is not being examined under another procedure of international investigation or settlement;

(f) that the individual has exhausted all available domestic remedies.

2. The Committee shall consider a communication, which is otherwise admissible, whenever the circumstances referred to in article 5(2) of the Protocol apply.

These matters are basically taken from the provisions in articles 1, 2, 3, and 5(2) OP. There was considerable discussion on what became rule 90(1)(*b*).

A literal construction which limited the competence of the HRC to receive communications only from the alleged victim would, in practice, be an enormous constraint. There was general agreement within the HRC that this construction should be rejected. However, it proved difficult to formulate an appropriate rule. A proposal that the HRC should receive communications from 'someone authorized' to act on the victims behalf proved unacceptable because it was thought to introduce complexity, rigidity, and domestic law requirements.[161] The HRC have taken a practical and relatively liberal view in the application of rule 90(1)(*b*). That practice is examined in the consideration of article 1 OP below.[162]

4.15 During the drafting of rule 90(2) a difficult question arose as to the interpretation of article 5(2) OP.[163] In the certified true English text article 5(2) OP provides that,

The Committee shall not consider any communication from an individual unless it is ascertained that:
(a) the same matter is not being examined under another procedure of international investigation or settlement;
(b) the individual has exhausted all available domestic remedies. This shall not be the rule where the application of the remedies is unreasonably prolonged.[164]

The difficult question that arose was whether the last sentence of article 5(2) applied to the whole of paragraph 2 or only to sub-paragraph (*b*). On the former interpretation it would be permissible for the HRC to declare admissible a communication being examined under another procedure of international investigation or settlement if it took the view that the procedure had been unreasonably prolonged. After some discussion the matter was referred for the expert opinion of United Nations Legal Counsel. That opinion was to the effect that the last sentence applied to both sub-paragraphs (*a*) and (*b*). Notwithstanding the clear opinion of UN Legal Counsel many of the HRC members were reluctant to accept the implications of the HRC having to pass judgment on another international body. Members pointed to the difficulty of establishing the correct interpretation before specific cases had been examined and the need to allow the HRC a certain amount of discretion.[165] Rule 90(2) as adopted merely repeats the terms of article 5(2) OP without clarification.

The reluctance of the HRC to pass judgment on another international organ is understandable. However, the delays evident in international petition systems render such a situation a distinct possibility.[166] Though the HRC would need to proceed with great circumspection it is submitted that if the delay is unreasonable by comparison with the admittedly lengthy norm in international procedures then the HRC should proceed to consider the communication.[167]

4.15.1 The OP does not expressly state the order in which the HRC should consider the conditions of admissibility. That members of the HRC take different views on this is clear from the decision in *C.L.D.* v. *France*.[168] C.L.D. claimed to be a victim of violations of various articles of the Covenant on the basis that the French Postal Administration had refused to issue him postal cheques printed in the Breton language, his mother tongue. Related complaints concerned the French fiscal authorities. All members of the HRC were agreed that the communication was inadmissible but three different arguments were adduced in the decision of the HRC and in two individual opinions. The majority of the members (though no vote is actually taken) decided that the communication was inadmissible for failure to exhaust domestic remedies. In the first individual opinion five members (Dimitrijevic, Higgins, Mavrommatis, Pocar, and Wennergren) argued that the communication was inadmissible *ratione materiae* under article 3 of the OP. The opinion argues that as between the articles 3 and 5(2)(*b*) of the OP,

There is an order of priority in those articles in the sense that the initial task of the Committee must necessarily be to ascertain whether a communication appertains to a claim which, if proved as to the alleged facts, could entail a violation of the Covenant. If it could not entail a violation, because *ratione materiae* it is not within the Covenant, the communication will be inadmissible under article 3 of the Optional Protocol . . . although in this preliminary phase of its work the Committee is not, of course, examining matters relating to the merits, it has to examine the claim to see whether it is 'incompatible with the Covenant' that is, whether or not it potentially relates to a right within the scope of the Covenant . . . the claims of the author reveal no facts which, even if proved, could occasion a violation of the Covenant . . . We therefore find it inappropriate to proceed to an examination of local remedies.

In the second individual opinion Mr Ndiaye also took the view that the communication should have been declared admissible *ratione materiae* rather than because of non-exhaustion of domestic remedies.[169] However, Mr Ndiaye very strongly took the view that the HRC should have considered the effect of a French Declaration on ratification of the Covenant that, 'In the light of article 2 of the Constitution of the French Republic . . . article 27 is not applicable as far as the republic is concerned'. Mr Ndiaye took the view that, on the basis of the rules in the Vienna Convention on the Law on Treaties (1969), France had excluded article 27 from its acceptance.

Accordingly, it is incomprehensible that the Committee, which of course has no power to object to the reservations of States parties, should have acted as though France was a party to article 27 . . . Unfounded in terms of the Covenant and the Protocol thereto, this decision is an inducement to internal and external proceedings which is particularly unjustifiable in that they will achieve nothing in the Committee.

The criticism of the other members by Mr Ndiaye is unjustified. As the first individual opinion made clear, 'no view is offered as to the legal effect of the French declaration regarding article 27'. The French Declaration does raise a number of difficult problems. These include, as the first individual opinion noted, whether it is legally a declaration or a reservation? Also, if it is a reservation, is the HRC competent to decide on its validity? What are the principles governing the validity of reservations? The Declaration has been discussed by the HRC during the consideration of the periodic reports of France.

4.15.2 The questions were directly considered in two decisions under the OP concerning the use of the Breton language in France (*M.K.* v. *France*, Doc. A/45/40, Apx., and *T.K.* v. *France*, Doc. A/45/40, Apx. After noting that the declaration had not been objected to by other States or been withdrawn and citing the definition of a reservation in article 2(1)(*d*) of the VCLT the HRC stated that,

The Convention does not make a distinction between reservations and declarations. The Covenant itself does not provide any guidance in determining whether a unilateral statement made by a State party upon accession to it should have a preclusionary effect regardless of whether it is termed a reservation or a declaration. The Committee observes in this respect that it is not the formal designation but the effect the statement purports to have that determines its nature. If the statement displays a clear intent on the part of the State party to exclude or modify the legal effect of a specific provision of a treaty, it must be regarded as a binding reservation, even if the statement is phrased as a declaration. In the present case, the statement entered into by the French Government upon accession to the Covenant is clear: it seeks to exclude the application of article 27 to France and emphasizes this exclusion semantically with the words 'is not applicable'. The statement's intent is unequivocal and thus must be given preclusionary effect in spite of the terminology used. Furthermore the State party's submission of 15 January 1989 also speaks of a French 'reservation' in respect of article 27. Accordingly the Committee considers that it is not competent to consider complaints directed against France concerning alleged violations of article 27 of the Covenant.

In an individual opinion Professor Higgins argued that a reference to article 2(1)(*d*) VCLT could not serve to turn interpretative declarations into reservations, that deliberately different language had been selected in the French notification to serve different legal purposes, and that the content in this case was clearly that of an interpretative declaration. Professor Higgins continued,

As noted in the decisions of the Committee, the Reports of France to the Committee under article 40 of the Covenant have explained that the prohibition in the Constitution of distinction on grounds of origin, race or religion means that there are no minorities in France; and therefore article 27 does not apply. As I believe the French notification concerning article 27 is a declaration and not a reservation, it is in my view ultimately for the Committee to see if the interpretation of the French Government accords with its own. The Committee has, in relation to several States parties, rejected the notion that the existence of minorities is in some way predicated on the admission of discrimination. Rather, it has insisted that the existence of minorities within the sense of article 27 is a factual matter; and that such minorities may indeed exist in States parties committed, in law and in fact, to the full equality of all persons within its jurisdiction. And many states parties whose constitutions, like that of the French Republic, prohibit discrimination, readily accept that they have minorities on whom they report under article 27.

Professor Higgins therefore concluded that the French declaration did not operate as a reservation although the communication was inadmissible for other reasons. The reasoning of Professor Higgins appears compelling.

4.16 After examining the material placed before it by the Secretariat the Special Rapporteur will decide to take one of a number of actions. He can decide to request from the author further additional written information or observations relevant to the question of admissibility.[170] Alternatively, he could decide to transmit the communication to the State party as well or only to the State party with a similar request.[171] Such requests must include a statement that the request does not imply that any decision has been reached on the question of admissibility.[172] In practice the time limit established by the HRC for the submission of observations and information is eight weeks.[173] The parties have a further four-week limit for the submission of comments on the information and observations if they choose to do so.[174]

It was established at the HRC's fourth session that to assist expediting the consideration of communications the above decisions could be taken by the Working Group without being placed before the HRC for approval.[175] In cases of doubt or uncertainty the Special Rapporteur will refer to the Working Group, and if the matter cannot be resolved, the decision will be taken by the HRC. A further option for the Special Rapporteur and the Working Group is to recommend to the HRC that the communication be declared inadmissible or be discontinued because of clear deficiencies that cannot be remedied by seeking further information from the author.

4.17 An important provision is that in rule 91(2) which states that a communication may not be declared admissible unless the State party concerned has received the text of the communication and has been given an opportunity to furnish information or observations relevant to the question of admissibility. Members stressed the fundamental importance of this rule in terms of procedural equality.

The decision on admissibility must be taken by the HRC as soon as possible. In another procedural innovation the HRC decided in July 1989 that a decision declaring a communication *admissible* could be taken by the Working Group alone but only if all five members of the group agreed. Inadmissibility decisions must still be taken by the HRC. In practice, the Working Group's recommendations are normally followed.[176]

4.18 During the first round of discussion the HRC considers the case documentation and the accompanying recommendations of the Working Group. It may adopt the WG recommendations or take a different course. It may also decide at this, or at a later stage, that the communication is of sufficient complexity to warrant the designation of a Special Rapporteur.[177] This step has been taken on a number of occasions to date.

Unless the communication is declared inadmissible by the HRC it is subject to further consideration at a subsequent session or sessions again based on the recommendations of the WG or the Special Rapporteur if one has been appointed. The HRC may adopt, change, or reject any such recommendation. Unless further information, observations, or comments are sought from the parties the HRC will take a decision on the question of admissibility at this point. The substantive determinations by the HRC on the grounds of admissibility are examined in detail below.[178]

4.19 The five options that have been developed to date have been to declare the communication:

4.19.1 *Inadmissible, in whole or in part.* This decision is communicated to the author of the communication and, where the communication has been transmitted to the State party, to that State party.[179] If the decision is based on article 5(2) OP (non-exhaustion of domestic or international remedies) the HRC may review this decision at a later date upon the receipt of a written request by or on behalf of the individual concerned containing information to the effect that the reasons for inadmissibility referred to in article 5(2) no longer apply.[180] One member justified the limitation in this rule to the grounds in article 5(2) on the basis that these were conditions of a 'temporary nature'.[181] Other members wanted the rule broadened because there could be grounds outside article 5(2) in which review was necessary.[182] It appeared to be accepted that the adoption of the rule does not preclude the author from re-submitting a communication held inadmissible on grounds other than those in article 5(2) OP.[183] The alternative course would be for the HRC to regard it as a new communication particularly as neither the OP nor the rules of procedure lay down any time limit for the submission of communications.[184] In practice there have been requests for the HRC to reconsider decisions declaring a communication inadmissible but to date the HRC have found no reason to justify reconsideration in any such case.[185]

4.19.2 *Discontinued.* This option is routinely used where final deadlines are not met. In one case the authors, despite repeated requests, failed to furnish the HRC with the necessary information without which the HRC was unable to arrive at a decision on admissibility.[186] In another case the HRC were informed that the authors wished to withdraw the case from consideration by the HRC on the ground that the same matter had been submitted to and was being considered under another procedure of international investigation or settlement.[187] Such a case would have been declared inadmissible in any event under article 5(2) OP.[188]

It has already been noted that the OP does not contain any provision for the securing of a friendly settlement similar to that in article 28 ECHR.[189] The procedure that the HRC should adopt if a settlement is reached is not spelt out in either the OP or the HRC's rules. In *Waksman* v. *Uruguay*[190] the approach of the HRC was to declare the communication 'Discontinued' after taking note that the State party had taken steps to remedy the matter complained of.

It would appear reasonable to suggest that certain conditions which lead to a communication being declared 'discontinued' may be of a temporary nature. For example, if the authors of the first communication noted above[191] were later to provide the requested information and provided a reasonable excuse for their earlier failure to do so, it should be open to the HRC to resume consideration of the communication.

4.19.3 *Suspended*. Consideration of a communication will be suspended if, for example, contact with the author has been lost because of the failure of the author to supply a return address.[192]

4.19.4 *Withdrawn*.[193] This has occurred, for example, when an individual has opted for another procedure of international investigation or settlement.[194]

4.19.5 *Wholly or partly admissible*.[195] In this event the texts of the decision of admissibility and any relevant documents are forwarded to the State party as soon as possible.[196] The author of the communication is also informed.[197]

6. The consideration of communications on the merits: procedures[198]

4.20 Any communication declared wholly or partly admissible is then subject to consideration on the merits. As already noted there is no intermediate stage between admissibility and merits for any attempt to reach a friendly settlement or for the exercise of good offices by the HRC.

Under article 4(2) OP the State party concerned then has six months to submit written explanations or statements clarifying the matter under consideration and any remedy, if any, that it has afforded.[199] This six-month time limit is the only time limit expressly provided for in the OP. The explanations or statements submitted by the State party are communicated to the author of the communication who may submit additional written information or observations within such time limits as the HRC directs.[200] The time limit commonly specified is six weeks.[201] Although not expressly provided for in the rules the HRC will receive further additional information and observations from either party in the light of any additional information and observations received.[202] This is in accordance with the general principle of procedural equality that the HRC seeks to apply to its considerations. The HRC may decide of its own motion to request specific additional information or replies to certain questions from either party.[203] It has done so on a number of occasions through the adoption of 'interim decisions' (sometimes referred to as 'interlocutory decisions').[204]

At its third session the HRC decided that it was necessary to amend its rules to make specific provision for the review of a decision declaring a communication admissible in the light of any additional information and observations submitted to it.[205] The rules now make provision for this and the rule was applied for the first time at the HRC's twenty-fourth session (1985).[206]

Unless the decision that a communication is admissible is reversed the HRC proceeds to consider the communication in the light of all written information made available to it by the author and the State party.[207] The final step is for the HRC to formulate its 'views' on the communication.[208] The HRC may refer the communication to the WG on Communications or to a Special Rapporteur for the consideration and formulation of views.[209] The WG or Special Rapporteur then makes recommendations to the HRC. The HRC may adopt, change, or reverse any recommendations of the WG or Special Rapporteur . The views of the HRC are then forwarded to the State party concerned and to the individual author.[210] The HRC has also requested the State party concerned to forward the views to the alleged victim if he or she is not the author.[211]

4.21 The HRC's views take the form of a collegiate view.[212] There was detailed discussion within the HRC on whether to permit members to attach individual opinions to the views of the HRC.[213] The main concern expressed was that these might undermine the moral authority of the HRC's views. It was stressed that the HRC's views were not legally binding and that it was therefore only through its 'moral and political impact' that the HRC's views could be enforced. The majority of members, however, took a different view. They argued that individual opinions could strengthen the HRC, that the minority should not be prevented from making its own views known, and that such a provision was in accordance with the freedom of expression established in article 19 of the ICCPR. The rule adopted states that, 'Any member of the Committee may request that a summary of his individual opinion shall be appended to the views of the Committee when they are communicated to the individual and to the state party concerned'.[214]

This rule provides only for a 'summary' of an individual opinion so members may be restricted from appending lengthy, detailed explanations of their opinions. In practice individual opinions have been appended to the HRC's views on a number of occasions.[215] To date they have normally been relatively brief. It is submitted that the decision to permit individual opinions was sensible and constructive. Such opinions can contribute to the development of the HRC's jurisprudence by, for example, making the view of the HRC clearer by revealing a further step or an alternative interpretation that the majority of the HRC felt unable to adopt.[216] The usefulness of individual opinions under the ECHR system and in the ICJ gives further support to this conclusion.[217]

7. Evidence[218]

1. *Admissibility*

4.22 It is difficult to determine any fixed rules that the HRC has applied. There has been no general statement on the types of evidence that the HRC will consider admissible.[219] Moreover, no piece of evidence has been stated to be excluded from the HRC's considerations in any particular case as inadmissible. It is possible to note the particular sources of evidence that the HRC has taken account of. These include:

(*a*) Testimonies from the authors;
(*b*) Testimonies from the alleged victims;
(*c*) Testimonies from alleged witnesses to the violations;
(*d*) Medical Reports;
(*e*) Psychiatric Reports;
(*f*) The text of legal judgments;
(*g*) The text of legislative, executive, and administrative acts;
(*h*) The texts of Codes of Practice or Guidelines connected with the texts in (*g*);
(*i*) The statements of a representative of the State party in proceedings before another United Nations body;
(*j*) The submissions from the State party.

One author has concluded after surveying international practice and relevant literature that, 'Subject to any rules of admissibility which may be specified in its constitutive instrument, fact-finding bodies may apply flexible admissibility criteria'.[220]

This conclusion seems to hold good for the HRC where the only express conclusion would appear to be that in article 3 OP providing for the exclusion of 'anonymous' communications.[221] This exclusion also seems to accord with the international practice of fact-finding bodies.[222] Apart from anonymous evidence then, it would appear open to the HRC to consider admissible evidence from whatever source and then decide as to its relevance and probative value.[223] Such an approach would accord with the general practice of international tribunals in the admission of evidence of adopting the liberal system of procedure of civil law countries.[224]

2. *Form*

4.23 The OP refers only to a 'written' procedure. Individuals may submit a 'written communication' to the HRC for consideration (article 2 OP). The State party must submit to the HRC 'written explanations or statements clarifying the matter and the remedy, if any, that may have been taken by that State' (article 4(2) OP). The HRC is directed to consider communications in the light of all 'written information made available to it by the individual and by the State party concerned' (article 5(1) OP).

The obvious question raised is whether it would be possible for the HRC to provide for a system of oral hearings through its rules of procedure or whether this possibility is excluded by the terms of the OP.[225] The HRC has discussed this question in private session[226] but no positive step has been taken in the direction of oral hearings and to date all communications have been considered on the basis of written information only.

4.24 The present limitation to written procedure is unsatisfactory.[227] It may be difficult for the HRC properly to resolve contradictions on the substance of the matter or to have a useful exchange of views when particular difficulties arise. Since the State party concerned in most communications to date, Uruguay, has not properly co-operated with the HRC, many of the HRC's views have effectively been judgments by default and so the full extent of these difficulties have not been exposed. They could only be resolved within a written procedure, if at all, by a lengthy process of submission and counter submission. As the proceedings of the HRC attain a greater degree of subtlety and complexity the deficiencies of a wholly written procedure are likely to become more acute.[228] Provisions for oral proceedings would then provide an eminently sensible procedure to assist the HRC.

If such provisions were made other difficulties would then present themselves. How would the travel expenses of communicants be defrayed if they were unable to pay for them?[229] Would legal representation be permitted?[230] Additional Secretariat staff and resources would almost certainly be necessary. Professor Tomuschat has pointed to another difficulty by posing the question, 'Can the stage of taking evidence take place differently according to the greater or lesser degree of preparedness of the State party concerned to allow for additional methods of proof?'[231] It is submitted that the answer must be yes. If at least some State parties are willing to co-operate in oral hearings the HRC should take advantage of that co-operation rather than reduce procedures to those dictated by States who do not wish to permit oral hearings. There should be no opposition to oral hearings as long as they only take place with the consent of the State party concerned.

4.25 It is submitted that in principle it is open to the HRC to make provision for the possibility of oral hearings with the consent of the State party concerned.[232] Such a procedure would parallel the successful practice under the article 40 reporting procedure of inviting State representatives to attend the consideration of national reports.[233] It is further submitted that the HRC should in fact make provision for oral hearings with the consent of the State party. However, the written procedure should remain the primary mode of obtaining evidence but when the HRC felt that an oral investigation would substantially assist its considerations that possibility should be open to it. Experience would indicate whether such a practice would become the exception or the rule. In practical terms, however, it is important to recognize that the HRC simply could not cope with oral hearings without a fundamental restructuring of its work and servicing. Indeed it could be argued that the present procedures for the consideration of reports from States parties are crucially important and more time should not be sacrificed for the consideration of individual communications.

Similar comments to the above can be made concerning the possibility of on-site inspections by the HRC concerning communications under the OP. Again there is nothing explicit in either the ICCPR or the OP. As Mose and Opsahl comment, 'Whether in the future this will be interpreted as a lacuna or a prohibition due to lack of competence remains to be seen'.[234] Again it is submitted that in principle it is open to the HRC to develop such practices with the consent of the State party concerned. The experience of the IACM,[235] the EUCM,[236] and the ILO[237] suggests that on-site investigations can assist human rights organs in their determinations and they provide useful models for the HRC to follow and develop.[238]

A less radical proposal would be for the HRC to develop a 'direct contacts' approach similar to that used with some success by the ILO.[239] This could provide the possibility of a more direct, informal, speedier process than a full scale on-site investigation. It would also almost certainly introduce the idea of friendly settlement into the OP proceedings. A similar direct contact approach has been developed to a limited extent under the article 40 process with some success.[240]

4.26 The basic submission behind each of these proposals is that the HRC has to have the flexibility to develop and adapt its procedures under the OP with the co-operation of the State parties concerned. In the long term it may well prove to have been sensible for the HRC to build up its practices and procedures carefully and cautiously. Over a period of time it can establish a bedrock of practice and allow States parties to acquire confidence in its impartiality and objectivity. With that confidence may come the degree of co-operation necessary for the implementation of the new practices suggested here.[241] Their adoption, particularly oral hearings, could be immensely important steps in making the OP procedure more effective.

3. *The burden and standard of proof*[242]

4.27 The approach of the HRC to the matters of the burden and standard of proof are of immense practical importance to the effective functioning of the OP. The initial burden of proof or persuasion would clearly seem to be on the alleged victim or the person acting on his behalf (both of whom will henceforth be referred to as the 'author'). An author is not obliged to prove his case at the admissibility stage. The obligation is only to submit sufficient evidence in substantiation of the allegations as will constitute a prima-facie case.[243] The HRC has declared a number of communications inadmissible on the ground of non-substantiation of allegations.[244] In a clear case a decision to declare a communication inadmissible or otherwise to terminate or suspend consideration of it may be taken without referring the case to the State party for its observations.[245] So, for example, if the author's evidence does not raise a prima-facie case the communication will not be referred to the State party at all. Conversely, however, a communication may not be declared admissible unless the State party has received the text and has been afforded an opportunity to furnish information or observations.[246] Thus it is open to the State party to refute the allegations and reduce the sufficiency of the authors' evidence below the required level of a prima-facie case. For example, in *J.M.* v. *Jamaica*[247] J.M. alleged that article 12(4) (the right to enter his own country) had been violated because he had been unable to obtain a new passport and thus unable to return to Jamaica. The State party submitted no information. The HRC declared the communication admissible. That decision was set aside when the State party submitted evidence which rebutted J.M.'s evidence. The HRC concluded that J.M. had failed to establish that he was a Jamaican citizen and had failed to substantiate that he was a victim of violations of the provisions of the ICCPR.

4.28 If a communication is declared admissible the State party is required to submit explanations or statements clarifying the matter under consideration (article 4(2) OP).[248] The explanations or statements must primarily relate to the substance of the matter under consideration and in particular the specific violations of the Covenant alleged to have occurred.[249] The HRC can also request further detailed information from the author or the State party and may specify particular questions and aspects of the communication as to which further information should be supplied.[250] These requests by the HRC represent one of the few positive roles in the OP proceedings taken by the HRC.

If the author fails to supply this information the HRC may hold that it can make no finding on all or part of the communication or that the allegations are unsubstantiated.[251] The effect of failure on the part of the State party is examined below.[252]

With regard to the consideration of communications on the merits the evidence supplied by the author has been sufficient when it has been of a specific, substantial, not insubstantial nature and of pertinent character. As for the obligations on the State party it is unfortunate that the HRC's approach can for the most part only be gleaned from cases in which the State party concerned has generally proved uncooperative.[253] Therefore, as noted earlier, many of the HRC's views effectively take the form of a judgment by default. This has been the situation since the HRC's very first expression of views in the *Massera* case.

4.29 In *J. L. Massera and Others* v. *Uruguay*[254] the communication alleged multiple violations of the Covenant to four victims. The explanations of the State party consisted of a 'Review of the rights of the accused in cases before a military criminal tribunal, and domestic remedies available to him for protecting and safeguarding his rights in the national courts of justice'.[255] The HRC decided that the submission of the State party was not sufficient to comply with the requirements of the OP (article 4(2)) since it contained 'No explanations on the merits of the case'.[256] A further request for observations met with no response. The HRC decided to base its views on the facts which had not been contradicted by the State party.[257] It expressed the view that there had been multiple violations to three of the alleged victims.

4.30 A different approach was taken to the problem of non co-operation from a State party in the HRC's second views. In *Santullo (Valcada)* v. *Uruguay*[258] S made specific allegations of ill-treatment and named the senior officers responsible. In its submissions the State party referred to the domestic legal provisions prohibiting any physical maltreatment in Uruguay. The submission did not give any further details but claimed that the authors' allegations were 'Unfounded, irresponsible and unaccompanied by the least shred of evidence and that they accordingly did not deserve further comment'.[259] The HRC decided to base its views on facts which had been 'essentially confirmed by the State party or are unrepudiated or uncontested except for denials of a general character offering no particular information or explanations'.[260] The HRC stated that,

The State party has adduced no evidence that his allegations of ill-treatment have been duly investigated in accordance with the laws to which it drew attention in its submission . . . A refutation of these allegations in general terms is not enough. A State party should investigate the allegations in accordance with its laws.[261]

Surprisingly, perhaps, the view that the majority of the HRC then went on to express was that,

As regards Article 7 of the Covenant[262] the Committee *cannot find that there has not been any violation of this provision*. In this respect the Committee notes that the State party has failed to show that it had ensured to the person concerned the protection required in article 2[263] of the Covenant.[264]

Obviously this negative finding does not carry the weight of a positive finding of a violation and represents a rather cautious and unsatisfactory jurisprudence.[265] Fortunately such a view has only ever been taken in the *Santullo (Valcada) Case*. In all subsequent cases the HRC has either expressed no view because, for example, of the generality of the allegations,[266] or expressed a positive view when the State party has only refuted allegations in general terms. In its third view, *Lanza and Perdoma* v.

Uruguay,[267] the HRC reiterated its view in the *Massera* case that denials of a general character would not suffice and stated that,

Specific responses and pertinent evidence (including copies of the relevant decisions of the courts and findings of any investigations which have taken place into the validity of the complaints made) in reply to the contentions of the author of a communication are required. The Government did not furnish the Committee with such information. Consequently, the Committee cannot but draw appropriate conclusions on the basis of the information before it.[268]

4.31 It is this approach to evidence which has since prevailed. The approach takes account of what may often be a factual inequality in evidential terms between the parties. The HRC's approach was further clarified in the case of *Bleir* v. *Uruguay*.[269] The authors[270] submitted detailed allegations that B had been arrested, detained incommunicado, and subjected to ill-treatment. These allegations were supported by the statements of family members and eyewitness testimonies. Uruguay submitted a brief categorical denial of B's detention. In the light of the 'overwhelming evidence' of the authors the HRC considered that the State party's submission was 'totally insufficient'.[271] The HRC concluded in an Interim Decision that,

13. The failure of the State party to address in substance the serious allegations brought against it and corroborated by unrefuted information, cannot but lead to the conclusion that Eduardo Bleir is either still detained, incommunicado, by the Uruguayan authorities or has died while in custody at the hands of the Uruguayan authorities.[272]

The State party objected to this part of the HRC's Interim Decision:

The Government of Uruguay wishes to state that, in paragraph 13 of that document, the Committee displays not only an ignorance of legal rules relating to the presumption of guilt, but a lack of ethics in carrying out the tasks entrusted to it, since it so rashly arrived at the conclusions that the Uruguayan authorities had put Eduardo Bleir to death. The Committee, whose purpose is to protect, promote and ensure respect for civil and political rights, should bear in mind that this task should always be carried out under the rule of law in accordance with its mandate and the universally accepted procedures concerning such matters as guilt and presumption of guilt.[273]

The HRC replied decisively,

The Human Rights Committee cannot accept the State party's criticism that it has displayed an ignorance of legal rules and a lack of ethics in carrying out the tasks entrusted to it or the insinuation that it has failed to carry out its task under the rule of law.
On the contrary, in accordance with its mandate under article 5(1) of the Optional Protocol, the Committee has considered the communication in the light of the information made available to it by the authors of the communication and by the State party concerned. In this connection the Committee has adhered strictly to the

principle audiatur et altera pars and has given the State party every opportunity to furnish information to refute the evidence presented by the authors.

The Committee notes that the State party has ignored the Committee's repeated requests for a thorough inquiry into the author's allegations.

With regard to the *burden of proof*, this cannot rest alone on the author of the communication, especially considering that the author and the State party do not always have equal access to the evidence and that frequently the State party alone has access to the relevant information. It is implicit in article 4(2) of the Optional Protocol that the State party has the duty to investigate in good faith all allegations of violation of the Covenant made against it and its authorities, especially when such allegations are corroborated by evidence submitted by the author of the communication, and to furnish to the Committee the information available to it. In cases where the author has submitted to the Committee allegations supported by substantial witness testimony, as in this case, and where further clarification of the case depends on information exclusively in the hands of the State party, the Committee may consider such allegations as substantiated in the absence of satisfactory evidence and explanations to the contrary submitted by the State party.[274]

4.32 This approach to the burden of proof has now become established as part of the HRC's standard jurisprudence. The statement above is the major precedent on this matter and the HRC frequently refers back to it.[275] In some subsequent decisions the HRC has indicated to the State party the appropriate evidence required, for example medical reports, inquiry reports, details of alleged charges, copies of court proceedings, and reports on the questioning of officials.[276]

4.33 In summary the HRC has interpreted article 4(2) OP as explicitly providing that the State party has the duty to contribute to clarification of the matter and an implicit duty to investigate in good faith all allegations of violations of the Covenant made against the State and its authorities, especially when corroborated by evidence, and to furnish to the HRC the information available to it. This represents a very positive interpretation of the OP by the HRC and prevents the lack of co-operation by a State party destroying the effective functioning of the OP. The effect is that no State party can benefit from its failure to co-operate fully with the HRC.[277]

4.34 There have, however, been occasions when it might have been expected that the HRC would go further in attempting to obtain substantiation or corroboration of the allegations. For example, in *Vasilskis* v. *Uruguay*,[278] the author (V's brother) based his statements on the testimony of ex-prisoners who were in the same prison as his sister, who were then in Europe as refugees, and who allegedly witnessed the torture and maltreatment at first hand and would have been prepared to testify to it, if necessary, to the HRC. The HRC could perhaps have requested the author to provide signed testimonies from these ex-prisoners. This would only impose a minimal burden on the author. Similarly, in *Quinteros and Quinteros* v. *Uruguay*,[279] it had been alleged, *inter alia*, that E.Q. had been arrested in the grounds of the Venezuelan embassy in Montevideo. Uruguay denied that the government had any part in the episode. Again it would seem to impose a minimal burden on the authors to submit signed testimonies from the witnesses in the Venezuelan embassy or at least to request such.

4.35 If the State party raises a defence under the particular limitation provisions of an article or under the general derogation provisions in article 4 the burden would seem to be on the State party to justify its limitation or derogation under the terms of the ICCPR.[280] For example, in *Hertzberg* v. *Finland*,[281] the onus was on the State party to show that the restrictions imposed on freedom of expression in connection with programmes concerning homosexuality were necessary for the protection of 'public morals'.[282] It should also be noted that the HRC will consider, *ex officio*, whether acts or omissions which are prima facie not in conformity with the Covenant could for any reasons be justified under the Covenant in the circumstances. The Committee then notes whether it would have been permissible to derogate from the rights concerned under article 4 OP, and, if so, whether the government has made any submissions of fact or law to justify such derogations.[283]

4.36 The HRC have not made any general comment on the matter of the appropriate *standard of proof* other than that of a prima facie requirement at the admissibility stage.[284] The general non-co-operation of and the failure to comply with the HRC's requests by Uruguay, the State party concerned in most communications when the HRC was seeking to develop appropriate standards, rendered the consideration of those communications a largely one-sided affair. However, the general approach of the HRC would suggest that it is applying something approximating to proof on a 'balance of probabilities' rather than a 'beyond reasonable doubt' standard. There may be some flexibility within this standard depending on the seriousness of the allegations involved.[285]

8. Final views under the OP[286]

4.37 After consideration and examination of the communication the HRC is directed to 'forward its views to the State party concerned and to the individual' (article 5(4)). The term 'views' was preferred in the Third Committee to the stronger terms 'suggestions' and 'recommendations'.[287] A number of commentators have regretted the weakness of the term 'views' and argued that the stronger terms rejected by the Third Committee would have been more precise and accorded greater authority to the HRC.[288] Professor Schwelb has noted that the French expression 'contestations' would suggest that the HRC would have stronger powers than are suggested by the term views.[289] M. Tardu has argued that, 'It seems that the HRC would have discretion as to the substance of its "views" which might include judgements as to the conformity of conduct of the state with the Covenant'.[290]

4.38 It was, therefore, very important to note how much authority the HRC considered that the term 'views' accorded to it. The practice of the HRC has been clear from its very first views. The HRC's views follow a judicial pattern and are effectively decisions on the merits.[291] The initial communication, the allegations of the author, the submissions of the State party, the decision on admissibility, and any interim decisions are recited in some detail. The facts upon which the HRC bases its views are set out. If the State party has not been co-operative the facts upon which the views are based are those which have been either essentially confirmed by the State party or are or appear to be uncontested except for denials of a general character offering no particular information or explanation.[292] The views often contain an indication of certain 'considerations' which the HRC has taken into account in formulating its views. These considerations have included, for example, the failure of either party to submit information requested by the HRC, particular matters arising during the consideration of the communication, the burden of proof, the obligations of either party under the Covenant or the general comments adopted by the HRC under article 40(4).[293] Many of the HRC's views contain substantive interpretations of the provisions of the Covenant and the OP.[294] The views then state whether in the HRC's view the facts as found disclose violations of the Covenant and why. However, the linkage between the facts and the violations found has not always been clearly spelt out by the HRC, particularly in its early views, with a consequent lack of clarity and legal precision.[295]

4.39 It is clear from the drafting work that the views of the HRC do not constitute a legally binding decision as regards the State party concerned.[296] In this respect the OP parallels the reports of the European Commission on Human Rights,[297] and the supervision systems of the International Labour Organization[298] and under the European Social Charter.[299] It contrasts markedly with the decisions of the European Court of Human Rights and the recommendations of the Committee of Ministers under the ECHR which are legally binding.[300] There is no higher organ expressly authorized to review or supervise the implementation of the HRC's views so these remain the last word on the communication.[301] Again this contrasts with the implementation systems under the ECHR,[302] the ILO,[303] and the European Social Charter.[304]

It is submitted that the HRC's views would obviously carry greater authority if they were legally binding on the State party. A legally non-binding view and the absence of any mechanisms of enforcement or execution afford a victim the most minimal degree of protection and relief. The strongest argument to support the OP system has been put by Professor Tomuschat:

Legally, the views formulated by the Human Rights Committee are not binding on the State party concerned which remains free to criticize them. Nonetheless, any State party will find it hard to reject such findings in so far as they are based on orderly proceedings during which the defendant party had ample opportunity to present its submissions. The views of the Human Rights Committee gain their authority from their inner qualities of impartiality, objectiveness and soberness. If such requirements are met, the views of the Human Rights Committee can have a far-reaching impact, at least vis-à-vis such Governments which have not outrightly broken with the international community and ceased to care anymore for concern expressed by international bodies. If such a situation arose, however, even a legally binding decision would not be likely to be respected.[305]

Much of this chapter on the OP has been directed to showing how the development of practices and procedures by the HRC enhance these very qualities of impartiality, objectiveness, and fairness. Many of these matters have been commented upon favourably and thus help to invest the HRC's views with greater authority and a legal rather than merely a 'political value'.[306]

4.40 It is arguable that the ambiguity of the term views and the fact that they are non-binding has allowed the HRC to go further in those views than might have been expected. The views do not end with the HRC's findings on the question of violations. Each view continues with a statement of the view of the HRC on the 'obligation' of the State party in the light of the HRC's findings. Among the general and particular obligations indicated by the HRC have been:

(*a*)   To take immediate steps to ensure strict observance of the provisions of the Covenant;[307]
(*b*)   To provide immediate and effective remedies to the victims (article 2(3) ICCPR);[308]
(*c*)   To provide adequate or appropriate remedies to the victims;[309]
(*d*)   To provide compensation to the victims;[310]
(*e*)   To immediately release the victims, or to commute a death sentence;[311]
(*f*)   To take steps with a view to enabling the victims to participate again in the political life of the nation;[312]
(*g*)   To adjust the provisions of legislation, sometimes specified, in order to implement its obligations under the Covenant;[313]
(*h*)   To give the victim permission to leave the country;[314]
(*i*)   To extend (to the victims) the treatment and rights of detained persons laid down in articles 7, 9, and 10 of the Covenant;[315]
(*j*)   To ensure that the victim receives and continues to receive all necessary medical care;[316]
(*k*)   To establish what has happened to the alleged victim, to bring to justice any persons found to be responsible for his death, disappearance, or ill-treatment, and to pay compensation to him or his family for any injury which he has suffered;[317]

(*l*) To ensure that the right to life is duly protected by amending the law;[318]

(*m*) To give the victim a trial or a fresh trial with all the procedural guarantees in article 14;[319]

(*n*) To provide the victim with effective remedies which would give her the possibility of enjoying the rights under article 12 of the Covenant (freedom of movement and residence) including a passport valid for travel abroad;[320]

(*o*) To investigate the allegations of torture;[321]

(*p*) To return property to the victim;[322]

(*q*) To take steps to ensure that similar violations do not occur in the future;[323]

(*r*) To transmit a copy of the views to the victim.[324]

It is interesting to note the specific nature and directness of some of these obligations, for example, to pay compensation or amend particular pieces of legislation.[325] This approach is very positive compared, for example, with that of the EUCT which simply states whether or not there has been a violation of the ECHR, though it has power under article 50 ECHR to award damages and costs in certain circumstances.[326]

4.41 Having declared a communication inadmissible or expressed its views as to the alleged violations and any resulting obligations the question remains whether the HRC has any competence to reconsider its views at the request of either party or follow up in any way its expression of views to ensure that they are respected by the State party.[327] These important matters have been considered by the Working Group on Communications and the plenary HRC. The extensive debate is well summarized in the HRC's annual report in 1983:

Some members were of the opinion that nothing in the Covenant and the Optional Protocol, which were the legal basis of the Committee's functions and limits, empowered the Committee to reconsider its views on communications or to ensure their implementation; that the Committee could have no inherent powers that had not been given to it explicitly by States parties and that it therefore had no competence to initiate the review of a case already concluded; that there was nothing in the Optional Protocol to prevent an individual from submitting a further communication if he was not satisfied with the Committee's views, or if he considered that there were facts or evidence to which attention should be drawn, and the question would then become one of admissibility of the new communication; that the Committee was a *sui generis* body, with no judicial powers and that the implementation of its views was left to the goodwill of the State party concerned; that the question of the monitoring of the implementation of those views in the absence of a clear legal mandate to that effect, might even be contrary to Article 2, paragraph 7, of the Charter of the United Nations relating to non-interference by the United Nations in the internal affairs of States; that States parties could, if they so wish, use the amendment procedure under Article 11 of the Protocol, an easy matter at the current stage, when there were only 28 States parties to the Protocol; that if the Committee took it upon itself to change procedures for which explicit ratification was required, its action could be taken as a warning to States to think twice before ratifying the Optional Protocol, since there was no prediction what additional obligations and procedures the Committee would attach to that instrument; and that no useful progress could be made in trying to press States to do what they were not obliged to do.

The majority of members, however, pointed out that the Committee could not let its work under the Optional Protocol degenerate into an exercise of futility; that due consideration had to be paid to both the letter and the spirit of the Covenant, and that whereas the Committee believed that certain appropriate action was reasonably open to it, or was not expressly prohibited, the Committee should take it and that the Optional Protocol allowed considerable latitude for interpretation since many issues were not specifically covered by its provisions. Several such issues were cited, as well as decisions and steps taken previously by the Committee, but which could not be traced directly back to the Committee or the Optional Protocol.[328] Considering that the Optional Protocol did not provide for the principle of *res judicata* as far as the Committee's decisions were concerned, and that the Committee's rules of procedure allowed for a review of a decision on admissibility, reconsideration of a communication should be possible, but only as an exception, not as a rule; that it should primarily be based on new facts, although legal arguments adduced at a later stage could not be entirely excluded; that a new rule to that effect may not be desirable at the present stage, but that if one was ultimately to be drawn up it should be an enabling rule whose effect would be to impose limitations and to discourage abuses. As to the question of whether the Committee was entitled to monitor the implementation of its decisions under the Optional Protocol, it was pointed out that, whereas the Committee had no executive powers enabling it to enforce its views, it could nevertheless do something to bring redress, or end continued violations, of the victim's rights after transmission of its views to the State party concerned. Moreover, it was clear from the preamble of the Protocol[329] and Article 2(3) of the Covenant[330] that the States parties intended the Covenant to be implemented. When a victim was clearly within the jurisdiction of a State and not in direct communication with the Committee, the Committee should indicate in its views that he might avail himself of certain remedies and the Committee should request the State party to communicate the entire decision to him and should also be requested to inform the Committee of any developments.[331]

The HRC have been pressed on the question of reconsideration and follow up of communications because in a number of cases authors have asked the Committee to take additional steps to persuade the States parties concerned to act in conformity with the views of the HRC. Similarly the HRC have been requested by authors to review a number of inadmissibility decisions.[332] The HRC has now expressed the opinion that,

Its role in the examination of any given case comes to an end by the adoption of views or by the adoption of another decision of a final nature. Only in exceptional circumstances may the Committee agree to reconsider an earlier final decision. Basically, this would only occur when the Committee is satisfied that new facts are placed before it by a party claiming that these facts were not available to it at the time of the consideration of the case and that these facts would have altered the decision of the Committee. The Committee, however, takes an interest in any action by the State party as a consequence of the Committee's views under the Optional Protocol, or in any action taken by the State party which concerns either the legal issues involved or the situation of the person concerned. Thus, when forwarding its views to a State party, the Committee invites the State party to inform it of any action pursuant to the views.[333]

The decision is clearly a compromise between the opposing views on these matters outlined above. It sets another important precedent of the HRC applying an interpretation of the OP which allows it some flexibility to take appropriate action, albeit modest, which is reasonably open to it, which is not expressly prohibited by the term of the OP. The most recent development is that on 25 July 1990 the HRC designated one member, Mr Fodor, as Special Rapporteur for Follow-Up on Views to seek and receive information on the action taken by the State party on the HRC's views.

4.42 Since the HRC's fifteenth session (March–April 1982) the letter of transmittal accompanying the Committee's views invites the State party to inform the HRC of any action pursuant to its views. A number of responses had been received from States parties. Responses were received from Canada in 1983,[334] Mauritius in 1983,[335] and from Finland in 1983 and 1989[336] informing the HRC of legislative or other measures that had been or were being taken in response to the HRC's views. Madagascar also informed the HRC that an individual whose case the HRC had considered had been released from imprisonment upon completion of his sentence and had left Malagasy territory.[337] In 1984 the Government of Uruguay requested that a list of persons released from imprisonment in 1983 and 1984 which had been furnished to the Secretary-General, be brought to the attention of the HRC. Included in the list were two persons whose cases had been considered by the HRC.[338] The HRC learned from other sources of the release of three other individuals whose cases it had considered.[339] Similar lists were provided by the Uruguayan Government in October 1984 and in February and March 1985.[340] Those lists included a number of persons whose cases were pending before the Committee or had been considered by it.[341]

4.43 In 1985 Canada informed the HRC that amending legislation had been passed to bring the Indian Act into conformity with the HRC's decision in the *Lovelace case*.[342] Finally Madagascar provided detailed comments and information concerning the decision in *Monja Jaona* v. *Madagascar*.[343] Madagascar maintained that the communication was inadmissible and in any event that no violations of the Covenant had occurred. The State party expressed its regret at not having made the information available to the HRC at an earlier stage and affirmed its intention to co-operate more fully with the HRC in the future.[344]

In response the HRC expressed its satisfaction at all measures taken by the States parties towards the observance of the Covenant and welcomed the positive responses and the co-operation of the States parties concerned.[345]

E. THE INTERPRETATION AND APPLICATION OF THE OP

1. The function of the HRC under the OP

4.44 There are no provisions in the ICCPR or the OP which expressly address this matter. However, the HRC has had a number of occasions on which to make clear its view of its function in relation to national courts and tribunals. In *Silva* v. *Uruguay* the HRC stated that, 'It is the function of the HRC, acting under the OP, to see to it that States parties live up to their commitments under the Covenant' (see ch. 7, pr. 7.40 below). In *Hertzberg et al.* v. *Finland*[346] the Committee pointed out that it was

not called upon to review the interpretation of paragraph 9(2) of chapter 20 of the Finnish Penal Code. The authors have advanced no valid argument which could indicate that the construction placed upon this provision by the Finnish tribunals was not made *bona fide*. Accordingly, the Committee's task is confined to clarifying whether the restrictions applied against the alleged victims, irrespective of the scope of the penal prohibitions under Finnish penal law, disclose a breach of any of the rights under the Covenant.[347]

Similarly, in *Pinkey* v. *Canada*[348] the Committee observed,

that allegations that a domestic court has committed errors of fact or law do not in themselves raise questions of violation of the Covenant unless it also appears that some of the requirements of article 14 have not been complied with.[349]

Again in *Maroufidou* v. *Sweden*,[350]

M claims that the decision to expel her was in violation of article 13 of the Covenant because it was not 'in accordance with the law'. In her submission it was based on an incorrect interpretation of the Swedish Aliens Act. The Committee takes the view that the interpretation of domestic law is essentially a matter for the courts and authorities of the State party concerned. It is not within the powers or functions of the Committee to evaluate whether the competent authorities of the State party in question have interpreted and applied the domestic law correctly in the case before it under the Optional Protocol, unless it is established that they have not interpreted and applied it in good faith or that it is evident that there has been an abuse of power.[351]

In the light of the information before it the HRC was

satisfied that in reaching the decision to expel Anna Maroufidou the Swedish authorities did interpret and apply the relevant provisions of Swedish law in good faith and in a reasonable manner and consequently that the decision was made 'in accordance with law' as required by article 13 of the Covenant.[352]

And again in *J.K.* v. *Canada*[353] the Committee observed that it was 'beyond its competence to review findings of fact made by national tribunals or to determine whether national tribunals properly evaluated new evidence submitted on appeal'.[354] The Committee 'does not deal with questions of constitutionality, but with the question whether a law is in conformity with the Covenant, as applied in the circumstances of the case . . .'.[355] Therefore, the application of a legal provision may violate the Covenant even though it has been held constitutional in the national courts of the State concerned.[356]

A related aspect is that the Committee

has only been entrusted with the mandate of examining whether an individual has suffered an actual violation of his rights. *It cannot review in the abstract whether national legislation contravenes the Covenant*, although such legislation may, in particular circumstances, produce adverse effects which directly affect the individual, making him thus a victim in the sense contemplated by article 2 of the Optional Protocol.[357]

The 'victim' requirement is dealt with in detail below (prs. 4.75–4.81).

4.44.1 The function of the HRC was acutely raised in *Hendriks* v. *Netherlands*.[358] H claimed a violation of article 23(4) of the Covenant (equality of spouses as to marriage and at its dissolution) because the courts in the Netherlands had granted exclusive custody of his son to his ex-wife without ensuring H's right of access as the father of his child. Access was refused because of the mother's refusal to co-operate. The HRC expressed the view that,

The courts of States parties are generally competent to evaluate the circumstances of individual cases. However, the Committee deems it necessary that the law should establish certain criteria so as to enable the courts to apply to the full the provisions of article 23 of the Covenant. It seems essential, barring exceptional circumstances, that these criteria should include the maintenance of personal relations and direct and regular contact between the child and both parents. The unilateral opposition of one of the parents, cannot, in the opinion of the Committee, be considered an exceptional circumstance.

The HRC then proceeded to note that the Netherlands court had made its appreciation of the best interests of the child in the light of all the circumstances and that, 'As a result, the Committee cannot conclude that the State party has violated article 23, but draws its attention to the need to supplement the legislation as stated in [the paragraph cited above]'. The difficulty of this approach is highlighted by two individual opinions. The first opinion, submitted by four members (Dimitrijevic, El Shafei, Higgins, and Zielinski), concluded that,

It is not for us to insist that the courts were wrong, in their assessment of the best interests of the child, in giving priority to the current difficulties and tensions rather than to the long-term importance for the child of contact with both its parents. However, we cannot but point out that this approach does not sustain the family rights to which Mr. Hendriks and his son were entitled under article 23 of the Covenant.

This opinion has great force. The function of the HRC should not be to review the correctness of the individual decision but to see whether the principles and criteria applied in reaching that decision were compatible with the Covenant, and in this case they clearly were not.

The second individual opinion, submitted by Mr Wako, argues that the Committee should have applied the criteria it established to the facts of the case to determine whether a violation of the Covenant had occurred. This, however, would make the HRC's function more like that of an appeal or 'fourth instance' body. This approach seems to have been clearly rejected by the HRC. Mr Wako also expressed concern that the Netherlands law did not include a statutory right of access nor any identifiable criteria under which the fundamental right of mutual contact between a non-custodial parent and his or her child could be denied. Such legislation (which was then being considered) would, in his view, better reflect the spirit of the Covenant.

4.45 It is notable that the views which the Committee has taken of its function under the OP closely parallel those taken by the EUCM and the EUCT under the ECHR.[359] Like those organs the HRC has also engaged in limited *ex officio* tasks, for example, raising of its own motion certain issues during the consideration of communications. However, there has as yet been no indication whether the HRC takes any view similar to that established under the ECHR of protecting the objective character of the obligations under the European Convention and 'l'ordre public de l'Europe'.[360]

2. The interpretation of the ICCPR and the OP [361]

4.46 The most important view of the HRC concerning the interpretation of the ICCPR and the OP is that in *Van Duzen* v. *Canada*.[362] The facts of the case raised complex issues concerning whether the provision in Article 15(1) of the ICCPR for the retroactivity of a 'Lighter Penalty' was applicable to a law amending the rules concerning the forfeiture of parole. The author raised the matter of the applicable principles of interpretation. He submitted that in a case of doubt a presumption of the liberty of the individual should be applied to article 15(1). He further argued that the meaning of article 15(1) he was advancing was assumed in reservations made by certain other States parties when they ratified the Covenant and was supported in the proceedings of the Third Committee in 1960 in which Canada had participated.[363] The State party agreed with the principle of interpretation advanced but submitted that there was no ambiguity in article 15(1). Therefore the author could not benefit from the presumption in favour of liberty.[364]

Unfortunately, the HRC made no comment or observation on such an alleged general principle of interpretation.[365] It did, however, make an important statement on the interpretation of the terms and concepts of the ICCPR and the OP,

> The Committee further notes that its interpretation and application of the ICCPR has to be based on the principle that the terms and concepts of the Covenant are *independent* of any particular national system of law and of all dictionary definitions. Although the terms of the Covenant are derived from long traditions within many nations, the Committee must now regard them as having an *autonomous meaning*. The parties have made extensive submissions, in particular as regards the meaning of the word 'Penalty' and as regards Canadian law and practice. The Committee appreciates their relevance for the light they shed on the nature of the issue in dispute. On the other hand, the meaning of the word 'Penalty' in Canadian law is not, as such, decisive. Whether the word 'Penalty' in Article 15(1) should be interpreted narrowly or widely, and whether it applies to different kinds of penalties, 'Criminal' and 'Administrative', under the Covenant, must depend on other factors. Apart from the text of Article 15(1) regard must be had, inter alia, to its object and purpose.[366]

It is interesting to note, first, that the HRC will regard at least some of the terms and concepts of the Covenant as having an 'autonomous', 'independent' meaning. A similar approach has been developed under the ECHR.[367] A clear example of the HRC adopting an autonomous interpretation of a provision of the Covenant is the case of *Lovelace* v. *Canada*.[368] At the time of submitting the communication L no longer qualified as an Indian under Canadian legislation. However, the HRC took the view that, 'Persons who are born and brought up on a reserve, who have kept ties with their community and wish to maintain these ties must normally be considered as belonging to that minority within the meaning of the Covenant'.[369] The HRC decided on the facts that L was entitled to be regarded as 'belonging' to the minority concerned and thus to claim the benefits of article 27 of the Covenant.[370]

4.47 Secondly, we can note that the direct reference to the text of the treaty and to its object and purpose mirrors the general rule of treaty interpretation in article 31 VCLT (1969).[371] Under the ECHR a teleological interpretation has increasingly been adopted and is now highly developed.[372] There has as yet been no parallel in the HRC's jurisprudence to the 'dynamic approach' to interpretation under the ECHR in accordance with which the institutions have identified their role as a protector of human rights in accordance with the changing perceptions of them in Western Europe as social values and attitudes evolve.[373] Clearly the HRC's comment does not rule out reference to the preparatory work on the Covenant and the OP, and indeed resort has been had to the preparatory work in a number of views. Notable examples were three Dutch cases concerning the scope of article 26 ICCPR.[374] In each case the HRC stated that it had 'perused' the *travaux préparatoires* of the ICCPR which provide a 'supplementary means of interpretation' (article 32 of the VCLT).[375] The HRC concluded that, 'The discussions, at the time of the drafting, concerning whether the scope of article 26 extended to rights not otherwise guaranteed by the Covenant, were inconclusive and cannot alter the conclusion arrived at by the ordinary means of interpretation . . .'.[376] The 'ordinary means' referred to by the HRC were those in article 31 VCLT.[377]

Finally, in *Lopez Burgos* v. *Uruguay*,[378] the HRC stated that it would not adopt an interpretation of the Covenant which was 'unconscionable'.[379]

4.48 It is convenient to note here that the 'Margin of Appreciation' (or 'Discretion') doctrine which has formed an important part of the jurisprudence under the ECHR has been introduced by the HRC. In *Hertzberg and Others* v. *Finland*,[380] the authors argued that the Finnish authorities, including the organs of the State controlled Finnish Broadcasting Corporation, had interfered with their right to freedom of expression and information (article 19) by imposing sanctions against participants in, or censoring, radio and television programmes dealing with homosexuality.[381] In its final views the HRC stated that, 'It has to be noted, first, that public morals differ widely. There is no universally applicable common standard. Consequently, in this respect, a certain *margin of discretion* must be accorded to the responsible national authorities'.[382]

It is as yet too early to know how widely the doctrine of the margin of appreciation will be interpreted in the HRC's jurisprudence. No subsequent decision or view has made reference to it. An unduly wide interpretation inevitably lowers the level of protection offered to alleged victims by reducing the level of international supervision. Though firmly established under the ECHR, and indeed of increasing significance, the doctrine has not been without its critics.[383]

3. Incompatibility with the provisions of the Covenant[384]

(a) *ratione temporis*[385]

4.49 The HRC has clearly stated that with respect to the original States parties to the OP it is only competent to consider alleged violations occurring on or after the date of the entry into force of the OP on 23 March 1976.[386] Similarly with respect to States which have later acceded to the OP the HRC is only competent to consider alleged violations occurring on or after the date of the entry into force of the OP for that State party.[387] Moreover, in *A.R.S.* v. *Canada*[388] the HRC expressed the view that, 'No action taken before the entry into force of the Covenant for the State party concerned can, as such, be judged in the light of the obligations deriving from the Covenant'.[389]

4.50 However, alleged violations occurring before the date of the entry into force of the State concerned can be considered by the HRC if the violations continue or have continuing effects after that date which themselves constitute a violation of the Covenant.[390] This approach has been consistently applied in a number of cases in which the HRC has declared communications or parts of communications inadmissible *ratione temporis*.[391] The HRC's final views in such cases commonly take the form that the facts as found by the HRC, 'In so far as they continued or occurred after the date of entry into force of the ICCPR and the O.P.' disclose certain violations or not.[392] In *Altesor* v. *Uruguay*[393] the HRC held that it could not establish with certainty what facts had occurred after the entry into force of the ICCPR and the OP. They would, therefore, make no finding as regards those allegations.[394]

The question of continuing violations has been raised in a number of communications. In *Carballal* v. *Uruguay*[395] the HRC concluded that although the date of C's arrest was prior to the entry into force of the ICCPR and the OP the alleged violations of articles 7, 9, 10, and 14 continued after that date.[396] In *Cabreira* v. *Uruguay*[397] it was argued that although the alleged torture of C took place before the entry into force of the ICCPR and the OP in Uruguay it had effects up to the date of the communication because it was on the basis of the confessions made under torture that C was sentenced to twelve years' imprisonment, which he continued to serve.[398] Unfortunately, the HRC did not reply to this argument but it would appear to have rejected it.

4.51 This question of the continuing effects of violations has been more directly considered in other cases. In *M.A.* v. *Italy*[399] the communication raised various possible violations of the ICCPR including the fair trial guarantee under article 14. Italy argued that the alleged violations occurred prior to the entry into force of the ICCPR and the OP in Italy on 15 December 1978 and that, therefore, the communication should be declared inadmissible *ratione temporis*.[400] M.A. raised the same point as in the *Cabreira* case.[401] He argued that, 'The violations did not come to an end prior to 15 December 1978, which is obvious since he is currently serving the sentence for which he was tried. Thus, the law applied is still in force and the sentence against M.A. is being carried out'.[402] The reply of the HRC was that, 'It must be shown that there were consequences which could themselves have constituted a violation of the Covenant. In the opinion of the Committee there were no such consequences in the circumstances in the present case'.[403]

The HRC's view seems to be a clear rejection of the argument advanced by M.A. It is submitted that the HRC's view was correct. The prison sentence was clearly a consequence of the alleged violations but that it is a necessary rather than a sufficient condition. The consequence itself, that is, the sentence, had to constitute a violation of the Covenant and on the facts it did not.

4.52 Other consequences of a prison sentence were raised in *J.K.* v.

Canada.[404] J.K. was convicted of arson prior to the entry into force of the ICCPR and the OP for Canada. He argued,

that the stigma of an allegedly unjust conviction and the social and legal consequences thereof, including the general prejudice in society against convicted persons, make him a victim today of Article 14, paragraphs 1 and 3 (a) to (c), and article 25 of the Covenant—of article 14 because he was allegedly denied a fair trial and of article 25, because his conviction bars him from equal access to public service and from running for public office and because his criminal record puts him at a disadvantage, in particular in the field of employment.[405]

Again the HRC took the view, correctly it is submitted, that, 'the consequences as described by the author do not themselves raise issues under the International Covenant on Civil and Political Rights'.[406]

(b) ratione materiae

4.53 The HRC is only competent to consider communications alleging violations of the rights 'set forth' in the ICCPR (article 1 OP).[407] The HRC has declared inadmissible *ratione materiae* communications alleging violations of rights or matters not contained in the ICCPR.[408] In *K.B.* v. *Denmark*[409] the communication was declared inadmissible, *inter alia*, on the ground that, 'The right to dispose of property, as such, is not protected by any provision of the ICCPR'.[410] In *C.E.* v. *Canada*[411] the communication related to C.E.'s claim for workman's compensation. It was declared inadmissible, *inter alia*, because the claim did not concern any of the rights referred to in the Covenant. In *I.M.* v. *Norway*[412] I.M. alleged that he had been overtaxed as a result of various acts and omissions of the Tax Office in Oslo allegedly based on racial discrimination against him and that the Olso authorities had failed to provide him with low rent accommodation, which failure contributed to his paying higher taxes.[413] The HRC stated that the communication did not reveal any evidence of violation of any of the rights in the ICCPR.[414] In particular the HRC pointed out that,

The assessment of taxable income and allocation of houses are not in themselves matters to which the Covenant applies; nor is there any evidence in substantiation of the author's claim to be a victim of racial discrimination.[415]

Accordingly, the HRC held the communication inadmissible as incompatible with the provisions of the ICCPR (article 3 OP). In *Stalla Costa* v. *Uruguay*[416] Uruguay argued that the communication should be declared inadmissible, 'on the ground that the author had no subjective right in law to be appointed to a public post, but only the legitimate aspiration to be so employed'.[417] The HRC decided that the question whether the author's claim was well-founded should be examined on the merits as he had made a reasonable effort to substantiate his claim and had invoked specific provisions of the Covenant in that respect.[418]

4.54 In *L.T.K.* v. *Finland*[419] the author claimed to be a victim of a violation of articles 18 and 19 ICCPR because his status as a conscientious objector to military service had not been recognized in Finland and he had been prosecuted because of his refusal to perform military service. The HRC expressed the view that,

The Covenant does not provide for the right to conscientious objection; neither Article 18 nor 19 of the Covenant, especially taking into account paragraph 3(c)(ii) of Article 8, can be construed as implying that right.[420]

Accordingly the claim was held inadmissible. More generally the HRC stated in *K.L.* v. *Denmark*[421] that it had no competence to examine allegations of violations of other international instruments. In *J.D.B.* v. *Netherlands*[422] the communication referred to the right to work in article 6 ICESCR.[423] The communication was declared inadmissible.

4.55 More difficult questions concerning the scope of the ICCPR and its relationship to other human rights instruments, in particular the International Covenant on Economic, Social, and Cultural Rights, were raised in three cases concerning the Netherlands. Those decisions concerned the scope of article 26 ICCPR which provides that,

All persons are equal before the law and are entitled without any discrimination to the equal protection of the law. In this respect, the law shall prohibit any discrimination and guarantee to all persons equal and effective protection against discrimination on any ground such as race, colour, sex, language, religion, political or other opinion, national or social origin, property, birth or other status.[424]

4.56 The three views, all issued on the same day, concerned various aspects of social security legislation in the Netherlands. In *S. W. M. Broeks* v. *Netherlands*[425] and in *F. H. Zwaan-de Vries* v. *Netherlands*[426] the authors complained that the Dutch Unemployment Benefit Act of 1976 violated article 26 of the Covenant. They argued that it was discriminatory in that, under it, benefits were discontinued to them because they had not proved that they were the 'breadwinners' of their respective families. This condition applied to them as married women but did not apply to married men. In *L. G. Danning* v. *Netherlands*[427] the author alleged a violation of article 26 in conjunction with article 2(1) on the basis that Dutch legislation on disability benefits was discriminatory in that it provided for higher benefits for married beneficiaries than for single, but cohabiting, beneficiaries. In each of these cases the Netherlands raised a number of similar arguments, some of which are considered elsewhere.

With respect to the scope of article 26 the Netherlands argued, first, that this article could only be invoked under the OP in the sphere of civil and political rights though not necessarily limited to the civil and political rights in the ICCPR. The example given by the Netherlands was that it could envisage the admissibility of a complaint concerning discrimination in the field of taxation.[428] Therefore, the Netherlands could not accept the admissibility of a complaint concerning the enjoyment of economic, social, and cultural rights. The State party referred to the rights concerning social security in the ICESCR, namely, articles 2, 3, and 9 and noted that the ICESCR had its own specific system and its own specific organ for the international monitoring of how States parties met their obligations and that it deliberately did not provide for an individual complaints procedure. 'The contracting parties deliberately chose to make this difference in international monitoring systems, because the nature and substance of social, economic and cultural rights make them unsuitable for judicial review of a complaint lodged by a State party or an individual.'[429] It was, therefore, incompatible with the aims of both the ICESCR and the ICCPR and its Optional Protocol for a complaint with respect to social security, as referred to in article 9 ICESCR, to be dealt with by way of an individual complaint under the OP based on article 26 ICCPR.

4.57 The view of the HRC was that,

the International Covenant on Civil and Political Rights would still apply even if a particular subject matter is referred to or covered in other international instruments, e.g., the International Convention on the Elimination of All Forms of Racial Discrimination, the Convention on the Elimination of All Forms of Discrimination Against Women, or, as in the present case, the International Covenant on Economic, Social and Cultural Rights. Notwithstanding the interrelated drafting history of the two Covenants, it remains necessary for the Committee to fully apply the terms of the International Covenant on Civil and Political Rights. The Committee observes in this connection that the provisions of article 2 of the International Covenant on Economic, Social and Cultural Rights do not detract from the full application of article 26 of the International Covenant on Civil and Political Rights.

... The discussions, at the time of the drafting, concerning the question whether the scope of article 26 extended to rights not otherwise guaranteed by the Covenant, were inconclusive and cannot alter the conclusion arrived at by the ordinary means of interpretation...

The Committee begins by noting that article 26 does not merely duplicate the guarantees already provided for in article 2. Its basis stems from the principle of equal protection without discrimination, as contained in article 7 of the Universal Declaration of Human Rights, which prohibited discrimination in law or in practice in any field regulated by public authorities. Article 26 is thus concerned with the obligations imposed on States in regard to their legislation and the application thereof.

Although article 26 requires that legislation should prohibit discrimination, it does not of itself contain any obligation with respect to matters that may be provided for by legislation. Thus it does not, for example, require any State to enact legislation to provide for social security. However, when such legislation is adopted in the exercise of a State's sovereign power, then such legislation must comply with article 26 of the Covenant.

The Committee observes in this connection that what is at issue is not whether or not social security should be progressively established in the Netherlands but whether the legislation providing for social security violates the prohibition against discrimination contained in article 26 of the International Covenant on Civil and Political Rights and the guarantee given therein to all persons regarding equal and effective protection against discrimination.

The right to equality before the law and to equal protection of the law without any discrimination does not make all differences of treatment discriminatory. A differentiation based on reasonable and objective criteria does not amount to prohibited discrimination within the meaning of article 26.[430]

Having established that article 26 applied the HRC expressed the view that there was a violation of article 26 in the *Broeks*[431] and *Zwaan-de Vries*[432] cases on the basis that the differentiation between married men and married women was not reasonable and therefore was discriminatory. By contrast in the *Danning* case[433] the HRC expressed the view that there was no violation of article 26 on the basis that it was 'persuaded that the differentiation complained of by Mr. Danning is based on objective and reasonable criteria ... By choosing not to enter into marriage, Mr. Danning and his cohabitant have not, in law, assumed the full extent of the duties and responsibilities incumbent on married couples. Consequently, Mr. Danning does not receive the full benefits provided for in Dutch law for married couples. The Committee concludes that the differentiation complained of by Mr. Danning does not constitute discrimination in the sense of article 26 of the Covenant.'[434]

4.58 The decision concerning the scope of article 26 is of great significance and resolves, to at least some extent, academic disagreements concerning prohibited discrimination.[435] As article 26 is stated to be 'concerned with the obligations imposed on States in regard to their legislation and the application thereof', 'in any field regulated and protected by public authorities', its scope is potentially extremely wide. It may cover, for example, taxation,[436] the whole range of social security and welfare legislation,[437] and immigration.[438] In all such areas the legislation will apparently be tested by reference to the test of whether the differentiations made are based on 'reasonable and objective criteria'. This may well pose severe problems for States. As the Netherlands argued in the above cases, 'Years of work are required in order to examine the whole complex of national legislation in search of discriminatory elements. The search can never be completed, either, as distinctions in legislation which are justifiable in the light of social views and conditions prevailing when they are first made may become disputable as changes occur in the views held in society.'[439] Although the HRC did not specifically respond to this point, presumably the answer to the latter part of it would lie in the concept of the 'margin of appreciation' (or discretion) under which a State party makes an initial assessment of the conditions obtaining in its national system and the consequent need to

restrict or limit rights.[440] The criterion of 'reasonable and objective' differentiations is that applied by the EUCT but it is clear that the prohibition on
discrimination under the ECHR has a more limited scope of application,
although it is not solely confined to situations where the rights set forth in the
ECHR have been infringed.[441] American jurisprudence in the area of discrimination and equal protection is immensely sophisticated.[442] Finally, we can
note the express application of the provisions of the Vienna Convention on
the Law on Treaties (1969) on the interpretation of treaties.[443]

4.59 In decisions on admissibility the HRC inevitably considers the
parameters of the relevant articles in the ICCPR. For example, in *A.S.* v.
Canada[444] the communication concerned the author's unsuccessful efforts
to obtain permission from the Canadian authorities for her daughter and
grandson to enter Canada to join her from Poland. The communication was
declared inadmissible *ratione materiae* on the basis that articles 12, 17, and
23 of the ICCPR were not applicable on the facts and with respect to article
26 there was no question in the circumstances of the case of any discrimination on any of the grounds referred to in the ICCPR.[445]

4.60 A more controversial decision was that in *J. B. et al. v. Canada*.[446]
The authors claimed that the general prohibition on strikes by public
employees in the Alberta Public Employee Relations Act of 1977 violated
article 22 of the ICCPR (freedom of association including the right to form
and join trade unions). Canada argued, *inter alia*, that article 22 did not contain a right to strike. The majority of the HRC expressed the view that the
communication was inadmissible *ratione materiae* because the right to strike
was not included in the scope of article 22. That view was based on a detailed
analysis of the *travaux préparatoires* and a comparison with article 8 of the
ICESCR which expressly guarantees the right to strike. Five members of the
HRC appended an important individual opinion. On their analysis of the
travaux préparatoires and a comparison with article 8 of the ICESCR they
considered the communication to be admissible. They stressed that, 'the
question that the Committee is required to answer at this stage is whether
article 22 alone or in conjunction with the other provisions of the Covenant
necessarily excludes, in the relevant circumstances, an entitlement to strike'.
On their view it did not. Therefore, 'Whether the right to strike is a necessary
element in the protection of the interests of the authors, and if so whether it
has been unduly restricted, is a question on the merits, that is to say, whether
the restrictions imposed in Canada are or are not justifiable under article
22(2)'. It is submitted that the decision on the substantive interpretation of
article 22 should have been taken at the merits stage.

4.61 Even more problematic with respect to the scope of admissibility
decisions is the approach to article 5 of the ICCPR and limitations clauses evident in the case of *M.A.* v. *Italy*.[447] There the HRC gave two grounds of inadmissibility in addition to the one noted above.[448] First, the HRC stated that,

Moreover, it would appear to the Committee that the acts of which M.A. was convicted (reorganizing the dissolved fascist party) were of a kind which are removed from the protection of the Covenant by Article 5 thereof and which were in any event justifiably prohibited by Italian law having regard to the limitations and restrictions applicable to the rights in question under the provisions of Articles 18(3), 19(3), 22(2) and 25 of the Covenant. In these respects therefore the communication is inadmissible under Article 3 of the Optional Protocol, as incompatible with the provisions of the Covenant, *ratione materiae*.[449]

Article 5 of the ICCPR to which the HRC refers provides that,

1. Nothing in the present Covenant may be interpreted as implying for any State, group or person any right to engage in any activity or perform any act aimed at the destruction of any of the rights and freedoms recognized herein or at their limitation to a greater extent than is provided for in the present Covenant.

The decision of the HRC parallels a controversial and much criticized early decision of the EUCM under the equivalent of article 5 of the ICCPR (article 17 of the ECHR) which declared inadmissible an aplication from the West German Communist Party alleging that government action banning it was contrary to articles 9, 10, and 11 of the ECHR.[450] It is submitted that the scope of article 5 should have been considered only at the merits stage. Similarly, it is submitted that the scope and application of permissible restrictions and limitation clauses under the ICCPR should normally be reserved for consideration at the merits stage.

4.62 Finally, in *M.A.* v. *Italy*[451] the HRC stated that,

M.A.'s additional claim that extradition proceedings, initiated by Italy while he was living in France, constitute a violation of the Covenant, is without foundation. There is no provision of the Covenant making it unlawful for a State party to seek extradition of a person from another country. The claim is therefore inadmissible under Article 3 of the Optional Protocol, as incompatible with the provisions of the Covenant, *ratione materiae*.[452]

M. A.'s claim with respect to a State seeking extradition is a novel one. There have been a number of applications under the ECHR concerning the sending state.[453] If on the facts of this case M.A. might have faced some danger on his return to Italy it would have been more appropriate to submit a communication concerning the sending State, France. The HRC would then have faced the question of whether to follow the jurisprudence under the ECHR concerning extradition.[454]

4.63 It remains to note that, like the EUCM,[455] the HRC does not require the communicant to specify accurately, or indeed at all, the particular rights in the ICCPR which he alleges have been violated. The HRC will conduct an examination, *ex officio*, of the articles of the ICCPR that appear to be relevant from the submissions of the parties.[456]

(c) ratione personae[457]

4.64 The matters to be considered here are the two basic questions of against whom and by whom may a communication be brought. The separate but related requirement that the communicant be a 'victim'[458] is also considered here for convenience.

(i) Against whom may a communication be brought?

4.65 The HRC is only competent to consider alleged violations by a State party to the ICCPR that has also become a party to the OP (article 1 OP).[459] So, for example, if a State validly denounces, terminates, suspends, or withdraws from the ICCPR or the OP the HRC would lose its competence in respect of that State under the OP.[460] Communications have been submitted concerning States that have not been party to the ICCPR or the OP. Under the HRC's Rules of Procedure the HRC do not receive such communications.[461]

4.66 Inevitably the HRC will have to deal with questions concerning the extent of the responsibility of a State party for acts or omissions committed 'within its jurisdiction' (article 1 OP) but committed by individuals, companies, corporations, or other bodies. For example in *B.d.B.* v. *Netherlands*[462] the State party expressed doubts as to whether an action by an Industrial Insurance Board could be attributed to its State organs when the Boards operate independently and there is no way in which the State party's authorities could influence concrete decisions. The HRC observed that, 'a State party is not relieved of its obligations under the Covenant when some of its functions are delegated to other autonomous organs'. The question was also raised in the case of *Hertzberg and Others* v. *Finland*.[463] The authors argued that the Finnish authorities, including organs of the State-controlled Finnish Broadcasting Corporation (FBC), had interfered with their right to freedom of information and expression in article 19 of the ICCPR by, 'Imposing sanctions against participants in, or censuring, radio and television programmes dealing with homosexuality'.[464] Criminal charges under the Finnish Penal Code had been brought against the editor of a programme dealing with homosexuality.[465] In its final views the HRC stated that it started from, 'The premise that the State party is responsible for actions of the Finnish Broadcasting Company (FBC), in which the State holds a dominant stake (90 per cent) and which is placed under specific government control'.[466] On these facts the finding of State responsibility was not too difficult a decision for the HRC. An alternative approach would have been to rest the responsibility of Finland on the legislative acts on which prosecutions had been brought. That was the approach taken by the EUCT in the *Young, James and Webster Cases*.[467] More difficult cases are sure to arise. For example, would the United Kingdom government be responsible for the activities of the British Broadcasting Corporation or Independent Television.[468] If in a particular case it proves impossible to hold the State party responsible for the acts concerned the possibility remains that the State party's responsibility can be based on its failure to secure the rights in the ICCPR (article 2(1) of the ICCPR) or to provide an effective remedy for the violation of rights (article 2(3) of the ICCPR).[469] The approach of the EUCT is to apply the general international law rules of State responsibility.[470] A similar approach from the HRC would seem sensible and desirable.

(ii) By whom may a communication be brought?

4.67 The HRC is only competent to receive and consider communications from 'individuals' who claim to be a victim of a violation by a State party of any of the rights set forth in the ICCPR (article 1 OP).[471] This clearly covers communications from one or more individuals.[472] It is also clear that the right to submit communications is not confined to the nationals of the State party concerned, nor only to the nationals of any State party. It is open to all 'individuals' whether nationals, aliens, or stateless persons provided they are 'subject to the jurisdiction' of the State party concerned.[473]

4.68 The HRC has held that an organization as such cannot submit a communication. In *Group of Associations for the Disabled* v. *Italy*[474] the communication was submitted by a group of associations for the defence of the rights of disabled and handicapped persons in Italy (a non-governmental organization referred to as 'Coordinamento') and the representatives of those associations. The representatives claimed that they themselves were disabled or handicapped or that their children were. The representatives acted primarily on behalf of 'Coordinamento' but also claimed to be acting on their own behalf.[475] The HRC held that,

According to Article 1 of the Optional Protocol, only individuals have the right to submit a communication. To the extent, therefore, that the communication originates from the 'Coordinamento', it has to be declared inadmissible because of lack of personal standing.[476]

In as far, however, as the communication was submitted on their own behalf by the representatives of the different associations forming the 'Coordinamento', those representatives did have personal standing under article 1 OP. The communication was, however, declared inadmissible on other grounds which are examined below.[477]

4.69 Similarly, in *J.R.T. and W.G. Party* v. *Canada*[478] the HRC held the communication inadmissible in so far as it concerned the W.G. Party (an unincorporated political party under the leadership of J.R.T.) because the W.G. Party was an association and not an individual.[479] As an individual J.R.T. had standing to submit the communication. The communication was declared inadmissible on other grounds.[480]

The OP's limitation of *locus standi* to individuals obliges organizations to hide behind the name of a person who does have the standing to submit a communication even when the alleged violations concern restrictions on the rights of groups or associations, for example, on the rights of assembly and association (articles 21 and 22 of the ICCPR).[481] The individual, or individuals, will also have to satisfy the OP's other requirements, for example, that he or they be 'victims' (article 1 OP). That requirement is dealt with below.[482]

4.70 The basic rule then under the OP is that a communication may only be submitted by one or more individuals. The HRC has stated its view that this does not mean that the individual must necessarily sign the communication himself.[483] We have already noted that during the drafting of its Rules the HRC recognized that provisions would have to be made for situations in which the alleged victim was unable to act.[484] The Rules provide then that,

Normally, the communication may be submitted by the individual himself or by his representative; the Committee may, however, accept to consider a communication submitted on behalf of an alleged victim when it appears that he is unable to submit the communication himself.[485]

Communications from duly authorized representatives have been accepted on a number of occasions but in practice the HRC has had to exercise its discretion under the above rule in a considerable number of cases. The person submitting the communication is identified in the HRC's jurisprudence as the 'author'.[486] The HRC regards a close family connection as sufficient to justify an author acting on behalf of an alleged victim.[487] Communications have been accepted on this basis, for example, from the alleged victims' father,[488] husband,[489] wife,[490] brother,[491] son-in-law,[492] niece,[493] daughter,[494] brother-in-law.[495] Generally, the HRC appears to have taken a fairly liberal approach as regards close family members. For example, in *Lanza and Perdoma* v. *Uruguay*[496] N submitted the communication on behalf of her aunt (L) and her uncle (P) concerning their detention and the conditions in which they were held. The HRC requested detailed information from N on the grounds and circumstances justifying her acting on behalf of L and P. N explained that the alleged victims were unable to act on their own behalf and that she was acting on their behalf as a close relative, believing, on the basis of her personal acquaintance with them that the alleged victims would agree to lodging a complaint.[497] The HRC decided that N was justified by reason of close family connection in acting on behalf of L and P.[498] If during the consideration of a communication by the HRC it becomes possible for the alleged victim to communicate with the HRC, for example, because they have been released, they are asked by the HRC whether they wish consideration of the communication to continue.

4.71 According to the HRC a communication submitted by a third party can only be considered if the author justifies his authority to submit the communication.[499] The onus of proof is on the author to establish that there is a sufficient link with the alleged victim or that he has justification to act.[500] As indicated above, in the case of close family members this burden may not be too difficult to discharge.[501] Generally though, to justify their acting on behalf of alleged victims who are not signatories, the authors must provide their reasons for believing that the alleged victims would approve of the authors' acting on their behalf and the authors' reasons for believing that they are unable to act on their own behalf.[502] For example, in *Massioti and Baritussio v. Uruguay*[503] M originally submitted the communication on behalf of herself and B. They had both been detained in the same prison. M submitted to the HRC that she had been informed by B's former defence counsel that B approved of M acting for her.[504] M claimed that B was not able to act on her own since that was impossible for someone detained under the 'prompt securities measures regime'.[505] She further claimed that B had no defence counsel at the time of the submission of the communication.[506] The HRC decided that M was acting on B's behalf.[507] It might be suggested that the HRC could have checked with B's former defence counsel that B did in fact approve of M acting for her. Presumably also the State party could have objected to the consideration of the communication on this point or have produced evidence to show that B could have acted on her own behalf. In fact the State party raised neither of these issues.

4.72 However, a number of communications have been declared inadmissible for failure to satisfy this onus of proof. In *Mbenge v. Zaire*[508] the HRC decided that M could act for his brothers and father-in-law but not for an unrelated pharmacist or the family driver because he had not established any grounds justifying his authority to act on their behalf.[509] In *L.A. on behalf of U.R.* v. *Uruguay*[510] L.A. submitted the communication on behalf of U.R., a medical student detained in Libertad prison in Uruguay. L.A. informed the HRC that as a member of the Swedish branch of Amnesty International he had been working on the case of U.R. for almost two years with no success. L.A. claimed to have authority to act because he believed, 'that every prisoner unjustly treated would appreciate further investigation of his case by the Human Rights Committee'.[511] The HRC decided that on the basis of this information it could not accept that the author had any authority to submit the communication on behalf of the alleged victim.[512]

4.73 In *S.G.F.* v. *Uruguay*[513] the communication was submitted by X (a non-governmental organization). X submitted that the request for it to act on behalf of S.G.F., a Uruguayan national living in Sweden, was made through close friends living in France whose identity it felt unable to disclose.[514] The HRC specifically pointed out that, 'No written evidence with regard to the authority of the organization (X) to act on behalf of the alleged victim has been provided'.[515] The HRC held that it could not accept, on the basis of the information before it; that X had the necessary authority to submit the communication on behalf of S.G.F.[516] In *J.F.* v. *Uruguay*[517] a parallel communication was received from X concerning J.F., the husband of S.G.F. J.F. was a Uruguayan national detained at Libertad prison in Uruguay. X claimed that the communication was submitted at the request of S.G.F. and that this request had been made through close friends whose names it felt unable to reveal.[518] Again the HRC pointed out that there was no written evidence with regard to the authority of X to act at the request of S.G.F. on behalf of J.F.[519] Accordingly, the communication was held inadmissible because the HRC could not accept that the author (X) had the necessary authority to act.[520]

4.74 These two decisions clearly indicate that if there were appropriate evidence of authority to act the non-governmental organization could have acted on behalf of the alleged victims. In this way non-governmental organizations can play an important, though limited, role under the OP procedure.[521] The greater resources and experience of non-governmental organizations could assist communicants who might otherwise find it immensely difficult to utilize the OP machinery effectively.

4.74.1 Finally, we can note that the HRC has expressed important views on who may bring a claim of a violation of article 1 of the Covenant (self-determination).[522]

(iii) The requirement that the individual has been a victim[523]

4.75 Under article 1 OP the 'individuals' submitting the communication or on whose behalf the communication is submitted must claim to be 'victims' of a violation by a State party. The HRC's most important pronouncement on the concept of a victim came in the case of *Shirin Aumeeruddy-Cziffra and Nineteen Other Mauritian Women* v. *Mauritius*[524] (hereinafter the *Mauritian Women Case*). The women claimed that the enactment of two legislative acts on immigration and deportation 'constituted discrimination based on sex against Mauritian women, violated the right to found a family and home, and removed the protection of the courts of law, in breach of articles 2, 3, 4, 17, 23, 25, and 26 of the ICCPR.[525] They claimed that,

Prior to the enactment of the laws in question, alien men and women married to Mauritian nationals enjoyed the same residence status, that is to say, by virtue of their marriage, foreign spouses of both sexes had the right, protected by law, to reside in the country with their Mauritian husbands or wives. The authors contend that, under the new laws, alien husbands of Mauritian women lost their residence status in Mauritius and must now apply for a 'residence permit' which may be refused or removed at any time by the Minister of Interior. The new laws, however, do not affect the status of alien women married to Mauritian husbands who retain their legal right to residence in the country. The authors further contend that under the new laws alien husbands of Mauritian women may be deported under a ministerial order which is not subject to judicial review.[526]

When the communication was submitted to the HRC seventeen of the co-authors were unmarried and three of the co-authors were married to foreign husbands.[527]

The State party argued, *inter alia*, that the authors of the communication did not allege that any particular individual had in fact been the victim of any specific act in breach of the provisions of the ICCPR.[528] The State party further argued that the communication was aimed at obtaining a declaration by the HRC that the two legislative acts complained of were capable of being administered in a discriminatory manner in violation of various provisions of the ICCPR.[529]

Before giving its views the HRC indicated the considerations upon which it based those views. The HRC stated that,

A person can only claim to be a victim in the sense of article 1 of the Optional Protocol if he or she is actually affected. It is a matter of degree how concretely this requirement is taken. However, no individual can in the abstract, by way of an *actio popularis*, challenge a law or practice claimed to be contrary to the Covenant. If the law or practice has not been concretely applied to the detriment of the individual, it must in any event be applicable in such a way that the alleged victim's risk is more than a theoretical possibility.[530]

Applying this approach the HRC sought to distinguish between the two groups of co-authors. The HRC noted that in the case of the seventeen unmarried co-authors there is,

No question of actual interference with, or failure to ensure equal protection by the law to any family. Furthermore there is no evidence that any of them is actually facing a personal risk of being thus affected in the enjoyment of this or any other rights set forth in the Covenant by the laws complained against. In particular it cannot be said that their right to marry under article 23(2) or the right to equality of spouses under article 23(4) are affected by such laws.[531]

Accordingly, the seventeen unmarried co-authors could not claim to be 'victims' of any breach of the rights under the ICCPR.[532]

As for the three married co-authors there is,

No doubt that they are actually affected by these laws, even in the absence of any individual measures of implementation (for instance, by way of a denial of residence, or an order of deportation, concerning one of the husbands). Their claim to be 'victims' within the meaning of the Optional Protocol has to be examined.[533]

The reasons given by the HRC as to why the three married co-authors were 'actually affected by these laws' included the precarious and uncertain residence situation of their foreign husbands, the years of delay with respect to one of the co-authors in the consideration of an application for a residence permit upon which also the granting of a work permit was dependent, and the possibility of deportation without judicial review at any time'.[534] The HRC then proceeded to examine the substance of their claims.[535]

4.76 The HRC's statement on the concept of a victim in the *Mauritian Women Case* clearly indicated its general approach while leaving it sufficient flexibility to assess whether the victim requirement has been satisfied on a case-to-case basis. In a number of subsequent cases the HRC has had the opportunity to shed further light on the concept of the victim. In *Hertzberg v. Finland*,[536] H, a lawyer, asserted in a radio interview that there was job discrimination in Finland on the ground of sexual orientation, and more particularly, to the detriment of homosexuals. Criminal charges were brought against the editor of the programme under the Finnish Penal Code. The editor was acquitted but H claimed that through these penal proceedings his right to seek, receive, and impart information under article 19 of the ICCPR was curtailed.[537]

The HRC concluded that H could not validly claim to be a victim on the grounds that the programme was actually broadcast, no sanctions were imposed against him, and H had not claimed that the programme restrictions applied would in any way personally affect him. The HRC added that, 'The sole fact that the author takes a personal interest in the dissemination of information about homosexuality does not make him a victim in the sense required by the Optional Protocol'.[538]

The HRC preceded its decision on H's claim to be a victim with a reference back to its decision in the *Mauritian Women Case*.[539] The HRC stressed that it had,

Only been entrusted with the mandate of examining whether an individual has suffered an actual violation of his rights. It cannot review in the abstract whether national legislation contravenes the Covenant, although such legislation may, in particular circumstances, produce adverse effects which directly affect the individual, making him thus a victim in the sense contemplated by articles 1 and 2 of the Optional Protocol.[540]

4.77 With respect to H's co-authors the HRC held that they did satisfy the victim requirement on the basis that their programmes had actually been censored by the Finnish Broadcasting Company.[541] It is interesting to note where the HRC drew the line in this case concerning the requirement of the individual claiming to be a victim. The provisions in the Finnish Penal Code had not been directly applied to any of the alleged authors. As Mr Opsahl pointed out in an individual opinion in the case, 'The question remains whether they have been more indirectly affected by it in a way which can be said to interfere with their freedom of expression'.[542] H's co-authors satisfied the victim requirement because their programmes had actually been censored. H did not because the programme with which he was involved had actually been broadcast and no sanctions had been imposed on him. It is important that the HRC noted that H had not claimed that the programme restrictions applied would in any way personally affect him. If H had so claimed, for example, on the basis that he was a journalist rather than a lawyer, he might then have satisfied the victim requirement on the bases of continuing interference with his right to freedom of expression, that prosecutions had taken place and thus inevitably the threat of prosecution would hang over his work in that field, and that he would be faced with the options of refraining from that area of work or becoming liable to criminal prosecution. In analogous circumstances the EUCT found the victim requirement satisfied in the case of *Dudgeon*.[543]

4.78 In *Group of Associations for the Disabled* v. *Italy*[544] the HRC gave some indication that the concept of the victim extended beyond persons actually and directly affected. The HRC stated that,

It is not the task of the Human Rights Committee, acting under the Optional Protocol, to review *in abstracto* national legislation as to its compliance with obligations imposed by the Covenant. It is true that in some circumstances, a domestic law may by its mere existence directly violate the rights of individuals under the Covenant.[545]

The communication was declared inadmissible because the authors had not demonstrated that they themselves were 'actually and personally affected' by the law concerned.[546] The obvious question is in what circumstances could a domestic law violate the Covenant by its very existence. The HRC may simply be referring to situations like that in the *Mauritian Women Case* where some actual effects of the laws concerned could be discerned even in the absence of actual implementation. The *Klass Case*[547] under the ECHR, concerning secret surveillance techniques, might suggest another situation where the HRC might find the victim requirement satisfied even in the absence of evidence of actual implementation.

4.79 To date, however, the HRC has stressed the need for the alleged victim to have been actually and personally affected. In *A.R.S.* v. *Canada*[548] the HRC referred to the requirement of an 'actual grievance'. The HRC stated that,

The mandatory supervision system is therefore not yet applicable to him. The possibility of the remission he has earned being cancelled after his release is still more hypothetical. In the present situation, therefore, he has no actual grievance such as is required for the admissibility of a communication by an individual under articles 1 and 2 of the Optional Protocol.[549]

The alleged violations must relate to specific individuals at a specific time. So in *J.H.* v. *Canada*[550] the HRC stated that,

An allegation to the effect that past or present promotion policies are generally to the detriment of English-speaking members of the Canadian Armed Forces is not sufficient in this respect.[551]

And in *Lovelace* v. *Canada*[552] the HRC stated that:

In the case of a particular individual claiming to be a victim of a violation, it cannot express a view on the law in the abstract, without regard to the date on which the law was applied to the alleged victim.[553]

4.80 The HRC has made it clear that the onus of proving in a substantiated manner that an individual has been a victim lies with the author.[554] The HRC will not engage in hypothetical or speculative assessments of potential violations. A person will not be a victim if he has in fact substantially obtained the benefit claimed. Two communications against Canada are instructive in this regard. Both of them raised very complex issues concerning the interpretation and application of article 15(1) of the ICCPR in relation to the effects of the Canadian Criminal Law Amendment Act 1977.[555] That Act removed the automatic forfeiture of parole for offences committed while on parole. The two authors claimed that by not making the Act retrospective Canada had contravened the last sentence of article 15 of the ICCPR.

In the first of these communications, *Van Duzen* v. *Canada*,[556] the HRC expressed the view that,

... regard must be had to the fact that the author has subsequently been released, and that this happened even before the date when he claims he should be free. Whether or not this claim should be regarded as justified under the Covenant, the Committee considers that, although his release is subject to some conditions, for practical purposes and without prejudice to the correct interpretation of article 15(1), he has in fact obtained the benefit he has claimed. It is true that he has maintained his complaint and that his status upon release is not identical in law to the one he has claimed. However, in the view of the Committee, since the potential risk of re-imprisonment depends upon his own behaviour, this risk cannot, in the circumstances, represent any actual violation of the right invoked by him.[557]

Accordingly, the HRC expressed the view that the case did not disclose a violation of the Covenant. As the HRC commented in the second case, *McIsaac* v. *Canada*,[558] *Van Duzen* had failed to '... clearly establish that his position in the end was substantially affected by the applicability or non-applicability of the new provision, and that therefore there was no violation of the Covenant'.[559] A similar result obtained in the *McIsaac Case* itself. There the HRC, in the absence of precise submissions from the author, attempted to examine in what way, if any, the alleged victim was affected by the situation of which he was in substance complaining. The HRC concluded that,

Mr. McIsaac has not established the hypothesis that if parole had not been forfeited, the judge would have imposed the same sentence of fourteen months and that he would therefore have been released prior to May of 1979. The HRC is not in a position to know, nor is it called upon to speculate, how the fact that his earlier parole was forfeited may have influenced the penalty meted out for the offence committed while on parole. *The burden of proving that in 1977 he has been denied an advantage under the new law and that he is therefore a 'victim' lies with the author.* It is not the Committee's function to make a hypothetical assessment of what would have happened if the new Act had been applicable to him.[560]

4.81 The HRC's jurisprudence with respect to the concept of the victim has now been examined. In summary, the HRC have stressed the requirement of the individual being 'actually and personally affected', or suffering an 'actual grievance'. While the review of the compatibility of legislation with the ICCPR *in abstracto* has been ruled out it is a 'matter of degree' how concretely the requirement of being personally affected is taken. There is clearly some degree of flexibility open to the HRC as it has recognized that there may be circumstances when the mere existence of a domestic law may violate the ICCPR. Again this is an area of the HRC's work where the experience with respect to the ECHR may be instructive.

4.81.1 Finally we can note that the HRC has issued important views concerning article 1 (self-determination) which are relevant in this context.[561]

(d) *ratione loci*[562]

4.82 A communication can only be submitted by 'individuals subject to [the] jurisdiction' of the State party (article 1 OP). Uruguay has argued in a series of cases that once an individual had left Uruguay he was 'outside the jurisdiction of the Uruguayan State'. Therefore, 'To consider the communication further would be incompatible with the purpose for which the Covenant and its Protocol were established, namely to ensure the effective protection of human rights and to bring to an end any situation in which these rights were being violated. The State party concluded that in this case no *de facto* situation existed to warrant findings by the Committee and that consequently, by intervening, the Committee would not only be exceeding its competence but would also be departing from normally established legal procedures'.[563]

The HRC has rejected the contentions of Uruguay on the ground that in each case the victims were under the jurisdiction of Uruguay while the alleged violations took place,

The Committee recalled that by virtue of article 2(1) of the Covenant, each State party undertakes to respect and to ensure to 'all individuals within its territory and subject to its jurisdiction' the rights recognized in the Covenant. Article 1 of the Optional Protocol was clearly intended to apply to individuals subject to the jurisdiction of the State party concerned at the time of the alleged violation of the Covenant, irrespective of their nationality. This was manifestly the object and purpose of article 1.[564]

The argument advanced by Uruguay accorded with that of Professor Schwelb[565] and noted by others.[566] Professor Schwelb has argued that the words 'within its territory' in article 2(1) of the ICCPR amount to a 'limitation of the substantive scope of the Covenant'.[567] Therefore, 'The conclusion seems inescapable that the scope of the procedural protection afforded by the Protocol cannot be wider than that of the substantive protection of the Covenant'.[568] Mose and Opsahl argue in response that the result of Professor Schwelb's view is not always convincing,

As an illustration, if a citizen's publications are seized or his passport annulled while he is abroad, he ought to be able to submit a communication invoking his freedom of expression or movement under the Covenant; and the travaux préparatoires to the Covenant suggest that the drafters in adopting the clause 'within its territory' did not have such cases in mind.[569]

The approach of the HRC as noted above[570] and below[571] has been clearly to reject the argument that once an individual has left the territory he had left the jurisdiction and therefore could not submit a communication. It is submitted that the HRC's approach is correct. It represents the most sensible interpretation from a human rights perspective and corresponds with the approach taken to the ECHR.[572]

4.82.1 It would, however, be premature to assume that the HRC have rejected altogether the view that the OP must be interpreted subject to the territorial limitation in article 2(1) of the ICCPR. The point can be illustrated by reference to the HRC's views in the case of *E. Quinteros and M. C. Almeida De Quinteros* v. *Uruguay*.[573] A.Q. alleged that her daughter, E.Q., had been arrested by military personnel and systematically tortured. A.Q. also claimed that she was a victim of violations of article 7 (psychological torture because she did not know where her daughter was) and of article 17 because of interference with her private and family life.[574] A.Q. was a Uruguayan national who was living in Sweden at the time she submitted the communication. The HRC specifically noted that the communication raised the matter of whether A.Q. was 'subject to the jurisdiction' at the time of the alleged violations.[575] The State party made no submissions on the point. In its final views the HRC noted that the statement of A.Q. that she was living in Uruguay at the time of the incident regarding her daughter was not contradicted by the State party. The HRC expressed the view that A.Q. had been a victim. It must therefore have accepted that she was within the jurisdiction.[576]

On the facts this decision follows those in the cases noted above.[577] It is interesting to consider, however, what approach the HRC would have taken if A.Q. had been temporarily resident outside Uruguay at the relevant time. It is submitted that the result should be the same, since the violations would be the same and it is hoped that the HRC would take this approach.

4.83 More difficult might be the situation where the alleged victim lived permanently abroad, for example, if in the alleged example given A.Q. had been permanently resident in Sweden at the time of the alleged violations. Here the HRC might be more willing to accept the argument of Professor

Schwelb concerning territorial limitation. In most cases there would be no problem because the alleged victim would not normally be subject to the State's jurisdiction at the time of the alleged violations in any event.

This situation of an alleged victim who is resident permanently or semi-permanently abroad has been considered by the HRC in a series of cases concerning the issuance of passports.[578] In *Lichtensztejn* v. *Uruguay*,[579] L, a Uruguayan citizen resident in Mexico since 1974 was refused issuance of a new passport when his passport expired on 23 October 1978. Uruguay argued that L failed to fulfil the minimum requirement of being 'subject to its [the State party's] jurisdiction', because he was outside the jurisdiction of the Uruguayan State when his petition was submitted. 'It is therefore inadmissible that the Committee should deal with communications of this kind, which run counter to its terms of reference and violate provisions of international instruments'.[580]

The HRC rejected Uruguay's argument that it was not competent under article 1 OP to consider the communication,

The issue of a passport is clearly within the jurisdiction of the Uruguayan authorities and he is 'subject to the jurisdiction' of Uruguay for that purpose. Moreover, a passport is a means of enabling him 'to leave any country, including his own', as required by article 12(2) of the Covenant. Consequently, the Committee found that it followed from the very nature of that right that, in the case of a citizen resident abroad, article 12(2) imposed obligations both on the State of residence and on the State of nationality and that, therefore, article 2(1) could not be interpreted as limiting the obligations of Uruguay under article 12(2) to citizens within its own territory.[581]

The difficult question which this decision raises is just which of the articles in the ICCPR are not of such a 'nature' that the HRC could interpret them as subject to the territorial limitation in article 2(1) of the ICCPR.[582] The examples drawn from the *Quinteros Case*[583] above might suggest that article 7 of the ICCPR (prohibition of torture and of inhuman or degrading treatment or punishment) should be subject to the territorial limitation in certain cases. On that basis A.Q. could not have claimed to be a victim if she had been permanently resident abroad. More directly, in *Lopez Burgos* v. *Uruguay*[584] the HRC had to consider its competence under article 1 OP to express its views on communications alleging violations of the Covenant by government agents but carried out in a foreign territory.[585]

4.84 In *Lopez Burgos* the author alleged that on 13 July 1976 her husband, L.B., was kidnapped in Buenos Aires, Argentina, by members of the 'Uruguayan security and intelligence forces', who were aided by Argentinian para-military groups, and secretly detained in Buenos Aires for two weeks. L.B. was then illegally and clandestinely transported to Uruguay. He was then officially arrested on 23 October 1976 and the Press was informed that, 'subversives have been surprised while conspiring'. He was detained incommunicado by the special security forces at a secret prison for three months. During approximately four months of detention in Argentina and Uruguay he was continuously subjected to physical and mental torture.[586]

In response to requests from the HRC the State party claimed that it had no information as to L.B.'s whereabouts between July and October 1976.[587] In its final views the HRC observed that,

> although the arrest and initial detention and mistreatment of Lopez Burgos allegedly took place on foreign territory, the Committee is not barred either by virtue of article 1 of the Optional Protocol ('... individuals subject to its jurisdiction' ...) or by virtue of article 2(1) of the Covenant ('... individuals within its territory and subject to its jurisdiction' ...) from considering these allegations, together with the claim of subsequent abduction into Uruguayan territory, inasmuch as these were acts perpetrated by Uruguayan agents on foreign soil.
>
> The reference in article 1 of the Optional Protocol to 'individuals subject to its jurisdiction' does not affect the above conclusion because the reference in that article is not to the place where the violation occurred, but rather to the relationship between the individual and the State in relation to a violation of any of the rights set forth in the Covenant, wherever they occurred.
>
> Article 2(1) of the Covenant places an obligation upon a State party to respect and to ensure rights 'to all individuals within its territory and subject to its jurisdiction', but it does not imply that the State party concerned cannot be held accountable for violations of rights under the Covenant which its agents commit upon the territory of another State, whether with the acquiescence of the Government of the State or in opposition to it. According to article 5(1) of the Covenant,
>
> > 'Nothing in the present Covenant may be interpreted as implying for any State, group or person any right to engage in any activity or perform any act aimed at the destruction of any of the rights and freedoms recognized herein or at their limitation to a greater extent than is provided for in the present Covenant'.
>
> In line with this, it would be unconscionable to so interpret the responsibility under article 2 of the Covenant as to permit a State party to perpetrate violations of the Covenant on the territory of another State, which violations it could not perpetrate on its own territory.[588]

The interpretation of article 1 OP as referring 'not to the place where the violation occurred, but rather to the relationship between the individual and **the State in relation to a violation of any of the rights set forth in the Covenant, wherever they occurred', and the view that article 2 does not** exclude accountability for violations by agents committed upon the foreign territory of another State, lend further weight to the argument against the incorporation of the territorial limitation of article 2(1) of the Covenant into article 1 OP.[589] More generally, an approach to jurisdiction based on the individual–State relationship significantly extends the ambit of the protection offered by the OP.

4.85 One member of the HRC, Professor Tomuschat, thought that the views of the HRC needed to be clarified and expanded and so appended an individual opinion.[590] He argued that the statement in the HRC's views that article 2(1) of the ICCPR does not imply that a State party cannot be held accountable for violations of the Covenant which its agents commit upon the territory of another State 'was too broadly framed and might therefore give rise to misleading conclusions'.[591] He argued, moreover, that,

In principle the scope of application of the Covenant is not susceptible to being extended by reference to article 5, a provision designed to cover instances where formally rules under the Covenant seem to legitimize actions which substantially run counter to its purposes and general spirit.[592]

On this point it is submitted that Professor Tomuschat is correct. However, it is worth noting that the HRC made reference to article 5(1) only to support an interpretation it would have adopted in any event. It does not constitute the basis of that interpretation.

4.86 Professor Tomuschat continued with his view of the proper interpretation of article 2(1) of the ICCPR:

To construe the words 'within its territory' pursuant to their strict literal meaning as excluding any responsibility for conduct occurring beyond the national boundaries would, however, lead to utterly absurd results. The formula was intended to take care of objective difficulties which might impede the implementation of the Covenant in specific situations. Thus, a State party is normally unable to ensure the effective enjoyment of the rights under the Covenant to its citizens abroad, having at its disposal only the tools of diplomatic protection with their limited potential. Instances of occupation of foreign territory offer another example of situations which the drafters of the Covenant had in mind when they confined the obligation of States parties to their own territory. All these factual patterns have in common, however, that they provide plausible grounds for denying the protection of the Covenant. It may be concluded, therefore, that it was the intention of the drafters, whose sovereign decision cannot be challenged, to restrict the territorial scope of the Covenant in view of such situations where enforcing the Covenant would be likely to encounter exceptional obstacles. Never was it envisaged, however, to grant States parties unfettered discretionary power to carry out wilful and deliberate attacks against the freedom and personal integrity against [sic] their citizens living abroad. Consequently, despite the wording of article 2(1), the events which took place outside Uruguay come within the purview of the Covenant.[593]

Here Professor Tomuschat's analysis is less convincing. The problem raised is not so much when protection should be denied as when there should be responsibility for violations. The 'tools of diplomatic protection' do limit the protection the national State can offer when a citizen is abroad but that does not bear on the question where the national State is itself the alleged violator. Similarly, with respect to the example of occupation of foreign territory, there is persuasive authority under the ECHR for holding a State responsible in such a situation for securing the rights in the ECHR 'to all persons under their actual authority and responsibility, whether that authority is exercised within their own territory or abroad'.[594]

4. The same matter is not being examined under another procedure of international investigation or settlement (art. 5(2)(*a*) OP)[595]

4.87 Under article 5(2)(*a*) OP the HRC is precluded from considering a communication only if the same matter *is* simultaneously being examined under another procedure of international investigation or settlement.[596] This is a notable departure from comparable international petitions procedures which preclude consideration of matters that have already been dealt with by other international procedures.[597] Obviously article 5(2)(*a*) will increase in importance as the number of States parties to the ICCPR and OP increases and the number of international procedures of investigation and settlement in operation expands. A number of the HRC decisions have given some content to the prohibition in article 5(2)(*a*) OP.

4.88 On a number of occasions the HRC has had to consider the situation of communications submitted to another procedure of international investigation or settlement by a third party. In *Antonaccio* v. *Uruguay*[598] the HRC took the view that it was not precluded from consideration of the communication as the third party had, at the author's request, asked the IACM to discontinue consideration of the case.[599] A similar approach was taken in *Altesor* v. *Uruguay*[600] even though the authors had made repeated efforts to conceal the fact that they were also the authors of the complaint to the IACM. When they withdrew their complaint to the IACM the HRC proceeded with its consideration.[601] In *Altesor* v. *Uruguay*,[602] in addition to the authors, an unrelated third party had also submitted a new complaint to the IACM. On this point the HRC concluded that, 'It was not prevented from considering the communication submitted to it by the authors . . . by reason of the subsequent complaint made by an unrelated third party under the procedures of the [IACM]'.[603]

This view was further explained in *Estrella* v. *Uruguay*.[604] There the HRC observed that the article 5(2)(*a*) OP could not be so

interpreted as to imply that an unrelated third party, acting without the knowledge and consent of the alleged victim, can preclude the latter from having access to the HRC. It therefore concluded that it was not prevented from considering the communication submitted to it by the alleged victim himself, by reason of a submission by an unrelated third party to the IACM. Such a submission did not constitute 'the same matter', within the meaning of article 5(2)(a) of the Optional Protocol.[605]

In *Cmn. No. 75/1980*[606] the HRC further explained that

the concept of the 'same matter' within the meaning of article 5(2)(a) of the Optional Protocol must be understood as including the same claim concerning the same individual, submitted by him or someone else who has standing to act on his behalf before the other international body.[607]

Similarly in *V.O.* v. *Norway*[608] the HRC stated that in its view the phrase 'the same matter' refers, 'with regard to identical parties, to the complaints advanced and facts adduced in support of them'.[609]

4.89 In *Sequeira* v. *Uruguay*[610] the HRC decided that a communication submitted to the IACM before the date of the entry into force of the ICCPR and the OP could not relate to events alleged to have taken place after that date.[611] Although the HRC did not explain the decision in these terms it seems reasonable to interpret its decision as stating that the complaints to the IACM were not the 'same matter' within the meaning of article 5(2)(*a*) OP as the complaints submitted to the HRC. Also in *Sequeira* the HRC decided that a two-line reference to the person concerned in a case before the Inter-American Commission on Human Rights, which listed in a similar manner the names of hundreds of other persons allegedly detained in the State party, 'did not constitute the same matter as that described in detail by the author in his communication to the HRC'.[612]

4.90 In three cases concerning the Netherlands published on the same date the HRC observed that the examination of State reports, submitted under article 16 of the ICESCR, does not, within the meaning of article 5(2)(*a*) OP, constitute an examination of the 'same matter' as a claim by an individual submitted to the HRC under the OP.[613]

4.91 The prohibition in article 5(2)(*a*) OP only covers 'procedures of international investigation or settlement'. HRC decisions have helped to clarify the kind of procedures covered. Of particular importance was the HRC's approach to the examination of a particular human rights situation in a given country under *Economic and Social Council Resolution 1503 (XLVIII)* which governs the procedures for the examination (by HRCion and Sub-Cion) of communications which appear to reveal 'a consistent pattern of gross and reliably attested violations of human rights and fundamental freedoms'.[614] The HRC determined that the Resolution 1503 procedure does not constitute a procedure of international investigation or settlement within the meaning of article 5(2)(*a*) OP because it is concerned with the examination of situations which appear to reveal a consistent pattern of gross violations of human rights and a situation is not 'the same matter' as an individual complaint.[615] The HRC stated that, 'The Protocol was not intended to deal with situations as such, but with individual complaints'.[616] Therefore, the Resolution 1503 procedure does not bar the HRC from consideration of an individual communication. The HRC's decision strengthens the case of those who argue that there are good legal grounds for the co-existence of the Resolution 1503 procedure and the OP.[617]

In an early decision the HRC decided that a procedure established by a non-governmental organization, such as the Inter-Parliamentary Council of the Inter-Parliamentary Union, does not constitute a procedure of international investigation or settlement within the meaning of article 5(2)(*a*) OP.[618] This decision was based on the HRC's determination that article 5(2)(*a*) OP can only relate to procedures implemented by inter-State or intergovernmental organizations on the basis of inter-State agreements or arrangements.[619] Subsequently the HRC explicitly stated that procedures established by non-governmental organizations such as Amnesty International, the International Commission of Jurists, or the International Committee of the Red Cross, irrespective of the latter's standing in international law, do not constitute procedures of international investigation or settlement within the meaning of article 5(2)(*a*) OP.[620]

In 1984 the HRC declared admissible a number of similar and related cases concerning the same country. The HRC observed that,

a study by an intergovernmental organization either of the human rights situation in a given country (such as that by the IACHR)[621] or a study of the trade union rights situation in a given country (such as the issues examined by the Committee on Freedom of Association of the ILO), or of a human rights problem of a more global character (such as that of the Special Rapporteur of the Commission on Human Rights on summary or arbitrary executions), although such studies might refer to or draw on information concerning individuals cannot be seen as being the same matter as the examination of individual cases within the meaning of article 5(2)(a) of the Optional Protocol.[622]

4.92 It may be open to States that are parties to various international procedures of investigation or settlement to determine which of those procedures to preclude consideration of a case by the HRC by making a reservation to article 5(2)(*a*) OP. This has been done by twelve of the fourteen contacting parties to the ECHR that have also ratified the OP.[623] Those reservations have been to the effect that the HRC shall not have competence if the same matter *has been* examined under another procedure of international investigation or settlement.[624] The validity and application of these reservations have been raised in communications before the HRC.

4.93 In *A.M.* v. *Denmark*[625] A.M. alleged violations of the Universal Declaration of Human Rights which the HRC said corresponded in substance to articles 7, 14, and 26 of the ICCPR.[626] A.M. had submitted the same matter to the EUCM. That application had been declared inadmissible as manifestly ill-founded under article 27(2) of the ECHR.[627] The HRC decided that in the light of Denmark's reservation to article 5(2)(*a*) OP the communication was inadmissible because the same matter had already been considered by the EUCM and therefore the HRC was not competent to consider it.[628]

4.94 One member of the HRC, Mr Graefrath, appended an individual opinion to the HRC's decision.[629] He argued that the reservation did not refer to matters the consideration of which had been denied under any other procedure by a decision of inadmissibility. An application which had been declared inadmissible had not, in the meaning of the reservation, been 'considered' in such a way that the HRC was precluded from considering it. His argument continued by noting that the conditions of admissibility and the substance of the rights in other instruments were different from those in the OP so that although a communication under the OP might lead to a similar result as under, for example, the ECHR, this was not necessarily so.

Mr Graefrath's view was based on his opinion that,

The reservation aims at preventing the HRC from reviewing cases that have been considered by another international organ of investigation. It does not seek to limit the competence of the HRC to deal with communications merely on the ground that the rights of the Covenant allegedly violated may also be covered by the European Convention and its procedural requirements. If that had been the aim of the reservation, it would, in my opinion, have been incompatible with the Optional Protocol.[630]

On the facts of the case it appears that the difference of opinion between the HRC's view and Mr Graefrath's turns on the question of whether the EUCM had 'considered' the application by A.M. It is submitted that the reservations should be interpreted as precluding consideration by the HRC only when the matter has been subject to substantive consideration under another procedure of international investigation or settlement. That consideration may have taken place at either the admissibility or merits stage. Though this submission seems clear it may in practice call for a degree of sophisticated analysis by the HRC.[631]

4.95 The HRC's approach to such reservations can be illustrated by reference to two other communications. In *V.O.* v. *Norway*[632] Norway argued that the communication was inadmissible because the inadmissibility decision of the EUCM on the basis of the application being manifestly ill-founded had involved an examination of the substance of the application.[633] The author of the application had argued, *inter alia*, that the provisions of the ICCPR differed in several respects from those of the ECHR.[634] The HRC declared the communication inadmissible because the same matter had been examined by the EUCM.[635] In *O.F.* v. *Norway*[636] the author had been informed by the EUCM that he was too late to submit an application.[637] The State party, however, informed the HRC that it would not object to the admissibility of the communication on the basis of its reservation because the case had not been examined by the EUCM.[638] It is submitted that on the basis of the argument above the HRC could have taken the view that it was competent to consider the matter notwithstanding the reservation because the matter had not received any substantive consideration by the EUCM.

4.96 Finally, on this matter, it is interesting to note Mr Graefrath's view that if the reservation had sought to limit the competence of the HRC in certain respects he considered that it would have been 'incompatible' with the OP[639] and thus presumably invalid.[640] In no decision to date has the HRC expressed the view that a reservation was incompatible with the OP although doubts have been expressed during the reporting procedure under article 40 concerning certain reservations.[641]

4.97 A difficult question of interpretation concerning article 5(2)(*a*) OP arose during the HRC's considerations of its draft Rules of procedure concerning the OP.[642] After the text of the rules on international remedies (art. 5(2)(*a*)) and domestic remedies (art. 5(2)(*b*)) the provision continues, 'This shall not be the rule where the application of the remedies is unreasonably prolonged'.

The question that arose was whether this provision applied to both article 5(2)(*a*) and (*b*), or only to (*b*). On the former interpretation it would be permissible for the HRC to declare admissible a communication being examined under another procedure of international investigation or settlement if it took the view that that procedure had been unreasonably prolonged. After some discussion the matter was referred for the expert opinion of United Nations Legal Counsel. That opinion, based mainly on the clarifications given by the sponsors of article 5(2) OP in the Third Committee,[643] was to the effect that the provision applied to both sub-paragraphs (*a*) and (*b*).[644] As we noted earlier, notwithstanding this clear opinion, many of the HRC members were reluctant to accept its implications in terms of the HRC having to pass judgment on other international bodies. They pointed to the difficulty of establishing the correct interpretation before specific cases had been examined and the need to allow the HRC a certain amount of discretion.[645] The Rule adopted by the HRC merely repeats the terms of article 5(2) without clarification.[646]

The reluctance of the HRC to pass judgment on another international body is understandable. However, the delays evident in international petition systems renders such a situation a distinct possibility. If faced with this problem the HRC should proceed with great circumspection and would clearly need to identify the source of the delay. It appears that no such situation has arisen to date.[647]

4.98 The decisions of the HRC noted above are very important. They have given clear indications of both the general and specific approach of the HRC to the considerations of other international procedures. Article 5(2)(*a*) OP could have been interpreted by the HRC in a way that would have greatly limited its competence. It could have taken the view that it was precluded from consideration of any matter that had been submitted to any other human rights institution or general investigation. It could similarly have taken a very expansive view of what constitutes 'the same matter' and which procedures qualify as 'procedures of international investigation or settlement'.

On the contrary, however, the general approach of the HRC has evinced a great reluctance to relinquish its competence. Restrictive interpretations have been applied to the expressions 'the same matter' and 'procedures of international investigation and settlement'.[648] The HRC has affirmed the principle of adjournment *pendente lite* at the expense of the principle *una via electa*.[649] This interpretation of the OP made it likely that at some stage the HRC would have to consider a communication which had already been the subject of substantive consideration by another international body and this happened in *Hendriks* v. *Netherlands* (pr. 4.44.1 above) where the issues had been previously considered by the EUCM. This eventuality raises acutely the difficulties concerning the co-existence of several procedures of international investigation or settlement. The reluctance of the HRC to follow the opinion of United Nations Legal Counsel when the application of the procedures of international investigation or settlement have been unduly prolonged bears testimony to the caution of the HRC concerning such co-existence and its desire to retain its flexibility while it gained further experience.

4.99 Certain aspects and problems of co-existence have been identified and analysed by commentators and suggestions have been made for their resolution.[650] No formal co-ordination procedures have been adopted by the HRC or other international institutions although procedures have been established for the exchange of information. It is very difficult to ascertain and provide solutions in the abstract for problems of co-existence. It would seem better not to establish any formal rules of procedure but to await the hopefully judicious resolution of particular difficulties as and when they arise. There is no reason to believe that the HRC cannot take a practical and flexible approach to each problem and accord to it the most appropriate solution.

Where States have made reservations aimed at preventing repeated consideration it has been submitted that these should be restrictively interpreted so as only to preclude reconsideration of the substantive determination of another international body.[651]

5. The individual has exhausted all available domestic remedies (articles 2 and 5(2)(*b*) OP)[652]

Introduction

4.100 The domestic remedies rule is an important feature of the international law concerning State responsibility for the treatment of aliens.[653] The rationale, purpose, and application of the rule were the subject of extensive debate during the drafting of both the ICCPR and the OP in relation to both inter-State and individual communications.[654] That debate has continued in the HRC.[655]

4.101 Before examining the HRC's practice some important matters must be noted. First, the OP does not expressly state that the domestic remedies rule shall be applied according to generally recognized rules of international law.[656] However, the HRC has stated that it, 'considers that this provision should be interpreted and applied in accordance with the generally accepted principles of international law with regard to the exhaustion of local remedies as applied in the field of human rights'.[657] It is therefore important to note that the most highly developed jurisprudence concerning domestic remedies is that under the ECHR, which does refer to public international law.[658] In one decision the HRC has expressly referred to the 'generally recognized rules of international law' concerning domestic remedies.[659]

Secondly, the OP does not contain any time limit within which a communication must be submitted after exhaustion of domestic remedies.[660] Such a time limit was debated during the drafting but was not adopted. The HRC also debated whether to include a time limit in its rules of procedure but no such rule was adopted.[661]

Thirdly, the experience under the ECHR suggests that the approach taken by the institution concerned to the question of domestic remedies can be of enormous importance in determining the impact of that institution.[662] The rule has already been the subject of a considerable body of jurisprudence in the HRC's views under the OP and a number of communications have been declared inadmissible on this ground. That jurisprudence will now be examined.

(a) The burden of proof as to exhaustion[663]

4.102 In a series of cases Uruguay argued that the authors had failed to exhaust domestic remedies and, moreover, that the burden of proof with regard to exhaustion was entirely upon the authors of the communication.[664] This argument was based on the submission that according to criminal law, dating back to the time of Roman law, the burden of proof 'in all cases' rested upon the plaintiff; for the party against which a charge was made, a reversal of the burden of proof would mean '*a probatio diabolica*'.[665] The HRC stated that it did not accept Uruguay's objection to admissibility, 'in the absence of specific information on local remedies available to the complainants in the particular circumstances of their cases'.[666] The general approach to the HRC has been that a communication would not be considered inadmissible for failure to exhaust domestic remedies unless the State party gave details of the particular remedies available in the circumstances of the case together with a reasonable prospect that such measures would be effective.[667] 'It is incumbent on the State party to prove the effectiveness of remedies the non-exhaustion of which it claims', and the availability of the alleged remedy must be 'reasonably evident'.[668]

It seems clear then that there is a burden on the State party to prove that local remedies are available and effective. However, there is also a burden on the author to show that he has exhausted any allegedly available remedies, that the alleged remedies are not effective or that there were special circumstances which absolved him from exhausting domestic remedies.

It is difficult to establish whether the initial burden is on the author to provide evidence that he has satisfied the domestic remedies rule or on the State party to prove that domestic remedies are available and effective. It is submitted that in principle the initial burden must rest with the author. However, the burden may not be very heavy.[669] If satisfied the onus of proof then moves to the State party. If the State party then provides evidence of available and effective remedies the onus may then return to the author to prove unavailability, ineffectiveness, or special circumstances.

(*b*) *The remedies to be exhausted*

4.103 The OP refers to the exhaustion of 'available' domestic remedies (arts. 2, 5 OP).[670] The HRC has clarified this requirement. First, the HRC has established that,

The Covenant provides that a remedy shall be granted whenever a violation of one of the rights guaranteed by it has occurred; consequently, it does not generally prescribe preventative protection, but confines itself to requiring effective redress *ex post facto*.[671]

It is important to understand the precise context of these words. On the facts of the case concerned the HRC expressed the view that, 'a subsequent judgement could nevertheless in principle have been an effective remedy in the meaning contemplated by article 2, paragraph 3, of the Covenant and article 5, paragraph 2(b), of the Optional Protocol'.[672] More generally, however, the undertaking in article 2(1) of the ICCPR to 'respect and ensure' the rights in the ICCPR may well prescribe some degree of 'preventative protection' for individuals.[673]

The HRC has expressed the view that, 'Exhaustion of domestic remedies can be required only to the extent that these remedies are effective and available'.[674] In a number of communications Uruguay has supplied a list of the local remedies allegedly available and submitted that the authors had failed to exhaust those remedies.[675] The typical response of the HRC has been to inform Uruguay that,

the communication would . . . not be considered inadmissible in so far as the exhaustion of domestic remedies was concerned, unless the State party gave details of the remedies which it submitted had been available to the author in the circumstances of his case, together with evidence that there would be a reasonable prospect that such measures would be effective.[676]

In reply Uruguay has submitted general descriptions of the remedies provided without, however, specifying which remedies were available in the particular circumstances.[677] The HRC has rejected such submissions as insufficient. It concluded, for example,

> that article 5(2)(b) of the Protocol did not preclude the Committee from considering a communication received under the Optional Protocol where the allegations themselves raise issues concerning the availability or effectiveness of domestic remedies and the State party when expressly requested to do so by the Committee did not provide details on the availability or effectiveness of domestic remedies in the particular case under consideration.[678]

4.104 The approach of the HRC is not that the domestic remedies rule does not apply as a condition of admissibility when the allegations themselves raise issues concerning the availability and effectiveness of those remedies. The decision is limited to the effects of the failure of a State party to provide details of the availability and effectiveness of domestic remedies in a particular case. Professor Trindade has applauded this approach of concentrating on 'the element of actual redress over a mechanistic process of exhausting local remedies'.[679]

If a matter is being actively considered within the domestic system then domestic remedies will not have been exhausted. For example, in *J.S.* v. *Canada*[680] J.S. had successfully applied to the Supreme Court of Ontario for judicial review of the decision of the Ontario Legal Aid Plan (OLAP), the legal aid authority in Ontario. The Supreme Court had set aside the decision and ordered that J.S.'s application be reconsidered. The OLAP had indicated that it was applying for leave to appeal to the Court of Appeal. The HRC noted that the matter was still *sub judice* and that, therefore, domestic remedies had not been exhausted.

4.104.1 In *A. and S.N.* v. *Norway*[681] the authors alleged violations of articles 18 and 26 of the Covenant in the application of the Norwegian Day Nurseries Act 1975 which provided that, 'the day nursery shall help to give the children an upbringing in harmony with basic Christian values'. The authors argued that they should not be required to exhaust domestic remedies because they were ineffective remedies on the basis that their child would have left nursery by the time of the domestic decision and because they doubted whether the Covenant would be applied to this national issue by a Norwegian court. The HRC accepted the submissions of the State party that the Covenant would be a source of considerable weight in interpreting the scope of the Christian objects clause and that the authors would have stood a reasonable chance of challenging the clause and the prevailing practice as to their compatibility with the Covenant had they submitted the case to the Norwegian courts. The HRC also noted that there was a possibility of the expeditious handling of the author's case before the local courts. Accordingly the HRC expressed the view, 'that the pursuit of the author's case before the Norwegian courts could not be deemed *a priori* futile and that the authors doubts about the effectiveness of domestic remedies did not absolve them from exhausting them' and therefore, the requirements of article 5(2)(*b*) OP had not been met.

Conversely, if the domestic remedies are no longer open to the alleged victim the domestic remedies rule will be satisfied. The effect of the doctrine of precedent on the availability of remedies was considered in *Pratt and Morgan* v. *Jamaica*.[682] The State party argued that while the doctrine of precedent was generally applicable it may be set aside on the grounds that a previous decision had been arrived at *per incuriam*. The HRC expressed the view: 'That the local remedies rule does not require resort to appeals that objectively have no prospect of success, is a well established principle of international law and of the Committee's jurisprudence ... A thorough consideration of the judgement of the Privy Council in the case of *Riley* [v. *Attorney-General*] does not lend itself to the conclusion that it was arrived at *per incuriam*'. It seems to be sufficient that the domestic remedies have been exhausted while the communication has been considered by the HRC.[683]

It is too early to determine the HRC's approach to extraordinary remedies. In one case the HRC stated that, 'an extraordinary remedy, such as seeking the annulment of decisions of the Ministry of Justice, does not constitute an effective remedy within the meaning of article 5(2)(b) of the Optional Protocol'.[684] There are conflicting decisions of the EUCM and in customary international law concerning the need to exhaust extraordinary remedies.[685] It might therefore be unwise to take the HRC's statement as a general practice. It simply represents the view of the HRC on the question of exhaustion of an extraordinary domestic remedy in the particular circumstances of one case. There may prove to be 'extraordinary remedies' in other legal systems of which the HRC will take the view that exhaustion is required.[686]

(*c*) *Relief from the duty of execution*[687]

4.105 Customary international law placed great importance on an exception to the domestic remedies rule for an injured party who proves the futility of exhausting domestic remedies.[688] The HRC has had a number of occasions on which to consider whether this exception should apply. Indeed, in the HRC's first published admissibility decision the authors argued that in the situation prevailing in Uruguay no local remedies existed. The HRC accepted that there were no effective local remedies and further indicated that in a communication complaining both of the prevailing situation and of an alleged violation of an individuals rights only the latter would be considered.[689]

4.106 The HRC has accepted that special security regimes may render a local remedy ineffective. For example, in *Santullo (Valcada)* v. *Uruguay*[690] Uruguay informed the HRC that the remedy of habeas corpus was not applicable under the regime of 'prompt security measures' then in operation.[691] Similarly the HRC may accept that the alleged remedy was factually unavailable in the particular case of the alleged victim. In *Bleir* v. *Uruguay*[692] the HRC accepted the submission that, 'All of the guarantees that could be invoked in penal proceedings were irrelevant, because he never appeared before any court; nor was he ever formally informed of the reasons for his arrest'.[693] In *G. Barbato* v. *Uruguay*[694] Uruguay submitted that G had not exhausted the domestic remedies available to him. However, no details were given of the remedies which could have been invoked in the particular circumstances of the case and it was not specified as to which of the violations could have been effectively remedied within the established military judicial process. The HRC expressed the view that it was unable to conclude that there were remedies available to G which he should have pursued.[695] Thus the communication was held admissible. Subsequently, the State party reiterated its submission and listed seven remedies allegedly available.[696]

The author, G's cousin, rejected the State party's assertions. His submission dealt with each of the alleged remedies and showed that each of them were either 'inapplicable', 'entirely theoretical and totally ineffective', or 'inappropriate'. The author then addressed the argument that as certain of the remedies might be applicable at a later stage they could be regarded as remedies which had not been exhausted. The author argued that it was essential to look at the entire procedure and noted that G had been detained for twenty months and that it would be a long time before a first instance decision would be made:

Accordingly, to claim that the proceedings must be completed in order to apply for— and exhaust—the remedies that are theoretically available would mean postponing action by the Committee for an unacceptable amount of time, particularly since failure to make a decision within a reasonable time is one of the violations that have been reported and one of the most obvious causes of what has happened. In other words, the possibility of instituting unacceptably lengthy proceedings, which is in itself a violation of the Covenant, would make the Government think that it was not subject to the Committee's jurisdiction. That could hardly be the intention of the Covenant.[697]

In its decision the HRC expressed the view that,

the remedies listed by the State party as unexhausted cannot be considered available to the alleged victim in the circumstances of his case. They are either inapplicable *de jure* or *de facto* and do not constitute an effective remedy, within the meaning of article 2(3) of the Covenant, for the matters complained of. There are, therefore, no grounds to alter the conclusion reached in the Committee's decision ... that the communication is not inadmissible under article 5(2)(b) of the Optional Protocol.[698]

The decision is of particular interest because of the direct reference to the obligations of the States parties to the ICCPR to provide an 'effective remedy' to any person who claims that his rights or freedoms under the ICCPR have been violated (article 2(3) of the ICCPR).[699] Professor Trindade has argued at length that the drafters of the Covenant envisaged the local remedies rule as directly related to the State's duty to provide effective local remedies as in article 2(3) of the ICCPR.[700]

4.107 An example of the legal, as distinct from the factual, unavailability of remedies is the case of *Guerrero* v. *Uruguay*.[701] Under the provisions of a legislative act it was not possible to institute a civil action for damages in conjunction with military criminal proceedings. An alternative action for compensation for persons injured by a police operation depended first on determining the criminal liability of the accused. As the accused had been acquitted no civil or administrative suit could be filed to obtain compensation. The HRC was unable to conclude that there were still effective remedies available that could be invoked on G's behalf.[702]

4.108 For remedies to be effective an alleged victim may need legal assistance. In *Lanza and Perdoma* v. *Uruguay*[703] the HRC noted that habeas corpus was not applicable and the State party had not shown the remedies available in the particular circumstances of the case.[704] The HRC then added that, 'Moreover, B.W.(L) and A.L.(P) have explained that they had no effective contact with lawyers to advise them of their rights or to assist them in exercising them'.[705]

This suggests that the HRC might take the view that when failure to exhaust the remedies available can be ascribed to the failure of the State party to permit, or provide if necessary, legal assistance that will constitute a 'special circumstance' which excuses the exhaustion of domestic remedies.[706] This argument might extend to failure to satisfy other requirements of the fair trial guarantee in article 14 of the ICCPR. Indeed the HRC has expressed the view on the facts of one case that the requirement of effective and available domestic remedies entails that the procedural guarantees for a fair and public hearing by a competent, independent, and impartial tribunal must be scrupulously observed.[707] It is submitted that this should not be read so widely as to suggest that all domestic remedies must conform with the requirements of article 14. Article 2(3) of the ICCPR clearly contemplates administrative and other non-judicial remedies.[708]

4.109 A State party may be estopped from raising the domestic remedies requirement in certain cases.[709] Thus in *Y.L.* v. *Canada*[710] the alleged victim had not been informed of the alleged remedy in the original decision complained of, or by his State appointed lawyer.[711] The HRC took the rather strict view that, 'The fact that the author was not advised that he could have resorted to judicial review is irrelevant in determining whether the claim of the author was of a kind subject to judicial control and supervision'.[712] However, in a joint individual opinion three members of the HRC took the view that Canada was 'estopped from asserting that either, procedurally, the author has failed to exhaust local remedies or that, substantively, the requisite guarantees under article 14(1) of the Covenant have been complied with'.[713]

Another interesting point concerning domestic remedies is suggested by the facts of *C.A.* v. *Italy*.[714] CA had opted for an exceptional administrative procedure rather than the normal court process. That option excluded the latter as a matter of law. It is submitted that on these facts the State party could not have relied on the domestic remedies rule.[715]

4.110 The effect of conditions attached to the exercise of remedies was raised in *Montero* v. *Uruguay*.[716] M was a Uruguayan citizen resident in West Berlin. She alleged that the ICCPR had been violated because the Uruguayan authorities had refused, without explanation, to renew her passport.[717] M was informed that there was a recourse by way of appeal against the government decision but that this had to be done in Uruguay. As M had no relatives in Uruguay to represent her the Uruguayan authorities offered her a safe-conduct to travel to Uruguay. M declined the offer because she did not have the financial means to undertake the journey and because her studies would have been unduly interrupted.[718]

The HRC expressed the view that it was unable to conclude that in the circumstances there were effective domestic remedies available to M which she had failed to exhaust.[719] The State party repeated its submission that M was free to return to Uruguay even without a valid passport. M replied that it was the normal procedure for Uruguayan citizens residing abroad to have their passport renewed by Uruguayan consulates, that she had applied to all the appropriate consular posts, and that the suggestion of the Uruguayan authorities that she travel to Uruguay was 'abnormal'.[720]

The HRC made no further comment on the matter of the exhaustion of domestic remedies. Again the HRC seems to have avoided a 'mechanistic application' of the rule. Presumably the approach of the HRC was that although a possible remedy existed the conditions attached to its use were so onerous, unreasonable, and unnecessary in the particular circumstances of M's case that it did not constitute an effective and available remedy. If this is the correct interpretation then it is submitted that it is to be commended.

4.111 The HRC would appear to have adopted the rule that the available domestic remedies must be properly exhausted.[721] This is particularly important because the result in such cases is not merely suspensory but precludes the admissibility of the communication.[722] In *N.S.* v. *Canada*[723] the communication concerned N.S.'s dismissal from work allegedly because of his race and religion. N.S. wished to appeal from a decision of the Adjudicator of the Public Service Staff Relations Board to the Canadian Federal Court of Appeal. However, the time for filing an appeal had passed. N.S. applied to the court for an extension but this was refused. N.S. submitted that he had exhausted all domestic remedies. The HRC rejected this submission. The HRC noted that the N.S. had failed to avail himself of the remedy of appeal in time. Moreover, the communication did 'not disclose the existence of any special circumstances which might have absolved the author, *according to generally recognized rules of international law*, from exhausting the domestic remedies at his disposal'.[724] Therefore, N.S. could not be considered to have exhausted the remedies available to him under Canadian law and the communication was declared inadmissible. In *J.R.T. v. Western Guard Party*[725] the HRC took the view that, 'It appears, however, in view of the ambiguity ensuing from the conflicting time limits laid down in the laws in question, that a reasonable effort was indeed made to exhaust domestic remedies in this respect and, therefore, the Committee does not consider that, as to this claim, the communication should be declared inadmissible under article 5(2)(b) of the Optional Protocol'.[726]

4.112 If the HRC does follow this approach the author must ensure that he has properly exhausted available domestic remedies. This will demand, for example, observance of time limits and the correct procedures and formalities of national law, making full use and advantage of the remedies available by pleading the important allegations, calling the necessary witnesses, and making appropriate objections.

4.113 It is open to the HRC to reverse a decision on non-exhaustion in the light of subsequent information.[727]

4.114 Finally, it is important to note that article 5(2)(*b*) contains an exception to the rule of exhaustion of domestic remedies, 'where the application of the remedies is unreasonably prolonged'.[728] The HRC could have expressly relied on this exception in this case of *G. Barbato* v. *Uruguay*.[729] It was expressly relied upon in *Pietroroia* v. *Uruguay*.[730] Referring to two remedies of an exceptional nature the HRC commented that it was 'not satisfied that they are applicable in the present case and, in any event, to require resort to them would unreasonably prolong the exhaustion of domestic remedies'.[731] In *Hammel* v. *Madagascar*,[732] a judicial decision on H's case was rendered while the HRC was considering the communication on the merits. The HRC expressed the view that as the applications had taken over four years the remedy had been unreasonably prolonged in the sense of article 5(2)(*b*) of the OP.[733] The HRC considered and rejected the application of the exception in *H.S.* v. *France*.[734] The case concerned a delay of six and half years in the decision depriving H.S. of his French nationality. The HRC expressed the view that,

the delays in the proceedings in 1984 and 1985 were caused by the author himself. For that reason the Committee is unable to conclude that domestic remedies, which according to both parties, are in progress, have been unduly prolonged in a manner that would exempt the author from exhausting them under article 5(2)(b) of the Optional Protocol.[735]

Accordingly, the requirement of exhaustion of domestic remedies had not been met by the author at the time of the submission and had still not been met. The communication was, therefore, inadmissible.

(d) Does the exhaustion rule apply where an application is directed against legislative measures or an administrative practice?[736]

4.115 This question is raised simply because of comparable international practice.[737] As we have already noted the HRC has stated that an individual cannot challenge *in abstracto* the compatibility of national legislation with the ICCPR. The individual must allege that the legislation has been applied in such a manner, or has produced 'adverse effects which directly affect' him, that he has actually been a 'victim' of a violation of the ICCPR.[738] An interesting point to note is that on some occasions the HRC has concluded that the questions of violation and of effective remedies can only be properly examined at the merits stage.[739]

A more difficult question for the HRC will be the application of the domestic remedies rule where the communication alleges the existence of an 'administrative practice'. Many of the communications concerning Uruguay have alleged that the violations concerned result from systematic practices and in response the HRC expressed the view that a 'practice' of inhuman treatment existed at La Libertad prison in Uruguay.[740] In none of these views though has the HRC made any comment on the effect of such a practice on the rule of exhaustion of domestic remedies. The question has been considered in the ECHR system most notably in the cases of *Donnelly and Others* v. *United Kingdom*[741] and *Ireland* v. *United Kingdom*.[742] The jurisprudence which has emerged is rather sophisticated, and has been criticized, but may at least provide some instructive points of reference for the HRC.[743]

(e) Domestic remedies: an appraisal

4.116 The placing of the burden of proof as regards the exhaustion of domestic remedies is a matter of great importance to the effectiveness of individual petition systems. It poses the choice between a strict application of the domestic remedies rule accompanied by an onerous burden of proof on the individual concerned or a shared burden of proof which takes account of the factual procedural equality of the individual. Professor Trindade has argued that, 'General international law (arbitral and judicial practice) provides ample and strong evidence in support of the sharing or distribution of the burden of proof between contending parties in inter-State litigation'.[744] *A fortiori* this approach should apply in respect of individual applications, 'since the local remedies rule per se already favours the more stronger party the Sovereign State'.[745] This sharing of the burden of proof has been the practice of the EUCM since the early 1960s.[746]

The relatively small amount of practice of the HRC has been noted above. With the proviso that the matter is a very difficult one, that all its aspects have not yet been considered, and that early approaches must necessarily be treated with some caution, it seems fair to comment that the HRC has taken an individual orientated approach, or at least not a State centred approach. It has avoided placing a heavy onus on the individual and placed the burden of showing that remedies are 'available and effective' squarely on the respondent State.[747] This approach is, in general terms, very much in line with that of the EUCM and the EUCT,[748] the IACM,[749] and the United Nations Sub-Commission on the Prevention of Discrimination and Protection of Minorities.[750] It represents a sensible, practical approach which recognizes the factual procedural inequality which will normally exist between the individual and the State party concerned and takes account of the complimentary undertaking on States parties under article 2(3) of the ICCPR to provide 'effective remedies'.[751]

More generally, the practice of the HRC in relation to the exhaustion of domestic remedies may provide some important international law precedents. However, as Professor Bowett has pointed out there is a danger in extrapolating from human rights claims to general international law claims.[752] In particular he notes Professor Trindade's argument that there may well be a duty on State parties to provide local remedies for violations of human rights on the basis of, for example, article 2(3) of the ICCPR,[753] and comments that, 'It is doubtful, however, that this can be extended to a more general proposition that a State is under a legal duty to provide local remedies for any breach of international law in relation to an alien'.[754]

6. Abuse of the right of submission (article 3 OP)[755]

4.117 Although raised by States parties on a number of occasions this ground has rarely operated to render a communication inadmissible.[756] It did so operate in *K.L.* v. *Denmark*.[757] There the HRC took into account that a similar complaint from the author had previously been declared inadmissible under the OP as devoid of any substantiation;[758] that the second complaint was similarly devoid of any substantiation in facts or law; and that the author had himself indicated that he still intended to pursue further domestic remedies. The HRC concluded that in these circumstances, the submission of the communication must be regarded as an abuse of the right of submission under article 3 OP.

7. Anonymous communications (article 3 OP)[759]

4.118 No communication has been declared inadmissible on this ground. In *Carballal* v. *Uruguay*[760] the HRC received no further correspondence from the author subsequent to his original communication. Letters addressed to him by the UN Secretariat were returned as unclaimed. The HRC based its final view on the information in the original communication.[761]

F. THE OPTIONAL PROTOCOL: SIGNIFICANCE, APPRAISAL, AND PROSPECTS

1. The status of the individual [762]

4.119 Although the International Convention on the Elimination of Racial Discrimination 1965 contained a provision on communications[763] the OP is perhaps of greater significance because it recognizes a right of individual petition in a universal instrument covering a wide range of civil and political rights. Commentators have described the OP as being revolutionary in terms of international law.[764] Over a decade of practice under the OP has demonstrated the feasibility of individual petition systems at the international level as the ECHR has at the regional level.[765] In this respect the OP represents a signal contribution to the recognition of the individual as a proper subject of international law.[766] Indeed, in theory at least, the OP represents an advance on the ECHR because the ECHR was intended primarily as a more general 'ordre public' guarantee than as providing individual remedies.[767]

2. The HRC under the OP

4.120 If the examination of communications by the HRC was to have credibility and be potentially effective then this task had to be carried out with objectivity, fairness, and procedural due process. There are a number of features of the OP that can be identified as affording credibility to the HRC in its work under the OP.[768] First, the members of the HRC are 'independent experts', rather than governmental representatives.[769] Practice has shown this to be a fundamental prerequisite for effective human rights organs.[770] Secondly, the HRC has a more secure existence in that it was established by a Treaty rather than a Resolution.[771] Thirdly, the HRC's mandate is defined by the OP and the legal norms it is to interpret and apply are established by the ICCPR. A major problem for United Nations human rights bodies conducting inquiries has been the lack of a defined set of legal norms against which to evaluate the facts as determined by them.[772] Fourthly, the OP is not open to the criticism of being a 'pre-judging' resolution, which often establishes international fact finding bodies.[773] Fifthly, the optional nature of the OP should protect the HRC from charges of political selectivity and 'ad-hocery' and thus avoid the development of alleged 'double standards' in the selection of cases to consider.[774] Sixthly, although the HRC's consideration and examination of communications is conducted in private its final 'views' are published.[775] Thus the damaging secrecy and excessive confidentiality of procedures like that under ECOSOC Resolution 1503 (XLVIII) are avoided.[776]

Thus the HRC has many distinct advantages in terms of the treaty status of the OP and in terms of the nature of the HRC as a body, its mandate, and the defined norms with which it is to operate. Other elements of the HRC's work examined above, for example, matters of access, admissibility, and form of evidence, the burden and standard of proof, the approach to the non-co-operation of some States parties, legal representation and legal aid, the nature and scope of the HRC's views, also have an important bearing on the credibility of the OP process. In general terms the HRC has proceeded cautiously on the basis of consensus. It has stressed the fundamental importance of individuals having access to it under the OP. It appears to have taken a liberal approach to the admissibility of evidence. It has recognized the factual inequality in evidential terms between the author and the State and adopted an approach to the burden of proof which has taken account of this. It has refused to allow the non-co-operation of a State party to defeat the object and purpose of the OP by effectively having an expression of views by default in such cases. Above all the HRC has consistently stated that it operates in accordance with the principle of 'equality of arms'.

4.121 The HRC has effectively understood 'views' as meaning a decision (or determination) on the merits.[777] Those views, both at admissibility and merits stages, have incorporated substantive interpretations of the provisions of the ICCPR and the OP. As the following chapters will illustrate the clarity and legal precision of some of the HRC's views has been open to criticism but to some extent this may be due to the initial caution of the HRC under a new procedure and its practice of operating on a consensus basis. The necessity for consensus inevitably reduces clarity and precision even if provision exists for the appending of individual opinions. Perhaps the most surprising aspect of the HRC's final views has been the clear and specific obligations spelt out in them for the State party concerned.[778] A State party is left in little or no doubt as to the necessary remedial action which may include, for example, amending legislation. The experience of the HRC in its consideration of communications under the OP can and has assisted it in its formulation of general comments under article 40(4) of the ICCPR. Such assistance can be gained both from the interpretation of the ICCPR in specific, concrete situations and in revealing the absence of procedural safeguards necessary to prevent human rights violations.

4.122 As noted, when the HRC discussed the issue a majority of the HRC indicated that they do not interpret the HRC's role as necessarily ending with its expression of views.[779] The HRC accepted the possibility of reconsideration of communications in exceptional circumstances and have now taken such action in respect of decisions on admissibility.[780] The HRC also stated that it has a continuing interest in any action taken by the State party in consequence of the HRC's expression of views. This decision is not only important in itself in the absence of any higher body to supervise implementation of the obligations of a State party, but also because of the approach to interpretation on which it is based. That approach to interpretation follows the precedent of other decisions of the HRC that were not expressly authorized by the ICCPR or the OP, for example, that on interim measures.[781] Such decisions have been taken on the basis that the HRC believed that certain appropriate action was reasonably open to it, or was not expressly prohibited.[782] Such an approach to interpretation allows the HRC to develop practices and procedures designed to secure the object and purposes of the ICCPR and the OP. The most recent development has been the appointment of the 'Special Rapporteur for Follow-Up on Views'.

4.123 It has been argued by Mose and Opsahl that it is open to the HRC to adopt an active, conciliatory, or mediatory function to bring about some kind of friendly settlement between the State party and the alleged victim.[783] They argue that the OP itself envisages some kind of settlement after admissibility because article 4(2) OP refers to the obligation of the State party to clarify 'the remedy, if any, that may have been taken by the State'. Their view is that 'remedy' cannot refer to existing domestic remedies because they must already have been exhausted under articles 2 and 5(2)(b) OP. 'It rather suggests that a State party which has been faced with an admissible claim, and perhaps has conceded some justification for it, may already have taken action to resolve it by way of remedying the situation'.[784] They further argue that it 'would be preferable and not contrary to the Protocol for the Committee to show some initiative at the stage of the merits ... It should not be seen as incompatible with the Committee functions to suggest, formally or informally, that it is at the disposal of the parties in order to reach a friendly settlement'.[785]

The authors' argument that 'remedy' in article 4(2) OP cannot mean domestic remedies is questionable bearing in mind Rule 93(4) of the HRC's Rules which allow it to review a decision declaring a communication admissible in the light of further explanations or statements from the State party under article 4(2) OP.[786] None the less, their general argument that the HRC could develop practices and procedures directed to the securing of friendly settlements is sound and sensible. Whether members of the HRC would be willing to take such steps will depend on their approach to the interpretation of the OP. The present consensus practice would prevent such a development if there is opposition to it within the HRC. The recent appointment of the 'Special Rapporteur for Follow-Up on Views' may evidence that members might now be more willing to accept that attempts to secure friendly settlements comes within their conception of the proper role of the HRC under the OP. Unfortunately, it appears that no proposals on these lines have been made and no public discussion of this matter has taken place in HRC meetings.

4.124 As there are no enforcement or supervisory mechanisms expressly envisaged by the OP—and none has been developed in practice—the pressure to observe the HRC's views must primarily come from their inherent authority as emanating from an independent body's objective assessment and from the accompanying publicity. Unfortunately, effective publicity for the HRC's work has been sadly lacking.[787] In part this no doubt stems from the fact that the work itself is carried out confidentially, in camera, and without oral hearings. It must also be observed that, ironically, the absence of overt politicization in the HRC renders it less likely to attract national and international publicity.[788] As a matter of practice it seems fair to note that the absence of United States participation deprives the HRC of the national and international publicity that inevitably seems to focus on any US involvement at the international level. Even within legal circles relatively scant attention has been paid to the actual practice of the HRC under the OP although this is now increasing.

4.125 The members of the HRC have consistently emphasized the need for greater publicity for all aspects of its work.[789] The Bureau of the HRC have met with the Director of the Information Services at Geneva to discuss ways of ensuring better publicity for the HRC and for the OP. Press conferences have been held for these purposes. An essential element of publicity at the international level is the availability of published material. Even within a confidential procedure the EUCM has shown that it is possible to publish a limited amount of information concerning communications. The greater the availability of published information the more likely the procedures concerned are to attract academic, professional, non-governmental, national, and international attention. The situation as regards the OP is improving in this respect particularly with the publication of a volume of selected decisions in 1985[790] and a second volume in 1990.[791] Recent academic publications are increasingly referring to decisions under the OP.[792] Similarly there is some evidence that some of the HRC's views have been influential in the States concerned and have attracted national publicity.[793]

There can be no doubt, however, that unless steps are taken to afford much greater publicity to the work of the HRC under the OP within the United Nations system, in national and international media, in national and international governmental and non-governmental institutions, then no matter how objective and authoritative the HRC's views the dearth of publicity for them will render them ineffective except as regards the most co-operative and committed of States parties.[794] It is a defect of the OP that there is no specific obligation on States parties to give publicity to it. Finally, as regards publicity, the best publicity for the OP would of course be its ratification by an increasing number of States parties to the ICCPR. Recommendations by the Human Rights Commission and the General Assembly along these lines must be accompanied by concerted pressure from national and international human rights bodies.[795]

4.126 In general terms this chapter has asserted that whatever the features of an international petition system its fate will ultimately be determined first, by the approach and attitude of the implementation body, and secondly, by the co-operation of the States parties concerned. With respect to the first determinant, though the work under the OP is still at a relatively early stage, it is submitted that on the basis of the foregoing examination the HRC can be commended for having adopted a positive approach and having fashioned a practicable and functional procedure. Though there are undoubted limitations in adopting a consensus approach the degree of consensus apparent in the HRC is remarkable in a universal body.[796] With time, patience, the continued cautious development of practices and procedures, continued consensus, and increased publicity, there can be at least some hope that the OP can develop into an effective counterpart on the universal level to the established regional systems.

3. The effectiveness of the OP for individuals

4.127 The ultimate concern of an alleged victim is of course with the observance of the HRC's views in an individual case rather than with the procedural merits of the OP system. It must be frankly admitted that compliance with the HRC's views by States parties has been disappointing. However, to make an informed appraisal it is important to put the situation into proper perspective.

4.128 As regards interim measures there have been some occasions on which States parties have complied with the HRC's views. This has had direct results for the individuals concerned in terms of them being accorded medical treatment or not being tortured or executed.[797] The interim measures indicated by the HRC are non-binding as a matter of law and depend totally on the co-operation and good faith of the State party concerned. Publicity might well add to their effectiveness although the HRC might think it could achieve more on a confidential basis. As a matter of contrast it is interesting to note that the record of compliance by contracting parties under the ECHR is notably good[798] while the record of the ICJ has been rather poor.[799]

4.129 The State party concerned in the majority of the HRC's final views has been Uruguay. The degree of co-operation afforded by the Uruguayan government has varied from minimal to non-existent,[800] although there was full co-operation by the new democratic government in Uruguay in the HRC's most recent decision.[801] Moreover, there is no evidence that any of the HRC's final views were observed prior to the installation of the new democratic government in March 1985. Representatives of the new government appeared before the HRC and promised co-operation both with respect to the reporting process and the OP procedure. The new government released many political prisoners including persons found by the HRC to be victims of human rights violations. The situation in Uruguay prior to March 1985 was characterized by a total breakdown of law and order. On that basis it can be argued that it gives a false and distorted impression of the effectiveness of the final views of the HRC.[802] It would be a gesture of faith in the HRC, and probably a matter of obligation under the OP, for the new Uruguayan government to comply with the HRC's final views, or at least those expressed after March 1985 but concerning events before that time.[803] There has to date been no evidence from Uruguay that it has taken such steps.

4.130 If the disappointing compliance record of Uruguay can perhaps partly be explained by the abnormal situation there the same cannot be said of other States that have either not co-operated with the HRC or have not complied with the HRC's final views. These States include Madagascar, Zaïre, Suriname.

4.131 There is, however, some evidence that States parties are willing to co-operate with the HRC in its examination of communications and to observe its final views. States which have co-operated in the examination of communications include Canada, France, Italy, Norway, Mauritius, Finland, Jamaica, Denmark, Netherlands, Sweden.

4.132 Three views in particular are important in showing that the HRC's final views can be influential and given effect to. First, in *Lovelace* v. *Canada*,[804] the HRC expressed the view that Canada had violated article 27 of the ICCPR in denying Lovelace the right to reside on an Indian reservation. Subsequently Canada informed the HRC that it had taken substantial steps towards amending the relevant legislation.[805] Although a Canadian commentator had expressed doubts as to whether the steps taken by the Canadian government were sufficient there is at least a strong element of respect and co-operation with the HRC.[806] Secondly, the *Mauritian Women Case* provides the clearest example of a State party taking measures in consequence of the HRC's final views.[807] The response of Mauritius was to amend the two pieces of legislation concerned so as to remove the discriminatory effect of those laws on the grounds of sex.[808] Thirdly, it is important to note the response of the government of Finland in *Hartikainen* v. *Finland*.[809] Although the HRC did not find a violation of article 18(4)[810] of the Covenant in the application of the relevant Finnish legislation it did note that certain difficulties had arisen in giving effect to those provisions but that it believed that appropriate action was being taken to resolve the difficulties.[811] The Finnish government subsequently informed the HRC of an amendment to the relevant Statute and further measures taken to solve the problems noted by the HRC.[812] Such a response is to be highly commended.

4.133 The most authoritative review of the OP to date concluded in 1981 that,

In principle it is revolutionary. In practice so far, it has had only limited, nearly negligible effects. The Covenant is a great document. Yet the Committee is a very modest entity for its implementation, and the Protocol does not give it much additional power. Despite all polite official comments about its importance, which reflect the overwhelmingly persuasive strength of the ideas of the Covenant rather than the realities which the Committee is facing, the Committee lacks support, publicity, and resources. Public opinion is hardly aware of it. The Protocol will only become effective if the Committee does. Both depend on being used, and being given means to work with, including assistance by a permanent Secretariat.

... The fact that only a few countries have accepted it, usually the ones with a record which gives them relatively little fear from individual complaints, is sometimes mentioned as a reason to be cautious. The countries with the most real problems are, however, likely to remain outside the reach of the Protocol in the all-foreseeable future. The Committee should not look to them, or what is acceptable to them, when establishing its own patterns and standards ... The procedures under the Protocol can no doubt be developed and improved. But the measure of its success should be the degree to which the Committee is able to convince and influence States, rather than condemn and expose them.[813]

To an extent it is important that the Optional Protocol is being kept alive as in the final analysis, though it is of little comfort to victims of human rights violations, progress in the international protection of human rights is likely to be identified over decades rather than years.[814] The broader significance of the Protocol in terms of the status of the individual in international law should also not be overlooked. As Prounis has commented,

The Human Rights Committee has not yet ushered in a new era in the observance of human rights. It neither provides an efficient forum for the vindication of individuals' human rights, nor addresses the remedial paradox of human rights violations. It does, however, stand as a historic first step towards providing a greater role for the individual in promoting protection of his or her rights. With a little initiative by the Committee members, the system created under the Optional Protocol could develop further.[815]

NOTES

1 For full text of the OP see appendix II below. There is a substantial amount of literature on the OP. Most of this deals with the drafting process or comments on the provisions of the OP. Very little of it is directed to the actual practices of the HRC. See Anon., 23 Rev. ICJ (1979) p. 26 at pp. 28–30; Anon., 25 Rev. ICJ (1980) p. 35 at pp. 37–8; Anon., 31 Rev. ICJ (1983) p. 42 at pp. 46–9; Anon., 35

Rev. ICJ (1985) p. 18 at pp. 21–5; Anon., 37 Rev. ICJ (1986) p. 25 at pp. 28–31; A. K. Ahmed, 'Analysis of the Decisions of the Committee on Human Rights', LLM thesis, c. 1982; Agarwal, ch. 1 n. 1 above, pp. 40–7; Bossuyt, *Guide*, pp. 793–818; M. Bossuyt, 'Le Règlement intérieur du Comité des Droits de l'Homme', XIV Revue belge de droit international (1978–9) p. 104 at 132–56; P. S. Brar, ch. 3 n. 1 above, ch. 3; P. S. Brar, 'The Practice and Procedures of the Human Rights Committee under the Optional Protocol of the International Covenant on Civil and Political Rights', 26 Ind. JIL (1986) pp. 506–43; F. Capotorti, ch. 2 n. 1 above, p. 131 at pp. 143–8 (1968); K. Das, 'United Nations Institutions and Procedures Founded on Conventions on Human Rights and Fundamental Freedoms', in K. Vasak (General editor), P. Alston (ed., English Edition), *The International Dimensions of Human Rights*, p. 303 at pp. 343–8; P. R. Ghandhi, 'The Human Rights Committee and the Right of Individual Communication', 57 BYIL 1986 (1987) pp. 201–51; W. P. Gormley, ch. 1 n. 1 above; M. Lippman, 'Human Rights Revisited: The Protection of Human Rights under the ICCPR', 26 NILR (1979) p. 221 at pp. 262–77; E. Mose and T. Opsahl, 'The Optional Protocol to the ICCPR', 21 Santa Clara Law Review (1981) pp. 271–331; M. Moscowitz, *Human Rights and World Order*, Chapters 9 and 10 (1958); M. Nowak, 'The Effectiveness of the ICCPR—Stocktaking after the First Eleven Sessions of the HRC', 1 HRLJ (1980) p. 136 at pp. 152–62, 168–9; M. Nowak, 'Survey of Decisions', 2 HRLJ (1981) p. 168 at 169–72; id., 3 HRLJ (1982) p. 207 at pp. 210–18; id., 5 HRLJ (1984) p. 199 at pp. 203–8; id., 7 HRLJ (1986) p. 287 at pp. 292–306; Othan A. Prounis, 'The Human Rights Committee: Toward Resolving the Paradox of Human Rights Law', 17 Col. HRLR (1985) pp. 103–19; R. S. Pathak, 'The Protection of Human Rights', 18 Ind. JIL (1978) pp. 265–73; B. G. Ramcharan, 'Implementing the International Covenants on Human Rights', in B. G. Ramcharan (ed.), *Human Rights: Thirty Years after the Universal Declaration*, p. 159 at pp. 187–95 (1979); B. G. Ramcharan, 'The Emerging Jurisprudence of the Human Rights Committee', 6 Dalhousie LJ (1980) p. 7 at pp. 33–40; A. H. Robertson, ch. 2 n. 1 above, p. 332 at 357–69 (1984); A. H. Robertson and J. G. Merrills, *Human Rights in the World*, pp. 54–73 (3rd, 1990); H. R. S. Ryan, 'Seeking Relief under the United Nations ICCPR', 6 Queens LJ (1981) pp. 389–407; E. Schwelb, 'Civil and Political Rights—The International Measures of Implementation', 62 AJIL (1968) p. 827 at pp. 860–68; E. Schwelb, 'The International Measures of Implementation of the ICCPR and of the O.P.', 12 Tex. ILJ (1977) pp. 141–86; D. L. Shelton, 'Individual Complaint Machinery under the United Nations 1503 Procedure and the O.P. to the ICCPR', in H. Hannum (ed.), *Guide to International Human Rights Practice*, p. 59 at pp. 67–72 (1984); L. B. Sohn, ch. 1 n. 1 above, p. 39 at 166–7 (1968); L. B. Sohn, 'Human Rights: Their Implementation and Supervision by the United Nations', in T. Meron (ed.), *Human Rights in International Law—Legal and Policy Issues*, Vol. ii, p. 369 at pp. 389–91; P. Sieghart, *The International Law of Human Rights*, Parts II–III *passim*, pp. 387–89 (1983); R. Starr, 'International Protection of Human Rights and the United Nations Covenant (1967) Wisconsin LR p. 841 at pp. 875, 881–3; M. Tardu, *Human Rights—The International Petition System*, Vol. i, pp. 2–25; Vol. ii, part I (1979–86); C. Tomuschat, 'Evolving Procedural

Rules: The United Nations Human Rights Committee's First Two Years of Dealing with Individual Communications', 1 HRLJ (1980) pp. 249–57; Ton J. M. Zuidjwick, *Petitioning the United Nations—A Study in Human Rights*, ch. 14 at pp. 348–69 and ch. 15 (1982); Ton J. M. Zuidjwick, 'The Right to Petition the United Nations because of Alleged Violations of Human Rights', 59 Can. Bar Rev. (1981) pp. 103–23; A. De Zayas and J. Th. Moller, 'Optional Protocol Cases Concerning the Nordic States before the United Nations Human Rights Committee', 4 Nordic Journal of International Law (1986) pp. 384–400; A. De Zayas, J. Th. Moller, T. Opsahl, 'Application of the International Covenant on Civil and Political Rights under the Optional Protocol by the Human Rights Committee', 28 GYIL (1985), pp. 9–64 updated in 26 Comparative Judicial Review (1989) pp. 2–52; M. J. Cote, 'Le Recours au comité des droits de l'homme de l'ONU—une illusion?', 26 Cahier de droit (1985) pp. 531–47; T. Meron, *Human Rights Law-Making in the United Nations*, ch. 3 (1986); A. J. Glenn Mower, Jr., 'Organizing to Implement the UN Civil/Political Rights Covenant', 3 HR Rev. (1978) pp. 122–31; M. Schmidt, 'The OP to the ICCPR: Procedure and Practice', 4 Interights Bull. (1989) pp. 27–30; Tyagi, ch. 5 and Addendum.

2 See n. 39 below. See generally on the right to petition in international law Zuidjwick, n. 1 above (1982); Gormley, ch. 1 n. 1 above; D. P. Parson, 'The Individual Right of Petition: A Study of Methods Used by International Organizations to Utilize the Individual as a Source of Information on the Violation of Human Rights', 13 Wayne L. Rev. (1967) pp. 678–705.

3 GA Resn. 421 (V), section F, cited in Doc. A/2929, ch. 1 n. 1 above, pr. 22. See Doc. A/2929, pr. 9. For summaries of the drafting work on the right to petition see Doc. A/2929, ch. 1 n. 1 above at ch. 7, prs. 59–89 (1955), Doc. A/6546, prs. 568–612 (1966), ibid. This account is largely drawn from those two documents.

4 See ch. 1, pr. 1.18 above.

5 See e.g. ECOSOC OR, 13th session, Supp. 9, pr. 84; Doc. A/2929, n. 3 above, pr. 75 *et seq*.

6 See e.g. ECOSOC OR, 16th session, Supp. 8, Ax. 3, prs. 132–43; Doc. A/2929, n. 3 above, pr. 76.

7 Doc. A/2929, n. 3 above, prs. 84–6. See Clark, ch. 1 n. 125 above.

8 See ch. 1, pr. 1.6 above.

9 See text to ch. 1 n. 38 above. On article 2 of the ICCPR see ch. 6 below.

10 See ch. 1, pr. 1.1 above. See also Zuidjwick, n. 1 above, ch. 3.

11 Doc. A/2929, n. 3 above, pr. 68. On the ECHR see *European Convention on Human Rights: Collected Texts*, (1986).

12 E/CN.4/SR.434, p. 6 (Turkey).

13 Doc. A/2929, n. 3 above, pr. 69. See the view of the HRC under the OP in *Antonaccio v. Uruguay*, pr. 4.11 below.

14 Doc. A/2929, n. 3 above, prs. 70–2. A proposal to insert a special article to the effect that States parties would not consider any steps taken by another party under the inter-State procedure as an unfriendly act was not received favourably, ibid., pr. 71.

15 See Doc. A/2929, n. 3 above, prs. 74–80.

16 See ECOSOC OR, 14th session, Supp. 4, Ax. IIIA.

17 See Doc. A/6546, n. 3 above, pr. 477.

18 Doc. A/6546, n. 3 above, pr. 485.

19 The vote was 59 for, 2 against, and 32 abstentions, Doc. A/6546, n. 3 above, pr. 597.

20 GA Resn. 2200 A (XXI), 21 UN GAOR (1496th meeting) pr. 60 at 6; A/PV 1496 (1966).

21 See ch. 1, pr. 1.3 above.

22 See pr. 4.119 below.

23 The HRC referred to the preamble in its decision in *Antonaccio v. Uruguay*, Doc. A/37/40, p. 114. See pr. 4.11 below.

24 See pr. 4.120 below.

25 There is no reference in the OP to any role in the implementation machinery of the OP for the ECOSOC or the Third Committee of the General Assembly. See the schemes of implementation machinery of the ECHR, the AMR, the original ICESCR system and the European Social Charter in Vasak/Alston (eds.), n. 1 above, pp. 684–5.

26 See the statement of Mr Kornyenko (Ukrainian SSR), Third Committee, A/C.3/SR 1441, pr. 51 (1966). See E. Schwelb, 'Civil and Political Rights', n. 1 above, p. 861 and n. 152 (1968).

27 So, for example, the two independent experts from the UK who have served on the HRC have taken part in the consideration of communications even though the UK is not a party to the OP.

28 This would include past and present members of the HRC of Russian, East German, Romanian, Bulgarian, Polish, and Yugoslavian nationality. See, however, the text to n. 35 below.

29 All members of the United Nations are *ipso facto* parties to the Statute of the ICJ (article 93 of UN Charter). However, members of the ICJ are to be elected regardless of their nationality (article 2, Statute of ICJ). Judges may sit on the court even if they are a national of a State which has not accepted the compulsory jurisdiction of the court under article 36(2) of the Statute.

30 See Van Dijk and Van Hoof, pp. 20–5.

31 Ibid., pp. 25–9.

32 See Lerner, ch. 3 n. 1 above, pp. 82–6.

33 See T. Buergenthal, R. Norris, and D. Shelton, *Protecting Human Rights in the Americas*, ch. 6 (2d, 1987).

34 Ibid.

35 For the USSR statement see Doc. E/CN.4/1989/SR.55, pr. 22. The statement was reaffirmed before the HRC in October 1989, SR 929 pr. 14. See Mose and Opsahl, p. 330.

36 Cf. Art. 31 of the Statute of the ICJ; Art. 10 of the Statute of the IACT. Under the ECHR all contracting parties have one member of the EUCM of their nationality or nominated by them, and all members of the Council of Europe have one judge of the EUCT of their nationality or nominated by them even if they have not accepted the right of individual petition (art. 25) or the compulsory jurisdiction (art. 46) of the EUCT. When a Chamber of the EUCM or the EUCT is formed

they include the Commission member or judge respectively of the national States concerned.

37 For example, most communications to date have concerned Uruguay which has never had one of its nationals or a person nominated by it serving as an independent expert on the HRC.

38 Under article 96 of the UN Charter an advisory opinion of the ICJ can be sought by organs of the UN and specialized agencies if they have been authorized by the General Assembly to do so. The autonomous status of the HRC would place it outside article 96 despite its strong links with the UN, see ch. 2, prs. 2.18–2.19 above. The General Assembly or the Security Council could obtain an advisory opinion concerning the ICCPR or the OP but such an opinion would not be binding on the States parties. See Sohn, ch 1 n. 1 above, p. 149 citing a Report of the Secretary-General (1950). We have already noted that all references to the ICJ in the ICCPR were deleted, see ch. 1, pr. 1.11 above. The EUCT has limited advisory jurisdiction under the 2nd Protocol to the ECHR which has never been invoked, see *ECHR—Collected Texts*, n. 11 above, pp. 27–30; Van Dijk and Van Hoof, pp. 187–90. The desirability of empowering the EUCT to give preliminary rulings at the request of a national court is being considered within the Council of Europe, see Information Sheet No. 18, Apx. XXIV, Council of Europe (1986) and Information Sheets No. 19, pp. 21–2 (1986); No. 24, p. 58 (1990). The IACT has issued a number of important advisory opinions, for example on reservations and the death penalty. See T. Buergenthal, 'The Advisory Jurisdiction of the Inter American Court of Human Rights', in T. Buergenthal (ed.), *Contemporary Issues in International Law*, pp. 127–47 (1984).

39 See the Netherlands proposal, A/C.3/L.1355, Report of the Third Committee, Doc. A/6546, pr. 474 (1966), and the ten-power amendment, Doc. A/C.3/L.1402/Rev. 2 (draft article 41 *bis*), ibid., pr. 477. For some of the different terminology used in some international instruments see Schwelb, 'Civil and Political Rights', n. 1 above, p. 864. 'The meaning of the term "petition" in continental and international legal usage is somewhat different from its meaning within the common law systems. ... The aim of the right of petition is especially to inform the relevant authorities of a certain problem or situation, and does not automatically lead to subsequent proceedings', Van Dijk and Van Hoof, p. 38.

40 The changes were suggested by France, Doc. A/C.3/SR.1418 pr. 8 (Mr Paolini). See also Doc. A/C.3/L.1394, later withdrawn. In the HRCion India proposed a 'petition' system under which the Committee might undertake an enquiry on receipt of complaints from groups of individuals and non-governmental organizations if it so decided. The proposal was rejected. This would have been a petition system in strict international law usage, see HRCion, Report of 7th session, ECOSOC OR, 13th session, Supp. 9, prs. 84–5.

41 See prs. 4.64–4.81 below. Cf. ECHR art. 25; ICERD art. 14; AMR art. 44.

42 See prs. 4.23–4.26 above.

43 Article 14(2) ICERD. For the background to this unusual provision see Humphrey, ch. 1 n. 1 above, p. 333 (1984); Lerner, ch. 3 n. 1 above, p. 84. See also article 14(3)–(6) ICERD. State representatives appearing before the HRC under the article 40 reporting process (see ch. 3 above) are sometimes asked whether

they would regard a particular remedy as constituting a domestic remedy requiring exhaustion under the OP.

44 See pr. 4.117 below.

45 See pr. 4.118 below.

46 See prs. 4.49–4.86 below.

47 See prs. 4.87–4.99 below.

48 See prs. 4.100–4.116 below.

49 This sentence has been the subject of an important decision by the HRC as to whether it applies to article 5(2)(*a*) OP as well as to article 5(2)(*b*) OP. See pr. 4.97 below.

50 Cf. articles 28 and 30 ECHR. See Van Dijk and Van Hoof, pp. 118–31. See also SR 502, pr. 8.

51 A good offices procedure is provided for in article 41(1)(*e*) ICCPR for inter-State complaints. On good offices in a human rights context generally see B. G. Ramcharan, *Humanitarian Good Offices in International Law* (1983).

52 For the importance of the HRC's Annual Report see ch. 3, pr. 3.40 above.

53 GA Resn. 1514(XV) (14 Dec. 1960), GAOR, 15th session, Supp. 16, p. 66.

54 Cf. article 15 ICERD. On the right of petition of such peoples see Zuidjwick, n. 1 above, ch. 4.

55 See pr. 4.6 below.

56 A discrepancy in the texts has been identified concerning article 5 OP, see pr. 4.87 below.

57 Mose and Opsahl, p. 276 argue that the speed of drafting has to be taken into account in interpreting and applying the OP.

58 In the Third Committee it was originally decided that the draft provisions on the right to individual petition would be included in a separate Protocol annexed to the Covenant. Subsequently the argument 'that it was impossible to have a Protocol that was both separate and annexed', was accepted, see SR A/C.3/SR.1451, pr. 62 (Saskena). See the comments at A/C.3/SR.1446 pr. 28 and SR 1451 pr. 54 (Schreiber, Director of the Human Rights Division). The ICCPR and the OP are listed as separate treaties by the Secretary-General of the UN. Professor Robertson has suggested that there is even some advantage in the OP being a separate treaty in terms of publicity, Robertson, ch. 2 n. 1 above, p. 360 (1981).

59 There were in fact twelve States parties as of that date.

60 See ch. 1, prs. 1.7, 1.24 above.

61 Article 29 VCLT (1969) provides that, 'Unless a different intention appears from the treaty or is otherwise established, a treaty is binding upon each State party in respect of its entire territory'.

62 'Human Rights—Status of International Instruments' (1987) p. 94, Doc. ST/HR/5.

63 See ch. 1, pr. 1.24 above.

64 See n. 62 above, pp. 91–4. See prs. 4.92–4.96 below.

65 Doc. A/44/40, Apx. I.

66 Of the twenty-three Contracting parties to the ECHR fourteen are also States parties to the OP. The UK has not signed or ratified the OP on the ground that, 'In

some respects it compares unfavourably from the individual's standpoint with the procedure established by article 25 of the European Convention on Human Rights, to which the United Kingdom has acceded', Hansard, HC Debs., Vol. 962, Written Answers, col. 262 (8 Feb. 1979). This view has recently been affirmed, see House of Lords Debates, Vol. 495, col. 591 (28 Mar. 1989) (Lord Glenarthur). See N. Grief, 'The International Protection of Human Rights: Standard-Setting and Enforcement by the United Nations and the Council of Europe' (1983) Bracton LJ pp. 41–65.

67 These States have traditionally not recognized the standing of the individual in international law, see ch. 1, prs. 1.18–1.21, 1.26 and ch. 4, pr. 4.2–4.4 above.

68 See ch. 1, pr. 1.25 above.

69 Doc. A/32/44 prs. 146–7.

70 Doc. A/44/40, pr. 614 as updated.

71 See Rules 78–81; Doc. A/32/44, prs. 52–4.

72 On behalf of the Secretary-General the Centre for Human Rights acts as the Secretariat to the HRC. The Secretariat staff for the work of the HRC under the OP is different from the staff which works with the HRC on the reporting process under article 40. The Communications Unit receives any submission, however addressed, provided it is intended for the UN and alleges some violation, Report of the Secretary-General, Doc. E/CN.4/1317 (1979). The Human Rights Centre employs nearly 50 professionals to serve the HRCion and related organs. On the HRC and the Secretariat see ch. 2, prs. 2.16–2.17 above. See also SD2 pp. 1–2.

73 The Secretariat refers as many communications as possible for consideration under the OP, Doc. E/CN.4/1317, n. 72 above, prs. 30–6 (1979).

74 SR 11 pr. 19 (Lallah).

75 SR 11 pr. 21 (Opsahl).

76 This point was consistently emphasized during the discussion and adoption of the HRC's Rules. The suggestion during the discussion by Mr Mazaud, Deputy Director of the then Division of Human Rights, that the Secretariat could take a decision on whether a communicant was under the jurisdiction of a State party to the OP must, it is submitted, be wrong (SR 11 pr. 32). Such a decision would clearly be one of substance that should be decided by the HRC.

77 SR 11 pr. 11 (Esperson).

78 SR 11 pr. 16 (Esperson).

79 SR 11 pr. 25 (Lallah).

80 R. 78(1). For example in *C.E.* v. *Canada*, SD, p. 16, C.E.'s letter was not explicitly addressed to the HRC but appeared to be submitted for consideration under the OP.

81 The CERD has adopted the same rule as the HRC but with the addition of the words, 'and who are subject to the jurisdiction of a State party bound by a declaration under article 14' (R. 83(1)). Under the ECHR procedures the Secretariat has the power to draw to the attention of potential applicants the possibility of rejection of the complaint in cases where the case law of the EUCM points in that direction, see Mikaelson, pp. 40–2; Van Dijk and Van Hoof, pp. 62–3. This does not occur under the OP.

82 See Doc. A/39/40, pr. 561.

83 R. 78(2).

84 Ibid.

85 R. 78(3). The CERD has adopted the same rule (R. 83(3)). A substantial number of applications to the EUCM have concerned States not a party to the ECHR. See EUCM, 'Survey of Activities and Statistics' (1989), p. 13.

86 See Doc. A/33/40, pr. 590.

87 See the comments of Graefrath at SR 11 pr. 27.

88 See Bossuyt, n. 1 above, pp. 130–3; Mose and Opsahl, p. 281.

89 The Secretariat model can be found in Apx. III below.

90 Doc. A/32/44, pr. 174. Cf. Rule 24 of the Rules of procedure of the EUCM, *ECHR—Collected Texts*, n. 11 above, p. 120.

91 Cf. article 14(2) ICERD (6 months); art. 26 ECHR (6 months); article 46 AMR (6 months).

92 Draft Rule 91(1), CCPR/C/L.2 and Add. 1 and 2.

93 See SR 20 prs. 51–60; SR 21 prs. 1–16.

94 SR 20 pr. 54 (Lallah).

95 SR 20 pr. 55 (Vincent-Evans).

96 SR 21 pr. 1 (Mr Mazaud, Deputy Director of the then Human Rights Division).

97 Article 26 ECHR.

98 SR 20 pr. 60 (Prado-Vallejo).

99 SR 21 pr. 5 (Opsahl).

100 SR 21 pr. 15 (Chairman).

101 See SR 20 pr. 57 (Vincent-Evans), SR 21 pr. 6 (Movchan), SR 21 pr. 8 (Esperson), SR 21 pr. 13 (Mora-Rojas). To the same effect see Mose and Opsahl, p. 310.

102 See Van Dijk and Van Hoof, pp. 113–14; Mikaelson, pp. 50–1.

103 For the HRC's discussion see SR 17 pr. 27–34, SR 34 pr. 60–74; Doc. A/32/44, prs. 90–4. See Mose and Opsahl, p. 315.

104 See prs. 4.19.4 below.

105 R. 79(1). For the HRC's discussion see SR 11 prs. 65–76.

106 R. 79(2).

107 R. 79(1). The numbering system used in the registration process was retrospectively changed at the HRC's eighteenth session, see Doc. A/37/40, note to pr. 381.

108 R. 81.

109 R. 80(1).

110 R. 80(2).

111 R. 80(1)(*a*)–(*g*). Under R. 80(3) the HRC may approve a questionnaire for the purpose of requesting this information from the author. Such a questionnaire is presently under consideration. When R. 80 (draft R. 81) was being adopted Mr Esperson stated that, 'It was possible for the State party to have entered a reservation when ratifying the Covenant and, in such cases, the Secretary-General had to determine whether its reservations applied to the communication under consideration' (SR 12 pr. 26). It is submitted that this view is incorrect. The applicability of a reservation must be a substantive question that is reserved to the HRC.

In fact the HRC has considered such a question in a number of cases. See e.g. *Fanali* v. *Italy*, ch. 10, pr. 10.52 below.

112 R. 80(4).

113 See Rules 82–6.

114 For the HRC's discussion see SR 12 pr. 28–34.

115 See e.g. the summary of the HRC's discussion of the question of follow-up to final views in prs. 4.41–4.43 below.

116 It is interesting to note, however, that a proposed rule referring to 'confidential' was not adopted.

117 If a communicant were to publicize this information the HRC might consider such action to be an abuse of the rights of submission and accordingly declare the communication inadmissible. See pr. 4.118 below.

118 These are published on the basis that they are 'final' decisions.

119 The identity of the authors and the State party concerned have sometimes been revealed in literature from the State party concerned. See e.g. the information published in Can. HRYB.

120 'Selected Decisions under the Optional Protocol (2nd–16th sessions)', Doc. CCPR/C/OP/1; (17th–32nd sessions), Doc. CCPR/C/OP/2 (1990).

121 The degree of publicity afforded by the HRC to its OP decisions has surprised and pleased the Secretariat (personal communication). None the less, the HRC can still look to the Council of Europe as a model of how to produce regular and detailed information concerning individual petitions.

122 R. 84(1)(*a*) and (*b*).

123 R. 84(2).

124 R. 85. In some views members have participated but not taken part in the adoption of the decision on admissibility or the view of the HRC. No explanation has been given for this practice. The explanation appears to lie in disagreement with the HRC on whether a member who is a national of the respondent State should take part in the consideration of such communications. The disagreement has not been definitively resolved to date, for example, Mr Aguilar Urbina took part in the admissibility decision in *J.R.C.* v. *Costa Rica*, Doc. A/44/40, p. 293.

125 For example, Mr Lallah did not take part in the *Mauritian Women Case* dealt with in pr. 4.75 below. Members who are nationals of the respondent State are not automatically precluded from consideration of the case. For example Mr Tarnopolsky took part in the decision in *McIsaac* v. *Canada*, Doc. A/38/40, p. 111. See n. 124 above.

126 Draft Rule 86, Doc. CCPR/C/L.2 and Add. 1 and 2, in Yb. HRC, Vol. ii, p. 1 at p. 7. See SR 13 prs. 26–59; SR 17 prs. 17–26; Mose and Opsahl, pp. 288–9. During the discussion it was debated whether the HRC could delegate to a working group any power concerning interim measures. In the result the power under R. 86 was reserved to the HRC. See, however, n. 130 below. Note also that there is no provision for interim measures in the inter-State procedure in the ICCPR nor has any such provision been made in the rules of procedure adopted by the HRC to deal with such complaints, Rules 72–7E. Interestingly, the HRCion's final draft contained an express provision on serious and urgent cases in the inter-State procedure, see article 40(3) in Doc. A/2929, p. 81 and p. 86, prs. 96–8. Mower,

n. 1 above, comments, 'For all practical purposes, the kind of approach this particular Committee takes to a State is irrelevant; what counts is that a Government
has been made aware of an international concern for the fate and well-being of an
individual, and of the feeling on the part of the international agency that interim
measures are necessary and desirable. What happens then depends on the
receptivity of a Government to international promptings, not the form in which
they are conveyed', p. 125. Cf. P. Mahoney, 'Development in the Procedure of the
EUCT: The Revised Rules of Procedure', 3 Yb. European Law (1983) p. 127 at
156–8; Van Dijk and Van Hoof, pp. 65–6, 152–3; article 48(2) AMR, Rule 26 of
The Rules of Procedure of the IACM, in 'Handbook', p. 130.

127 SR 17 pr. 25.

128 Even final views of the HRC are not binding, see prs. 4.37–4.40 below; Doc.
A/43/40, pr. 645.

129 During the HRC's debate it was suggested that this should be permissible to deal
with urgent cases. The draft rule 86 had provided that interim measures could be
requested 'at any time'. This was amended to 'prior to forwarding its final views'.
The International Court of Justice has had to face the same problem of whether to
issue interim measures before a decision on jurisdiction.

130 '... he mentioned the case of an alleged victim of violations of human rights
whose life had probably been saved by the fact that the Committee had asked for
her to be examined by a doctor. Another case, about eighteen months earlier, was
that of a person who had eventually not been extradited to a country where she
was in danger of being sentenced to death. Another victim of alleged violations of
human rights would be—or had already been—released. These cases showed that
action taken by the Committee was effective, even if it could not change political
systems or situations from one day to the next', SR 179 pr. 35 (Chairman). See
also SR 731 pr. 13 (Pocar). The HRC has requested a number of stays of
execution in respect of a number of individuals from Jamaica. Stays of execution
were granted, see Doc. A/43/40, pr. 655. The HRC appointed Mr Mavrommatis
to be Special Rapporteur on death penalty cases and authorized him to take rule
86 decisions on behalf of the Committee, ibid., pr. 656. Mrs Higgins, the Special
Rapporteur on new communications, now performs this role. See also *C.J.* v.
Jamaica, Doc. A/43/40, p. 267, pr. 6: 'The State party shall be requested, taking
into account the spirit and purpose of rule 86 ..., not to carry out the death
sentence against the author before he has had a reasonable time, after completing
the effective domestic remedies available to him, to request the Committee to
review the present decision'. See the decisions on Rule 86 in SD2, pp. 2–3.

131 See below, prs. 4.41–4.43.

132 Doc. A/37/40, p. 114. *See also Birindwa and Tshisekedi v. Zaïre*, Doc. A/45/40,
Apx., pr. 12.5.

133 Doc. A/37/40, p. 114, pr. 2.6.

134 Ibid., pr. 10.

135 Ibid., pr. 11 at 3.

136 Ibid., pr. 14.

137 Ibid.

138 Ibid.

139 Ibid., pr. 18. Antonaccio was still not permitted to communicate with the HRC. The HRC made a similar request in *Bequio* v. *Uruguay*, Doc. A/38/40, p. 180.

140 See Van Dijk and Van Hoof, pp. 49–52; Mikaelson, pp. 24–33. See also the 'European Agreement Relating to Persons Participating in Proceedings of the European Commission and Court of Human Rights', (1969), *ECHR—Collected Texts*, n. 11 above, pp. 100–9.

141 On the principle of effective interpretation see A. McNair, *Law of Treaties*, ch. 23; I. Brownlie, *Principles of Public International Law* (4th edn., 1990), p. 631; D. J. Harris, *Cases and Materials on International Law* (3rd edn., 1983), pp. 595–601.

142 A general proposition that individuals had status under international law was rejected by opponents of an individual right of petition, see ch. 4, pr. 4.2 above. Presumably such a proposition would still be objectionable to certain members of the HRC.

143 Doc. A/42/40, p. 130.

144 Ibid., pr. 15. See e.g. *Marais* v. *Madagascar*, Doc. A/38/40, p. 141.

145 Ibid., pr. 19.3.

146 See R. Clark, 'Legal Representation', in B. G. Ramcharan, (ed.), *International Law and Fact-Finding in the Field of Human Rights*, pp. 104–36 (1982); Ryan, n. 1 above; Zuidjwick, n. 1 above. See also *Hammel* v. *Madagascar*, pr.4.11 above.

147 Cf. R. 94(5) of CERD's Rules of Procedure which provides that 'The Committee may invite the presence of the petitioner or his representative and the presence of representatives of the State party concerned in order to provide additional information or to answer questions on the merits of the communication', UN Doc. CERD/C/35/Rev. 3, p. 28. There was some discussion in the CERD as to whether the Rule exceeded CERD's mandate and how the travel expenses of the petitioner would be defrayed if he was unable to pay them, see A/38/18, pr. 45 (1983). R. 30(1) of the revised rules of the EUCT (1982) allow an individual to play a much more significant role than hitherto in EUCT proceedings, see Mahoney, n. 126 above, pp. 127–41; P. T. Muchlinksi, 'The Status of the Individual under the ECHR and Contemporary International Law', 34 ICLQ (1985) pp. 376–82.

148 See pr. 4.14 below.

149 This rule is considerably relaxed in some cases, see prs. 4.70–4.74 below.

150 Ibid.

151 See prs. 4.23–4.26 below.

152 'Bearing in mind the admixture of adversarial and inquisitorial elements usually found in fact-finding it may be valuable for fact-finding bodies to consider ways and means of drawing upon legal expertise in the examination of witnesses and in the marshalling of evidence', Clark, n. 146 above, p. 130. Clark also notes 'the predilection to adopt civil law rather than common law modes of doing legal business', ibid., pp. 129–30. Further matters that would present themselves would be the possibility of submissions from interested third parties as has happened under the ECHR on a number of occasions, see Mahoney, n. 126 above, pp. 141–54; Van Dijk and Van Hoof, pp. 154–5.

153 Under the ECHR provision for legal aid is dealt with on the basis of administra-

tive measures devised by the Council of Europe. The provisions are set out in the Addendum to the EUCM's Rules of Procedure, see *ECHR—Collected Texts*, n. 11 above, pp. 134–5; Van Dijk and Van Hoof, pp. 63–4. In 1989 41 applicants received legal aid from the EUCM. The total sum expended was 300,000 French Francs, EUCM, 'Survey of Activities' (1989), p. 10.

154 Zuidjwick, n. 1 above, describes the present OP procedures as 'inexpensive and simple', p. 121 (1981).

155 On NGOs see ch. 1, pr. 1.15 above. A recent example of a body offering such assistance is INTERIGHTS, the International Centre for the Legal Protection of Human Rights (London). INTERIGHTS assisted in the case of *Robinson* v. *Jamaica*, Doc. A/44/40, p. 241.

156 See Rules 87–92. See in particular, Brar, n. 1 above (1986).

157 Doc. A/32/44, prs. 58–9; SR 20 prs. 3, 5, 6, and 8.

158 R. 89(1). The rules of procedure of the HRC apply as far as possible to the Working Group, R. 89(2).

159 Rule 89, Doc. A/44/40, prs. 618–20; Apx. IX. The Special Rapporteur has also assumed functions with respect to interim measures in death penalty cases, see pr. 4.10, n. 130 above.

160 Rules 78(2) and 80. One or more communications may be merged for joint consideration, R. 88(2). See, e.g., *Lanza and Perdoma* v. *Uruguay*, SD, p. 45, pr. 10; Doc. A/43/40, pr. 644.

161 For the discussion see SR 21 prs. 17–42, SR 22 prs. 1–45.

162 See prs. 4.70–4.74 below.

163 See SR 22 prs. 46–64; SR 33 prs. 21–52; Doc. A/32/44, prs. 68–73.

164 SR 33 pr. 23 (Mr Mazaud, Assistant Director, Division of Human Rights). The individual communications procedure in article 14 ICERD makes no reference to procedures of international investigation or settlement, see art. 14(7) ICERD.

165 Ibid. It is interesting to note the comments of Mr Movchan (USSR) 'The Legal Counsel's interpretation, based on semantic and historical considerations, should obviously be taken into account, but that did not mean that other interpretations, which might give more weight to ethics, psychology or the law and be based on the practice of international bodies, should be dismissed', SR 33 pr. 27. See also ibid., pr. 28. The comparable rule in the ICERD clearly only refers to domestic remedies, art. 14(7)(*a*) ICERD.

166 The Council of Europe has recently adopted an eighth Protocol to the ECHR with a view to speeding up the consideration of applications by the EUCM, see *ECHR—Collected Texts*, n. 11 above, pp. 57–62. See also 'Colloquy Report on Merger of the EUCM and EUCT', 8 HRLJ (1987) pp. 1–216; Council of Europe, Human Rights—Information Sheet No. 23, pp. 60–61.

167 It is worth noting here that the reservations made by all of the Contracting parties to the ECHR who have ratified the OP, bar the Netherlands and Portugal, would exclude such an eventuality by barring the HRC's jurisdiction *ab initio*, see prs. 4.93–4.96 below. See Van Dijk and Van Hoof, p. 59.

168 Doc. A/43/40, p. 252.

169 '... the Committee was unable to see that the only right which seemed to be involved was that provided for in article 27. However, article 27 has a precise

content. ... This article certainly does not demand of States parties that they require their postal administrations to issue postal cheques in a language other than the official language, nor does it stipulate that the authorities should accept information provided in another language. The Covenant is indifferent to the centralized or decentralized character of States, to the existence or non-existence of an official language. By apparently overlooking that point, the Committee arrived at a decision which is all the more open to criticism in that the question of national languages has enormous political significance for third world States, particularly in Africa. But whatever its legitimacy, the problem of such languages cannot be solved by acts of the Committee and in any case not beyond the content of article 27', ibid., appendix II, pr. 2.

170　See e.g. *A et al.* v. *S*, SD, p. 3.

171　See e.g. *Ramirez* v. *Uruguay*, Doc. A/35/40, p. 121; SD, p. 3.

172　R. 91(1).

173　Doc. A/32/44, p. 154; Doc. A/40/40, pr. 29.

174　Ibid. There is no specific rule of procedure on this point, see Mose and Opsahl, p. 287; Bossuyt, n. 1 above, p. 148. The time limits are often exceeded by both authors and States parties, see Schmidt, n. 1 above.

175　Doc. A/33/40, pr. 588.

176　R. 87. See n. 159 above.

177　It is clear, therefore, that a Special Rapporteur may be appointed before a decision as to admissibility is taken. The HRC's practice in this respect is similar to that of the EUCM, see Van Dijk and Van Hoof, pp. 64–5.

178　See prs. 4.49–4.118 below.

179　R. 92(1).

180　R. 92(2).

181　SR 33 pr. 9 (Opsahl).

182　See SR 24 pr. 62 (Tomuschat), SR 33 pr. 8 (Graefrath).

183　SR 33 pr. 15 (Graefrath).

184　See pr. 4.9 below.

185　Doc. A/38/40, pr. 395. See pr. 4.41 below on reconsideration of communications.

186　See *V* v. *S*, SD, p. 35; *B, C, D and E* v. *S*, SD, pp. 11–12. See also Doc. A/34/40, pr. 449.

187　*O.E.* v. *S*, SD, p. 35.

188　At least until those proceedings have been completed, see prs. 4.87–4.99 below (on art. 5(2)).

189　See pr. 4.5 above.

190　Doc. A/35/40, p. 120; SD, p. 36.

191　*V* v. *S*, n. 186 above.

192　See *A et al.* v. *S*, SD, pp. 35–6.

193　See text to notes 102–4 above. In *LSN* v. *Canada* the communication was withdrawn after legislative reform by Canada, SD2, p. 6. See also *MMQ* v. *Uruguay*, SD2, p. 8 and *NG* v. *Uruguay*, SD2, p. 9.

194　See e.g. *V* v. *S*, SD, p. 35. The communication was discontinued.

195　As noted above, in certain circumstances the Working Group may be able to take a decision declaring a communication admissible, see pr. 4.17 above. For examples of communications held partly admissible see *B, C, D and E* v. *S*, SD, pp. 11–12; *Pinkey* v. *Canada*, SD, pp. 12–15. For examples of admissibility decisions see *Waksman* v. *Uruguay*, SD, pp. 9–10; *Lovelace* v. *Canada*, SD, p. 10.

196 R. 93(1).

197 Ibid.

198 See Rules 93 and 94.

199 R. 93(2). If the facts are sufficiently clear and the parties agree the HRC can proceed immediately from the admissibility decision to a decision on the merits.

200 R. 93(3). See SR 34 prs. 2–13. They should also be communicated to the alleged victim if different, see pr. 4.11 above.

201 Doc. A/36/40, pr. 397.6.

202 SR 34 prs. 4–5.

203 Doc. A/36/40, pr. 397.7.

204 See e.g. *Massera and Others* v. *Uruguay*, SD, p. 37; *Lovelace* v. *Canada*, SD, pp. 37–9; *B* v. *S*, SD, p. 39; *Bleir* v. *Uruguay*, Doc. A/37/40, p. 130, prs. 11.1–13.1; *Hammel* v. *Madagascar*, Doc. A/42/40, p. 130, prs. 1a and 13.1.

205 See the discussion at SR 72 prs. 19–26.

206 R. 93(4). See *C.F. et al.* v. *Canada*, Doc. A/40/40, p. 217. Recourse to R. 93(4) was again made in *J.M.* v. *Jamaica*, Doc. A/41/40, p. 164; *Croes* v. *Netherlands*, Doc. A/44/40, p. 259. For cases where the HRC found no justification to review its decision declaring a communication admissible see *Hammel* v. *Madagascar*, Doc. A/42/40, p. 130, pr. 17, *Reid* v. *Jamaica*, Doc. A/45/40, Apx. See Mose and Opsahl, pp. 316–17.

207 Article 5(1) OP; R. 94(1).

208 Article 5(4) OP; R. 94(1).

209 R. 94(1).

210 Article 5(4) OP; R. 94(2). Both these provisions refer to the 'individual' rather than to the victim or the author.

211 The State party would seem to be under an obligation to allow the victim to receive the HRC's views, see pr. 4.11 above.

212 The same is true of the EUCM, the EUCT, the European Court of Justice, and the ICJ. The same used to be true of the Privy Council prior to 1966, see Lord Reid, 'The Judge as Law Maker' (1972) 12 JSPTL (NS) pp. 22–9.

213 See SR 34 prs. 14–47; Bossuyt, n. 1 above, pp. 152–3 (1978–9).

214 R. 94(3).

215 In most cases there has been only one individual opinion although more than one member may have associated themselves with that opinion. A number of individual opinions are noted as relevant points in this work.

216 Professor Robertson has commented that they 'should strengthen the quasi-judicial character of the HRC and should contribute to the development of its jurisprudence', in Henkin (ed.), n. 1 above, p. 363. Similarly, Bossuyt, n. 213 above.

217 See I. Hussain, *Dissenting and Separate Opinions in the World Court* (1984). Note also Lauterpacht, *The Development of International Law by the International Court* (1958), who quotes the following comment by Hughes CJ, 'A

dissent in a court of last resort is an appeal to the brooding spirit of the law, to the intelligence of a future day, when a later decision may possibly correct the error into which the dissenting judge believes the court to have been betrayed', p. 66 pr. 23, n. 10. This passage was adopted by Judge Jessup in his dissenting judgment in the South West Africa Cases and recalled by Judge Schwebel in his recent dissent in the *Case Concerning Military and Paramilitary Activities in and against Nicaragua*, (*Nicaragua* v. *US*), ICJ Reports, 1986, p. 14 at p. 167.

218 See generally B. G. Ramcharan, 'Evidence', in B. G. Ramcharan (ed.), *International Law and Fact-Finding in the Field of Human Rights*, p. 64 at pp. 68–83; H. Cohn, 'International Fact-Finding Processes', 18 Rev. ICJ (1977), p. 40; D. Sandifer, *Evidence before International Tribunals* (Rev. Edition) (1975).

219 Cf. the statement of the EUCT that, 'The Court is not bound, under the Convention or under general principles applicable to international tribunals, by strict rules of evidence. In order to satisfy itself, the Court is entitled to rely on evidence of every kind including, in so far as it deems them relevant, documents or statements emanating from Governments, be they respondent or applicant, or from their institutions or officials', *Ireland* v. *United Kingdom*, EUCT, Series A, Vo. 25, pr. 209.

220 Ramcharan, n. 218 above, p. 72.

221 See below pr. 4.118.

222 Ramcharan, n. 218 above, p. 73.

223 See Sandifer, n. 218 above, ch. 4.

224 See Clark, n. 146 above. On the ICJ see G. Schwarzenberger, *International law*, Vol. iv, pp. 636–40.

225 For some comment on this question see Schwelb, n. 1 above (1968), p. 867; Mose and Opsahl, pp. 279, 289–90; Tomuschat, n. 1 above, p. 254; Robertson, n. 1 above in Henkin (ed.), p. 361; A. Dieye, 'Hearings', in Ramcharan (ed.), n. 218 above, ch. 5.

226 See SR 138 prs. 105–21 (Confidential Document), referred to by Tomuschat, n. 1 above.

227 In 1980 Mr Tomuschat commented that 'Since it is confined to "written information", the Human Rights Committee finds itself in an extremely delicate situation. *To date, the procedure provided for in the Optional Protocol has not stood the test of viability*. And it is difficult to see how this unsatisfactory state of affairs could be improved', n. 225 above, p. 254 (my emphasis).

228 Members have indicated that matters raised in communications are becoming more complex and raising difficult questions of interpretation, see SR 731 pr. 14 (Chairman). In *Lubicon Lake Band* v. *Canada* the HRC observed that 'persistent disagreement between the parties as to what constitutes the factual setting for the dispute at issue has made the consideration of the claim on the merits most difficult', UN Doc. A/45/40, Apx., pr. 30.

229 See pr. 4.12 above. The question has been raised by members of the CERD with respect to the procedures recently adopted by them.

230 Ibid.

231 Tomuschat, n. 1 above, p. 254.

232 Mr Dieye, a former member of the HRC, has argued that, 'If it is not expressly

provided for, it is submitted that as a general principle, fact-finding bodies possess inherent competence to conduct hearings', n. 225 above, p. 94.

233 R. 68. See ch. 3, pr. 3.19 above.

234 Mose and Opsahl, p. 290, n. 98.

235 See Edmundo Vargas Carreno, 'Visits on the Spot—The Experience of the Inter-American Commission of Human Rights', in Ramcharan (ed.), n. 146 above, pp. 137–50; R. E. Norris, 'Observations *In Loco*—Practice and Procedure of the Inter-American Commission on Human Rights', 15 Texas ILJ (1980) pp. 46–95.

236 See H. C. Kruger, 'Visits on the Spot—The Experience of the European Commission of Human Rights', in Ramcharan (ed.), n. 146 above, pp. 151–9; Van Dijk and Van Hoof, pp. 109–12. Visits on the spot by the EUCM have generally concerned complaints under article 3 ECHR regarding the treatment of prisoners or other detained persons and the conditions of their detention. For example Commissioners have visited Broadmoor prison in the UK. A delegation from the EUCM visited Turkey (27 Jan. 1985–2 Feb. 1985) at the initiation of the Turkish Government to investigate violations of the ECHR alleged by Denmark, France, Netherlands, Norway, and Sweden, A. 9940–9944/82. A friendly settlement has recently been agreed which involves continuing supervision by the EUCM of the human rights situation in Turkey, see EUCM, Report on the Applications of Denmark, France, Netherlands, Norway and Sweden against Turkey and the Conclusion of a Friendly Settlement, 25 ILM (1986) pp. 308–18.

237 See G. Von Potobsky, 'Visits on the Spot—the Experience of the I.L.O', in Ramcharan (ed.), n. 146 above, pp. 160–75.

238 See also Sandifer, n. 218 above, s. 80.

239 See G. Von Potobsky, n. 237 above; F. Wolf, 'Human Rights and the International Labour Organisation', in T. Meron (ed.), *Human Rights in International Law—Legal and Policy Issues*, p. 273 at pp. 285–6 (1984).

240 See ch. 3, pr. 3.9 above.

241 Cf. the development of practices under the ECHR on the status of the individual and submissions from third parties, see Mahoney, n. 126 above, pp. 141–54.

242 See generally Sandifer, n. 218 above, ss. 29–32. See also pr. 4.102 below on the burden of proof as regards the exhaustion of domestic remedies.

243 Doc. A/39/40, pr. 588.

244 See e.g. *O.F.* v. *Norway*, Doc. A/40/40, p. 204; *M.F.* v. *Netherlands*, Doc. A/40/40, p. 213; *J.D.B.* v. *Netherlands*, Doc. A/40/40, p. 226; *K.L.* v. *Denmark*, SD, p. 24.

245 See Doc. A/36/40, pr. 397.3 at (*d*).

246 R. 91(2). Commentators regard this rule as of fundamental importance, see Cohn, n. 218 above.

247 Doc. A/41/40, p. 164.

248 In *Fals Borda and Others* v. *Colombia*, Doc. A/37/40, p. 193 and SD, p. 139, the HRC stated that the State party was not under a duty to address new allegations introduced only after a communication had been held admissible, pr. 13.5.

249 See e.g. *De Bouton* v. *Uruguay*, Doc. A/38/40, p. 143 and SD, p. 72, pr. 5 at 3. See below on how this approach has developed. For a case in which the HRC did accept the submission of the State party see *Scarrone* v. *Uruguay*, Doc. A/39/40,

p. 154. There the HRC found that in the light of information provided by the State party with regard to the treatment of Scarrone it could not justify a finding of a violation of article 10(1) of the Covenant (pr. 10.3).

250 See pr. 4.14 above. Such requests are usually made either within the HRC's admissibility decisions or by means of Interim (Interlocutory) Decisions. See e.g. *Lovelace v. Canada*, Doc. A/36/40, p. 166, prs. 7–8.

251 See e.g. *Bequio v. Uruguay*, Doc. A/38/40, p. 180, pr. 11.4; *Montejo v. Colombia*, Doc. A/37/40, p. 168 and SD, p. 127, pr. 9.2; *Cabriera v. Uruguay*, Doc. A/38/40, p. 209, pr. 10.3; *Vidal Martins v. Uruguay*, Doc. A/37/40, p. 157, and SD, p. 122, pr. 8.

252 See prs. 4.29–4.36.

253 The ICJ has faced the similar and related problem of non-appearance, see G. Fitzmaurice, 'The Problem of the Non-Appearing Defendant Government', 51 BYIL 1981 (1982) p. 89; J. B. Elkind, *Non-Appearance before the International Court of Justice: A Functional and Comparative Analysis* (1984); H. W. A. Thirlway, *Non-Appearance Before the International Court of Justice* (1985).

254 Doc. A/34/40, p. 124; SD, p. 40.

255 Ibid., pr. 6.

256 Ibid., pr. 7.

257 Ibid., pr. 9. Tomuschat, n. 1 above, p. 252, adds, 'Nor discloses any *prima facie* appearance of being false or inaccurate'. Note, however, that this sentence does not appear in the HRC's view.

258 Doc. A/35/40, p. 107; SD, p. 43.

259 Ibid., pr. 8.

260 Ibid., pr. 10.

261 Ibid., pr. 11.

262 Article 7 contains a prohibition on torture and inhumane or degrading treatment or punishment. See ch. 9 below.

263 Article 2 provides, *inter alia*, that States parties must respect and ensure to all individuals within their jurisdiction the rights in the ICCPR. See ch. 6 below.

264 Doc. A/35/40, p. 107; SD, p. 43.

265 See Mose and Opsahl, pp. 324–5; Anon., 23 Rev. ICJ (1979) p. 26 at 29–30.

266 See n. 251 above.

267 Doc. A/35/40, p. 111; SD, p. 45.

268 Ibid., pr. 15.

269 Doc. A/37/40, p. 130; SD, p. 109.

270 The alleged victim's father and mother.

271 Doc. A/37/40, p. 130, pr. 11.2 at 11.

272 Ibid., pr. 11.2 at 13.

273 Ibid., pr. 12.

274 Ibid., prs. 13.1–13.3. In *Birindwa and Tshisekedi v. Zaire*, Doc. A/45/40, Apx., the HRC took 'the opportunity to reiterate that while partial and incomplete information provided by States parties may assist in the examination of communications, it does not satisfy the requirement of article 4, paragraph 2, of the Optional Protocol', pr. 12.4.

275 See e.g. *Romero v. Uruguay*, Doc. A/39/40, p. 159, pr. 12.3.

276 See e.g. *Solorzano* v. *Uruguay*, Doc. A/41/40, p. 134; *Vasilskis* v. *Uruguay*, Doc. A/38/40, p. 173, prs. 10.3 and 10.4; *Pietraroia* v. *Uruguay*, Doc. A/36/40, p. 153 and SD, p. 76, pr. 15.

277 See Tomuschat, n. 1 above, pp. 252–3; Nowak, n. 1 above, pp. 159–60. See also the comments of the HRC in *Scarrone* v. *Uruguay*, Doc. A/39/40, p. 154, pr. 10.2.

278 Doc. A/38/40, p. 173.

279 Doc. A/38/40, p. 216.

280 See e.g. on derogations, *Silva* v. *Uruguay*, Doc. A/36/40, p. 130, dealt with in ch. 7, prs. 7.37–7.41 below.

281 Doc. A/37/40, p. 161.

282 See ch. 11, prs. 11.19–11.19.1 below.

283 See e.g. *Lanza and Perdoma* v. *Uruguay*, Doc. A/35/40 p. 111, pr. 15.

284 See text to n. 243 above.

285 In *Ireland* v. *United Kingdom*, the EUCT adopted a standard of beyond reasonable doubt in relation to allegations of violations of article 3 ECHR, EUCT, Series A, Vol. 25, prs. 160–1. See *Cross on Evidence*, pp. 141–8 (6th, 1985).

286 See R. S. Pathak, 'The Protection of Human Rights', 18 Ind. JIL (1978) pp. 165–73; C. Tomuschat, 'International Courts and Tribunals with Regionally Restricted and/or Specialized Jurisdiction', in H. Mosler and R. Bernhardt (eds.), *Judicial Settlement of International Disputes*, p. 285 at pp. 305–6 (1974); Schwelb, 'Civil and Political Rights', n. 1 above, pp. 857–9, 867–8; Capotorti, ch. 2 n. 1 above, p. 144; Saskena, ch. 1, n. 144 above, p. 596 at p. 610; Brar, n. 1 above, pp. 538–41; Mose and Opsahl, pp. 317–31; Tardu, n. 650 below, p. 781.

287 Cf. UN Doc. A/C.3/L.1402/Rev. 2 ('suggestions') with the revised text A/C.3/L.1411/Rev. 2 ('views'). See A/C.3/SR 1440, pr. 9 and SR 1441 pr. 40.

288 See n. 286 above. The Chairman of the CERD has suggested that the power of the CERD to make 'suggestions' and 'recommendations' under the petition procedure in article 14 ICERD gives the CERD greater competence than article 5(4) OP gives the HRC, see Report of the CERD, Doc. A/38/18, pr. 25 (1983). For the first opinion of the CERD see *Yilmaz-Dogan* v. *Netherlands*, Doc. CERD/C/36/D/1/1984. A second communication is under consideration.

289 n. 286 above.

290 n. 286 above.

291 'The HRC has managed to make its "views" under article 5(4) an efficient tool of its evaluation. None of the decisions hitherto handed down reads like a diplomatic communiqué. Obviously, they have all been drafted on the pattern of a judicial decision', Tomuschat, n. 1 above, p. 255. See also Nowak, n. 1 above (1980), p. 54; B. Graefrath, 'Trends emerging in the practice of the HRC', 3/80 Bulletin of the GDR Committee for Human Rights (1980) pp. 3–32.

292 See prs. 4.27–4.36 above.

293 Ibid. For example, in *Hammel* v. *Madagascar*, Doc. A/42/40, p. 130, pr. 19.2, the HRC took account of its general comment under article 40(4) on the position of aliens. States parties have also relied on the HRC's general comments in their submissions under the OP.

294 See chs. 5–12 below.

295 See e.g. ch. 9 below (on articles 7 and 10(1)).

296 See n. 1 above. The HRC specifically notes this in SD2, pr. 8.

297 See Van Dijk and Van Hoof, ch. 2.

298 See N. Valticos, *The International Labour Organization* (1979).

299 See. D. Harris, *The European Social Charter* (1984).

300 See Van Dijk and Van Hoof, chs. 3 and 4.

301 'States parties to the OP endeavour to observe the views, but in case of non-compliance the OP does not provide for an enforcement mechanism or for sanctions', SD2, pr. 8. It is uncertain whether the General Assembly or the ECOSOC could play any role in communications under their general jurisdictional powers. Brar, n. 1 above (1986) comments, 'It is hoped that the Third Committee of the General Assembly will be increasingly used as a forum to bring pressure to bear upon States parties to comply with the final views adopted by the Human Rights Committee', p. 541.

302 See n. 297 above.

303 See n. 298 above.

304 See n. 299 above.

305 Tomuschat, n. 1 above, p. 255. Unfortunately, this was perhaps the case with Uruguay prior to the new government in March 1985.

306 Capotorti, ch. 2 n. 1 above, p. 144.

307 See e.g. *Ambrosini, Massera and Massera* v. *Uruguay*, Doc. A/34/40, p. 124, pr. 10 at (iii).

308 See e.g. *Lopez Burgos* v. *Uruguay*, Doc. A/36/49, p. 176, pr. 14. In *Carballal* v. *Uruguay*, Doc. A/36/40, p. 125, pr. 14 the obligation specified was to provide effective remedies, 'If applied for'. There is no explanation of why this requirement only appears in that view.

309 See e.g. *De Montejo* v. *Uruguay*, Doc. A/37/40, p. 168, pr. 12; *Broeks* v. *Netherlands*, Doc. A/42/40, p. 139, pr. 16.

310 See e.g. *Carballal* v. *Uruguay*, Doc. A/36/40, p. 125. In a number of cases the HRC has specifically referred to 'compensation in accordance with article 9(5) of the Covenant'. See e.g. *Santullo (Valcada)* v. *Uruguay*, Doc. A/35/40, p. 107, pr. 13. Mose and Opsahl, comment that, 'The specific provision referred to here does not exclude other remedies, but since neither the Protocol nor the Covenant prescribe what kind of measures are required in the various situations of violations, the Committee apparently felt it could not be more precise', p. 324.

311 See e.g. *Lopez Burgos* v. *Uruguay*, Doc. A/36/40, p. 176; *Robinson* v. *Jamaica*, Doc. A/44/40, p. 241; *Pratt and Morgan* v. *Jamaica*, Doc. A/44/40, p. 222.

312 See e.g. *Silva and Others* v. *Uruguay*, Doc. A/36/40, p. 130, pr. 10.

313 See e.g. *Aumeeruddy-Cziffra and Others* v. *Mauritius*, Doc. A/36/40, p. 134, pr. 11; *Fals Borda* v. Colombia, Doc. A/37/40, p. 193, pr. 15.

314 See e.g. *Lopez Burgos* v. *Uruguay*, Doc. A/36/40, p. 176.

315 See e.g. *Barbato* v. *Uruguay*, Doc. A/38/40, p. 124, pr. 11.

316 See e.g. *Antonaccio* v. *Uruguay*, A/37/40, p. 114, pr. 21.

317 See e.g. *Bleir* v. *Uruguay*, Doc. A/37/40, p. 130, pr. 15; *Barbato* v. *Uruguay*, Doc. A/38/40, p. 124, pr. 11.

318 See e.g. *De Guerrero* v. *Uruguay*, Doc. A/37/40, p. 137, pr. 15.

319 See e.g. *Antonaccio* v. *Uruguay*, Doc. A/37/40, p. 114, pr. 21.

320 See e.g. *Vidal Martins* v. *Uruguay*, Doc. A/37/40, p. 157, pr. 10. In three parallel cases concerning passports the HRC referred only to an obligation to provide effective remedies pursuant to article 2(3) of the Covenant, *Lichtenszteijn* v. *Uruguay*, Doc. A/38/40, p. 166, pr. 10; *Montero* v. *Uruguay*, Doc. A/38/40, p. 186, pr. 11; *Nuñez* v. *Uruguay*, Doc. A/38/40, p. 225, pr. 11.

321 See e.g. *Muteba* v. *Uruguay*, Doc. A/39/40, p. 182, pr. 13. In *Baritussio* v. *Uruguay*, Doc A/37/40, p. 187, pr. 14, the HRC urged the State party 'to investigate the allegations of torture made against named persons in this case'.

322 See e.g. *Ex-Philibert* v. *Zaïre*, Doc. A/38/40, p. 197, pr. 9.

323 See e.g. *Lopez Burgos* v. *Uruguay*, Doc. A/36/40, p. 176. This obligation has been expressed in the majority of views to date.

324 See e.g. *Barbato* v. *Uruguay*, Doc. A/38/40, p. 124, pr. 11.

325 Note that in *Marais* v. *Madagascar*, Doc. A/38/40, p. 141, pr. 20, the HRC's views included the statement that, 'The Committee would welcome a decision by the State party to release Mr Marais, prior to completion of his sentence, in response to his petition for clemency'. Mr Marais was not released until the completion of his sentence.

326 On the powers of the EUCT under article 50 ECHR see Van Dijk and Van Hoof, pp. 171–85, and R. 53 of the EUCT's Rules of Procedure. There is now a substantial jurisprudence on article 50 ECHR. See also article 32 ECHR for the role of the Committee of Ministers when a case is not referred to the EUCT. See generally on State responsibility for human rights violations Meron, ch. 1 n. 225 above, part III.

327 In two cases the HRC has had recourse to R. 93(4) of its rules which provides for a review of a decision declaring a communication admissible in the light of any explanations or statements submitted by the State party. See *C.F. et al.* v. *Canada*, Doc. A/40/40, p. 217; *J.M.* v. *Jamaica*, Doc. A/41/40, p. 164. In both cases the authors made no comments on the information subsequently provided by the State party.

328 See e.g. pr. 4.10 above on interim measures under the OP.

329 For the text of the Preamble see Apx. II below.

330 See ch. 6 below.

331 Doc. A/38/40, prs. 392–3.

332 Doc. A/39/40, pr. 621.

333 Ibid.

334 Doc. A/38/40, pr. 394 and Apx. XXXI.

335 Ibid., Apx. XXXIII.

336 Ibid., Apx. XXXII. In 1989 Finland informed the HRC that the necessary steps would be taken to alter the law to comply with the view of the HRC in *Vuolanne* v. *Finland*, Doc. A/44/40, p. 249: violation of article 9(4) of the Covenant because V unable to challenge his detention before a court. See Doc. A/44/40, Apx. XII.

337 Doc. A/39/40, pr. 624.

338 Doc. A/39/40, pr. 623.

339 Doc. A/39/40, pr. 623. The three individuals were J. L. Massera, Doc. A/34/40, p. 124; L. Celiberti de Casariego, Doc. A/36/40, p. 185; R. Pietraroia, Doc. A/36/40, p. 153. Professor Tolley has noted that J. L. Massera, a distinguished mathematician, was released three days before the situation in Uruguay was to be subject to a private discussion in the Human Rights Commission. He comments that, 'a procedure fashioned to redress patterns of gross violations thus produced an isolated individual remedy granted for symbolic effect', 'The Concealed Crack in the Citadel: The United Nations Commission on Human Rights' Response to Confidential Communications', 6 HRQ (1984), p. 420 at p. 457.

340 Doc. A/40/40, pr. 703. The newly elected government came to power on 1 March 1985. The new government provided the HRC with part of the text of a general amnesty law of 8 March 1985 under which all political prisoners had been released and all forms of political banishment had been lifted. In *Conteris* v. *Uruguay*, Doc. A/40/40, p. 196, pr. 9.2, the HRC noted that Conteris has been released pursuant to this general amnesty.

341 Ibid. The individuals concerned have included Antonaccio, Izquierdo, Bequio, Vasilskis, Nieto, Machado, Scarrone, and Romero, cited in Nowak, n. 1 above (1986) p. 305 n. 74.

342 Doc. A/40/40, pr. 704. *Lovelace* v. *Canada*, Doc. A/36/40, p. 166; SD, p. 83.

343 *Monja Jaona* v. *Madagascar*, Doc. A/40/40, p. 179.

344 Doc. A/40/40, pr. 705.

345 Doc. A/39/40, pr. 625; Doc. A/40/40, pr. 706.

346 Doc. A/37/40, p. 161; SD p. 24.

347 Ibid., pr. 9.2.

348 Doc. A/37/40, p. 101; SD p. 12.

349 Ibid., pr. 11. See also the arguments raised by both the State party and the author in *M.A.* v. Italy, Doc. A/39/40, p. 190.

350 Doc. A/36/40, p. 160; SD p. 80.

351 Ibid., pr. 10.1.

352 Ibid., pr. 10.2. The Committee had established that article 13 requires compliance with both the substantive and the procedural requirements of the law, ibid., pr. 9.3. For article 13 see Apx. I. On the interpretation of 'in accordance with the law' under the ECHR see Van Dijk and Van Hoof, pp. 578–83.

353 Doc. A/40/40, p. 215.

354 Ibid., pr. 7.2. Similarly in *Muhonen* v. *Finland*, Doc. A/40/40, p. 164, pr. 11.1, as regards the evaluation by Finnish authorities of an application for exemption from armed or unarmed service in the Finnish Armed Forces.

355 *Fals Borda* v. *Colombia*, Doc. A/37/40, p. 193, pr. 13.3.

356 An example is the *Fals Borda* case, ibid.

357 *Hertzberg and Others* v. *Finland*, Doc. A/37/40, p. 161; SD p. 124, pr. 9.3. See also *McIsaac* v. *Canada*, Doc. A/38/40, p. 111, pr. 10.

358 Doc. A/43/40, p. 230 and 2 appendices. See also *J.H.* v. *Finland*, Doc. A/44/40, p. 298, in which the HRC noted, *inter alia*, that it is 'not an appellate court . . .', pr. 6.4. 'While article 14 of the Covenant guarantees the right to a fair trial, it is for the appellate courts of the States parties of [*sic*] the Covenant to evaluate facts and evidence in a particular case', *A. W.* v. *Jamaica*, Doc. A/45/40, Apx., pr. 8.2,

and *G.S.* v. *Jamaica*, Doc. A/45/40, Apx., pr. 3.2. See also the individual opinions of Ms Chanet in these two decisions.

359 'the Committee applies the provisions of the Covenant and of the OP in a judicial spirit and, performs functions similar to those of the EUCM, in as much as the consideration of applications from individuals is concerned. Its decisions on the merits (of a communication) are, in principle, comparable to the reports of the EUCM, non-binding recommendations', SD2, p.1. See Fawcett, pp. 323–9.

360 See *Ireland* v. *UK*, EUCT, Series A, Vol. 25 (1978), pr. 239, *Austria* v. *Italy*, EUCM, decn. admiss., 4 YBECR (1961) p. 116; Fawcett, pp. 330–5. Cf. the 2nd Advisory Opinion of the IACT on *The Entry into Force of the American Convention for a State Ratifying or Adhering with a Reservation*, 3 HRLJ (1982) pp. 153–65. 'In concluding these human rights treaties, the States can be deemed to submit themselves to a legal order within which they, for the common good, assume various legal obligations, not in relation to other States, but towards all individuals within their jurisdiction', ibid., pr. 29.

361 See P. Hassan, 'The International Covenants on Human Rights: An Approach to Interpretation', 19 Buffalo LR (1969) pp. 35–50; id., 'The International Covenant on and Political Civil Rights: Background and Perspective on Article 9(1)', 3 Denver JILP (1973) pp. 153–83. See generally, articles 31–2 VCLT (1969).

362 Doc. A/37/40, p. 150. See T. Opsahl and A. De Zayas, 'The Uncertain Scope of Article 15(1) of the International Covenant on Civil and Political Rights' (1983) Can. HRYB pp. 237–54.

363 Doc. A/37/40, p. 150, pr. 6.2.

364 Ibid., pr. 8.6.

365 See I. Brownlie, *Principles of Public International Law*, pp. 288–9, 626–32 (4th, 1990).

366 Doc. A/37/40, p. 150, pr. 10.2 (my emphasis). See also *Maroufidou* v. *Sweden*, Doc. A/36/40, p. 160, on article 13 ICCPR, 'The reference to "law" in this context is to the domestic law of the State concerned, which in the present case is Swedish law, though of course the relevant provisions of domestic law must themselves be compatible with the provisions of the Covenant', ibid., pr. 9.3.

367 See e.g. the decision of the EUCT in the *Engel Case* (1978) on the concept of 'criminal charge' in article 6(1) ECHR. The equivalent of article 15(1) ICCPR can be found in article 7 ECHR. The EUCM has deemed itself competent to review the interpretation and application of the provisions of municipal law by the national court, A.1852/63, *X.* v. *Austria*, Yearbook VIII (1965) p. 190 at p. 198. See Van Dijk and Van Hoof, pp. 358–68, who comment, 'As a matter of fact the case law of the Commission shows that the national authorities hardly have to fear an autonomus interpretation of that municipal law by the Commission', p. 360.

368 Doc. A/36/40, p. 166; SD p. 83.

369 Ibid., pr. 14.

370 Ibid.

371 'A Treaty shall be interpreted in good faith in accordance with the ordinary meaning to be given to the terms of the treaty in their context and in the light of its object and purpose', article 31(1) VCLT (1969).

372 See e.g. *Wemhoff* v. *FRG*, EUCT, Series A, Vol. 7 (1968); *Golder* v. *UK*, ibid., Vol. 18 (1981); *Airey* v. *Ireland*, ibid., Vol. 32 (1979); *Young, James and Webster*, v. *UK*, ibid., Vol. 44 (1981).

373 See e.g. *Dudgeon* v. *UK*, EUCT, Series A, Vol. 45 (1981); *Marcxx* case, ibid. Vol. 31 (1979); *Weeks* v. *UK*, ibid., Vol. 114 (1987). See generally C. C. Morrisson, *The Dynamics of Development in the European Human Rights Convention System* (1981); Merrills, chs. 4, 5.

374 *Broeks* v. *Netherlands*, Doc. A/42/40, p. 139; *Danning* v. *Netherlands*, ibid., p. 151; *Zwaan-de Vries* v. *Netherlands*, ibid., p. 160. See prs. 4.55–4.58 below.

375 Ibid., pr. 12.2 of each view.

376 Ibid., pr. 12.3 of each view.

377 See n. 371 above.

378 Doc. A/36/40, p. 176.

379 Ibid., pr. 12.3.

380 Doc. A/37/40, p. 161; SD p. 124.

381 Ibid., pr. 2.1.

382 Ibid., pr. 10.3. For the HRC's view see ch. 11 below.

383 See C. Morrisson, 'Margin of Appreciation in European Human Rights Law', 6 RDH/HRJ (1973) pp. 263–86; T. O'Donnell, 'The Margin of Appreciation Doctrine: Standards in the Jurisprudence of the European Court of Human Rights', 4 HRQ (1982) pp. 474–96; Van Dijk and Van Hoof, pp. 585–606; C. Feingold, 'The Little Red Schoolbook and the European Convention on Human Rights', 3 HR Rev. (1978) pp. 263–86; H. C. Yourow, 'The Margin of Appreciation in the Dynamics of European Human Rights Jurisprudence', 3 Connecticut JIL (1987) pp. 111–59.

384 See Brar, n. 1 above, pp. 507–31; Mose and Opsahl, pp. 295–302.

385 Generally see article 28 of the Vienna Convention on the Law of Treaties (1969). For the practice under the ECHR see Van Dijk and Van Hoof, pp. 9–11. For recent decisions see *Baggetta* v. *Italy*, EUCT, Series A, Vol. 119 (1987); *Milasi* v. *Italy*, ibid., Vol. 119 (1987).

386 See e.g. *Sequeira* v. *Uruguay*, Doc. A/35/40, p. 127; *De Touron* v. *Uruguay*, Doc. A/36/40. p. 120. This also applies to the right to a remedy under article 2 of the ICCPR, see *R.A.V.N.* v. *Argentina*, Doc. A/45/40, Apx., and the accompanying individual opinion of Wennergren.

387 See e.g. *C.E.* v. *Canada*, SD, p. 16.

388 SD, p. 29.

389 Ibid., pr. 5.1. The communication concerned certain provisions of the Parole Act 1970 and article 15 of the ICCPR.

390 Doc. A/33/40, pr. 581. See e.g. *A et al.* v. *S*, SD, p. 3 and p 17. Cf. the decision of the EUCM in the *De Becker* case, 2 YBECHR (1958–9), p. 214 at pp. 233–4.

391 See e.g. *De Bazzano* v. *Uruguay*, SD, p. 40; *L.P.* v. *Canada*, SD, p. 21.

392 See e.g. *De Bazzano* v. *Uruguay*, ibid., pr. 10.

393 Doc. A/37/40, p. 122.

394 Ibid., prs. 8(2), 9(2). See also *Acosta* v. *Uruguay*, Doc. A/39/40, p. 169, pr. 14.

395 Doc. A/36/40, p. 125.

396 Ibid., pr. 5(*a*).

397 Doc. A/38/40, p. 209.

398 Ibid., pr. 2.3.

399 Doc. A/39/40, p. 190.

400 Ibid., pr. 7.2.

401 See Doc. A/38/40, p. 209.

402 Doc. A/39/40, p. 190, pr. 9.

403 Ibid., pr. 13.2.

404 Doc. A/40/40, p. 215.

405 Ibid., pr. 4.

406 Ibid., pr. 7.3. Note also *Gueye and Others* v. *France*, Doc. A/44/40, p. 189, in which the HRC considered an interpretative declaration by France purporting to limit the HRC's competence *ratione personae*.

407 Under article 5 of the OP2 the competence of the HRC under the OP extends to OP2 unless the State party has stated to the contrary on ratification or accession. 'The OP provides a procedure under which individuals can claim that their individual rights have been violated. These rights are set out in part III of the Covenant, articles 6 to 27 inclusive', *Lubicon Lake Band* v. *Canada*, Doc. A/45/40, Apx. Cf. the practice under the parallel article 25 ECHR as to which see Van Dijk and Van Hoof, pp. 78–80; *Digest of Strasbourg Case Law Relating to the ECHR*, Vol. i (articles 1–5), pp. 22–73, Council of Europe (1984). By contrast the inter-State procedure under article 24 ECHR covers alleged violations of any of the provisions of the ECHR, not just its Section I. The position would probably be the same under the inter-State procedure in article 41 of the ICCPR.

408 Doc. A/39/40, pr. 587. See e.g. *J.J.* v. *Denmark*, SD, p. 26, in which the author's complaint concerned the refusal of the Ombudsman to censure a decision of the Ministry of Justice; *H.M.C.A.* v. *Netherlands*, Doc. A/44/40, p. 267, pr. 11.6: 'The Covenant does not provide for the right to see another person criminally prosecuted'; *V.R.M.B.* v. *Canada*, Doc. A/43/40, p. 258, pr. 6.3: the Committee 'observes that a right of asylum is not protected by the Covenant'.

409 SD, p. 24.

410 Ibid. The HRC also found no facts to substantiate the author's claims that she was a victim of a breach of articles 2(1), 3, or 26 or of any other rights protected by the Covenant. A right to property was proposed in both the HRCion and the Third Committee of the General Assembly, see ch. 1 n. 200 above.

411 SD, p. 16.

412 Doc. A/38/40, p. 241.

413 Ibid., prs. 1 and 2.

414 Ibid., pr. 5.

415 Ibid. The reference to racial discrimination raises the important question of whether the ICCPR contains a prohibition on certain forms of discrimination or only a prohibition on certain forms of dicrimination with respect to the rights contained in the ICCPR. See now the important decisions of the HRC noted in prs. 4.55–4.58 below. Under article 14 ECHR there is only the more limited protection as regards the rights in section I. Cf. the admissibility decision of the EUCM in the *East African Asians Cases*, 13 YBECHR 928 at 994 (1970), where

the EUCM stated that, 'Quite apart from any consideration of article 14, discrimination based on race could, in certain circumstances, of itself amount to degrading treatment within the meaning of article 3 of the Convention'. See Morrisson, *The Dynamics of Development in the European Human Rights Convention System Rights* (1981).

416 Doc. A/42/40, p. 170.

417 Ibid., pr. 7.3. See ibid., prs. 4 and 6.1.

418 Doc. A/42/40, p. 170.

419 Doc. A/40/40, p. 240.

420 Ibid., pr. 5.2. See also *M.J.G. v. Netherlands*, Doc. A/43/40, p. 271 and *Järvinen v. Finland*, n. 437 below. For the provisions of the Covenant see Apx. I. For a recent report see A. Eide and C. Mubanga-Chipoya, 'Conscientious Objection to Military Service', UN Doc. E/CN.4/Sub.2/1983/30/Rev. 1 (1985). See also Recommendation No. R(87)8 of the Committee of Ministers of the Council of Europe (April, 1987); HRCion Resn. 1989/59, Report on 45th Session, ECOSOC OR, 1989, Supp. 2, p. 139.

421 SD p. 24. The position is the same under the ECHR.

422 SD p. 24. The author had occasionally worked as a television repairman without the required licence from the Chamber of Commerce. He claimed that he was 'discriminated against by Dutch legislation which prevents him from gainful employment and which punishes him for seeking an alternative to being unemployed'.

423 On the right to work see D. Harris, *The European Social Charter*, pp. 21–37 (1985).

424 On the drafting of article 26 see Bossuyt, *Guide*, pp. 479–92. For academic views on the interpretation of article 26 see Ramcharan and Tomuschat, in ch. 6 n. 1 below. More generally see C. Scott, 'The interdependence and permeability of human rights norms: towards a partial fusion of the international Covenants on human rights', 27 Osgoode Hall LJ (1989) pp. 769–878.

425 Doc. A/42/40, p. 139. See also *P.P.C. v. Netherlands*, Doc. A/43/40, p. 244.

426 Doc. A/42/40, p. 160.

427 Doc. A/42/40, p. 151.

428 *Broeks v. Netherlands*, Doc. A/42/40, p. 139, pr. 8.3.

429 Ibid., pr. 8.5. See ch. 1, prs. 1.8–1.12, 1.18–1.21 above.

430 Doc. A/42/40, p. 139, prs. 12.1–1.13.

431 Ibid., prs. 14–15.

432 Doc. A/42/40, p. 160, prs. 14–15.

433 Doc. A/42/40, p. 151.

434 Ibid., pr. 14.

435 See n. 424 above.

436 See *I.M. v. Norway*, pr. 4.53 above.

437 See *Gueye and Others v. France*, Doc. A/44/40, p. 189, pr. 6, concerning alleged discrimination in respect of pension rights; *Vos v. Netherlands*, Doc. A/44/40, p. 232, concerning alleged discrimination in respect of welfare legislation. *H.A.E.d.j. v. Netherlands*, and *Jarvinen v. Finland*. The EUCT has recently dealt with social security cases in terms of article 6 ECHR, see *Feldbrugge Case v.*

Netherlands, EUCT, Series A, Vol. 99, (1986); *Deumeland* v. *FRG*, ibid., Vol. 100 (1986).

438 It is often alleged that UK immigration legislation and practice is discriminatory though this is rejected by the present government. See A. Owers, 'Immigration', in P. Sieghart (ed.), *Human Rights in the United Kingdom*, pp. 18–28 (1988).

439 *Broeks* v. *Netherlands*, Doc. A/42/40, p. 139, pr. 8.3.

440 The HRC have applied the concept under the OP, see ch. 11 below. On the margin of appreciation see n. 383 above.

441 See the *Belgian Linguistics Case*, EUCT (1968); Van Dijk and Van Hoof, pp. 532–48; Merrills, pp. 152–9.

442 See R. D. Rotunda, J. E. Nowak, and J. N. Young, *Treatise on Constitutional Law*, Vol. ii, ch. 18 (1986).

443 See prs. 4.46–4.48 above on the interpretation of the Covenant and the Optional Protocol.

444 SD, p. 27.

445 For these provisions see Apx. I below.

446 Doc. A/41/40, p. 151.

447 Doc. A/39/40, p. 190.

448 See pr. 4.51 above.

449 Doc. A/39/40, p. 190, pr. 13.3.

450 A.250/47, 1 YBECHR 222 (1955–7). On article 17 ECHR see Van Dijk and Van Hoof, pp. 562–87

451 Doc. A/39/40, p. 190.

452 Ibid., pr. 13.4.

453 See Fawcett, pp. 51–3, 119–20; *Soering* v. *UK*, EUCT, Series A, Vol. 161 (1989).

454 On the facts, however, this would not have assisted M.A. because the OP did not enter into force with respect to France until 17 May 1984.

455 See Van Dijk and Van Hoof, p. 80.

456 See e.g. the approach of the HRC in the case of *A.S.* v. *Canada*, SD, p. 27, pr. 4.

457 See Mose and Opsahl, pp. 298–302; Meron, n. 1 above, pp. 100–6; Brar, n. 1 above pp. 509–15. On the practice under the ECHR see Van Dijk and Van Hoof, pp. 76–8.

458 Article 1 OP.

459 See ch. 1, pr. 1.33.

460 There is no denunciation clause in the ICCPR although one was considered, see ch. 1, n. 210 above. There is a denunciation clause in the OP (article 12). Generally see articles 42–72 of the Vienna Convention on the Law of Treaties (1969).

461 See ch. 4, pr. 4.9 above.

462 Doc. A/44/40, p. 286, pr. 6.5. For the practice under the ECHR see Van Dijk and Van Hoof, pp. 76–8. On the general rules of State responsibility see I. Brownlie, *Systems of the Law of Nations—State Responsibility* (Part I), chs. 7 and 8, (1983).

463 Doc. A/37/40, p. 161. The case is discussed in ch. 11, prs. 11.19–11.19.2 below.

464 Doc. A/37/40, p. 161, pr. 2.1.

465 Ibid., pr. 2.2.

466 Ibid., pr. 9.1.

467 *Young, James and Webster* v. *UK*, EUCT, Series A, Vol. 44, prs. 48–9 (1981). Accordingly, the EUCT did not examine whether, as the applicants had argued, the State might also be responsible on the ground that it should be regarded as employer or that British Rail was under its control.

468 See A.4515/50, *X and Association of Z* v. *UK*, Coll. 38, p. 86 (1972). The application concerned complaints about the BBC. The EUCM expressly left the question of State responsibility open. See also A.6586/74, *X* v. *Ireland* (unpublished).

469 F. Jacobs, *The European Convention on Human Rights* (1975) made this suggestion with respect to the ECHR. However, the EUCT has decided that article 1 of the ECHR is not capable of independent violation, *Ireland* v. *United Kingdom*, EUCT, Series A, Vol. 25 (1978), pr. 13. The precise effect of article 13 of the ECHR has not yet been fully resolved, see Van Dijk and Van Hoof, pp. 520–32, Fawcett, pp. 289–94, who comments that, 'The fact is that there is basic confusion of thought as to the real purpose and function of the Article', (p. 294).

470 See also A. 852/60, *X* v. *FRG*, 4 YBECHR (1961), p. 346 at pp. 350–2; Merrills, pp. 100–3.

471 In *EHP and Others* v. *Canada* the HRC stated that 'the question of whether a communication can be submitted on behalf of "future generations" does not have to be resolved in the circumstances of the present case', SD2, p. 20, pr. 8. Cf. article 25(1) ECHR. See Brown Weiss, *In Fairness to Future Generations* (1990).

472 For example, in the *Mauritian Women* case the communication was submitted by twenty Mauritian women, Doc. A/38/40, p. 145; SD, p. 67. Initially the authors requested that their identity should not be disclosed to the State party. Subsequently, one of the authors agreed to the disclosure of her name. Such requests could cause difficulties if acceded to because it may not be possible for the State party to properly defend itself unless it knows the particular circumstances of the individual or individuals concerned. In *Gueye and Others* v. *France*, Doc. A/44/40, p. 189, the communication was submitted on behalf of the author and 742 other retired Senegalese members of the French Army.

473 For example, in *Marais* v. *Madagascar*, Doc. A/38/40, p. 141, M was a South African national. South Africa is not a party to the ICCPR. On the requirement that the individual be 'subject to the jurisdiction' of the State party (article 1) see prs. 4.82–4.86 below.

474 Doc. A/39/40, p. 197.

475 Ibid., pr. 1.

476 Ibid., pr. 5. 'A company incorporated under the laws of a State party to the Optional Protocol, as such, has no standing under article 1, regardless of whether its allegations appear to raise issues under the Covenant', *A Newspaper publishing company* v. *Trinidad and Tobago*, Doc. A/44/40, p. 307, pr. 3.2.

477 See pr. 4.78 below. Cf. the decision of the EUCM in the case of A.3798/68, *Church of Scientology* v. *UK*, 12 YBECHR p. 306. The decision is criticized by Jacobs, n. 469 above, p. 148.

478 Doc. A/38/40, p. 231.

479 Ibid., pr. 8.

480 These are examined in ch. 12 below.

481 Mose and Opsahl, p. 302. 'It may be noted that the Committee has not been authorized to receive communications from organizations. In a world where individuals can generally act effectively only through organizations, this omission is significant', Pathak, n. 1 above, p. 270. Professor Buergenthal has suggested that measures taken against a juridical person may amount to a violation of the ICCPR if they infringe upon rights of individuals, for example, the right of association, Buergenthal in Henkin (ed.), n. 1 above, p. 73. See also n. 407 above.

482 See prs. 4.75–4.81 below.

483 Doc. A/35/409, pr. 393.

484 See pr. 4.14 above.

485 R. 90(1)(*b*).

486 So, for example, in *Guerrero* v. *Colombia*, Doc. A/37/40, p. 137, the communication was submitted on behalf of the alleged victim's wife by a Professor of International Law from Colombia; in *Hertzberg* v. *Finland*, Doc. A/37/40, p. 161, the five authors and alleged victims were represented by SETA (Organization for Sexual Equality); in *Nunez* v. *Uruguay*, Doc. A/38/40, p. 225, the communication was submitted by the author with the assistance of the International League for Human Rights. On the concept of the 'author' see Mose and Opsahl, p. 300.

487 Doc. A/33/40, pr. 580. An objection to this approach was made in the Third Committee of the General Assembly by the representative of Argentina, UN Doc. A/C.3/32/SR.30 at 13, pr. 59 (1977).

488 *Bleir* v. *Uruguay*, Doc. A/37/40, p. 130. In *Croes* v. *Netherlands*, Doc. A/44/40, p. 259, the communication was submitted by C who subsequently passed away. C's heirs requested the Committee to continue its examination of the case.

489 *Bleir* v. *Uruguay*, ibid.

490 *Touron* v. *Uruguay*, Doc. A/36/40, p. 120.

491 *Mbenge* v. *Zaïre*, Doc. A/38/40, p. 134.

492 Ibid.

493 *Lanza and Perdoma* v. *Uruguay*, Doc. A/35/40, p. 111.

494 *Bleir* v. *Uruguay*, Doc. A/37/40, p. 130.

495 A member of the HRC has indicated that the status of a brother-in-law as a relative raised some discussion in the HRC, see V. Dimitrijevic, *The Roles of the Human Rights Committee*, p. 22 (1986).

496 Doc. A/35/40, p. 111.

497 Ibid., prs. 3 and 4.

498 Ibid., pr. 6.

499 Doc. A/39/40, pr. 571.

500 See e.g. *Hartikainen* v. *Finland*, Doc. A/36/40, p. 147; SD, p. 74, prs. 3–4.

501 See pr. 4.70 above.

502 See *A et al.* v. *S*, SD, pp. 3 and 17–18.

503 Doc. A/37/40, p. 187; SD, p. 136.

504 Doc. A/37/40, p. 187, pr. 2.1.

505 Ibid.

506 Ibid.

507 Ibid., pr. 4.

508 Doc. A/38/40, p. 134. Note that at the time of the submission M was resident in

Belgium. The alleged violations occurred after M had left Zaire in 1974. See also *A.S. v. Canada*, pr. 4.59 above, in which the author was resident in Canada and the communication concerned the failure by A.S. to obtain permission from the Canadian authorities for her daughter and grandson, who were resident in Poland, to enter Canada to join her.

509 Doc. A/38/40, p. 134, pr. 5.
510 Doc. A/38/40, p. 239.
511 Ibid., pr. 2.
512 Ibid., pr. 4. Similarly in *D.F. v. Sweden*, Doc. A/40/40, p. 228, concerning alleged discrimination and abuse of Arabs in Sweden.
513 Doc. A/38/40, p. 245. SD2, p. 43.
514 Ibid., pr. 1.
515 Ibid.
516 Ibid., pr. 3.
517 Doc. A/38/40, p. 247.
518 Ibid., pr. 1.
519 Ibid.
520 Ibid., pr. 3.
521 See Mose and Opsahl, pp. 301–2. On NGOs see ch. 1, pr. 1.15 above.
522 See ch. 5, pr. 5.22 below.
523 The victim requirement also appears in article 25 ECHR as to which see Van Dijk and Van Hoof, pp. 33–7.
524 Doc. A/36/40, p. 134; SD, p. 67.
525 Doc. A/36/40, p. 134, pr. 1. The two Acts concerned were the Immigration (Amendment) Act 1977 and the Deportation (Amendment) Act 1977.
526 Doc. A/36/40, p. 134, pr. 1.1.
527 Ibid., pr. 1.2.
528 Ibid., pr. 7.3.
529 Ibid., pr. 5.5.
530 Ibid., pr. 9.2. In the *South West Africa Cases* the ICJ stated that 'actio popularis', although known to certain legal systems, was not a general principle of law, ICJ Reports (1966), p. 6, at p. 47.
531 Ibid., pr. 9.2(*a*).
532 Ibid., pr. 10.3. Meron, n. 1 above comments that, 'This conclusion was not inevitable. The Committee could have reasoned that the statutes affected the right of the women to marry persons of their choice and that, therefore, these women could claim to be affected by a violation of article 23 when considered in conjunction with the provisions of the Political Covenant prohibiting discrimination', p. 105.
533 Doc. A/36/40, p. 134, pr. 9.2(*b*)2.
534 Ibid., pr. 9.2(*b*)2(i)3.
535 The HRC expressed the view that the facts disclosed violations of articles 2(1) and 3 in conjunction with articles 17, and of articles 2(1), 3, and 26 in conjunction with article 23, ibid., prs. 9.2(*b*)2(i)8 and 9.2(*b*)(2)(ii)4. Note that pr. 10.1 of the HRC's view is misleading in this respect. The case is considered in ch. 6 below.
536 Doc. A/37/40, p. 161.

537 Ibid., pr. 2.2.

538 Ibid., pr. 10.1.

539 See pr. 4.75 above. Note that the question of whether H was a victim was decided at the merits stage. The communication had been held admissible, Doc. A/36/40, p. 134, pr. 5.

540 Doc. A/37/40, p. 161, pr. 9.3.

541 Ibid., pr. 10.2.

542 Ibid., Appendix.

543 EUCT, Series A, Vol. 45 (1982).

544 Doc. A/39/40, p. 197.

545 Ibid., pr. 6.2.

546 Ibid.

547 EUCT, Series A, Vol. 28 (1978).

548 SD, p. 29.

549 Ibid., pr. 5.2.

550 Doc. A/40/40, p. 230.

551 Ibid., pr. 4.2.

552 Doc. A/36/40, p. 166; SD, p. 83.

553 Ibid., pr. 10.

554 See *Group of Associations for the Disabled* v. *Italy*, pr. 4.78 above.

555 Article 15(1) of the ICCPR provides, *inter alia*, that, 'If subsequent to the commission of the offence, provision is made for the imposition of a lighter penalty, the offender shall benefit thereby'.

556 Doc. A/37/40, p. 150.

557 Ibid., pr. 10.3.

558 Doc. A/38/40, p. 111.

559 Ibid., pr. 10.

560 Ibid., pr. 11 (my emphasis). 'These considerations led to the conclusion that it cannot be established that in fact or law [as to which see paragraph 12] the alleged victim was denied the benefit of a 'lighter' penalty to which he would have been entitled under the Covenant', ibid., pr. 13. See also *A.D.* v. *Canada*, Doc. A/39/40, p. 200, pr. 8.2.

561 See ch. 5, pr. 5.22 below.

562 See Meron, n. 1 above, pp. 106–9; T. Meron, *Human Rights in Internal Strife: Their International Protection*, pp. 40–3 (1987); K. Widdows, 'The Application of a Treaty to Nationals of a Party Outside its Territory', 35 ICLQ (1986) pp. 724–30.

563 See *Massioti and Baritussio* v. *Uruguay*, Doc. A/37/40, p. 187; SD p. 136, pr. 7.1 (M had left for the Netherlands, B for Sweden); *Estrella* v. *Uruguay*, Doc. A/38/40, p. 150 (E had left for France).

564 *Estrella*, pr. 4.1; *Massioti and Baritussio*, pr. 7.2.

565 Schwelb, 'Civil and Political Rights', n. 1 above, pp. 862–3 (1968). See also D. Schindler, 'Human Rights and Humanitarian Law', 31 Am. ULR (1982) p. 935 at p. 939.

566 See Lippman, n. 1 above, p. 226.

567 See n. 1 above (1968). Although concern was expressed about this limitation in

both the HRCion and the Third Committee the words were retained in a separate vote in the Third Committee. It was suggested that the words be deleted and the term 'jurisdiction' be qualified to show that the guarantee extended to individuals subject to the territorial and personal jurisdiction of the State, Doc. A/5655, prs. 18 and 29 (1965).

568 See n. 1 above (1968).

569 Mose and Opsahl, pp. 298–9.

570 See pr. 4.82 above.

571 See pr. 4.82.1–4.86 below.

572 See Van Dijk and Van Hoof, pp. 7–9.

573 Doc. A/38/40, p. 216. The decision is considered in ch. 9, pr. 9.23 below.

574 Doc. A/38/40, p. 216, p. 1.9.

575 Ibid., pr. 2.

576 Ibid., pr. 14.

577 See pr. 4.82 above.

578 *Lichtensztejn* v. *Uruguay*, Doc. A/38/40, p. 166; *Nunez* v. *Uruguay*, ibid., p. 225; *Montero* v. *Uruguay*, ibid., p. 186; *Martins* v. *Uruguay*, Doc. A/3740 p. 157. See Anon., 31 Rev. ICJ (1983) p. 42 at pp. 47–8; Meron, n. 1 above, p. 109; H. Hannum, *The Right to Leave and Return in International Law and Practice*, pp. 20–1 (1987). See also *Mbenge* v. *Zaïre*, Doc. A/38/40, p. 134, where the alleged victims were resident in Belgium and all the alleged violations occurred after they had left the territory of Zaïre. The requirement of M being within the territory and subject to the jurisdiction of Zaïre was not discussed by the HRC. On the case see ch. 8 below and ch. 10 below.

579 Op. cit.

580 Ibid., pr. 4.

581 Ibid., pr. 6.1.

582 Article 13, concerning the expulsion of aliens, might be an example. For text see Apx. I.

583 See pr. 4.82.1 above.

584 Doc. A/36/40 p. 176; SD p. 88.

585 See generally I. Brownlie, *Systems of the Laws of Nations—State Responsibility* (Part I), ch. 10 (1983).

586 Doc. A/36/40, p. 176, prs. 2.2–2.3.

587 Ibid., pr. 7.3.

588 Ibid., prs. 12.1–12.3.

589 See prs. 4.82–4.83 above.

590 Doc. A/36/40, p. 184.

591 Ibid., first para.

592 Ibid. See also *M.A.* v. *Italy*, pr. 4.61 above.

593 Doc. A/36/40, p. 184.

594 *Cyprus* v. *Turkey*, EUCM, 2 D. & R. p. 125 at p. 136 (1975). See also A.8007/77, *Cyprus* v. *Turkey*, EUCM, 13 D. & R. p. 85 at pp. 148–9 (1979). More generally see T. Meron, 'Applicability of Multilateral Conventions to Occupied Territories', 72 AJIL (1978) pp. 542–57; E. R. Cohen, *Human Rights in the Israeli Occupied Territories* (1985).

595 Mose and Opsahl, pp. 305–9; Lippman, n. 1 above; Schwelb, n. 1 above, pp. 866–7; Brar, n. 1 above, pp. 520–4; Tardu, n. 650 below; Trindade, n. 650 below. Article 5(2)(*a*) OP only deals with the effects of consideration by another international procedure. It does not address the question of whether the HRC could reconsider a communication which it has already considered, and if so, in what circumstances. This question is dealt with in pr. 4.41 above. Cf. article 27(1)(*b*) ECHR as to which see Mikaelson, pp. 144–52. There is no co-ordination rule in respect of the inter-State procedures under the ICCPR. Note though article 44 of the ICCPR, text in Apx. I below.

596 While considering communications under the OP the HRC became aware of a language discrepancy in the text of article 5(2)(*a*) OP. The Chinese, English, French, and Russian texts provide that the HRC shall not consider any communication from an individual unless it has ascertained that the same matter 'is not being *examined*' under another procedure of international investigation or settlement. However, the Spanish text refers to any communication which '*has not been examined*'. The HRC ascertained that the discrepancy was due to an oversight in the preparation of the Spanish text of the OP. The HRC decided to base its work on the other language versions. See Doc. A/35/40, pr. 385, n. 8. The HRC's decision was clearly correct in the light of the *travaux préparatoires*. In the Third Committee of the General Assembly the principle *una via electa* had been abandoned in favour of a system of adjournment of proceedings *pendente lite*. See Lippman, n. 1 above; Tardu, n. 650 below; and the discussion in A/C.3/SR.1432 and 1433.

597 See e.g. article 27 ECHR.

598 Doc. A/37/40, p. 114; SD, p. 101.

599 Ibid., prs. 5–8.

600 Doc. A/37/40, p. 122; SD, p. 105.

601 Ibid., prs. 7.1–7.2.

602 Doc. A/37/40, p. 122; SD, p. 105.

603 Ibid., pr. 5.

604 Doc. A/38/40, p. 150.

605 Ibid., pr. 4.3.

606 Referred to in Doc. A/39/40, pr. 580.

607 Ibid.

608 Doc. A/40/40, p. 232.

609 Ibid., pr. 4.4.

610 Doc. A/35/40, p. 127; SD, p. 52.

611 Ibid., pr. 6(*a*).

612 Ibid., pr. 9(*a*).

613 *Broeks* v. *Netherlands*, Doc. A/42/40, p. 139; *Zwaan-de Vries* v. *Netherlands*, ibid., p. 160; *Danning* v. *Netherlands*, ibid., p. 151. The cases are considered in prs. 4.55–4.58 above.

614 *A et al.* v. *S*, SD, p. 17. The State party also argued that the HRC could not consider the communication with respect to one alleged victim, D, because his case had already been submitted to UNESCO. The HRC found, however, that, 'UNESCO has at present no procedure of international investigation or

settlement, as referred to in article 5(2)(a) of the Protocol, relevant to this case', ibid., pp. 17–18. See now the UNESCO communication procedure noted in *UN Action*, ch. 1 n. 6 above, pp. 333–4. On HRCion procedures see M. J. Bossuyt, 'The Development of Special Procedures of the United Nations Commission on Human Rights', 6 HRLJ (1985) pp. 179–210. On UNESCO procedures see S. Marks, 'The Complaint Procedure of UNESCO', In H. Hannum (ed.), *A Guide to International Human Rights Practices*, pp. 94–107 (1984).

615 SD, p. 17.

616 Ibid.

617 The Sub-Commission for the Prevention of Discrimination and the Protection of Minorities has debated whether Resolution 1503 should be reviewed by ECOSOC in the light of the entry into force of the OP, see Zuidjwick, n. 1 above (1982).

618 Doc. A/33/40, pr. 582.

619 Ibid. This would presumably cover proceedings by, for example, the Russell Tribunal or Permanent Peoples Tribunals, as to which see M. Dixon (ed.), *On Trial: Reagan's War Against Nicaragua—Testimony of the Permanent Peoples' Tribunal* (1985).

620 Doc. A/39/40, pr. 582.

621 See T. Buergenthal, R. Norris, and D. Shelton, *Protecting Human Rights in the Americas* (2d, 1986).

622 Doc.A/39/40, pr. 582. The communication concerned was *Baboeram and Others* v. *Suriname*, Doc. A/40/40, p. 187, pr. 9.1.

623 See the reservations of Denmark, France, Iceland, Italy, Luxembourg, Norway, Spain, and Sweden, in *Human Rights—Status of International Instruments*, pp. 90–4 (1987). The exceptions are Portugal, and the Netherlands whose position is explained in Van Dijk and Van Hoof, p. 59. Thus, for example, the HRC could consider the case of *H.v.D.P.* v. *Netherlands*, Doc. A/42/40, p. 185, which had been declared inadmissible *ratione materiae* by the EUCM, ibid., pr. 2.2. The reservations are in accordance with a resolution of the Committee of Ministers of the Council of Europe, see 13 YBECHR (1970), pp. 74–6.

624 *Human Rights—Status*, n. 623 above.

625 Doc. A/37/40, p. 212; SD, p. 32.

626 Ibid., pr. 3.2.

627 Ibid., prs. 2.2–3.2. The expression 'manifestly ill-founded' does not appear in the OP although it was present in early draft versions in the Third Committee, see e.g. Doc. A/6546, n. 1 above, pr. 474. On a number of occasions States parties have argued that communications should be rejected as 'ill-founded'.

628 Doc. A/37/40, p. 212, prs. 6–7.

629 Ibid., Appendix.

630 Ibid., fourth paragraph.

631 See Mikaelson, who takes a similar view concerning article 27 ECHR. See the four examples he gives, pp. 144–50.

632 Doc. A/40/40, p. 232.

633 Ibid., pr. 4.2.

634 Ibid., pr. 2.5–2.6.

635 Ibid., pr. 4.4.

636 Doc. A/40/40, p. 204; Doc. A/39/40, pr. 583.

637 Doc. A/40/40, p. 204, pr. 1.4.

638 Ibid., pr. 3.3.

639 Doc. A/40/40, p. 232, Appendix.

640 See article 19 VCLT (1969). See also the views considered in prs. 14.15.1–14.15.2 above.

641 See ch. 6 below.

642 See SR 21, prs. 46–64; SR 33, prs. 21–52; Doc. A/32/44, prs. 68–73.

643 See Doc. A/C.3/L.1411/Rev. 2 in Doc. A/6546, n. 1 above, pr. 568 (1966). Cf. article 14(7) ICERD which clearly only covers domestic remedies.

644 SR 33 pr. 23.

645 It is interesting to note the comments of Mr Movchan (USSR national) cited in n. 165 above. See also his comments at SR 33, pr. 28.

646 R. 90(2). Mose and Opsahl, p. 309, comment, 'The intention was clearly to leave the scope of the prolongation clause still open to discussion'.

647 An Eighth Protocol to the ECHR has recently been adopted with a view to speeding up the procedures of the EUCM, see *ECHR—Collected Texts*, pp. 57–62 (1986).

648 See pr. 4.88–4.96 above.

649 See pr. 4.97 above.

650 Anon, 31 Rev. ICJ (1983) pp. 43–4; T. Buergenthal, 'International and Regional Human Rights Law and Institutions: Some Examples of their Interaction', 12 Tex. ILJ (1977) pp. 114–17; Council of Europe, Report of the Committee of Experts to the Committee of Ministers on the Problem of the Co-existence of the Two Systems of Control, Doc. CM. (68) 39 (February 1968); Council of Europe, Report of the Committee of Experts to the Committee of Ministers, Human Rights: Problems Arising from the Co-existence of the United Nations Covenants on Human Rights and the ECHR, Doc. CE/H 70(7) (1970); J. De Meyer, 'International Control Machinery in the ECHR in Relation to Other International Instruments for the Protection of Human Rights', Colloquy on Human Rights, Athens (Sept. 1978), Doc. H/Coll. 78(5), pp. 45–58; A. Eissen, 'The ECHR and the U.N. Covenant on Civil and Political Rights: Problems of Co-existence', 22 Buffalo LR (1972) pp. 181–216; Lippman, n. 1 above, who suggests that, 'The solution to the problem of priority among competing international procedures would seem to lie in standardization of international organizational practices', p. 268; A. H. Robertson, 'The UN Covenant on Civil and Political Rights and the ECHR' (1968–9) 43 BYIL, pp. 21–48 (1970); A. H. Robertson and J. G. Merrills, *Human Rights in the World*, pp. 141–5 (3rd., 1990); E. Schwelb, 'The ICERD', 15 ICLQ (1966) p. 996 at pp. 1046–8; Sieglerschmidt, 'Report to the Consultative Assembly of the Council of Europe, on the Protection of Human Rights in the U.N. Covenant on Civil and Political Rights and its Optional Protocol and in the ECHR', Council of Europe, Consultative Assembly, Doc. 3773, 28th Ordinary Session (1976); L. Sohn, 'Human Rights: Their Implementation and Supervision by the U.N.', in T. Meron (ed.), *Human Rights in International Law—Legal and Policy Issues*, Vol. ii, pp. 390–4, who

suggests that, 'The Optional Protocol may, however, be interpreted as giving precedence to regional procedures', p. 394; L. Sohn, 'A Short History of U.N. Documents on Human Rights', in *18th Report of the Commission to Study the Organization of Peace*, pp. 174–9 (1968); M. Tardu, 'The Protocol to the U.N. Covenant on Civil and Political Rights and the Inter-American System: A Study of Coexisting Petition Procedures', 70 AJIL. (1976) pp. 778–800; A. A. C. Trindade, 'The Domestic Jurisdiction of States in the Practice of the United Nations and Regional Organizations', 25 ICLQ (1976) pp. 715–65; A. A. C. Trindade, 'Co-existence and Co-ordination of Mechanisms of International Protection of Human Rights (at global and regional levels)', 202 Recueil des cours (1987–II); Van Dijk and Van Hoof, *Theory and Practice of the ECHR*, pp. 52–60; see also 62 UN ESCOR., Supp. (No. 6), 15–16, UN Doc. E/5927, E/CN.4/1257 (1977).

651 See prs. 4.92–4.96 above.

652 See A. A. C. Trindade, *The Application of the Rule of Exhaustion of Local Remedies in International Law* (1983); A. A. C. Trindade, 'Exhaustion of Local Remedies under the UN Covenant on Civil and Political Rights and its Optional Protocol', 28 ICLQ 734–65 (1979); Mose and Opsahl, pp. 302–5; Brar, n. 1 above, pp. 524–7. C. F. Amerasinghe, *Local Remedies In International Law* (1990); Brownlie, pp. 494–504.

653 See generally Trindade, n. 652 above (1983). In the *Interhandel Case (U.S. v. Switzerland)*, 1959 ICJ Rep., p. 6 the Court stated that, 'The domestic remedies rule is a fixture of international law'. See also *Case Concerning Elettronica Sicula S.p.A. (ELSI)* (United States v. Italy), ICJ Rep. (1989) p. 15.

654 See article 41(1)(c) ICCPR. On the drafting see Bossuyt, *Guide*, pp. 666–9.

655 The HRC has recently stated that 'The purpose of article 5, paragraph 2(b) of the Optional Protocol is, *inter alia*, to direct possible victims of violations of the provisions of the Covenant to seek, in the first place, satisfaction from the competent State party authorities and, at the same time, to enable States parties to examine, on the basis of individual complaints, the implementation, within their territory and by their organs, of the provisions of the Covenant and, if necessary, remedy the violations occurring, before the Committee is seized of the matter', *T.K. v. France*, Doc. A/45/40, Apx., pr. 8.3. See Trindade, n. 652 above (1979), pp. 757–9.

656 Cf. article 41(1)(c) ICCPR and article 26 ECHR where this reference to international law does appear. On the practice under the ECHR see Mikaelsen, pp. 105–40; Van Dijk and Van Hoof, pp. 81–98.

657 Doc. A/33/40, pr. 586.

658 Note Mikaelsen's comment that, 'Especially in the earlier practice of the Commission frequent references are found to generally recognized rules of international law as defined in the various decisions by various tribunals. However, as the practice of the Commission on this rule developed rapidly, the reference in article 26 to generally recognized rules of international law became almost futile as the most important contribution of the international evolution of the exhaustion doctrine came from the Commission itself', p. 107.

659 *X v. Canada*, SD, p. 19. Referred to by Trindade (1979), n. 652 above, p. 763.

The HRC referred to special circumstances which according to 'generally recognized rules of international law' absolved an author from exhausting the domestic remedies requirement. See pr. 4.105–4.114 below and n. 688 below.

660 See Trindade (1983), n. 652 above, ch. 5; A. A. C. Trindade, 'The Time Factor in the Application of the Rule of Exhaustion of Local Remedies in International Law', 61 Rivista di Diritto Internazionale (1978) pp. 232–57. Mose and Opsahl suggest that, 'The term "available" in the Protocol may be used to soften some of the harsher effects of the strict application of non-exhaustion as a ground of inadmissibility', p. 304.

661 See pr. 4.9 above.

662 See Mikaelsen n. 656 above.

663 See Trindade (1983) n. 652 above, ch. 3; Trindade (1979) n. 652 above, pp. 761–2; A. A. C. Trindade, 'The Burden of Proof with Regard to the Exhaustion of Local Remedies in International Law', 9 RDH/HRJ (1976) pp. 81–121. On the practice under the ECHR see Mikaelsen, pp. 108–11. See also Robertson, 39 ICLQ (1990) pp. 191–6.

664 See e.g. *Lanza and Perdoma* v. *Uruguay*, Doc. A/35/40, p. 111, prs. 8, 13.

665 Cited in Trindade (1979), n. 652 above, p. 761.

666 *Ramirez* v. *Uruguay*, Doc. A/35/40, p. 121; SD, p. 49.

667 Ibid.

668 *C.F. et al.* v. *Canada*, Doc. A/40/40, p. 217, prs. 6.2, 10.1. Similarly in *Croes* v. *Netherlands*, Doc. A/44/40, p. 259, pr. 10, '. . . remedies, the availability of which is not evident, cannot be invoked by the State party to the detriment of the author'.

669 'Article 5(2)(*b*) . . . is a general rule which applies unless the remedies are unreasonably prolonged, or the author of a communication has convincingly demonstrated that domestic remedies are not effective, i.e. do not have any prospect of success', *T.K.* v. *France*, Doc. A/45/40, Apx., pr. 8.2. See also the individual opinion of Mr Wennergen appended to this decision. Under the ECHR the applicant has only to provide prima-facie evidence (*commencement de preuve*) that the requirement has been complied with, Trindade (1983), n. 652 above, ch. 3, p. 145.

670 In the HRCion it was explained with regard to the expression 'available domestic remedies' in the draft inter-State provisions that, 'The absence of a specific reference to "domestic, judicial and administrative remedies" was to take account of the fact that there might be remedies other than judicial and administrative ones just as there were cases where no available remedies existed', Doc. A/2929, ch. 7, pr. 99. Note that under article 2(3) of the ICCPR each State party undertakes to 'develop the possibilities of judicial remedy'. On article 2 see ch. 6 below.

671 *C.F. et al.* v. *Canada*, Doc. A/40/40, p. 217, pr. 6.2.

672 Ibid., 'The Committee has stressed in other cases that remedies the availability of which is not reasonably evident cannot be invoked to the detriment of the author in proceedings under the Optional Protocol. According to the detailed legal explanations . . ., however, the legal position appears to be sufficiently clear in that the specific remedy of a declaratory judgement was available, and if granted,

would have been an effective remedy against the authorities concerned. In drawing this conclusion, the Committee also takes note of the fact that the authors were represented by legal counsel', ibid., pr. 10.1.

673 On article 2 see ch. 6 below.

674 Doc. A/39/40, pr. 584. This notion of effectiveness was apparently stressed in the HRC's private discussions on the domestic remedies rule, see Trindade (1979), n. 652 above, pp. 757–9.

675 *Ramirez* v. *Uruguay*, Doc. A/35/40, p. 121; *Sequeira* v. *Uruguay*, Doc. A/35/40, p. 127. For this list see Trindade (1979), n. 652 above, p. 760, n. 155.

676 See e.g. *Ramirez* v. *Uruguay*, Doc. A/35/40, p. 121, pr. 5.

677 The authors of one communication submitted that the list of remedies was 'a mimeographic reproduction in every single case, regardless of the completely different situations involved ... In practice the legal remedies fail to operate because of the restrictive interpretations they receive ... that contention cannot be defeated by a series of quotations from legal codes. All this does is to deprive the argument of any reality', UN Doc. CCPR/C/FS/R.8/Add. 5 prs. 3 and 4. Cited by Trindade (1979), n. 652 above, p. 760.

678 *Ramirez* v. *Uruguay*, Doc. A/35/40, p. 121, pr. 9; SD, pp. 4, 49.

679 Trindade (1979), n. 652 above, p. 761. The HRC's subsequent practice has maintained this approach of concentrating on the availability and effectiveness of local remedies.

680 Doc. A/38/40, p. 243. Similarly see *F.G.G.* v. *Netherlands*, Doc. A/42/40, p. 180.

681 Doc. A/43/40, p. 246. For a similar decision see *C.L.D.* v. *France*, Doc. A/43/40, p. 252, pr. 5.3. See also *O.W.* v. *Jamaica*, Doc. A/43/40, p. 250, one of a number of communications declared inadmissible under article 5(2)(*b*) OP on the basis that the author had not exhausted his remedy of appeal to the Privy Council. Subsequently, the HRC declared two communications admissible on the basis that the remedy of appeal to the Privy Council was not an effective remedy. The decisions appear inexplicable. See Schmidt, n. 1 above, p. 28.

682 Doc. A/44/40, p. 222, prs. 12.3, 12.5. Similarly if the alleged victim has been refused leave to appeal, as in *Z.Z.* v. *Canada*, SD, p. 19. The communication was declared inadmissible on the basis that, 'A thorough examination by the Committee of the dossier submitted by the author has not revealed any facts in substantiation of his allegations, and the communication is thus found to be manifestly devoid of any facts requiring further consideration'.

683 *Pietraroia* v. *Uruguay*, Doc. A/36/40, p. 153.

684 Doc. A/39/40, pr. 584. See *Pietraroia* v. *Uruguay*, n. 686 below. By implication all ordinary judicial, administrative, and arbitral remedies must be exhausted.

685 See Mikaelsen, pp. 118–21, particularly on the decisions in the *Nielsen Case*, A.347/57, 2 YBECHR (1958–9) p. 412 at 438–42, and *X* v. *Denmark*, A.4311/69, 14 YBECHR (1971) p. 280 at pp. 316–20. Cf. the decision in the *Salem Case* (*Egypt* v. *US*) 2 RIAA, p. 1161 (1932). See Trindade (1983), n. 652 above, pp. 89–94.

686 See *Pietraroia* v. *Uruguay*, Doc. A/36/40, p. 153, pr. 12 concerning two exceptional remedies.

687 See generally Trindade (1983), n. 652 above, ch. 2, B and ch. 4, II.

688 See Manke, n. 750 below, p. 645; *The Ambatielos Case* (*Greece* v. *UK*) 12 RIAA p. 83.

689 R. 1/1 (1976–8), Doc. CCPR/C/FS/R.1/Add. 1, 2–3 (unpublished), cited in Trindade, n. 652 above (1979), p. 762.

690 Doc. A/35/40, p. 107; SD p. 43.

691 Ibid., pr. 8. Similarly see *Lanza and Perdoma* v. *Uruguay*, Doc. A/35/40, p. 111, pr. 13; *Sequeira* v. *Uruguay*, Doc. A/35/40, p. 127, pr. 3.

692 Doc. A/34/40, p. 130; SD p. 109.

693 Ibid., pr. 2.5.

694 Doc. A/38/40, p. 124.

695 Ibid., pr. 5.2.

696 Ibid., pr. 6.2.

697 Ibid., pr. 7.4.

698 Ibid., pr. 9.4.

699 On article 2 see ch. 6 below.

700 See Trindade (1983), n. 652 above; Ibid. (1979). See also A. A. C. Trindade, 'Exhaustion of Local Remedies in International Law and the Role of National Courts', Archiv Des Volkerrechts (1977–8) pp. 333–70. See also pr. 4.116 below.

701 Doc. A/37/40, p. 137.

702 Ibid., prs. 4.2, 6.2, 6.3, 7.2, 7.3, 8.2, 9, and 11.8.

703 Doc. A/35/40, p. 111; SD p. 45.

704 Ibid., pr. 13.

705 Ibid.

706 See also *Simones* v. *Uruguay*, Doc. A/37/40, p. 174 concerning the failure of a court appointed counsel to make alleged exceptional domestic remedies known to the alleged victim. The HRC noted that they were 'exceptional in character' and that, 'the officially appointed defence counsel had not invoked them on behalf of (S) although more than a year has passed since the Supreme Military Court rendered judgement against her. They could not therefore be regarded as having, in effect, been "available" within the meaning of article 5(2)(*b*) of the Optional Protocol'. Cf. Fawcett, p. 360, 'the failure of the lawyer may, if proved, be a special circumstance excusing compliance with the rule in article 26 (ECHR) provided he has sought and failed to obtain restitutio in integrum' (1987). See also the *Artico Case*, EUCT, Series A, Vol. 37 (1980).

707 *Gilboa* v. *Uruguay*, Doc. A/41/40, p. 128, pr. 7.2.

708 On article 2 see ch. 6 below.

709 Cf. *Foti* v. *Italy*, EUCT (1982); *Corigliano* v. *Italy*, EUCT (1982); *Van Oosterwijk* v. *Belgium*, EUCT (1980). Van Dijk and Van Hoof, pp. 144–6.

710 Doc. A/41/40, p. 145.

711 Ibid., prs. 3.1, 7.

712 Ibid., pr. 9.4. In the view of the HRC the provisions of the Federal Court Act did contain provisions to ensure to the author the right to a fair hearing in the situation. Therefore, the communication was inadmissible because the basic allegations did not reveal the possibility of any breach of the Covenant, ibid., prs. 9.5, 10.

713 Doc. A/41/40, p. 150 (Graefrath, Fausto Pocar, and Tomuschat).

714 Doc. A/38/40, p. 237.

715 The decision in *C.A.* v. *Italy* is considered in ch. 10, pr. 10.27 below.

716 Doc. A/38/40, p. 186.

717 Ibid., pr. 1.2.

718 Ibid., pr. 2.10. Cf. under the ECHR lack of financial means is not regarded, *per se*, as a special circumstance which absolves the applicant from exhaustion of domestic remedies, see A.181/56 (1957), 1 YBECHR (1955–7) pp. 139–41; A.2257/64, *Soltikow* v. *FRG* (1968), 27 CD p. 1 at pp. 27–8.

719 Doc. A/38/40, p. 186, pr. 6.1.

720 Ibid., prs. 8.3, 8.4.

721 See *R.T.* v. *France*, Doc. A/44/40, p. 277, prs. 5.3, 7.4. Cf. Mikaelson, pp. 131–2; The *Ambatielos Case*, n. 688 above.

722 See R. 92(2) discussed in pr. 4.19.1 above.

723 SD p. 19. See also *S.H.B.* v. *Canada*, Doc. A/42/40, p. 174, pr. 7.2 in which the HRC took the view that the author's doubts about the effectiveness of the particular domestic remedies were not warranted and did not absolve him from exhausting them under article 5(2)(*b*) OP. See also *R.T.* v. *France*, Doc. A/44/40, p. 277, prs. 5.3, 7.4.

724 SD p. 19 (my emphasis).

725 Doc. A/38/40, p. 231.

726 Ibid., pr. 8(*b*). The communication was declared inadmissible on other grounds which are examined in ch. 12 below. In two decisions concerning the refusal of French courts to register complaints drafted in the Breton language the HRC stated that, 'In view of the fact that the author has demonstrated his proficiency in French, the Committee finds that it would not be unreasonable for him to submit his claim in French to the French courts. Further, no irreparable harm would be done to the author's substantive case by using the French language to pursue his remedy. The objection raised by the author, that he is not sufficiently acquainted with French legal terminology to prepare submissions to courts cannot be entertained by the Committee; the same difficulty is faced by citizens in all countries, even when using their mother tongue, and is the principal reason for seeking professional legal assistance', *M.K.* v. *France*, Doc. A/45/40, Apx., pr. 8.4. In *B.d.B.* v. *Netherlands* Doc. A/44/40, p. 286, the HRC expressed the view that, 'whereas authors must invoke the substantive rights contained in the Covenant, they are not required, for purposes of the Optional Protocol, necessarily to do so by reference to specific articles of the Covenant', pr. 6.3.

727 See *C.F. et al.* v. *Canada*, Doc. A/40/40, p. 217.

728 See pr. 4.15 above for HRC's discussion on this.

729 See pr. 4.106 above.

730 Doc. A/39/40, p. 153. See also *Hermoza* v. *Peru*, Doc. A/44/40, p. 200, pr. 10.2.

731 Doc. A/39/40, p. 153, pr. 12. See also *Weinberger* v. *Uruguay*, Doc. A/36/40, p. 114, pr. 11 and *Solorzano* v. *Uruguay*, Doc. A/41/40, p. 134, pr. 5.6.

732 Doc. A/42/40, p. 130.

733 Ibid., pr. 17.

734 Doc. A/41/40, p. 169.

735 Ibid., pr. 9.4. See also *N.A.J.* v. *Jamaica*, Doc. A/45/40, Apx., pr. 10.3.

736 See Trindade (1983), n. 652 above, pp. 157–8, 187–212; Mikaelsen, pp. 122–31.

737 Ibid. Mikaelsen suggests the following summary of the EUCM's approach, 'If an individual application is directed against the governing rules of a country in the form of legislation or administrative practice tolerated at a high level, the exhaustion rule does not apply unless the legal system of the country concerned offers a possibility to test the legal provisions or the adminstrative practice concerned against the Constitution of the country, including the Convention if this is incorporated as Constitutional law. If an individual application is directed against an administrative practice tolerated at lower level the Commission will ascertain whether or not the domestic remedies available are effective', p. 129.

738 See prs. 4.64–4.81.1 above, in particular *Hertzberg* v. *Finland*, pr. 4.76.

739 See e.g. *Fals Borda* v. *Colombia*, Doc. A/37/40, p. 193, pr. 7.2. This approach parallels that under the ECHR.

740 See ch. 9, prs. 9.18–9.18.1 below.

741 A.5577–5583/72, 16 YBECHR p. 212 at 262 (1973), 19 YBECHR p. 84 (1975). See K. Boyle and H. Hannum, 'Individual Applications under the ECHR and the Concept of an Administrative Practice: The Donnelly Case', 68 AJIL (1974), pp. 440–53; ibid., 'The Donnelly Case, Administrative Practice and Domestic Remedies under the European Convention: One Step Forward and Two Steps Back', 71 AJIL (1977) pp. 316–21.

742 EUCT, Series A, Vol. 27 (1978).

743 See the literature in notes 736, 737, and 741 above.

744 Trindade (1983), n. 652 above, p. 169.

745 Ibid.

746 Ibid.

747 See prs. 4.102–4.103 above.

748 See Trindade (1983), n. 652 above; and the literature cited in n. 656 above.

749 See A. A. C. Trindade, 'Exhaustion of Local Remedies in the Inter American System', 18 Ind. JIL (1978) pp. 345–51.

750 See H. I. Manke, 'The Exhaustion of Domestic Remedies in the U.N. Sub-Commission on the Prevention of Discrimination and the Protection of Minorities', 24 Buff. LR (1968) pp. 643–81; Trindade (1983), n. 652 above, pp. 163–8; see also A. A. C. Trindade, 'Exhaustion of Local Remedies under ICERD', 22 Germ. YIL (1979) pp. 374–83.

751 On article 2 see ch. 6 below.

752 Bowett, Book Review of Trindade (1983), n. 652 above, 55 BYIL 1984 (1985) pp. 268 at p. 269.

753 See Trindade (1979) and (1983), n. 652 above.

754 Bowett, n. 752 above.

755 See Mose and Opsahl, pp. 294–5. On the ECHR see Van Dijk and Van Hoof, pp. 69–71.

756 For submissions of States parties see e.g. *L.P.* v. *Canada*, SD p. 21 at p. 22(*a*); *Pinkey* v. *Canada*, SD p. 95 pr. 24–5. In *Lubicon Lake Band* v. *Canada* the HRC dismissed as an abuse of the right of submission allegations that Canada had conspired to create an artificial Indian Band with competing claims to land, UN Doc. A/45/40, Apx., pr. 32.2.

757 SD pp. 26–7.

758 For that decision see *K.L.* v. *Denmark*, SD p. 24.

759 See Brar, n. 1 above, pp. 530–1. On practice under ECHR see Mikaelsen, p. 72; Van Dijk and Van Hoof, pp. 68–9.

760 Doc. A/36/40, p. 125, pr. 8.

761 Ibid., pr. 8.

762 See ch. 1, pr. 1.1 above. See ECHR Protocol 9 (1990).

763 See article 14 ICERD. The provision did not enter into force until 3 Dec. 1982. See Reports of the CERD Doc. A/38/18, pp. 7–13 (1983), Doc. A/42/18, p. 159 (1987), Doc. A/44/18, p. 84 (1990).

764 Mose and Opsahl, text to n. 813 below.

765 See F. Jacobs, *The European Convention on Human Rights*, p. 272 (1975).

766 See n. 762 above.

767 See *Austria* v. *Italy*, n. 360 above. See generally, A. H. Robertson, *Human Rights in Europe*, ch. 2 (2nd, 1977).

768 See generally, B. G. Ramcharan (ed.), n. 218 above; H. Cohn, ibid.; F. Ermacora, 'International Enquiry Commissions in the Field of Human Rights', 1 RDH/HRJ (1968) pp. 180–218; id., 'United Nations and Human Rights in Chile', 1 HR Rev. (1976) pp. 145–56; T. F. Franck and H. S. Fairley, 'Procedural Due Process in Human Rights Fact-finding by International Agencies', 74 AJIL (1980) pp. 308–45; Theo. C. Van Boven, 'Fact-Finding in the Field of Human Rights', 3 Isr. YHR (1973) pp. 93–117; W. Miller, 'United Nations Fact-Finding Missions in the Field of Human Rights', Australian YIL (1970–3) pp. 40–50.

769 See ch. 2 above.

770 Cf. The EUCT, EUCM, IACM, IACT, CERD, CEDAW, CESCR, Committee against Torture, Sub-Commission on the Prevention of Discrimination and the Protection of Minorities, are all composed of independent experts. The HRCion, the most controversial and criticized international human rights body, is composed of governmental representatives. See H. Tolley, *The UN Human Rights Commission* (1987).

771 Cf. the new Committee on Economic, Social, and Cultural Rights which is solely based on an ECOSOC Resolution. See Alston, and Alston and Simma in ch. 1 n. 108 above.

772 See the literature in n. 768 above.

773 Ibid.

774 This is one of the principal criticisms levelled at the United Nations and at the HRCion in particular, see Tolley, n. 770 above, ch. 9; T. Franck, 'Of Gnats and Camels: Is There a Double Standard at the United Nations?' 78 AJIL (1984) pp. 811–33, which also appears in Franck's book, *Nation against Nation: What Happened to the UN Dream and What the U.S. Can Do About It* (1985).

775 The admissibility decisions and views are initially notified in press releases which are issued simultaneously in Geneva and New York. They are available on request. The decisions and views are included as appendices in the HRC's Annual Reports. Two volumes of selected decisions have been published. See pr. 4.124 below.

776 See Tolley, n. 770 above, ch. 4; Bossuyt, n. 614 above.

777 See prs. 4.37–4.43 above.
778 See pr. 4.40 above.
779 See pr. 4.41 above.
780 Ibid.
781 See pr. 4.10 above.
782 See Mose and Opsahl, pp. 276–80.
783 Ibid., pp. 321–2.
784 Ibid., p. 321.
785 Ibid., pp. 321–2.
786 See pr. 4.20 above.
787 The Council of Europe has a highly developed publicity system for the work of the EUCM and the EUCT.
788 By contrast the HRCion gets a great deal of national and international publicity.
789 See ch. 2, pr. 2.9 above.
790 See n. 1 above.
791 See n. 120 above. A digest of the HRC's jurisprudence is promised in the coming years, SD2, p. 2.
792 See e.g. B. G. Ramcharan, *The Right to Life in International Law* (1985); N. Rodley, *The Treatment of Prisoners in International Law* (1987); H. Hannum, *The Right to Leave and Return in International Law and Practice* (1987); S. R. Chowdhury, ch. 7 n. 1 below.
793 See A. Bayefsky, 'The Human Rights Committee and the Case of Sandra Lovelace', 20 Can. YIL (1982) pp. 244–66. Views of the HRC also appear to have attracted national publicity in Uruguay and Colombia.
794 A number of States have not co-operated with the HRC under the OP.
795 See e.g. HRCion Resn. 1989/17, HRCion, Report of the 45th session, ECOSOC OR, 1989, Supp. 2, p. 58; GA Resns. 41/32 (3 Nov. 1986), 41/119, 41/120, and 41/121 (4 Dec. 1986).
796 On consensus see ch. 2, pr. 2.7 above. A more cynical view might note that the co-operation of experts from Eastern Europe is risk free in terms of Eastern European states who are not parties to the OP. We have noted the importance of the accession of Hungary to the OP in 1988 and of the proposed accession of the USSR.
797 See pr. 4.10 above.
798 See Van Dijk and Van Hoof, pp. 65–6, 152–3. See N. Price, 'Human Rights, "Death Row", and Administrative Remedies', 34 ICLQ (1985) pp. 162–7.
799 See G. Schwarzenberger, *International Law—International Courts*, Vol. iv, pp. 527–54. See also G. Naldi, 'Case Concerning the Frontier Dispute between Burkina Faso and Mali: Provisional Measures of Protection', 35 ICLQ (1986) pp. 970–5.
800 See prs. 4.27–4.36 for the approach of the HRC.
801 *Stalla Costa* v. *Uruguay*, Doc. A/42/40, p. 170.
802 Similar comments might apply with respect to the situation in Colombia.
803 Cf. the recent decision of the Iran–United States Claims Tribunal in *Short* v. *Islamic Republic of Iran* (1987), noted in 82 AJIL (1988) pp. 140–3.
804 Doc. A/36/40, p. 166.

805 Doc. A/38/40, Apx. XXXI; SD p. 83. After amendments in 1985 to the Indian Act significant numbers of people were reinstated or registered as status Indians. Additional funding had to be provided.

806 See Bayefsky, n. 793 above.

807 See pr. 4.75 above and ch. 6 below. Note also that after the Dutch social security cases, dealt with in prs. 4.55–4.58 above, legislation was passed to ensure conformity with article 26 of the Covenant, see 3 Interights (1988) pp. 38–9.

808 Doc. A/38/40 Apx. XXXII; SD p. 67. Cf. the response of the UK to the judgment of the EUCT in *Abdulaziz, Cabales and Balkandales Case* (1985) which was to remove the advantages enjoyed by foreign wives and fiancées, see Statement of Changes in Immigration Rules, Parliamentary Papers, 1985, HC, Paper 503.

809 Doc. A/36/40, p. 147. In July 1989 Finland also indicated that it would alter its law to remedy the violation of article 9(4) of the Covenant found by the HRC in *Vuolanne* v. *Finland*, Doc. A/44/40, p. 249 and Apx. XII.

810 Article 18 (4) provides, 'The States parties to the present Covenant undertake to have respect for the liberty of parents and, when applicable, legal guardians to ensure the religious and moral education of their children in conformity with their own convictions'.

811 Doc. A/36/40, p. 147 pr. 10.5.

812 Doc. A/38/40, Apx. XXXIII; SD, p. 74.

813 Mose and Opsahl, pp. 329–31. However, since 1981 the number of States parties to the OP has doubled. As of 27 July 1990 there were 50 States parties to the OP. See also Doc. A/44/40, pr. 618. See also Tyagi, ch. 5, section III, E.

814 An assessment of the first decade or so of experience under the ECHR would not have suggested its present success.

815 Prounis, n. 1 above, p. 118.

5

Article 1[1]

1. All peoples have the right to self-determination. By virtue of that right they freely determine their political status and freely pursue their economic, social and cultural development.

2. All peoples may, for their own ends, freely dispose of their natural wealth and resources without prejudice to any obligations arising out of international economic co-operation, based upon the principle of mutual benefit, and international law. In no case may a people be deprived of its own means of subsistence.

3. The States Parties to the present Covenant, including those having responsibility for the administration of Non-Self-Governing and Trust Territories, shall promote the realization of the right of self-determination, and shall respect that right, in conformity with the provisions of the Charter of the United Nations.

Introduction

5.2 The concept of self-determination has been one of the dominant political forces of the twentieth century. It did not expressly appear in the Covenant of the League of Nations (1919) but by 1945 the pressure for the inclusion of the 'principle' of self-determination in the United Nations Charter proved irresistible. As we noted in chapter 1 the inclusion of a 'right' of self-determination in the international covenants was the subject of prolonged controversy.[2]

Article 1 is not covered by the non-derogation provision in article 4(2).[3] It has been the subject of a General Comment under article 40.[4] A small number of States have made reservations to article 1.[5] Article 1 has generally been considered separately but on occasions it has been linked with article 25 which deals with certain political rights of citizens and article 19 concerning freedom of opinion and expression.[6]

5.3 The HRC has stressed the importance of article 1 in a General Comment:

In accordance with the principles and purposes of the Charter of the United Nations, article 1 of the International Covenant on Civil and Political Rights recognises that all peoples have the right of self-determination. The right of self-determination is of particular importance because its realization is an *essential condition* for the effective guarantee and observance of individual human rights and for the promotion and strengthening of those rights. It is for that reason that States set forth the right of self-determination in a provision of positive law in both Covenants and placed this provision as article 1 apart from and before all of the other rights in the two Covenants.[7]

The importance attached here by the HRC contrasts markedly with the minimal information provided by States parties in their national reports.[8] As the HRC commented,

Although the reporting obligations of all States parties include Article 1, only some reports give detailed explanations regarding each of its paragraphs. The Committee has noted that many of them completely ignore Article 1, provide inadequate information in regard to it or confine themselves to a reference to election laws. The Committee considers it highly desirable that States parties' reports should contain information on each paragraph of Article 1.[9]

5.4 The HRC's approach to each paragraph of article 1 is outlined below. A few general issues concerning self-determination raised by the HRC members must briefly be noted first. Members have questioned State representatives on the relationship between self-determination and the proposed New International Economic Order[10] and the Right to Development.[11] Similar questions have related to the relationship between self-determination and certain general principles of international law, for example, non-intervention, non-interference, and the prohibition on the use of force.[12] For instance, the Iranian representative was asked how the advocacy of the export of revolution could be reconciled with article 1 and the principle of non-interference in the internal affairs of States.[13]

5.5 In its General Comment the HRC referred to 'Other international instruments concerning the right of all peoples to self-determination in particular the Declaration on Principles of International Law concerning Friendly Relations and Co-Operation Amongst States in accordance with the Charter of the United Nations'.[14] This is an interesting reference because it has been argued that the concept of self-determination in the 1970 Declaration is much narrower than that in the Covenant.[15] However, the mere reference by the HRC in its General Comment to the 1970 Declaration could not sensibly be taken to suggest either that the two instruments are of the same scope or that the scope of the ICCPR has been narrowed by the 1970 Declaration. A narrower view that the right of self-determination does not apply to a sovereign independent State or to a section of the people or nation but only to a people under foreign or alien domination has been argued for by India and Sri Lanka, who have made reservations or interpreted article 1 to this effect.[16] These views were criticized by some HRC members as being too restrictive[17] and formal objections were made by France, FRG and the Netherlands.[18] When faced with such interpretations or reservations it would be particularly helpful in determining the scope of the ICCPR if the HRC was to express a Committee view on its validity rather than individual members simply expressing isolated views that other members may or may not agree with.[19]

Finally, we must note that the HRC has stated that it 'considers that history has proved that the realization of and respect for the right of self-determination of peoples contributes to the establishment of friendly relations and co-operation between States and to strengthening international peace and security'.[20]

A. ARTICLE 1 UNDER THE REPORTING PROCESS

Article 1(1)

5.6 The questions most consistently put to State representatives have concerned how the right of peoples to self-determination was understood, promoted, and given effect.[21] Was self-determination seen as a continuing right or did a people achieve self-determination once and for all upon attaining independence or with the uniting of the constituent political entities of the State?[22] Was it possible to argue for changes in the present constitutional structures and political processes of the State? For example, the representatives of the German Democratic Republic and the Democratic Republic of Korea were questioned as to the possible reunification of Germany[23] and Korea respectively.[24] Another matter frequently raised has been the possibility of advocating and achieving secession.[25] For example, the representatives of the USSR, the Belorussian SSR, and the Ukrainian SSR were all asked similar questions concerning the right to secession guaranteed in their respective constitutions.[26] In reply the representative of the USSR, for example, stated that,

In the first place, it should be realized that it was absolutely inconceivable that a Republic would want to secede, since there was a solid and unshakeable bond uniting all the peoples and nations of the state, which attributed their well-being to the fact that they formed part of the Soviet Union. Nevertheless, the right to secede did exist and could be exercised.[27]

5.7 A number of questions put by the HRC have concerned the beneficiaries of article 1. Who was entitled to the right of self-determination? What criteria were applied in making that decision?[28] During consideration of the report of Canada[29] one member asked whether the word 'peoples' in article 35 of the Canadian Charter of Rights and Freedoms 1982[30] (concerning the 'aboriginal peoples') cast a light on the application of article 1 of the Covenant.[31] The representative of the USSR was asked 'whether, under the Soviet system, there was any difference between nations and nationalities as such and the concept of the Soviet people. Who had the right to self-determination: nations and nationalities, or only the Soviet peoples within the meaning of the Constitution?'[32]

Similarly members have asked whether the people had been consulted concerning the present constitutional structure or any changes in that structure and whether a people had the right to choose another political system.[33] Related questions have concerned the relevance of self-determination to minorities in States parties.[34] What was the status of those minorities?[35] How did the State party view the relationship between article 1 and article 27 concerning the rights of minorities?[36] Was the aim to assimilate indigenous populations or to assist them in preserving their identity?[37] We have already noted that the *travaux préparatoires* would suggest that minorities, as such, do not have a right of self-determination.[38] The language of article 1 though is not clear and literally would not preclude a right of self-determination for a minority if that minority constituted a 'people'. A central issue then is what constitutes a 'people' and on that issue the HRC has not even attempted to provide a definition or any governing criteria. Although it must be recognized that the drafters deliberately did not define a 'people'[39] the HRC is open to criticism for its failure to address this central issue. The HRC is in a unique position to provide some guidance to States on this issue. While the central issues of self-determination remain undefined and without guiding criteria the dangers of explosive self-determination claims arising will continue.

5.8 In a General Comment the HRC stated that,

Article 1 enshrines an inalienable right of all peoples as described in its paragraphs 1 and 2. By virtue of that right they 'freely determine their political status and freely pursue their economic, social and cultural development'. The article imposes on all States parties corresponding obligations. This right and the corresponding obligations concerning its implementation are interrelated with other provisions of the Covenant and rules of international law.[40]

The General Comment does not specify the 'corresponding obligations' or identify the 'other provisions of the Covenant' or the 'rules of international law' referred to.[41] The HRC's General Comment also stated that States parties 'should describe the constitutional and political processes which in practice allow the exercise of this right'.[42]

Article 1(2)

5.9 Article 1(2) has been the subject of relatively minimal consideration by the HRC. Occasionally questions have been raised concerning the distribution of property,[43] limitations on the right to use property,[44] and government measures affecting property and natural resources, for example, agrarian reform,[45] nationalization, and expropriation measures.[46] Members have also requested information on the State's view of the new international economic order, the extent and influence of multinational companies in the economy generally, and more specifically concerning the exploitation of natural resources.[47]

5.10 During consideration of the report of France[48] one member suggested that article 1(2) implied the right to protect a State's natural resources from pollution. In that respect he asked the French representative how France reconciled the right of the peoples of its Territories in the South Pacific to protect themselves from atmospheric pollution with the carrying out of atomic weapons tests in the Muraroa Atoll.[49] The French representative did not reply.

5.11 Commenting on article 1(2) the HRC has stated that,

Paragraph 2 affirms a particular aspect of the economic content of the right of self-determination; namely the right of peoples, for their own ends, freely to 'dispose of their natural wealth and resources without prejudice to any obligations arising out of international economic co-operation, based upon the principle of mutual benefit, and international law. In no case may a people be deprived of its own means of subsistence'. This right entails corresponding duties for all States and the international community. States should indicate any factors or difficulties which prevent the free disposal of their natural wealth and resources contrary to the provisions of this paragraph and to what extent that affects the enjoyment of other rights set forth in the Covenant.[50]

Again the HRC does not indicate the specific nature of the 'corresponding duties' on other States and the international community.[51] That the arguments for a new international economic order and a right to development are often couched in terms of the obligations on developed States and the international community might suggest that the HRC had such matters in mind.[52]

5.12 It remains to note that no member of the HRC has yet commented on the relationship between article 1(2) and article 47, nor does the HRC's General Comment address this issue. As we have noted some commentators have suggested that article 47 radically affects article 1(2).[53]

Article 1(3)

5.13 The most consistent request to State representatives on article 1(3) has been for a clear statement on the international application of self-determination.[54] Three members of the HRC in particular, Mr Al Douri, Mr Bouziri, and Mr Graefrath took the lead concerning article 1(3). States have been asked what practical and concrete steps they have taken to help peoples to achieve self-determination.[55] Particular attention has been given to the Palestinian[56] and Namibian peoples.[57] The matters raised by HRC members have included support for and diplomatic relations with Israel[58] and South Africa;[59] maintaining an embassy in Jerusalem;[60] the economic or military assistance given to national liberation movements and to the peoples concerned;[61] support for and application of economic and military sanctions against South Africa;[62] ratification of International Conventions against Apartheid;[63] the promotion of self-determination in overseas territories, dependencies, and departments and the situation if such territories desired independence but did not have the economic resources to sustain it.[64]

5.14 Mr Graefrath has regularly asked State representatives whether individuals or companies subject to the State's authority were permitted to contribute by their trade, co-operation and activities to the support of the South African regime or the occupation of Namibia.[65] He has argued that States parties could not evade their obligations under article 1(3) in this manner.[66] It is submitted that Mr Graefrath is correct in terms of article 1(3) with respect to the responsibility of States parties for individuals and companies 'within their jurisdiction' (article 2(1)). There is, however, considerable disagreement between States concerning the effectiveness of, for example, political and economic sanctions against South Africa.[67] It is doubtful, therefore, that article 1(3) could oblige States to impose sanctions or other measures against South Africa or other States as the only way to promote the realization of the right of self-determination.

5.15 Many of the major current international disputes have arisen before the HRC. While often expressing great concern members have generally been very restrained in their comments. Among the conflicts adverted to have been those in the Lebanon,[68] Sri Lanka,[69] the Western Sahara,[70] New Caledonia,[71] the Falkland Islands,[72] Northern Ireland,[73] and Afghanistan.[74] Though restrained members have often made very clear the importance of the application of self-determination to these situations and it would seem clear, therefore, that members of the HRC view article 1 as having an application outside the colonial situation.[75]

5.16 The comments of Professor Higgins concerning Afghanistan are not untypical:

Her second question concerned the underlying and preliminary question of self-determination, in which connection the Committee relied heavily on information from United Nations institutions.[76] The Commission on Human Rights adopted an annual resolution speaking of the denial of the right to self-determination in Afghanistan. The presence of 100,000 occupying troops and the participation of foreign advisors in various ministries and in the Khad, the security apparatus, had been verified by Professor Ermacora's report (E/CN.4/1985/21).[77] It was difficult to see how that situation or the fact that 4 million refugees had chosen to flee the country after the 1979 events, were compatible with self-determination. She had listened with interest to the Afghan representative's remarks on the Loya-Jirgah.[78] In her view, however, it was questionable whether any system short of election on the basis of the 'one-person, one-vote' principle could be a satisfactory expression of self-determination, and in that connection she referred to her own country's experience in Southern Rhodesia. Furthermore, according to her information, one quarter of the representatives in the Loya-Jirgah in fact consisted of party officials and persons sympathetic to the Government and there was little discussion beyond the ratification of Government policies.[79]

5.17 In its General Comment on article 1 the HRC stated that,

Paragraph 3, in the Committee's opinion, is particularly important in that it imposes specific obligations on States parties, not only in relation to their own peoples but *vis-à-vis* all peoples which have not been able to exercise or have been deprived of the possibility of exercising their right to self-determination. The general nature of this paragraph is confirmed by its drafting history. It stipulates that 'The States Parties to the present Covenant, including those having responsibility for the administration of Non-Self-Governing and Trust Territories, shall promote the realization of the right of self-determination, and shall respect that right, in conformity with the provisions of the Charter of the United Nations'. The obligations exist irrespective of whether a people entitled to self-determination depends on a State party to the Covenant or not. It follows that all States parties to the Covenant should take positive action to facilitate realization of and respect for the right of peoples to self-determination. Such positive action must be consistent with the States' obligations under the Charter of the United Nations and under international law: in particular, States must refrain from interfering in the internal affairs of other States and thereby adversely affecting the exercise of the right to self-determination. The reports should contain information on the performance of these obligations and the measures taken to that end.[80]

5.18 Again the HRC does not attempt to spell out the 'specific obligations' on States parties. It seems clear though that the HRC takes the view that those obligations exist whenever a people (though that term is not defined) are being deprived of their right to self-determination, and are not dependant on the people concerned being under the jurisdiction of another State party to the Covenant.[81] The HRC's view seems to go further than the undertaking on States parties in article 2 of the Covenant, 'To respect and ensure to all individuals within its territory and subject to its jurisdiction the rights recognized in the present Covenant'. As interpreted by the HRC article 1 calls for positive action to support the right of self-determination of individuals who are not within its territory or subject to its jurisdiction. The obligation to take action though is limited to measures over legal persons and matters within its territory or subject to its jurisdiction.

5.19 Although the General Comment calls for 'positive action', that action must be consistent with the United Nations Charter and international law. That of course hides the differences of opinion among States as to the legitimacy of, for example, the use of force to achieve self-determination, and of the kinds of assistance that it is permissible to afford to national liberation movements.[82] The particular reference to 'interference in the internal affairs' of States reflects the concern of many States at such interference and the continuing debate as to what constitutes purely internal affairs.[83] Finally, it is interesting to note the express reference to the drafting history of article 1. Such references have been relatively rare in the practice of the HRC. The preparatory work appears to have been of greater relevance to the preparation of general comments, and views under article 5(4) OP,[84] than within the context of the reporting procedure under article 40(1) of the ICCPR.

B. ARTICLE 1 UNDER THE OPTIONAL PROTOCOL

5.20 Article 1 has been raised in a small number of communications under the OP. In *A.D.* v. *Canada*[85] the author, a Grand Captain of the Mikmaq tribal society, claimed that the Mikmaqs had been denied and were continuing to be denied the right of self-determination by the government of Canada. It was further submitted that Canada had deprived the alleged victims of their means of subsistence and had enacted and enforced laws and policies destructive of the family life of the Mikmaqs and inimical to the proper education of their children.[86] The stated objective of the communication was that the traditional government of the Mikmaq tribal society be recognized as such and that the Mikmaq nation be recognized as a State.[87]

The HRC declared the communication inadmissible because the author had not proved that he was authorized to act as a representative on behalf of the Mikmaq tribal society and had failed to support his claim that he personally was a victim of a violation of any rights contained in the Covenant.[88]

5.21 Mr Errera appended an interesting individual opinion to the HRC's views.[89] He argued that the examination on admissibility raised three questions that were fundamental to the interpretation of article 1(1) and to the HRC's jurisprudence relating to individual communications alleging violations of article 1(1). The three questions were:

1. Does the right of 'all peoples' to 'self-determination', as enunciated in article 1, paragraph 1, of the Covenant, constitute one 'of the rights set forth in the Covenant' in accordance with the terms of article 1 of the Optional Protocol?

2. If it does, may its violation by a State party which has acceded to the Optional Protocol be the subject of a communication from *individuals*?

3. Do the Mikmaq constitute a 'people' within the meaning of the above-mentioned provisions of article 1, paragraph 1, of the Covenant?

As the HRC's decision did not answer any of these questions he could not endorse it.

As for the HRC's view it is normal practice for judicial or administrative rulings to avoid answering substantive questions and even procedural questions if the matter can be dismissed by reference to other procedural requirements.[90] As to the three questions raised, comments by individual

HRC members during the drafting of the General Comment on article 1 might suggest that the first two should be answered in the affirmative.[91] The HRC's decision itself would suggest that the second question should be answered in the affirmative as it would appear that the communication would not have been declared inadmissible if A.D. had been properly authorized to act as a representative of the Mikmaqs.[92] The more interesting question perhaps was not whether individuals could bring a communication in a representative capacity but whether an individual could bring a self-determination claim *qua* individual. It is interesting to speculate how an individual could show that he personally was a victim of a violation of the right of a people to self-determination.[93] Would simple denial of the right to vote be sufficient[94] or would a more general denial of civil and political rights be necessary?[95] The case of *Mpaka-Nsusu* v. *Zaïre*[96] below might have suggested another possibility in terms of restrictions on the establishment of political parties.

5.22 The HRC's view is now clearer after two recent admissibility decisions. In the first of these the HRC stated that,

the author, as an individual, cannot claim to be a victim of a violation of the right of self-determination enshrined in article 1 of the Covenant. Whereas the Optional Protocol provides a recourse procedure for individuals claiming that their rights have been violated, article 1 of the Covenant deals with rights conferred upon peoples, as such.[97]

Similarly, in the second admissibility decision, *Lubicon Lake Band* v. *Canada*, concerning a communication submitted by an individual acting on his own behalf and claiming to act on behalf of others, the HRC observed,

that the Covenant recognizes and protects in most resolute terms a people's right of self-determination and its right to dispose of its natural resources, as an essential condition for the effective guarantee and observance of individual human rights and for the promotion and strengthening of those rights. However, the Committee observes ... that the author, as an individual, cannot claim under the Optional Protocol to be a victim of a violation of the right to self-determination enshrined in article 1 of the Covenant, which deals with rights conferred upon peoples as such.[98]

The view of the HRC then appeared to be that an individual can only bring a self-determination claim in a representative capacity and only for violation of the peoples' right to self-determination though no indication is given of what that right includes.[99]

As for Mr Errera's third question this is clearly a substantive matter that could only be determined on a full consideration. We have noted above that the HRC has not attempted to define or establish criteria for a 'people' under the article 40 reporting procedure or in its general comment on article 40.[100] Moreover, in its final views in *Lubicon Lake Band* v. *Canada* (above) the

HRC stated that 'the question whether the Lubicon Lake Band constitutes a "people" is not an issue for the Committee to address under the OP to the Covenant'. The decisions in the *Lubicon Lake Case* effectively take the right of self-determination out of the OP system.

5.22.1 In *Kitok* v. *Sweden*[101] the communication concerned restrictions on reindeer breeding rights. Kitok was a Swedish citizen of Sami ethnic origin. Sweden argued that 'the Sami do not constitute a "people" within the meaning given to that word in article 1', but admitted 'that the Sami form an ethnic minority in Sweden'.[102] The HRC considered the issues under article 27 of the Covenant and expressed the view that there was no violation.[103]

5.23 In *Mpaka-Nsusu* v. *Zaïre*[104] the author, again an individual communicant, alleged that although the people of Zaïre had declared themselves in favour of a bipartisan constitutional system he had been prevented from establishing a second political party.[105] The HRC declared the communication inadmissible. They observed that the information before it did not justify a finding as to the alleged violation of article 1.[106] The observation is not very helpful. It could be interpreted simply as there being insufficient evidence on the facts or that the allegations did not even raise an issue of self-determination. The latter interpretation would be of particular significance bearing in mind the large number of one-party States and the question of the compatibility of such regimes with the ICCPR.[107] In the light of the importance of this issue it is submitted that the latter interpretation should not necessarily be assumed to be the correct one. However, in the light of the decisions noted above (prs. 5.22–5.22.1), individuals could not raise such alleged violations under the OP as a self-determination issue.

APPRAISAL

5.24 On reflection the practice of the HRC under article 1 seems somewhat disappointing. Many national reports have contained little if any information. Questions have been spasmodic and often there has been no reply from the State representative in any event, although the situation is often better during the consideration of second and third periodic reports. The General Comment adopted by the HRC on article 1 was vague, uninformative, and went little beyond a bare call for more information from States parties rather than an attempt at interpretation. The adoption of general comments affords the HRC an important opportunity to give some content to the right to self-determination. The HRC is open to criticism for not using that opportunity to attempt to provide some definitions and criteria in terms, for example, of the meaning of 'peoples', the relationship between self-determination and the preservation of territorial integrity, and the relationship between article 1 and article 27 of the ICCPR on minority rights. It is instructive to consider why the HRC appears to have made little constructive progress with respect to article 1.

5.25 First, the criticisms of those who argued that self-determination should not have been in the ICCPR because it was a political principle rather than a legal right may have proved to have been correct.[108] In this regard it is interesting to note the comment of Mr Opsahl during consideration of the Report of Sri Lanka, 'In article 1, the Covenant had given a legal aspect to self-determination, but it was primarily a political ideal that needed to be adjusted to the realities of the situation. The Covenant was not helpful in suggesting how the indispensable political solution might be achieved'.[109] Of course, it is that adjustment to reality that causes the greatest controversy between protagonists. Mindful of the difficult political conflicts that are usually associated with calls for self-determination the HRC has generally treaded very warily in this area. Similarly, as was noted by the United Kingdom representative before the HRC, self-determination issues are generally addressed in a number of other, and arguably more appropriate, international forums.[110]

5.26 Secondly, since the proposal to include self-determination in the Covenants was made by the General Assembly (1952) most trust and non-self-governing territories have achieved independence.[111] The decolonization era is now largely complete. The attentions of those newly independent States have now turned to other matters, for example, a New International Economic Order[112] and the Right to Development and other 'Third Generation' rights.[113] While self-determination remains a cardinal principle for these States in the external sense of independence from colonial, alien, or foreign domination there is distinctly less enthusiasm for the internal aspects of self-determination in terms of the free choice of domestic political institutions and authorities and respect for the international human rights of the people of the State.[114] Similarly, the fears of claims for secession based on self-determination for minority and other groups remains an overriding concern for many States.[115]

5.27 Thirdly, the very concept of self-determination remains a controversial one. The central difficulties of reconciling the right of self-determination with the preservation of the 'territorial integrity' of the State, of identifying the beneficiaries and content of the right, and the consequences of the international recognition of the right of self-determination in terms of international support remain.[116] The practice of the HRC to date has done little or nothing to shed light on these fundamental problems and appears unlikely to do so. That may in part reflect the inherent limitations of working only on the basis of consensus.[117]

5.28 It is perhaps unfair to be too critical of the HRC's performance concerning article 1. In the light of difficulties outlined above a minimalist, cautious, and uncontroversial approach to article 1 may ultimately appear to have been the only sensible avenue open to it. As Mr Tomuschat commented during the consideration of the HRC's draft comment on article 1,

The comments prepared by the Committee might seem rather insubstantial, but they reflected its experience with regard to the application of article 1, which was rather limited. Furthermore, a large number of United Nations bodies dealt with the implementation of that fundamental article, and the Committee's action could only be modest or marginal.[118]

NOTES

1 Cf. arts. 1, 55 UN Charter; ICESCR art. 1; AFR arts. 19 and 20. For summaries of the drafting history of article 1 see ch. 1 n. 134 above; Bossuyt, *Guide*, pp. 19–48. There is an extensive literature on the right to self-determination. Particularly useful are Y. Alexander and R. A. Friedlander (eds.), *Self-Determination: National, Regional and Global Dimensions* (1980); A. K. Ahmed, 'Analysis of the Decisions of the Committee on Human Rights', pp. 10–13, (LLM. thesis, London); K. N. Blay, 'Self-Determination Versus Territorial Integrity in Decolonization Revisited', 25 Ind. JIL (1985) pp. 386–410; L. C. Buchheit, *Secession: The Legitimacy of Self-Determination* (1978); A. Cassese, 'The Self-Determination of Peoples', in L. Henkin (ed.), *The International Bill of Rights— The International Covenant on Civil and Political Rights*, pp. 92–113 (1981); L. Chen, 'Self-Determination as a Human Right', in M. Reisman and B. Weston (eds.), *Towards World Order and Human Dignity*, pp. 198–261 (1976); J. Crawford, *The Creation of States in International Law*, pp. 84–118, 219–27, 257– 68, 335–83 (1979); J. Crawford (ed.), *The Rights of Peoples* (1988); A. Cristescu, 'The Right to Self-Determination: Historical and Current Development on the Basis of United Nations Instruments', UN Doc. No. E/CN.4/Sub. 2/404/Rev. 1, (1981), UN Sales No. E.80.XIV.3; J. Fawcett, 'The Role of the United Nations in the Protection of Human Rights—Is It Misconceived?', in A. Eide and A. Schou (eds.), *International Protection of Human Rights*, pp. 95–101 and 282–88 (1968); T. M. Franck and P. Hoffman, 'The Right of Self-Determination in Very Small Places', 8 NYUJILP (1975–6) pp. 331–86; H. Gros-Espiell, 'The Right to Self-Determination: Implementation of United Nations Resolutions' (1980), UN Sales No. E.79.XIV.5; H. Hannum, *Autonomy, Sovereignty and Self-Determination* (1990); A. Kiss, 'The Peoples' Right to Self-Determination', 7 HRLJ (1986) pp. 165–75; S. Morphet, 'The Development of Article 1 of the Human Rights Covenants', in D. M. Hill (ed.), *Human Rights and Foreign Policy—Principles and Practice*, pp. 67–88 (1989); K. J. Partsch, 'Fundamental Principles of Human Rights, Self-Determination, Equality and Non-Discrimination', in K. Vasak (ed.), P. Alston, (rev. edn.), *The International Dimensions of Human Rights*, Vol. i, pp. 61–8 (1982); M. Pomerance, *Self-Determination in Law and Practice* (1982); M. N. Shaw, *Title to Territory in Africa: International Legal Issues* (1986); M. Rafiqul Islam, 'Use of Force in Self-Determination Claims', 25 Ind. JIL (1985) pp. 424–47; A. Rigo-Sureda, *The Evolution of the Right of Self-Determination: A Study of United Nations Practice* (1973); E. Suzuki, 'Self-Determination and World Public Order', 16 Virg. JIL (1976) pp. 781–862; U. O. Umozurike, *Self-Determination in International Law* (1972); *United Nations Action in the Field of*

Human Rights, Ch. 3 (1988); V. Van Dyke, *Human Rights, the U.S., and the World Community*, ch. 5 (1970); R. C. A. White, 'Self-Determination: A Time for Re-Assessment', 28 NILR (1981) pp. 147–70; M. Whiteman, *Digest of International Law*, Vol. v, pp. 38–87, Vol. xiii, pp. 701–68; Brownlie, pp. 595–98.

The principal international instruments on political and economic self-determination are 'The Declaration on the Granting of Independence to Colonial Territories and Peoples', GA Resn. 1514 (XV), 15 UN GAOR Supp. 66, p. 66, Doc. A/4684 (1960); GA Resn. 1541, 15 UN GAOR, Supp. 16, p. 29, Doc. A/4684 (1960); 'The Resolution on Permanent Sovereignty over Natural Resources', GA Resn. 1803 (XVII), 17 UN GAOR Supp. 17, p. 15, Doc. A/5217 (1962); 'The Declaration on Principles of International Law Concerning Friendly Relations and Co-Operation amongst States in Accordance with the Charter of the United Nations', GA Resn. 2625 (XXV) (1970); 'The Charter of Economic Rights and Duties of States', GA Resn. 3281, 29 UN GAOR Supp. No. 31, p. 50, Doc. A/9631 (1974). See also the 'Declaration on the Enhancement of the Effectiveness of the Principle of Refraining from the Threat or Use of Force in International Relations', GA Resn. 42/22, 27 ILM (1988) pp. 1672–9.

2 See ch. 1, prs. 1.22–1.23 above.

3 Nicaragua is the only State to have derogated from article 1. See *Human Rights—Status of International Instruments*, p. 64 (1987). A number of HRC members commented on the derogation, see SR 422 pr. 17 (Al Douri), pr. 38 (Dimitrijevic). The State representative explained that the decree relating to the state of emergency, instead of listing the rights and guarantees that had been suspended because of the state of emergency, had included all the provisions of the Covenant except those relating to guarantees which were not subject to suspension. He acknowledged that the procedure was mistaken and was due to his government's inexperience in such matters, SR 429 pr. 33. Revised Declarations did not include derogation from article 1, *Human Rights—Status*, above, pp. 65–8. Notwithstanding that article 1 is derogable under the terms of the Covenant it would be impermissible to derogate from the right of self-determination if self-determination is *jus cogens*. See H. Gros-Espiell, 'Self-Determination and Jus Cogens', in A. Cassese (ed.), n. 1 above; Pomerance, n. 1 above, ch. 9.

4 GC 12(21), UN Doc. A/39/40, Ax. VI. Also in Doc. CCPR/C/21/Add. 3. For the HRC's discussions see SR 476, 478, 503, 504, 513, 514, 516, 537. The English version of the GC was adopted at the HRC's 516th meeting. The other language versions were adopted at the 537th meeting.

5 See *Human Rights—Status*, n. 3 above. States making reservations or interpretative declarations have included the UK and India.

6 See e.g. SR 128 pr. 19 (Tomuschat on Chile). For the text of article 25 see Apx. I.

7 GC 12(21), pr. 1 (my emphasis). Mr Ndiaye was concerned at the attribution of the importance of article 1 to its place in the Covenant. For comments by individual members on the importance of article 1 see e.g. SR 294 pr. 4 (Bouziri on Portugal). During the preparation of the GC there were discussions on whether to include a reference to the UN Charter, whether self-determination was a principle or a purpose of the Charter, and whether it was an individual or a

collective right. Note the UK declaration in respect of article 1, 'The Government of the United Kingdom declare their understanding that, by virtue of article 103 of the Charter of the United Nations, in the event of any conflict between their obligations under article 1 of the Covenant and their obligations under the Charter (in particular, under articles 1, 2 and 73 thereof) their obligations under the Charter shall prevail', *Human Rights—Status*, n. 3 above, p. 46. In response to questioning from HRC members, SR 594 prs. 34–46, the UK representative commented that, 'He would, however, note unofficially that the reservation seemed to do more than what was already provided in the Charter, namely, that in any conflict between obligations under the Charter and any other international obligations, those under the Charter would in any event take priority', SR 594 pr. 50.

8 Many of the early national reports included no information on article 1. More recent reports have contained much fuller information. See, for example, the report of Nicaragua, Doc. CCPR/C/42/ Add. 8, pp. 20–4 (1989).

9 GC 12(21), pr. 3. For critical comments by individual members see e.g. SR 294 pr. 4 (Bouziri on Portugal).

10 See e.g. SR 214 pr. 54 (Graefrath on Senegal), reply at SR 217 pr. 46; SR 476 pr. 17 (Hanga on Iran). On the New International Economic Order see K. Hossain (ed.), *Legal Aspects of the New International Economic Order* (1980); A. Cassesse, *International Law in a Divided World*, ch. 13 (1986); M. Bulajic, *Principles of International Development Law* (1986); J. Makarczyk, *Principles of a New International Economic Order* (1988); 'The NIEO and the Promotion of Human Rights', UN Doc. E/CN.4/Sub.2/1990/19.

11 See e.g. SR 440 pr. 9 (Prado-Vallejo on France). See the 'Declaration on the Right to Development', GA Resn. 41/128 (4 Dec. 1986) noted in 38 Rev. ICJ (1987) pp. 53–6; 'Report of the Secretary-General on the Realization in All Countries of Economic and Social Rights and on a Human Right to Development in Relation to Peace and the Requirements of a New International Economic Order', UN Doc. E/CN.4/1334 (1979); S. K. Baruah (Rapporteur), 'The Right to Development and its Implications for Development Strategy', Human Rights and Development Working Papers No. 3 (1979); P. Alston, 'Making Space for New Human Rights', 1 Harv. HRY (1988) pp. 3–40; C. G. Weermantry, 'The Right to Development', 25 Ind. JIL (1985), pp. 482–505; G. Abi-Saab, 'Analytical Study on Progressive Development of the Principles and Norms of International Law Relating to the New International Economic Order', Doc. A/39/504, Add. 1 (23 Oct. 1984); 'Human Rights in Development Series', Papers by Brownlie, Addo, Adelman, Ghai, Thomas, Hill, Tomasevski, and Muchlinski, (Commonwealth Secretariat, November 1989); 'Global Consultation on the Realization of the Right to Development as a Human Right', Report of the Secretary-General, UN Doc. E/CN.4/1990/9, parts i–iv. F. Snyder & P. Slinn, *International Law of Development: Comparative Perspectives* (1987). 'In the post-colonial era the rights to self-determination manifests itself as the right to development', Graefrath, ch. 6 n. 1 below, p. 13.

12 See e.g. SR 98 pr. 23 (Mora-Rojas on Yugoslavia), reply at SR 102 pr. 28; SR 214 pr. 11 (Vincent-Evans on Senegal); SR 282 pr. 9 (Sadi on Tanzania); SR 468

pr. 25 (Prado Vallejo on El Salvador), reply at ibid., pr. 36; SR 421 pr. 1 (Hanga on Nicaragua). See *Military and Paramilitary Activities in and against Nicaragua* (*Nicaragua* v. *US*), Merits, 1986 ICJ Rep. p. 14.

13 See SR 365 pr. 46 (Al Douri on Iran). There was no direct response from the State representatives, SR 368. See also in the context of self-determination and revolution SR 472 pr. 2 (Movchan on El Salvador); SR 224 pr. 9 (Tarnopolsky on Suriname); SR 366 prs. 24–7 (Graefrath on Iran).

14 GC 12(21), pr. 7. See G. Arangio-Ruiz, *The United Nations Declaration on Friendly Relations and the System of the Sources of International Law*, pp. 131–41 (1979).

15 See Cassese in Henkin (ed.), n. 1 above, who suggests that the 1970 Declaration indicates to the HRC how article 1(3) should be interpreted, p. 110; and Cassese, 'Political Self-Determination—Old Concepts and New Developments', in A. Cassese (ed.), *U.N. Law/Fundamental Rights*, pp. 137–65 (1979).

16 *Human Rights—Status*, n. 3 above, p. 9 (India); Doc. CCPR/C/14/Add. 6, pr. 2 (Sri Lanka).

17 See SR 472 prs. 32 (Bouziri) and 38 (as corrected) (Graefrath), SR 477 pr. 67 (Bouziri on Sri Lanka); reply at SR 477 prs. 51, 71; Doc. A/39/40, pr. 269 (India). Cf. the comments of the Indian representative in 1952 to the effect that the field of application of the draft self-determination article was wider than the colonial situation, Doc. E/CN.4/SR 399 pr. 4. Note also the view expressed by Professor Graefrath in an article that self-determination keeps the way open for the next step of the emancipation of mankind, i.e. the prohibition of exploitation by capital, ch. 6 n 1 below, p. 12.

18 See Doc. CCPR/C/2/Add. 1, pp. 37–9.

19 For an example of the view of an individual member note the following comment by Sir Vincent-Evans during consideration of the report of Sri Lanka, 'Article 1 of the Covenant clearly stated that all peoples had the right of self-determination. He took the view that reference to "peoples" meant the whole of the people within the independent sovereign people, including minority sections of the population. The right of self-determination was a right of a continuing character . . .', SR 477 pr. 68.

20 GC 12(21), pr. 8.

21 See e.g. SR 392 pr. 15 (Bouziri on Iceland); SR 222 pr. 4 (Sadi on Colombia); '. . . paragraph 11 of the report appeared to attribute the right of self-determination to the State and not, as was usually the case, to the people who exercised that right by voting in elections', SR 897 pr. 30 (Ndiaye on Bolivia).

22 See SR 532 pr. 23 (Ermacora on GDR). Cassese, n. 1 above, argues that internal self-determination is a continuing right that cannot be considered as implemented once and for all, p. 98.

23 SR 92 pr. 50 (Graefrath on FRG); SR 532 pr. 23 (Ermacora on GDR). The consideration of the third periodic report of the GDR was postponed in October 1989 because of political events in the GDR which ultimately led to reunification on 3 October 1990. See also the 'Treaty at the Final Settlement with respect to Germany' of 12 September 1990.

24 See SR 509, 510, and 516; Doc. A/39/40 pr. 370; reply at pr. 388. See K. L. Kow,

'The Korean Unification Question and the United Nations', in T. Buergenthal (ed.), *Contemporary Issues in International Law*, pp. 541–58 (1984).

25 See e.g. SR 99 pr. 20 (Tarnopolsky on Yugoslavia); SR 136 pr. 57 (Tomuschat on Romania). On secession see Buchheit, n. 1 above, ch. 2.

26 See SR 109 pr. 51 (Tomuschat on USSR); reply at SR 112 pr. 7–8; SR 117 pr. 27 (Lallah on Belorussian SSR); reply at SR 119 pr. 64; SR 154 pr. 37 (Tarnopolsky) and SR 155 pr. 29 (Opsahl on Ukrainian SSR); reply at SR 159 pr. 11. See generally Buchheit, n. 1 above, pp. 121–7 on 'Soviet policy and practice'. The USSR faces increased demands for autonomy from its nationalities. Political developments in Eastern Europe in 1989–90 have raised the spectre of secession in the USSR, particularly in the Baltic States.

27 SR 112 pr. 8. In July 1990 it seems more inevitable than 'inconceivable'.

28 See e.g. SR 206 pr. 26 (Graefrath on Canada); SR 472 pr. 20 (Dimitrijevic on El Salvador); SR 109 pr. 51 (Tomuschat on USSR).

29 UN Doc. CCPR/C/1/Add. 43.

30 Canada Act 1982, 'The Constitution Act 1980', Schedule B.

31 SR 559 pr. 46 (Ermacora); reply at SR 562 pr. 8. See pr. 5.22 below.

32 SR 565 pr. 10 (Ermacora).

33 See Doc. A/39/40 pr. 323 (on the Gambia).

34 Minorities dealt with have included the Tamils in Sri Lanka, Aborigines in Australia, Amerindians in Colombia, Macedonians in Bulgaria. A number of States parties have argued that they do not have any minorities at all. France made a reservation that, 'in the light of article 2 of the Constitution of the French Republic, the French Government declares that article 27 is not applicable so far as the Republic is concerned', *Human Rights—Status*, n. 3 above, p. 35. The FRG declared that it interpreted this, 'declaration as meaning that the Constitution of the French Republic already fully guarantees the individual rights protected by article 27', ibid., p. 88. In response to questioning from HRC members the French representative commented, *inter alia*, that, 'the concept of a "minority" had come from Central Europe, where the interplay of different languages, ethnic groups and cultures has caused it to be developed in certain well-defined geographical and historical circumstances. In France, however, the concept had always seemed dangerous, since the establishment of a minority could lead to its isolation, to the establishment of ghettos, and to persecution ... If the issue were analysed in depth, the provisions of article 27 of the covenant would be seen to run counter to the provisions of article 26, since the concept of a "minority" was closely connected with the concept of discrimination. France was opposed to all forms of discrimination and therefore could not accept the concept of a legal "minority", since it intended to grant to everybody the same degree of freedom in conditions of equality and fraternity ... Liberty and equality did not imply uniformity, and it was by virtue of the concepts of liberty and equality, and not of the concept of legally organized minorities, that the rights of citizens to live in their different ways were recognized', SR 455 prs. 80–2. It is a defect in the HRC's procedures that the HRC does not respond as a whole to such fundamental arguments concerning the interpretation and implementation of the Covenant. A general comment would be the obvious place for the HRC to respond. See now the

important views of the HRC in *M.K.* v. *France*, Doc. A/45/40, Apx., *T.K.* v. *France*, Doc. A/45/40, Apx., and the accompanying individual opinion of Professor Higgins in each view, considered in ch. 4, pr. 4.15.2 above.

35 See e.g. SR 365 pr. 47 (Al Douri on Iran).

36 See e.g. SR 109 pr. 12 (Opsahl on USSR); SR 206 pr. 3 (Hanga on Canada).

37 See e.g. SR 206 pr. 26 (Graefrath on Canada). On Indigenous Peoples see R. L. Barsh, 'Indigenous Peoples: An Emerging Object of International Law', 80 AJIL (1986) pp. 369–85; Crawford, n. 1 above (1988). The UN Sub-Commission on the Prevention of Discrimination and the Protection of Minorities is drafting a 'Declaration on the Rights of Indigenous Populations', see 39 Rev. ICJ (1987) p. 28. See also E. I. Daes, 'Discrimination against Indigenous Populations', Doc. E/CN.4/Sub. 2/1990/42. In June 1989 the ILO adopted the Convention Concerning Indigenous and Tribal Peoples in Independent Countries, 28 ILM (1989) pp. 1382–92. See also 'The Rights of Indigenous Peoples', Human Rights Fact Sheet No. 9 (UN, Geneva, 1990).

38 See ch. 1, pr. 1.22 above.

39 See Doc. A/2929, ch. 4, prs. 9, 15 (1954); Doc. A/3077, pr. 31 (1955). Many of the works in n. 1 above attempt to define self-determination or aspects of it. During the drafting of the GC on article 1 the Chairman commented that, 'The difficulties in the field could not be avoided indefinitely', SR 476 pr. 34. See also pr. 5.22 below.

40 GC 12(21), pr. 2.

41 See the international instruments cited in n. 1 above.

42 GC 12(21), pr. 4. Cassese, n. 1 above, comments that, 'Self-determination presupposes freedom of opinion and expression (article 19), the right of peaceful assembly (article 21), the freedom of association (article 22), the right to vote (article 25(b)), and more generally the right to take part in the conduct of public affairs, directly or through freely chosen representatives (article 25(a)). Whenever these rights are recognized for individuals, the people as a whole enjoy the right of internal (political) self-determination; whenever those rights are trampled upon, the right of the people to self-determination is infringed', p. 97. See H. J. Steiner, 'Political Participation as a Human Right', 1 Harv. HRY (1988) pp. 77–134.

43 See e.g. SR 129 pr. 14 (Bouziri on Chile).

44 We have already noted that there is no right to property in the ICCPR, ch. 1 n. 200 above.

45 See e.g. SR 469 pr. 7 (Bouziri on El Salvador).

46 See e.g. SR 386 pr. 28 (Graefrath) and SR 387 pr. 41 (Hanga on Columbia).

47 See e.g. SR 199 pr. 10 (Hanga on Iraq); SR 422 pr. 4 (Hanga on Nicaragua). See n. 10 above.

48 UN Doc. CCPR/C/22/Add. 2.

49 SR 440 pr. 10 (Prado-Vallejo). The International Court of Justice declined to consider the legality of the French nuclear testing in the *Nuclear Tests Cases* (*Australia* v. *France*), ICJ Reps. 1974, p. 253; (*New Zealand* v. *France*) ICJ Reps., p. 457. See N. Grief, 'Nuclear Tests and International Law', in I. Pogany (ed.), *Nuclear Weapons and International Law*, pp. 217–44 (1987).

50 GC 12(21), pr. 5.
51 Cf. *The Trail Smelter Arbitration*, 3 RIAA (1905). Ahmed, n. 1 above, suggests that in the light of the question asked by Mr Prado-Vallejo, n. 49 above, 'the right of a country to freely dispose of its natural wealth entails the corresponding duty of protection to all peoples, both citizens of its own territories and others', p. 12.
52 See M. G. K. Nayar, 'Human Rights and Economic Development: The Legal Foundations', 2 Univ. HR (1980) pp. 55–81. A number of HRC members had reservations about making an express reference to a new international economic order in the general comment, see e.g. SR 476 pr. 21 (Vincent-Evans), SR 478 pr. 11 (Bouziri).
53 See ch. 1 n. 144. Cf. E. N. Luttwak, 'Intervention and Access to Natural Resources', in H. Bull (ed.), *Intervention in World Politics*, pp. 79–94 (1984).
54 See e.g. SR 528 pr. 39 (Prado-Vallejo on Chile).
55 See e.g. SR 392 pr. 15 (Bouziri on Iceland).
56 See e.g. SR 257 pr. 27 (Graefrath on Italy); SR 331 pr. 40 (Tarnopolsky on Jordan). See S. Morphet, 'The Palestinians and their Right to Self-Determination', in R. J. Vincent (ed.), *Foreign Policy and Human Rights*, pp. 85–103 (1986); M. C. Bassiouni, 'Self-Determination and the Palestinians', ASIL Proc. (1971) pp. 31–40; L. C. Green, 'Self-Determination and the Settlement of the Arab-Israeli Conflict', ASIL Proc. (1971) pp. 40–48.
57 See e.g. SR 469 pr. 8 (Bouziri on El Salvador). See I. I. Dore, 'Self-Determination of Namibia: Paradigm of a Paradox', 27 Harv. ILJ (1986) pp. 159–91. An agreement that led Namibia to independence was initiated on 1 April 1989. See 'Interim Reports of the *Ad Hoc* Working Group of Experts on Southern Africa', UN Doc. E/CN.4/1990/7, and Add. 1.
58 See e.g. SR 356 pr. 41 (Al Douri on Uruguay).
59 See e.g. SR 322 pr. 62 (Sadi on Netherlands).
60 See e.g. SR 222 p. 12 (Bouziri on Colombia).
61 See e.g. SR 257 pr. 67 (Sadi on Italy); SR 291 pr. 12 (Hanga on Jamaica). See pr. 5.19, n. 83 below.
62 See e.g. SR 257 pr. 26 (Graefrath on Italy), reply at SR 261 prs. 35–7; SR 440 pr. 12 (Prado-Vallejo on France).
63 See e.g. SR 293 prs. 25–6 (Movchan on Portugal); SR 482 pr. 38 (Graefrath on NZ). The principal Convention is the International Convention on the Suppression and Punishment of the Crime of Apartheid, 1973. The Swedish representative replied that, 'although his Government considered *Apartheid* to be a serious violation of human rights and fundamental freedoms, it took the view that defining *Apartheid* as an international crime entailed international legal obligations which could not be fully understood or implemented', SR 635 pr. 40.
64 See e.g. SR 439 pr. 27 (Bouziri on France); SR 440 pr. 9 (Prado-Vallejo on France); SR 69 pr. 28 (Tarnopolsky), pr. 43 (Prado-Vallejo on UK); reply at SR 70 prs. 20–1.
65 See e.g. SR 441, pr. 34 (on France); SR 594 pr. 37 (on UK). See A. M. Khalifa, 'Adverse Consequences for the Enjoyment of Human Rights of Political, Economic and Other Forms of Assistance Given to the Racist and Colonialist Regime of South Africa' (1985), UN Doc. E/CN.4/Sub.2/1984/8/Rev. 1; UN

Sales No. E.85.XIV.4; referred to by Graefrath at SR 594 pr. 37 (on UK); updated report in UN Doc. E/CN.4/Sub.2/1990/13/and Add. 1. See also 'Implementation of Decree No. 1 for the Protection of the Natural Resources of Namibia', 80 AJIL (1986) pp. 442–91; M. C. Gosiger, 'Strategies for Disinvestment from United States Companies and Financial Institutions Doing Business in South Africa', 8 HRQ (1986) pp. 517–39; *Transnational Corporations in South Africa and Namibia: U.N. Public Hearings*, Vol. i, *Reports of the Panel of Eminent Persons and of the Secretary-General* (1986). See n. 57 above.

66 See e.g. SR 635 pr. 38 (Graefrath on Austria).

67 For important recent developments see the US Comprehensive Anti-Apartheid Act 1986 and other measures in 26 ILM (1987) pp. 77–133; *Mission to South Africa: The Commonwealth Report* (1986); *UN Hearings*, n. 65 above.

68 See SR 365 pr. 35 and 366 pr. 3 (Bouziri on Iran); SR 442 pr. 12 (Al Douri on Lebanon), reply at SR 446 pr. 13. See 'Lebanon—A Conflict of Minorities' (1983), Minority Rights Group, report n. 61; J. P. Gasser, 'Internationalized Non-International Armed Conflicts: Case Studies of Afghanistan, Kampuchea and Lebanon', 33 Am. ULR (1983) p. 145–61.

69 See SR 473 pr. 8 (Opsahl or Sri Lanka); SR 472 pr. 20 (Dimitrejevic on Sri Lanka). See 'The Tamils of Sri Lanka', Minority Rights Group, report no. 25 (revised, 1984); Report of Amnesty International Mission to Sri Lanka, 31 Jan–9 Feb 1982 (1983) and Updating Statement, July–September 1983 (1983); P. Hyndman, 'Human Rights, the Rule of Law and the Situation in Sri Lanka', 8 Univ. NSWLJ (1985) pp. 337–61. India–Sri Lanka, Agreement to Establish Peace and Normalcy in Sri Lanka, 26 ILM (1987) pp. 1175–85.

70 See SR 327 pr. 13 (Ermacora on Morocco); See G. J. Naldi, 'The Statehood of the Saharan Arab Democratic Republic', 25 Ind. JIL (1985) pp. 448–81; M. Shaw, 'The Western Sahara Case', 49 BYIL 1978 (1979) pp. 118–54; T. Franck, 'The Stealing of the Sahara', 70 AJIL (1976) pp. 694–721; *The Western Sahara Case*, Advisory Opinion, ICJ Reports, 1975, p. 12. The UN Secretary-General is exercising his good offices in seeking a peaceful resolution of the issue, see GA Resn. 44/88 (1989).

71 See SR 441 pr. 43 (Al Douri on France).

72 See SR 594 pr. 40 (Prado-Vallejo) and pr. 45 (Pocar) on UK; reply at pr. 54. On self-determination with respect to the Falkland Islands see D. Dunnett, 'Self-Determination and the Falklands', 59 International Affairs (1983) pp. 415–28; M. Pomerance, n. 1 above, pp. 16, 21–2, 27, 29, 44; A. R. Coll and A. C. Arendt, *The Falklands War—Lessons for Strategy, Diplomacy and International Law*, pp. 19, 25, 29–30, 82–3, 94, 99 (1985); H. E. Chebabi, 'Self-Determination, Territorial Integrity and the Falkland Islands', 100 PSQ (1985) pp. 215–25; P. Beck, *The Falkland Islands as an International Problem* (1988); L. Gustafson, *The Sovereignty Dispute over the Falkland (Malvinas) Islands* (1988). See the UK–Argentina Joint Statement of 15 February 1990.

73 See SR 594 pr. 42 (Wako on UK); reply at pr. 53. See C. Townshend, 'Northern Ireland', in R. J. Vincent (ed.), n. 56 above, pp. 119–40; A. Guelke, 'International Legitimacy, Self-Determination, and Northern Ireland', 11 Rev. Int. St. (1985) pp. 37–52; 'The Two Irelands—the Problem of the Double Minority—A

Dual Study of Inter-Group Tensions', Minority Rights Group, Report no. 2 (Rev. edn., 1982). The most important recent constitutional development in respect of Northern Ireland was the Anglo-Irish Agreement, which was unsuccessfully challenged in *Ex. p. Molyneaux* [1986] 1 WLR p. 331. See T. Hadden and K. Boyle, *The Anglo-Irish Agreement: Commentary, text and official review* (1989).

74 See SR 565 pr. 8 (Opsahl on USSR); SR 608 pr. 26 (Afghan State representative). See Ermacora's report, n. 77 below and Higgins, pr. 5.16 below. See A. G. Noorani, 'Afghanistan and the Rule of Law', 24 Rev. ICJ (1980) pp. 37–52; Gasser, n. 68 above. An agreement for, *inter alia*, withdrawal of Soviet troops was signed on 14 April 1988, 27 ILM (1988), p. 577. The agreement on withdrawal was complied with but severe human rights problems continue, see n. 77 below.

75 See pr. 5.5 above on India and Sri Lanka.

76 See ch. 3, prs. 3.12–3.18 on 'Sources of information'.

77 See 'Report on the Situation in Afghanistan', 6 HRLJ (1985) pp. 29–76. For his latest report see UN Doc. E/CN.4/1990/25.

78 The Loya Jirgah is a 'supreme council composed of the most respected representatives of the people', SR 603 pr. 14 (State representative).

79 SR 604 pr. 44.

80 GC 12(21), pr. 6.

81 For the HRC's discussion on this see SR 537. On article 2 see ch. 6 below.

82 See Crawford, n. 1 above (1979); M. Akehurst, *A Modern Introduction to International Law*, pp. 299–302 (6th, 1987); Pomerance, n. 1 above, ch. 8; Blay, n. 1 above; Cassese, n. 1 above, p. 100; P. Rubino, 'Colonialism and the Use of Force by States', in A. Cassese (ed.), *The Current Legal Regulation of the Use of Force*, pp. 133–45 (1986); R. Higgins, 'The Attitude of Western States towards Legal Aspects of the Use of Force', in Cassese (ed.), ibid., p. 435 at pp. 448–50; H. Bokor-Szego, 'The Attitude of Socialist States toward the International Regulation of the Use of Force', in Cassese (ed.), ibid., p. 453 at pp. 469–76; M. Rafiqul Islam, 'Use of Force in Self-Determination Claims', 25 Ind. JIL (1985) pp. 424–77; R. A. Falk, 'Intervention and National Liberation Claims', in H. Bull (ed.), n. 53 above, pp. 119–34; H. Wilson, *International Law and the Use of Force by National Liberation Movements* (1988). See also the UN Convention against the recruitment, use, financing, and training of mercenaries, GA Resn. 44/34 (1989).

83 See n. 82 above and ch. 1, prs. 1.18–1.21 above.

84 See ch. 4, prs. 4.46–4.48 above.

85 Doc. A/39/40, pp. 200–4. SD2, p. 23.

86 Ibid., pr. 2.1. The territory concerned was the lands allegedly possessed and governed by the Mikmaq's when they entered into a protection treaty with Great Britain in 1752 and which are known today as Nova Scotia, Prince Edward Island, and parts of Newfoundland, New Brunswick, and the Gaspe peninsula of Quebec, ibid., pr. 1, as corrected in SD2, p. 23.

87 Ibid., pr. 2.2. The Mikmaqs have purported to ratify the ICCPR and, indeed, have sent an Article 40 report to the HRC.

88 Ibid., pr. 8.2. The specific allegations made by A.D. related to self-government,

education, enfranchising of aboriginal peoples, property rights, and subsistence, ibid., pr. 3. See further UN Doc. E/CN.4/1990/NGO/43.

89 Doc. A/38/40, p. 200 at p. 204.

90 Famous examples are the judgments of the ICJ in the *Nuclear Tests Cases*, n. 49 above, and the *South West Africa Cases*, ICJ Reps. 1966, p. 6.

91 '... the expression "collective right" seemed to him to be poorly chosen, since it gave the impression that an individual alone could not invoke a violation of article 1 of the Covenant', SR 476 pr. 36 (Graefrath). In response Mr Bouziri commented, 'In the Working Group that expression had caused no difficulty. It implied that a people could take advantage of that right but did not thereby prevent an individual from invoking it in a communication under the Optional Protocol', SR 478 pr. 9.

92 On the facts the HRC took the view that A.D. had merely authorized himself. It appears that the only body which could properly have authorized A.D. was the 'Grand Council' of the Mikmaqs, the traditional Government of the Mikmaqs.

93 The HRC's view appears to assume that it is open to an individual to advance evidence to show that he personally was a victim of a violation of the right to self-determination. It is interesting to note that the State party argued, *inter alia*, that the author could not claim because self-determination is a collective right; that the communication was inadmissible, *ratione materiae*, on the basis that article 1 could not affect the territorial integrity of a State (reference was made to the Declarations of 1960 and 1970 in n. 1 above); and because the remedy sought, namely the recognition of Statehood, goes beyond the competence of the HRC. Unfortunately, the HRC view did not address these arguments.

94 Note that article 25(*b*) ICCPR contains a right for citizens to take part, *inter alia*, in the conduct of public affairs and to vote. For text see Apx. I below. See Steiner, n. 42 above.

95 See Cassese, n. 42 above.

96 Doc. A/41/40, p. 142. See pr. 5.23 below.

97 Doc. A/42/40, pr. 401. For the final views subsequent to this decision see *Kitok v. Sweden*, Doc. A/43/40, p. 221, noted in pr. 5.22.1 below.

98 Doc. A/42/40, p. 106. 'The Committee decided, however, that the communication could be considered, in so far as it might raise issues under article 27 and other articles of the Covenant', ibid. The first sentence quoted in the text is almost taken directly from the HRC's General Comment on article 1, see pr. 5.3 above. For the HRC's final view in the *Lubicon Lake Band* case see Doc. A/45/40, Apx.

99 Note the criteria in the 1970 Declaration, n. 1 above, which refers under the principle of equal rights and self-determination to, 'independent States conducting themselves in compliance with the principle of equal rights and self-determination of peoples as described above and thus possessed of a government representing the whole people belonging to the territory without distinction as to race, creed or colour'. See also Brar, ch. 4 n. 1 above, p. 515.

100 See pr. 5.7 above.

101 Doc. A/43/40, p. 221.

102 Ibid., prs. 4.1, 4.2.

103 The HRC decided that an individual could not claim to be a victim of a violation of article 1 as an individual, see n. 97 above.

104 Doc. A/41/40, pr. 142.

105 Ibid., pr. 9.2.

106 Ibid., pr. 9.2.

107 See ch. 6 below on article 2 of the ICCPR.

108 See ch. 1, prs. 1.22–1.23.

109 SR 473 pr. 8.

110 See SR 594 pr. 34.

111 The major exception was South West Africa/Namibia. See n. 57 above.

112 See n. 10 above.

113 See n. 11 above; P. Alston, 'Conjuring up New Human Rights: Proposals for Quality Control', 78 AJIL (1984) pp. 607–21; S. Marks, 'Emerging Human Rights: A New Generation for the 1980s?', in R. Falk *et al*. (eds.), *International Law: A Contemporary Perspective*, pp. 501–13 (1985).

114 A number of members stressed the non-limitation of article 1 to colonial situations during discussion of the draft General Comment on article 1, see SR 478. Mr Bouziri stated that the HRC was unanimous on this question, SR 477 pr. 67. Note also the comment of Professor Harris, 'The 1966 Covenants do not limit the principle of self-determination to the colonial situation. It seems unlikely that they reflect customary international law in this respect', D. J. Harris, *Cases and Materials on International Law*, p. 101 (3rd, 1983). Professor Cassese has argued that the more limited doctrine of self-determination may be *jus cogens*, n. 1 above, pp. 109–11. On external and internal self-determination see H. Gros-Espiell, n. 1 above.

115 See Buchheit, n. 1 above. During consideration of the report of Senegal Mrs Higgins, 'sought more specific information about demands for autonomy in Casamance, which the Senegal government seemed inclined to interpret as a demand for secession that must be opposed', SR 722 pr. 10. In reply the State representative 'stressed that the right to secession ought not to be likened to a principle of international law. As for the first element of article 1, it in fact referred to a colonial situation. However, no colonial situation existed in Casamance', SR 722 pr. 13.

116 'Above all, the determination of which "self" is entitled to determine "what", "when", and "how", remain the central question which elude simple objective answers', Pomerance, n. 1 above, p. 73.

117 The comments of the Chairman of the Working Group that drafted the general comment would seem to support this view, see SR 476 prs. 11–14, SR 478 prs. 7–15 (Bouziri).

118 SR 478 pr. 2.

6

Article 2[1]

6.1

1. Each State party to the present Covenant undertakes to respect and to ensure to all individuals within its territory and subject to its jurisdiction the rights recognized in the present Covenant, without distinction of any kind, such as race, colour, sex, language, religion, political, or other opinion, national or social origin, property, birth, or other status.

2. Where not already provided for by existing legislative or other measures, each State party to the present Covenant undertakes to take the necessary steps, in accordance with its constitutional processes and with the provisions of the present Covenant, to adopt such legislative or other measures as may be necessary to give effect to the rights recognized in the present Covenant.

3. Each State party to the present Covenant undertakes:

(a) To ensure that any person whose rights or freedoms as herein recognized are violated shall have an effective remedy, notwithstanding that the violation has been committed by persons acting in an official capacity;

(b) To ensure that any person claiming such a remedy shall have his right thereto determined by competent judicial, administrative or legislative authorities, or by any other competent authority provided for by the legal system of the State, and to develop the possibilities of judicial remedy;

(c) To ensure that the competent authorities shall enforce such remedies when granted.

Introduction

6.2 Article 2 is critically important as it contains the key general undertakings to 'respect and ensure' the rights in the ICCPR, to adopt the legislative and other measures necessary to 'give effect' to those rights, and to ensure an 'effective remedy' in the event of a violation. These general undertakings would seem to apply with respect to all of the rights recognized in the ICCPR (articles 1–27). Article 2 has been the subject of a general comment by the HRC.[2]

A. ARTICLE 2 UNDER THE REPORTING PROCESS

Article 2(1)

6.3 The starting point in the consideration of every State report under article 40 has been an attempt by the HRC to discern the precise effect that ratification of the Covenant has had on the State's legal and constitutional order.[3] The fundamental point here, following from the universality of the Covenant and its non-assumption of a single socio-political order,[4] is that article 2 leaves it to the discretion of each State party as exactly how 'to give effect to the rights recognized'. In its General Comment on article 2 the HRC noted, 'that Article 2 of the Covenant generally leaves it to the States parties concerned to choose their method of implementation in their territories within the framework set out in that article'.[5]

To facilitate their understanding of this matter Committee members often request information concerning the circumstances of ratification or accession in terms of whether any body or organ carried out any systematic review of the compatibility of the State's laws, regulations and practices with the Covenant[6] and, if so, whether any divergences or inconsistencies were revealed and action taken or proposed thereon, for example, constitutional, legal, or administrative changes.[7] If reservations or declarations had been made on ratification or accession the typical approach of members of the HRC has been to ask for clarification of their precise scope, an explanation as to why they had been made, and whether their withdrawal was being considered.[8]

6.4 A consistent theme of the HRC's considerations then has been its insistence upon a clear and detailed exposition of the exact status of the Covenant within the respective constitutional and legal regimes of the States parties.[9] At times very technical attention has thus been concentrated on the relationship between the Covenant and the Constitution and the internal laws of the State party enacted prior to and subsequent upon ratification or accession. States are requested to explain how their respective legal regimes would resolve the problems of conflict between the provisions of the Covenant and those of its Constitution and internal laws including the role of customary laws, traditional institutions, and tribal traditions.[10] Details are sought of the account taken of the Covenant for the purpose of interpreting provisions of domestic legislation and as a standard for the administrative authorities in the exercise of discretionary powers.[11] If State representatives are unable to give a definitive exposition of the relationship between the State's international obligations and its municipal law because of uncertainty they often give the latest theoretical conceptions as advanced by its academics and jurists and the principles of interpretation applied by its courts.[12]

6.5 From the questions put by HRC members and its general comment noted above[13] a number of points seem clear. First, States are not obliged by the terms of the ICCPR formally to incorporate the terms of the ICCPR into their domestic law. The vast majority of States parties have not incorporated the ICCPR and have not attracted criticism from HRC members on that basis.[14] States parties that have not incorporated the ICCPR include Australia, Denmark, the GDR, the UK, the USSR, and Poland. States parties that have incorporated the ICCPR at some level of domestic law include Colombia, FRG, Hungary, Japan, Italy, the Netherlands, Peru, and Yugoslavia. Secondly, however, it is open to States to incorporate the ICCPR and if they do so it is possible that at least some of the provisions of the ICCPR could be held to be self-executing. Certainly such a possibility is not precluded by the ICCPR. Moreover, during the drafting of article 2 a US proposal that 'the provisions of the Covenant shall not themselves become effective as national law', was decisively rejected.[15] Academic commentators seem in general agreement on these questions of incorporation and self-execution.[16]

6.6 Further development of article 2 has prompted requests for specific information on the exercise of governmental and executive powers affecting human rights. For example, explanations have been sought as to the jurisdictional competence on matters affecting human rights in federal States, how the necessary uniformity to comply with international obligations is attained in federal States, and how conflicts would be resolved.[17] We have already noted that the provisions of the Covenant 'extend to all parts of federal States without any limitations or exceptions'.[18] Considerable doubts were expressed by HRC members concerning Australia's original 'general reservation that article 2, paragraphs 2 and 3, and article 50 shall be given effect consistently with and subject to the provisions in article 2, paragraph 2'.[19] The original Australian reservation was withdrawn and replaced with the following Declaration,

Australia has a federal constitutional system in which legislative, executive and judicial powers are shared or distributed between the Commonwealth and the constituent States. The implementation of the treaty throughout Australia will be effected by the Commonwealth, State and Territory authorities having regard to their respective constitutional powers and arrangements concerning their exercise.[20]

The HRC has not yet had an opportunity to comment on the new Declaration and its legal effect.[21] Similarly searching questions have been asked concerning the territorial applicability of the Covenant in respect of States with dependent or overseas territories.[22]

6.7 A number of States have been questioned concerning the application of article 2(1) with respect to situations where the government may not be in control over the whole of the national territory[23] and or when its armed forces are deployed outside the national territory.[24] Such questioning has not been attended by the controversy that has surrounded the Committee on the Elimination of Racial Discrimination which has adopted formal decisions concerning a number of such situations.[25]

6.8 The HRC has recognized the need for its considerations to go beyond the realms of constitutional theory. In a General Comment the HRC stated that it recognized, 'in particular, that the implementation [of the ICCPR] does not solely depend on constitutional or legislative enactments, which in themselves are often not *per se* sufficient'.[26] Similarly, Mr Tomuschat has commented that,

> The abstract rules about the settlement of conflicts between different kinds of legal sources needed to be implemented in judicial practice. Were judges competent to give effect to such rules, declaring invalid a legal norm which would be inconsistent with the Covenant? Could they themselves take such decisions concerning inconsistency or would they refer the issue to the Supreme Court? Lastly, since the rights and freedoms enshrined in the Constitution were largely similar to the rights and freedoms enshrined in the Covenant, did Finland have an effective system for controlling the Constitutionality of laws?[27]

Article 2(2)

6.9 The second aspect of the HRC's approach to article 2 has been for it to seek the kind of information which will allow it to review the national implementation of a state's international obligations under the Covenant to 'respect and ensure to all individuals within its territory and subject to its jurisdiction the rights recognized in the present Covenant, without distinction of any kind'. It is by now trite comment that rights proclaimed in international instruments may be worthless unless they are effectively implemented through national provisions and by organs operating at the domestic level. [28] It is this national dimension which is the supreme aspect of the system of international control and underlies article 2, paragraph 2 which provides that,

> Where not already provided for by existing legislative or other measures each State party to the present Covenant undertakes to take the necessary steps, *in accordance with its constitutional processes* and with the provisions of the present Covenant, to adopt such legislative or other measures as may be necessary to give effect to the rights recognized in the present Covenant.[29]

6.10 It is evident that any body, such as the HRC, attempting to review the national implementation of international obligations must be prepared to go beyond mere formal legal texts and try to look at the practical measures taken to 'give effect' to and to 'respect and ensure' the rights in the ICCPR.[30] The diversity of constitutional processes, socio-legal traditions, and national implementation techniques necessitates this.[31] In intensively pursuing this objective Committee members have sought substantive factual information on and clarification of, for example, judicial, executive, administrative, and other bodies having jurisdiction affecting human rights or responsibility for ensuring human rights; the legal bases, procedures, and practices of any special type of court or organ having exceptional jurisdiction, for example, military tribunals,[32] special criminal or economic courts;[33] the role of Ombudsmen,[34] Mediateurs,[35] Civil Liberties Commissioners,[36] and National Human Rights Commissions;[37] executive or administrative measures which more precisely define and delineate Constitutional and legislative norms or the rights in the Covenant;[38] the prohibitive effect of unwritten principles such as 'the principle of legality'[39] or 'socialist legality';[40] the role of public and social organizations such as trade unions in the protection of human rights; the effects of collectivism on the enjoyment of civil and political rights; general freedoms that play a significant role in the implementation of the Covenant, for example, freedom of the press, association, and scientific research,[41] the existence of limitations and restrictions on the enjoyment of rights.[42] Requests for statistical information have become more and more frequent and many national reports contain statistical information.[43] This pursuit of detailed information on national implementation is obviously more specifically directed with respect to each of the substantive rights in the Covenant. The approach to a selection of rights is illustrated in this work.[44]

6.11 We have already noted that during the drafting of the Covenant there was extensive discussion concerning whether the obligation to implement the Civil and Political Covenant would be of an immediate or progressive nature.[45] That discussion has since been echoed in academic writings.[46] The HRC has not made any clear statement on that question as a Committee in a General Comment but it is fair to note that individual members have generally stressed the immediacy of the obligation and contrasted it with the progressive obligation in article 2 of the ICESCR.[47] However, this stress on immediacy has been accompanied by the clear acknowledgement that there are many obstacles to the full achievement of the rights in the Covenant.[48] A number of specific problems have been discussed including, economic conditions, under-development, unemployment, drought, illiteracy.[49] That sense of realism has persisted throughout the HRC's considerations to date. One can perhaps best summarize the approach that seems to have emerged from individual members by saying that they have generally viewed the obligation in article 2 as an immediate one but that they are sympathetic to States parties who can point to specific factors and difficulties which prevent or hinder the full and immediate implementation of the rights in the Covenant. In effect the burden of proof is on a State party which is not immediately implementing the Covenant to provide some specific justification or explanation. There has been no suggestion that the HRC would accept any argument to the effect that the obligation in article 2 is a progressive one in the sense that a State party could choose not to implement a particular right as a matter of policy and justify this by arguing that article 2 does not contain an immediate obligation. Mr Tomuschat has commented,

The Human Rights Committee has never had any doubts about the true meaning of article 2(2) of the CCPR. No member has ever maintained that States enjoyed a margin of discretion concerning the time limits during which full conformity of their conduct with their international obligations could be brought about. Nor has any government appearing before the Human Rights Committee defended such an understanding of the CCPR. Even more conclusive are the views adopted by the Human Rights Committee on the merits of cases brought to its attention under the Optional Protocol. The Human Rights Committee has chosen a format for such views according to which, on an article-by-article basis, findings are made as to violations which have occurred. If the CCPR had not intended to impose on States a strict duty of compliance, no such findings could have been made.[50]

6.12 What the HRC have chosen to make clear is that the Covenant does place active obligations on States:

The Committee considers it necessary to draw the attention of States parties to the fact that the obligation under the Covenant is not confined to the respect of human rights, but that States parties have also undertaken to ensure the enjoyment of these rights to all individuals under their jurisdiction. This aspect calls for *specific activities* by the States parties to enable individuals to enjoy their rights. This is obvious in a number of articles (e.g. article 3 [on the equal rights of men and women to the enjoyment of the rights in the ICCPR]), but in principle this undertaking relates to all rights set forth in the Covenant.[51]

... Article 3, as articles 2(1) and 26 in so far as those articles primarily deal with the prevention of discrimination on a number of grounds, among which sex is one, requires not only measures of protection but also *affirmative action* designed to ensure the positive enjoyment of rights. This cannot be done simply by enacting laws. Hence more information has generally been required regarding the role of women in practice with a view to ascertaining what measures, in addition to purely legislative measures of protection, have been or are being taken to give effect to the precise and positive obligations under article 3 and to ascertain what progress is being made in this regard ... the positive obligation undertaken by States parties under that article may itself have an inevitable impact on the legislation or administrative measures designed to regulate matters other than those dealt with in the Covenant. One example, among others, is the degree to which immigration laws which distinguish between a male and a female citizen may or may not adversely effect the scope of the right of the woman to marriage to non-citizens or to hold public office.[52]

... the implementation of this provision (article 24) entails the adoption of special measures to protect children, in addition to the measures that States are required to take under article 2 ... In most cases, however, the measures to be adopted [to protect children] are not specified in the Covenant and it is for each State to determine in the light of the protection needs of children in its territory and within its jurisdiction. The

Committee notes in this regard that such measures, although intended primarily to ensure that children fully enjoy the other rights enunciated in the Covenant, may also be economic, social and cultural. For example, every possible economic and social measure should be taken to reduce infant mortality and to eradicate malnutrition among children and to prevent them from being subjected to acts of violence and cruel and inhuman treatment or from being exploited by means of forced labour or prostitution, or by their use in illicit trafficking of narcotic drugs, or by other means. In the cultural field, every possible measure should be taken to foster the development of their personality and to provide them with a level of education that will enable them to enjoy the rights recognized in the Covenant, particularly the right to freedom of opinion and expression. Moreover, the Committee wishes to draw the attention of States parties to the need to include in their reports information on measures adopted to ensure that children do not take a direct part in armed conflicts.[53]

6.13 In the Third Committee there had been no objection to the interpretation of draft article 2 under which special measures for the advancement of any socially and educationally backward sections of society should not be construed as 'distinction' within the meaning of article 2. In its General Comment on 'non-discrimination' the HRC stated that 'Reports of States parties . . . very often lack information which would reveal discrimination in fact . . . the Committee wishes to know if there remain any problems of discrimination in fact, which may be practised either by public authorities, by the community, or by private persons or bodies. The Committee wishes to be informed about legal provisions and administrative measures directed at diminishing or eliminating such discrimination. The Committee also wishes to point out that the principle of equality sometimes requires States parties to take affirmative action in order to diminish or eliminate conditions which cause or help to perpetuate discrimination prohibited by the Covenant. For example, in a State where the general conditions of part of the population prevent or impair their enjoyment of human rights, the State should take specific action to correct those conditions. Such action may involve granting for a time to the part of the population concerned preferential treatment in specific matters as compared with the rest of the population. However, as long as such action is needed to correct discrimination in fact, it is a case of legitimate differentiation under the Covenant.'[54] However, the HRC's call for 'specific activities' and 'affirmative action' seems to go well beyond this context and asserts a more general positive obligation to ensure the rights recognized in the ICCPR.[55] Unfortunately, the call for 'specific activities' and 'affirmative action' does not resolve the debate as to whether the obligation under article 2 is immediate or progressive but as noted the HRC has striven for a 'constructive dialogue' with States parties rather than to use the article 40 procedure to condemn States for their possible failures to implement the ICCPR when they are faced with genuine difficulties.[56] In terms of a constructive dialogue between the HRC and the States parties the question of the immediacy or otherwise of the obligation in article 2 has assumed less importance than the legal analyst would inevitably attach to it. The general comments contrast sharply with the passive attitude of many State parties which have argued that their respective systems fully guarantee the rights in the Covenant, for example, the GDR,[57] the UK[58] and the USSR.[59] Doubts have been expressed as to the correctness of such claims both by HRC members[60] and academic commentators.[61]

6.14 With respect to the non-discrimination (or non-distinction) aspect of article 2 the general practice of the HRC has been to request detailed information as to the constitutional or other legal provisions, and administrative measures which embody and give effect to the principle of non-discrimination. In its General Comment on non-discrimination the HRC noted that the Covenant neither defined the term 'discrimination' nor indicated what constituted discrimination. After referring to the definition of 'racial discrimination' in the ICERD and 'discrimination against women' in the CEDAW, the HRC commented that, 'While these conventions deal only with cases of discrimination on specific grounds, the Committee believes that the term "discrimination" as used in the Covenant should be understood to imply any distinction, exclusion, restriction or preference which is based on any ground such as race, colour, sex, language, religion, political or other opinion, national or social origin, property, birth or other status, and which has the purpose or effect of nullifying or impairing the recognition, enjoyment or exercise by all persons, on an equal footing, of all rights and freedoms. The enjoyment of rights and freedoms on an equal footing, however, does not mean identical treatment in every instance.'[62] Attention is usually drawn to and comment requested in respect of non-correlation of the terms of a State's laws and practices with the series of distinctions set forth in article 2(1): such as race, colour, sex, language, religion, political or other status, national or social origin, property, birth or other status.[63]

6.15 In particular attention has been drawn to the importance of provisions prohibiting discrimination on the grounds of political opinion. For example, during consideration of the Report of Poland[64] Mr Tarnopolsky commented that,

In connection with Article 2 of the Covenant, the report made no mention of the existence of guarantees of equal rights irrespective of political opinion. Such an omission assumed considerable importance in a country in which a specific ideology was enshrined in the Constitution. While under Article 1 of the Covenant, all peoples were free to opt for such a socio-political system, there remained the question of the protection of the various fundamental freedoms in such a context.[65]

6.16 Questions concerning non-discrimination are often related to other substantive rights, for example, concerning access to the public service under article 25 of the Covenant. Another matter to which HRC members have accorded some significance concerns the issue of the ownership of property in terms of its role both in the realization of rights and more specifically as coming within 'other status' in article 2(1).[66] Its potential importance was clearly indicated by the HRC's leading proponent of this view, Mr Hanga,

Everyone knew that equality of rights needed to be buttressed by social and economic structures. What, then, was the role of ownership of property? In what ways did property rights ensure such equality, in view of the fact that in the USSR there was State property, group property, and personal property? In what way did those various forms of ownership contribute to guaranteeing the *de jure* and *de facto* equality of citizens in economic, political and social life?[67]

6.17 Other matters commonly raised have concerned any distinctions made between aliens and citizens other than those provided for in the Covenant[68] and whether any organ existed which was specifically charged with the task of monitoring or eliminating the existence of discrimination, for example, the Race Relations Board (now the Commission for Racial Equality) in the UK.[69] Another matter which has attracted some attention has been the seemingly privileged position of the 'working class'[70] and the 'Communist Party'[71] in some of the Socialist countries, for example, Romania.[72]

6.18 Notwithstanding its jurisprudence to the effect that the Covenant assumes no primacy on the part of any one form of legal or political order, Committee members have on occasions raised some doubts as to whether the very nature of a constitutional or political regime, or at least certain aspects of it, are in compliance with the terms of the Covenant. A few examples will suffice to indicate how far HRC members have seen fit to make their views known.

During consideration of the report of Togo Mr Fodor observed that,

One might ask whether it was actually the Togolese people or only the President of Togo who had ruled out the multi-party system and whether such a system was in strict compliance with the Covenant. He wondered whether the fact that the statutes of the sole party formed part of the basic legislation that provided for the enjoyment of civil and political rights by citizens . . . meant that the party was a legislative body. What was its relationship with the National Assembly where legislation was concerned, what position did its statutes occupy in the hierarchy of legislative texts and could the statutes conflict with the Penal code or other existing codes?[73]

During consideration of the report of Chile[74] Mr Graefrath commented that, 'The report now before the Committee had come from an authority whose very existence was based on the elimination of the democratic rights of the Chilean people'.[75] That attitude was generally echoed by the other members of the HRC, including Mr Opsahl, who suggested that, 'The Committee should not be too conciliatory when examining dictatorships which on various pretexts declared that they did not accept or restricted fundamental civil and political rights ... What was needed was not reports conforming to Article 40 but Governments conforming to Article 25'.[76]

6.19 A particularly interesting and pertinent example of the HRC's approach is the case of Iran. Subsequent to the Islamic revolution in February 1979 the Iranian authorities denounced the reports[77] submitted to the HRC by the Shah's regime as 'failing to reflect the reality of the situation in Iran regarding the status of civil and political rights' and 'constituted an [sic] conscious attempt to cover up the gross and widespread violations of fundamental human rights and individual freedoms'.[78] The new authorities promised that once a new Constitution had been drafted and elections for a constituent assembly held, a new report would be submitted in conformity with article 40. In introducing that new report the Iranian representatives made statements indicating the general principles of the Iranian Islamic State and referring extensively to the provisions of the new Constitution.[79] One representative then stated that, 'He felt bound to emphasize that although many of the articles of the Covenant were in conformity with the teachings of Islam, there could be no doubt that the tenets of Islam would prevail whenever the two sets of laws were in conflict'.[80]

While a number of HRC members expressed the view that they believed that there was no inherent contradiction between the teachings of the Koran and the principles of the Covenant, there was some concern expressed at this statement and it was suggested that if there was any presumption it should be to the effect that the Covenant should prevail in the event of conflict.[81] More generally a number of members raised questions as to the difficulties encountered by a theocracy in ensuring conformity with the rule of law and with its modern international obligations.[82] These questions are of the greatest importance for the implementation of the Covenant as up to thirty countries are either totally or partially Islamic[83] and it has been reported that Iran has become the first country to question the philosophical basis of the Universal Declaration of Human Rights (1948).[84] Moreover, international concern over the human rights situation in Iran might suggest that there are a number of issues as to which the 'teachings of Islam', as interpreted and applied by Iran, and the provisions of the ICCPR may be in conflict, for example, as regards the status of women, religious tolerance, and the punishment of criminals.[85]

6.20 The United Kingdom constitutional system has not escaped criticism:

In view of the rather fragmentary character of the case law, he concluded that it was highly probable that the substance of the Covenant was not entirely protected by the domestic legal rules of the United Kingdom. It would therefore have been advisable to confer upon the Covenant the legal force of statutory law. He agreed in principle that States were free to decide how they would discharge their international obligations. However, as States parties had undertaken, in Article 2, to respect all the rights recognized in the Covenant, he considered that it should be possible, even in the United Kingdom, to invoke the provisions of the Covenant before tribunals and administrative agencies. In the absence of any constitutional provisions under which an Act of Parliament designed to curtail such rights could be opposed, it would appear that machinery should be introduced to prevent their curtailment.[86]

Similarly, during consideration of the periodic reports of the UK a number of members expressed severe doubts as to the compatibility of the heredity element of membership of the House of Lords with the terms of articles 2(1) and 25 of the Covenant on the basis that it constituted a distinction on the grounds of birth.[87]

Article 2(3)

6.21 In practical terms whatever the nature of the situation with respect to the theoretical existence of the rights and freedoms recognized in the Covenant their true enjoyment ultimately depends on securing the existence of an 'effective remedy' for anyone who claims that there has been a violation of his rights and freedoms. Commensurate with this importance members have devoted considerable and painstaking attention to paragraph 3 of article 2. The breadth of their considerations can vividly be illustrated in a schematic outline of the aspects of remedies dealt with: was there a specific remedy for violation of the rights in the Covenant or did a person have to initiate a civil action and claim damages;[88] was there any kind of *actio populais*;[89] the difference between ordinary and special remedies and the possibilities of appeal;[90] could an individual initiate proceedings invoking the Covenant directly before a court, administrative tribunal, or authority and call for the annulment of a law which ran counter to the Covenant, and make the matter one of public debate, without such a claim having a detrimental effect on him;[91] were there any cases in which courts or other authorities had made specific pronouncements in proceedings involving or based on interpretation of the Covenant;[92] details of the legal bases of the authorities in a State competent to deal with human rights violations and the possibility of conflict between them; could the Covenant be invoked in preventative as well as enforcement proceedings;[93] were there any legal doctrines whereby the remedies did not apply and what limitations and restrictions conditioned the exercise of remedies;[94] in what cases could an appeal be ruled out by statute;[95] in what circumstances could an individual appeal against an administrative decision and would the appellate body be different from the one whose decision was being challenged;[96] was there a system of free legal aid and assistance;[97] was the legal profession open to everyone, what qualifications were required, how many people used its services and were such services available to persons in prison or held in detention;[98] how many cases were dealt with by the different authorities and what was the average length of time taken;[99] were various remedies available and were different types of damages available, for example, indirect, loss of earnings, moral;[100] the effectiveness of a civil remedy against a public official especially in the case of insolvency on the official's part.[101] More specific and particular considerations have prompted the raising of matters such as the role of Ombudsmen,[102] the exclusion of illegally obtained evidence,[103] the formal or substantive nature of the examination of a claim of human rights violation, the general principles concerning the accountability of the police and other State organs, and whether remedies called for in individual cases under the Optional Protocol had been granted to the party or parties concerned.[104]

6.22 Considerable importance has been attached to the determination of remedies by 'competent judicial, administrative, legislative or other authorities provided for by the legal system of the State'. In assessing the existence of such authorities the matters raised have included, *inter alia*, provisions for the election of and the terms of tenure of the judiciary, particularly when there is an element of popular election, for example, Comrades Courts in the USSR,[105] Self-Management Courts in Yugoslavia.[106] It is frequently asked how judicial independence and impartiality are ensured and administrative influence resisted.[107] Similar questions have been raised in the consideration of the provisions of article 14 of the ICCPR.[108]

6.23 A consistent theme of the HRC's deliberations has been that for people to exercise their rights they must be aware of their existence. Thus States parties have been requested to provide information concerning their efforts to publicize the terms of the Covenant,[109] to disseminate human rights information, translate the Covenant into the national and minority languages,[110] improve literacy rates,[111] and encourage the monitoring of the implementation of the Covenant by national human rights groups. In a General Comment the HRC stated that,

It is very important that individuals should know what their rights under the Covenant (and the Optional Protocol, as the case may be) are and also that all administrative and judicial authorities should be aware of the obligations which the State party has assumed under the Covenant. To this end, the Covenant should be publicized in all the official languages of the State and steps should be taken to familiarize the authorities concerned with its contents as part of their training. It is desirable also to give publicity to the State party's co-operation with the Committee.[112]

Where a State party has publicized its report and made it available to its citizens the HRC has been quick to commend such a practice, for example, by Canada, the FRG, and the GDR.[113]

B. ARTICLE 2 UNDER THE OPTIONAL PROTOCOL

6.24 Article 2 has been raised in a substantial number of communications under the OP. Many of those decisions and views noted in the chapter on the Optional Protocol[114] or in the chapters dealing with the application of particular rights under the OP.[115] A high proportion of the allegations of violation of article 2 have been declared inadmissible for various reasons and are therefore only briefly noted as indicators of the potential scope of article 2.

Article 2(1)

6.25 We have already noted the HRC's view in *Santullo (Valcada)* v. *Uruguay*[16] in which after stating that 'it could not find that there had not been a violation of article 7', the HRC's view continued, 'In this respect the Committee notes that the State party has failed to show that it has ensured to the person concerned the protection required by article 2 of the Covenant'.[117] The view suggests a positive obligation on the State party to 'ensure' protection.[118] In *S.S.* v. *Norway*,[119] the author argued that Norway had not afforded him sufficient protection against attacks and interference with his person and his property. The author had been found guilty of violations of various provisions of the Penal Code in defending himself against attacks. He claimed that repeated requests for protection and proper investigation had gone unheeded by the police. The communication was declared inadmissible for failure to exhaust domestic remedies. In *C.F.* v. *Canada*[120] the HRC expressed the view that the Covenant 'does not generally prescribe preventive protection ...'.[121] It has been submitted above that this does not mean that the Covenant will never require preventative protection to comply with the obligation to 'respect and ensure' the rights protected. The question of positive obligations under the Covenant was also raised by Canada in *A.S.* v. *Canada*.[122] Canada argued, *inter alia*, that article 17, 'should be interpreted primarily as negative and therefore could not refer to an obligation by the State positively to re-establish conditions of family life already impaired'.[123] The HRC took the view that article 17 was not applicable on the facts.[124]

In the *Mauritian Women Case*[125] the HRC considered the protection to which a 'family' was entitled from society and the State under article 23 of the Covenant.[126] The HRC expressed the opinon that, 'the legal protection or measures a society or a State can afford to the family vary from country to country and depend on different social, economic, political and cultural conditions and traditions'.[127] The view would appear to be specific to article 23 rather than a general statement concerning permissible variations in the level of protection demanded by the Covenant.[128]

6.26 For a State party the obligation under article 2 applies 'to all individuals within its territory and subject to its jurisdiction'. Therefore, it is not confined to nationals of the State concerned.[129] We have also considered the territorial applicability of the Covenant and the OP.[130] Similarly we examined the requirement of being 'subject to [the] jurisdiction' of the State concerned.[131] The issue of jurisdiction was also raised in *H.v.d.P.* v. *Netherlands*.[132] The author was an international civil servant with the European Patent Office (EPO) based in Munich, West Germany. He claimed to be a victim of discrimination in the promotion practices of the EPO and that the appeals procedures within the EPO did not constitute an effective remedy. The author, a national of the Netherlands, brought the communication against the Netherlands. He claimed that the HRC was competent to consider the case on the basis that five States parties to the EPO (France, Italy, Luxembourg, the Netherlands, and Sweden) were also parties to the OP and that the 'E.P.O., though a public body common to the Contracting States, constitutes a body exercising Dutch public authority'.[133] The HRC took the view that the author had no claim under the OP on the basis that,

The author's grievances ... concern the recruitment policies of an intenational organization, which cannot, in any way, be construed as coming within the jurisdiction of the Netherlands or of any other State party to the International Covenant on Civil and Political Rights and the Optional Protocol thereto.[134]

The approach of the HRC parallels that of the EUCM in an application concerning a decision of the Council of the European Communities.[135]

6.27 A considerable number of communications have raised the non-discrimination (distinction) aspect of article 2(1). Many of those communications raised the question of the relationship between articles 2 and 26 (equality before the law and equal protection of the law). We have already noted the jurisprudence of the HRC to the effect that article 26 does not merely duplicate the guarantees in article 2 but constitutes an independent principle of equal protection.[136] The Covenant therefore represents an important advance on article 14 of the ECHR which only prohibits discrimination in the enjoyment of the rights and freedoms in the ECHR.[137]

The principles of non-discrimination and equal protection apply both to the securing of rights and in respect of restrictions on rights. In the *Mauritian Women Case*[138] the HRC stated that, 'Where the Covenant requires a substantial protection as in article 23, it follows from those provisions that such protection must be equal, that is to say not discriminatory, for example on the basis of sex'.[139] Similarly,

Where restrictions are placed on a right guaranteed by the Covenant, this has to be done without discrimination on the ground of sex. Whether the restriction in itself would be in breach of that right regarded in isolation, is not decisive in this respect. It is the enjoyment of rights which must be secured without discrimination. Here it is sufficient, therefore, to note that in the present position an adverse distinction based on sex is made, affecting the alleged victims in their enjoyment of one of their rights. No sufficient justification for this difference has been given. The Committee must then find that there is a violation of articles 2(1) and 3 of the Covenant, in conjunction with article 17(1).[140]

6.28 Discrimination on the basis of sex was also alleged in the case of *Lovelace* v. *Canada* concering L's loss of rights and status as an Indian when she married a non-Indian.[141] An Indian man who married a non-Indian woman did not lose his Indian status. In the light of its finding of a violation of article 27 of the Covenant when read in the context of articles 12, 17, and 23 and 2, 3, and 26 of the Covenant the HRC found it unnecessary to examine the general provisions against discrimination in articles 2, 3, and 26.[142] In an individual opinion Mr Bouziri took the view that articles 2(1), 3, 23(1) and (4), and 26 of the Covenant had also been breached on the basis that some of the provisions of the Indian Act were discriminatory, particularly as between men and women.[143]

6.29 The HRC have indicated when a distinction or differentiation will constitute discrimination: 'A differentiation based on reasonable and objective criteria does not amount to prohibited discrimination within the meaning of article 26'.[144] As we noted in chapter 4[145] in two of the cases on Dutch social security law the HRC found the differentiation to be unreasonable and therefore discriminatory on the basis of sex[146] while in the third it found that the differentiation based on marital status did not constitute discrimination in the sense of article 26 of the Covenant because it was based on 'objective and reasonable criteria'.[147]

6.29.1 The HRC has now had a number of views in which to apply the 'objective and reasonable criteria' test to alleged discrimination. In *Gueye and Others* v. *France*[148] the alleged victims were 743 retired soldiers of Senegalese nationality who had served in the French Army prior to the independence of Senegal in 1960. They claimed that they had been discriminated against in respect of pension rights. The HRC found that there had been a differentiation by reference to nationality acquired upon independence and that this fell within the reference to 'other status' in article 26 (the same expression appears in article 2(1) of the Covenant). The HRC then considered whether the differentiation was based on reasonable and objective criteria:

A subsequent change in nationality cannot by itself be considered as a sufficient justification for the different treatment, since the basis for the grant of the pension was the same service which both they and the soldiers who remained French had provided. Nor can differences in the economic, financial and social conditions as between France and Senegal be invoked as a legitimate justification. If one compared the case of retired soldiers of Senegalese nationality living in Senegal with that of retired soldiers of French nationality living in Senegal, it would appear that they enjoy the same economic and social conditions . . . In the Committee's opinion, mere administrative convenience or the possibility of some abuse of pension rights cannot be invoked to justify unequal treatment. The Committee concludes that the difference in treatment of the authors is not based on reasonable and objective criteria and constitutes discrimination under the Covenant.[149]

The HRC's view indicates that the 'reasonable and objective criteria' test will be applied in a strict manner and will require convincing evidence from the State party trying to satisfy it. The view also confirms that the implementation of the Covenant can involve considerable financial obligations for States parties.

  6.29.2 In *Vos* v. *Netherlands*[150] Mrs V argued that the application of the Dutch social security legislation had discriminated against her on grounds of sex and marital status. The HRC took the view that the unfavourable result complained of by Mrs V followed

from the application of a uniform rule to avoid overlapping in the allocation of social security benefits. This rule is based on objective and reasonable criteria, especially bearing in mind that both statutes under which Mrs. Vos qualified for benefits aim at ensuring to all persons falling thereunder subsistence level income. Thus the Committee cannot conclude that Mrs. Vos has been a victim of discrimination within the meaning of article 26 of the Covenant.[151]

Presumably the HRC will apply the same criteria in the context of article 2(1) as in the context of article 26.

  6.29.3 In *Vuolanne* v. *Finland*[152] the State party argued that article 9(4) of the Covenant (right of persons deprived of liberty by arrest or detention to take proceedings before a court to determine the lawfulness of the detention) did not apply to detention in military procedure and noted in support of this view that the HRC's General Comment on article 9[153] omitted military disciplinary procedure from a list of types of detention.[154] The HRC rejected the view of the State party:

The Committee considers that this question must be answered by reference to the express terms of the Covenant as well as its purpose. It observes that as a general proposition, the Covenant does not contain any provision exempting from its application certain categories of persons. According to article 2, paragraph 1, 'each State party to the present Covenant undertakes to respect and to ensure to all individuals . . .'. The all-encompassing character of the terms of this article leaves no room for distinguishing between different categories or persons, such as civilians and members of the military, to the extent of holding the Covenant to be applicable in one case but not in the other. Furthermore, the *travaux préparatoires* as well as the Committee's general comments indicate that the purpose of the Covenant was to proclaim and define certain human rights for all and to guarantee their enjoyment. It is, therefore, clear that the Covenant is not, and should not be conceived in terms of whose rights shall be protected but in terms of what rights shall be guaranteed and to what extent. As a consequence the application of article 9, paragraph 4, cannot be excluded in the present case.[155]

The reasoning of the HRC is convincing. To have upheld the submission of the State party would have opened potentially dangerous loopholes in the protection offered by the Covenant.

6.30 Communications have been submitted alleging discrimination on the basis of sex,[156] marital status,[157] political opinion,[158] race,[159] nationality,[160] age,[161] membership of the Romany minority,[162] and because of the authors' ethnic, religious, and national background and for political reasons.[163]

Article 2(2)

6.31 No communications have specifically raised article 2(2). When the HRC expresses the view that there has been a violation of the Covenant it has on a number of occasions stated that the State party should adjust or review the operation of its legislation as well as granting remedies to the individual victims concerned.[164] It is also interesting to note the view of the HRC in *Hartikainen* v. *Finland*[165] in which the authors alleged that compulsory classes for children on religion and ethics violated 18(4) of the Covenant.[166] There the HRC took the view that although the State party admitted that difficulties were being experienced in regard to the existing teaching plan the HRC, 'believes that appropriate action is being taken to resolve the difficulties and it sees no reason to conclude that this cannot be accomplished, compatibly with the requirements of article 18(4) of the Covenant, within the framework of existing laws'.[167] Here the HRC displays a sensible degree of flexibility in the application of the Covenant and an understanding of the difficulties faced by States parties in giving effect to the Covenant.[168]

Article 2(3)

6.32 In *Hermoza* v. *Peru*[169] three members of the HRC appended an individual opinion in which they expressed the view that there had been violations of article 2(3)(*a*) and (*c*) because 'neither the administrative nor the judicial authorities of the State party found it possible, over a period spanning a decade, to provide the author with an appropriate remedy and to enforce that remedy'.[170] In its views under the OP the HRC has consistently stressed the requirement of an effective remedy in terms of the measures necessary to remedy the violations, pay adequate compensation, and to take steps to ensure that similar violations do not occur in the future.[171] The approach of the HRC to the exhaustion of domestic remedies and the kind of remedies required in the event of violation have already been examined in chapter 4.[172] The HRC appears to have followed the jurisprudence under the

ECHR in only requiring a person to 'claim' that his rights have been violated rather than that they must actually have been violated before article 2(3) can apply.

6.33 An important question is whether article 2(3) is capable of independent violation. In *S.H.B.* v. *Canada*,[173] Canada argued that, 'Articles 2(1–3) and 3 of the Covenant are relevant to a determination of whether other articles of the Covenant have been violated, they are not capable of independent violation in their own right'.[174] The HRC did not reply to this submission. However, in *Ex-Philibert* v. *Zaïre*[175] the Committee found a separate violation of article 2(3). P had been arrested and detained for over nine months and had no effective remedy under the domestic law of Zaïre in respect of the violations of the law complained of.[176]

6.34 Article 2(3) is obviously related to other articles of the Covenant which provide for specific remedies. In *Baritussio* v. *Uruguay*[177] despite a decision granting her provisional release B remained in detention for another three years. Although her defence lawyer made representations to the military judges concerned he was informed that, if the prison authorities did not comply with the court order, the judges could do no more.[178] The HRC expressed the view that article 2(3) had been violated in conjunction with article 9(4) (right to take proceedings to challenge the lawfulness of detention).[179] A situation in which court orders are ignored represents a serious threat to the enforcement of rights under article 2(3) of the Covenant and must demand immediate action on the part of the authorities of the State. In *Hammel* v. *Madagascar*[180] the HRC expressed the view that article 9(4) of the Covenant had been violated but expressed no view on other claims including article 2(3) of the Covenant.[181]

6.35 A more helpful view of the HRC on the relationship between article 2(3) and other articles providing for remedies is that in *Fanali* v. *Italy*.[182] Italy had made a reservation to article 14(5) of the Covenant (right to review of conviction and sentence by a higher tribunal). The author argued, *inter alia*, that his right of appeal was none the less confirmed by article 2(3) to which Italy had made no reservation. The HRC was

unable to share this view which seems to overlook the nature of the provisions concerned. It is true that article 2(3) provides generally that persons whose rights and freedoms, as recognized in the Covenant, are violated 'shall have an effective remedy'. But this general right to a remedy is an accessory one, and cannot be invoked when the purported right to which it is linked is excluded by a reservation, as in the present case. Even had this not been so, the purported right, as in the case of article 14(5), consists itself of a remedy (appeal). Thus it is a form of *lex specialis* besides which it would have no meaning to apply the general right in article 2(3).[183]

Presumably the same approach could be taken to articles providing specific remedies or procedural guarantees, for example, article 9(4),[184] article 13 (procedure for the expulsion of aliens lawfully in the territory),[185] and, of great importance, the right to a fair and public hearing by a competent, independent, and impartial tribunal established by law for the determination of any 'criminal charge' or of 'rights and obligations in a suit at law' (article 14).[186] The HRC's view does not answer the question of whether article 2(3) is capable of independent violation.

6.36 In *Stalla Costa* v. *Uruguay*[187] the State party argued that there could be no remedy because S.C. had no right under domestic law to be appointed to a public post. S.C. argued that the relevant Act was discriminatory because its effect was that only former employees were being admitted to the public service. The Act sought to restore the rights of those who had been dismissed on ideological, political, or trade union grounds or for purely arbitrary reasons by the previous *de facto* regime, to reinstate them in their jobs, and allow them to resume their careers in the public service and to receive a pension. The HRC took the view that the enactment was a measure of redress for public officials who were victims of violations of article 25 of the Covenant.[188] and as such were entitled to have an effective remedy under article 2(3)(*a*) of the Covenant.

The Act should be looked upon as such a remedy. The implementation of the Act, therefore, cannot be regarded as incompatible with the reference to 'general terms of equality' in article 25(c) of the Covenant. Neither can the implementation of the Act be regarded as an invidious distinction under article 2, paragraph 1, or as prohibited discrimination within the terms of article 26 of the Covenant.[189]

Clearly the communication concerned an exceptional situation where a legitimate aim of providing the only effective remedy for one set of victims involved a limitation on the rights of other individuals. While the view is comprehensible in that light the HRC could usefully have stressed the requirement of proportionality between the means sought and the aim sought to be realized. So, for example, the application of the Act should not be indefinite but only for so long as necessary to afford an adequate opportunity to remedy the original violations.

APPRAISAL

6.37 The approach of the HRC to article 2 was always going to be crucial. In the consideration of State reports it has been accorded central importance. Members have acknowledged the discretion States parties have as to how to implement the rights in the Covenant.[190] However, they have generally stressed the immediacy of the obligation while being sympathetic to genuine difficulties in implementing the Covenant.[191] In the General Comment on article 2 and in other general comments the HRC has clearly established that

States parties are obliged to take positive measures to 'respect and ensure' the rights in the Covenant.[192] Close and critical attention has been given to the relevant terms of national laws and the practices of national organs as the HRC members have sought to ascertain the practical implementation of the Covenant on a non-discriminatory basis.[193] Reservations and interpretations have been considered and commented upon although the HRC has made no formal determination of their competence in respect of them.[194] The HRC has acknowledged the vital function of 'effective remedies' in giving effect to the Covenant and its consideration of the range of possible remedies has been most impressive.[195]

As regards the HRC's jurisprudence under the OP the fundamental determination has concerned not so much article 2 but the relationship between article 2 and article 26. The interpretation of article 26 as an independent equal protection guarantee adds considerably to the scope and importance of the Covenant.[196]

NOTES

1 For similar provisions see UDHR art. 8; ECHR arts. 1, 13, and 14; AMR arts. 1, 2, and 25; ADRD art. XVIII; AFR arts. 7 and 26; Human Rights International Instruments, Part D (1983). For a summary of the drafting of article 2 see UN Docs. A/2929, ch. 5, and A/5655 prs. 6–36; Bossuyt, *Guide*, pp. 49–73. On article 2 ICCPR in particular see T. Buergenthal, 'To Respect and to Ensure: State Obligation and Permissible Derogations', in L. Henkin (ed.), *The International Bill of Rights—The ICCPR*, pp. 72–8 (1981); B. Graefrath, 'How Different Countries Implement International Standards on Human Rights' (1984–5) CHRYB pp. 3–30; F. Jhabvala, 'The Practice of the Covenant's Human Rights Committee, 1976–82: Review of State Party Reports', 6 HRQ (1984) pp. 81–106 at 95–106; F. Jhabvala, 'On Human Rights and the Socio-Economic Context', 31 NILR (1984) pp. 149–82; F. Jhabvala, 'Domestic Implementation of the Covenant on Civil and Political Rights', 32 NILR (1985) pp. 461–86; R. B. Lillich, 'Civil Rights', in T. Meron (ed.), *Human Rights in International Law— Legal and Policy Issues*, Vol. i, p. 115 at 132–6 (1984); T. Meron, *Human Rights Law-Making in the United Nations*, pp. 119–23 (1986); T. Opsahl, 'Human Rights Today: International Obligations and National Implementation', 23 Scandinavian Studies in Law (1979) pp. 149–76; O. Schachter, 'The Obligation of Parties to Give Effect to the Covenant on Civil and Political Rights', 73 AJIL (1979) pp. 462–5; O. Schachter, 'The Obligation to Implement the Covenant in Domestic Law', in L. Henkin (ed.), above, pp. 311–31 (1981); E. Schwelb, 'The Nature of the Obligations of the States Parties to the ICCPR', in *René Cassin Amicorum Discipulorumque Liber*, pp. 301–24 (1969); E. Schwelb, 'Some Aspects of the International Covenants on Human Rights of December 1966', in A. Eide and A. Schou (eds.), *International Protection of Human Rights*, p. 103 at

107–10 (1968); B. G. Ramcharan, 'Equality and Non-Discrimination', in Henkin (ed.), above, pp. 246–69 (1981); C. Tomuschat, 'Equality and Non-Discrimination under the International Covenant on Civil and Political Rights', in von Ingo von Munch (ed.), *Staatsrecht—Volkerrecht—Europarecht, Festschrift für Hans-Jurgen Schlochauer*, pp. 691–716 (1981); C. Tomuschat, 'National Implementation of International Standards on Human Rights' (1984–5) CHRYB pp. 31–61. More generally on Equality and Non-Discrimination see I. Brownlie, *Principles of Public International Law*, pp. 598–601 (4th, 1990); J. Greenberg, 'Race, Sex and Religious Discrimination in International Law', in T. Meron (ed.), above, Vol. ii, ch. 8 (1984); W. McKean, *Equality and Non-Discrimination under International Law* (1983); J. F. Partsch, 'Fundamental Principles of Human Rights: Self-Determination, Equality and Non-Discrimination', in K. Vasak (gen. ed.), P. Alston (Eng. ed.), *The International Dimensions of Human Rights*, vol. i, p. 61 at pp. 68–86 (1982); P. Sieghart, *The International Law of Human Rights*, pp. 56–9, 67–71, 72–84 (1983); *United Nations Action in the Field of Human Rights*, ch. 4 (1988); E. W. Vierdag, *The Concept of Discrimination in International Law* (1973).

2 GC 3(13), Doc. A/36/40, p. 108. The HRC has recently adopted a general comment on 'non-discrimination' which is of importance to article 2', see Doc. CCPR/C/21/Rev. 1/Add. 1 (21 Nov. 1989); SR 901 prs. 31–67, 914 prs. 7–37, 938, 939, and 948.

3 'The Committee should therefore focus its attention primarily on the reality of human rights practices. One of the basic factors on which the effectiveness of the Covenant depended was its position in the legal order of the State', SR 128 pr. 16*a* (Tomuschat).

4 See ch. 1, pr. 1.34 above.

5 GC 3(13), n. 2 above, pr. 1; Doc. A/36/40, p. 109; also in Doc. CCPR/C/21. The corollary of this is the customary international law rule that a State may not invoke the provisions of its internal law as justification for its failure to perform a treaty, see Article 27 VCLT 1969. See also the exchange between Mr Movchan (SR 69 pr. 68) and the UK representative (SR 70 pr. 12) concerning the obligation under article 2(2). The ICCPR parallels the ECHR in not requiring States parties to formally incorporate it into domestic law, see ch. 1, pr. 1.18–1.21 above and A. Drzemczewski, *European Human Rights Convention in Domestic Law*, ch. 1 (1983).

6 A good example of such a body is the Interministerial Committee on human rights established by the Italian government in 1977. The Committee prepared the initial Italian report and its second periodic report, Docs. CCPR/C/6/Add. 4, CCPR/C/37/Add. 9. The Committee systematically examines and discusses human rights problems, ensuring continuous co-operation between the competent State authorities. See also the reports of Australia, Doc. CCPR/C/14/Add. 1, p. 16 (1981) and Canada, Doc. CCPR/C/Add. 43, Vol. i, pp. 6–7 (1979). Note also the case of Suriname. After being informed that following the *coup d'état* of February 1980 a Committee would be appointed to study the amendments to be made to the Constitution the Human Rights Committee thought that the best role that it could play would be to highlight some of the matters to be

taken into account to ensure compatibility with its obligations under the Covenant. See SR 223, 224, and 227.

7 For an account of some such changes see SR 416 pr. 4 (Australian State representative); SR 481 pr. 4 (New Zealand State representative).

8 See e.g. SR 69 prs. 13 (Graefrath), 44 (Prado-Vallejo), and 65 (Movchan) concerning the UK reservation to article 12(4) so as to preserve immigration controls. For reply see SR 70 pr. 43. A number of States have made reservations to or deposited interpretative declarations on the Covenant, see *Human Rights— Status of International Instruments* (1987); 'Reservations, Declarations, Notifications and Objections Relating to the International Covenant on Civil and Political Rights and the Optional Protocol Thereto', Doc. CCPR/C/2/Rev. 2 (12 May 1989). No formal decision has been taken by the HRC concerning their competence with respect to reservations, see D. Shelton, 'State Practice on Reservations to Human Rights Treaties' (1983) CHRYB p. 204 at pp. 230–1. For CEDAW's practice see Byrnes, ch. 3 n. 1 above, pp. 51–56.

9 See e.g. SR 345 pr. 33 (Opsahl on Rwanda). 'The Covenant requires both *respect* for its rights *and their ensurance*. And the incorporation of the Covenant into domestic law, *per se*, will achieve neither of these objectives although it may clear away some of the obstacles to their achievement', Jhabvala, n. 1 above, p. 483 (1985). See also Tomuschat, text to n. 86 below (on UK).

10 See e.g. SR 345 prs. 24 (Tomuschat) and 40 (Graefrath) on Rwanda; SR 365 pr. 39 (Hanga on Iran), SR 402 pr. 40 (Ermacora on Australia), SR 481 pr. 20 (Movchan on New Zealand).

11 See e.g. SR 77 pr. 9 (Vincent-Evans on Norway). Interesting examples of rules of presumption and interpretation are those applied by Denmark, see Doc. CCPR/ C/Add. 4 and 19; SR 54 prs. 11 (Hanga), 40 (Opsahl), and 53 (State representative). The ECHR is increasingly referred to by UK courts. For a notable example, see *Attorney-General* v. *Guardian Newspapers Ltd.* [1987] 3 All ER 316; *Attorney-General* v. *Guardian Newspapers (No. 2)* [1988] 3 All ER 545. See also *R* v. *Secretary of State for the Home Department, ex p Brind* [1990] 1 All ER 469 (CA).

12 See e.g. the report of Portugal, Doc. CCPR/C/6/Add. 6, pp. 9–22.

13 See text to n. 5 above.

14 'Subsequent practice has lent further support to the interpretation that incorporation into domestic law is not required by the Covenant', Schachter, n. 1 above, p. 314 (1981). While incorporation may not be required members may suggest that it is advisable. During consideration of the report from Hong Kong many members of the HRC suggested to the UK representatives that consideration be given to solving as many human rights problems as possible, or to enacting the Covenant into law, before 1997. See SR 855–7. Recent events in China add weight to these suggestions. See ch. 1 n. 257 above.

15 Doc. A/2929, pr. 12. See also Doc. E/600, ch. 1 n. 1 above, Report of Working Group on Implementation.

16 See e.g. Graefrath, n. 1 above; Tomuschat, ibid. (1984–5); Schachter, ibid. (1981); Jhabvala, n. 1 above (1985); Lillich, ch. 1 n. 231 above (1985); Green, ch. 1, n. 1 above, p. 46.

17 See e.g. SR 94 pr. 16 (Koulishev on FRG).

18 Article 50. See ch. 1, pr. 1.24 above.

19 See *Human Rights—Status*, n. 8 above, p. 86. For the HRC's consideration see SR 401, 402, 403, 407, and 408. See, for example, SR 402 prs. 11 (Prado-Vallejo), 28 (Movchan), and 37 (Ermacora). For academic comment see G. Triggs, 'Australia's Ratification of the International Covenant on Civil and Political Rights: Endorsement or Repudiation?', 31 ICLQ (1982) pp. 278–306; H. Burmeister, 'Federal Clauses: An Australian Perspective', 34 ICLQ (1985) pp. 522–37.

20 *Human Rights—Status*, n. 8 above, p. 29.

21 See D. McRae, 'The Legal Effect of Interpretative Declarations' (1978) 49 BYIL pp. 155–73; Marks, ch. 1 n. 154 above.

22 See e.g. SR 69 pr. 12 (Graefrath) and SR 70 pr. 19 (State representative) concerning the UK; SR 439 pr. 46 (Vincent-Evans on France). On the territorial application of the Covenant see ch. 1, pr. 1.24 above.

23 See e.g. SR 443 prs. 2 (Vincent-Evans), 37 (Ermacora), 55 (Tomuschat), SR 444 prs. 12 (Opsahl), 27 (Aguilar), and 40 (Bouziri) on Lebanon; reply at SR 446 pr. 44; SR 468 pr. 23 (Prado-Vallejo on El Salvador); reply at SR 468 prs. 36–8, SR 474 pr. 15; SR 165 prs. 19–21 and SR 166 pr. 52 (Prado-Vallejo on Cyprus); reply at SR 165 prs. 33–45 and SR 166 prs. 57–8.

24 See e.g. SR 160 prs. 44 (Opsahl), 62 (reply), 70 (Opsahl), 73 (Chairman) on Syria; See also SR 444 pr. 13 as corrected (Opsahl on Lebanon). The EUCM has taken the view that under the ECHR a State is responsible for securing the rights and freedoms in the Convention to all persons under their 'Actual authority and responsibility, whether that authority is exercised within the national territory or abroad', *Cyprus* v. *Turkey*, 2 D. & R. p. 125, Decn. Admiss. (1975).

25 See N. Lerner, *The United Nations Convention on the Elimination of Racial Discrimination*, Pt. IV, ch. 4 (2nd, 1980); N. Lerner, 'The Golan Heights Case and the U.N. Committee on Racial Discrimination', 3 Isr. YHR. (1973) pp. 118–35; T. Meron, 'The International Convention on the Elimination of all Forms of Racial Discrimination and the Golan Heights', 8 Isr. YHR. (1978) pp. 222–39; T. Meron, 'The Meaning and Reach of the ICERD', 79 AJIL (1985) pp. 283–318.

26 GC 3(13), n. 2 above, pr. 1.

27 SR 170 pr. 38 on Finland's report, Doc. CCPR/C/Add. 32.

28 See Opsahl, n. 1 above; Jhabvala, n. 1 above (1985); K. Vasak, 'Human Rights: As a Legal Reality', in Vasak/Alston (eds.), n. 1 above, pp. 3–10; M. Sorenson, 'Report Concerning Obligations of a State Party to a Treaty as Regards its Municipal Law', in A. H. Robertson (ed.), *Human Rights in National and International Law*, pp. 11–46 (1968).

29 My emphasis. See SR 370 prs. 20–1 (Vincent-Evans). On the essentially supplementary nature of international human rights protection see the EUCT in *The Belgian Linguistics Case*, EUCT, Series A, Vol. 6, pr. 10 (1968), 11 YBECHR p. 832.

30 See e.g. Tomuschat, text to n. 27 above.

31 See Jhabvala, n. 1 above, 31 NILR (1985).

32 See e.g. SR 357 pr. 29 (Opsahl on Uruguay).

33 See e.g. SR 603 prs. 51–2 (Serrano-Caldera on Afghanistan), SR 84 pr. 4 (Lallah on Madagascar).

34 See e.g. SR 354 pr. 2 (Graefrath on Guyana).

35 See e.g. SR 441 pr. 42 (Al Douri on France).

36 See e.g. SR 319 pr. 12 (Opsahl), 35 (Vincent-Evans on Japan); reply at SR 324 pr. 10.

37 See e.g. SR 420 pr. 26 (Prado-Vallejo on Nicaragua); SR 870 pr. 39 (Serrano-Caldera on Togo). See ch. 1 n. 119 above. The General Assembly has repeatedly called for the establishment of national and private human rights organizations.

38 See e.g. SR 31 pr. 38 (Vincent-Evans on Ecuador).

39 See e.g. SR 77 pr. 9 (Vincent-Evans on Norway). See also O. Garibaldi, 'General Limitations on Human Rights: The Principle of Legality', 17 Harv. ILJ (1976) pp. 503–57.

40 See e.g. SR 108 pr. 29 (Mora Rojas on USSR).

41 Generally see J. Ziman, P. Sieghart, and J. P. Humphrey, *The World of Science and the Rule of Law* (1986).

42 See ch. 11 below on freedom of expression.

43 See e.g. SR 628 pr. 34 (Movchan on Luxembourg); SR 871 pr. 35 (Higgins on Togo seeking comparative data on education levels). For an example of the provision of such information see SR 581 pr. 31 (Dominican Republic).

44 See ch. 5 above and chs. 7–12 below.

45 See ch. 1, pr. 1.17 above.

46 See the articles by Jhabvala, n. 1 above HRQ (1984), and subsequent correspondence at 6 HRQ (1984) pp. 539–40 (Humphrey) and 7 HRQ (1985) p. 565 (Y. Iwasawa); Schwelb, n. 1 above (1969); Schachter, n. 1 above (1981); Tomuschat, n. 1 above, p. 694 (1981); SR 206 prs. 16–18 (Tomuschat). P. Alston and G. Quinn, n. 47 below, p . 173, comment, 'In practice it can be strongly argued that, in at least some states parties to the Covenant on Civil and Political Rights, certain of those rights are by no means susceptible of immediate realization. Moreover, the standard that is in fact being applied, with the implicit (but certainly unstated) endorsement of the HRC, is one of progressive achievement', p. 173.

47 See e.g. SR 54 pr. 18 (Vincent-Evans on Denmark), SR 402 pr. 29 (Movchan on Australia), SR 551 pr. 4 (Opsahl on Trinidad and Tobago). Cf. though the comment that, 'it was clear that implementation could be gradual', SR 198 pr. 35 (Movchan on Mongolia). On article 2 of the ICESCR see E. W. Vierdag, 'The Legal Nature of the Rights Granted by the International Covenant on Economic, Social and Cultural Rights', 9 NYIL (1978) pp. 69–105; P. Alston and G. Quinn, 'The Nature and Scope of States Parties' Obligations under the International Covenant on Economic, Social and Cultural Rights', 9 HRQ (1987) pp. 156–229; Y. Klerk, 'Working Paper on Article 2(2) and Article 3 of the International Covenant on Economic, Social, and Cultural Rights', 9 HRQ (1987) pp. 250–73; Principles 16–34 of the Limburg Principles, ibid., pp. 122–35; M. K. Addo, 'The Justiciability of Economic, Social and Cultural Rights', 14 CLB (1988) pp. 1425–32.

48 See e.g. SR 284 prs. 33–5 (Aguilar on Mali); SR 473 pr. 29 (Aguilar on Sri Lanka).

49 See e.g. SR 282 pr. 2 (Tarnopolsky on Mali); SR 345 pr. 37 (Graefrath on Rwanda).

50 Tomuschat, n. 1 above (1984–5), p. 42.

51 GC 3/13, n. 2 above, pr. 1. See also SR 109 pr. 13 (Opsahl on USSR), SR 440 pr. 66 (Opsahl on France).

52 GC 4(13), prs. 2–3; Doc. A/36/40, pp. 109–10; also in Doc. CCPR/C/21.

53 GC 17 (35) (article 24), Doc. A/44/40, p. 173, prs. 1, 3.

54 GC 18 (37), n. 2 above, prs. 9, 10. Tomuschat, n. 1 above (1981), comments that, '. . . articles 2(1) and 26 do not prohibit affirmative action designed to further the interests of traditionally disadvantaged minority groups [citing, *inter alia*, Doc. A/C.3/1259, prs. 33, 34] provided that granting such privileges does not amount to overt discrimination of the majority. In the field covered by the CCPR, such instances will rarely happen, civil and political rights being directed against governmental interference in private affairs. Such freedom "from" the State cannot be enhanced for the benefit solely of specific groups', pp. 715–16. In a note to this comment Tomuschat adds, 'It would certainly be unwise to contend that the CCPR provides a solution to the issue of "adverse discrimination" as dealt with by the U.S. Supreme Court in the famous case Bakke case, see *Regents of the University of California v. Bakke*, 438 U.S. 265 (1978)'. See also the important recent decision of the US Supreme Court in *Johnson v. Transportation Agency of Santa Clara County*, California, 480 US 616; 107 S. Ct. 1442; 55 US Law Week 4379.

55 The jurisprudence on positive obligations under the ECHR has been rather limited to date. See *Marcxx v. Belgium*, EUCT, Series A, Vol. 31 (1979); *Airey v. Ireland*, EUCT, Series A, Vol. 32 (1979); *Platform 'Ärzte für das Leben' v. Austria*, ibid., Vol. 139 (1988) pr. 32. Cf. article 1(4) ICERD and article 4 CEDAW which expressly state that certain special measures shall not be deemed or considered discrimination.

56 See pr. 6.11 above.

57 See Docs. CCPR/C/1/Add. 13 and C/28/Add. 2; SR 65, 532 (State representatives). See also UN Doc. CCPR/C/52/Add. 1 (1988).

58 See Docs. CCPR/C/1/Add. 17, and C/32/Add. 5; SR 67 and 593 (State representatives). For the UK's third periodic report see UN Doc. CCPR/C/58/Add. 6 (1990).

59 See Docs. CCPR/C/1/Add. 22 and C/28/Add. 3; SR 108 and 564 (State representatives). See also UN Doc. CCPR/C/52/Add. 2 (1988).

60 See SR 65, 67, 68, 532–4 and 536 (GDR): SR 67, 69, 70, 593–8 (UK); SR 108, 109, 112, 564–7, and 570, 928–31 (USSR).

61 See Jhabvala (1985), Opsahl, and Schachter (1981) at n. 1 above.

62 GC 18 (37), n. 2 above, prs. 7, 8. HRC members have generally referred to discrimination rather than to distinction. Commentators seem in agreement that there is in this context no difference in substance between the two terms, see e.g. Klerk, n. 47 above. The ICESCR uses the term 'discrimination' in its article 2. In the Third Committee the suggestion that 'distinction' in the draft ICCPR be replaced by 'discrimination' was not accepted as some members of the Committee felt that the term 'discrimination' had acquired a shade of meaning which rendered it less

appropriate in the context of the ICCPR. It was also noted that the term 'distinction' had also been used in both the UN Charter and the Universal Declaration, Doc. A/5655, pr. 19. The French expression 'sans distinction aucune', appears in both article 2 of the ICCPR and article 2 of the ICESCR. The European Court of Human Rights faced this problem of interpretation in the *Belgian Linguistics Case*, Series A, Vol. 6, 11 YBECHR p. 832, pr. 10 (1968), where it followed the more restrictive term 'discrimination' in the English text.

63 See e.g. SR 361 pr. 24 (Ermacora on Jordan), SR 431 pr. 4 (Tarnopolsky on Peru). 'The Committee . . . would like to receive information from States parties as to the significance of such omissions', GC 18 (37), n. 2 above, pr. 11.

64 Doc. CCPR/C/4/Add. 2.

65 SR 187 pr. 44. See also SR 108 pr. 48 (Vincent-Evans on USSR); SR 483 pr. 42 (Tomuschat on Yugoslavia). To the last comment the State representative replied that, 'Expert opinion on constitutional law considered that the Constitution prohibited discrimination on grounds of political opinion. That was also the practice of the Constitutional courts', ibid., pr. 43. It is understood that this issue had been widely discussed in Yugoslavia over a number of years in the light of the ICCPR.

66 We have already noted that no right to property was included in the Covenant, see ch. 1 n. 200 above.

67 SR 109 pr. 37.

68 See ch. 1, pr. 1.35 above. See also the HRC's important general comment GC 15(27) on the 'Position of aliens under the Covenant', Doc. A/41/40, pp. 117–19.

69 See SR 110 pr. 5 (Tomuschat on Mauritius).

70 See e.g. SR 131 pr. 37 (Bouziri on Bulgaria).

71 See e.g. SR 108 pr. 46 (Vincent-Evans on USSR) and SR 109 pr. 57 (Tomuschat on USSR). Jhabvala, n. 1 above (1985), comments that, 'It would appear that political discrimination in favour of the respective communist parties, and correspondingly against those holding different political views, is given a constitutional foundation in these countries (referring to the Soviet-bloc States). In as much as these constitutional provisions reflect the socio-political philosophies of these States, it would seem to be clear that for these parties to conform, even "formally", to the norms of the Covenant, they would have to radically revise their social and political philosophy and their constitutions . . .', pp. 473–4. Cf. the comment of Graefrath, n. 1 above, '. . . at times attempts are made to suggest that the Covenant was a treaty which made the capitalist model of fundamental freedoms binding on its states parties. Such an interpretation denies the universal character of the Covenant and borders on the absurd assumption that the socialist states agreed to a treaty amounting to the abandonment of the socialist system', p. 6. Cf. R. Falk, 'Comparative Protection of Human Rights in Capitalist and Socialist Third World Countries', 1 Univ. HR (1979) pp. 3–29.

72 See the consideration of its report in SR 133, 136, 137, and 140. The political changes in Eastern Europe in 1989–90 may lead to the removal of the dominant constitutional positions of Communist parties and see the introduction of multi-

party democracies. See K. Sword (ed.), *Guide to Eastern Europe—The Changing Face of the Warsaw Pact* (1990).

73 SR 870 pr. 34, reply in SR 874 prs. 1–4. See also, e.g. SR 283 pr. 25 (Sadi on Mali) and SR 345 pr. 19 (Tomuschat on Rwanda) concerning one-party States.

74 Docs. CCPR/C/1/Add. 25 and 40.

75 SR 128 pr. 2.

76 SR 129 pr. 51. 'The burden was on States parties to show that the form of government they adopted was not an obstacle to the enforcement of those important provisions [of the Covenant]', SR 283 pr. 25 (Opsahl on Mali).

77 See Docs. CCPR/C/Add. 16 and 26 and Corr. 1.

78 SR 149 prs. 26–8.

79 See SR 368.

80 SR 364 pr. 4.

81 See SR 366 pr. 10.

82 See SR 364 pr. 55 (Opsahl), SR 366 pr. 10 (Tomuschat). For reply see SR 368.

83 C. Humana, *World Human Rights Guide*, p. 5 (2nd, 1986).

84 See ch. 1, pr. 1.34 above. Generally see International Commission of Jurists, *Human Rights in Islam* (1982); D.E.Artz, 'The Application of International Human Rights Law in Islamic States', 12 HRQ (1990) pp. 202–30; Report on Iran by the Special Representative of the HRCion, UN Doc. E/CN.4/1990/24.

85 See n. 84 above; Humana, n. 83 above, p. 131. As of July 1990 no second periodic report has been submitted by Iran (due 1983).

86 SR 69 pr. 83. See generally, S. H. Bailey, D. J. Harris, and B. Jones, *Civil Liberties—Cases and Materials*, ch. 1 (2nd, 1985). See also the comments at SR 93 pr. 66 (Lallah on FRG).

87 See e.g. SR 69 pr. 3 (Lallah); reply in Doc. CCPR/C/1/Add. 35, pr. 2; SR 147 prs. 6 (Lallah), 22 (Tomuschat), 23 (Graefrath), and 25 (Sadi); replies at prs. 15 and 35.

88 See e.g. SR 84 pr. 6 (Lallah on Madagascar).

89 See e.g. SR 349 pr. 39 (Vincent-Evans on France).

90 See e.g. SR 356 pr. 3 (Dieye on Uruguay).

91 See e.g. SR 64 pr. 57 (Prado-Vallejo on Czechoslovakia), SR 67 pr. 59 (Tomuschat on GDR).

92 See e.g. SR 64 pr. 63 (Tomuschat on Czechoslovaka). In reply State representatives often claim that the ICCPR is being invoked but are unable to cite any examples.

93 See Doc. A/35/40, pr. 125 (Iraq).

94 See e.g. SR 98 pr. 26 (Mora-Rojas on Yugoslavia).

95 See e.g. SR 99 pr. 33 (Koulishev on Czechoslovakia): SR 879 pr. 50 (Fodor on Uruguay concerning the compatibility with article 2 of the Amnesty Act and the Law of Expiry).

96 See e.g. SR 187 pr. 17 (Tomuschat on Poland).

97 See e.g. SR 132 pr. 30 (Opsahl on Bulgaria).

98 See e.g. SR 187 pr. 25 (Lallah on Poland).

99 See e.g. SR 109 pr. 30 (Hanga on USSR).

100 See e.g. SR 109 pr. 30 (Hanga on USSR); SR 430 pr. 47 (Tomuschat on Peru).

101 See e.g. SR 205 pr. 47 (Hanga on Canada); SR 69 pr. 30 (Tarnopolsky on UK). See also SR 441 pr. 23 (Tomuschat on France concerning the 'Act of Government' theory).

102 See e.g. SR 353 pr. 28 (Tomuschat on Guyana).

103 See e.g. SR 69 pr. 30 (Tarnopolsky on UK).

104 See e.g. SR 355 pr. 29 (Prado-Vallejo on Uruguay). At the conclusion of the consideration of the second periodic report of Uruguay the Chairman of the HRC presented the Uruguayan delegation with a list of all the cases concerning Uruguay which had been examined under the OP, together with the HRC's final recommendations on the cases. He hoped the Uruguayan government would study the cases and take appropriate action, SR 879 pr. 59.

105 See SR 109 pr. 70 (Lallah). For details see Doc. CCPR/C/1/Add. 22.

106 See SR 99 pr. 15 (Hanga). For details see Doc. CCPR/C/1/Add. 23.

107 See e.g. SR 67 pr. 13 (Tarnopolsky on GDR), SR 84 pr. 3 (Lallah on Madagascar), SR 109 pr. 70 (Lallah on USSR).

108 See ch. 10 below.

109 See e.g. SR 355 pr. 18 (Prado-Vallejo on Uruguay).

110 See e.g. SR 98 pr. 46 (Vincent-Evans on Yugoslavia). See also 'Human Rights Bill in Eight African Languages', 2(1) Human Rights Newsletter p. 9 (March, 1989, United Nations).

111 See e.g. SR 421 pr. 6 (Hanga on Nicaragua), SR 345 pr. 37 (Graefrath on Rwanda).

112 GC 3(13), n. 2 above, pr. 2. See also SR 345 pr. 27 (Vincent-Evans on Rwanda). The HRCion has repeatedly called on governments to publish the texts of the two Covenants and the OP in as many languages as possible and to distribute them as widely as possible in their territories. It has also urged the Secretary-General of the UN to give more publicity to the work of the HRC and ensure that the necessary administrative and related support is provided, see e.g. HRCion Resn. 1989/17, prs. 12–13 HRCion, Report on 45th session, ECOSOC, OR, Supp. 2, p. 58 (1989).

113 See Tomuschat, n. 1 above, p. 60 (1984–5). See the criticisms of Chan and Lau, ch. 1 n. 257 above, p. 151 on consultation and publicity for the U.K.'s report on Hong Kong.

114 See ch. 4 above.

115 See ch 5 above and chs. 7–12 below.

116 Doc. A/35/40, p. 107. See pr. 4.30 above.

117 Doc. A/35/40, p. 107, pr. 12.

118 See pr. 6.12 above and ch. 8 below on article 6.

119 SD, p. 30.

120 Doc. A/40/40, p. 217. See ch. 4, pr. 4.103 above.

121 Doc. A/40/40, p. 217, pr. 6.2.

122 SD, p. 27. See ch. 4, pr. 4.59 above.

123 SD, p. 27, pr. 5.1.

124 See ch. 4, pr. 4.59 above. See also General Comment 16(32) on article 17, Doc. A/43/40, p. 181.

125 *Aumeeruddy-Cziffra and Others* v. *Mauritius*, Doc. A/36/40, p. 134. See ch. 4, pr. 4.75 above.

126 For the text of article 23 see Apx. I below.

127 Doc. A/36/40, p. 134, pr. 9.2(*b*)2(ii)1.

128 See also GC 18 (37), n. 2 above, pr. 5. See ch. 6, prs. 6.11–6.12 above on the immediacy of the general obligation under article 2 of the Covenant and ch. 1, pr. 1.34 on the universality of the Covenant.

129 See ch. 4, pr. 4.67 above.

130 See ch. 4, prs. 4.82–4.85 and ch. 6, pr. 6.7 above.

131 See ch. 4, prs. 4.66, 4.82–4.86 above.

132 Doc. A/42/40, p. 185.

133 Ibid., pr. 2.3.

134 Ibid., pr. 3.2.

135 *C.F.D.T.* v. *European Communities/Their Member States*, A.8030/77, 13 D. & R. 231. See also A.235/56, 2 YBECHR 256 at 288–304, concerning the responsibility of West Germany for the Supreme Restitution Court (an international tribunal) in West Germany. The jurisdiction of a national State over an international organization has recently been considered in the UK following the collapse of the International Tin Council. For a review see C. Greenwood, All ER Rev 1989 pp. 240–46.

136 See ch. 4, prs. 4.55–4.58 above. The point was reiterated in GC 18 (37), n. 2 above, pr. 12.

137 See Van Dijk and Van Hoof, pp. 532–48; Fawcett, pp. 294–306.

138 See n. 125 above.

139 Ibid., pr. 9.2(*b*)2(ii)2.

140 Ibid., pr. 9.2(*b*)2(i)8. Similarly the HRC found the variation in the protection of the family under article 23 on the basis of sex to be discriminatory with respect to Mauritian women and that it could not be justified by security requirements, ibid., pr. 9.2(*b*)2(ii)3. For the action taken by Mauritius see pr. 4.132 above.

141 Doc. A/36/40, p. 166.

142 Ibid., prs. 13.2–19.

143 Ibid., p. 175.

144 *Broeks* v. *Netherlands*, Doc. A/42/40, p. 139, pr. 13. 'The Committee observes that not every differentiation of treatment will constitute discrimination, if the criteria for such differentiation are reasonable and objective and if the aim is to achieve a purpose which is legitimate under the Covenant', GC 18(37), n. 2 above, pr. 13. Under the ECHR a distinction is discriminatory if it has no objective and reasonable justification, that is, if it does not pursue a legitimate aim or if there is not a reasonable relationship of proportionality between the means employed and the aim sought. See Van Dijk and Van Hoof n. 137 above. For a recent decision on article 14 of the ECHR see *Rasmussen* v. *Denmark*, 7 EHRR p. 371.

145 See ch. 4, prs. 4.55–4.58 above.

146 *Broeks* v. *Netherlands*, Doc. A/42/40, p. 139, prs. 14–15; *Zwaan-de Vries* v. *Netherlands*, Doc. A/42/40, p. 160, prs. 14–15. See ch. 4, prs. 4.56–4.58 above.

147 *Danning* v. *Netherlands*, Doc. A/42/40, p. 151, pr. 14. See ch. 4, prs. 4.56–4.58 above.

148 Doc. A/44/40, p. 189.

149 Ibid., pr. 9.5.

150 Doc. A/44/40, p. 232.

151 Ibid., pr. 12. In an accompanying individual opinion two members of the HRC expressed the view that a differentiation on the sole ground of marital status as a widow cannot be based on reasonable and objective criteria and, therefore, constituted prohibited discrimination within article 26, ibid., Appendix, pr. 5.

152 Doc. A/44/40, p. 249.

153 GC 8/16, Doc. A/37/40, pp. 95–6.

154 Doc. A/44/40, p. 249, pr. 6.3.

155 Ibid., pr. 9.3. The HRC proceeded to express the view that article 9(4) had been violated because Mr Vuolanne was unable to challenge his detention before a court. The Finnish government subsequently informed the HRC that legislation would be enacted to remedy the situation. See Doc. A/44/40, p. 311. See also *Giry* v. *Dominican Republic*, Doc. A/45/40, Apx., pr. 5.3.

156 *Mauritian Women Case*, n. 125 above; *Broeks* v. *Netherlands*, n. 146 above; *Zwaan-de Vries* v. *Netherlands*, n. 146 above; *Vos* v. *Finland*, Doc. A/44/40, p. 232, considered in pr. 6.29.2 above. In *Avellanal* v. *Peru*, Doc. A/44/40, p. 196, the HRC expressed the view that there was a violation of articles 3, 14(1), and 26 of the Covenant in the application to A of article 168 of the Peruvian Civil Code which only permitted a husband to represent matrimonial property before the courts.

157 *Danning* v. *Netherlands*, n. 147 above; *Vos.* v. *Finland*, Doc. A/44/40, p. 232, considered in pr. 6.29.2 above.

158 *Wienberger Weisz* v. *Uruguay*, Doc. A/36/40, p. 114. The HRC stated that, 'In no case, however, may a person be subjected to sanctions solely because of his or her political opinion (arts 2(1) and 26), ibid., pr. 15.

159 *Pinkey* v. *Canada*, Doc. A/37/40, p. 101, pr. 26. The HRC found that it did not have any verifiable information before it to substantiate P's allegations of wrongful treatment. In *Gueye and Others* v. *France*, Doc. A/44/40, p. 189, dealt with in pr. 6.29.1 above, the authors claimed, *inter alia*, that they had been discriminated against on racial grounds. The HRC found no evidence to support the allegation that the State party had engaged in racially discriminatory practices *vis-à-vis* the authors, ibid., pr. 9.4. In *Bhinder* v. *Canada*, Doc. A/45/40, Apx., B's labour contract was terminated because he wore a turban and therefore refused to wear safety headgear. The HRC took the view that the requirement was reasonable and directed toward objective purposes that are compatible with the Covenant.

160 See *Wight* v. *Madagascar*, Doc. A/39/40, p. 171. The HRC observed that the information available to it was insufficient to show that W was arrested and charged primarily because of his South African nationality and the South African nationality of his aircraft, ibid., pr. 16. See also *F.G.G.* v. *Netherlands*, Doc. A/42/40, p. 180 (alleged discrimination in dismissal of foreign sailors): inadmissible for failure to exhaust domestic remedies; *H.v.d.P.* v. *Netherlands*, Doc. A/42/40, p. 185 (alleged discrimination in promotion policies), see pr. 6.26 above. In *V.R.M.B.* v. *Canada*, Doc. A/43/40, p. 258, the HRC expressed the

view that, 'With respect to articles 2 and 26 of the Covenant, the author has failed to establish how the deportation of an alien on national security grounds constitutes discrimination', pr. 6.3.

161 *L.T.K.* v. *Finland*, Doc. A/39/40, p. 240, concerning the application of an age limit to alternative service which prevented L.T.K. from substituting military service with alternative service. The communication was declared inadmissible as not raising an issue under the Covenant. No specific reference was made to the alleged discrimination.

162 *E.H.* v. *Finland*, Doc. A/41/40, p. 168. E.H. claimed that a heavier sentence had been imposed on her for a criminal offence than that imposed on another Finnish woman in a similar case. The communication was held inadmissible as an examination did not reveal any facts in substantiation of the author's claim.

163 *K. L.* v. *Denmark*, SD, p. 24. Declared inadmissible on the ground of non-substantiation of allegations. See also *Gueye and Others* v. *France*, Doc. A/44/40, p. 189, considered in pr. 6.29.1 above on 'other status'.

164 See e.g. *Fals Borda* v. *Colombia*, Doc. A/37/40, p. 193, pr. 15; *Mauritian Women Case*, Doc. A/36/40, p. 134, pr. 11.

165 Doc. A/36/40, p. 147; SD, p. 74.

166 For the text of article 18(4) see Apx. I below.

167 Ibid., pr. 10.5. Cf. the recent decision of the EUCM on religious education in A.10491/83, *Angelini* v. *Sweden*, 10 EHRR (1988) pp. 123–9.

168 The reports submitted to the HRC under article 40 should cover, *inter alia*, the 'progress made in the enjoyment' of the rights (article 40(1)) and 'indicate the factors and difficulties, if any, affecting the implementation of the Covenant' (article 40(2)). See ch. 3 above.

169 Doc. A/44/40, p. 200.

170 Ibid., Appendix I, pr. 4.

171 See e.g. *Mpandanjila et al* v. *Zaïre*, Doc. A/41/40, p. 121, pr. 11; *Hermoza* v. *Peru*, Doc. A/44/40, p. 200, pr. 13.1.

172 See ch. 4, prs. 4.100–4.116 above. In *Boyle and Rice* v. *UK*, A.9659/82 and A.9658/82, the EUCM stated that article 13 of the ECHR (the equivalent of article 2(3) of the ICCPR) provides the counterpart of the requirement to exhaust domestic remedies under article 26 and reflects the subsidiary character of the Convention system to the national systems safeguarding human rights.

173 Doc. A/42/40, p. 174.

174 Ibid., pr. 5.3. In *M.G.B. and S.P.* v. *Trinidad and Tobago*, the HRC stated that articles 2(3)(*a*) and (*b*) and 5 of the Covenant are general undertakings by States and cannot be invoked, in isolation, by individuals under the OP, Doc. A/45/40, Apx., pr. 6.2. See also *R.A.V.N.* v. *Argentina*, and the important accompanying individual opinion of Wennergren on the requirements of article 2 of the Covenant, Doc. A/45/40, Apx.

175 Doc. A/38/40, p. 197.

176 Ibid., pr. 8. The HRC also found violations of articles 9(1)–(4) and 10(1).

177 Doc. A/37/40, p. 187.

178 Ibid., pr. 12.

179 Ibid., pr. 13. The HRC stated that there was no competent court to which B could have appealed during her arbitrary detention.
180 Doc. A/42/40, p. 130.
181 Ibid., prs. 1, 20.
182 Doc. A/38/40, p. 160.
183 Ibid., pr. 13. See ch. 10, pr. 10.52 below.
184 See the cases cited in prs. 6.33–6.34 above.
185 For the text of article 13 see Apx. I.
186 On article 14 see ch. 10 below. Cf. the decision of the EUCT in *Airey* v. *Ireland*, Series A, Vol. 32, p. 18 (1979).
187 Doc. A/42/40, p. 170.
188 See Apx. I below.
189 Ibid., pr. 11.
190 See pr. 6.3 above.
191 See pr. 6.11 above.
192 See prs. 6.12–6.13 above.
193 See prs. 6.9–6.10, 6.14–6.17.
194 See prs. 6.3, 6.6 above.
195 See prs. 6.21–6.22.
196 See prs. 6.27, and ch. 4, prs. 4.56–4.58 above.

7

Article 4[1]

7.1

1. In a time of public emergency which threatens the life of the nation and the existence of which is officially proclaimed, the States parties to the present Covenant may take measures derogating from their obligations under the present Covenant to the extent strictly required by the exigencies of the situation, provided that such measures are not inconsistent with their other obligations under international law and do not involve discrimination solely on the ground of race, colour, sex, language, religion or social origin.

2. No derogation from articles 6, 7, 8 (paragraphs 1 and 2), 11, 15, 16 and 18 may be made under this provision.

3. Any State party to the present Covenant availing itself of the right of derogation shall immediately inform the other States parties to the present Covenant, through the intermediary of the Secretary-General of the United Nations, of the provisions from which it has derogated and of the reasons by which it was actuated. A further communication shall be made, through the same intermediary, on the date on which it terminates such derogation.

Introduction

7.2 Article 4 is self-evidently a key provision of the ICCPR. Its terms regulate the measures open to States parties in the most critical of human rights situations, public emergencies. Experience demonstrates that such situations are commonly characterized by severe human rights violations.[2] The practice of the HRC is then significant in a number of respects. First, it is an important indicator of how the HRC envisages its role under the reporting procedure because a provision concerning derogation acutely raises the issues of the scope of international implementation procedures and their relationship with the concept of State sovereignty.[3] Secondly, the response of a State to a public emergency is an acid test of its commitment to the effective implementation of human rights.[4] Thirdly, the problems engendered by states of emergency and their effects on human rights have increasingly attracted attention in recent years, particularly within the United Nations. There now exists some important international case law, analyses of state practice, and academic analysis which have given much greater content to the terms used in article 4.[5] This jurisprudence can supply useful guidance to the HRC in its considerations of article 4.

There follows a brief distillation of the practice of the HRC under article 4. That practice includes the adoption of a general comment under article 40(4) of the Covenant.[6] The considerations of the United Kingdom reports provide an instructive example and so are dealt with more particularly.[7]

A. ARTICLE 4 UNDER THE REPORTING PROCESS

7.3 When the HRC was preparing guidelines for the submission of reports under article 40(1)(*a*) a number of members expressed the view that the subject of derogations should not be mentioned because, in particular, to do so might be misinterpreted as weakening the provision in article 4(3) of the Covenant which requires that notification to the Secretary-General of any derogation and of the reasons therefore be made immediately. Unfortunately, it was decided, therefore, not to refer expressly to derogations in the General Guidelines.[8] It is submitted that the objecting members confused the two separate obligations to report (article 40(1)) and to notify (article 4(3)). It would have been more sensible to indicate clearly to States parties the information the HRC required concerning derogation practice and procedure.

7.4 It appears from the comments of members of the HRC that very few reports have given adequate information on article 4 and in almost all cases members have asked questions, made comments, and requested further additional informaton.[9] Indeed, at times, the primary emphasis of much of the considerations of the HRC has appeared to be the collection of further detailed information relevant to article 4.

Article 4(1)

7.5 An interesting feature of the approach of members to article 4 is that they have not strictly confined their considerations to events after the entry into force of the ICCPR for the State concerned.[10] State representatives have frequently been asked for information concerning any state of emergency occurring at any time since the existence of the State or in a more recent period, for example, the last twenty years.[11] Members have then used those examples, if any, to determine whether the appropriate national procedures and mechanisms exist to ensure compliance with the terms of article 4 and whether any elements of emergency regimes have subsisted after their termination.[12]

7.6 Members have asked how a public emergency is officially proclaimed, who is entitled to make the proclamation, on what grounds and by what procedures.[13] Was the official proclamation of a state of emergency a precondition to the constitutionality or legality of the measures taken thereunder?[14] Particular attention has been directed to the circumstances which permit of the proclamation of a public emergency, for example, political, social, economic factors, or natural disasters.[15] This has generally involved a kind of comparative analysis between the terms of the Covenant and the terms of the respective State Constitution and legislative acts.[16] There has been no attempt by the HRC, however, to provide a definition of or criteria for a 'public emergency'.[17] Members have sought to determine the role and function of national authorities charged with the implementation of the state of emergency.[18] They have expressed concern at the concentration of powers in the hands of a single individual, for example, the President or Prime Minister, or in the hands of a single organ of Government, for example, the executive or the armed forces, particularly where this has been at the expense of a parliamentary body.[19]

7.7 The search for additional information has concentrated on attempting to determine the precise legal effects of the different forms and degrees of public emergency encountered by the HRC, for example, state of siege,[20] state of alarm,[21] economic state of emergency,[22] state of war,[23] state of national necessity.[24] Members have wanted to know whether constitutional or legislative provisions were partially suspended or abrogated altogether. They have indicated their concern at general restrictions and limitations based on vague and undefined concepts such as public order, public safety, public security, necessity, national security, international terrorism, latent subversion, and perverse delinquency, and requested explanations as to the domestic understandings of these concepts.[25] In its General Comment the HRC stated that it held 'the view that measures taken under article 4 are of an exceptional and temporary nature and may only last as long as the life of the nation concerned is threatened'.[26]

7.8 State representatives have often been invited to explain how the legal regime under a public emergency conforms to the requirements of the Covenant. Were there any controls or restrictions upon the organs concerned with implementing the state of emergency?[27] In particular, was there any parliamentary supervision or legislative control over the proclamation of a public emergency, its continuance, extension, or termination?[28] Could the constitutionality or legality of the emergency measures be challenged in a constitutional court or in the ordinary courts?[29] Was judicial review available and did remedies exist for those who alleged that their rights under the ICCPR had been violated?[30] How would conflicts between the constitutional powers and the terms of the Covenant be resolved?

7.9 It is of course important to note that emergency situations potentially affect all of the other rights in the ICCPR. The HRC's considerations must then be seen in the context of its detailed consideration of other rights in the ICCPR. However, even within the specific context of article 4 members have frequently required information and explanations of the effect of measures taken under public emergencies on the exercise and enjoyment of the rights and remedies in the ICCPR, from article 1 to article 27, including articles from which derogation had been made.[31] For example, during consideration of the second periodic report of Spain[32] a number of members expressed concern about the effect on articles 9 and 14 of the ICCPR of the operation of Organic Law No. 8/1984 concerning the extension of the permissible period of police detention and limitations on access to counsel.[33] Similarly, during consideration of the report of Sri Lanka[34] a number of members expressed doubts about the compatibility of the Prevention of Terrorism Act 1979 with the provisions of the Covenant, particularly articles 9, 14, and 15.[35]

7.10 There has been no real indication from members as to what is covered by the expression 'other obligations under international law' with which derogation measures must not be inconsistent.[36] The only indication of what might be covered have been the occasional suggestion from an HRC member that the terms of the 1949 Geneva Conventions on the Law of War and the 1977 Protocols thereto[37] are of relevance to the situation concerned, for example, in Afghanistan[38] and in El Salvador.[39] Commentators have indicated that the expression would cover, for example, obligations for States parties under the United Nations Charter, humanitarian law treaties, regional human rights conventions, and customary international law.[40]

7.11 Criticism has been directed to national provisions which appear to violate the provision in article 4(1) that derogation measures must not 'involve discrimination solely on the ground of race, colour, sex, language, religion or social origin'. For example, article 23(3)(d) of the Constitution of Barbados was objected to on the basis that it allowed distinctions to be made in terms of a public emergency on some prohibited grounds.[41]

7.12 The approach of France to article 4 attracted some interesting comments. France's ratification was accompanied by the following reservation:

First, the circumstances enumerated in article 16 of the Constitution in respect of its implementation, in article 1 of the Act of 3 April 1978 and in the Act of 9 August 1849 in respect of the Declaration of a state of siege, in article 1 of Act No. 55–385 of 3 April 1955 in respect of a declaration of a state of emergency and which enable these instruments to be implemented, are to be understood as meeting the purpose of article 4 of the Covenant; and secondly, for the purposes of interpreting and implementing article 16 of the Constitution of the French Republic, the terms 'to the extent strictly required by the exigencies of the situation' cannot limit the power of the President of the Republic to take 'the measures required by circumstances'.[42]

Mr Herdocia-Ortega commented that, 'the provisions of article 16 of the French constitution appeared to be in conformity with the requirements of article 4 of the Covenant, as were the arrangements with regard to states of siege and emergency'.[43] Mr Tarnopolsky requested clarification of the first part of the reservation. Did it mean that the Covenant would apply only to the extent that it was possible under the Constitution or that the Constitution could normally be applied to the extent permitted by article 4 of the Covenant?[44] Mr Al Douri commented that, 'with due regard for the reservations entered by France in respect of that article, he would like to know who was responsible for exercising control over the acts of the President in that case'.[45] Mr Graefrath commented,

France had made a reservation with regard to article 4, thereby confirming that reservations concerning article 4 were possible and that, by the entering of a reservation, the scope of emergency measures could be broadened considerably. It seemed clear from the text submitted that article 16 of the French Constitution and the relevant legislation had a far wider range of application than article 4 of the Covenant. Furthermore, the French reservation stated that it was the responsibility of the President of the Republic to decide what measures were strictly necessary. That was not a reservation, but a correct interpretation of the Covenant, which did not subject such powers of a State party to foreign control.[46]

The French representative replied,

As for the extent of France's reservation to article 4, he repeated that the reservation only applied to paragraph 1, which was quite legitimate under the Vienna Convention on the Law of Treaty [*sic*]. It seemed to him that the question of whether reservations could be made to other paragraphs of that article was one for the Committee to decide.[47]

7.13 It is submitted that the HRC should take a stricter approach to reservations to a derogation provision than this. It is difficult to reconcile a considerable broadening of the scope of emergency powers with the object and purpose of the ICCPR. It has been argued that a similar French reservation to the ECHR is invalid as incompatible with the objects and purposes of the ECHR.[48] This submission implies that the HRC should consider the validity of reservations made by States within the context of the article 40 reporting procedure.

7.14 In the HRC's considerations under article 4 there have been no clear indications of the application of any criteria by members to the declaration of a public emergency although there is useful comparative jurisprudence under the ECHR in this respect.[49] In specific cases individual members have expressed doubts as to the justification for a particular emergency regime or its continuation,[50] and suggested that article 4 allowed States parties considerable latitude in deciding when a public emergency justified derogation[52] and that the decision concerning the emergency situation was a sovereign act.[52] There has not, however, been any clear statement by the HRC on the scope of its jurisdiction under article 4 or on the existence of any doctrine similar to that of the 'margin of appreciation' developed under the ECHR.[53]

7.15 The HRC has summed up its experience under the reporting procedure as follows:

States parties have generally indicated the mechanism provided in their legal system for the declaration of a state of emergency and the applicable provisions of the law governing derogations. However, in the case of a few States which had apparently derogated from Covenant rights, it was unclear not only whether a state of emergency had been officially declared but also whether rights from which the Covenant allows no derogation had in fact been derogated from and further whether the other States parties had been informed of the derogations and of the reasons for the derogations.[54]

Article 4(2)

7.16 The HRC has stated that it holds the view that, 'in times of emergency, the protection of human rights becomes all the more important, particularly those rights from which no derogation can be made'.[55] State representatives are asked to explain how the relevant domestic provisions ensure that the non-derogable rights in article 4(2) are protected in times of public emergency.[56] On a number of occasions members have clearly stated their view that non-derogable rights were being violated, for example, in Chile,[57] Uruguay,[58] Iran,[59] and El Salvador.[60]

7.17 Only one State, Trinidad and Tobago, has made a reservation to article 4(2). That reservation stated that,

The Government of the Republic of Trinidad and Tobago reserves the right not to apply in full the provision of paragraph 2 of article 4 of the Covenant since section 7(3) of its Constitution enables Parliament to enact legislation even though it is inconsistent with sections (4) and (5) of the said Constitution.[61]

During consideration of the report of Trinidad and Tobago this reservation was criticized. For example, Mr Tomuschat commented that,

The matter was a serious one, since the drafters of the Covenant had stressed in the wording of the article their understanding that there should be limits to restrictions on specific rights even in situations of crisis. It was a serious inconsistency with the objectives and purposes of treaty law, for the Government of Trinidad and Tobago to have found it expedient to make such a reservation. The Government should be asked to consider withdrawing it.[62]

The Federal Republic of Germany had also lodged a formal objection to the reservation stating that in its opinion, 'it follows from the text and the history of the Covenant that the said reservation is incompatible with the object and purpose of the Covenant'.[63] The State representative replied that in view of the serious nature of the question it would have to be put to the relevant Ministry.[64] The approach of Mr Tomuschat represents a much more active view of the role of the HRC in the context of article 4 as regards reservations than that of Mr Graefrath noted above (pr. 7.12) and is to be preferred. Again it would be much better if the HRC as a body expressed a view on the validity of the reservation in question. Similarly, there needs to be an established mechanism to ensure that a prompt reply is received from the State concerned rather than waiting until consideration of that State's next periodic report.[65]

7.18 Although article 4(2) indicates which of the articles are non-derogable, members of the HRC have indicated that it would be difficult to justify derogations from some of the other articles of the Covenant, for example, concerning suspension of the political rights in article 25.[66]

Article 4(3)

7.19 Members of the HRC have consistently referred to the requirements of article 4(3) of the ICCPR and stressed that they are not a 'mere formality'.[67] In its General Comment on article 4 it stated that along with the protection of human rights, 'it was important that States parties, in times of public emergency, inform other States parties of the nature and extent of the derogations they have made and of the reasons therefore, and further, to fulfil their reporting obligation under article 40 of the Covenant by indicating the nature and extent of each right derogated from together with the relevant documentation'.[68] The General Comment does not indicate whether or when States parties who have made derogations are required to report on them to the HRC and, as we have already noted, there has been some disagreement within the HRC as to the relationship between article 4 and the reporting obligation in article 40.[69] It has been submitted that it is patently inadequate for the HRC to be unable to consider derogations made by States parties except in accordance with the established five-year schedule for reporting.[70] Moreover, States parties often request a postponement of the consideration of their report if a state of emergency exists.

7.20 Although members have stressed the importance of notification of derogations and indicated on a number of occasions that notifications have not satisfied the requirements of article 4(3), there has been no real suggestion that derogations made under article 4(1) have been invalid on the basis of failure to comply or fully comply with the notification requirements in article 4(3).[71] The furthest that individual members have gone has been to state their view that the derogations made have not satisfied the requirements of article 4(1) as to, for example, proportionality, necessity, and official proclamation. For instance, during consideration of the second periodic report of Chile[72] a number of members were severely critical of measures taken under the state of emergency. For example, Mr Graefrath commented, *inter alia*, that,

In order to permit continuing violations of human rights, the unconstitutional state of emergency had been institutionalized during an interim period and subsequently in the new Constitution. As a result, the Junta now disposed of various levels of emergency measures which could be used whenever necessary to protect the existing regime. What was called an emergency in Chile had nothing to do with what was intended by the same term in Article 4 of the Covenant. The so-called state of emergency was being used to justify the discriminatory measures provided for in article 8 of the 1980 Constitution, which condemned as illegal any action by an individual or group intended to propagate doctrines of a totalitarian character or based on class warfare.[73]

7.21 Inevitably in its consideration of States of emergency under article 4, whether proclaimed officially or *de facto*, members of the HRC have had to consider the wider political context of inter-State disputes and civil wars with or without the involvement of outside States, for example, with regard to the situations in Afghanistan,[74] Colombia,[75] Cyprus,[76] Egypt,[77] El Salvador,[78] Jordan,[79] the Lebanon,[80] Nicaragua,[81] Sri Lanka.[82] It is notable that during consideration of these situations members have generally, though not always, avoided commenting on the political aspects and the relevance of actions of other States.[83] Normally members have simply confined themselves to asking how these factual situations affected the implementation of the rights in the ICCPR in the States concerned.[84] Such an approach is to be commended in the light of the HRC's membership and status and the politicized nature of most other United Nations human rights bodies.[85]

7.22 The stress put on article 4(3) by HRC members seems to be bearing fruit. It appears that States parties are increasingly complying with the notification obligations in article 4(3) particularly after the State has appeared before the HRC.[86]

The United Kingdom and Article 4

7.23 It is instructive to look a little more closely at an example of the HRC's considerations under article 4. The example chosen is that of the United Kingdom because it most usefully illustrates the workings of the HRC.

7.24 The UK ratified the ICCPR on 20 May 1976.[87] By a note dated 17 May 1976 the UK gave notice under article 4(3) of the ICCPR to the Secretary-General of the United Nations of the existence in the UK of a public emergency threatening the life of the nation arising from campaigns of organized terrorism related to Northern Irish affairs. The notice indicated the intention of the government to take and continue measures which might be inconsistent with certain provisions of the Covenant and would, to that extent, derogate from the UK's obligations. In so far as any of the measures taken were inconsistent with the provisions of articles 9, 10(2), 10(3), 12(1), 14, 17, 19(2), 21, or 22 of the Covenant the UK derogated from those provisions.[88]

7.25 The UK submitted its initial report under article 40(1)(*a*) on 21 September 1977.[89] In a single paragraph concerning article 4 the report recapitulated the reasons for derogations.[90] During the 'first round'[91] consideration of the UK report as regards article 4 it was noted that the report provided no substantial information on the measures which derogated from the obligations in the ICCPR.[92] Two members raised questions concerning the territorial applicability of the emergency measures.[93] Finally, Mr Movchan commented that he was not convinced that the events in question threatened the life of the nation and said that he would appreciate information on the juridical considerations that had influenced the decision to make the derogations.[94]

7.26 The State representative from the UK replied that the UK considered that a threat to the life of the nation did exist and indicated that the European Court of Human Rights had unanimously agreed on this point.[95] He also gave further information with respect to certain of the emergency measures and how they might be considered to be incompatible with the relevant provisions of the ICCPR.[96]

7.27 In a Supplementary report the UK stated that the derogations applied to the UK as a whole and that they would not be withdrawn until the emergencies giving rise to them came to an end.[97] During consideration of that Supplementary report in 1979 questions were put concerning the use of internment,[98] interrogation procedures, and the use of confessions, the right to consult with counsel, and the availability of habeas corpus. Reference was also made to the report of the Bennett Committee on Police Interrogation Procedures in Northern Ireland.[99] The State representative replied to the questions put and gave some details on the recommendations of the Bennett Committee.[100]

7.28 At this point of its work it was difficult to conclude otherwise than that the HRC's consideration of the situation in Northern Ireland was manifestly inadequate. From any perspective the situation there is clearly open to much greater scrutiny than the HRC had accorded to it. The International Commission of Jurists' study on states of emergency suggested that the inadequacy of the HRC's consideration was due to its not having a greater awareness of the prevailing situation in Northern Ireland and of details of the *Ireland* v. *UK* litigation under the ECHR.[101]

7.29 On 4 December 1984 the UK submitted its second periodic report to the HRC under article 40(1)(*b*).[102] As regards article 4 the report referred briefly to a letter of 22 August 1984 notifying the Secretary-General of the United Nations that the UK had withdrawn, from the date of notification, its notice of derogation. The notification stated, *inter alia*, that,

the United Kingdom Government, taking account of developments in the situation since the notice . . . [of derogation] . . . and in measures taken to deal with it, have come to the conclusion that it is no longer necessary, in order to comply with its obligations under the Covenant, for the United Kingdom to continue, at the present time, to avail itself of the right of derogation under article 4.[103]

7.30 For the consideration of the second periodic report the 'state of emergency' was one of the specific issues upon which the HRC decided that it would focus attention.[104] Prior to appearing before the HRC the State representatives were forwarded, *inter alia*, a number of questions and issues concerning the state of emergency upon which the HRC wanted further information and explanation.[105]

7.31 Before the HRC the State representative stated that the

Government had withdrawn the notice of derogation because it believed that the rights in the Covenant were fully observed throughout the United Kingdom. That did not mean that there was no longer an emergency but simply that there had been changes in the situation in Northern Ireland and in the measures taken to deal with it.[106]

Reference was made to the two Acts of Parliament giving special powers,[107] the recommendations of Sir George Baker on Northern Ireland emergency legislation,[108] and the system for investigating complaints against police officers in Northern Ireland.[109]

7.32 After the statement of the State representative a number of members made comments and put questions. The range of views and issues was much wider and more critical than hitherto. Questions were raised concerning the Diplock Courts;[110] convictions based on confessions or on the evidence of accomplices;[111] progress towards resolution of the 'Irish Question'; Police Complaints Boards; the control of the actions of and the use of force by the police and security forces;[112] inquiries into civilian deaths;[113] why it was thought possible to work within the provisions of the Covenant rather than derogating from them;[114] the implementation of the recommendations of the Bennett Committee;[115] parliamentary control over the emergency powers of the executive; the consequences of the period of derogation;[116] the possibility of recourse to the Covenant to determine the legitimacy of measures taken by the government; action being taken in the social and political fields to solve the problems of Northern Ireland and the current situation of violence in Northern Ireland;[117] and the matter of self-determination in Northern Ireland.[118]

7.33 The State representative replied to the range of questions put and indicated why the UK felt able to withdraw its derogations under the ICCPR.[119] Two members of the HRC continued to make their concerns felt. Mr Graefrath again raised the matter of the practice of the use of firearms under the law.[120] The right to life (article 6) is, of course, one of the non-derogable provisions of the ICCPR.[121] In his concluding comments Mr Movchan clearly indicated that he was not persuaded by the views of the State representative:

The handling of the emergency situation in Northern Ireland demonstrated a clear departure from the provisions of Article 4 in so far as the United Kingdom representative had admitted that the security forces were not under active control and that they supervised their own acts. There had been no court proceedings in relation to the loss of life, including the lives of children, which had occurred.[122]

7.34 On the basis of the foregoing review it is submitted that the consideration of the implementation of article 4 of the ICCPR with respect to the UK and Northern Ireland was much more impressive and critical during consideration of the UK's second periodic report than during consideration of the UK's initial report. This bodes well for the HRC in light of the fact that in practical terms it appears that the consideration of second and subsequent periodic reports will dominate the HRC's future work under article 40.[123]

B. ARTICLE 4 UNDER THE OPTIONAL PROTOCOL

7.35 Article 4 of the ICCPR has been considered in a number of the HRC's views under article 5(4) OP. A high proportion of those views have concerned the situation in Uruguay where multiple violations of rights under the ICCPR have been alleged. The communications have generally concerned the application of 'prompt security measures' under the state of emergency in Uruguay.[124] Uruguay has often made general reference to the state of emergency in its submissions. The now established approach of the HRC is exemplified by its view in *Ramirez* v. *Uruguay*:[125]

The Human Rights Committee has considered whether any acts and treatment, which are prima facie not in conformity with the Covenant, could for any reason be justified under the Covenant in the circumstances. The Government has referred to provisions of Uruguayan law, including the Prompt Security Measures. However, the Covenant (article 4) does not allow national measures derogating from its provisions except in strictly defined circumstances, and the Government has not made any submissions of fact or law to justify such derogation. Moreover, some of the facts referred to above raise issues under provisions from which the Covenant does not allow derogation under any circumstances.[126]

7.36 This view clearly indicates that the HRC will consider *ex officio* the possible application of article 4 even when the State party does not specifically rely upon it. The obvious question raised is what the approach of the HRC would be if there were possible justifications under the Covenant for alleged violations. The above view clearly places the burden of proof on the State party so presumably the HRC could do no more than invite the State party to submit evidence of fact or law justifying the derogations concerned. Such an approach on the part of a human rights body of inviting justifications for derogations would have little to commend it.[127] The HRC's view in *Silva* v. *Uruguay*[128] below suggests that if a State party could justify its derogations under the terms of article 4(1) and (2) of the ICCPR the fact that it had not complied with the notification requirements under article 4(3) of the ICCPR would not preclude it from raising a defence based on its derogations.

7.37 In *Silva and Others* v. *Uruguay*[129] the State party expressly relied on the terms of article 4. The alleged victims claimed that Uruguay had violated article 25 of the ICCPR (the right of citizens to take part in public affairs, to vote and have access to the public service).[130] Under article 1(*a*) of Institutional Act No. 4 of 1 September 1976 the alleged victims had been deprived of the right to engage in any activity of a political nature, including the right to vote for fifteen years, because they had been candidates for elective office on the lists of certain political groups in the 1966 and 1971 elections.[131] The groups concerned had subsequently been declared illegal by the Uruguayan government.

7.38 Uruguay submitted to the HRC that it had derogated from the ICCPR and had informed the Secretary-General of the United Nations of this in accordance with article 4(3) of the ICCPR.[132] Moreover, 'Article 25, on which the authors of the communication argue their case, is not mentioned in the text of article 4(2). Accordingly, the Government of Uruguay, as it has a right to do, has temporarily derogated from some provisions relating to political parties.'[133]

7.39 The government submitted no further information to the HRC. The HRC expressed the view that it felt unable to accept that the requirements set forth in article 4(1) had been met. After noting the terms of article 4(1) and the notification submitted by Uruguay under article 4(3) the HRC stated that,

The Government of Uruguay has made reference to an emergency situation in the country which was legally acknowledged in a number of 'Institutional Acts'. However, no factual details were given at that time. The note confined itself to stating that the existence of the emergency situation was 'a matter of universal knowledge'; no attempt was made to indicate the nature and the scope of the derogations actually resorted to with regard to the rights guaranteed by the Covenant, or to show that such derogations were strictly necessary. Instead, the Government of Uruguay declared that more information would be provided in connection with the submissions of the country's reports under article 40 of the Covenant. To date neither has this report been received, nor the information by which it was to be supplemented.[134]

This approach indicates that the HRC will take account of information concerning article 4 submitted in the reports of States parties under article 40. This approach would seem to accord with common sense as it allows the HRC to take account of all relevant information known to it.

7.40 The HRC continued with the following critically important passage:

Although the sovereign right of a State party to declare a state of emergency is not questioned, yet, in the specific context of the present communication, the Human Rights Committee is of the opinion that a State, by merely invoking the existence of exceptional circumstances, cannot evade the obligations which it has undertaken by ratifying the Covenant. Although the substantive right to take derogation measures may not depend on a formal notification being made pursuant to article 4(3) of the Covenant, the State party concerned is duty-bound to give a sufficiently detailed account of the relevant facts when it invokes article 4(1) of the Covenant in proceedings under the Protocol. It is the function of the Human Rights Committee, acting under the Optional Protocol, to see to it that States parties live up to their commitments under the Covenant. In order to assess whether a situation of the kind described in article 4(1) of the Covenant exists in the country concerned, it needs full and comprehensive information. If the respondent Government does not furnish the required justification itself, as it is required to do under article 4(2) of the Optional Protocol and article 4(3) of the Covenant, the Human Rights Committee cannot conclude that valid reasons exist to legitimize a departure from the normal legal regime prescribed by the Covenant.[135]

This passage represents a strong assertion of the HRC's assessment function under the OP, a clear statement that the burden of proof is on the respondent State to provide 'full and comprehensive information' to the HRC, and a definite warning that, in default of justification, the respondent State's derogations will not be accepted as legitimate under the terms of the Covenant.[136] More generally, the HRC, while acknowledging the sovereign right of a State to declare a state of emergency, asserts a measure of international supervision over that national determination.[137] This approach closely parallels that of the EUCT.[138]

7.41 The HRC then proceeded to consider the situation on the assumption that a State of emergency did exist in Uruguay. It expressed the view that even on that assumption it could not see

What ground could be adduced to support the contention that, in order to restore peace and order, it was necessary to deprive all citizens, who as members of certain political groups had been candidates in the elections of 1966 and 1971, of any political rights for a period as long as 15 years. This measure applies to everyone, without distinction as to whether he sought to promote his political opinions by peaceful means or by resorting to, or advocating the use of, violent means. The Government of Uruguay has failed to show the interdiction of any kind of political dissent is required in order to deal with the alleged emergency situation and pave the way back to political freedom.[139]

Here the HRC is assessing the actions of the State party in terms of the necessity and proportionality of the measures applied and the onus is on the State party to justify its measures in those terms. On the basis of the foregoing the HRC expressed the view that the prohibition on the authors unreasonably restricted their rights under article 25 of the ICCPR and that the State party was, therefore, under an obligation to take steps with a view to enabling them to participate again in the political life of the nation.[140]

7.42 In *Guerrero* v. *Colombia*[141] the author (G's husband) alleged that G and seven other persons had been arbitrarily killed by the police in a raid, that the police action was unjustified and had been inadequately investigated by the Colombian authorities. Criminal investigations into the cases were defeated by recourse to a Legislative Decree No. 0070 which justified actions taken by the police in the course of certain operations.[142] The Decree Law had been introduced in the context of an existing state of siege in Colombia and had been upheld as constitutional by the Supreme Court.[143] The State party had referred to that decision in its submissions to the HRC. In an 'Interim Decision' the HRC decided to request information as to 'how, if at all, the state of siege proclaimed in Colombia affected the present case'.[144] The State party replied that the state of siege would affect the case only if those involved in the police operation invoked the Decree Law in justification of the act and if this was accepted by the Military Tribunal trying the case. It was submitted that the state of siege had no effect on either criminal or civil proceedings or on any administrative action brought by the injured party, although it was acknowledged that no civil action could be instituted in conjunction with military proceedings. The ultimate acquittal of all the accused precluded the filing of a civil or an administrative suit.

7.43 The HRC stated that in formulating its views it took account of the reference to a situation of disturbed public order in Decree No. 0070 and took note of the notification of Colombia under article 4(3) of the ICCPR.[145] That notification referred to the existence of a state of siege in all the national territory since 1976 and to the necessity of adopting extraordinary measures to deal with such a situation. The notification declared that, 'temporary measures have been adopted that have the effect of limiting the application of articles 19 paragraph 2 (freedom of expression) and article 21 (right of peaceful assembly)'.[146] The HRC observed that the case was not concerned with either of those articles and that under article 4(2) of the Covenant several rights were non-derogable including articles 6 and 7 which had been invoked by the author.[147] The HRC then examined the facts and expressed the view that article 6(1) (the right to life) had been violated in two respects and that any further violations had been subsumed within the more serious violations of article 6.[148]

APPRAISAL[149]

7.44 Of the 92 States parties to the ICCPR (as of 27 July 1990) 15 of them have given notification of derogations under article 4(3) while states of emergency are known to exist or have existed since entry into force of the ICCPR for the State concerned in a number of other States parties.[150] The HRC's work under article 4 then is obviously of major importance as regards its role in the implementation of the ICCPR. However, as noted, its General Guidelines on the form and content of initial reports adopted contained no reference to derogations.[151] This absence must bear an element of responsibility for the inadequate information submitted with respect to article 4. The absence could, to some extent, have been made good by the General Comments adopted by the HRC under article 40(4) of the ICCPR. Unfortunately, the HRC has to date only adopted one rather brief and inadequate General Comment on article 4. Its terms have been noted above. It would be of immense help to States parties if in its General Comment the HRC had indicated more of its understanding of the content of article 4 and the applicable principles and limitations concerning its application. The unofficial attempts to do just this in the Siracusa Principles[152] and the Paris Standards[153] represent invaluable aids to the interpretation and application of article 4 and facilitate a more critical analysis of the implementation of article 4 by States parties. It is submitted that on the basis of its considerable experience under the reporting procedure the HRC should attempt to do something similar when it comes to preparing a second general comment on article 4.[154]

7.45 We have already noted the HRC's summary of its experience under article 4 (up to 1981) in its General Comment in which it noted the lack of clarity in the information provided by States parties.[155] In the light of this much of the work of the HRC has been directed to obtaining a clearer picture of the situation in the States concerned. Moreover, we have already noted that the HRC's considerations of article 4 of the ICCPR must be understood in the context of its consideration of other articles of the ICCPR.[156] Notwithstanding this point, however, the foregoing review indicates the best and the worst of the procedures adopted by the HRC. At its worst can be found no information in the State report;[157] no questions made or comments put by members regarding article 4; inadequate and sporadic questioning; inadequate replies by State representatives or no reply at all;[158] the failure of States to supply such information in Supplementary reports;[159] the absence of HRC procedures to determine whether or not questions have received a satisfactory reply; the failure of the HRC to develop procedures for requesting *ad hoc* reports from States parties undergoing states of emergency;[160] no formal determinations of whether the requirements of article 4(1) and (3) have been satisfied or the terms of article 4(2) have been violated.[161]

7.46 The HRC procedures appear in a better light during consideration of second periodic reports. There attention can be more adequately focused on a state of emergency and the situation can therefore be subjected to a more critical and exacting analysis as, for example, was the case with the United Kingdom examined above.[162] More generally, individual members have on occasions made it quite clear that they took the view that article 4 was being violated.[163] The range of questions put by members has been extensive but, unfortunately, until the consideration of second periodic reports they are not put in an intelligible and systematic manner. Members have also clearly made use of outside sources of information when considering states of emergency.[164] It is also worth noting that the continued stress on the importance of article 4(3) appears to be eliciting more response from States parties than was evident in the HRC's earlier years.[165]

7.47 It is quite clear then that the HRC sees its role as that of examining the compliance of States parties with the provisions of article 4 of the ICCPR.[166] There has been no question of simply accepting the judgment and determinations of the national authorities as conclusive.[167] However, it is difficult to foresee more effective international supervision of the implementation of article 4 by the HRC unless progress is made on resolving two of the fundamental jurisdictional questions that were raised in chapter 3.[168]

7.48 First, whether the HRC has jurisdiction to request *ad hoc* reports from States parties undergoing states of emergency. The HRC's failure to resolve this matter meant, for example, that the state of emergency in Poland was never considered by the HRC while it was in force.[169] The recent decision of the HRC to make a specific request for information to El Salvador on the basis of article 40(1)(*b*) of the Covenant could have been an important development in the jurisprudence of the HRC but it now appears unlikely that the HRC will make such a request again and certainly not on a regular basis.[170] It would be preferable for the HRC to take a formal decision on when it will consider exercising its jurisdiction under article 40(1)(*b*).[171] The second jurisdictional question which awaits resolution is whether the HRC has competence under article 40(4) to make General Comments addressed to specific individual States parties to the ICCPR. However harsh and critical the comments of individual members they could not compare with a determination by the HRC as a body that article 4 was not being complied with. The considerations of the HRC in this respect compare unfavourably with the review of certain selected States (a number of which have been considered by the HRC) in the International Commission of Jurists, 'Study on States of Emergency'.[172] The latter presented much more critical and structured appraisals.

7.49 The approach of the HRC under the OP has complemented that under the reporting process. The HRC has clearly put the burden of proof on the derogating State to show compliance with the requirements of article 4.[173] Such an approach is necessarily dictated by the HRC's minimal fact-finding opportunities in the absence of oral hearings and fact-finding missions.[174] An international supervisory role is assumed, 'to see to it that States parties live up to their commitments under the Covenant'.[175] Derogation provisions are strictly examined in terms of necessity, proportionality, and the specific limitations in article 4.[176]

7.50 It was crucially important for the HRC to take a critical and restrictive approach to the implementation of article 4 for two reasons. First, as we have already noted, public emergencies present grave problems for the securing of human rights.[177] Secondly, in view of its very lmited powers both under the reporting[178] and individual communications procedures,[179] '[t]he most the implementation bodies can do is to adopt a scrupulous judicial attitude that will influence world opinion by its objectivity and thoroughness'.[180] Despite the criticisms made of the HRC's work above the HRC has established itself as an independent and respected international human rights body[181] which can bring a constructive analysis to bear on public emergencies. That analysis can be of considerable assistance to a government acting in good faith and in co-operation with the HRC. Where those elements of good faith and co-operation are lacking the most the HRC's considerations can achieve is to stimulate international pressure through national and international publicity.

NOTES

1 For other derogation provisions see art. 15 ECHR, art 27 AMR, art. 30 ESC. Note that there are no derogation provisions in the ICESCR and the AFR. On the drafting of article 4 see A/2929, ch. 5, prs. 35–47; A/5655, prs. 37–56; Bossuyt, *Guide*, pp. 81–102. On derogation and public emergencies see T. Buergenthal, 'To Respect and to Ensure—State Obligations and Permissible Derogations', in L. Henkin (ed.), *The International Bill of Rights—The Covenant on Civil and Political Rights*, p. 72 at pp. 78–86 (1981); B. Buzan, *People, States and Fear— The National Security Problem in International Relations* (1983); A. Carty, 'Human Rights in a State of Exception: the I.L.A. Approach and the Third World', in T. Campbell *et al.* (eds.), *Human Rights—From Rhetoric to Reality*, pp. 60–79 (1986); E. I. Daes, *The Individual's Duties to the Community and the Limitations on Human Rights and Fundamental Freedoms under Article 29 of the U.D.H.R.*, Part 3, Doc.E/CN.4/Sub. 2/432/Rev. 2 (1983); L. C. Green, 'Derogations of Human Rights in Emergency Situations', 16 Can. YIL (1978) pp. 92–115; J. Hartman, 'Derogations from Human Rights Treaties in Public Emergencies', 22 Harv. ILJ (1981) pp. 1–52; J. Hartman, 'Working Paper for the Committee of Experts on Article 4', 7 HRQ (1985) pp. 89–131; R. Higgins, 'Derogations under Human Rights Treaties', 48 BYIL (1978) pp. 281–320; International Commission of Jurists', *States of Emergency—Their Impact on Human Rights* (1983); S. R. Chowdhurry, *Rule of Law in a State of Emergency—The Paris Minimum Standards of Human Rights Norms in a State of Emergency* (1988), referred to below as the 'Paris Standards'; ILA, 'Enforcement of Human Rights', ILA Report, pp. 108–97, 62nd Conference (Seoul, 1986); B. Mangan, 'Protecting Human Rights in National Emergencies: Shortcomings in the European System and a Proposal for Reform', 10 HRQ (1988) pp. 372–94; T. Meron, *Human Rights Law-Making in the United Nations*, pp. 86–100 (1986); T. Meron, *Human Rights in Internal Strife: Their International Protection* (1987); R. Norris, 'The Suspension of Guarantees', 30 Am. ULR (1980) pp. 189–223; D. O'Donnell, 'States of Exception', 21 Rev. ICJ (1978)

pp. 52–60; id., 'States of Siege or Emergency and their Effects on Human Rights: Observations and Recommendations of the ICJ', UN Doc. E/CN.4/Sub. 2/NGO 93 (August 1983); N. Questiaux, 'Study of the Implications for Human Rights of Recent Developments Concerning Situations Known as States of Siege or Emergency', Doc. E/CN.4/Sub. 2/1982/15 (July 1982); P. Sieghart, *The International Law of Human Rights*, pp. 110–18 (1983); A. M. Singhvi, 'The State of Emergency and the Law of Nations', 25 Ind. JIL (1985) pp. 554–75; P. Stein, 'Derogations from Guarantees Laid Down in Human Rights Instruments', in I. Maier (ed.), *Protection of Human Rights in Europe—Limits and Effects* (1982) pp. 123–33; Symposium on 'Security of the Person and Security of the State: Human Rights and Claims of National Security', 9 Yale JWPO (1982) part I; Symposium, 'Limitation and Derogation Provisions in the ICCPR', 7 HRQ (1985) part I, the set of principles adopted by the Conference entitled 'The Siracusa Principles on the Limitation and Derogation Provisions in the ICCPR' are referred to below as the 'Siracusa Principles' (they have also been published in UN Doc. E/CN.4/1985/4 (Sept. 1984); C. Warbrick, 'The Protection of Human Rights in National Emergencies', in F. E. Dowrick (ed.), *Human Rights—Problems, Perspectives, Texts*, pp. 89–106 (1979).

2 See n. 1 above and R. Falk, 'Responding to Severe Violations', in Jorge I. Dominquez *et al.*, *Enhancing Global Human Rights*, pp. 207–57 (1979).

3 See ch. 1, prs. 1.18–1.21; Hartman, n. 1 above (1981), pp. 1–4.

4 See Hartman, ibid., p. 11.

5 See n. 1 above. The Sub-Commission on the Prevention of Discrimination and the Protection of Minorities now prepares an annual report of the respect for rules governing the declaration of states of exception. The report is to follow the definition and guidelines in the study by Questiaux, n. 1 above and attempt to evaluate the effects of states of emergency on the practical observance of human rights. The first report by Despouy covered twenty-eight countries, see 39 Rev. ICJ (1987) p. 29. For the latest report see Doc. E/CN.4/Sub.2/1989/30/Rev. 1.

6 GC 5/13, Doc. A/36/40, p. 110, adopted by the HRC at its 311th meeting (July 1981).

7 See prs. 7.23 *et seq*.

8 See the discussion in SR 43 prs. 54–7; SR 44 prs. 1–9; Doc. A/32/44, pr. 138. The guidelines do, however, impliedly cover derogations, see part II, *b*, at ch. 3, pr. 3.3 above.

9 See GC 5/13, pr. 2, cited in pr. 7.15 below.

10 See ch. 4, prs. 4.49–4.52 above on '*ratione temporis*' under the OP.

11 See e.g. SR 199 pr. 13 (Vincent-Evans on Iraq), SR 200 pr. 2 (Lallah on Iraq), SR 222 pr. 49 (Koulishev on Colombia), SR 387 pr. 11 (Tomuschat on Mexico).

12 SR 118 pr. 13 (Lallah on Ecuador).

13 SR 29 pr. 6 (Lallah on Tunisia). See Siracusa Principles 42–3, and 62, n. 1 above.

14 SR 170 pr. 58 (Hanga on Finland). The requirement of an official proclamation in article 4 ICCPR represents an important advance on article 15 ECHR. In *Lawless* v. *Ireland*, EUCT, Series A, Vol. 3 (1961), the EUCT noted that, 'the Convention does not contain any special provision to the effect that the Contracting State concerned must promulgate in its territory the notice of derogation

addressed to the Secretary-General of the Council of Europe', pr. 47. The absence of such a requirement has been criticized, e.g., by Fawcett, p. 313. See Resolution 56(16) of the Council of Ministers, *ECHR—Collected Texts*, p. 200 (1987).

15 See e.g. SR 84 pr. 11 (Uribe-Vargas on Madagascar), SR 87 pr. 11 (Madagascan State representative); SR 258 pr. 48 (Tarnopolsky on Italy), SR 222 pr. 3 (Sadi on Colombia). Derogations in the event of natural disasters were envisaged during the drafting, see Doc. A/2929, ch 5, pr. 39. Siracusa Principle 41, n. 1 above, states that, 'Economic difficulties *per se* cannot justify derogation measures'.

16 For an academic analysis of the AMR on similar lines see Norris, n. 1 above (1980).

17 Cf. The criteria adopted by the EUCT in the *Lawless Case*, n. 14 above, prs. 23–30. See Siracusa Principles 39–41, n. 1 above. It is interesting to note the following explanation in the second periodic report of Australia concerning whether a state of emergency in Queensland as a result of a strike by electricity supply workers in the south-east of that State should have resulted in a notification of derogation under article 4(3) of the Covenant: 'as the Queensland situation was confined to that State, it was not an emergency threatening "the life of the nation" within the terms of article 4, paragraph 3 of the Covenant', Doc. CCPR/C/42/Add. 2, p. 36.

18 See e.g. SR 213 pr. 11 (Tarnopolsky on Senegal).

19 See e.g. SR 248 pr. 30 (Bouziri on Venezuela), SR 265 pr. 35 (Ermacora on Barbados), SR 327 pr. 40 (Tarnopolsky on Morocco), SR 128 pr. 66 (Vincent-Evans on Chile), SR 442 pr. 19 (Bouziri on Lebanon).

20 See pr. 7.12 below (on France).

21 See SR 142 pr. 5 (Tarnopolsky on Spain).

22 See SR 422 pr. 7 (Al Douri on Nicaragua).

23 See SR 170 pr. 84 (Prado-Vallejo on Finland), reply at SR 172 pr. 7.

24 See SR 83 pr. 27 (Hanga on Madagascar), SR 84 pr. 11 (Uribe-Vargas on Madagascar), SR 222 pr. 3 (Sadi on Colombia). See Singhvi, n. 1 above, at n. 2.

25 See e.g. SR 355 pr. 28 (Prado-Vallejo on Chile), SR 356 prs. 31–2 (Ermacora on Uruguay), SR 127 prs. 23–44 (Prado-Vallejo) and 128 pr. 17 (Tomuschat) on Chile, SR 888 pr. 44 (Prado-Vallejo) and pr. 48 (Myullerson on New Zealand). See Siracusa Principles 22–34, n. 1 above.

26 GC 5/13, n. 6 above, pr. 3. See Siracusa Principle 48, n. 1 above. The EUCM stated in the *De Becker Case* that continued derogation of rights will not be justifiable under the Convention after the emergency has ceased, A.214/56, 2 YBECHR p. 214. The institutionalization of emergency measures into ordinary laws is a technique increasingly favoured by governments, see pr. 7.20 below (Graefrath on Chile).

27 See e.g. SR 29 pr. 6 (Lallah on Tunisia). See also the Siracusa Principles, n. 1 above.

28 See e.g. SR 52 pr. 49 (Lallah on Sweden). See Siracusa Principles 49–50, 55, n. 1 above. In the *Lawless Case*, n. 14 above, the EUCT noted the number of safeguards designed to prevent abuses in the operation of the system of administrative detention, pr. 37.

29 See Siracusa Principles 56 and 60, n. 1 above. See also G. J. Alexander, 'The

Illusory Protection of Human Rights by National Courts during Periods of Public Emergency', 5 HRLJ (1984) pp. 1–65.

30 See e.g. SR 331 pr. 39. See IACT, 'Judicial Guarantees in States of Emergency', Advisory Opinion OC-9/87, 9 HRLJ (1988) pp. 204–12.

31 See e.g. SR 224 pr. 77 (Lallah on Suriname), SR 282 pr. 21 (Lallah on Tanzania), SR 442 pr. 15 (Al Douri on Nicaragua), SR 128 pr. 66 (Vincent-Evans on Chile), SR 221 pr. 23 (Prado-Vallejo on Colombia).

32 Doc. CCPR/C/32/Add. 3.

33 See SR 586 prs. 34–44, SR 587 prs. 1–33.

34 Doc. CCPR/C/14/Add. 4 and 6 (1984).

35 See SR 471, 472, 473, and 477. Similarly see the summary of the HRC's discussion on the special powers in the Indian Constitution in Doc. A/39/40, pr. 251.

36 See Doc. A/2929, ch. 5, pr. 43. In the *Lawless Case*, n. 14 above, the EUCT considered the same expression. The EUCT stated that no facts had come to its knowledge to suggest that this condition had not been satisfied, prs. 39–41. Similarly in *UK* v. *Ireland*, EUCT, Series A, Vol. 25, pr. 222 (1978).

37 For the text of these see A. Roberts and R. Guelff, *Documents on the Laws of War*, pp. 169–337 (1949) and 387–468 (1977) (2nd, 1989). See H. Montealegre, 'The Compatibility of State Party's Derogations under Human Rights Instruments with its Obligations under Protocol II and Common Article 3', 33 Am. ULR (1983) pp. 41–51; C. Lysaght, 'The Scope of Protocol II and its Relation to Common Article 3 of the Geneva Conventions of 1949 and Other Human Rights Instruments', ibid., pp. 9–27; Siracusa Principle 67, n. 1 above. As of 1 October 1990 Iraq had made no derogation from article 4 in respect of its invasion of Kuwait.

38 See SR 604 pr. 36 (Tomuschat), reply at SR 608 pr. 25 ('there was no civil war in Afghanistan') and SR 608 pr. 51 (Tomuschat).

39 See SR 469 pr. 33 (Graefrath).

40 See SR 444 pr. 12 (Opsahl). See also Siracusa Principles 66–9, n. 1 above; Gasser, ch. 5, n. 68 above. See also the advisory opinion of the IACT on 'Other Treaties Subject to the Advisory Jurisdiction of the Court', 3 HRLJ (1982) p. 146.

41 See e.g. SR 265 pr. 6 (Tarnopolsky on Barbados). See also the second periodic report of Barbados, Doc. CCPR/C/42/Add. 3 pp. 4–5. A. P. Blaustein and G. H. Flanz, *Constitutions of the Countries of the World*, vol. ii (Dec. 1987). Similarly see SR 292 pr. 39 (Vincent-Evans on Jamaica), Doc. A/39/40, pr. 326 (on Gambia).

42 *Human Rights—Status of International Instruments*, pp. 34–5 (1987). For the French Report see Doc. CCPR/C/22/Add. 2. Further information is provided in France's second periodic report, Doc. CCPR/C/46/Add. 2 pp. 17–19 (1987). See also McRae, ch. 6 n. 21 above.

43 SR 440 pr. 23.

44 SR 440 pr. 55.

45 SR 441 pr. 47.

46 SR 441 pr. 35 (as corrected).

47 SR 445 pr. 32. As noted in ch 6, pr. 6.3 above the HRC has made no formal

determination on the question of the HRC's competence in respect of reservations.

48 See *ECHR—Collected Texts*, p. 77 (1987); Van Dijk and Van Hoof, pp. 611–13; Higgins, n. 1 above, p. 317 n. 5. Article 64 ECHR permits reservations other than those of a general character. See P. H. Imbert, 'Reservations to the European Convention on Human Rights Before the Strasbourg Commission: The Temeltasch Case', 33 ICLQ (1984) pp. 558–95; Marks, ch. 1, n. 154 above.

49 See *Lawless Case*, n. 14 above; *UK* v. *Ireland*, n. 36 above; *The Greek Case*, 12 YBECHR (1969) pp. 41–2.

50 See SR 127–30, 527–31, and 546–8 on Chile. See M. J. Bossuyt, 'The United Nations and Civil and Political Rights in Chile', 27 ICLQ (1978) pp. 462–71. On the situation in Chile after the ending of the state of emergency in 1988 see SR 942–45.

51 See e.g. SR 128 pr. 40 (Tarnopolsky on Chile). See the judgments of the EUCT in the cases of *Lawless*, n. 14 above, and *Ireland* v. *UK*, n. 36 above.

52 See e.g. SR 284 pr. 34 (Aguilar on Mali), SR 421 prs. 36–8*a* (Graefrath on Nicaragua). See also SR 224 prs. 47 (Lallah on Suriname).

53 Reference to this doctrine was made during the discussions of the Third Committee in 1963, see Doc. A/5655, pr. 49. On the doctrine of the margin of appreciation see ch. 4 n. 383 above.

54 GC 5/13, n. 6 above, pr. 2.

55 GC 5/13, n. 6 above, pr. 3. See Siracusa Principles 59–60, n. 1 above.

56 See e.g. SR 248 pr. 4 (Prado-Vallejo on Venezuela), SR 271 pr. 28 (Tarnopolsky on Kenya).

57 See n. 51 above.

58 See SR 355, 356, 357, 359, and 373.

59 See SR 364, 365, 366, and 368.

60 See SR 468, 469, 474, and 485.

61 See *Human Rights—Status*, n. 42 above, pp. 44–5. For the relevant provisions of the Constitution of Trinidad and Tobago see Blaustein and Flanz, n. 41 above, Vol. xvi (1977, 1983).

62 SR 555 pr. 1.

63 See *Human Rights—Status*, n. 42 above, p. 51. On reservations see articles 19–23 of the VCLT (1969).

64 SR 555 pr. 2. It is difficult to see how a reservation to a derogation provision could be other than contrary to the object and purpose of a human rights treaty. When presenting the second periodic report of Trinidad and Tobago the State representative indicated that her government had not deemed it necessary to withdraw the reservation to article 4(2), SR 765 pr. 15. The reservation again attracted criticism, ibid., prs. 16–18 (Higgins), 20 (Cooray), 22 (Lallah).

65 See n. 64 above.

66 See e.g. SR 160 pr. 51 (Vincent-Evans on Syria), SR 430 pr. 32 (Prado-Vallejo on Peru), SR 528 pr. 11 (Vincent-Evans on Chile). Some studies have suggested that the list of non-derogable rights in article 4(2) should be extended, see ICJ study, n. 1 above, p. 463, pr. 38, and Siracusa Principle 70, n. 1 above. Article 27 of the AMR contains a longer list of non-derogable rights than article 4(2). For States

parties to the AMR these would be covered by 'other obligations under international law' in article 4(2) of the ICCPR. Cf. the third Advisory Opinion of the IACT, n. 40 above.

67 SR 469 pr. 9 (Tomuschat on El Salvador). See also SR 355 pr. 24 (Prado-Vallejo on Uruguay).

68 GC 5/13, n. 6 above, pr. 3. See also Siracusa Principles 44–7.

69 See ch. 3, prs. 3.8–3.8.1 above.

70 Ibid. For example the initial report of Poland (Doc. CCPR/C/3/Add. 2 (1979) was considered by the HRC in 1979 (SR 186, 187, and 190). A state of emergency was declared in Poland on 13 December 1981. The state of emergency was finally terminated on 22 July 1983. The second periodic report of Poland, which reviews the state of emergency, was submitted to the HRC in October 1985 (Doc. CCPR/C/32/Add. 9 and Add. 13). It was considered by the HRC in March 1987 (SR 708–711). Therefore the HRC had no opportunity to enter into a dialogue with Poland until the state of emergency had been terminated. For UN Reports on the state of emergency in Poland see Doc. E/CN.4/1983/18 (Gobbi), Doc. E/CN.4/1984/26 (Gobbi and Patricio Ruedas), criticized by Franck, 78 AJIL (1984) p. 811 at pp. 829–30. See principle 73 of the Siracusa Principles, n. 1 above.

71 See e.g. SR 355 pr. 24 (Prado-Vallejo on Uruguay). Cf. the view expressed on this matter by the HRC under the OP in pr. 7.40 below.

72 Doc. CCPR/C/32/Add. 1 (1981). See also n. 50 above.

73 SR 528 pr. 28. See also his comments on Chile at SR 128 prs. 8–9 and on Iran at SR 366 pr. 27. In the *Greek Case* the EUCM rejected the applicants' view that a revolutionary government is barred from derogating under article 15 of the ECHR because it created the crisis, *Greek Case*, 12 YBECHR (1969) pp. 31–2. Only Mr Ermacora, now a member of the HRC, dissented from this view, ibid., pp. 102–3.

74 See SR 603, 604, and 608. For the recent international agreement on Afghanistan see ch. 5, n. 74 above.

75 See SR 221, 222, 223, and 226.

76 See SR 27, 28, 165, and 166.

77 See SR 499, 500, and 505.

78 See SR 468, 469, 474, 485, 716, 717, and 719.

79 See SR 103, 331, and 332.

80 See SR 442, 443, 444, and 446.

81 See SR 420, 421, 422, 428, and 429. See also *Case Concerning Military and Paramilitary Activities in and against Nicaragua* (*Nicaragua* v. *United States of America*), Merits, Judgment, ICJ Reports 1986, p. 14; 25 ILM (1986) pp. 1023–289. See also the material at 25 ILM (1986) pp. 1290–325, 1337–65.

82 See SR 471, 472, 473, and 477. See P. Hyndman, 'Human Rights, the Rule of Law and the Situation in Sri Lanka', 8 Univ. NSWLJ (1985) pp. 337–61.

83 A good example of the judicious but critical approach of HRC members is the consideration of the report of Afghanistan, n. 74 above. A less successful consideration took place of the report of the post-1979 regime in Iran, see SR 364, 365, 366, and 368. See also SR 430 pr. 46 (Tomuschat on Peru).

84 For some exceptions to the HRC's general approach see the comments at SR 442 prs. 9–19 (Al Douri), prs. 29–34 (Movchan), SR 443 prs. 15–36, 40 (Bouziri) and prs. 40–2 (Errera) concerning the Israeli presence in the Lebanon; SR 468 pr. 25 (Prado-Vallejo concerning US interference in El Salvador), reply at SR 468 pr. 36; SR 604 pr. 64 (Graefrath on Afghanistan); SR 604 pr. 44 (Higgins on the Soviet Occupation of Afghanistan).

85 Particularly the UN Human Rights Commission, see H. Tolley, ch. 1 n. 1 above.

86 See *Human Rights—Status*, n. 42 above, pp. 58–85, covering twelve States parties; 'Reservations, Declarations, Notifications and Objections Relating to the ICCPR and the OP Thereto—Note by the Secretary-General', Doc. CCPR/C/2/ Rev. 2 (12 May 1989) listing fifteen states parties. The USSR derogated from articles 12 and 21 of the Covenant in response to nationalistic clashes in Azerbaydzhan, ibid., p. 73. The UK reintroduced a derogation to article 9 as a result of the judgment of the EUCT in the case of *Brogan and Others* v. *UK*, EUCT, Series A, Vol. 145-B (1989), see ibid., p. 74. For an example of detailed information see that provided by Chile in Doc. CCPR/C/32/Add. 2 (1984). The ICJ study, n. 1 above, suggests that during the first five years the Covenant was in force at least fifteen States parties failed to give any or timely notice of states of emergency including Colombia, Peru, and Uruguay, p. 454.

87 The UK had signed the Covenant on 16 Sept. 1968. See E. Schwelb, 'The United Kingdom Signs the Covenants on Human Rights', 18 ICLQ (1969) pp. 457–68.

88 *Human Rights—Status*, n. 42 above, p. 84. Hartman (1981), n. 1 above, pp. 19–20, criticizes the Covenant's requirements that notice only need be given of the provisions from which there have been derogations rather than of the derogation measures taken as under article 15(3) ECHR. Hartman also refers to the, 'U.K.'s "shotgun" approach of suspending all articles even remotely implicated by the emergency measures', p. 20 n. 102.

89 Doc. CCPR/C/1/Add. 17 (1977).

90 Ibid., p. 3.

91 See ch. 3, pr. 3.20 above.

92 SR 69 pr. 26 (Graefrath).

93 Ibid., and SR 69 pr. 31 (Tarnopolsky).

94 SR 67 pr. 27.

95 '. . . [T]he existence of such an emergency was perfectly clear . . .', *Ireland* v. *UK*, EUCT, n. 36 above, pr. 205.

96 SR 70 prs. 29–32.

97 **Doc. CCPR/C/1/Add. 35, pr. 10 (1978).**

98 **The practice of internment was ended in December 1975. The question of its reintroduction has been raised recently after the bombings in Enniskillen in November 1987.**

99 Cmnd. 7497 (1979).

100 See SR 148.

101 ICJ study, n. 1 above. For material and literature on the situation in Northern Ireland see S. H. Bailey, D. J. Harris, and B. L. Jones, *Civil Liberties—Cases and Materials*, ch. 4 (2d, 1985); K. Boyle and T. Hadden, n. 117 below; ICJ study, n. 1 above, pp. 217–46; K. Boyle, 'Human Rights and Political Resolution in Northern

Ireland', in Symposium, Yale JWPO, n. 1 above, pp. 156–77; A. Jennings (ed.), *Justice under Fire: The Abuse of Civil Liberties in Northern Ireland* (1988); S. Bailey, *Human Rights and Responsibilities in Britain and Ireland* (1988); K. D. Ewing and C. A. Gearty, *Freedom Under Thatcher*, ch. 7 (1990).

102 Doc. CCPR/C/32/Add. 5 (1984).

103 Doc. CCPR/C/2/Add. 8, Apx. II, p. 2. The UK derogations under article 15 ECHR were withdrawn at the same time. See now n. 86 above.

104 See ch. 3, prs. 3.25–3.27.

105 Ibid.

106 SR 594 pr. 3.

107 Ibid., pr. 4. The Northern Ireland (Emergency Provisions) Act 1978 and the Prevention of Terrorism (Temporary Provisions) Act 1984. See *Brogan and Others* v. *UK*, EUCT, Series A, Vol. 145-B, (1989); *Fox, Campbell and Hartley* v. *UK*, EUCT, Judgement of 30 August 1990. For the more recent legislation see the Northern Ireland (Emergency Provisions) Act 1987; Prevention of Terrorism (Temporary Provisions) Act 1989.

108 SR 594 pr. 4. Review of the Operation of the Northern Ireland (Emergency Powers) Act 1978, Cmnd. 9222 (1984). See also Review of the Operation of the Prevention of Terrorism (Temporary Provisions) Act 1984 by Viscount Colville of Culross, Cmnd. 264 (1987); id., 1988 Review (30 January 1989). See generally D. P. J. Walsh, *The Use and Abuse of Emergency Legislation* (1983); C. Walker, *The Prevention of Terrorism in British Law* (1986); D. Bonner, *Emergency Powers in Peacetime* (1985).

109 SR 594 pr. 5.

110 SR 594 pr. 6 (Lallah), 8 (Graefrath). See S. C. Greer and A. White, *Abolishing the Diplock Courts—The Case for Restoring Jury Trial to Scheduled Offences in Northern Ireland* (1986). Recent suggestions that Diplock courts would be reformed have apparently been rejected by the Home Office, see *The Times*, 21 July 1987.

111 See T. Gifford, *Supergrasses—The Use of Accomplice Evidence in Northern Ireland* (1984); S. C. Greer, 'Supergrasses and the Legal System in Britain and Northern Ireland', 102 LQR (1986) pp. 198–249; S. C. Greer, 'The Rise and Fall of the Northern Ireland Supergrass System', 1987 Crim. LR pp. 663–70.

112 SR 594 pr. 7 (Lallah), 9 (Movchan), 12 (Opsahl). See RUC Stalker–Sampson Investigations, 1435 Hansard (House of Commons) (25 Jan. 1988) col. 21–3.

113 See n. 112 above.

114 SR 594 pr. 11 (Opsahl).

115 SR 594 pr. 13 (Cooray).

116 SR 594 pr. 14 (Pocar).

117 SR 594 pr. 15 (Prado-Vallejo). The most important political step since the consideration of the UK's second periodic report has been the conclusion and implementation of the Anglo-Irish Agreement, see ch. 5 n. 73 above. See also K. Boyle and T. Hadden, *Ireland—A Positive Proposal* (1985).

118 SR 594 pr. 42 (Wako). See ch. 5 n. 73 above.

119 SR 594 prs. 16–33.

120 SR 596 pr. 2. A number of applications to the EUCM have concerned the use of firearms in Northern Ireland, see ch. 8 below on article 6 under the OP.

121 Article 4(2) of the Covenant, see pr. 7.1 above. See W. P. Gormley, 'The Right to Life and the Rule of Non-Derogability: Peremptory Norms of Jus Cogens', in B. G. Ramcharan (ed.), *The Right to Life*, pp. 120–59 (1985).

122 SR 598 pr. 30.

123 See ch. 3, prs. 3.25–3.28 above. Since the examination of its second periodic report the UK has derogated from article 9(3) of the Covenant in response to the judgment of the EUCT in *Brogan and Others* v. *UK*, n. 107 above. The third periodic report of the UK was submitted in October 1989 and deals very briefly with article 4, see UN Doc. CCPR/C/58/Add.6, prs. 57–60.

124 See also the consideration of the Uruguayan reports in SR 355, 356, 357, 359, and 373. See also the ICJ Study, n. 1 above.

125 Doc. A/35/40, p. 121.

126 Ibid., pr. 17.

127 In *McVeigh et al* v. *UK*, the EUCM stated that where there is a critical situation in the country concerned, it will not take article 15 into consideration if it has not been relied upon by the respondent government, A.8022/77, 25 D. & R. p. 15.

128 Doc. A/36/40, p. 130. See prs. 7.37–7.41 below.

129 Doc. A/36/40, p. 130.

130 For the text of article 25 see Apx. I below.

131 Doc. A/36/40, p. 130 at p. 131, note (*a*).

132 See *Human Rights—Status*, n. 42 above, pp. 84–5.

133 Doc. A/36/40, p. 130, pr. 6.

134 Ibid., pr. 8.2.

135 Ibid., pr. 8.3. Similarly in *De Montejo* v. *Colombia*, 'The State party concerned is duty bound, when it invokes article 4(1) of the Covenant in proceedings under the Optional Protocol, to give a sufficiently detailed account of the relevant facts to show that a situation of the kind described in article 4(1) of the Covenant exists in the country concerned', Doc. A/37/40, p. 168, pr. 10.3.

136 See generally on the burden of proof under the OP, ch. 4, prs. 4.27–4.35 above.

137 See pr. 7.41 below. For a comparable approach to other provisions see *Maroufidou* v. *Sweden*, Doc. A/36/40, p. 160 (expulsion law applied and interpreted in good faith and in a reasonable manner: no violation of article 13), prs. 10.1–10.2; *Aumeeruddy-Cziffra* v. *Mauritius*, Doc. A/36/40, p. 134, ('the legislation . . . is discriminatory with respect to Mauritian women and cannot be justified by *security* requirements', pr. 9.2(*b*)2(ii)3; *Hammel* v. *Madagascar*, Doc. A/42/40, p. 130 (H's expulsion violated article 13 because the grounds of expulsion were not those of compelling *national security*), pr. 20; *V.R.M.B.* v. *Canada*, Doc. A/43/40, p. 258, 'It is not for the Committee to test a sovereign State's evaluation of an alien's security rating' (in the context of deportation), pr. 6.3.

138 'It falls in the first place to each contracting State, with its responsibility for the "life of [its] nation", to determine whether that life is threatened by a "public emergency" and, if so, how far it is necessary to go in attempting to overcome the

emergency. By reason of their direct and continuous contact with the pressing needs of the moment, the national authorities are in principle in a better position than the international judge to decide both on the presence of such an emergency and on the nature and scope of derogations necessary to avert it. In this matter, Article 15(1) leaves those authorities a wide margin of appreciation. Nevertheless, the States do not enjoy an unlimited power in this respect. The Court, which, with the Commission, is responsible for ensuring the observance of the States' engagements (Art. 19), is empowered to rule on the question of whether the States have gone beyond the "extent strictly required by the exigencies" of the crisis. The domestic margin of appreciation is thus accompanied by a European supervision', *UK* v. *Ireland*, n. 36 above, pr. 207.

139 Doc. A/36/40, p. 130, pr. 8.4.
140 Ibid., prs. 9–10.
141 Doc. A/37/40, p. 137. The case is also considered in ch. 8, prs. 8.17–8.20 below.
142 For the text of the Decree see ibid., pp. 148–9.
143 Ibid., pr. 3.2.
144 Ibid., pr. 5.
145 Doc. CCPR/C/2/Add. 4.
146 Doc. A/37/40, p. 137, pr. 12.2.
147 Ibid. See chs. 8 (article 6) and 9 (article 7) below.
148 See ch. 8, prs. 8.17–8.20 below.
149 See Hartman, n. 1 above (1981) pp. 40–52; Jaap A. Walkate, 'The Human Rights Committee and Public Emergencies', in Yale JWPO, n. 1 above, pp. 133–47.
150 See n. 86 above and GC 5/13 pr. 2, cited in pr. 7.15 above.
151 See pr. 7.3 above.
152 See n. 1 above.
153 See n. 1 above.
154 Members have suggested that a second General Comment on article 4 should be adopted. However, no such comment is in preparation.
155 GC 5/13, pr. 2, cited in pr. 7.15 above.
156 See pr. 7.9 above.
157 e.g. the initial USSR report, Doc. CCPR/C/1/Add. 2.
158 e.g. the representative of Iraq (SR 203, 204) did not reply to questions concerning article 4, SR 199 pr. 13 (Vincent-Evans).
159 States parties have often failed to supply promised Supplementary reports.
160 See ch. 3, prs. 3.8–3.8.1 above.
161 Cf. ICJ study, n. 1 above.
162 See prs. 7.23–7.34 above.
163 See pr. 7.16 above.
164 See ch. 3, prs. 3.12–3.18 above. See Siracusa Principle 72, n. 1 above.
165 See prs. 7.19–7.22 above.
166 See Siracusa Principle 71, n. 1 above.
167 See Siracusa Principle 57, n. 1 above.
168 See ch. 3, prs. 3.29–3.38 above.
169 See n. 70 above.
170 See ch. 3, pr. 3.8.1 above.

171 See e.g. the proposals of Opsahl in SR 349 prs. 16–17 and Tarnopolsky in SR 404 prs. 95–9.
172 See n. 1 above. It is interesting to note that the Siracusa Principles, n. 1 above, do not cover this question of general comments addressed to individual States parties.
173 See prs. 7.35–7.36, 7.40 above.
174 See ch. 4, prs. 4.23–4.26.
175 See pr. 7.40 above.
176 See prs. 7.41–7.43 above.
177 See pr. 7.2 above.
178 See ch. 3 above.
179 See ch. 4 above.
180 Hartman, n. 1 above (1981), p. 49.
181 See ch. 2 above.

8

Article 6[1]

8.1

1. Every human being has the inherent right to life. This right shall be protected by law. No one shall be arbitrarily deprived of his life.
2. In countries which have not abolished the death penalty, sentence of death may be imposed only for the most serious crimes in accordance with the law in force at the time of the commission of the crime and not contrary to the provisions of the present Covenant and to the Convention on the Prevention and Punishment of the Crime of Genocide. This penalty can only be carried out pursuant to a final judgement of a competent court.
3. When deprivation of life constitutes the crime of genocide, it is understood that nothing in this article shall authorize any State party to the present Covenant to derogate in any way from any obligation assumed under the provisions of the Convention on the Prevention and Punishment of the Crime of Genocide.
4. Anyone sentenced to death shall have the right to seek pardon or commutation of the sentence. Amnesty, pardon or commutation of the sentence of death may be granted in all cases.
5. Sentence of death shall not be imposed for crimes committed by persons below eighteen years of age and shall not be carried out on pregnant women.
6. Nothing in this article shall be invoked to delay or prevent the abolition of capital punishment by any State party to the present Covenant.

Introduction

8.2 The right to life is the only right in the ICCPR which is expressly stated to be 'inherent' in every human being.[2] In its first General Comment on article 6, under article 40(4), the HRC described it as 'the supreme right'.[3] It is one of the rights under the ICCPR from which no derogation is permitted even in a 'time of public emergency which threatens the life of the nation'.[4] Only one State has made a reservation to article 6 and that was subsequently withdrawn.[5]

The importance which the HRC has attached to article 6 can be gauged from the fact that it is the only article which has been the subject of two general comments.[6] The work of the HRC under article 6 has coincided with the increased concern of regional and international human rights institutions for the protection of the right to life in the face of widespread violations.[7]

A. ARTICLE 6 UNDER THE REPORTING PROCESS

8.3 In the consideration of State reports article 6 has been accorded critical importance and a wide interpretation that has permitted discussion of many vital and wide-ranging matters whose inclusion within the realms of article 6 is perhaps not immediately apparent.[8] Within the bounds of the ICCPR itself the articles identified as having a particular relationship with article 6 include articles 7, 9, 10, 14, and 20.[9]

The following words of a former HRC member, Mr Ganji, are a useful precursor to an examination of the HRC's approach to article 6 because they indicate the rationale behind the wide perspective brought to bear on the right to life:

In order to exercise any of the rights with which the Committee was concerned an individual had to exist, and in order to exist, he must die neither before nor after birth and he must receive a minimum of food, education, health care, housing and clothing. There was undoubtedly an interconnexion between the right to life, the requirements of which were material and the right to exercise all other freedoms.[10]

In its General Comment the HRC supported this broad approach to article 6:

... the Committee has noted that quite often the information given concerning article 6 has been limited to only one or other aspect of this right. It is a right which should not be interpreted narrowly.
... the Committee has noted that the right to life has been too often narrowly interpreted. The expression 'inherent right to life' cannot properly be understood in a restrictive manner, and the protection of this right requires that States adopt *positive measures*. In this connexion, the Committee considers that it would be *desirable* for States parties to take all possible measures to reduce infant mortality and to increase life expectancy, especially in adopting measures to eliminate malnutrition and epidemics.[11]

8.4 The right to life has been dealt with by almost all of the reports submitted to the HRC but the information supplied by States parties, particularly in the early years, has generally been confined to an indication of how their respective legal systems outlaw the taking of life.[12] In its consideration of State reports HRC members have attempted to gain a much deeper understanding of how States have approached and dealt with their undertaking to 'protect' the right to life and in particular what 'positive measures' had been adopted.[13] As Mr Tomuschat commented during consideration of the report of the Lebanon, 'it was not only for the legislator, but for all State authorities, the executive, the police, the military—actively to protect life'.[14] Information has consistently been sought on the measures taken to reduce maternal and infant mortality and to raise life expectancy.[15] Along the same lines the

HRC's considerations have extended to such matters as measures taken in the public health and environmental fields, for example, concerning labour safety measures, industrial accidents, the combating of occupational diseases, the control of food and pharmaceutical products, combating crime and drug abuse, the development of a nutritional policy and the establishment of health centres, efforts to eradicate malnutrition and eliminate epidemics, reduce unemployment, and implement agrarian reforms, and more recently, the regulation of the transportation and dumping of nuclear waste.[16]

This broad approach and the consequent call for 'positive measures' including those indicated by the HRC as 'desirable' raises some legal difficulties. The approach inevitably leads the HRC to consider matters covered by the parallel International Covenant on Economic, Social, and Cultural Rights.[17] The obligations under the ICESCR are clearly of a progressive nature.[18] There is nothing necessarily illogical in interpreting article 6 as containing both immediate and progressive obligations with respect to the right to life but if this is accepted then the argument that all of the obligations under the ICCPR are immediate is no longer sustainable.[19] This in turn would raise problems concerning the consideration of a communication under the OP alleging a violation of a broader, progressive aspect of the right to life.[20] By comparison a very cautious attitude has been adopted to the question of any 'positive' obligation in article 2 ECHR.[21] Finally, in terms of the HRC, it is worth noting that two members of the HRC were particularly influential in developing the HRC's approach to article 6, Mr Graefrath (expert from the GDR), and Sir Vincent-Evans (expert from the UK).

8.5 Abortion[22] and euthanasia[23] have only been spasmodically dealt with by HRC members. The ICCPR contains no express provision concerning the points in time at which life commences and terminates and thus the precise extent of a State's obligation is uncertain.[24] Draft proposals that would have covered a right to life 'from conception' were not adopted.[25] A number of HRC members have commented that the question of abortion was a peculiarly moral and controversial one and that it would therefore be difficult to achieve a Committee view on it.[26] However, individual members have felt free to express their own personal views on the subject. For example, during consideration of the abortion law adopted in Italy in 1978 Mr Bouziri commented that he 'thought the abortion laws so strict that they infringed, perhaps on religious grounds, the woman's freedom in that respect which it was essential to respect'.[27] When dealing with the question of abortion the principal concern of the members has been to determine the circumstances in which abortions were authorized.[28] This could be taken to suggest that abortions are not *per se* contrary to the ICCPR or at least that they might be compatible with the ICCPR in certain circumstances. The jurisprudence under the ECHR and of the United States Supreme Court would suggest that the right to privacy in article 17 of the ICCPR would be relevant to the determination of those circumstances.[29] Similarly with respect to euthanasia.[30] Questions concerning birth control have been exceptional.[31]

8.6 Of particular concern to the HRC has been the taking of life by, and the use of firearms by, the police and security forces. In its first General Comment the HRC stated that,

The protection against arbitrary deprivation of life which is explicitly required by the third sentence of article 6(1) is of paramount importance. The Committee considers that States parties should take measures not only to prevent deprivation of life by criminal acts, but also to prevent arbitrary killing by their own security forces. The deprivation of life by the authorities of the State is a matter of the utmost gravity. Therefore, the law must strictly control and limit the circumstances in which a person may be deprived of his life by such authorities.[32]

In accordance with this approach members have sought information on any legislation, regulations, or administrative orders concerning the circumstances in which the police and security forces are entitled to open fire, for example, in cases of riots, political disturbances, arrests and escapes from prison, how they were enforced and what safeguards existed against the arbitrary use of such arms.[33] The representative of the GDR was questioned as to whether its laws and practices concerning the use of firearms by security forces at its borders could be reconciled with the requirements of article 6 on the non-arbitrary deprivation of life and proportionality in the use of force.[34]

8.7 The growing world phenomenons of so-called 'disappeared persons' and extra-legal killings have increasingly attracted the attention of the HRC.[35] Generally, members have avoided making direct accusations but rather have concentrated on whether specific and effective measures existed to prevent the disappearance and killing of individuals.[36] Moreover, by linking article 6 with the guarantee of the right to a fair hearing in article 14 of the ICCPR the HRC has stressed that, 'States should establish effective facilities and procedures to investigate thoroughly cases of missing and disappeared persons in circumstances which may involve a violation of the right to life'.[37] During consideration of the report of Sri Lanka a number of members expressed great concern at emergency regulations which authorized police officers to take possession of deceased persons and to bury or cremate them without an inquest.[38] On occasions HRC members have referred to international reports[39] alleging violations of the right to life or to notorious cases concerning particular individuals[40] or groups[41] and those dealt with in views under the OP.[42]

If violations of the right to life have been alleged the HRC members have indicated that it is the responsibility of the government to investigate the allegations irrespective of whether it is alleged that the government is responsible.[43] This accords with the approach of the HRC under the OP[44] and complements the general rules of State responsibility concerning the treatment of aliens.[45]

8.8 One matter that has been subjected to scrupulously close and punishing analysis has been the use of the death penalty.[46] Members have comprehensively dealt with all facets of this matter including the six express limitations on the imposition and implementation of a sentence of death. Such a sentence (*a*) may only be imposed for the most serious crimes;[47] (*b*) must be in accordance with the law in force at the time of the commission of the crime;[48] (*c*) must not be contrary to the other provisions of the Covenant[49] or the Genocide Convention;[50] (*d*) can only be carried out pursuant to a final judgment rendered by a competent court;[51] (*e*) shall not be imposed for crimes committed by persons below 18 years of age[52] and shall not be carried out on pregnant women;[53] (*f*) any person sentenced to death shall have the right to seek pardon or commutation of the sentence.

The notably consistent approach of the HRC to the death penalty, as compared with the rather spasmodic treatment of abortion and euthanasia noted above,[54] stems largely from the clearly perceived abolitionist philosophy behind the provisions of paragraphs (2) and (6) of article 6. In its General Comment the HRC stated that,

> While it follows from article 6(2) and (6) that States parties are not obliged to abolish the death penalty totally, they are obliged to limit its use and, in particular, to abolish it for other than the 'most serious crimes'. Accordingly, they ought to consider reviewing their criminal laws in this light and, in any event, to restrict the application of the death penalty to the 'most serious crimes'. The article also refers generally to abolition in terms which strongly suggest (paras. (2) and (6)) that abolition is desirable.[55]

As regards the limitation of the application of the death penalty to the 'most serious crimes' the HRC has expressed the view that this 'must be read restrictively to mean that the death penalty should be quite an exceptional measure'.[56] Members have looked closely at the offences for which the death penalty is prescribed and questioned State representatives as to the categorization of certain offences as 'most serious'.[57] Members have expressed concern at the possible imposition of the death penalty for vague, generalized, or economic crimes, for example, 'crimes against the State';[58] 'sabotage';[59] 'murder committed for gain or for leading a parasitic way of life';[60] 'armed operations', 'corruption on earth', and 'offences against the Constitution';[61] 'misuse of public funds';[62] double membership of political parties or for political activities;[63] for non-violent crimes, for example, drug offences,[64] for minor sexual crimes,[65] and for violations of the basic duties of command in a military context.[66] Representatives are asked how many persons have been sentenced and executed for such crimes. Some importance has been attached by HRC members to the need for the relevant provisions of law to be expressed in sufficiently explicit terms to enable everyone to understand what activities are prescribed.[67]

To understand the practical application of the relevant provisions of a State's laws and regulations members have further requested some statistics on the use of the death penalty within a given period, particularly for political offences,[68] whether the death penalty was the exclusively prescribed punishment for those offences or whether alternatives existed,[69] the frequency of the commutation of sentences and whether, as required by article 6(2), the imposition of the death penalty was in accordance with the law at the time of the commission of the crime and not contrary to the provisions of the Covenant particularly with respect to the vitally important procedural guarantees in articles 9 and 14 of the ICCPR.[70] As the HRC stated in its General Comment,

It also follows from the express terms of article 6 that it can only be imposed in accordance with the law in force at the time of the commission of the crime and not contrary to the provisions of the Covenant. The procedural guarantees therein prescribed must be observed, including the right to a fair hearing by an independent tribunal, the presumption of innocence, the minimum guarantees for the defence, and the right to review by higher tribunal. These rights are applicable in addition to the particular right to seek pardon or commutation of sentence.[71]

Again only rarely have members put specific allegations to States of the abuse of the death penalty.[72] On the limitation that the death penalty should not be imposed contrary to the provisions of the Genocide Convention the standard approach has been to ask whether the State party's national law contains provisions in conformity with the Genocide Convention.[73]

8.9 Notwithstanding the express provision that 'Amnesty, pardon or commutation of the sentence may be granted in all cases', at least one member has suggested that a State party cannot abuse this provision. During consideration of the report of Chile, Mr Graefrath commented that,

States parties to the Covenant had an obligation to ensure the realization of the rights recognized in that instrument. It was generally recognized, and had been affirmed by all the reports hitherto dealt with in the Committee, that the obligation extended to penal prosecution and punishment for grave breaches of human rights. The present occasion was the first on which a regime had boasted that it had pardoned those who had committed grave breaches of human rights and had discontinued penal prosecutions against them. He fully shared the view expressed in paragraph 326 of the Working Group's report[74] to the effect that an amnesty declared by a Government in favour of officials who engaged in systematic and gross violations of human rights was legally ineffective as contrary to the generally accepted principles of law and that on the international level persons responsible for such violations were liable for crimes committed by them. Such conduct was a clear violation of the Covenant.[75]

The question of amnesties at the end of prolonged and violent civil disorders is a controversial one. The conflict between bringing offenders to justice and the need for national reconciliation is a difficult one to resolve. The situation in Chile, however, is a different one because the regime in power sought to grant an amnesty while remaining in power for the foreseeable future.[76] It is submitted that in such circumstances the purported amnesty should not be recognized as legally effective at either the national or international level.[77]

8.10 In accordance with the abolitionist philosophy of article 6 information has been sought on any consideration given by a State party to abolition of the death penalty,[78] the state of public opinion on that question, and the reasoning behind a particular State's retention of the death penalty.[79]

After consideration of a substantial number of reports the HRC expressed the following conclusion in 1982:

> The Committee concludes that all measures of abolition should be considered as progress in the enjoyment of the right to life within the meaning of article 40, and should as such be reported to the Committee. The Committee notes that a number of States have already abolished the death penalty or suspended its application. Nevertheless, States' reports show that progress made towards abolishing or limiting the use of the death penalty is quite inadequate.[80]

8.11 The relationship between war and the right to life has only rarely been directly referred to within the context of specific State reports.[81] However, the HRC still chose to include a paragraph in its first General Comment on article 6 explicitly dealing with this question, if only in somewhat generalized terms,

> The Committee observes that war and other acts of mass violence continue to be a scourge of humanity[82] and to take the lives of thousands of human beings every year. Under the Charter of the United Nations the threat or use of force by any State against another State, except in the exercise of the inherent right of self-defence, is already prohibited.[83] The Committee considers that States have the supreme duty to prevent wars, acts of genocide and other acts of mass violence causing arbitrary loss of life. Every effort they make to avert the danger of war, especially thermo-nuclear war, and to strengthen international peace and security would constitute the most important condition and guarantee for the safeguarding of the right to life. In this respect, the Committee notes, in particular, a connection between article 6 and article 20, which states that the law shall prohibit any propaganda for war (paragraph 1) or incitement to violence (paragraph 2) as therein described.[84]

8.12 The broader relationship between the right to life and war was taken a step further in the HRC's second General Comment. Its importance justifies a substantial extract:

> 2. In its previous general comment, the Committee also observed that it is the supreme duty of States to prevent wars. Wars and other acts of mass violence continue to be a scourge of humanity and take the lives of thousands of innocent human beings every year.

3. While remaining deeply concerned by the toll of human life taken by conventional weapons in armed conflicts, the Committee has noted that, during successive sessions of the General Assembly, representatives from all geographical regions have expressed their growing concern at the development and proliferation of increasingly awesome weapons of mass destruction, which not only threaten human life but also absorb resources that could otherwise be used for vital economic and social purposes, particularly for the benefit of developing countries, and thereby for promoting and securing the enjoyment of human rights for all.

4. The Committee associates itself with this concern. It is evident that the designing, testing, manufacture, possession and deployment of nuclear weapons are amongst the greatest threats to the right to life which confront mankind today. This threat is compounded by the danger that the actual use of such weapons may be brought about, not only in the event of war, but even through human or mechanical error or failure.

5. Furthermore, the very existence and gravity of this threat generates a climate of suspicion and fear between States, which is in itself antagonistic to the promotion of universal respect for and observance of human rights and fundamental freedoms in accordance with the Charter of the United Nations and the International Covenants on Human Rights.

6. *The production, testing, possession, deployment and use of nuclear weapons should be prohibited and recognized as crimes against humanity.*

7. The Committee accordingly, in the interests of mankind, calls upon all States, whether parties to the Covenant or not, to take urgent steps, unilaterally and by agreement, to rid the world of this menace.[85]

8.13 This General Comment raises a number of key points and issues. Clearly the HRC recognized that a comment relating to nuclear weapons was going to be politically sensitive and so it proved.[86] The French expert on the HRC, who was not present when the comment was adopted, felt compelled to register a number of objections.[87] A number of States in the Third Committee also criticized the comment.[88] The obvious question is why the HRC felt it necessary to broach the issue of nuclear weapons, which had not featured prominently in its questioning under the article 40 reporting process.[89] The General Comment itself points to a number of reasons including the views in successive sessions of the General Assembly and the resources absorbed by nuclear weapons that could be used for developing countries.[90] We noted in consideration of self-determination under article 1 of the ICCPR the increasing demands made by developing countries for a legal right to more resources from the developed countries as part of the proposed New International Economic Order and the Right to Development.[91] The comment also responds to the much wider application of the human rights concept in recent years in terms of alleged rights to peace, development, and a healthy environment.[92] In general terms this also raises the problem of how to respond to changing conceptions of the contents of human rights over time.[93] Note that the HRC makes its call 'in the interest of mankind' and to all

States whether parties to the Covenant or not. The States most obviously concerned who are not parties are the United States and China.[94]

As for the content of the General Comment the most controversial aspect is that in paragraph 6, that the 'production, testing, possession, deployment and use of nuclear weapons should be prohibited and recognized as crimes against humanity'. This was the comment that attracted criticism, particularly from Western States in the Third Committee. It is difficult to accept that the term 'should' suggests anything other than a desirable goal to be achieved rather than a statement of immediate legal obligation derived from article 6 of the ICCPR. If it were a statement of the HRC's view of present international law then a number of States parties, including the UK, the USSR, France, and India, would clearly be in breach of the Covenant. If this interpretation of the HRC's view is correct the criticism of the HRC is that it is stepping outside its role of supervising the immediate implementation of the rights in the ICCPR.[95] Similarly, the ICCPR is being interpreted to contain progressive as well as immediate obligations.[96] Equally, however, it is difficult to dispute the HRC's assertion that nuclear weapons are 'amongst the greatest threats to the right to life which confront man today'.

As a matter of international law 'crimes against humanity' derive from the Charter of the Nuremberg Tribunal.[97] In more general terms the comment raises again the question of the relationship between the two 'International Covenants'.[98] Finally, we can again note a reference to the obligations in the United Nations Charter.[99]

B. ARTICLE 6 UNDER THE OPTIONAL PROTOCOL

8.14 Violations of article 6 have been alleged in a small number of communications. On all but one occasion the HRC expressed the view that there had been a violation. The one case in which the HRC did not actually state that article 6 had been violated is dealt with first.

8.15 In *Bleir* v. *Uruguay*[100] it was alleged that B was arrested in October 1975, detained incommunicado, and subjected to cruel treatment and torture.[101] The State party submitted that a warrant for B's arrest had been issued since August 1976 but that his whereabouts were unknown.[102] No information, explanations, or observations were offered by the State party in reply to various submissions, including eyewitness testimony, concerning B's detention.[103]

In an interim decision the HRC stated that it considered,

that it is the clear duty of the Government of Uruguay to make a full and thorough inquiry (a) into the allegations concerning Mr. Bleir's arrest and his treatment while in detention prior to 26 August 1976, and (b) as to his apparent disappearance and the circumstances in which a warrant for his arrest was issued on 26 August 1976. The Committee urges that this should be done without further delay and that the Committee should be informed of the action taken by the Government of Uruguay and of the outcome of the inquiry.[104]

The jurisprudence of the HRC under the OP, examined in chapter 4 above, would indicate that the 'clear duty' referred to by the HRC is a legal duty deriving from the terms of the OP.[105] The HRC's opinion is clearly of great practical importance and mirrors the asserted position under customary international law concerning the treatment of aliens.[106] It is also interesting to note the use of the device of an 'interim decision' by the HRC which, as we suggested above, can be a useful device for indicating to the State party the approach the HRC is likely to take and the information and co-operation it expects.[107]

After outlining the considerations on which it based its interim decision[108] the HRC stated that,

The failure of the State party to address in substance the serious allegations brought against it and corroborated by unrefuted information, cannot but lead to the conclusion that Eduardo Bleir (B) is either still detained, incommunicado, by the Uruguayan authorities or has died while in custody at the hands of the Uruguayan authorities.[109]

The Uruguayan government strongly objected to this part of the HRC's interim decision and those objections are noted elsewhere.[110] In its final views the HRC expressed itself a little more cautiously. The HRC found violations of articles 7, 9, and 10(1) and stated, 'that there are serious reasons to believe that the ultimate violation of article 6 has been perpetrated by the Uruguayan authorities'.[111]

The HRC took the approach that although it could not conclusively express the view that article 6 had been violated it could and should state that there were 'serious reasons' to believe that there had been a violation. The view adopted by the HRC shows a flexible approach to its work under the OP. A strictly judicial organ might have felt obliged to make a clear determination as to the alleged violation. The HRC's view ended by urging Uruguay to reconsider its position and to take effective steps to establish what had happened to B since October 1975, to bring to justice any persons found to be responsible for his death, disappearance, or ill-treatment, and to pay compensation to him or his family for any injury suffered and to ensure that similar violations did not occur in the future.[112]

8.16 In *H. Barbato* v. *Uruguay*,[113] H completed an eight-year term of imprisonment in July 1980 but was kept in detention thereafter under the 'prompt security measures regime'.[114] His release was to be conditioned on him leaving the country.[115] He was informed that he would be released to leave for Sweden but this decision was revoked. At the end of November

1980 H was transferred to Montevideo Police Headquarters. His where-abouts were then unknown until 28 December 1980. He was allegedly seen at the quarters of a cavalry regiment and was reportedly in good spirits. He was last seen alive on 24 December 1980. On 28 December his mother was called to the Military Hospital without any explanation and shown H's body for identification purposes. The death certificate stated as the cause of death 'acute haemorrhage resulting from a cut of the carotid artery' and his mother was told that he had committed suicide with a razor blade. The author (H's cousin) alleged that this explanation was false and that H had died as a consequence of the mistreatment and torture to which he had allegedly been subjected.

In its admissibility decision the HRC held the communication admissible and made its standard request for written explanations or statements clarifying the matter, court orders, and relevant decisions.[116] It also requested copies of the death certificate and medical report and of the reports on whatever inquiries were held into the circumstances surrounding H's death.[117]

The State party forwarded a transcript of the autopsy report concerning H.[118] The author replied that the State party had given no explanations concerning his numerous complaints; that the autopsy in no way indicated beyond any doubt that the cause of H's death was suicide as claimed; that the autopsy was conducted by military personnel (it was conducted by a Lieutenant in the Medical Corps) and not by doctors chosen by relatives; the body showed signs of having undergone a tracheotomy and having been kept refrigerated; there was no explanation of the circumstances in which death was certified; there was no information on any investigation into the circum-stances of death; the official explanation was implausible and unacceptable and represented a cover-up; and that even if the victim did commit suicide it could only have been because of compulsion by threats of violence.[119]

In its expression of views the HRC stated that it had taken into account the following considerations:

Only a transcript of the autopsy report had been submitted. The State party has not submitted any report on the circumstances into which Hugo Dermit (H) died or any information as to what inquiries have been made or the outcome of such inquiries. Consequently, the Committee cannot help but give appropriate weight to the informa-tion submitted by the author, indicating that a few days before Hugo's death he had been seen by other prisoners and was reported to have been in good spirits, in spite of the interruption of the preparations for his release and departure from Uruguay. While the Committee cannot arrive at a definite conclusion as to whether Hugo Dermit committed suicide or was killed by others while in custody; yet, the inescapable conclusion is that in all the circumstances the Uruguayan authorities either by act or by omission were responsible for not taking adequate measures to protect his life, as required by article 6(1) of the Covenant.[120]

In this case the HRC felt that this 'inescapable conclusion' allowed them to express the view that article 6 had been violated because 'the Uruguayan authorities had failed to take appropriate measures to protect H's life while in custody'.[121] The HRC's view then was that the circumstances allowed them to go further than stating that there were 'serious reasons' to believe that article 6 had been violated, as they had in *Bleir* v. *Uruguay*,[122] even though the HRC acknowledged that they could not arrive at a 'definite conclusion' as to what had happened to H. According to the HRC's view an 'act' or 'omission' can violate article 6 as the obligation is to take 'adequate' or 'appropriate' measures to 'protect' the life of a person held in custody. The approach of the HRC would seem to mirror the customary international law obligation of a State to account for an individual held in custody although there is no reference in the HRC's view to any relevant international jurisprudence.[123] The HRC's approach would seem to indicate that if an author establishes a prima-facie case the State party concerned is obliged to conduct an inquiry into the circumstances of death and submit that report to the HRC. Failure to comply with that obligation will mean that the allegations made will form the basis of a finding of violation against the State party. In practical terms this is probably the only sensible approach open to the HRC as the State party is clearly in a situation in which the relevant evidence is either in its exclusive control or only available to it.[124]

After expressing the view that article 6 had been violated the HRC again expressed the view that the State party was under an obligation, *inter alia*, to take effective steps to establish the facts of Hugo Dermit's (H's) death and to pay appropriate compensation to his family.[125]

8.17 In *Guerrero* v. *Colombia*[126] the author's wife died in the course of a police raid on a house where it was believed that a kidnapped ambassador was being held prisoner. The ambassador was not found but the police patrol waited in the house for the arrival of the suspected kidnappers. Seven persons who subsequently entered the house were shot by the police and died. Among these was the author's wife, G. Although the police initially claimed that the victims had died while resisting arrest the forensic, ballistic, and other reports repudiated this account. The reports showed that none of the victims had fired a shot and that they had all been killed at point blank range, some of them shot in the back or in the head. It was also established that the victims were not all killed at the same time, but at intervals, as they arrived at the house, and that most of them had been shot while trying to save themselves from the unexpected attack. With respect to G the forensic report showed that she had been shot several times after she had already died from a heart attack.[127]

The Office of the State Counsel for the National Police instituted an administrative inquiry into the case.[128] The dismissal of all members of the patrol involved in the operation was requested and was ordered on 16 June

1980.[129] Two criminal investigations into the case were defeated by recourse to Decree-Law No. 0070 of 1978.[130] This Decree amended article 25 of the Penal Code, 'for so long as the public order remains disturbed and the national territory is in a state of siege'.[131] The Decree established a new ground of defence that could be pleaded by members of the police force to exonerate them if an otherwise punishable act was committed, 'in the course of operations planned with the object of preventing and curbing the offences of extortion and kidnappings ...'.[132] The Supreme Court of Colombia had held the Decree to be constitutional.[133] At no time could a civil action for damages be instituted in conjunction with military criminal proceedings.[134]

8.18 Before dealing directly with the facts of the case the HRC indicated its approach to article 6:

The right enshrined in this article is the supreme right of the human being. It follows that the deprivation of life by the authorities of the State is a matter of the utmost gravity. This follows from the article as a whole and in particular is the reason why paragraph 2 of the article lays down that the death penalty may be imposed only for the most serious crimes. The requirements that the right shall be protected by law and that no one shall be arbitrarily deprived of his life mean that the law must strictly control and limit the circumstances in which a person may be deprived of his life by the authorities of a State.[135]

The HRC's description of the right to life as the 'supreme right' accords with the importance attached to article 6 under the reporting process.[136] As we noted, the HRC has looked very closely at the domestic laws and regulations authorizing the taking of life by the authorities of the State.[137] The terms of the above paragraph are almost exactly recited in the HRC's first General Comment on article 6.[138]

8.19 The HRC then proceeded to deal with the facts of the case:

In the present case it is evident from the fact that seven persons lost their lives as a result of the deliberate action of the police that the deprivation of life was *intentional*. Moreover, the police action was apparently taken without warning to the victims and without giving them any opportunity to surrender to the police patrol or to offer any explanation of their presence or intentions. There is no evidence that the action of the police was necessary in their own defence or that of others, or that it was necessary to effect the arrest or prevent the escape of the persons concerned. Moreover, the victims were no more than suspects of the kidnapping which had occurred some days earlier and their killing by the police deprived them of all of the protections of due process of law laid down in the Covenant. In the case of Mrs. Maria Fanny Suarez De Guerrero (G), the forensic report showed that she had been shot several times after she had already died from a heart attack. There can be no reasonable doubt that her death was caused by the police patrol. For these reasons it is the Committee's view that the action of the police resulting in the death of Mrs. Maria Fanny Suarez De Guerrero was *disproportionate* to the requirements of law enforcement in the circumstances of the case and that she was arbitrarily deprived of her right to life contrary to article 6(1) of the International Covenant on Civil and Political Rights. Inasmuch as the police action was made justifiable as a matter of Colombian law by Legislative Decree No. 0070 of 20 January 1978, the right to life was not adequately protected by the law of Colombia as required by article 6(1).[139]

A number of important points can be noted. It is unclear exactly how the HRC determined that G's death was 'caused' by the action of the police patrol when the medical report revealed that she had already died from a heart attack before being shot several times. It could be that G's heart attack was caused by the unexpected attack by the police patrol and the accompanying shock but no process of causation is clearly spelt out. When the allegation is of a violation of the right to life the process of causation is fundamental and the HRC's explanation is defective in this respect.

On its view of the facts the HRC was of the opinion that article 6(1) had been violated in two respects. First, G had been arbitrarily deprived of her life. It is interesting that the HRC characterized this deprivation of life as 'intentional'. This term was proposed during the drafting as a substitute for 'arbitrarily' but the proposal was not accepted.[140] An intentional killing is obviously more difficult to justify in terms of necessity and proportionality. However, it is submitted that 'arbitrary' deprivation is probably not limited to intentional killing and would probably include negligent or reckless killing in certain circumstances.[141]

The HRC then proceed to indicate some of the circumstances in which the taking of life might not violate article 6(1), namely, when necessary in self-defence or the defence of others or necessary to effect an arrest or to prevent an escape.[142] The circumstances of the case are then closely scrutinized. In this case the HRC pointed out the factual elements suggesting that the police action was not necessary: the victims were given no warning, no opportunity to surrender or to offer any explanation, and were only suspects. In this way the HRC introduces the principle of 'proportionality to the requirements of law enforcement' as an element in the evaluation of the circumstances allegedly constituting a violation of article 6(1). Presumably in the application of this important principle it would only be in extremely rare cases that it would be permissible to use lethal force.[143]

8.20 The second basis on which the HRC expressed the view that article 6 had been violated in the *Guerrero Case*[144] was that G's right to life was not adequately protected by law. The mere existence of Legislative Decree No. 0070 amounted to a failure to protect the right to life because it could effectively be invoked to justify in law the arbitrary deprivation of life contrary to article 6.[145] The HRC expressed the view that the State party was obliged to compensate G's husband and to ensure that the right to life was duly protected by amending the law.[146] The HRC's view is a clear expression of the obligation on a State party whose law is found to be in violation of the

Covenant notwithstanding its constitutionality in domestic law.[147] The approach of the HRC is commendably positive in this respect. Finally, taking the two bases of the HRC's view together it can also be argued that 'arbitrary' covers more than just illegal killings as the offenders had a legal defence under a domestic law that had been adjudged constitutional by the Colombian Supreme Court.[148]

8.21 During the drafting of the Covenant it was argued in the HRCion that the text of article 6 should state specifically and exhaustively the circumstances in which the taking of life would not violate the right to life.[149] Against this approach it was argued that any such enumeration would necessarily be incomplete and would tend to give the impression that greater importance was being given to the exceptions than to the right.[150] The final HRCion text contained a general formulation of the right without exceptions.[151] It was explained that a clause providing that no one should be deprived of his life 'arbitrarily' would indicate that the right was not absolute and obviate the necessity of setting out possible exceptions in detail. Others criticized the use of the term 'arbitrary' because it failed to express a generally recognized idea and was ambiguous. It was argued that the term 'arbitrarily' meant 'illegally' or 'unjustly' or both and that it should be retained as it had been used in several articles in the Universal Declaration of Human Rights and in certain articles of the draft Covenant.[152] The term again prompted differences of opinion in the Third Committee of the General Assembly where various meanings were suggested, for example, 'fixed or done capriciously or at pleasure; without adequate determining principle; depending on the will alone; tyrannical; despotic; without cause based upon law; not governed by any fixed rule or standard'.[153] It was proposed by the Netherlands that article 6 should follow the formulation of article 2 ECHR in specifying the cases in which deprivation of life would be deemed lawful.[154] The majority, however, did not favour such a formulation.[155] It is also interesting to note that the HRC drew attention to the fact that the police action deprived the suspects of all the 'protections of due process laid down in the Covenant'.[156] During the discussions in the Third Committee some representatives argued that the term 'arbitrarily' was synonymous with the expression 'without due process of law' and implied such guarantees as the right to a fair trial and protection against false arrest.[157]

8.22 In their considerations under the OP the HRC have the task of determining in what circumstances the deprivation of life will be characterized as arbitrary and thus violate article 6.[158] It is difficult to conclude other than that no clearly defined meaning of the term emerged from the drafting process.[159] In the *Guerrero Case*[160] the HRC revealed some indications of its approach to 'arbitrary' by reference to matters of intention, necessity in particular circumstances, and proportionality to the requirements of law enforcement. In determining its approach the albeit limited jurisprudence under article 2 ECHR can provide the HRC with persuasive comparative material.[161] However, there is little doubt that the terms of article 6 and the inconclusiveness of the *travaux préparatoires* leave the HRC with the flexibility to develop and apply its own understanding of 'arbitrary' on a case-by-case basis. There seems to be no ordinary meaning or clear evidence from the *travaux préparatoires* to restrict that flexibility.[162]

8.22.1 The HRC has recently completed a General Comment on article 17 of the Covenant.[163] In that General Comment the HRC gave some definition to the terms of article 17:

The term 'unlawful' means that no interference can take place except in cases envisaged by the law. Interference authorized by States can only take place on the basis of law, which itself must comply with the provisions, aims and objectives of the Covenant.

The expression 'arbitrary interference' is also relevant to the protection of the right provided for in article 17. In the Committee's view the expression 'arbitrary interference' can also extend to interference provided for under the law. The introduction of the concept of arbitrariness is intended to guarantee that even interference provided for by law should be in accordance with the provisions, aims and objectives of the Covenant and should be, in any event, reasonable in the particular circumstances.[164]

This interpretation of 'arbitrary' as having an autonomous, Covenant meaning is of immense importance.[165] The term clearly goes beyond what is lawful under national laws. This definition is consistent with the approach of the HRC to the interpretation of article 6 under the OP, for example in the *Guerrero Case*, discussed above.[166]

8.23 In *Baboeram and Others* v. *Suriname*[167] the HRC had to consider a notorious incident in which fourteen persons were arrested, subjected to violence, and executed.[168] The State party argued that a coup attempt had been foiled and that a number of arrested persons had been killed while trying to escape.[169] After repeating part of its General Comment on article 6,[170] the HRC took the same view as in the *Guerrero Case*[171] that, 'it was evident from the fact that 15 prominent persons had lost their lives as a result of deliberate action by the military police that the deprivation of life was intentional.[172] The State party has failed to submit any evidence proving that these persons were shot while trying to escape.'[173] Thus the HRC took the view that the victims were arbitrarily deprived of their life in violation of article 6(1).[174] As regards the 'intentional' deprivation of life the same comments as in the *Guerrero Case* apply.[175] It is also interesting to note the HRC using its general comments under article 40(4) of the Covenant in a view under the Optional Protocol.

8.24 The HRC has had to consider the problems of disappearances and killings. In *Herrera Rubio* v. *Colombia*[176] H.R. was allegedly arrested and tortured by Colombian military authorities, who also threatened him that unless he signed a confession his parents would be killed. Subsequently persons in civilian clothes and others wearing military uniforms, identifying themselves as members of the counter-guerrillas, went to the home of H.R.'s parents and took them away by force. A week later the corpses of H.R.'s parents were discovered. A judicial investigation was carried out concerning the killings which the State party claimed established that no member of the Armed Forces had taken part in the killings.[177] As regards article 6 the HRC expressed the following view:

Whereas the Committee considers that there is reason to believe, in the light of the author's allegations, that Colombian military persons bear responsibility for the deaths of José Herrera and Emma Rubio de Herrera, no conclusive evidence has been produced to establish the identity of the murderers. In this connection the Committee refers to its general comment 6(16) concerning article 6 of the Covenant, which provides *inter alia*, that States parties should take specific and effective measures to prevent the disappearance of individuals and establish effective facilities and procedures to investigate thoroughly, by an appropriate impartial body, cases of missing and disappeared persons in circumstances which may involve a violation of the right to life. The Committee has duly noted the State party's submissions concerning the investigations carried out in this case which, however, appear to have been inadequate in the light of the State party's obligations under article 2 of the Covenant.[178]

On this basis the HRC expressed the view that there had been a violation of 'article 6, because the State party failed to take appropriate measures to prevent the disappearance and subsequent killing of José Herrera and Emma Rubio de Herrera and to effectively investigate the responsibility for their murders'.[179] The HRC stated that the obligations on the State party included further investigation of the offences.[180]

The HRC's view is interesting in a number of respects. First, it clearly suggests that there is a preventative or positive aspect to the right to life.[181] Unfortunately it does not indicate what the HRC considered the appropriate measures the State party could have taken to prevent the disappearance and killing of H.R.'s parents. This is a particularly important omission when, as will usually be the case, the State party denies the involvement of official personnel in the incidents concerned. In such circumstances the HRC's view that the responsibility for murders must be thoroughly and effectively investigated, and that it is competent to determine the adequacy of those investigations, assumes critical importance.[182] Again, however, the HRC is open to criticism for not being more specific as to the particular inadequacies of the investigation and not elucidating on a State party's obligations under article 2 of the Covenant.[183]

8.24.1 In *Miango* v. *Zaïre*[184] M was allegedly kidnapped, taken to a military camp, and tortured. M was later seen in a precarious physical condition in a hospital at Kinshasa. M's relatives were subsequently brought to the hospital to identify M's body. The explanation in the report of the traffic police was that M died as a result of a traffic accident. The HRC did not accept this. They preferred the explanation in a report by a forensic physician that M had died as a result of traumatic wounds probably caused by a blunt instrument. The author's family had requested the public prosecutor's office to conduct an inquiry into the death of M, and in particular that the military officer who delivered M to the hospital be summoned for questioning. However, the officer concerned, with the consent of his superiors, had refused to be questioned.[185]

After noting the failure of the State party to furnish any information and clarifications concerning the matter in accordance with the duty in article 4(2) of the Optional Protocol[186] the HRC expressed the view that the facts disclosed a violation of article 6(1) of the Covenant. However, the HRC made no attempt to explain this violation, for example, in terms of the responsibility to account for persons held in official custody[187] or in terms of the obligation thoroughly and effectively to investigate the responsibility for murders.[188]

8.25 The most significant decision of the HRC concerning article 6 is perhaps that in *Mbenge* v. *Zaïre*.[189] M, a Zaïrian citizen and former Governor of the Shaba region, left Zaïre in 1974 and thereafter resided in Belgium as a political refugee. In his absence he was twice sentenced to capital punishment by Zaïrian tribunals. The HRC examined the information before it and expressed the view that the facts disclosed violations, *inter alia*, of articles 14(3)(*a*), (*b*), (*d*), and (*e*) because M was charged, tried, and convicted in circumstances in which he could not effectively enjoy the safeguards of due process enshrined in those provisions.[190] This aspect of the decision is dealt with elsewhere.[191] M had also alleged a breach of article 6. On this the HRC expressed the view that,

Paragraph 2 of that article provides that the sentence of death may be imposed only 'in accordance with the law (of the State party) in force at the time of the commission of the crime and not contrary to the provisions of the Covenant'. This requires that both the substantive and the procedural law in the application of which the death penalty was imposed was not contrary to the provisions of the Covenant and also that the death penalty was imposed in accordance with that law and therefore in accordance with the provisions of the Covenant. Consequently, the failure of the State party to respect the relevant requirements of article 14(3) leads to the conclusion that the death sentences pronounced against the author of the communication were imposed contrary to the provisions of the Covenant, and therefore in violation of article 6(2).[192]

It is understood that before reaching this decision the HRC referred to the *travaux préparatoires* to ascertain whether it was the intention of the drafters to etablish this double protection aspect in relation to article 6 of the Covenant. Certain members of the HRC were only willing to accept this interpretation after that referral. It is unfortunate that in its expression of views the HRC does not acknowledge this referral and thereby facilitate a more informed understanding of how a particular interpretation was adopted.[193]

In terms of the decision itself the HRC states that the failure of the substantive or procedural law of a State party to comply with any provision of the Covenant will render any death penalty imposed a violation of article 6(2). Considering the wide range of rights protected by the Covenant the HRC's decision is of enormous significance. Thus, for example, a death penalty might violate article 6(2) if it were imposed in a discriminatory manner (articles 2, 3, 26),[194] if the mode of execution were inhuman or degrading (article 7),[195] if it were imposed on a person who had been arbitrarily arrested or detained (article 9), if imposed after a trial which did not satisfy all the demands of article 14,[196] if the evidence to ground the conviction had been obtained in violation of the person's right to privacy (article 17), if the crime concerned a freedom guaranteed by the Covenant, for example, if the death penalty was imposed for some of the vague generalized offences noted during the consideration of article 6 under the reporting process.[197] The HRC's approach accords with that of the Supreme Courts of the United States[198] and India[199] but the EUCT has yet to rule on this question.[200]

In *Mbenge*[201] M claimed that he had been the victim of purely politically motivated and substantially unfounded charges. The HRC expressed no view on these allegations because of lack of sufficient information.[202] On its approach to article 6(2) a death penalty imposed for political reasons would violate article 6(2) if the HRC were of the view that the substantive or procedural law of the State breached any provisions of the Covenant, for example, article 2, 3, or 26.[203]

8.26 In *Lafuente Penarrieta et al.* v. *Bolivia*[204] the authors alleged that there had been a violation, *inter alia*, of article 6(4) because, notwithstanding a Presidential Decree granting them an amnesty, the alleged victims were not released.[205] Although the HRC referred to this matter in its finding of facts it inexplicably expressed no view in respect of it.[206]

8.26.1 In *EHP* v. *Canada* (SD2, p. 20) the authors alleged that the storage of radioactive waste near their residences threatened the right to life of present and future generations in the area. The HRC stated that the communication raised 'serious issues with regard to the obligation of States parties to protect human life'. The communication was declared inadmissible for non-exhaustion of domestic remedies.

APPRAISAL

8.27 Under the reporting procedure the HRC has interpreted article 6 as encompassing wide-ranging positive obligations, some of which are clearly of a progressive nature. For example, matters such as infant mortality, malnutrition, and public health schemes have been raised.[207] This approach was echoed in the collective opinion of the HRC as expressed in its first General Comment on article 6.[208] Views under the Optional Protocol have also suggested that there is a preventative or positive aspect to article 6.[209] While many academic commentators have pressed for a liberal and positive interpretation of the right to life,[210] in the context of the ECHR Professor Fawcett has stressed,'the fact that it is not life, but the right to life, which is to be protected by law'.[211] If a liberal interpretation is given to the right to life this inevitably introduces the concept of progressive obligations into the Covenant.[212] It also inevitably leads to some overlapping between civil and political and social and economic rights.[213] This in turn raises the question of the applicability of the Optional Protocol procedure to a liberally interpreted right to life. For example, how would the HRC respond if a communication alleged a violation of the right to life on the basis of the failure of the State authorities to reduce infant mortality or reduce malnutrition?[214] The matter could hardly be declared inadmissible *ratione materiae*[215] in the light of its practice under the reporting procedure and its first General Comment on article 6.[216] What would be the nature of the obligation of a State party? Who could petition the HRC as a victim? How, if at all, could the process of causation be established? The much debated general problem concerns the justiciability of economic and social rights.[217] The EUCT has had to deal with cases involving overlaps between the ECHR and the European Social Charter in matters of trade union rights and illegitimate children.[218]

8.28 The duty of any human rights organ in the interpretation of human rights guarantees is to approach its task in good faith and to interpret in accordance with the general rules of treaty interpretation.[219] If that approach results in rights being interpreted to contain obligations that were not realized or perhaps even not intended by the drafters no reproach may be levelled at the interpreting organ.[220] The danger of too positive and liberal an interpretation of rights is that it may leave States parties uncertain of their obligations and discourage other States from undertaking the obligations at all. Similarly, States parties may balk at the indirect introduction of aspects of social and economic rights into a petitions system when this was clearly contrary to their intentions.[221]

The liberal interpretation of article 6 is also manifested in the HRC's general comments concerning the right to life and war, and in particular, thermo-nuclear war.[222] We have already considered those general comments.[223]

8.29 Already within the small number of cases it has considered the HRC has had to deal with some important aspects of article 6. There is a 'clear duty' to make full, thorough, and effective inquiries concerning alleged violations.[224] The HRC will state that there are 'serious reasons' to believe that article 6 has been violated even if it cannot be conclusively proved.[225] There are obligations to account for and to take 'adequate' or 'appropriate' measures to 'protect' the life of persons held in custody.[226] There are obligations, though not spelt out, to prevent the disappearance and killing of potential victims.[227] There are various obligations attendant upon a finding of a violation of the right to life, for example, to compensate the family[228] and to amend a law which does not adequately protect the right to life.[229] More specifically, in interpreting 'arbitrarily' the HRC has introduced the concepts of intention, necessity, proportionality to the requirements of law enforcement, and justification.[230] The General Comment on article 17 supports an autonomous interpretation on 'arbitrary'.[231] The HRC has interpreted article 6(2) as requiring that the substantive and procedural laws in the application of which a death penalty is imposed are not contrary to the provisions in the Covenant.[232] Finally, the HRC has made use of its general comments and stressed that the right to life is the 'supreme right'[233] and that article 6 requires strict controls and limitations on the circumstances on which a person may be deprived of life by the authorities of the State.[234]

NOTES

1   The right to life is also recognized in art. 3 UDHR, art. 2 ECHR, art. 1 ADRD, art. 4 AMR, art. 4 AFR. On the drafting of article 6 see in general Docs. A/2929, ch. 6, prs. 1–10, A/3764, prs. 85–121; Bossuyt, *Guide*, pp. 113–46. On the right to life see Amnesty International, *Political Killings by Governments* (1983); Y. Dinstein, 'The Right to Life, Physical Integrity and Liberty', in L. Henkin (ed.), *The International Bill of Rights—The ICCPR*, pp. 114–27 (1981); G. P. Fletcher, 'The Right to Life', 13 Georgia Law Review (1979) pp. 1371–94; E. Lane, 'Mass Killings by Governments: Lawful in the World Legal Order?', 12 NYUJILP (1979) pp. 239–80; L. E. Landerer, 'Capital Punishment as a Human Rights Issue before the United Nations', 4 RDH/HRJ (1971) pp. 511–34; R. Lillich, 'Civil Rights', in T. Meron (ed.), *Human Rights in International Law*, p. 115 at pp. 120–4 (1984); L. J. MacFarlane, *The Theory and Practice of Human Rights*, ch. 2 (1985); F. Przetacznik, 'The Right to Life as a Basic Human Right', 9 RDH/HRJ (1976) pp. 585–609; B. G. Ramcharan, 'The Right to Life', 30 NILR (1983) pp. 297–329; B. G. Ramcharan (ed.), *The Right to Life in International Law* (1985); N. Rodley, *The Treatment of Prisoners under International Law*, chs. 6–8 (1987); P. Sieghart, *The International Law of Human Rights*, pp. 128–35 (1983); *UN Action in the Field of Human Rights*, pp. 184–90 (1988); Reports of UN Rapporteur, nn. 7 and 35 below; ECOSOC Safeguards Guaranteeing Protection of the Rights of Those Facing the Death Penalty, ECOSOC Resn. 1984/50, ECOSOC 'Principles on the Effective Protection and Investigation of Extra-Legal, Arbitrary and Summary Executions', ECOSOC Resn. 1989/65, endorsed by the GA in Resn. 44/144. The GA has recently adopted a second Optional Protocol to the ICCPR aimed at abolishing the death penalty, see GA Resn. 44/

128 (15 Dec. 1989), text in Apx. IV below. Cf. Protocol No. 6 to the ECHR, in *ECHR—Collected Texts*, pp. 46–9 (1987).

2 Many of the commentators in n. 1 above suggest that the right to life is part of customary international law.

3 GC 6(16), Doc. A/37/40, pp. 93–4; also in Doc. CCPR/C/21/Add. 1. Adopted by the HRC at its 378th meeting (July 1982). For the HRC's discussion see SR 369, 370, 371, and 378 Add. 1.

4 See article 4 of the ICCPR, which is dealt with in ch. 7 above. Cf. article 15 ECHR. Professor Gormley has argued that the right to life in article 6(1) represents *jus cogens*, see W. P. Gormley, 'The Right to Life and the Rule of Non-Derogability: Peremptory Norms of Jus Cogens', in Ramcharan (1985),n. 1 above, pp. 120–59.

5 See *Human Rights—Status of International Instruments*, p. 88 n. 8 (1987).

6 GC 6(16), n. 3 above; GC 14(23), Doc. A/40/40, pp. 162–3; also in Doc. CCPR/C/21/Add. 4. Adopted by the HRC at its 563rd meeting (November 1984).

7 See *UN Action*, n. 1 above; Reports of the Special Rapporteur of the Human Rights Commission on Summary or Arbitrary Executions, latest reports, Docs. E/CN.4/1987/20, E/CN.4/1988/22 and Add. 1 and 2, E/CN.4/1989/25, E/CN.4/1990/22 and Corr. 1, which includes, ECOSOC Resn. 1989/25, n. 1 above; E. Lane, n. 1 above; E. Kaufman and P. Weiss Fagen, 'Extrajudicial Executions: An Insight into the Global Dimensions of a Human Rights Violation', 3 HRQ (1981) pp. 81–100; HRCion Resn. 1989/64.

8 See in particular the works by Ramcharan, n. 1 above.

9 See chs. 9–12 below.

10 SR 67 pr. 78, during consideration of the report of the GDR. Cf. the decision of the Indian Supreme Court in n. 20 below.

11 GC 6(16), n. 3 above, prs. 1, 5 (my emphasis). A number of other general comments make reference to the requirement on States to take positive measures, see e.g. ch. 6, prs. 6.11–6.12 above on article 2. The HRC again referred to the reduction of infant mortality and malnutrition in its General Comment on article 24 (rights of children), see GC 17 (35), pr. 3, in Doc. A/44/40, p. 173 cited in ch. 6, pr. 6.12, text to n. 53 above. See also SR 30 pr. 32 (Tomuschat on Finland) who contrasts the respective obligations (art. 2) under the two international Covenants. On art. 2 of the ICCPR see ch. 6 above. See also F. Menghistu, 'The Satisfaction of Survival Requirements', in Ramcharan (ed.), n. 1 above, pp. 63–83.

12 See text to preceding note. For examples of inadequate information see the reports of Portugal (Doc. C/C/6/Add. 6) and Jordan (Doc. C/1/Add. 24). For much more adequate information see the reports of Canada (Doc. C/1/Add. 43) and the second periodic report of Australia (Doc. C/42/Add. 2 (1987). The information in the latter covers criminal law, murder, manslaughter/negligent driving, abortion, suicide, aboriginal customary law, penalties, emergency medical treatment, civil law, AIDS, capital punishment, and genocide.

13 See Ramcharan, n. 1 above (1983); H. A. Kabaalioglu, 'The Obligations to 'Respect' and to 'Ensure' the Right to Life', in Ramcharan (ed.), n. 1 above, pp. 160–81; A. Redelbach, 'Protection of the Right to Life by Law and Other Means', ibid., pp. 182–220.

14 SR 443 pr. 55.
15 See e.g. SR 65 pr. 31 (Graefrath on Czechoslovakia), and GC 6(16), in pr. 8.3 above. For examples of States parties responding to requests for such information see e.g. Hungarian Report, Doc. CCPR/C/1/Add. 44; Syrian Report, Doc. CCPR/C/1/Add. 31. A criteria of assessment often used in the PQI Index, see e.g. J. I. Dominguez, 'Assessing Human Rights Conditions', in J. I. Dominguez *et al.*, *Enhancing Global Human Rights*, pp. 21–116 (1979).
16 See e.g. SR 54 pr. 90 (Graefrath on Finland); SR 92 pr. 52 (Graefrath on FRG); SR 199 pr. 10 (Hanga on Iraq); SR 257 pr. 38 (Hanga on Italy); SR 319 pr. 27 (Graefrath), 52 (Hanga on Japan); SR 386 pr. 32 (Graefrath on Mexico); SR 431 pr. 21 (Cooray on Peru); SR 441 pr. 36 (Graefrath on France); SR 845 pr. 13 (Lallah on Norway). See generally K. Tomasevski and P. Alston (eds.), *The Right to Food* (1984); K. Tomasevski, *The Right to Food: Guide through Applicable International Law* (1987); R. J. Dupuy (ed.), *The Right to Health as a Human Right* (1979). See also HRCion Resn. 1989/42 on the 'Movement and dumping of toxic and dangerous products and wastes'.
17 UKTS 6 (1977). See ch. 1, pr. 1.16 above, and Scott, ch. 4 n. 424 above.
18 See article 2 ICESCR, n. 17 above.
19 See ch. 1, pr. 1.16 and ch. 6, prs. 6.11–6.12 above.
20 It is interesting to speculate how the HRC would have responded to the alleged violations of the right to life in the decision of the Indian Supreme Court in *Tellis and Others* v. *Bombay Municipal Corporation and Others* [1987] LRC (Const) 351. 'The right to life . . . includes the right to livelihood', ibid., p. 371.
21 See ch. 6, n. 55 above and the cases cited in article 6 under the OP, below.
22 See e.g. SR 412 pr. 5 (Herdocia-Ortega on Austria), reply at SR 416 pr. 25; SR 391 pr. 40 (Prado-Vallejo on Iceland). Where abortion has been dealt with it has sometimes been linked to articles 23 and 24 of the Covenant, see Apx. I below, or to the more general question of the role of women in society, see e.g. SR 897 pr. 16 (Dimitrijevic on Bolivia). In July 1989 the HRC deleted a question on abortion from its list of issues concerning the Italian report but without prejudice to it being raised by any individual member of the HRC. The issue was raised with the Italian representatives, see SR 909. See also J. K. Mason and R. A. McCall Smith, *Law and Medical Ethics*, ch. 5 (2d, 1987); T. Ritterspach, 'Abortion Law in Italy', 5 HRLJ (1984) pp. 385–8.
23 See Mason and McCall Smith, op. cit., ch. 15.
24 See Lillich, n. 1 above, pp. 123–4.
25 See Doc. E/CN.4/SR.140 pr. 11; E/CN.4/SR.149 prs. 10–11; Doc. A/3764, pr. 113. Cf. article 4(4) AMR which provides that the right to life exists, 'in general, from the moment of conception'. See the *Baby Boy Case*, IACM, Case No. 2141 (United States), 2 HRLJ (1981) 110. The ECHR does not expressly cover the point but see A. 867/60, *X* v. *Norway*, 4 YBECHR p. 270; A.6959/75, *Bruggemann and Scheuten* v. *FRG*, 5 D. & R. p. 103, in which the EUCM noted article 6(5) ICCPR, and A.8416/79, *X.* v. *UK*, 19 D. & R. p. 244 (1980).
26 For some support for this view see SR 369 prs. 22, 33, 26 and SR 370 pr. 12. Part of the draft General Comment on article 6, which was not kept in the final version, reads, 'The Committee notes, on the other hand, that the extent of the protection

of the right to life of the unborn is a controversial issue in many States parties and cannot be resolved by reference to this article. This would also appear to be the position as regards voluntary euthanasia and, in particular, when death is permitted to take its natural course'. No explanation appears of why this text was dropped but it is submitted that its omission was more concerned with not prejudging the question rather than saying that the Covenant provides no assistance at all. See Graefrath, ch. 6 n. 1 above (1984–5), p. 6, who comments on abortion, 'Obviously, this cannot be decided by invoking article 6 of the Covenant'. The jurisprudence under the ECHR would suggest that the right to privacy (art. 17 Covenant) would also be relevant to the determination of such issues. See *Bruggemann and Scheuten Case*, n. 25 above. Similarly the US approach in *Roe* v. *Wade*, 93 S.Ct. 705 (1973). For a recent US Supreme Court ruling see *Webster* v. *Reproductive Health Services*, 57 USLW 5023 (1989). See also *Borowski* v. *Attorney-General of Canada* (1983) DLR (4th) 112 and *R.* v. *Morgentaler* (1988) 44 DLR (4th) 385.

27 SR 258 pr. 58 commenting on the Italian Report, Doc. C/6/Add. 4, pr. 29. Similarly at SR 110 pr. 19, SR 292 prs. 9–10, SR 369 pr. 25 (on Portugal). For a parallel example concerning euthanasia see the critical remarks at SR 222 pr. 6 and SR 223 pr. 5 on a provision of the Colombian Penal Code permitting mitigation of sentence in the case of mercy killings.

28 See e.g. SR 206 pr. 11 (Bouziri on Canada); SR 439 pr. 29 (Bouziri on France); SR 481 pr. 41 (Bouziri on New Zealand).

29 See n. 26 above on these cases. Article 17 is not dealt with in this thesis. The HRC's General Comment on article 17 makes no reference to abortion or euthanasia, Doc. A/43/40, p. 181.

30 See the decision in the *Matter of Quinlan*, Supreme Court of New Jersey, 70 NJ 10, 355 A 2d 664 (1976). See also *Cruzan* v. *Missouri Dept. of Health*, 110 S.Ct. 2841 (1990).

31 See SR 551 pr. 110 (Bouziri on Trinidad and Tobago).

32 GC 6(16), n. 3 above, pr. 3. The GC was echoed in the HRC's views in the *Guerrero Case*, prs. 8.17–8.20 below.

33 See e.g. SR 65 pr. 2 (Tomuschat on Czechoslovakia); SR 67 pr. 60 (Tomuschat on GDR); SR 92 pr. 31 (Opsahl on FRG); SR 155 pr. 9 (Ukranian SSR); SR 110 pr. 18 (Opsahl on Mauritius); SR 292 pr. 18 (Tarnopolsky on Jamaica); SR 353 pr. 20 (Vincent-Evans on Guyana); SR 431 pr. 66 (Opsahl on Peru); ch. 7, pr. 7.32, n. 112, 113 above (on UK). On the use of force by security forces in Northern Ireland see K. Asmal (Chairman), *Shoot to Kill—International Lawyers' Inquiry* (1985); R. Spjut, 'The "Official" Use of Deadly Force by the Security Services against Suspected Terrorists: Some Lessons from Northern Ireland' [1986] PL pp. 38–64. During consideration of the report of the UK for the Dependent Territories Mr Lallah asked the UK representatives for more details on the deaths of three Irishmen in Gibraltar, including the results of any inquiry, SR 856 pr. 70, reply at pr. 72.

34 SR 533 prs. 16 (Ermacora), 18 (Tomuschat on GDR); reply at SR 534 pr. 1–6.

35 See e.g. SR 128 pr. 69 (Vincent-Evans on Chile); SR 421 pr. 16 (Ermacora on Nicaragua); SR 468 pr. 28 (Prado-Vallejo on El Salvador); SR 421 pr. 16

(Ermacora on Nicaragua); SR 475 pr. 35 (Aguilar on Mali); SR 364 pr. 73 (Vincent-Evans on Iran); SR 878 pr. 21 (Chanet on Uruguay). The massacres at the Sabra and Chatila camps in the Lebanon were raised by a number of members, see SR 443 prs. 8 (Vincent-Evans), 22 (Bouziri), 39 (Ermacora), 42 as corrected (Errera), 55 (Tomuschat), SR 446 pr. 19 (State representative). Generally see Rodley, n. 1 above, chs. 6 and 8; N. Rodley, 'U.N. Action against "Disappearances", Summary or Arbitrary Executions and Torture', 8 HRQ (1986) pp. 700–30; D. Kramer and D. Weissbrodt, 'The 1980 U.N. Commission on Human Rights and the Disappeared', 3 HRQ (1981) pp. 18–33; 10th Report of the HRCion Working Group on Enforced or Involuntary Disappearances, UN Doc. E/CN.4/1990/13. E. Kaufman and P. Weiss Fagen, n. 7 above; Reports of the UN Special Rapporteur, n. 7 above, Docs. E/CN.4/1983/16 and Add. 1 and Add. 1, Corr. 1; E/CN.4/1984/29; E/CN.4/1985/17; E/CN.4/1986/21, n. 7 above; D. Weissbrodt, 'Protecting the Right to Life: International Measures against Arbitrary or Summary Killings by Governments', in Ramcharan (ed.), n. 1 above, pp. 297–314. See also pr. 8.24 below.

36 See the discussion concerning questions raised during consideration of the second periodic report of Iraq, SR 746 prs. 6 (Higgins), 17 (State representative), 19–20 (Lallah), 21 (Pocar), SR 747 pr. 1 (Lallah).

37 GC 6(16), n. 3 above, pr. 4. See e.g. SR 469 pr. 37 (Dimitrijevic on El Salvador).

38 SR 472 pr. 9 (Vincent-Evans), pr. 29 (Errera); reply at SR 477 prs. 26–7.

39 See e.g. SR 356 pr. 15 (Tarnopolsky on Chile referring to reports of the IACM; reply at SR 359 pr. 12; SR 421 pr. 16 (Ermacora on Nicaragua); SR 746 pr. 19 (Lallah on Iraq referring to the report of the Special UN Rapporteur). During consideration of the report of Chile members made constant reference to the reports of the *Ad Hoc* Working Group of the HRCion and to UN resolutions.

40 See e.g. SR 354 pr. 18 (Tarnopolsky on Guyana concerning the death of Walter Rodney, a political activist); SR. 128 pr. 10 (Graefrath on Chile concerning the assassination of Orlando Letelier); SR 475 pr. 46 (Tomuschat on Guinea concerning the death of Dialo Telli, former Secretary-General of the OAU, caused by the so-called 'black-death' or starvation diet); SR 709 pr. 18 (Dimitrijevic on Poland referring to the killing of Father Popieluszko).

41 See e.g. SR 364 pr. 76 and 365 pr. 7 concerning the alleged execution of a number of leaders of the Bahai' faith in Iran; reply at SR 368 prs. 11, 53; SR 472 pr. 15 (Ermacora on Sri Lanka); SR 431 pr. 8 (Tarnpolsky on Peru).

42 See e.g. SR 355 pr. 29 (Uruguay).

43 See e.g. SR 469 pr. 32 (Graefrath on El Salvador); SR 746 pr. 6 (Higgins on Iraq); SR 354 pr. 188 (Tarnopolsky on Guyana concerning the mass killings at the Jonestown religious community). See also 128 pr. 32 (Tomuschat on Chile) on the jeopardizing of a persons health or life by a penalty of banishment.

44 See pr. 8.24 below.

45 See I. Brownlie, *Systems of the Laws of Nations—State Reponsibility*, Part I, chs. 7 and 8 (1983).

46 See *The Death Penalty*, Amnesty International Report (1979); D. Pannick, *Judicial Review of the Death Penalty* (1982); Landerer, n. 1 above; Rodley, n. 1

above, ch. 7; R. Sapienza, 'International Legal Standards on Capital Punishment', in Ramcharan (ed.), n. 1 above, pp. 284–96; *Advisory Opinion of the IACT on Restrictions to the Death Penalty* (arts. 4(2) and (4) AMR), Advisory Opinion OC-3/83, (Sept. 1983), 4 HRLJ (1983) p. 345–63. See now OP2 in Apx. IV below.

47 During the drafting the phrase 'most serious crimes' was criticized as lacking legal precision, since the concept of 'serious crime' differed from one country to another, Doc. A/2929, ch. 6, pr. 6.

48 This limitation is a specific application of the general principle in article 15 ICCPR.

49 For example, imposed in an inhuman or degrading manner contrary to article 7 ICCPR. Cf. the joint dissenting judgment of Lord Scarman and Lord Brightman in *Riley and Others* v. *Attorney-General of Jamaica*, [1983] 1 AC 719. Similarly if the death penalty is imposed after proceedings which do not comply with article 14 of the ICCPR, see *Mbenge* v. *Zaïre*, pr. 8.25 below.

50 Convention on the Prevention and Punishment of the Crime of Genocide, 1948, UKTS 58 (1970); 78 UNTS 277.

51 The word 'competent' also appears in article 14 of the ICCPR, see ch. 10 below.

52 See SR 402 pr. 18 (Prado-Vallejo on Australia). Cf. article 4(5) AMR prohibits the imposition of capital punishment where the person was under 18 years of age at the time the crime was committed. Cf. *Roach and Pinkerton* v. *United States*, Case No. 9647, IACM, 8 HRLJ (1988) pp. 145–55.

53 The text does not make it clear whether it would be permissible to carry out the death penalty on the mother after the child is born. The point was raised but not resolved during the drafting, Doc. A/2929, n. 1 above, pr. 10. Even if not prohibited by article 6(5) such action might constitute inhuman treatment with respect to both the mother and the child. See SR 468 pr. 29 (Prado-Vallejo on El Salvador); SR 443 pr. 25 (Bouziri on Lebanon). Cf. art. 4(5) AMR. See also Meron, ch. 6 n. 1 above, pp. 99–100.

54 See pr. 8.5 above.

55 GC 6(16), n. 3 above, pr. 6. Other general comments have called for the review of applicable laws, e.g. GC 4(13) pr. 4 on article 3, Doc. A/36/40, pp. 109–10. See also the Preamble to OP2.

56 GC 6(16), n. 3 above, pr. 7. This interpretation has though been present since the inception of the HRC's work. See n. 47 above.

57 SR 482 pr. 22 (Prado-Vallejo on New Zealand). Cf. art. 4(3) AMR which forbids the re-establishment of the death penalty in States which have abolished it.

58 SR 117 pr. 40 (Tomuschat on Belorussian SSR).

59 SR 198 pr. 8 (Bouziri on Mongolia); reply at SR 202 prs. 6–7.

60 SR 64 pr. 38 (Tarnopolsky on Czechoslovakia).

61 SR 364 prs. 38 (Sadi), 56 (Opsahl) on Iran.

62 SR 135 pr. 54 (Vincent-Evans), SR 136 pr. 28 (Sadi on Romania).

63 SR 200 pr. 19 (Opsahl on Iraq). See also SR 746 pr. 5 (Higgins on Iraq concerning the death penalty for Zionists and Freemasons). Cf. art. 4(4) AMR, 'In no case shall capital punishment be inflicted for political offences or related common crimes'.

64 See SR 322 pr. 68 (Tomuschat on the Netherlands); reply at SR 325 pr. 19.

65 SR 364 pr. 39 (Sadi), SR 365 pr. 8 (Tarnopolsky on Iran).

66 SR 257 pr. 70 (Sadi on Italy).

67 See e.g. SR 366 pr. 15 (Tomuschat on Iran). Cf. *Restrictions of the Rights and Freedoms of the American Convention—The Word 'Laws' in Article 30*, Advisory Opinion No. OC-6/86 of the IACT, 7 HRLJ (1986) pp. 231–67.

68 See e.g. SR 283 pr. 11 (Tarnopolsky on Mali); SR 735 pr. 4 (Mommersteeg on Zaïre).

69 The principle of proportionality would demand that the death sentence should only be the penalty for the most serious of crimes. It might also require that it not be the mandatory penalty.

70 See e.g. SR 364 pr. 73 (Vincent-Evans on Iran).

71 GC 6(16), n. 3 above, pr. 7. See the *Mbenge Case*, pr. 8.25 below.

72 For some exceptional cases see the consideration of the reports of Chile, SR 127–30; of Iran, SR 364–6, 368.

73 'The information from various official sources ... pointed to the existence of genocide in El Salvador', SR 474 pr. 4 (Movchan on El Salvador); reply, ibid., pr. 5. On Genocide see L. Kuper, 'Genocide and Mass Killings: Illusion and Reality', in Ramcharan (ed.), n. 1 above, pp. 114–19.

74 Doc. E/CN.4/1310.

75 SR 128 pr. 5. See *Judgement on Human Rights Violations by Former Military Leaders (Argentina)*, 26 ILM (1987) pp. 317–72. See L. Joinet, 'Amnesty Laws', 35 Rev. ICJ (1985) pp. 27–30.

76 A new President was elected in Chile in December 1989 but General Pinochet remains head of the armed forces. Note also the comment of Professor Higgins, 'she felt that it was for a democratically elected Government to declare a general amnesty and not the Government responsible for the violations', SR 945 pr. 61 (on Chile).

77 See Joinet, n. 75 above, pp. 28–30.

78 See e.g. SR 292 pr. 18 (Tarnopolsky on Jamaica).

79 See e.g. SR 197 pr. 17 (Vincent-Evans on Mongolia).

80 GC 6/16, n. 3 above, pr. 6.

81 SR 414 pr. 21 (Hanga, referring to general disarmament).

82 Cf. the reference to the 'scourge of war' in the preamble to the United Nations Charter.

83 See *Military and Paramilitary Activities in and Against Nicaragua (Nicaragua v. U.S.)*, Merits, 1986 ICJ Rep. p. 14.

84 GC 6(16), n. 3 above, pr. 2. On article 20 see ch. 12 below. See also SR 414 pr. 21 (Hanga on general disarmament).

85 GC 14(23), n. 6 above, prs. 2–7 (my emphasis).

86 See SR 545 pr. 15. The HRC sent the General Comment straight to the General Assembly in view of its importance, Doc. A/40/40, pr. 683.

87 See SR 571 prs. 2–7 (Errera). See also SR 563 pr. 6 (Ermacora).

88 See Doc. A/C.3/39/SR.46, 48, 49, 50, 51.

89 The issue has been dealt with more often since the adoption of the second General Comment. See e.g. SR 532 pr. 65 (GDR State representative). See also SR 533 pr. 13 (Prado-Vallejo on GDR on the 'right to live in peace').

90 See e.g. GA Resn. 37/189A (18 Dec. 1982). See also HRCion Resn. 1982/7 (19 Dec. 1982).

91 See ch. 5, prs. 5.4, 5.11 above. We also noted that nuclear testing by France has been raised but in context of article 1, see ibid., pr. 5.10.

92 See ch. 5 n. 111 above. See also P. J. M. De Waart, 'The Inter-Relationship between the Right to Life and the Right to Development', in Ramcharan (ed), n. 1 above, pp. 84–96; A. A. Tikhonov, 'The Inter-Relationship between the Right to Life and the Right to Peace', ibid., pp. 97–113; Brown Weiss, ch. 4 n. 471 above.

93 See C. C. Morrisson, *The Dynamics of Development in the European Human Rights Convention System* (1981).

94 One of the objections of Errera, n. 87 above, was this reference to non-States parties.

95 See ch. 6, prs. 6.11–6.13 above on art. 2 of the Covenant.

96 Ibid.

97 The Charter is annexed to the Agreement for the Establishment of an International Military Tribunal, UKTS 4 (1945); 5 UNTS 251. See also GA Resn. 95(1), GAOR Resolutions, First Session, Part II, p. 188, affirming the principles of international law recognized by the Charter and the judgment of the Tribunal.

98 See ch. 1, pr. 1.16 and ch. 6, prs. 6.11 above.

99 References to the UN Charter have appeared in other general comments, see e.g. the comment on article 1, see ch. 5, prs. 5.3, 5.17 above.

100 Doc. A/37/40, p. 130. See Rodley, n. 1 above, pp. 192–3.

101 Ibid., pr. 2.2.

102 Ibid., pr. 4.9.

103 Ibid., pr. 9. The authors were B's husband and father.

104 Ibid., pr. 11. See GC 6(16), pr. 4 in pr. 8.7, text to n. 37 above.

105 See ch. 4, prs. 4.28–4.33 above.

106 See e.g. the decisions in the *Janes Claim*, *US* v. *Mexico* (1926) 4 RIAA p. 82; *Noyes Claim*, *US* v. *Panama* (1933), 6 RIAA p. 308. See Brownlie, ch. 6 n. 1 above, ch. 23.

107 See ch. 4, pr. 4.4 above.

108 Doc. A/37/40, p. 130, pr. 11.2.

109 Ibid.

110 Ibid., pr. 12, noted at ch. 4, pr. 4.31 above.

111 Ibid., pr. 14. 'The IACM has said that where individuals have "disappeared" but the Government concerned refused to provide any information about them or about the progress of any investigations aimed at determining their whereabouts, it is legitimate to presume that the (American Declaration on the Rights and Duties of Man) has been violated, and that agents of the Government, or individuals protected or tolerated by it, have not been uninvolved in the violation', Sieghart, n. 1 above, pp. 133–4, citing Cases 1702, 1745, and 1755 (Guatemala), IACM Annual Report (1975) p. 67. See *Velasquez Rodriguez* v. *Honduras*, IACT, Judgment of 29 July 1988, 9 HRLJ (1988) pp. 212–49; *Fairen Garbi and Solis Corrales* v. *Honduras*, IACT, Series C, No. 6 (1989). See also *Rubio* v. *Colombia*, pr. 8.24 below.

112 Doc. A/37/40, pr. 15. See also n. 123 below.

113 Doc. A/38/40, p. 124.

114 Doc. A/38/40, pr. 1.6. This regime was subjected to close analysis by HRC members under the article 40 reporting process. See also ICJ Study, ch. 7, n. 1 above, pp. 43–68 (1983).

115 It is not uncommon for such an offer to be made in Latin American countries.

116 See ch. 4, pr. 4.4 above.

117 Doc. A/38/40, p. 124, pr. 5.3.

118 Ibid., pr. 6.1.

119 Ibid., pr. 7.2.

120 Ibid., pr. 9.2.

121 Ibid., pr. 10(a).

122 See pr. 8.15 above.

123 See e.g. the *Quintanilla Claim, Mexico* v. *US* (1926) 4 RIAA p. 101; the *Turner Claim, US* v. *Mexico* (1927) 4 RIAA p. 278.

124 See ch. 4, prs. 4.27–4.33 above. See also *Sanjuan Aravelo* v. *Colombia*, Doc. A/45/40, Apx. Two brothers had disappeared in March 1982. None of the investigations had suggested that the disappearances had been caused by persons other than Government officials. The investigations and judicial procedures were continuing. The HRC expressed the view that the right to life and to liberty and security of the person had not been effectively protected by the State of Colombia. See also the individual opinion of Mr Ando in this case.

125 Doc. A/38/40, p. 124, pr. 11. See the cases cited in n. 123 above.

126 Doc. A/37/40, p. 137. See Rodley, n. 1 above, pp. 149–50. See also ch. 7, prs. 7.42–7.43 above.

127 Doc. A/37/40, p. 137, pr. 1.2.

128 Ibid., pr. 6.4. This Office was responsible for exercising judicial supervision over the system of military criminal justice with regard to proceedings against national police personnel.

129 Ibid., prs. 3.4, 6.5.

130 Ibid., prs. 1.4, 7.1, 7.2. The first criminal investigation was annulled as a result of an *ex officio* review by a Higher Military Court. The full text of Decree-Law No. 0070 is appended to the HRC's view, ibid., pp. 148–9.

131 Ibid., pr. 1.5.

132 Ibid., pr. 11.2.

133 Ibid., pr. 3.2 citing extracts from the Supreme Court's judgment. Cf. the ICJ Study, ch. 7, n. 1 above, pp. 53–4, which describes the effect of the Decree and the judgment as a 'licence to kill'.

134 Ibid., pr. 11.8.

135 Ibid., pr. 13.1.

136 See pr. 8.2 above at n. 3.

137 See pr. 8.6 above at n. 32.

138 GC 6.16, pr. 3, see pr. 8.6 above.

139 Doc. A/37/40, p. 137, prs. 13.2, 13.3 (my emphasis).

140 See Doc. A/2929, ch. 6, pr. 3; Doc. A/3746, pr. 94. See pr. 8.22.1 below on the General Comment on article 17.

141 The term 'intentionally' does appear in art. 2 ECHR. It is interesting to compare the decision of the HRC in *Guerrero* with the opinion of the EUCM in A.2758/66, *X* v. *Belgium*, admiss. decn., 12 YBECHR p. 174 (1969). The applicants husband, an innocent bystander, was killed by a bullet fired (it was assumed *arguendo*) at short range by a constable engaged in quelling a riot. The EUCM held that the Constable did not intend to kill and therefore did not violate article 2(1) and that his action could be justified as self-defence under article 2(2) ECHR. See also *Farrell* v. *UK*, EUCM, 5 EHRR 465; *Stewart* v. *UK*, EUCM, n. 181 below.

142 These circumstances are specifically provided for in article 2 ECHR. They were also among the exceptions proposed during the drafting of the Covenant. The exceptions proposed in the HRCion were: (*a*) execution of death sentence imposed in accordance with the law; (*b*) killing in self-defence or defence of another; (*c*) death resulting from action lawfully taken to suppress insurrection, rebellion, or riots; (*d*) killing in attempting to affect lawful arrest or preventing the escape of a person in lawful custody; (*e*) killing in the case of enforcement measures authorized by the Charter; (*f*) killing in defence of persons, property or State or in circumstances of grave civil commotion; (*g*) killing for violation of honour. For more details see Bossuyt, *Guide*, pp. 115-19.

143 The kidnapping of an ambassador, particularly if accompanied by death threats, might in some circumstances be viewed as a serious enough offence to justify lethal force if necessary, for example, to effect the arrest of the kidnappers. On the facts of the *Guerrero* case, however, the police action was clearly unnecessary. Cf. the decision of the Federal Constitutional Court of the FRG, B VerfGE 46 p. 160, cited in *UN Yearbook of Human Rights* 1977-8, p. 53 (1982), on the obligation of a State to protect human life where an individual has been abducted by terrorists.

144 Doc. A/38/40, p. 137.

145 Ibid., pr. 13.3. In the HRCion it was stated that the draft provision that 'everyone's right to life shall be protected by law' was intended to emphasize the duty of States to protect life, Doc. A/2929, ch. 6, pr. 4.

146 Ibid., pr. 15. According to the ICJ Study, ch. 7, n. 1 above, p. 67, the relevant law ceased to have effect when the state of siege was lifted in June 1982. Subsequent states of siege were imposed in 1984, see *Human Rights—Status of International Instruments*, pp. 60-2 (1987). Extra-judicial killings and disappearances continue while investigations are obstructed by death threats, see e.g. the accounts in the Amnesty International Annual Reports.

147 See n. 133 above.

148 Ibid.

149 See n. 142 above.

150 Doc. A/2929, ch. 6, pr. 2.

151 Ibid., at p. 29.

152 Ibid., pr. 3. The other articles of the Covenant in which the terms 'arbitrary' or 'arbitrarily' appear are articles 9(1), 17(1), and 12(4).

153 Doc. A/3746, pr. 114. See Bossuyt, *Guide*, pp. 123-4.

154 Doc. A/C.3/L.651.

155 Doc. A/3764, pr. 115. The proposal was rejected by 50 votes to 9, with 11 abstentions.

156 See pr. 8.19 above.

157 Doc. A/3764, pr. 114.

158 See C. K. Boyle, 'The Concept of Arbitrary Deprivation of Life', in B. Ramcharan (ed.) (1985), n. 1 above, pp. 221–44.

159 See pr. 8.21 above and notes thereto.

160 Doc. A/38/40, p. 137.

161 See Fawcett, pp. 33–40. Similarly the jurisprudence of the IACM and IACT in respect of article 1 ADRD and article 4 AMR. See the *Baby Boy Case*, n. 25 above; D. Shelton, 'Abortion and the Right to Life in the Inter-American System: The Case of the "Baby Boy"', 2 HRLJ (1981) pp. 309–18; D. Weissbrodt and R. Andrus, 'The Right to Life during Armed Conflict: Disabled Peoples International v. U.S.', 29 Harv. ILJ (1988) pp. 59–83.

162 See articles 31 and 32 of the Vienna Convention on the Law of Treaties (1969).

163 GC 16 (32) (article 17), Doc. A/43/40, pp. 181–3, also in Doc. CCPR/C/21/ Add. 6, adopted by the HRC at its 791st meeting (23 March 1988).

164 Ibid., prs. 3–4. See also *von Alphen* v. *Netherlands*, Doc. A/45/40, Apx., pr. 5.8, and the individual opinion of Mr Ando thereon. 'Arbitrariness is not so much something opposed to a rule of law, as something opposed to the rule of law. This idea was expressed by the Court in the *Asylum* case, when it spoke of "arbitrary action" being "substituted for the rule of law" (*Asylum, Judgement, I.C.J. Reports 1950, p. 284*). It is a wilful disregard of due process of law, an act which shocks, or at least surprises, a sense of judicial propriety', *Electronica Sicula S.P.A. (ELSI)* (*U.S.* v. *Italy*), ICJ Reps. 1989 p. 15, pr. 128; 28 ILM 1109 (1989).

165 An autonomous interpretation has also been given to the expression 'suit at law' in article 14 of the Covenant, see ch. 10 below.

166 See prs. 8.17–8.20 above.

167 Doc. A/40/40, p. 187. See Rodley, n. 1 above, pp. 155–6.

168 The incident was also considered in a number of reports by individuals and bodies investigating the human rights situation in Suriname, see e.g., IACM Report on a Visit to Suriname in June 1983, OAS/Ser.L/II.61, Doc. 6 Rev. 1. (1983), ch. 2; Report of the Special Rapporteur of the HRCion on Summary and Arbitrary Executions, Doc. E/CN.4/1985/17, Ax. 5; Report of the Dutch Lawyers Committee for Human Rights, Doc. E/CN.4/1983/55.

169 Doc. A/40/40, p. 187, pr. 6.3, 13.2.

170 See pr. 8.6 above.

171 See prs. 8.17–8.20 above.

172 Ibid., pr. 8.19.

173 Doc. A/40/40, p. 187, pr. 14.1.

174 Ibid., pr. 15.

175 See pr. 8.19 above.

176 Doc. A/43/40, p. 190.

177 Ibid., pr. 10.2.

178 Ibid., pr. 10.3.

179 Ibid., pr. 11.

180 Ibid., pr. 12. See also *A. V.R.N.* v. *Argentina* and the important individual opinion on disappearances by Wennergren, Doc. A/45/40, Apx.

181 Cf. in A.6040/73, *X.* v. *Ireland*, admiss. decn., 16 YBECHR p. 388 (1973), the applicant complained that the refusal of the authorities to give her severely disabled daughter a medical card and thus free treatment and other welfare benefits constituted a breach of her daughter's right to life. The EUCM raised but did not pursue the question of whether the scope of article 2 is limited to the negative prohibition of the taking of life or could, in certain circumstances, call for more positive action. In A.7154/75, *Association X.* v. *UK*, 14 D. & R. p. 31 (1979), the EUCM examined the risks of a programme of voluntary vaccination and concluded that the system of control and supervision established by the State was sufficient to comply with its obligation to protect life under article 2 of the Convention. In its opinion the EUCM stated that it considered that, 'the first sentence of article 2 imposes a broader obligation on the State than that contained in the second sentence. The concept that "everyone's life shall be protected by law" enjoins the State not only to refrain from taking life "intentionally" but, further, to take appropriate steps to safeguard life.' This interpretation was affirmed in *Stewart* v. *UK*, A.10044/82, 7 EHRR p. 409. See also on positive obligations A.9360/81 v. Ireland, 32 CD 211; A.9825/82 v. UK and Ireland, 8 EHRR 49; A.10565/83 v. FRG, 7 EHRR 152.

182 Cf. The obligation under customary international law, see n. 123 above.

183 On article 2 see ch. 6 above.

184 Doc. A/43/40, p. 218.

185 Ibid., pr. 8.2.

186 See ch. 4, prs. 4.27–4.33 above.

187 See n. 123 above.

188 See pr. 8.24 above.

189 Doc. A/38/40, p. 134. The view in *Mbenge* was re-affirmed in *Pinto* v. *Trinidad and Tobago* and *Reid* v. *Jamaica*, Doc. A/45/40, Apxs. See the individual opinion of Mr Wennergren in each view.

190 Ibid., pr. 21(*b*).

191 See ch. 10, prs. 10.33, 10.40 below.

192 Doc. A/38/40, p. 134, pr. 17. See also GC 6(16), n. 3 above, pr. 7, text to n. 56 above.

193 The text of the HRCion's draft had referred in article 6(2) to a death penalty not being contrary to the 'principles of the Universal Declaration of Human Rights' rather than to the Covenant, Doc. A/2929, ch. 6, and p. 29. Article 6(2) as adopted was largely that proposed in a report of a Working Group of the Third Committee (A/C.3/L.655 and Corr. 1), A/3764, prs. 102, 116–17.

194 Cf. The recent decision of the United States Supreme Court in *McClesky* v. *Kemp*, 95 L Ed. 2d 262 (1987), 107 S. Ct. 1756 (1987) in which M argued unsuccessfully that the death penalty was applied in racially discriminatory manner. See R. L. Kennedy, 'McClesky v. Kemp: Race, Capital Punishment and the Supreme Court', 101 Harv. LR (1988) pp. 1388–443.

195 See the decisions concerning the extradition of applicants to face the death

penalty in the US, A.10497/83, *Kirkwood* v. *UK*, 6 EHRR 373; *Soering* v. *UK*, EUCT, Series A, Vol. 161 (1989). See also *VRMB* v. *Canada*, Doc. A/43/40, p. 258, pr. 6.3, 'With regard to article 6 of the Covenant, the author has merely expressed fear for his life in the hypothetical case that he should be deported to El Salvador. The Committee cannot examine hypothetical violations of the Covenant rights which might occur in the future; furthermore, the Government of Canada has publicly stated on several occasions that it would not extradite the author to El Salvador and has given him the opportunity to select a safe third country'.

196 In *Pratt and Morgan* v. *Jamaica*, Doc. A/44/40, p. 222, the HRC expressed its view that, 'in capital punishment cases, States have an imperative duty to observe rigorously all the guarantees for a fair trial set out in article 14 of the Covenant. Although in this case article 6 is not directly at issue, in that capital punishment is not *per se* unlawful under the Covenant, it should not be imposed in circumstances where there have been violations by the State party of any of its obligations under the Covenant. The Committee is of the view that the victims of the violations of article 14, paragraph 3 (c), and 7 are entitled to a remedy; the necessary prerequisite in the particular circumstances is the commutation of sentence', pr. 15.

197 See pr. 8.8 above.

198 See Pannick, n. 46 above, pp. 26–7, citing, *inter alia*, *Herbert* v. *Louisiana* 272 US 312 (1926). See also the decision of the Privy Council in *Mootoo* v. *Attorney-General* [1979] 1 WLR 1334, cited in Pannick, ibid., p. 36.

199 See Pannick, ibid., pp. 27–29, citing, *inter alia*, *Maneka Gandhi* v. *Union of India* [1978] 1 SCC 248.

200 Article 2 ECHR does not contain any equivalent to article 6(2) of the Covenant. Pannick, ibid., p. 30, cites from the judgments of the EUCT in the *Sunday Times Case*, EUCT, Series A, Vol. 30, pr. 49 (1979), and the *Winterwerp Case*, EUCT, Series A, Vol. 33, pr. 45 (1979), and comments that, 'It is uncertain whether the European Court will, like the American and Indian Supreme Courts, develop the concept of "law" to embrace substantive criteria of the rule of law and due process of law. What is certain is that the three most prestigious constitutional courts in the world have accepted that, in the context of a constitutional document, a statute is not necessarily 'law'. See also the decision of the IACT in n. 67 above.

201 Doc. A/38/40, p. 134.

202 Ibid., prs. 9, 15.

203 The Covenant does not contain any 'political offence' exception to capital punishment. Such an exception was proposed in the HRCion but was not adopted, Doc. A/2929, ch. 6, pr. 6. Cf. article 4(4) AMR which provides that, 'In no case shall capital punishment be inflicted for political offences or related common crimes'. See Advisory Opinion OC/3/83 of the IACT, n. 46 above.

204 Doc. A/43/40, p. 199.

205 Ibid., prs. 1.9, 10.3. The detainees were subsequently released, ibid., pr. 15.2.

206 Ibid., prs. 15.2. The HRC's view states that it lacked sufficient evidence to make findings with regard to other claims made by the authors, ibid., pr. 17.

207 See prs. 8.3–8.4 above.
208 GC 6/16, pr. 5. Text in pr. 8.3 above.
209 See pr. 8.24 above at n. 181.
210 See in particular Ramcharan, n. 1 above.
211 Fawcett, p. 37.
212 See pr. 8.4 above. See also ch. 6 above on article 2 and ch. 1, pr. 1.16 on the immediacy of the obligations in the Covenant.
213 See the literature cited in ch. 1, pr. 1.16 above, and Scott, ch. 4 n. 424 above.
214 Cf. the decision of the EUCM in A.7154/75, n. 181 above.
215 See ch. 4, prs. 4.53–4.63 above.
216 See prs. 8.3–8.4 above.
217 See ch. 1, pr. 1.16 above.
218 See D. Harris, *The European Social Charter*, p. 271 (1984).
219 See Hassan, ch. 4, n. 361 above. Cf. Merrills, *passim*.
220 For a very significant view under the HRC in this respect see the cases concerning article 26 of the Covenant considered in ch. 4, pr. 4.55–4.58 above. It has been argued that the decision of the EUCT in *Young, James and Webster* v. *U.K.*, EUCT, Series A, Vol. 44 (1981) contradicted the clear intentions of the drafters concerning closed shops.
221 Note that both the European Social Charter and the ICESCR do not make any provision concerning petitions. The Constitution of the ILO, articles 24 and 26, provides for complaints from trades unions, employers, and States, but not individuals.
222 See prs. 8.11–8.12 above.
223 See pr. 8.13 above.
224 *Bleir* v. *Uruguay*, pr. 8.15 above, at n. 104.
225 Ibid., pr. 8.15.
226 *Barbato* v. *Uruguay*, pr. 8.16 above, at nn. 120 and 121.
227 *Rubio* v. *Colombia*, pr. 8.24 above.
228 See e.g. *Miango* v. *Zaïre*, pr. 8.24.1 above, pr. 11.
229 See *Guerrero* v. *Colombia*, prs. 8.17–8.20 above at n. 146.
230 See *Guerrero* v. *Colombia*, ibid.
231 See pr. 8.22.1 above.
232 See *Mbenge* v. *Zaïre*, pr. 8.25 above.
233 GC 6/16, pr. 8.2 above, at n. 3. *Guerrero* v. *Colombia*, pr. 8.18.
234 See pr. 8.6 above.

9

Article 7[1]

9.1

Article 7
No one shall be subjected to torture or to cruel, inhuman or degrading treatment or punishment. In particular, no one shall be subjected without his free consent to medical or scientific treatment.

Article 10
1. All persons deprived of their liberty shall be treated with humanity and with respect for the inherent dignity of the human person.

2.(a) Accused persons shall, save in exceptional circumstances, be segregated from convicted persons and shall be subject to separate treatment appropriate to their status as unconvicted persons.

(b) Accused juvenile persons shall be separated from adults and brought as speedily as possible for adjudication.

3. The penitentiary system shall comprise treatment of prisoners the essential aim of which shall be their reformation and social rehabilitation. Juvenile offenders shall be segregated from adults and be accorded treatment appropriate to their age and status.

Introduction

9.2 Article 7 is non-derogable in any circumstances.[2] It has been the subject of a General Comment under article 40(4).[3] In that General Comment the HRC stated that the purpose of article 7 was 'to protect the integrity and dignity of the individual'.[4] Article 7 has featured consistently in the 'views' adopted by the HRC under article 5(4) of the OP.[5]

A. ARTICLE 7 UNDER THE REPORTING PROCESS

In the consideration of State reports under article 40 article 7 has been linked in particular with articles 9[6] and 10(1). In its General Comment the HRC stated that,

For all persons deprived of their liberty, the prohibition of treatment contrary to article 7 is supplemented by the positive requirement of article 10(1) of the Covenant that they shall be treated with humanity and with respect for the inherent dignity of the human person.[7]

Similarly, in its General Comment on article 10 the HRC recalled that, 'this article supplements article 7 as regards the treatment of all persons deprived of their liberty'.[8] More generally article 7 has been linked in differing contexts with various articles of the Covenant including articles 6, 8, 9, 14, 23, and 24.[9] Comments often link, for example, disappearances, torture and ill-treatment, extra-judicial killings, and the destruction of family life.[10] Moreover, since its inception the HRC has taken a broad view of the scope of article 7. In its view article 7, 'clearly protects not only persons arrested or imprisoned, but also pupils and patients in educational and medical institutions'.[11] Similarly in its General Comment on article 10 the HRC stated that, 'the wording of paragraph 1, its context—especially its proximity to article 9, paragraph 1, which also deals with all deprivations of liberty—and its purpose support a broad application of the principle expressed in that provision'.[12] This broad approach also parallels that taken to article 3 ECHR under which there is now substantial jurisprudence, and is to be strongly commended as it adds considerably to the protection offered by the ICCPR.[13]

9.3 In the course of their considerations under article 40 HRC members have generally limited their questions, comments, and observations to matters stemming from information provided by the State reports or from cases considered under the Optional Protocol. However, members have not refrained from making specific charges of torture against a number of States, for example, Iran,[14] Afghanistan,[15] El Salvador,[16] Uruguay,[17] Chile.[18] Obviously the prohibition in article 7 covers matters of extreme political sensitivity at both the domestic and international levels. HRC members have recognized this by showing restraint and diplomacy in the framing of their questions and comments to State representatives. In general they have successfully followed a difficult line in establishing and maintaining a condition of 'constructive dialogue' while at the same time making clear their concerns and reservations to State representatives.[19] However, there has been no question of members glossing over or evading the issues. Many comments have been precisely formulated and critical, for example,

Reports had been published of healthy persons being interned in Soviet psychiatric institutions for political or punitive reasons, which would appear to be a clear violation of the terms of that article. He asked whether those reports were being investigated and what precautions were being taken in the Soviet Union to ensure that such treatment did not occur ... some of the sentences meted out in previous years to persons convicted of political offences seemed excessively severe to observers in other countries. It would be appreciated if some comments could be made to assist the Committee in its understanding of this matter.[20]

9.4 The information provided by most State reports has generally been limited to an indication of the major constitutional and legislative provisions embodying the proscription in article 7. The HRC noted that, it is not sufficient for the implementation of this article to prohibit such treatment or punishment or make it a crime. Most States have Penal provisions which are applicable to cases of torture or similar practices. Because such cases nevertheless occur, it follows from article 7, read together with article 2 of the Covenant, that States must ensure an effective protection through some machinery of control. Complaints about ill-treatment must be investigated effectively by competent authorities. Those found guilty must be held responsible, and the alleged victims must themselves have effective remedies at their disposal including the right to obtain compensation.[21]

Accordingly, HRC members have requested more details on the practical workings of those provisions and other aspects within the ambit of article 7. States have been questioned as to whether their laws and practices with respect to accused and convicted persons, those held in preventative detention, and the imposition and execution of punishments and penalties, correspond to the United Nations Minimum Standard Rules for the Treatment of Prisoners,[22] the United Nations Code of Conduct for Law Enforcement Officials, and the Standard Minimum Rules for the Administration of Juvenile Justice.[23] More specifically members have raised such issues as the physical conditions of detention,[24] the discriminatory treatment of political detainees,[25] the conditions, procedures, and safeguards applicable in cases of psychiatric detention,[26] and the general principle of proportionality as regards punishments.[27]

9.4.1 In its General Comment the HRC drew on its experience in dealing with article 7 to indicate to States parties the kinds of safeguards which it considered could make control machinery effective. These were

provisions against detention incommunicado, granting, without prejudice to the investigation, persons such as doctors, lawyers, and family members access to the detainees; provisions requiring that detainees should be held in places that are publicly recognized and that their names and places of detention should be entered on a central register available to persons concerned, such as relatives; provisions making confessions or other evidence obtained through torture or other treatment contrary to article 7 inadmissible in court; and measures of training and instruction of law enforcement officials not to apply such treatment.[28]

This kind of General Comment is particularly useful from the point of view of States parties. It gives practical, concrete indications of how the HRC views the demands of article 7 in terms of national laws and practices by which the performance of each State can be measured. That this aspect of the General Comment adopts many of the safeguards suggested by international non-governmental organizations such as Amnesty International suggests that such organizations are having an input into the HRC's work in this respect.[29]

9.5 The HRC has stated that article 7 has a wide scope of application. However, the HRC has refrained from defining or providing clear criteria for the application of article 7. The General Comment stated that,

As appears from the terms of this article, the scope of the protection required goes far beyond torture as normally understood. It may not be necessary to draw sharp distinctions between the various prohibited forms of treatment or punishment. These distinctions depend on the kind, purpose and severity of the particular treatment.[30]

9.6 Among the particular forms of punishments and practices the application of which have attracted the attention and sometimes the criticism of HRC members have been certain interrogation methods,[31] the evidential use of illegally obtained information,[32] virginity testing of immigrants,[33] the treatment of the so called 'blanket people' in Northern Ireland,[34] stoning and flogging,[35] whipping,[36] 30–40 years' rigorous imprisonment,[37] loss of nationality,[38] and deprivation of civil and political rights for extended periods.[39]

9.7 The HRC has consistently probed State representatives on their practices of solitary confinement and corporal punishment. Matters canvassed have included the determination of the authorities with power to authorize these practices, for what periods, for what offences or conduct, in what circumstances, and the conditions governing the confinement and punishment.[40] As regards solitary confinement the HRC has expressed the view that, 'even such a measure as solitary confinement may, according to the circumstances, and especially when the person is kept incommunicado, be contrary to this article'.[41] This approach seems to accord with that of the EUCM to such cases.[42] As regards corporal punishment the individual members of the HRC have generally taken an anti-corporal punishment stance, often suggesting that it may contravene both article 7 and article 24(1) of the ICCPR which provides that, 'Every child shall have, without any discrimination . . . the right to such measures of protection as are required by his status as a minor, on the part of his family, society and the State'.[43] In its General Comment the HRC was more equivocal and ambiguous. After referring to the various prohibited forms of treatment or punishment the Comment continued, 'in the view of the Committee the prohibition must extend to corporal punishment, including excessive chastisement as an educational or disciplinary measure'.[44] The obvious ambiguity is as to whether the prohibition in article 7 extends to corporal punishment *per se* and to excessive chastisement as an educational or disciplinary measure, or only to corporal punishment which amounts to such excessive chastisement. In view of the doubt it is probably only safe to assume the latter at the present time.[45]

9.8 During its consideration of State reports the HRC has emphasized the fundamental role in the implementation of the prohibition in article 7 of 'an effective remedy, notwithstanding that the violation has been committed by persons acting in an official capacity' (article 2(3)).[46] State representatives have been requested to provide examples, if any, of recent investigations and prosecutions for contravention of the domestic provisions corresponding to article 7.[47] Reference has been made to views adopted under article 5(4) OP concerning violations of articles 7 and 10(1).[48] Similarly questions have been raised concerning arrangements for visits by the International Red Cross[49] and the possibility of establishing prison inspection services.[50] In its General Comment on article 7 the HRC stated that, 'it is the duty of public authorities to ensure protection by the law against such treatment even when committed by persons acting outside or without any official authority'.[51] There is no explanation of 'official authority'. The 'duty' to 'ensure protection' suggests a positive and active role for the State in this context. In practical terms the HRC's comment would cover the activities of so-called 'death squads', which operate in certain countries. Such groups are often allegedly linked to, if not comprised of, State security forces.[52]

9.9 The prohibition on medical and scientific experimentation without the free consent of the person concerned has been the subject of consistent but rather limited consideration.[53] A matter commonly raised has concerned the regulations, if any, governing the removal and transplant of human organs or tissue.[54] The Mexican representative was asked whether it could be concluded from a provision of the Health Code permitting authorized clinical research of human beings 'only when ... there is no foreseeable possibility of causing death', that medical experiments which did not endanger the life of the subject could be carried out without his consent. If so, it was suggested that the provision was in conflict with the Covenant.[55]

9.10 During the drafting process it was recognized that medical and scientific experimentation were very complex matters raising many difficult questions.[56] Though the provision was drafted with the atrocities of the Nazi concentration camps during World War II in mind it was clearly recognized that the provision as formulated went much wider.[57] Among the particular issues discussed were exceptions to this principle where the health of the individual or the community were involved, the problem of the consent of the sick or unconscious person, the need to outlaw criminal experimentation without hindering legitimate scientific or medical practices, the distinction between treatment and experimentation.[58] Modern practices such as psycho-surgery,[59] research on children, research concerning pharmaceutical products,[60] the AIDS virus, fetal and embryo experimentation,[61] and fluoridation might well raise issues for the HRC to consider. The fundamental issue to note will be the HRC's approach to and interpretation of 'free consent' and the distinction between treatment and experimentation.[62] No real assistance on these issues has been gained from the HRC's practice to date.

In its General Comment on article 7 the HRC noted the paucity of information received on the second sentence of article 7 and commented that it took the view that, at least in countries where science and medicine are highly developed, and even for peoples and areas outside their borders if affected by their experiments, more attention should be given to the possible need and means to ensure the observance of this provision. Special protection in regard to such experiments is necessary in the case of persons not capable of giving their consent.[63]

B. ARTICLES 7 AND 10 UNDER THE OPTIONAL PROTOCOL[64]

9.11 Articles 7 and 10(1) have featured prominently in the HRC's final views. In many of these the HRC found that both articles had been violated. This is accounted for the fact that these views have concerned the treatment of detainees, which is a subject covered by both articles 7 and 10(1).[65] All of the HRC's views on article 7 have concerned the first sentence of article 7. No final view has dealt with the matter of consent to medical and scientific experimentation.[66] Many of the HRC's important decisions on evidential and procedural matters under the OP have been developed in cases concerning article 7 and 10(1). These have been dealt with in chapter 4 above.

9.12 The main features of the HRC's views under articles 7 and 10(1) will now be reviewed. Their usefulness in facilitating an understanding of the HRC's approach to its work has been reduced by a number of factors. The great majority of the HRC's views have concerned Uruguay. The factual allegations have been relatively confined and consistent focusing on methods of torture and mistreatment and conditions of detention. Thus the scope for the HRC to develop the borderline of articles 7 and 10(1) has been restricted. A much wider range of issues have been considered under article 3 ECHR.[67] Even within its limited scope the HRC's analyses have been rather sparse, cautious, and unhelpful. This is partly explicable by the consistent failure of the Uruguayan authorities to co-operate with the HRC, for example, with respect to the production of evidence or the specific rebuttal of allegations.[68] The result is that the HRC's jurisprudence has been developing in a rather abstract, academic manner without the benefit of detailed counter argument. Often the HRC's views have simply consisted of a recitation of the factual allegations and the HRC's stating that those facts form the basis of findings of violations of, *inter alia*, articles 7 and 10(1) of the Covenant. Accordingly, many of the HRC's views are unsatisfactory with regard to an understanding of a particular decision and also, more generally, in terms of facilitating a comprehensible development of the meaning of the Covenant. The following cases are examples of the unsatisfactory nature of the HRC's approach in these regards.

9.12.1 In *Ambrosini* v. *Uruguay*[69] it was alleged that A was held incommunicado in an unidentified place, confined with four other political prisoners in a cell measuring 4.2 by 2.5 metres in conditions seriously detrimental to his health. The HRC expressed the view that the facts revealed, *inter alia*, violations of articles 7 and 10(1) because A was detained under conditions seriously detrimental to his health.[70] Article 10(1) was also violated because A was held incommunicado for months and was denied the right to be visited by any family member.[71] Presumably the conditions of detention did not amount to torture but there is no indication whether the conditions amounted to 'cruel treatment', 'inhuman treatment', or 'degrading treatment'. Article 10(1) provides little assistance as each of these limbs of article 7 might be covered by the requirement for detainees to be 'treated with humanity and respect for their inherent dignity'. The HRC also does not explain the source of the 'right' to be visited by any family member. It does not expressly appear in the ICCPR but it may be implied by a combination of other articles.[72] Visits by family members were mentioned as a safeguard by the HRC in its General Comment on article 7 but was not referred to as a right.[73]

9.12.2 In *Antonaccio v. Uruguay*[74] the HRC expressed the view that there had been violations of article 7 and 10(1) because A was held in solitary confinement for three months in an underground cell, was subjected to torture over a period of three months, and was being denied the medical treatment his condition required.[75] There is no further explanation of the HRC's views so it is uncertain whether such a period of and circumstances of solitary confinement alone would have violated article 7 or article 10(1) or both.[76] We noted above that in its General Comment on article 7 the HRC stated that solitary confinement 'may, according to the circumstances, and especially when the person is kept incommunicado, be contrary to this article'.[77] It is unfortunate that the HRC does not comment on or explain the circumstances of solitary confinement in this case and thereby afford a useful example of the scope of its General Comment.[78] Similar criticism can be made with regard to the denial of medical treatment to A.[79]

9.12.3 Another unhelpful finding is that in *Lanza and Perdoma v. Uruguay*.[80] L and P made detailed allegations of ill-treatment (L) and physical and mental torture (P). The HRC simply expressed the view that the facts disclosed violations of articles 7 and 10(1) because of the 'treatment which they received while in detention'.[81] No attempt is made to be more specific. No comment is made on the allegations of mental as distinct from physical torture.[82] Even more inexplicable are cases where the HRC makes no finding of facts and expresses no view on the allegations at all. An example is *M. V. Massera v. Uruguay*[83] where it was alleged that while in detention M suffered from an inadequate diet and unhealthy working conditions so that her state of health was weakened.[84]

9.13 To turn to the substance of the HRC's views, there have been a substantial number of views in which the HRC has specifically categorized allegations as constituting torture.[85] The first of these was in the HRC's first expression of views. In *J. L. Massera* v. *Uruguay*[86] it was alleged that M had been forced to remain standing with his head hooded for many hours, had lost his balance, fallen down, and broken his leg. The injury was not immediately taken care of with the result that the leg was left several centimetres shorter than the other one. The HRC found that as a result of the maltreatment received M had suffered permanent injury, and expressed the view that the facts disclosed violations of articles 7 and 10(1) because during his detention M was tortured as a result of which he suffered permanent physical damage.[87] There is no definition or explanation of the term 'torture'. The only factual evidence of M's mistreatment was that he was hooded and forced to remain standing for long hours. If this treatment alone constituted torture then the threshold has been set at a much lower level than that indicated by the EUCT in the *Ireland* v. *United Kingdom Case*.[88] In that case 'wall-standing' and 'hooding' were only two of five techniques which the EUCT held to constitute a practice of inhuman and degrading treatment but specifically not a practice of torture because the technique 'did not occasion suffering of the particular intensity and cruelty implied by the word torture'.[89] Alternatively, the HRC's view may have been that it was the fact that permanent physical injury resulted from M's treatment that rendered it torture. On that basis a State party is being held responsible for any injury resulting from the mistreatment of an individual even if the extent of injury was not intended. Interesting questions of foreseeability and liability for omissions would inevitably be raised if this approach was pursued.[90] Other findings of torture by the HRC would reject the possible argument that a finding of 'permanent physical damage' is a precondition to a finding of torture.[91]

9.14 The factual allegations in the communications in which the HRC has made a finding of torture have included practices which would clearly have come within any conception of torture: application of electric shocks, use of submarino (putting the detainee's hooded head into foul water), insertion of bottles or barrels into detainee's anus, being forced to remain standing, hooded, and handcuffed with a piece of wood in the mouth for several days and nights;[92] physical beatings[93] or treatment which results in permanent physical damage[94] or a broken jawbone and perforated eardrums,[95] being forced to do the 'planton' (standing upright with eyes blindfolded throughout the day), being buried and walked over;[96] beatings with rubber truncheons, near asphyxiation in water, psychological torture including threats of torture or violence to friends or relatives, or of dispatch to Argentina to be executed, threats of having to witness the torture of friends, mock amputations;[97] beatings, electric shocks, and mock executions.[98] Despite a number of opportunities the HRC has failed to state explicitly that mental or psychological suffering can amount to torture.[99]

9.14.1 In other cases of seemingly comparable severity, however, the

HRC has refrained from using the term torture. In *Lanza* v. *Uruguay*[100] L was almost constantly kept blindfolded with her hands tied and subjected to various forms of mistreatment such as 'cabellete', 'submarino seco', 'picano', and 'planton'.[101] The HRC expressed the view that there had been violations of articles 7 and 10(1) because of the 'treatment' received during detention.[102] In *Weinberger* v. *Uruguay*[103] the allegations were of torture, being kept blindfolded with hands tied, and treatment leaving the detainee with serious physical injuries (one arm paralysed, leg injuries, and infected eyes). The HRC used the expression 'severe treatment'.[104] In *Izquierdo* v. *Uruguay*[105] similar allegations were termed 'ill-treatment'.[106] 'Severe treatment' was again used in *Conteris* v. *Uruguay*.[107] This was accompanied by a finding that article 14(13)(*g*) of the ICCPR had been violated because C had been 'forced by means of torture to confess guilt'. Why the article 7 finding does not also refer expressly to torture is not explained. Finally, in other cases the HRC has combined expressions basing its views on evidence of 'torture and inhuman treatment'[108] and the 'treatment (including torture) suffered'.[109]

9.14.2 In no case then has the HRC sought to define or delineate the boundaries between 'torture' and 'inhuman treatment' or to explain why certain allegations have been designated torture while others of similar severity have not.[110] A remarkable view is that in *Acosta* v. *Uruguay*.[111] The HRC found the allegations of torture to be unsubstantiated but, nevertheless, expressed the view that the information before it evidenced that A had been subjected to inhuman treatment and that Uruguay had thereby violated articles 7 and 10(1). This view is extraordinary since the only evidence identified by the HRC was A's being held incommunicado for various periods.[112]

9.15 The term 'degrading treatment' has only appeared in a small number of cases. In *De Bouton* v. *Uruguay*[113] B alleged that she was subjected to 'moral and physical ill-treatment' including once being forced to stand for thirty-five hours with minor interruptions, that her wrists were bound causing pain and that her eyes were continuously kept bandaged. The conditions of detention grew worse with B allegedly kept sitting on a mattress, blindfolded, not allowed to move for many days, and only being allowed to take a bath every ten or fifteen days. The HRC expressed the view that there had been violations of articles 7 and 10(1) on the basis of evidence of 'inhuman and degrading treatment'.[114] There was no discussion or explanation of the term 'degrading treatment' or how it was to be distinguished from inhuman treatment[115] or why other cases concerning similar factual allegations have been designated only as 'inhuman treatment', 'severe treatment', or 'ill-treatment' but not 'degrading treatment'. It is only possible to speculate that the distinctions between the cases may turn on particular evidential details which remain unexplained. No reference to 'moral' ill-treatment was made.

9.15.1 Similar comments can be made regarding the only other view in which the expression 'degrading treatment' appears, which also contains one of only three uses by the HRC of the expression 'cruel treatment'. In *Gilboa v. Uruguay*[116] the HRC expressed the view that G had been subjected to 'torture and to cruel and degrading treatment'. In its statement of facts the HRC refers to the torture (beatings, 'electric prod', stringing up) to which G had been subjected. There is no explanation of 'cruel and degrading treatment'. The allegations included 'various forms of continuous degradation and violence, such as always having to remain naked with the guards and torturers, threats and insults and promises of further acts of cruelty'.[117] Finally in one view, *Conteris v. Uruguay*[118] the HRC referred to 'harsh' conditions of detention. This expression does not appear in articles 7 or 10(1).

9.16 The basic thrust of the argument above is that the HRC has failed to define or establish criteria for distinguishing between the terms in article 7. This accords with the approach of the HRC in its General Comment on article 7 in which it stated its view that, 'It may not be necessary to draw sharp distinctions between the various prohibited forms of treatment and punishment. These distinctions depend on the kind, purpose and severity of the particular treatment'.[119] Similarly it can be argued that the criticism is academic because violation of any element of article 7 is totally and unequivocally prohibited. It must also be recognized that on the basis of the experience under parallel article 3 ECHR the boundaries of article 7 of the ICCPR are likely to be complex and fluid and may change over time.[120] None the less, communications under the OP afford the HRC opportunity to give content to articles 7 and 10(1) by permitting analysis of the 'kind, purpose and severity of the particular treatment' in individual, concrete cases. In response the HRC has failed to draw intelligible and comprehensible distinctions between the various limbs of article 7. Even apart from the contribution that this would make to developing the content of the ICCPR from the point of view of States parties, the distinctions between the prohibitions are crucial in terms of reputation, international standing, the level of reparation to be afforded, and propaganda value.[121] It may then be very important for a State party to avoid having its actions categorized as torture as distinct from a lesser violation of article 7. Conversely, findings of torture from a body of international human rights experts like the HRC should carry great weight and moral force. Unfortunately, the HRC has not afforded to States parties a clear understanding of the scope of the respective prohibitions. The resulting categorization of findings as 'torture', or as 'inhuman', 'ill', or 'severe' treatment thus appears to have an element of arbitrariness attached to it which must inevitably reduce the potency and standing of the HRC's views. In practical terms the absence of definition is particularly important with respect to the lower reaches of the article 7 prohibitions because that is where the difficult line must be drawn between permissible and impermissible treatment and conduct by States.[122] Common State practices on which the HRC could have provided more guidance include solitary confinement, incommunicado detention, and prison conditions.[123]

As a living instrument of human rights protection the ICCPR will only develop as a guide to States parties and an effective recourse for individuals if in its general comments and its views under the OP the HRC gives much more of an indication of its understanding of the terms used in the Covenant. Even if it is accepted that the formulation of definitions is a difficult task in the early years of a human rights body, what must at least be demanded is that the HRC articulate a much more intelligible link between the facts it finds and the violations which in its view they reveal. For example, which of a number of findings of fact constitutes the essential element in the view that there has been a violation of article 7? Or is it a particular combination of findings?[124] What renders a particular set of facts serious enough to constitute torture as distinct from any other prohibited form of treatment? As noted in chapter 4 these criticisms are not confined to views concerning article 7. The form and substance of many of the HRC's views are such that it is difficult to state exactly what, if anything, the HRC has decided and interpretation is often reduced to speculation.[125]

9.17 In a line of cases the HRC has expressed the view that conditions of detention can violate articles 7 and 10(1).[126] The alleged conditions in particular cases have included solitary confinement for three months and denial of medical treatment;[127] incommunicado detention in a small cell (1 m. by 2 m.) in solitary confinement for eighteen months;[128] solitary confinement for several months in a cell almost without natural light;[129] detention in a garage with open doors, sleeping uncovered on the floor, with no change of clothing, blindfolded, hands bound, having only two cups of soup per day;[130] detention in overcrowded cells with 5 cm. to 10 cm. of water on the floor, being kept indoors all day, insufficient sanitary conditions, hard labour, poor food,[131] periods of incommunicado detention, chained to a bed spring on the floor with minimal clothing, and severe rationing of food. The HRC described these as inhuman conditions.[132]

9.18 In *Estrella* v. *Uruguay*[133] the HRC found that the 'inhuman conditions of detention' violated article 10(1) but no reference was made to article 7 with respect to the conditions of detention. Why conditions in one case violate articles 7 and 10(1) when in another they violate only article 10(1) is not explained.[134] The *Estrella* case is important in other respects and bears more detailed consideration.

Estrella, a concert pianist, was allegedly kidnapped by fifteen strongly armed individuals and subjected to physical and psychological torture and other ill-treatment which had lasting effects particularly on his arms and hands. He was threatened with death and denied necessary medical attention. In January 1978 he was taken to Libertad prison. He spent the first ten days in a cell which was a kind of cage. He remained imprisoned there until February 1980. At Libertad E was subjected to further ill-treatment and to arbitrary punishments including thirty days' solitary confinement in a punishment cell and seven months without mail or recreation. He was also subjected to harassment. His mail was subjected to severe censorship. E provided a detailed description of prison conditions at Libertad.[135]

The HRC expressed the view that Uruguay had violated article 7 because E was subjected to torture during his first few days of detention.[136] The HRC's view refers only to 'torture' but its statement of facts refers to 'physical and psychological torture'.[137] The HRC's views contained a very important statement with respect to the alleged prison conditions at Libertad:

On the basis of the detailed information submitted by the author (see in particular paras. 1.10 to 1.16 above) the Committee is in a position to conclude that the conditions of imprisonment to which Miguel Angel Estrella was subjected at Libertad were inhuman. In this connection the Committee recalls its consideration of other communications (see for instance its views on R. 16/66 adopted at its seventh session) which confirm the existence of a *practice of inhuman treatment* at Libertad.[138]

9.18.1 The HRC repeated this view concerning a practice at Libertad in *Nieto* v. *Uruguay*[139] and stated that it had come to this conclusion 'on the basis of specific accounts by former detainees themselves'.[140] In both *Estrella* and *Nieto* the inhuman prison conditions were held to constitute a violation of article 10(1). Again there is no explanation of the absence of a reference to article 7 in this respect, which would have been a more potent finding.

The concept of a practice does not appear in the ICCPR. It has, however, figured in the jurisprudence under the ECHR.[141] In terms of the practice of the HRC Uruguay might justifiably have some complaint with the HRC's introduction of this concept. E had not expressly claimed that there was a practice of inhuman treatment at Libertad in violation of the Covenant. Therefore, the Uruguayan authorities were not afforded the opportunity to deny that a practice of inhuman treatment existed, as distinct from violations of E's rights under the ICCPR.[142] Moreover, the Committee's decision appears to be based on a relatively small number of cases. The European Commission has by contrast demanded, for example, 'a substantial number of acts of torture or ill-treatment which are the expression of a general situation'.[143] The HRC also makes no reference to the additional element identified in ECHR jurisprudence of 'official tolerance'. The finding of a practice might have implications as regards the exhaustion of domestic remedies under article 5 of the OP. This has been noted in chapter 4.[144]

9.19 In *Estrella* the HRC also expressed a view concerning the restriction and censorship of E's mail. The HRC stated that,

With regard to the censorship of (E's) correspondence, the Committee accepts that it is normal for prison authorities to exercise measures of control and censorship over prisoners' correspondence. Nevertheless, article 17 of the Covenant provides that 'no one shall be subjected to arbitrary or unlawful interference with his correspondence'. This requires that any measures of control or censorship shall be subjected to satisfactory legal safeguards against arbitrary application (see para. 21 of the Committee's views of 29 October 1981 on communication No. R. 14/63). Furthermore the degree of restriction must be consistent with the standard of humane treatment of detained persons required by article 10(1) of the Covenant. In particular, prisoners should be allowed under necessary supervision to communicate with their family and reputable friends at regular intervals, by correspondence as well as receiving visits. On the basis of the information before it, the Committee finds that (E's) correspondence was censored and restricted at Libertad prison to an extent which the State party has not justified as compatible with article 17 read in conjunction with article 10(1) of the Covenant.[145]

9.20 In its General Comment on article 10 the HRC established some important points concerning the conditions of detention and the humane treatment of detainees:

3. The humane treatment and the respect for the dignity of all persons deprived of their liberty is a basic standard of universal application which cannot depend entirely on material resources. While the Committee is aware that in other respects the modalities and conditions of detention may vary with the available resources, they must always be applied without discrimination, as required by article 2(1).

4. Ultimate responsibility for the observance of this principle rests with the State as regards all institutions where persons are lawfully held against their will, not only in prisons but also, for example, hospitals, detention camps or correctional institutions.[146]

Paragraph 3 of the comment represents a clear recognition by the HRC of the resource implications of article 10(1). That the HRC can envisage a variable, but non-discriminatory, standard as regards the 'modalities and conditions of detention' would support the argument of those who suggest that the Covenant contains progressive obligations.[147] Paragraph 4 of the comment is a clear statement of the 'ultimate responsibility' of the State and reaffirms the wide application of article 10(1) noted above.[148] So the treatment of detainees in private prisons, hospitals, clinics, and other institutions remains the responsibility of the State.

9.21 No final view to date has dealt with the interpretation and application of the expressions 'cruel punishment' and 'inhuman punishment'. With respect to 'degrading punishment' the HRC has recently expressed the view that, 'for punishment to be degrading, the humiliation or debasement involved must exceed a particular level and must, in any event, entail other elements beyond the mere fact of deprivation of liberty'.[149] The issue of whether corporal punishment as a judicial punishment or as a disciplinary measure constitutes degrading treatment has been considered by the EUCT.[150] We have noted the anti-corporal punishment approach of some

HRC members during the consideration of article 40 reports and the HRC's statement in its General Comment on article 7 that, 'In the view of the Committee the prohibition must extend to corporal punishment, including excessive chastisement as an educational or disciplinary measure'.[151] Whether corporal punishment constitutes a violation of article 7 depends on whether this statement in the General Comment is read as an outright prohibition or only as a prohibition on corporal punishment which constitutes 'excessive chastisement'.[152] Consideration of article 10(1) might also be relevant in the context of corporal punishment administered to detainees.

9.22 Three communications have raised some interesting points concerning article 7 that are worthy of comment. In *Valcada* v. *Uruguay*[153] it was alleged that V has been tortured, ill-treated, and subjected to conditions of detention which violated the Covenant.[154] In its final views the HRC stated that,

11. As regards the allegations of ill-treatment, the Committee noted that in his communication the author named the senior officers responsible for the ill-treatment which he alleged he received. The State party adduced no evidence that his allegations of ill-treatment have been duly investigated in accordance with the laws to which it drew attention... A refutation of these allegations in general terms is not enough. The State party should investigate the allegations in accordance with its laws.

12. ... As regards article 7 of the Covenant the Committee cannot find that there has not been any violation of this provision. In this respect the Committee notes that the State party has failed to show that it had ensured to the person concerned the protection required by article 2 of the Covenant.[155]

The evidential points of the HRC's finding and its decision on article 2 ICCPR are dealt with elsewhere.[156] Of interest to article 7 is the individual opinion in this case of Mr Tarnopolsky to which five other members associated themselves. That opinion reads, in full:

Although I agree with the view of the Committee that it could not find that there has not been any violation of article 7 of the Covenant, I also concluded, for the reasons set out in paragraph 11 of the Committee's views, that there has been a violation of article 7 of the Covenant.[157]

In this opinion the minority appears to have found a violation of article 7 in the failure of the State party to investigate in accordance with its laws the allegations made against named senior officers. In a number of cases under the OP the HRC have established the obligation of a State party under the OP to investigate in good faith all allegations of violation of the Covenant made against it and its authorities.[158] The minority view that the failure to investigate allegations of a violation of article 7 itself constitutes a violation of article 7 contrasts then with the view consistently taken by the HRC of the obligation imposed by the Covenant and the OP to investigate. The minority finding could be based on the notion of presumed complicity. If so, such an approach was rejected in the arbitral opinion in the *Janes Claim*[159] although that concerned the responsibility of the State with respect to the actions of a private killer. There the Commission held the government concerned liable for its failure to measure up to its duty diligently to prosecute and properly punish the offender.[160] It is submitted that this approach of holding the State responsible for the breach of its obligation to investigate rather than of the substantive prohibition in article 7 (or any other article concerned for that matter) is preferable to the view adopted by the minority. The minority view has not appeared in any subsequent decision. It would have been more helpful if the minority opinion had been set out in more detail with an accompanying explanation.

9.23 The second case of note concerning article 7 is *E. Quinteros and M. C. Almeida de Quinteros* v. *Uruguay*.[161] A.Q. submitted the communication on behalf of her daughter E.Q. and on her own behalf. It was alleged that E.Q. was arrested by military personnel in the grounds of the Venezuelan Embassy in Montevideo and systematically tortured.[162] The Uruguayan authorities denied that the government had any part in the episode and stated that the authorities were still searching for E.Q. throughout Uruguay.[163]

The HRC found that on 28 July 1976 E.Q. was arrested in the grounds of the Embassy of Venezuela at Montevideo by at least one member of the Uruguayan police force and that in August 1976 she was held in a military detention centre in Uruguay where she was subjected to torture.[164] The HRC expressed the view that there had been violations of articles 7, 9, and 10(1) of the Covenant (as regards E.Q.).[165] A.Q. had also claimed, *inter alia*, that she was a victim of violations of article 7 (psychological torture because she did not know where her daughter was) and of article 17 because of interference with her private and family life.[166] The HRC stated that,

With regard to the violations alleged by the author on her own behalf, the Committee notes that, the statement that she was in Uruguay at the time of the incident regarding her daughter, was not contradicted by the State party.[167] The Committee understands the anguish and stress caused to the mother by the disappearance of her daughter and the continuing uncertainty concerning her fate and whereabouts. The author has a right to know what has happened to her daughter. In these respects, she too is a victim of the violations suffered by her daughter in particular, of article 7.[168]

The HRC appears to state that the violations were suffered by E.Q. but that A.Q. is also a victim of them.[169] On this approach the requirement in article 1 OP that the communication comes from an individual claiming to be a 'victim of a violation' of a right set forth in the Covenant does not necessarily mean that the violation must have been suffered by that individual but only that the individual was a 'victim' of that violation whether suffered by himself or someone else.[170] One commentator noted that,

The most important aspect of the Quinteros decision is that it recognizes as a violation of the Covenant a State's acts which cause anguish and suffering to the immediate relatives of disappeared persons. This has never been done before in a human rights case. By expanding the class of victims of human rights violations by State parties to the Covenant, the decision increases the number of persons who may be afforded a remedy by the Committee.[171]

This commentator appears to assume that A.Q. was a victim of violations of the Covenant herself as distinct from the violations suffered by E.Q.[172] It is certainly possible to read the HRC's view in this way on the basis that the 'anguish and stress' caused to A.Q. by the disappearance come within the prohibitions in article 7.[173] Another aspect of this may be that this anguish and stress resulted from the denial to A.Q. of her 'right to know' of E.Q.'s whereabouts.[174] The last sentence quoted begins, 'In these respects', perhaps suggesting that this was a second aspect of the case. The HRC's view is open to criticism in that it gives no indication of the nature of this right, legal or moral, or its source, perhaps any one or more of articles 7, 10(1), 17, or 23 of the ICCPR.[175] In *Simones* v. *Uruguay*[176] the HRC expressed the view that article 10(1) had been violated because S had been held incommunicado for three months and during this period the authorities, 'wrongfully denied that she was detained'.[177] If 'wrongfully' is understood as in violation of the Covenant this gives further support to the view that a right to know of a relative's whereabouts if he is in the custody of the State is protected by the Covenant.[178]

If the correct reading of the HRC's view is that there was a violation of article 7 with respect to A.Q. then that is certainly a positive step by the HRC and represents a wide interpretation of the ICCPR and the OP. In previous communications raising questions of suffering to detained relatives because of the alleged failure to acknowledge detention, the application of torture or ill-treatment, and the absence or denial of medical treatment, the HRC has refrained from any ruling other than as regards the violations of the Covenant suffered by the direct victims of these acts or omissions though this may simply be because the relatives submitting the case have not claimed to be victims themselves.[179]

The HRC's view could simply be limited to the phenomenon of disappeared persons on the basis that the failure of the State to acknowledge detention necessarily causes anguish and distress to relatives. Alternatively, the HRC's view may be open to extensive development if read literally as covering the suffering caused to an immediate person by the violation of any right in the Covenant. Imprisonment following the denial of the right to a fair trial or for the expression of political or religious views offer obvious examples. It is difficult to speculate where the HRC might draw the line if it pursues this analysis at all. No subsequent decision has discussed this issue.

It remains to note that, unfortunately, the HRC made no express comment on A.Q.'s allegations of violation of article 17 because of interference with her private and family life. It is only possible to speculate that either the HRC rejected the allegation, found it unnecessary to decide the point in the light of its view that there had been a violation of article 7 in respect of A.Q., or found any possible violation of article 17 to be subsumed within the article 7 violation.

9.23.1 The third important case is *Pratt and Morgan* v. *Jamaica*.[180] The case raised two issues concerning article 7:

the first is whether excessive delays in judicial proceedings constituted not only a violation of article 14, but 'cruel, inhuman and degrading treatment'. The possibility that such a delay as occurred in this case could constitute cruel and inhuman treatment was referred to by the Privy Council. In principle prolonged judicial proceedings do not *per se* constitute cruel, inhuman or degrading treatment even if they can be a source of mental strain for the convicted prisoners. However, the situation can be otherwise in cases involving capital punishment and an assessment of the circumstances of each case would be necessary. In the present cases the Committee does not find that the authors have sufficiently substantiated their claim that delay in judicial proceedings constituted for them cruel, inhuman and degrading treatment under article 7.

The second issue under article 7 concerns the issue of warrants for execution and the notification of the stay of execution. The issue of a warrant for execution necessarily causes intense anguish to the individual concerned. In the authors' case, death warrants were issued twice by the Governor General, first on 13 February 1987 and again on 23 February 1988. It is uncontested that the decision to grant a first stay of execution, taken at noon on 23 February 1987, was not notified to the authors until 45 minutes before the scheduled time of the execution on 24 February 1987. The Committee considers that a delay of close to 20 hours from the time of stay of execution was granted to the time the authors were removed from their death cell constitutes cruel and inhuman treatment within the meaning of article 7.[181]

The first of these issues was recently considered by the EUCT in *Soering* v. *UK*.[182] The EUCT unanimously held that the extradition of S to the United States would in the circumstances violate article 3 ECHR.[183] On the second issue the view of the HRC clearly indicates that psychological pressure can constitute 'cruel and inhuman treatment'.[184]

9.24 It has already been noted that the HRC have found violations of both articles 7 and 10(1) in a large number of cases.[185] In over a dozen cases the HRC has found a violation of article 10(1) alone. A number of these have already been noted. The most common violation of article 10(1) has been incommunicado detention for periods ranging from six weeks to many months.[186] In one case the HRC commented on how incommunicado detention can prevent the effective exercise of other rights.[187] In other findings of violation of article 10(1) the HRC has specifically referred to the denial of visits by family members,[188] wrongful denial of the fact of detention,[189] and possibly also the denial of medical treatment.[190] In

Mpandanjila and Others v. Zaïre[191] the HRC expressed the view that article 10(1) had been violated because the authors had been subjected to 'ill-treatment' during their period of banishment but no view is expressed as regards the deprivation of adequate medical attention which the HRC found as fact.[192] Similar comments can be made of the view in *Solorzano* v. *Uruguay*.[193] In *Izquierdo* v. *Uruguay*[194] the 'ill-treatment' founded a violation of article 7. Again there is no explanation of the material distinctions between the cases. The important views in which the HRC found that a practice of inhuman treatment which existed at Libertad prison in Uruguay violated article 10(1) has already been noted.[195]

9.25 The final view to note on article 10 is that in *Pinkey* v. *Canada*.[196] P alleged, *inter alia*, that article 10(2)(*a*) had been violated on the grounds that during his pre-trial detention he was not segregated from convicted prisoners and that his treatment as an unconvicted prisoner was worse than that given to convicted prisoners.[197] The State party submitted that,

The practice at the Lower Mainland Regional Correction Centre is for some sentenced prisoners in protective custody to serve as food servers and cleaners in the remand area of the prison. This arrangement is designed to keep them away from other sentenced prisoners who might cause them harm. The sentenced prisoners in the remand unit are not allowed to mix with the prisoners on remand except to the extent that it is inevitable from the nature of their duties. They are accommodated in separate tiers of cells from those occupied by remand prisoners.

The Government of Canada is of the view that lodging convicted prisoners in the same building as remand prisoners does not violate article 10, paragraph 2, of the ICCPR. This was recognized in the annotations on the text of the draft international covenant on human rights prepared by the Secretary-General of the United Nations. In paragraph 43 of the said annotations, it was indicated that,

'Segregation in the routine of prison life and work could be achieved though all prisoners might be detained in the same building. A proposal that accused prisoners should be placed in separate quarters was considered to raise practical problems; if adopted, States parties might be obliged to construct new prisons'.

Further, the Government of Canada does not consider that casual contact with convicted prisoners employed in the carrying out of menial duties in a correction centre results in a breach of the provisions of the Covenant.[198]

P replied that the contacts resulting from such employment of convicted prisoners were by no means 'casual' but were 'physical and regular' since they did in fact bring unconvicted and convicted prisoners together in physical proximity on a regular basis.[199] In its final view the HRC stated that,

The Committee is of the opinion that the requirement of article 10(2)(a) of the Covenant that 'accused persons shall, save in exceptional circumstances, be segregated from convicted persons' means that they shall be kept in separate quarters (but not necessarily in separate buildings). The Committee would not regard the arrangements described by the State party whereby convicted persons work as food servers and cleaners in the remand area of the prison as being incompatible with article 10(2)(a), provided that contacts between the two classes of prisoners are kept strictly to a minimum necessary for the performance of those tasks.[200]

As the HRC did not express the view that article 10(2)(*a*) had been violated it seems to have taken the view that accommodation 'in separate tiers of cells' constitutes 'segregation' for the purposes of article 10(2)(*a*). The end result comes close to reading into article 10(2)(*a*) the requirement of 'separate quarters' that the drafters did not adopt. That this does not 'necessarily' mean in separate buildings leaves open the possibility that in some circumstances it might be necessary to have separate buildings. The decision on contacts between the two classes of prisoners appears to set a sensible and practical standard for States parties. Unfortunately, the HRC expressed no view on P's allegations that his treatment as an unconvicted prisoner was worse than that given to convicted prisoners.[201] Finally, it is interesting to note that the case represents one of the few occasions on which a State party has referred to the *travaux préparatoires* in its submissions. The recent publication of a 'Guide to the Travaux Préparatoires of the ICCPR' may help to make this a more frequent practice.[202]

APPRAISAL

9.26 The HRC's work on article 7 under the reporting procedure has provided a useful opportunity for obtaining information on and critically probing and examining how States parties apply the prohibition in article 7 in their domestic systems. The members individually and the HRC collectively have recognized and emphasized the vital importance of some domestic 'machinery of control' through procedural safeguards and the need for an effective remedy, through investigation and compensation in the event of a violation.[203] Having obtained the basic information during the consideration of first and second periodic reports allows the HRC to proceed to the practical implementation and effectiveness of these procedures.[204] We have also suggested that the HRC could have been more dynamic in its consideration of the second sentence of article 7 which covers matters of continuing contemporary concern.[205]

9.27 The effectiveness of a reporting procedure ultimately depends on the co-operation and good faith of the States parties. Similarly, national and international publicity for the work of the HRC is of immense importance. It is very difficult to assess whether the HRC's consideration of article 7 has had any effect. Certainly the States parties could take account of the constructive comments and criticisms of the HRC and reappraise their relevant domestic laws and practices. The dialogue between the HRC and the representatives of

States parties focuses on more specific and detailed matters with the consideration of each subsequent periodic report. While judgment may be reserved in an institution's early years, as time passes the effectiveness or otherwise of the HRC's work will become more apparent.

9.28 Certainly there has been much to commend in the HRC's work to date. It has subjected State representatives and their reports to testing and critical examination. Moreover, it has managed to do so without unduly offending or antagonizing State sensitivity.[206] It is unfortunate that national and international publicity for the HRC's work in this area has been sadly lacking. Such publicity is often a potent force for change and progress.[207]

9.29 Similar considerations apply in assessing the effectiveness of the HRC's work under the OP on article 7 and 10. The vast majority of this has concerned Uruguay, which had manifested an attitude of non-cooperation with the HRC.[208] Again publicity for the HRC's views has been minimal. There is no real evidence to date that any of the HRC's recommendations as to remedies for violations of article 7 or 10(1) have been followed.[209] We have considered a number of constructive aspects of the HRC's jurisprudence on these provisions while criticizing others. The final views are often unhelpful, incomprehensible, or ambiguous.[210] In some the HRC has, without explanation, failed to comment on important allegations. The HRC has failed to develop a consistent, intelligible categorization of its views leading to a certain element of arbitrariness in its findings. Incommunicado detention, solitary confinement, and denial of medical treatment have been the object of violations of the Covenant but there has been no clear statement on exactly which provisions of the Covenant they violate or any accompanying explanation. Similarly, there has been no clear statement on mental or psychological as distinct from physical torture. More constructive developments have been the views that conditions of detention can violate articles 7 and 10(1), the finding of a 'practice of inhuman treatment' at Libertad prison in Uruguay, and possibly also the finding of an article 7 violation in the stress and anguish caused by the disappearance of a relative and the continuing uncertainty of his fate and whereabouts. The HRC's experience in examining communications concerning articles 7 and 10(1) can also inform and improve its consideration under the reporting procedure. However, in the final analysis, it seems difficult to conclude otherwise than that the views of the HRC on these provisions have only been of marginal significance in terms of effective human rights protection.

9.30 There exists a panoply of national and international measures directed to the suppression and elimination of torture. These include national criminal and civil laws and administrative provisions, a range of national institutions for protecting human rights, an array of international instruments and codes, a large number of international governmental and non-governmental organizations which consider and monitor torture and similar practices. The watershed decision of the United States Court of Appeals in *Filartiga* v. *Pena-Irala* has highlighted another method of human rights protection, namely the use of international human rights standards by national courts.[211]

The considerations of the HRC under the reporting procedure and its views under the OP represents further developments in this seemingly impressive regime of protection. The reality, however, is that the complex phenomenon of torture and related practices continues to flourish and survive in every geographic region of the world. In its report *Torture in the Eighties*, Amnesty International cites reports of torture and ill-treatment from ninety-eight countries for the period January 1980 to mid-1983.[212] The need for more effective protection was recognized within the United Nations, the Council of Europe, and the Organization of American States. Each organization has now produced a Convention on torture and related practices.[213]

9.31 The United Nations Convention (UNCAT) contains a definition of torture and a series of obligations and undertakings.[214] These provisions address in detail the principal features of a domestic regime which can play an effective role in facilitating the prevention and suppression of torture and other practices of ill-treatment. Many of these provisions cover matters raised by the HRC under the reporting process. The Convention also provides for the establishment of a Committee against Torture.[215] Under a reporting procedure the Committee may make such 'comments and suggestions on the report as it may consider appropriate'.[216] This provision would appear to give the new Committee more scope directly to address particular deficiencies in specific States parties than the HRC has assumed to date in its general comments under article 40(4).[217] The UNCAT also provides optional procedures for inter-State and individual communications to the Committee against Torture.[218] The major advance in the UN Convention, however, was to have been a mandatory confidential inquiry system to be operated by the Committee in co-operation with the State party and on the basis of 'any reliable information' received by the Committee 'which appears to it to contain well-founded indications that torture is being systematically practised'.[219] Unfortunately, the final text permits States parties to opt out of the visiting procedures.[220] The European Convention against Torture marks the most important advance in that it provides for compulsory visits with no provisions for opting out, making reservations or derogation.[221] Whether the work of the HRC on torture and ill-treatment will effectively be overtaken by that of the new Committee against Torture depends on the interpretation by that Committee of its jurisdiction, the level of ratification of the UN Convention, whether States parties opt out of the visiting procedures, and whether they opt into the individual and inter-State communication procedures.

NOTES

1 See n. 64 below on the scope of this chapter. For similar prohibitions see art. 5 UDHR, art. XXVI ADRD, art. 3 ECHR, art. 5(2) AMR, art. 5 AFR. On the drafting of articles 7 and 10 see Doc. A/2929, ch. 6, prs. 11–16, 39–44; Doc. A/4045, prs. 3–22, 68–86; M. Bossuyt, *Guide*, pp. 147–60. See Amnesty International, *Torture in the Eighties* (1984); S. Ackerman, 'Torture and other Forms of Cruel and Unusual Punishment in International Law', 11 Vand. J. Trans. L. (1978) pp. 653–707; C. Bassiouni and D. Derby, 'An Appraisal of Torture in International Law and Practice: The Need for an International Convention for the Suppression and Prevention of Torture', 48 Revue internationale de droit pénal (1977) pp. 17–114; Y. Dinstein, 'The Right to Life, Physical Integrity and Liberty', in L. Henkin (ed.), *The International Bill of Rights—The Covenant on Civil and Political Rights*, pp. 122–6 (1981); B. H. Klayman, 'The Definition of Torture in International Law', 51 Temple LQ (1978) pp. 449–515; P. Koojimanns, 'Torture and other Cruel or Degrading Treatment or Punishment', Docs. E/CN.4/1986/15, E/CN.4/1987/13, E/CN.4/1988/17, E/CN.4/1989/15, E/CN.4/1990/17; H. Noor Mohammed, 'Due Process of Law for Persons Accused of a Crime', in L. Henkin (ed.), above, pp. 122–6; E. Peters, *Torture* (1985); N. Rodley, *The Treatment of Prisoners under International Law* chs. 1–5 (1987); P. Sieghart, *The International Law of Human Rights*, pp. 159–74 (1983); *UN Action in the Field of Human Rights*, pp. 199–216 (1988).

The following Conventions have recently been concluded, United Nations Convention against Torture (1985), UN Doc. A/Res. 39/46, 23 ILM 1027 (1984) and 24 ILM 535 (1985); European Convention for the Prevention and Suppression of Torture and Inhuman or Degrading Treatment or Punishment, 1987, ETS No. 126; Inter-American Convention to Prevent and Punish Torture (1985), OASTS 67, 25 ILM 519 (1986). See also the following international instruments, Standard Minimum Rules for the Treatment of Prisoners, approved by ECOSOC in Resn. 663C (XXIV) (1957) and with an additional article in ECOSOC Resn. 2076 (LXII) (1977); Declaration on the Protection of All Persons from Being Subjected to Torture and other Cruel, Inhuman or Degrading Treatment or Punishment, GA Resn. 3542 (XXX) (1975); Code of Conduct for Law Enforcement Officials, GA Resn. 34/169 (1979); Principles of Medical Ethics Relevant to the Role of Health Personnel, Particularly Physicians, in the Protection of Prisoners and Detainees against Torture and other Cruel, Inhuman or Degrading Treatment or Punishment, GA Resn. 37/194 (1982). These international instruments are collected in *Human Rights—A Compilation of International Instruments* (1988), and in the appendices to Rodley, above. See also the 'United Nations Body of Principles for the Protection of All Persons under any Form of Detention or Imprisonment', GA Resn. 43/197 (9 Dec. 1988).

2 Art. 4(2) Covenant. See ch. 7 above.

3 GC 7(16), Doc. A/37/40, p. 94. Also in Doc. C/21/Add. 1. For the HRC's discussion see SR 371, 373, and 378 Add. 1. The HRC is in the process of updating its general comments on articles 7, 9 and 10, see Doc. A/44/40, p. 137.

4 Ibid., pr. 1.

5 See prs. 9.11–9.25 below.

6 See e.g. SR 327 pr. 31 (Aguilar on Morocco). Article 9 concerns the liberty and security of the person, see Apx. I below. The HRC has adopted a General Comment on article 9, see GC 8(16), Doc. A/37/40, p. 95. Also in Doc. C/21/Add. 1.

7 GC 7(16), n. 3 above, pr. 2.

8 GC 9(16), pr. 2, Doc. A/37/40, p. 96. Also in Doc. C/21/Add. 1.

9 See e.g. SR 327 pr. 43 (Tarnopolsky on Morocco). For these articles see Apx. I below.

10 See e.g. SR 475 pr. 18 (Opsahl on Guinea); SR 884 prs. 23–4 (Prado-Vallejo on the Philippines).

11 GC 7(16), n. 3 above, pr. 2.

12 GC 9(16), n. 8 above, pr. 2. On treaty interpretation see articles 31, 32 VCLT (1969).

13 See Fawcett, pp. 41–53; Van Dijk and Van Hoof, pp. 226–41; C. C. Morrisson, *The Dynamics of Development in the European Human Rights Convention System* (1981); P. J. Duffy, 'Article 3 of the European Convention on Human Rights', 32 ICLQ (1983) pp. 316–46.

14 See Doc. A/37/40, pr. 309.

15 See Doc. A/40/40, pr. 598.

16 See Doc. A/42/40, pr. 160.

17 See Doc. A/37/40, prs. 272, 278.

18 See Docs. A/34/40, pr. 80; A/39/40, prs. 463–64.

19 See ch. 3, pr. 3.3 above.

20 SR 108 pr. 50 (Sir Vincent-Evans). See also the discussion of this issue during consideration of the second periodic report of the USSR, summary in Doc. A/40/40, prs. 275–81. See C. Yeo, 'Psychiatry, the Law and Dissent in the Soviet Union', 14 Rev. ICJ (1975) pp. 34–41; A. Koryagin, 'Involuntary Patients in Soviet Psychiatric Hospitals', 26 Rev. ICJ (1981) p. 49. It is reported that the matter has now been officially recognized in the USSR. See *The Times*, 5–6 January 1988. A United States delegation of psychiatrists visited the USSR in 1989. In October 1989 the USSR was granted full membership of the World Psychiatric Association subject to confirmation in a year's time. See also SR 930.

21 GC 7(17), n. 3 above, pr. 1. On article 2 see ch. 6 above. Cf. in *Ireland* v. *UK*, EUCT, Series A, Vol. 25 (1978), the EUCT took the view that it could not order the UK to institute criminal or disciplinary proceedings, prs. 62, 82. In the *Greek Case*, 12(2) YBECHR (1969), the EUCM transmitted remedial proposals to the Committee of Ministers which approved them by Resolution, see pp. 514–15.

22 See n. 1 above. Doc. A/4045, pr. 84 (Report of the Third Committee, 1958). Cf. the decision of the EUCM in *Eggs* v. *Switzerland*, A.7341–76, 6 D. & R. 176. See also D. L. Skoler, 'World Implementation of the U.N. Standard Minimum Rules for the Treatment of Prisoners', 10 J. Int. L. & Econ. (1975) pp. 453–82; ECOSOC Resn. 1984/47 on procedures for the effective implementation of the SMR for the treatment of prisoners.

23 See n. 1 above. See e.g. SR 65 pr. 3 (Tomuschat on Czechoslovakia); SR 67 pr. 61

(Tomuschat on GDR); SR 249 pr. 74 (Tomuschat on Venezuela); SR 878 pr. 19 (Cooray on Uruguay).

24 See e.g. SR 346 pr. 7 (Tarnopolsky on Rwanda).

25 See e.g. SR 67 pr. 61 (Tomuschat on GDR); SR 99 pr. 11 (Lallah on Yugoslavia). See *Bleir* v. *Uruguay*, notes to pr. 9.24 below.

26 See e.g. text to pr. 9.3, n. 20 above (on USSR); SR 126 pr. 5 (Lallah on Romania); SR 264 pr. 23 (Vincent-Evans on Barbados). See the leading cases under the ECHR of *Winterwerp* v. *Netherlands*, EUCT, Series A, Vol. 33 (1979); *X.* v. *UK*, EUCT, Series A, Vol. 46 (1981); *Van der Leer* v. *Netherlands*, ibid., Vol. 170 (1990). *Simon Herald* v. *Austria*, 14 YBECHR p. 352.

27 See e.g. SR 440 pr. 57 (Tarnopolsky on France); SR 560 pr. 7 (Tomuschat on Canada), reply at SR 562 pr. 5.

28 GC 7(16), n. 3 above, pr. 1.

29 See Amnesty International Report, n. 1 above, pp. 247–51. See ch. 3, prs. 3.12–3.18 above on the sources of information used under the reporting process.

30 GC 7(16), n. 3 above, pr. 2. See articles 1 and 16 of the UN Convention against Torture (UNCAT), n. 1 above.

31 See e.g. SR 65 pr. 3 (Tomuschat on Czechoslovakia); SR 69 pr. 18 (Graefrath), SR 148 prs. 3–6 (Lallah on UK). For the UK reply see SR 148 prs. 23–7 and Supplementary Report, Doc. C/1/Add. 35 prs. 14–17.

32 See e.g. SR 69 pr. 32 (Tarnopolsky on UK); SR 98 pr. 64 (Tomuschat on Yugoslavia); SR 413 pr. 28 (Tomuschat on Austria). See also article 15 of the UNCAT, n. 1 above.

33 SR 148 pr. 3 (Lallah on UK). Reply at SR 148 pr. 21.

34 SR 69 pr. 7 (Lallah on UK). Cf. *McFeely* v. *UK*, A.8317/78, 3 EHRR (1981) p. 161.

35 SR 365 pr. 10 (Tarnopolsky on Iran).

36 SR 403 pr. 19 (Graefrath on Australia). 'Whipping as a punishment has been abolished in all States but Western Australia', Second periodic report of Australia, Doc. C/42/Add. 2 (1987), prs. 209–10. That report also raises the problem of traditional laws enforced by aboriginal communities which involved punishments which could be regarded as unacceptable and cruel, including, 'thigh spearing, forms of corporal punishment, initiation or putting young offenders "through the law", exile to an outstation or another community and public "shaming" or "growling"', ibid., pr. 205. The report continued by noting the view of the Australian Law Reform Commission that, 'what would be degrading in one community or culture might not be degrading, indeed might be fully accepted in another', and the general view of the Commission that, 'while the general law did not and should not condone or sanction "unlawful" (in the general sense) punishments, courts should take account of the traditional law basis of the unlawful action in determining the existence of a criminal intent and in sentencing. In many instances this already occurs', ibid., pr. 207.

37 SR 142 pr. 6 (Tarnopolsky on Spain).

38 SR 129 pr. 5 (Bouziri on Chile).

39 See the comments on Tomuschat at SR 128 pr. 22 (on Chile). Such deprivation

has, in certain circumstances, been held to violate article 25 of the Covenant, see e.g. *J. L. Massera* v. *Uruguay*, Doc. A/34/40, p. 124, pr. 10.2. See also Fawcett, p. 49.

40 See e.g. SR 111 pr. 18 (Esperson on Mauritius); SR 153 pr. 41 (Vincent-Evans on Ukrainian SSR); SR 213 pr. 14 (Tarnopolsky on Senegal); SR 386 pr. 33 (Graefrath on Mexico).

41 GC 7(16), n. 3 above, pr. 2. The keeping of persons incommunicado has, in certain circumstances, been held to be a violation of article 10(1) of the Covenant, see pr. 9.24 below.

42 See Fawcett pp. 47–8. See e.g. *Hilton* v. *UK*, A.5613/72, 4 D. & R. p. 177; *Bonzi* v. *Switzerland*, A.7854/77, 12 D. & R. p. 185 at 189.

43 See e.g. SR 162 pr. 91 (Tarnopolsky on UK Dependencies).

44 GC 7(16), n. 3 above, pr. 2. During the drafting of this general comment Mr Tarnopolsky stated that references to chastisement as an educational measure and protecting pupils in educational institutions, 'tended to trivialize the prohibition of torture or cruel, inhuman or degrading treatment or punishment', SR 371 pr. 16.

45 See the decisions of the EUCT in *Tyrer* v. *UK*, EUCT, Series A, Vol. 26 (1978); *Campbell and Cosans* v. *UK*, EUCT, Series A, Vol. 48 (1982). In *Warwick* v. *UK*, Report of 18 June 1986, the EUCM ruled by 12 votes to 5 that corporal punishment as a disciplinary measure constituted 'degrading treatment' under the ECHR. The Committee of Ministers was unable to attain the two-thirds majority necessary for a determination as to whether there had or had not been a violation of article 3, Resolution DH(89) 5 (2 Mar. 1989).

46 On article 2(3) see ch. 6 above.

47 SR 469 pr. 38 (Dimitrijevic on El Salvador).

48 SR 356 pr. 14 (Tarnopolsky on Uruguay).

49 See e.g. SR 364 pr. 74 (Vincent-Evans on Iran).

50 See e.g. SR 366 pr. 16 (Tomuschat on Iran).

51 GC 7(16), n. 3 above, pr. 2.

52 See e.g. the view of the HRC in *Baboeram* v. *Suriname*, ch. 8, pr. 8.23 above. See also AI Report on *Political Killings*, ch. 8, n. 1 above; Reports of the UN Special Rapporteur, ibid., notes 7 and 35.

53 See e.g. SR 92 pr. 53 (Graefrath on FRG); SR 779 pr. 35 (Higgins on Denmark). The limited consideration is perhaps surprising given that the provision was controversial at the drafting stage, see n. 1 above. See also A. C. Ivy, 'The History and Ethics of the Use of Human Subjects in Medical Experiments', (1948) 108 Science pp. 1–5; H. Saba, 'Les Droits de l'homme et de l'expérimentation biomedicale sur l'homme', *Mélanges offerts à Polys Modinos*, pp. 260–6 (1968); J. K. Mason and A. McCall-Smith, *Law and Medical Ethics*, chs. 17–18 (2d, 1983). See also the texts on human experimentation in (1980) Revue internationale de droit pénal at pp. 419, 445, and 459.

54 See e.g. SR 77 pr. 27 (Hanga on Norway); SR 170 pr. 60 (Hanga on Finland); SR 205 pr. 51 (Hanga on Canada).

55 SR 386 pr. 10 (Prado-Vallejo). For reply see SR 404 pr. 36.

56 See n. 1 above for the drafting records.

57 Ibid. There is no comparable express provision in other international human rights texts.
58 Ibid.
59 SR 92 pr. 53 (Graefrath on FRG). See Mason and McCall-Smith, n. 53 above, pp. 293–6.
60 See e.g. SR 441 pr. 37 (Graefrath on France).
61 See Mason and McCall-Smith, n. 53 above, chs. 16–17; Human Fertilisation and Embryology: A Framework for Legislation, Cmd. 259 (1987); The Fifth Report of the Voluntary Licensing Authority for Human in Vitro Fertilisation and Embryology (1990); Human Fertilization and Embryology Act 1990. B. M. Knoppers, 'Modern Birth Technology and Human Rights', 33 Am. J. Comp. L. (1985) pp. 1–31; R. Lee and D. Morgan (eds.), *Birthrights—Law and Ethics at the Beginning of Life* (1989); P. Sieghart, *AIDS and Human Rights: A U.K. Perspective* (1989).
62 See Mason and McCall Smith, n. 53 above, chs. 9 and 16.
63 GC 7(16) n. 3 above, pr. 3.
64 This section covers both articles 7 and 10 of the Covenant because, in terms of the views of the HRC, it was not sensible to consider article 7 in isolation.
65 We have noted that in its general comments on articles 7 and 10 the HRC made reference to the relationship between the two articles, see pr. 9.2 above.
66 In *Acosta* v. *Uruguay*, A alleged that, 'he was subjected to psychiatric experiments (giving the name of the doctor) and that for three years, against his will, he was injected with tranquillizers every two weeks', Doc. A/39/40, p. 169, pr. 2.7. The HRC noted that these allegations concerned a period before the entry into force of the Covenant and the OP for Uruguay, ibid., pr. 14.
67 See n. 13 above.
68 For the HRC's approach to these problems see ch. 4, prs. 4.27–4.36 above. A number of States have shown little co-operation to the HRC, see ch. 4, prs. 4.42–4.43, 4.127–4.132 above.
69 Doc. A/34/40, p. 124.
70 Ibid., pr. 10 at (i).
71 Ibid.
72 See also *Simones* v. *Uruguay*, pr. 9.23 below.
73 See pr. 9.4.1. above, and *Quinteros* v. *Uruguay* and *Simones* v. *Uruguay* in pr. 9.23 below.
74 Doc. A/37/40, p. 114.
75 Ibid., pr. 12.
76 See pr. 9.24 below.
77 See pr. 9.7 above.
78 A number of cases under the ECHR have concerned solitary confinement, see n. 42 above.
79 See the cases below on art. 10(1). Cf. *Kotalla* v. *Netherlands*, A.7994/77, 14 D. & R. p. 238.
80 Doc. A/35/40, p. 111.
81 Ibid., pr. 16.
82 See the *Estrella Case*, pr. 9.18 below.

83 Doc. A/34/40, p. 124.

84 Ibid., pr. 2. The HRC did express the view that article 10(1) had been violated but on other grounds. Similarly, in *Machado* v. *Uruguay*, Doc. A/39/40, p. 148, pr. 1.7, concerning allegations of ill-treatment. In *Ireland* v. *UK*, A.5301/71, Report of the EUCM (1978), the EUCM stated that restrictions on diet, if considered separately, may not as such constitute inhuman treatment, p. 401.

85 See *J. L. Massera* v. *Uruguay*, Doc. A/34/40, p. 124; *Grille Motta* v. *Uruguay*, Doc. A/35/40, p. 132; *Lopez Burgos* v. *Uruguay*, Doc. A/36/40, p. 176; *Antonaccio* v. *Uruguay*, Doc. A/37/40, p. 114; *Bleir* v. *Uruguay*, Doc. A/37/40, p. 130; *Estrella* v. *Uruguay*, Doc. A/38/40, p. 150; *E. Quinteros* v. *Uruguay*, A/38/40, p. 216; *Muteba* v. *Zaïre*, Doc. A/39/40, p. 182; *Gilboa* v. *Uruguay*, Doc. A/41/40, p. 128; *O. B. Acosta* v. *Uruguay*, Doc. A/44/40, p. 183. See also *Conteris* v. *Uruguay*, pr. 9.14.1. below, and *Baboeram* v. *Suriname*, pr. 8.23 above, in which in the light of its view that article 6(1) of the Covenant had been violated it did not consider it necessary to consider assertions that other provisions of the Covenant (including articles 7 and 10) were violated. In *Lubicon Lake Band* v. *Canada* allegations that the devastation wrought on the Band constituted cruel, inhuman and degrading treatment were not substantial, Doc. A/45/40, Apx., pr. 32.2.

86 Doc. A/34/40, p. 124. See Rodley, n. 1 above, p. 80. J. L. Massera, a distinguished Uruguayan mathematician, was subsequently released.

87 Doc. A/34/40, p. 124, pr. 9(ii).

88 See n. 21 above.

89 Ibid., pr. 173. For the EUCT's understanding of torture see ibid., pr. 167. There were four dissents from the EUCT's judgment. The EUCM had held unanimously that the combined use of the five techniques constituted a practice of inhuman treatment and torture, Report of the EUCM, n. 84 above, p. 401. The EUCT's understanding of torture has been criticized, see Fawcett, p. 46; Klayman, n. 1 above, pp. 497–500, 504–5.

90 See *Pratt and Morgan* v. *Jamaica*, Doc. A/44/40, p. 222, dealt with in pr. 9.23.1 below, on a failure to communicate the granting of a stay of execution to the prisoners concerned until shortly before their scheduled execution. The definition of torture in article 1 of the UN Convention against Torture, n. 1 above, refers to any 'act' by which severe pain or suffering, whether physical or mental, is intentionally inflicted on a person.

91 In many of the cases cited in n. 85 above there was no evidence submitted of permanent physical injury. In his separate opinion in *Ireland* v. *UK*, n. 21 above, Judge Zekia argued that whether the injuries were transitory or permanent in duration was one of the relevant factors to be taken into account in determining whether the conduct concerned constituted torture. Many modern torture techniques leave no permanent signs of injury, see Amnesty International Danish Medical Group, *Evidence of Torture* (1977).

92 *Grille Motta* v. *Uruguay*, Doc. A/35/40, p. 132.

93 *Lopez Burgos* v. *Uruguay*, Doc. A/36/40, p. 176; *O. B. Acosta* v. *Uruguay*, Doc. A/44/40, p. 183.

94 See *J. L. Massera* v. *Uruguay*, pr. 9.13 above.

95 *Lopez Burgos* v. *Uruguay*, Doc. A/36/40, p. 176.

96 *Bleir* v. *Uruguay*, Doc. A/37–40, p. 130; *Estrella* v. *Uruguay*, Doc. A/38/40, p. 150; *E. Quinteros* v. *Uruguay*, Doc. A/38/40, p. 216.

97 *Estrella* v. *Uruguay*, Doc. A/38/40, p. 150. The EUCT has held that, 'provided it is sufficiently real and immediate, a mere threat of conduct prohibited by article 3 [ECHR] may itself be in conflict with it', see *Campbell and Cosans* v. *UK*, EUCT, Series A, Vol. 48, pr. 26 (1982).

98 See *Muteba* v. *Zaire*, Doc. A/39/40, p. 182. See also *Gilboa* v. *Uruguay*, Doc. A/41/40, p. 128. Mock executions were among the treatments features in the *Greek Case*, n. 21 above, p. 500, 504.

99 However, this does seem to be the clear implication from *Estrella* v. *Uruguay*, see pr. 9.18 below. See also the *Quinteros Case*, pr. 9.23 below; *Pratt and Morgan* v. *Jamaica*, Doc. A/44/40, p. 222, considered in pr. 9.23. 1 below. In the *Greek Case*, n. 21 above, the Sub-Commission of the EUCM defined non-physical torture as 'the infliction of mental suffering by creating a state of anguish and stress by means other than bodily assault', and gave as one of their examples mock executions, pp. 461–3.

100 Doc. A/35/40, p. 111.

101 Ibid., pr. 9. See Rodley, n. 1 above, pp. 87–8.

102 Ibid., pr. 16. Similarly in *Ramirez* v. *Uruguay*, Doc. A/35/40, p. 121.

103 Doc. A/36/40, p. 114.

104 Ibid., pr. 16.

105 Doc. A/37/40, p. 179.

106 Ibid., pr. 9.

107 Doc. A/40/40, p. 196, pr. 10.

108 *Grille Motta* v. *Uruguay*, Doc. A/35/40, p. 132, pr. 16.

109 *Lopez Burgos* v. *Uruguay*, Doc. A/36/40, p. 176, pr. 13; *O. B. Acosta* v. *Uruguay*, Doc. A/44/40, p. 183, pr. 11 ('O.B.A. subjected to torture and to cruel, inhuman and degrading treatment and punishment').

110 See GC 7(16), n. 3 above, pr. 2, cited in pr. 9.5 above. See also n. 36 above.

111 Doc. A/39/40, p. 169.

112 Ibid., prs. 13.2–15.

113 Doc. A/36/40, p. 143.

114 Ibid., pr. 13.

115 In *Ireland* v. *UK*, n. 21 above, the finding of the EUCT was that the use of the five techniques constituted a practice of 'inhuman and degrading treatment' (finding 3). Another finding was that there existed at Palace Barracks a practice of 'inhuman treatment' (finding 6). See Sieghart, n. 1 above, pp. 167–70.

116 Doc. A/41/40, p. 128. The other views referring to cruel treatment are *O. B. Acosta* v. *Uruguay*, Doc. A/44/40, p. 183, n. 109 above; *Pratt and Morgan* v. *Jamaica*, Doc. A/44/40, p. 222, dealt with in pr. 9.23.1 below.

117 Doc. A/41/40, p. 128, pr. 4.3. Cf. in *Tyrer* v. *UK*, n. 45 above, the EUCT stated that for a punishment to be degrading the humiliation or debasement must be more than that which exists in the case of generally accepted forms of punishment imposed by courts for criminal offences. See also the *Greek Case*, n. 21 above, p. 186.

118 Doc. A/40/40, p. 196.

119 GC 7(16), n. 3 above, pr. 2. See pr. 9.5 above, text to n. 30.

120 'Movement and development in article 3 [ECHR] is obvious and will likely grow more intense and more frequent. However basic this human right may seem, it is most complex indeed', Clovis C. Morrisson, *The Dynamics of Development in the European Human Rights Convention System*, p. 72 (1981).

121 Hence the importance for the UK of the EUCT's decision, n. 21 above, that it had not 'tortured' detainees. On compensation for torture see *Filartiga II—The Damages Opinion*, 7 HRQ (1985) pp. 245–53; Anon., 'Torture: Prosecution and Compensation in Columbia', 35 Rev. ICJ (1985) pp. 5–6.

122 See Meron, ch. 7 n. 1 above (1986), p. 114.

123 See Ackerman, n. 1 above, pp. 682–3 on US law.

124 'The language of the Human Rights Committee has been especially inconsistent in its many cases dealing with violations of article 7', Rodley, n. 1 above, p. 87.

125 In a recent view the HRC was much more reasoned in its approach to alleged violations of articles 7 and 10(1), 'In no case was severe pain or suffering, whether physical or mental, inflicted upon A.V. by or at the instigation of a public official; nor does it appear that the solitary confinement to which the author was subjected, having regard to its strictness, duration and the end pursued, produced any adverse effects on him. Furthermore, it has not been established that V. suffered any humiliation or that his dignity was interfered with apart from the embarrassment inherent in the disciplinary measure to which he was subjected. In this connection, the Committee expressed the view that for punishment to be degrading, the humiliation or debasement involved must exceed a particular level and must in any event, entail other elements beyond the mere fact of deprivation of liberty': no violation of article 7 or 10(1), *Vuolanne v. Finland*, Doc. A/44/40', p. 249, pr. 9.2. On the HRC's 'views' generally see ch. 4, pr. 4.38 above.

126 See e.g. *Ambrosini* v. *Uruguay*, Doc. A/34/40, p. 124; *Carballal* v. *Uruguay*, Doc. A/36/40, p. 125; *Massiotti* v. *Uruguay*, Doc. A/37/40, p. 187; *Marais* v. *Madagascar*, Doc. A/38/40, p. 141; *Antonaccio* v. *Uruguay*, Doc. A/37/40, p. 114. Cf. *Estrella*, pr. 9.18 below. See also the *Greek Case*, n. 21 above, p. 489.

127 *Antonaccio* v. *Uruguay*, n. 126 above.

128 *Marais* v. *Madagascar*, Doc. A/38/40, p. 141.

129 *De Voituret* v. *Uruguay*, Doc. A/39/40, p. 164.

130 *Carballal* v. *Uruguay*, Doc. A/36/40, p. 125.

131 *Massiotti* v. *Uruguay*, Doc. A/37/40, p. 187. See also *Muteba* v. *Zaïre*, Doc. A/38/40, p. 182.

132 *Wight* v. *Madagascar*, Doc. A/40/40, p. 171. See also *Tshisekedi* v. *Zaïre*, Doc. A/45/40, Apx.: 'inhuman treatment' where T was deprived of food and drink for four days after his arrest and was subsequently kept interned under unacceptable insanitary conditions.

133 Doc. A/38/40, p. 150.

134 A possible rationalization could have been that article 7 would concern individual cases while article 10(1) would concern situations or practices. However, the HRC's views do not accord with such an explanation.

135 E was expelled from Uruguay in February 1980.

136 Doc. A/38/40, p. 150, pr. 10.

137 Ibid., pr. 8.3. See also the *Quinteros Case*, pr. 9.23 below.

138 Ibid., pr. 9.1 (my emphasis). The communication referred to is *Schweizer* v. *Uruguay*, Doc. A/38/40, p. 117 in which the HRC expressed the view that article 10(1) had been violated because S had been detained under inhuman prison conditions.

139 Doc. A/38/40, p. 201.

140 Ibid., pr. 10.4.

141 See the literature cited in ch. 4, pr. 4.115, n. 474 above. See also Klayman, n. 1 above, pp. 509–12.

142 Similar criticisms have been made of the International Court of Justice on occasions. See J. Dugard, 'The Nuclear Tests Cases and the South West Africa Cases: Some Realism about the International Judicial Decision', 16 Virg. JIL (1975–6) pp. 463–504.

143 The *Greek Case* 12(2) YBECHR (1969) pp. 194–6.

144 See ch. 4, pr. 4.115 above.

145 Doc. A/38/40, p. 150, pr. 9.2. The communication referred to by the HRC is *Antonaccio* v. *Uruguay*, Doc. A/37/40, p. 114 although the cross reference appears mistaken. The reference should presumably have been to *Pinkey* v. *Canada*, Doc. A/38/40 p. 101, pr. 34, in which the HRC stated that 'a legislative provision in the very general terms of this section did not . . . in itself provide satisfactory legal safeguards against arbitrary application . . .'. Cf. *Golder* v. *UK*, EUCT, Series A, Vol. 18 (1975); *Silver* v. *UK*, EUCT, Series A, Vol. 61 (1983); *Boyle and Rice* v. *UK*, EUCT, Series A, Vol. 131 (1988).

146 GC 9(16), prs. 3, 4. On article 2 of the Covenant see ch. 6 above. In *Bleir* v. *Uruguay*, Doc. A/37/40, p. 130, it was alleged that B was singled out for especially cruel treatment because he was a Jew, ibid., pr. 2.3. The HRC found, *inter alia*, a violation of articles 7 and 10(1) but made no reference to the alleged discriminatory treatment.

147 See ch. 6, pr. 6.11–6.13 above.

148 See pr. 9.2 above.

149 *Vuolanne* v. *Finland*, Doc. A/44/40, p. 249, pr. 9.2: no violation of article 7 or 10(1).

150 See n. 45 above.

151 See pr. 9.7 above.

152 Ibid.

153 Doc. A/35/40, p. 107.

154 Ibid., pr. 2.

155 Ibid., prs. 11, 12.

156 See ch. 4, pr. 4.30 above and ch. 6, pr. 6.25 on article 2.

157 Doc. A/35/40, p. 110.

158 See ch. 4, prs. 4.27–4.33 above.

159 *US* v. *Mexico*, 4 RIAA 82 (1926).

160 Ibid., pr. 20. See also the *Noyes Claim*, *US* v. *Panama*, 6 RIAA 308 (1933).

161 Doc. A/38/40, p. 216. See the Note by Camille Jones, 25 Harv. ILJ (1984) pp. 440–77; Anon., 37 Rev. ICJ p. 42 at p. 46 (1986).

162 It was alleged by the author that due to this event Venezuela suspended its diplomatic relations with Uruguay, Doc. A/38/40, p. 216, pr. 1.3.

163 Doc. A/38/40, p. 216, pr. 6.

164 Ibid., pr. 12.3.

165 Ibid., pr. 13.

166 Ibid., prs. 1.9 and 7.3.

167 See ch. 4, pr. 4.34 above.

168 Doc. A/38–40, p. 216, pr. 14.

169 This is the literal reading of the last sentence of the quoted paragraph. The comma after 'particular' is ungrammatical. However, even if a comma is placed after 'daughter' the sentence would still state that A.Q. is a victim of the violations 'suffered by her daughter' rather than clearly stating that A.Q. is herself a victim of violations of the Covenant.

170 See ch. 4, prs. 4.75–4.18.1 on the 'victim' requirement. Note that the HRC had already decided that A.Q. was entitled to act on behalf of E.Q., Doc. A/38/40, p. 216, pr. 3. Cf. the concept of the indirect victim under the ECHR, see Mikaelson, pp. 79–82.

171 Jones, n. 161 above, p. 476. In the *Greek Case*, n. 21 above, the Sub-Commission of the EUCM stated that deliberate or unnecessary emotional suffering caused to the families of detainees was prohibited by article 3 ECHR, p. 466. See also Anon., n. 161 above.

172 Ibid.

173 Perhaps as psychological torture, as A.Q. had alleged, or inhuman treatment.

174 Jones, n. 161 above, makes no comment on this point.

175 For the texts of these articles see Apx. I.

176 Doc. A/37/40, p. 174.

177 Ibid., pr. 12.

178 Cf. the customary international law duty to account for persons held in custody, see ch. 8, n. 123. See also The Principles on Detention and Imprisonment, n. 1 above, in particular principles 14, 17–18.

179 See e.g. *Bleir* v. *Uruguay*, Doc. A/37/40, p. 130; *Nieto* v. *Uruguay*, Doc. A/38/40, p. 201.

180 Doc. A/44/40, p. 222.

181 Ibid., prs. 13.6, 13.7.

182 EUCT, Series A, Vol. 161 (1989). The HRC reaffirmed its jurisprudence in *Pratt and Morgan* in *Reid* v. *Jamaica*, Doc. A/45/40, Apx., pr. 11.6.

183 The EUCT indicated that a relevant consideration in its finding was that S could have been sent for trial to the Federal Republic of Germany. It is interesting to speculate what the EUCT would have decided if there had been no such option available. The judgment suggests that the finding would have been the same, see ibid., prs. 100–1.

184 Cf. See text to n. 99 above.

185 See pr. 9.17 above.

186 *Ambrosini, J. L. Massera and M. V. Massera* v. *Uruguay*, Doc. A/34/40, p. 124 ('months'); *Pietraroia* v. *Uruguay*, Doc. A/36/40, p. 153 ('many months'); *De Casariego* v. *Uruguay*, Doc. A/36/40, p. 185 ('four months'); *Simones* v.

Uruguay, Doc. A/37/40, p. 174 ('three months'); *Caldas* v. *Uruguay*, Doc. A/38/ 40, p. 192 ('six weeks'); *Machato* v. *Uruguay*, Doc. A/39/40, p. 148 ('five months'); *Romero* v. *Uruguay*, Doc. A/39/40, p. 159 ('several months'). For a case in which the HRC found no violation of article 10(1) see *Vuolanne* v. *Finland*, Doc. A/44/40, p. 249, noted in n. 125 above.

187 *Caldas* v. *Uruguay*, n. 186 above. See ch. 10, pr. 10.34.3 below.

188 In *Ambrosini* v. *Uruguay*, pr. 9.12 above, the HRC referred to the 'right' to be visited by a family member. Similarly in *Massera* v. *Uruguay*, Doc. A/34/40, p. 124, pr. 10(ii).

189 *Simones* v. *Uruguay*, pr. 9.23 above.

190 *Antonaccio* v. *Uruguay*, pr. 9.12.2 above. In *Pinto* v. *Trinidad and Tobago*, the HRC reaffirmed that the obligation in article 10(1) 'encompasses the provision of adequate medical care during detention', Doc. A/45/40, Apx., pr. 12.7.

191 Doc. A/41/40, p. 121.

192 Ibid., prs. 8.2, 10. The administrative banishment was held to violate the freedom of movement in article 12(1) of the Covenant.

193 Doc. A/41/40, p. 134.

194 Doc. A/37/40, p. 179.

195 See pr. 9.18 above.

196 Doc. A/37/40, p. 101. See also ch. 10, prs. 10.36–37 below.

197 Doc. A/37/40, p. 101, pr. 23.

198 Ibid., pr. 28 at B.

199 Ibid., pr. 29.

200 Ibid., pr. 30.

201 For the submissions of the State party on this point see, ibid., pr. 28 at A.

202 See Bossuyt, *Guide*.

203 See prs. 9.4–9.4.1 above.

204 See *Torture in the Eighties*, n. 1 above, ch. 6.

205 See prs. 9.9–9.10 above.

206 See pr. 9.3 above.

207 See generally ch. 2, pr. 2.9 above.

208 See pr. 9.12 above.

209 See pr. 9.12, n. 68 above.

210 See the cases cited in prs. 9.12.1–9.12.3 above.

211 630 F. 2d. 876 (1980), 19 ILM 966 (1980). See generally ch. 1, pr. 1.37 above.

212 See n. 1 above.

213 Ibid.

214 UNCAT, n. 1 above, articles 1–16. See J. Donnelly, 'The Emerging International Regime against Torture', 33 NILR (1986) pp. 1–23. See also A. Cassese, 'The New Approach to Human Rights: The European Convention for the Prevention of Torture', 83 AJIL (1989) pp. 128–53. Members of the HRC have inquired as to the effect of the ratification of the CAT on the domestic legal system, see e.g. SR 878 pr. 18 (Fodor on Uruguay).

215 The Committee has now been elected and includes one member of the HRC, Ms Christine Chanet (France), see 2 Interights Bulletin p. 31 (1987). The

Committee's meetings are closed. Its second session was held in April 1989, see 4 Interights Bulletin p. 3 (1989).

216 Article 19, UNCAT.

217 See ch. 3, prs. 3.29–3.35 above.

218 Articles 21 and 22 UNCAT respectively. For the CAT's first decision see *O.R., M.M. and M.S.* v. *Argentina*, UN Doc. CAT/C/3/D/1, 2 and 3/1988.

219 Article 20 UNCAT. With the agreement of the State party the inquiry could include a visit to the State concerned, article 20(3).

220 Article 28 UNCAT.

221 See n. 1 above and the accompanying Explanatory Report (1987).

Article 14[1]

1. All persons shall be equal before the courts and tribunals. In the determination of any criminal charge against him, or of his rights and obligations in a suit at law, everyone shall be entitled to a fair and public hearing by a competent, independent and impartial tribunal established by law. The press and the public may be excluded from all or part of a trial for reasons of morals, public order (*ordre public*) or national security in a democratic society, or when the interest of the private lives of the parties so requires, or to the extent strictly necessary in the opinion of the court in special circumstances where publicity would prejudice the interests of justice; but any judgement rendered in a criminal case or in a suit at law shall be made public except where the interest of juvenile persons otherwise requires or the proceedings concern matrimonial disputes or the guardianship of children.

2. Everyone charged with a criminal offence shall have the right to be presumed innocent until proved guilty according to law.

3. In the determination of any criminal charge against him, everyone shall be entitled to the following minimum guarantees, in full equality:

(a) To be informed promptly and in detail in a language which he understands of the nature and cause of the charge against him;

(b) To have adequate time and facilities for the preparation of his defence and to communicate with counsel of his own choosing;

(c) To be tried without undue delay;

(d) To be tried in his own presence, and to defend himself or through legal assistance of his own choosing; to be informed, if he does not have legal assistance, of this right; and to have legal assistance assigned to him, in any case where the interests of justice so require, and without payment by him in any such case if he does not have sufficient means to pay for it;

(e) To examine, or have examined, the witnesses against him and to obtain the attendance and examination of witnesses on his behalf under the same conditions as witnesses against him;

(f) To have the free assistance of an interpreter if he cannot understand or speak the language used in court;

(g) Not to be compelled to testify against himself or to confess guilt.

4. In the case of juvenile persons, the procedure shall be such as will take account of their age and the desirability of promoting their rehabilitation.

5. Everyone convicted of a crime shall have the right to his conviction and sentence being reviewed by a higher tribunal according to law.

6. When a person has by a final decision been convicted of a criminal offence and when subsequently his conviction has been reversed or he has been pardoned on the ground that a new or newly discovered fact shows conclusively that there has been a miscarriage of justice, the person who has suffered punishment as a result of such conviction shall be compensated according to law, unless it is proved that the non-disclosure of the unknown fact in time is wholly or partly attributable to him.

7. No one shall be liable to be tried or punished again for an offence for which he has already been finally convicted or acquitted in accordance with the law and penal procedure of each country.

Introduction

10.2 Article 14 is not covered by the non-derogation provision in article 4(2) ICCPR.[2] It has been the subject of a General Comment under article 14(4).[3] During the consideration of State reports it has generally been dealt with alone although its relationship with article 9 has often been noted.[4] The right to a fair hearing has long been regarded as a central feature of the rule of law and in its General Comment the HRC stated that the provisions of article 14 are 'aimed at ensuring the proper administration of justice'.[5]

It is not surprising, therefore, that members of the HRC have attached great importance to article 14. The appropriate parts of State reports and the relevant texts of accompanying Constitutions, penal codes, civil codes, and procedural codes have been closely and critically examined for compliance with the complex of rights guaranteed by article 14.[6] HRC members have sought to understand how practical effect is given to its various aspects in the domestic law of the State concerned.[7]

The HRC has noted that the 'article 14 of the Covenant is of a complex nature and that different aspects of its provisions will need specific comments', but that, 'Not all reports provided details on the legislative and other methods adopted specifically to implement each of the provisions of article 14'.[8] The HRC's considerations of article 14 have involved an enormous number of questions and comments of which only a schematic outline and a few illustrative examples can be given. It is instructive, though somewhat artificial, to break down the HRC's work into a paragraph-by-paragraph analysis.

A. ARTICLE 14 UNDER THE REPORTING PROCESS

Article 14(1)

10.3 Members of the HRC have sought to ascertain how the equality of 'all persons' before courts and tribunals and the entitlement to a 'fair and public hearing' are guaranteed in the domestic law of the States parties.[9] Particular scrutiny has been directed to the terms of any distinctions between citizens and aliens[10] and any discrimination against political offenders[11] or on grounds of political opinion.[12] Similarly, questions have been put concerning restrictions on legal capacity.[13] Members have stressed the difficulty in securing equality before courts and tribunals and emphasized the need to take practical steps. For example,

With reference to article 14 of the Covenant, equality before the courts was not achieved simply by avoiding discrimination in legislation as mentioned in paragraph 46 of the report. There were many serious social, cultural and language barriers that could make access to the courts extremely unequal and there was also the question of cost. It would be interesting to hear, therefore, what Iceland had done and was doing to ensure that equality before the courts really meant equal access to those courts and to the legal profession.[14]

Some members of the HRC have indicated their view that the principle of equality before the law 'meant not merely equality between one citizen and another but also the equality of the citizen vis-à-vis the executive'.[15] There has though been little specific discussion in terms of the procedural equality of parties.[16] In its General Comment the HRC stated that it would find useful, 'more detailed information on the steps taken to ensure that equality before the courts, including equal access to courts, fair and public hearings and competence, impartiality and independence of the judiciary are established by law and guaranteed in practice. In particular, States parties should specify the relevant constitutional and legislative texts which provide for the establishment of the courts and ensure that they are independent, impartial and competent, in particular with regard to the manner in which judges are appointed, the qualifications for appointment, and the duration of their terms of office; the conditions governing promotion, transfer and cessation of their functions and the actual independence of the judiciary from the executive branch and the legislature.'[17] The final sentence of this comment is clearly in terms of the classic separation of powers doctrine.[18]

10.4 There has also been little specific discussion under the reporting procedure of the key terms 'criminal charge' and 'rights and obligations in a suit at law'.[19] This is perhaps surprising bearing in mind the jurisprudence under article 6 of the ECHR where parallel expressions have been developed as 'autonomous concepts' but this is probably simply a reflection on the nature of article 40 as a reporting process rather than a petitions procedure.[20] The scope of the latter expression has indeed been the subject of an important decision under the Optional Protocol.[21]

The HRC did, however, address the issues in its General Comment:

In general, the reports of states parties fail to recognize that article 14 applies not only to procedures for the determination of criminal charges against individuals but also to procedures to determine their rights and obligations in a suit at law. Laws and practices dealing with these matters vary widely from State to State. This diversity makes it all the more necessary for States parties to provide all relevant information and to explain in greater detail how the concepts of 'criminal charge' and 'rights and obligations in a suit at law' are interpreted in relation to their respective legal systems.[22]

This comment is open to the obvious criticism that it fails to give any criteria or definition to the key concepts in article 14(1). If practices vary widely from State to State the HRC should indicate its understanding of the concepts so that compliance with article 14(1) can be more meaningfully assessed not only by the HRC itself but also by States parties. This criticism would appear to be valid even if it is recognized that the problems occasioned by the interpretation of article 6 ECHR at the regional level might be greatly compounded at the universal level in giving autonomous content to article 14(1).

10.5 Two important matters of general relevance to a fair hearing that have been raised by members concern the legal profession and the availability of legal aid. They have sought information on how the legal profession is organized, the restrictions and limitations applicable or operating in practice, and their freedom to exercise their profession.[23] A typical approach is that of Mr Tomuschat, who

wished to know how the legal profession was organized. Was it free and independent, or were lawyers public servants who required State authorization before practising their profession? Were they required only to have certain qualifications or was there any discretionary control on the grounds of public interest?[24]

With regard to legal aid members have sought information on its availability, the conditions necessary to secure it, and the problems the application of a legal aid scheme raised.[25] For example, during consideration of the report of France, Sir Vincent-Evans commented that,

In connection with article 14 of the Covenant, which applied to both civil and criminal proceedings, he observed that the costs involved in a court case might sometimes prevent a person from obtaining justice not only in a criminal case but even more so with regard to the recognition of a civil right. Mr. Guillame had referred to legal aid in France but that was often not granted except to the very poorest and it would be interesting to know what the current situation was in France for a middle class individual.[26]

Matters concerning the legal profession and legal aid systems have also been raised in connection with paragraph 3 of article 14.[27] HRC members have recognized, however, that mechanisms other than an individual's lawyer may be useful in securing respect for article 14. For example, the representative of the Dominican Republic was asked whether the offices of the Ombudsman or the *defensor del pueblo* could be used to improve the administration of justice particularly in rural areas.[28]

10.6 The requirement of a 'fair and public hearing by a competent, independent and impartial tribunal established by law' has attracted detailed attention. Discussion and comment has primarily focused on (*a*) the nature and jurisdiction of courts and tribunals; (*b*) the separation of powers; (*c*) the judiciary in all its forms; and (*d*) the 'public hearing' guarantee and the limitations thereon.

(*a*) The nature and jurisdiction of courts and tribunals

10.7 Members have sought to determine the existence, organization, nature, and jurisdiction of special or extraordinary courts[29] or tribunals that dealt, for example, with labour disputes or economic, social, or administrative matters,[30] or that applied special rules or procedures.[31] Of particular concern has been the operation of military or revolutionary tribunals.[32] Members have sought details of their jurisdiction, particularly in respect of civilian matters, and assurances that such tribunals operated in accordance with the guarantees in article 14.[33] If such tribunals did exercise civilian jurisdiction members have requested explanations of the removal of that jurisdiction from civilian authorities and asked whether the possibility of returning the matter concerned to the civilian authorities was being considered.[34] Among the kind of bodies that have attracted close and often critical attention have been 'Special Courts',[35] 'Public Security Committees',[36] 'Self-Management Courts',[37] 'Comrades Courts',[38] 'Sharia Courts',[39] 'State Security Courts',[40] and 'Gun Courts'.[41]

Consideration of the situation in Suriname raised the question of the compatibility with the Covenant of the establishment of special courts to try members of the previous administration.[42] One member of the Committee clearly thought that such a step would contravene the Covenant:

With regard to article 14 ... he had noted, in the aforementioned Declaration by the Government, that it was planned to set up special courts, outside the judicial order, to try members of the previous administration charged with corruption. Any Government had, of course, the right to punish such crimes, but the creation of tribunals foreign to the judicial order would certainly be contrary to the provisions of the Covenant, and he would like to have further details about those plans.[43]

In its General Comment the concern of the HRC at the operation of special courts and tribunals was expressed at length:

The provisions of article 14 apply to all courts and tribunals within the scope of that article whether ordinary or specialized. The Committee notes the existence, in many countries, of military or special courts which try civilians. This could present serious problems as far as the equitable, impartial and independent administration of justice is concerned. Quite often the reasons for the establishment of such courts is to enable exceptional procedures to be applied which do not comply with normal standards of justice. While the Covenant does not prohibit such categories of courts, nevertheless the conditions which it lays down clearly indicate that the trying of civilians by such courts should be very exceptional and should take place under conditions which genuinely afford the full guarantees stipulated in article 14. The Committee has noted a serious lack of information in this regard in the reports of some States parties whose judicial institutions include such courts for the trying of civilians. In some countries such military and special courts do not afford the strict guarantees of the proper administration of justice in accordance with the requirement of article 14 which are essential for the effective protection of human rights. If States parties decide in circumstances of a public emergency as contemplated by article 4 to derogate from normal procedures required by article 14, they should ensure that such situations do not exceed those strictly required by the exigencies of the actual situation, and respect the other conditions in paragraph 1 of article 14.[44]

This aspect of the HRC's General Comment represents a useful response to the HRC's experience under the article 40 process and is a clear recognition of the abuses commonly practised by such special courts. Although it is possible to derogate from article 14, failure to comply with article 14 may result in violations of provisions of the Covenant from which it is not possible to derogate, for example, article 6.[45] Although the comment only expressly deals with the problem of the trial of civilians by special courts and tribunals, during the discussion of the draft comment concern was also expressed at the lack of fair trial guarantees for military personnel in such bodies.[46]

(b) The separation of powers and the judiciary

10.8 These matters are clearly related and will be dealt with together. HRC members have been quick to express serious concern when the lines of demarcation between executive and judicial power have appeared indiscernible.[47] For example, during consideration of the report of Nicaragua Mr Opsahl commented that,

Under the Sandinista Police Jurisdiction Act the police were granted the jurisdiction to apply the police regulations and laws through police examining magistrates. He asked whether in that event the police functioned as courts and why offenders could not be brought before ordinary courts.[48]

Similarly Sir Vincent-Evans asked the Yugoslavian representatives,

Could one hope to obtain a fair trial when the Courts were so closely integrated in the political system, especially in cases of political offences? Was a Judge liable to be dismissed or disciplined if other agencies of the system felt he had adjudicated in a manner detrimental to its interests, for example, in a political case?[49]

By contrast on a number of occasions Mr Graefrath indicated a somewhat different conception of the separation of powers,

He did not think that the separation of powers and the establishment of professional and irremovable Judges were of themselves guarantees for the establishment of an independent judiciary. Furthermore, the irremovability of Judges could be seen as a kind of discrimination and privilege vis-à-vis other professions on the grounds of social status and could be dangerous to the establishment of a democratic society.[50]

Another matter consistently raised has been the role of the Official Public Prosecutor,[51] Procurator,[52] or People's Advocate,[53] and his precise powers in terms of investigation, prosecution, and adjudication.

10.9 A lengthy catalogue of questions have been developed in respect of the judiciary in all its forms. What rules and procedures governed the appointment,[54] election,[55] nomination,[56] dismissal, recall,[57] suspension,[58] transfer,[59] and retirement[60] of judges? What were the terms and conditions of tenure? Who or which authority or institution applied the appropriate rules?[61] How was the judiciary organized and composed? Were particular qualifications or legal training required?[62] What was the nature and extent of the role played by the lay judiciary and assessors? What disciplinary regime was applicable and was it possible for a judge to commit offences in his official capacity?[63] What general and specific legal and other guarantees existed to ensure the independence and impartiality of the judiciary?[64] Could the legislative or the executive set aside judicial decisions?[65] How could the impartiality of judges be ensured?[66] Was access to the judiciary limited by, for example, social origin, the educational process, or financial constraints?[67] Was the independence or impartiality of judges affected by the need to follow a particular party line,[68] an ideological limitation such as 'socialist justice',[69] or a government conception of public order.[70] During consideration of the report of Nicaragua Mr Bouziri warned against the dangers of abuse of extensive discretionary powers vested in judges and its implications for their impartiality.[71]

In its General Comment the HRC stated that,

States parties should specify the relevant constitutional and legislative texts which provide for the establishment of the courts and ensure that they are independent, impartial and competent, in particular with regard to the manner in which judges are appointed, the qualifications for appointment, and the duration of their terms of office; the conditions governing promotion, transfer and cessation of their functions and the actual independence of the judiciary from the executive and legislative branch.[72]

A question which has occasionally been put by members but rarely accorded the importance it deserves is how, in practice, an individual could actually challenge the independence or impartiality of a judge or tribunal.[73] Similarly, only rarely have questions of structural limitations and deficiencies, for example, lack of resources and shortage of judicial power,[74] access to and the administration of justice in small communities been put.[75]

The willingness of members to try and discern the actual practices of States rather than be content with general assurances and explanations is well illustrated in the comments of Mr Opsahl during consideration of the report of El Salvador:

With regard to the present state of the judicial system in El Salvador, a fact-finding mission from the New York Bar had stated that the system of Penal justice in El Salvador was in general disarray and that senior members of the judiciary were corrupt. Such statements compelled the Committee to raise certain questions especially concerning the initiation of judges, jurors and witnesses. He pointed out that insufficient resources were allocated to education and training in the legal profession which, consequently, left much to be desired.[76]

From this comment it is possible to note both the use of outside information by a HRC member and a clear recognition that the implementation of the Covenant requires the allocation of resources by the State.[77]

(c) *The public hearing guarantee and its limitations*[78]

10.10 Members of the HRC have not, under the article 40 process, subjected the guarantee and its limitations to detailed analyses and there has been little real discussion of the meaning of the specified grounds of limitation.[79] Similarly no assistance on this matter is provided by the HRC's General Comment.[80] This perhaps reflects the fact that the nature of the article 40 process is not one of precise definition but one of general content and meaning. Members have requested detailed clarification on the given grounds of limitation in a particular State both in law and in practice.[81] They have asked how those grounds are defined or understood and as to their compatibility with the limitations in the Covenant.[82] The United Kingdom representative was asked whether the 'concept of public security had evolved in any way since 1920, particularly from the point of view of jurisprudence and administrative practice'.[83] The representative of the USSR was asked how a limitation to cover cases of 'State Secrets' was consistent with the Covenant.[84] The representative of Czechoslovakia was asked, 'Could proceedings be closed to the public for reasons of State security in general and not only for reasons of national security as mentioned in article 14'.[85] The representative of Romania was asked to define the limitation in terms of cases prejudicial to socialist morality.[86] The Swedish representative was asked about the frequency of the use of the in camera procedure.[87] What restrictions, if any, were there on the admission of the mass media to court hearings.[88] Members have occasionally asked whether it was possible for members of an accused's family to be present during trial,[89] and, more rarely, of the possibility of foreign observers or non-governmental organizations attending trials.[90]

During consideration of the report of Uruguay Mr Tomuschat made use of the HRC's experience with regard to communications concerning Uruguay under the Optional Protocol to indicate the extent of a State party's obligations under article 14(1):

It was implicit in the right to a fair trial that sentences of long periods of detention should be handed down in writing. In that connection, the Committee had never been provided with the text of any court decisions despite repeated requests.[91]

In its General Comment on article 14 the HRC stated that,

The publicity of hearings is an important safeguard in the interest of the individual and of society at large. At the same time, article 14, paragraph 1, acknowledges that courts have the power to exclude all or part of the public for reasons spelt out in that paragraph. It should be noted that, apart from such exceptional circumstances, the Committee considers that a hearing must be open to the public in general, including members of the press, and must not, for instance, be limited only to a particular category of persons. It should be noted that, even in cases in which the public is excluded from the trial, the judgement must, with strictly defined exceptions, be made public.[92]

It is notable that the HRC regards the public hearing requirement as an 'important safeguard'. As such it would have been helpful if the HRC had provided some criteria for the assessment of the permissible limitations. The reference to particular categories of persons may be inspired by the alleged practice in some States of packing the courts with persons paid by the State. Admission of members of the press is obviously of particular importance in terms of bringing effective publicity to bear on possible deficiencies in court proceedings. A number of recent applications to the EUCM have concerned exclusion of the press from or restrictions on the reporting of proceedings in the UK.[93] Finally, even where the trial legitimately does not take place in public there is a back-up safeguard in the form of a requirement of a public judgment.[94]

It remains to note that in its General Comment the HRC stated that in order to safeguard the rights of accused persons under, *inter alia*, article 14(1), judges should have the authority to consider any allegations made of violations of these rights during any stage of the prosecution.[95] It is difficult to understand why the comment does not expressly extend to alleged violations of article 14(1) in the determination of 'rights and obligations in a suit at law'.

Article 14(2): the presumption of innocence[96]

10.11 Members have inquired as to how the presumption of innocence is given effect in domestic law. Was it clearly and expressly provided for in the Constitution, Penal Code, or in other legislation?[97] In any event, how was the presumption given effect in practice, for example, with respect to restrictions on the media?[98] Generally members have confined their considerations to the basic matters of the burden and standard of proof[99] and the operation of statutory exceptions to the burden of proof.[100] The related issue of the use of confessions has also been raised.[101] They have pointed to apparent inconsistencies and requested further explanation.[102] In its General Comment on article 14 the HRC noted the lack of information from States parties on article 14(2) and stated that it, 'in some cases, has even observed that the presumption of innocence, which is fundamental to the protection of human rights, is expressed in very ambiguous terms or entails conditions which render it ineffective'.[103]

Occasionally it has been stated or suggested that the presumption of innocence has a wider significance than the matters of the burden and standard of proof. During consideration of the report of Canada Mr Opsahl commented that,

> The provisions might be considered to have other implications than those concerning the burden of proof. It might be asked for example, whether an accused person who had been acquitted had to pay the costs of the proceedings; whether the public prosecutor should refrain from taking legal action but declare publicly that he considered the person guilty; whether an accused person could accept a penalty in order to avoid being sent to trial; and whether authorities other than the courts respected the presumption of innocence.[104]

Mr Janca has pointed to the possibility of the regime of detention under which an accused is held violating the presumption of innocence:

> He did not fully understand the information provided in the report on article 10.[105] It seemed that not only convicted persons but also persons under preliminary investigation could be placed in corrective labour institutions and subjected to corrective labour measures, although they had not been sentenced. If that was so, such a measure would be in contradiction with article 14, paragraph 2, of the Covenant . . .[106]

Mr Tomuschat has even gone so far as to suggest that the terms of a criminal offence may itself be a violation of the presumption of innocence:

> The vague and general definition of such criminal offences as subversive association might violate the presumption of innocence required by article 14(2) of the Covenant in as much as any individual hostile to the government would be liable to criminal sanction merely by discussing political issues with friends. Much fuller information was needed on the scope of such offences and on the practice of the courts in dealing with them. It needed to be demonstrated that such broadly framed provisions were truly necessary and not intended solely to criminalize political dissent.[107]

In its General Comment the HRC as a whole adopted a broader interpretation of article 14(2) than simply matters relating to proof but did not expressly go as far as Mr Janca or Mr Tomuschat. The HRC commented,

> By reason of the presumption of innocence, the burden of proof of the charge is on the prosecution and the accused had the benefit of the doubt. No guilt can be presumed

until the charge has been proved beyond reasonable doubt. Further, the presumption of innocence implies a right to be treated in accordance with this principle. It is therefore a duty for all public authorities to refrain from prejudging the outcome of a trial.[108]

This broad approach to the presumption of innocence is to be welcomed as the presumption, which in the words of the HRC 'is fundamental to the protection of human rights',[109] is increasingly under attack and the subject of a growing number of cases under the ECHR.[110]

Article 14(3): minimum guarantees in criminal cases

10.12 As with the first sentence of article 14(1), members have sought to determine whether the 'minimum guarantees' of article 14(3) are secured in 'full equality'.[111] Clearly paragraphs 1 and 3 are related, the latter being the minimum, though not exhaustive, preconditions of a fair criminal trial. As the HRC stated in its General Comment, 'the requirements of paragraph 3 are minimum guarantees, the observance of which is not always sufficient to ensure the fairness of a hearing as required by article 1'.[112] In this sense then the concept of a fair hearing is ultimately a residual one.[113] In its General Comment the HRC also stated that, 'In order to safeguard the rights of the accused under paragraph 3 of article 14, judges should have authority to consider any allegations made of violations of the rights of the accused during any stage of the prosecution'.[114]

Some important general matters such as procedural equality, the legal profession and the legal aid system which have been raised under article 14(3), have already been noted above under article 14(1).[115] Members have often indicated to State representatives the desirability of dealing with article 14(3) on a point-by-point basis.[116] They have pointed to apparent gaps or inconsistencies, expressed doubts, and asked for further clarifications.

10.13 Article 14(3)(*a*) has attracted little attention or discussion. Members have done little more than note the relevant provisions of domestic law and point to any possible inadequacies. In its General Comment the HRC stated that,

State reports often do not explain how this right is respected and ensured. Article 14, subparagraph 3 (a) applies to all cases of criminal charges, including those of persons not in detention. The Committee notes further that the right to be informed 'promptly' requires that information is given in the manner described as soon as the charge is first made by a competent authority. In the opinion of the Committee this right must arise when in the course of an investigation a court or an authority of the prosecution decides to take procedural steps against a person suspected of a crime or publicly names him as such. The specific requirements of subparagraph 3 (a) may be met by stating the charge either orally or in writing, provided that the information indicates both the law and the alleged facts on which it is based.[117]

The reference to the taking of 'procedural steps' against a person suspected of a crime as constituting a charge is obviously important as exactly when a person is charged can be a difficult question to determine.[118] However, it may still be difficult to determine what in practice constitutes a 'procedural step', particularly in States with inquisitorial systems of procedure. The requirement that the information given relate to both the law and the alleged facts parallels the jurisprudence under the ECHR.[119]

10.14 In respect of article 14(3)(*b*) members have requested clarification and justification of any general or specific limitations on the preparation of the defence.[120] For example, during consideration of the report of Poland Mr Janca commented,

The report indicated that the accused had the right to counsel of his own choosing and could communicate with him directly without any other person being present. However, that freedom was limited by the fact that, during the preparatory proceedings, the Prosecutor, while authorising the accused to confer with his lawyer, could nonetheless reserve the right to be present at the meeting or to designate another person to attend it and that, in exceptional cases, he could even refuse such authorization. That limitation of the right of the accused did not seem to be in conformity with the spirit of article 14, paragraph 3 (b), of the Covenant.[121]

Similarly members have asked whether the right to communicate was secured at the stage of preliminary hearings[122] and whether there were circumstances when only written communication was permissible.[123] A serious restriction on the right to communicate was indicated in the report of Romania concerning article 172 of its Criminal Code:

An accused person may contact defence counsel. Where the interests of the investigation so require, the prosecuting authority may, by an order stating the reasons on which it is based, prohibit an accused person under arrest from contacting his defence counsel for a period of not less [*sic*] than thirty days. If necessary, the prohibition may be extended for a period of not more than thirty days. Contact with defence counsel may not be prohibited where the period of detention is extended by the court or once the prosecution's material has been submitted.[124]

A number of the HRC members expressed concern about this provision and doubted its compatibility with article 14(3)(*b*) and (*d*).[125]

10.14.1 Only rarely has the difficulty of securing the right to communicate with counsel when the accused is held in some form of isolation been touched upon.[126] The scope and meaning of 'facilities' has not been discussed in terms during the consideration of State reports notwithstanding some clear opportunities to do so, for example, in response to a reservation by Australia concerning the provision of 'adequate facilities' to prisoners.[127] Fortunately, the HRC's General Comment was more helpful:

What is 'adequate time' depends on the circumstances of each case, but the facilities must include access to documents and other evidence which the accused requires to prepare his case, as well as the opportunity to engage and communicate with counsel. When the accused does not want to defend himself in person or request a person or an association of his choice, he should be able to have recourse to a lawyer. Furthermore, this subparagraph requires counsel to communicate with the accused in conditions giving full respect for the confidentiality of their communications. Lawyers should be able to counsel and to represent their clients in accordance with their established professional standards and judgement without any restrictions, influences, pressures or undue influences from any quarter.[128]

The requirement of access to documents and evidence and communication with counsel parallels the jurisprudence under the ECHR.[129] Obvious problems of public interest privilege and professional privilege present themselves. The reference to legal representation without undue interference is a key aspect of the protection afforded by article 14. Many of the communications under the Optional Protocol concerning article 14 have referred to the difficulties and restrictions faced by defence lawyers, particularly in political cases.[130] It is interesting to note though that the representation must be in accordance with 'established professional standards' so that abuses by defence lawyers could legitimately lead to restrictions by the State with respect to those lawyers.

10.15 Members have asked how the requirement of article 14(3)(*c*) is guaranteed in the practice of its domestic courts. Concern has been expressed both over unduly lengthy trial procedures and over accelerated procedures.[131] One member even suggested to the State representative from the Federal Republic of Germany the advisability of streamlining its procedures, for example, by introducing a system whereby the prosecution might pursue certain charges and drop others which caused particular difficulties with regard to investigation and proof.[132] State representatives have been asked to indicate the average and maximum periods of pre-trial detention and, more rarely, to give statistics on the normal duration of trials.[133]

The Australian report raised an interesting problem concerning the interpretation of article 14(3)(*c*) as it applied to remote areas:

In the more remote and sparsely populated areas of Australia, a special problem of delay before trial arises in that a court may not always be immediately available to hear charges and language difficulties may present a barrier to commencement of proceedings. However, every effort is made to keep such delays to a minimum ... Although this delay before trial is longer than would be the ideal, in these special circumstances the delays are not considered to be unreasonable or 'undue' and are considered therefore not to be inconsistent with the requirements of this paragraph.[134]

Again members of the HRC failed to take a golden opportunity to indicate their views on a matter of some importance bearing in mind the wide geographical spread of States parties to the ICCPR.[135]

In its General Comment the HRC stated that,

> This guarantee relates not only to the time by which a trial should commence, but also the time by which it should end and judgement be rendered; all stages must take place 'without undue delay'. To make this right effective, a procedure must be available in order to ensure that the trial will proceed 'without undue delay', both in first instance and on appeal.[136]

The HRC does not indicate when the period begins. If it runs from the point of the charge then according to the HRC this will be when the court or the prosecution authorities take procedural steps against the suspected person or publicly names him as such.[137] As for the end of the relevant period this would clearly seem to be at the end of any possible appeal.[138] It appears that not only must the whole trial period be 'without undue delay' but that each individual stage must take place 'without undue delay'. If so this again follows the practice under the ECHR.[139]

10.16 Article 14(3)(*d*) has attracted consistent attention and various members have stressed its vital role and importance.[140] Members have asked for details of any rules or procedures excluding or restricting a defendant's presence at trial.[141] Doubts have been raised about trials *in absentia* before military tribunals and appeals *in absentia*.[142] One member has taken the view that the right to be tried in his presence also applies to juveniles.[143]

A number of matters have been raised concerning the right to legal assistance.[144] Were there restrictions or limitations on the choice of legal assistance?[145] Could a foreign lawyer be chosen?[146] Could the chosen person be rejected and, if so, on what grounds?[147] What remedies existed for a denial of access?[148] Was it possible to contact a legal assistant before proceedings had commenced,[149] for example, in respect of a preliminary hearing?[150] The approach of Mr Tomuschat, during consideration of the report of Guinea, is typical of that taken by many members:

> Further information on the institutional aspect of assistance by legal counsel would be welcome. The fact that the Covenant spoke of such assistance presupposed the existence of independent lawyers not acting under Government instructions but responsible only to accused persons. According to some reports, lawyers in Guinea were organized as public officials. If that were the case, and if they were placed under the instructions of the Government, that would be a serious obstacle to providing accused persons with the services required for the defence of their rights under the Covenant?[151]

Members have inquired as to who bore the responsibility for paying for legal assistance. Some members have stressed the desirability of the cost being met by the State even when the defendant has been convicted.[152] Others have suggested that a practice under which the defendant was liable for costs would be inconsistent with article 14(3)(*d*).[153] It is interesting to note that Australia made an interpretative declaration regarding the consistency of means-tested legal aid with the obligation in article 14(3)(*d*).[154]

In its General Comment the HRC stated that,

Not all reports have dealt with all aspects of the right of defence as defined in sub-paragraph 3(d). The Committee has not always received sufficient information concerning the protection of the right of the accused to be present during the determination of any charge against him nor how the legal system assures his right either to defend himself in person or to be assisted by counsel of his own choosing, or what arrangements are made if a person does not have sufficient means to pay for legal assistance. The accused or his lawyer must have the right to act diligently and fearlessly in pursuing all available defences and the right to challenge the conduct of the case if they believe it to be unfair. When exceptionally for justified reasons trials in absentia are held, strict observance of the rights of the defence is all the more necessary.[155]

Again the HRC stresses the key role of lawyers in the implementation of article 14.[156]

10.17 With regard to article 14(3)(*e*) members have asked for information regarding the grounds for rejecting or restricting[157] the witnesses on behalf of the defence and whether the State met their expenses.[158] Again members have pointed to inconsistencies or inadequacies. For example, during consideration of the report of Uruguay, Mr Tomuschat commented,

The guarantee provided in article 14(3)(e) of the Covenant had to be interpreted broadly, as extending to all stages in the taking of evidence. There were considerable difficulties in enforcing the right in Uruguay since evidence was taken primarily in the preliminary investigation when the accused had little opportunity of influencing the proceedings. The provisions of article 176 of the Code of Military Penal Procedure (CCPR/C/1/Add. 57, p. 5) were dangerous in that they seriously limited the opportunity given to the accused to challenge evidence gathered by the prosecution.[159]

It has been asked whether the authorities could rely on written evidence alone.[160] It is difficult to see how such a situation could comply with article 14(3)(*e*) or indeed the general fair hearing requirement in article 14(1).[161]

In its General Comment the HRC stated that article 14(3)(*e*) was 'designed to guarantee to the accused the same legal powers of compelling the attendance of witnesses and of examining or cross-examining any witnesses as are available to the prosecution'.[162] There is no comment on who may be a witness, any right to be confronted with witnesses, restrictions on calling witnesses, or the admittance of different classes of evidence, for example, hearsay evidence.[163]

10.18 With respect to article 14(3)(*f*) members have laid great stress on the importance of the assistance of an interpreter being 'free'.[164] Members have stated that if a defendant is obliged to pay that practice is contrary to the Covenant.[165] For example, the Hungarian report stated that, 'The expenses on interpreter's service shall be advanced by the prosecuting authority and shall be charged as cost to the defendant if found guilty'.[166] Mr Opsahl questioned whether this was still the position.[167] The reply of the State representative did not cover the specific point.[168]

In its General Comment the HRC stated that, 'This right is independent of the outcome of the proceedings and applies to aliens as well as to nationals. It is of basic importance in cases in which ignorance of the language used by a court or difficulty in understanding may constitute a major obstacle to the right of defence'.[169]

10.19 With respect to article 14(3)(*g*) members have done little more than satisfy themselves that this right is embodied in the Constitution, penal code, or criminal practice and inquired as to the existence of a remedy for a violation of this right.[170] Mr Dimitrijevic has raised the question of convictions based on confessions and the possible relevance of violations of the right to privacy in article 17. He 'wondered whether there were any cases in which a conviction could be based solely on the basis of confessions and whether evidence could be obtained by means which constituted a violation of privacy (surveillance methods)'.[171] In its General Comment the HRC pointed to the relevance of other provisions of the Covenant:

In considering this safeguard the provisions of article 7 and article 10, paragraph 1, should be borne in mind. In order to compel the accused to confess or to testify against himself frequently methods which violate these provisions are used. The law should require that evidence provided by means of such methods or any other form of compulsion is wholly unacceptable.[172]

This invocation of other articles accords with the HRC's practice of raising questions of confessions under articles 7 and 10 during the reporting procedure.[173]

Article 14(4): procedure for juveniles [174]

10.20 In general terms members have engaged in relatively little comment or discussion of article 14(4). They have largely confined themselves to requesting further details of the information provided in State reports concerning, for example, the composition and nature of any specialized institutions in operation and the kind of social rehabilitation measures taken.[175] The limited consideration is perhaps surprising given the obvious importance of the subject and the no doubt varied practice of States parties.[176]

In its General Comment the HRC stated that,

Not many reports have furnished sufficient information concerning such relevant matters as the minimum age at which a juvenile may be charged with a criminal offence, the maximum age at which a person is still considered to be a juvenile, the existence of special courts and procedures, the laws governing procedures against juveniles and how all these special arrangements for juveniles take account of 'the desirability of promoting their rehabilitation'. Juveniles are to enjoy at least the same guarantees and protection as are accorded to adults under article 14.[177]

The last sentence of this comment might suggest that in some circumstances extra safeguards and procedures for juveniles will be necessary to comply with article 14(4).

Article 14(5): right of review [178]

10.21 HRC members have sought further information on the appeal or review procedures of States parties, for example, concerning whether the review was limited to the law or extended to the facts and the sentence imposed,[179] the composition of the reviewing body,[180] and whether there were any exclusions, exceptions, or limitations on those procedures.[181] They have pointed to apparent inadequacies or non-compliance.[182]

During the consideration of the report of Iraq attention was focused on the practice and procedure of its Revolutionary Court.[183] The State representative stated that,

The Revolutionary Court, created in 1969 to protect the Revolution was not a truly exceptional court . . . the Court differed from the ordinary courts, however, in that its findings were final and not subject to appeal. There was no recourse except in the case of capital punishment; the death sentence must in fact be ratified by a presidential decree. In practice, however, the person condemned could request the President of the Republic to review the sentence, and in such a case the President of the Republic referred the matter to a special legal commission which looked into the case and made recommendations.[184]

Mr Tomuschat immediately pointed to the 'contradiction' between this information and the terms of article 14(5) and requested an explanation.[185] The representative replied that any Iraqi citizen could appeal to the President who thus served in a way as a court of appeal.[186] Mr Tomuschat replied that,

despite the replies provided by the representative of Iraq, it still appeared that Iraqi legislation failed to provide the full coverage and protection of the rights of the accused and convicted persons under article 14, paragraph 5, of the Covenant. He hoped that the Committee would soon obtain further information of Iraqi efforts to improve that situation.[187]

This question was again turned to during consideration of Iraq's second periodic report.[188] This process of information, comment, request for explanation and further information, reply, and comment is highly typical of the workings of the article 40 process.

During the consideration of the report of Austria, Sir Vincent-Evans suggested that Austria reconsider its reservation to article 14(5) because it undermined a very important humanitarian principle of criminal law.[189]

In its General Comment on article 14 the HRC stated as regards paragraph 5 that,

Particular attention is drawn to the other language versions of the word 'crime' ('*infraction*', '*delito*', '*prestuplenie*') which show that the guarantee is not confined only to the most serious offences. In this connection, not enough information has been provided concerning the procedures of appeal, in particular the access to and powers of reviewing tribunals, what requirements must be satisfied to appeal against a judgement and the way in which the procedures before review tribunals take account of the fair and public hearing requirements of paragraph 1 of article 14.[190]

The comment is helpful in explicitly referring to the applicability of the fair and public hearing guarantees in article 14(1) to appeal and review proceedings.[191]

Article 14(6): compensation for miscarriages of justice[192]

10.22 Members have sought details of how the right to compensation for miscarriages of justice is given effect in domestic law, if at all?[193] Was the right specifically established, for example, in the Constitution or the Penal Code?[194] Was there some form of extra-statutory scheme in operation?[195] Could information be supplied on specific cases of the application of the compensation laws?[196] Were there any means of moral compensation?[197]

A number of members expressed doubts as to whether the United Kingdom system of *ex gratia* payments was in conformity with article 14(6).[198] The United Kingdom representative replied, *inter alia*, that,

Although the scheme was an extra-statutory one, the Home Secretary did not in practice refuse to make payment. His Government therefore considered that the practice accorded with the spirit of the Covenant, and it would see whether it could not be made to accord more closely with the letter also.[199]

HRC members again raised the issue during consideration of the UK's second periodic report. Subsequently the UK resisted domestic calls for institutional reforms, though it did concede a number of important procedural reforms.[200] The UK government has now established a statutory scheme to cover compensation for miscarriages of justice.[201]

In its General Comment the HRC stated that,

It seems from many State reports that this right is often not observed or insufficiently guaranteed by domestic legislation. States should, where necessary, supplement their legislation in this area to bring it into line with the provisions of the Covenant.[202]

Article 14(7): *non bis in idem*[203]

10.23 With respect to article 14(7) members have asked whether the domestic rules were compatible with it and whether practical examples of its effect could be given. They have pointed to apparent inconsistencies and requested details of relevant case law.[204] For example, the view was expressed that the power of the President or Prime Minister of Egypt to order a retrial before another court of persons acquitted by a State Security Court was contrary to article 14(7) and should be reviewed.[205] The Netherlands report raised the question of whether article 14(7) had international or only domestic application but no conclusive reply was received.[206] The point has now been resolved in a communication under the Optional Protocol.[207] In response to the Australian report HRC members raised the interesting question of the application of punishment under both criminal and aboriginal customary law.[208]

Article 14(7) has been the subject of reservations by a number of States including Austria, Denmark, Finland, France, Iceland, Netherlands, Norway, and Sweden.[209] This is not surprising as the provision in article 14(7) was not included in the Human Rights Commission's text and proved controversial when proposed in the Third Committee.[210] On a number of occasions during the consideration of reports HRC members have expressed concern at these reservations and suggested that they should be reconsidered.[211] The HRC as a body responded to these reservations in its General Comment:

> In considering State reports differing views have often been expressed as to the scope of paragraph 7 of article 14. Some States parties have even felt the need to make reservations in relation to procedures for the resumption of criminal cases. It seems to the Committee that most States parties make a clear distinction between a resumption of a trial justified by exceptional circumstances and a retrial prohibited pursuant to the principle of *ne bis in idem* as contained in paragraph 7. This understanding of the meaning of *ne bis in idem* may encourage States parties to reconsider their reservations to article 14, paragraph 7.[212]

It is very useful for the HRC to respond in this way to reservations made by States parties as it continues the dialogue under article 40 of the ICCPR and should encourage States parties to reconsider and withdraw reservations which may now appear unnecessary in the light of the HRC's expressed understanding of article 14(7).

B. ARTICLE 14 UNDER THE OPTIONAL PROTOCOL

Introduction

10.24 The breadth of the HRC's considerations of article 14 under the reporting process has testified to its central importance in the view of members of the HRC.[213] That importance is further attested to by the frequent invocation of article 14 under the OP. The majority of the HRC's views on article 14 have concerned Uruguay. In a substantial number of views the HRC has expressed the view that one or more of the provisions of article 14 have been violated.

The scope of article 14

10.25 Although the determination of the scope of the parallel expressions in article 6 of the ECHR have had a dominant role in the jurisprudence of the EUCM and the EUCT, no decision on the merits under the OP has occasioned any discussion of the scope of the expressions 'criminal charge' and 'rights and obligations in a suit at law'.[214] However, three admissibility decisions do offer some assistance.

10.26 The most important of these is undoubtedly that in *Y.L.* v. *Canada*.[215] Y.L. was dismissed from the Canadian army on the basis of alleged medical disorders. His application for a disability pension was rejected by a Pension Commission which held that Y.L.'s disability neither arose out of, nor was directly connected with, his military service, as required by the Pension Act (1952). That decision was confirmed on appeal. Two subsequent applications were rejected. An application to an Entitlement Board of the Commission was unsuccessful. Finally, the author appealed to the Pension Review Board which confirmed the earlier rulings.

The author alleged that the proceedings before the Pension Review Board violated the guarantees in article 14(1) in a number of respects. The State party argued that the communication was inadmissible *ratione materiae* because the proceedings did not constitute a 'suit at law' as envisaged by article 14(1). In addition the State party claimed that domestic remedies had not been exhausted because the decision of the Board had not been challenged before the Federal Court of Appeal.[216]

The HRC's Working Group on Communications (WGC) decided that it needed further information from the author and the State party. It noted, 'that the decision might require a finding as to whether the claim which the author pursued in the last instance before the Pension Review Board was a "suit at law" within the meaning of article 14(1) of the Covenant'.[217] To assist it the WGC requested answers, *inter alia*, to the following questions:

(a) How does Canadian domestic law classify the relationship between a member of the Army and the Canadian State? Are the rights and obligations deriving from such a relationship considered to be civil rights and obligations or rights and obligations under public law?

(b) Are there different categories of civil servants? Does Canada make a distinction between a statutory regime (under public law) and a contractual regime (under civil law)?

(c) Is there a distinction, in Canadian domestic law, between persons employed by private employers under a labour contract, and persons employed by the Government?[218]

There are strong echoes here from the jurisprudence under the ECHR and clearly some importance was attached to the classification and regulation of the relationship by the domestic Canadian law.[219]

With reference to the expression 'suit at law' the HRC stated that,

The … expression is formulated differently in the various language texts of the Covenant and each and every one of those texts is, under article 53, equally authentic.

The *travaux préparatoires* do not alone resolve the apparent discrepancy in the various language texts. In the view of the Committee the concept of a 'suit at law' or its equivalent in the other language texts is based on the nature of the right in question rather than on the status of one of the parties (governmental, parastatal or autonomous statutory entities), or else on the particular forum in which individual legal systems may provide that the right in question is to be adjudicated upon, especially in common law systems where there is no inherent difference between public and private law and where the courts normally exercise control over the proceedings either at first instance or on appeal specifically provided by statute or else by way of judicial review. In this regard, each communication must be examined in the light of its particular features.

In the present communication, the right to a fair hearing in relation to the claim for a pension by the author must be looked at globally, irrespective of the different steps which the author had to take in order to have his claim for a pension finally adjudicated.[220]

On the facts of the case the HRC concluded that Y.L.'s basic allegations 'do not reveal the possibility of any breach of the Covenant' because in the HRC's view, 'it would appear that the Canadian legal system does contain provisions in the Federal Court Act to ensure to the author the right to a fair hearing in the situation'.[221]

10.26.1 Again the HRC's decision echoes the jurisprudence of the ECHR in stressing the 'nature of the right' or the particular adjudication forum as the dominant factors. It is interesting to note that three members of the HRC added an individual opinion in which they argued that the dispute did not constitute a 'suit at law'. They seem, however, to accept that the nature of the right or obligation concerned and the adjudication forum are the 'two criteria which would appear to determine conjunctively the scope or article 14'.[222] Their individual opinion is based on the view that in this case neither criteria was met. First, because in Canada the relationship between a soldier and the Crown had many specific features differing essentially from a labour contract under Canadian law. Secondly, the Pension Review board was an administrative body functioning within the executive branch of the government in Canada, lacking the quality of a court. The latter argument would have given article 14 a much narrower scope that has been given to article 6 of the

ECHR. It is submitted the HRC's view is the better one. On the facts of the case the critical factor in the HRC's determination appears to be that the claim was of a kind subject to judicial supervision and control.[223]

10.27 In *C.A.* v. *Italy*[224] C.A. had sought to challenge the limited authority given to him to teach under a certificate issued by an education office. C.A. chose to appeal to the President of the Republic under an exceptional (administrative) recourse procedure. C.A. alleged that article 14 had been violated on various grounds, *inter alia*, that the relevant legislation excluded the possibility for those who chose to use the exceptional procedure of having their rights determined in a suit at law by a judicial tribunal. The HRC took the view that,

> According to the author's own submission, it was open to him to pursue his case by means of proceedings before domestic courts. Instead, he chose to avail himself of the procedure by way of appeal to the President of the Republic. In these circumstances, the author cannot validly claim to have been deprived of the right guaranteed under article 14(1) of the Covenant to have the determination of 'rights . . . in a suit at law' made by a competent, independent and impartial tribunal.[225]

The decision suggests that if a State party provides an alleged victim with two mutually exclusive recourse procedures, one of which may well satisfy the requirements of article 14, and the alleged victim chooses the alternative procedure, he cannot thereafter claim to have been deprived of the rights guaranteed by article 14(1). By electing for the administrative remedy C.A. effectively waived his right to the article 14(1) guarantee. It is submitted that the waiver must not be tainted by constraint although his ignorance of the exclusionary nature of the remedies may not be a bar.[226] Thus the HRC held the communication inadmissible, 'without having to determine whether article 14(1) is at all applicable to a dispute of the present nature'.[227]

10.28 Finally, in *Pinkey* v. *Canada*[228] P, a citizen of the United States, claimed, *inter alia*, that he had been denied a fair hearing and review of his case in regard to a deportation order which was to come into effect on his release from prison.[229] The State party argued that the case did not involve the determination of a criminal charge but there is no indication as to whether it could involve the determination of rights or obligations in a suit at law.[230] In *V.R.M.B.* v. *Canada*[231] the author argued that public law disputes also fall under the scope of the application of article 14 and so cover immigration hearings and deportation proceedings.[232] The HRC did not decide the point of interpretation but expressed the view that there was in any event no facts to substantiate a violation of article 14.[233]

Fair hearing; competent, independent, and impartial tribunal

10.29 In many communications under the OP there have been both general and specific allegations of violation of the 'fair hearing' guarantee. In *Pinkey*

v. *Canada*[234] P's argument mainly concerned an allegedly missing briefcase containing vital defence evidence. The HRC expressed the view that it had not found any support for P's allegation that material evidence had been withheld. We noted in chapter 4 that the HRC has taken the view that it is not its function under the OP to provide a judicial appeal from or judicial review of the decisions of national authorities. In *Hermoza* v. *Peru*[235] the HRC noted that,

the concept of a fair hearing necessarily entails that justice be rendered without undue delay ... A delay of seven years constitutes an unreasonable delay ... delays in implementation have continued and two and a half years after the judgement ... the author has still not been reinstated in his post ... This delay ... constitutes a further aggravation of the violation of the principle of a fair hearing ... Such seemingly endless sequence of instances and the repeated failure to implement decisions are [in]compatible with the principle of a fair hearing'.[236]

Similarly in *Morael* v. *France*[237] the HRC expressed the view that 'Although article 14 does not explain what is meant by a "fair hearing" in a suit at law (unlike paragraph 3 of the same article dealing with the determination of criminal charges), the concept of a fair hearing in the context of article 14(1) of the Covenant should be interpreted as requiring a number of conditions, such as equality of arms, respect for the principle of adversary proceedings, preclusion of *ex officio reformatio in pejus* (*ex officio* correction worsening an earlier verdict), and expeditious procedure.[238]

In *Conteris* v. *Uruguay*[239] the HRC expressed the view that there had been a violation of article 14(1) because there had been no fair and public hearing. Along with the lack of public hearing there were also violations of, *inter alia*, article 14(3)(*b*), (*c*), (*d*), and (*g*). The only seeming additional violation which grounded the article 14(1) finding was perhaps that C's own statements to the military court at first instance were ignored and not entered into the court records.[240] Alternatively the HRC may simply be using the fair hearing violation as a residual concept.[241]

General allegations of the absence of a fair hearing in the operation of military tribunals have not, *per se*, founded article 14 violations. However, in *Cariboni* v. *Uruguay*[242] the HRC found a violation of article 14(1) on the basis that C had been denied a fair and public hearing, without undue delay, by an independent and impartial tribunal.[243] The only specific matter raising the question of the independence and impartiality of the military tribunal was perhaps that although the prosecutor requested a nine-year sentence for C he was in fact sentenced to fifteen years' imprisonment. We have already noted that the HRC expressed strong concern about the operation of military or special courts in its General Comment on article 14.[244]

Equality before courts and tribunals

10.29.1 In *B.d.B.* v. *Netherlands*[245] the HRC considered the nature of the equality guarantee in article 14(1). The HRC expressed the view that, 'Article 14 of the Covenant guarantees procedural equality but cannot be interpreted as guaranteeing equality of results or absence of error on the part of the competent tribunal'.[246] In *Robinson* v. *Jamaica*[247] the trial judge had refused to order an adjournment to allow R to have legal representation when several adjournments had already been ordered because the prosecution's witnesses were unavailable or unready. The HRC expressed the view that this 'raises issues of fairness and equality before the courts. The Committee is of the view that there has been a violation of article 14, paragraph 1, due to inequality of arms between the parties'.[248] In *Avellanal* v. *Peru*[249] the HRC found a violation of the requirement in article 14(1) that all persons be equal before the courts and tribunals on the basis that under Peruvian law only a husband could represent matrimonial property before the courts.[250]

Public hearing and public judgment[251]

10.30 It is convenient to consider these two requirements together. Most of the alleged violations of these requirements have concerned the operation of military tribunals in Uruguay.[252] They reveal a consistent pattern of alleged violations of article 14: closed trials, conducted in writing with neither the alleged victim, his counsel, if any, nor close relatives allowed the right to be present, and a failure to make the judgment public. In *Touron* v. *Uruguay*[253] T had been charged with offences of conspiracy and subversion. There were no public hearings during the whole procedure at first instance. T was not allowed to be present or to defend himself. The judgment was not made public. The State party made the following submission to the HRC:

It must be explained that public hearings do not exist under the Uruguayan legal order. The trial is conducted in writing and the accused has the opportunity to express himself through his counsel and by means of formal statements before the judge.[254]

The HRC did not specifically refer to this submission but simply expressed the view that, *inter alia*, article 14(1) had been violated because T had no public hearing. The submission of the State party seems to assume that a trial in writing does not amount to a public hearing. If so, the submission suggests an institutionalized violation of article 14 in the operation of the Uruguayan legal order. If the HRC was of this view it could include a statement to this effect in its expression of views under the OP. If members thought this inappropriate[255] it would still be open to them to raise such questions of institutional violations during the article 40 reporting process in respect of the State party concerned and indeed this has happened. In this way the HRC's experience under the OP can inform and guide its approaches under the article 40 procedure. In its final views on the *Touron*[256] case the HRC commented that,

> The State party has not responded to the Committee's request that it should be furnished with the texts of any court orders or decisions relevant to the matter. The Committee is gravely concerned by this omission. Although similar requests have been made in a number of other cases, the Committee has never yet been furnished with the texts of any court decisions. This tends to suggest that judgements, even of extreme gravity, as in the present case, are not handed down in writing. In such circumstances, the Committee feels unable, on the basis of the information before it, to accept . . . that the proceedings against Luis Touron amounted to a fair trial . . .[257]

Members of the HRC took up this rather cautiously phrased allegation of a failure to hand down judgments in writing with the State representative of Uruguay when he appeared before the Committee during the reporting process.[258]

10.31 In *Estrella* v. *Uruguay*[259] E was told by an official whom he met at the prison where he was detained that he had been sentenced to four and a half years' imprisonment for 'conspiracy to subvert action to upset the Constitution and criminal preparations'. The HRC expressed the view that the facts disclosed, *inter alia*, a violation of article 14(1) because E was tried without a public hearing and no reason had been given by the State party to justify this in accordance with the Covenant.[260] In fact, to date, no State party has ever raised any of the exceptions to the public hearing requirement in answer to an allegation against it.

10.31.1 In *R.M.* v. *Finland*[261] the HRC stated that it 'believe[d] that the absence of oral hearings in the appellate proceedings raises no issue under article 14 of the Covenant'.[262]

Article 14(2): The presumption of innocence

10.32 It appeared from two early decisions[263] taken by the HRC that it took the view that violations of article 14(1) and (3) which deprive an accused person of the safeguards of a fair trial also constitute à violation of the presumption of innocence although there is no attempt to explain the reasoning behind this.[264] However, in subsequent similar cases in which the Committee has held there to have been violations of article 14(1) and (3) there has been no suggestion that these violations also constituted a violation of the presumption of innocence.[265] We have already noted the broad approach of the HRC to the presumption of innocence evident in its General Comment.[266] In *Hermoza* v. *Peru*[267] three members of the HRC appended an individual opinion finding a violation of article 14(2) where H had been dismissed from the Guardia Civil:

(H) appears to have all the time been treated as guilty while officially being temporarily suspended. This amounted to a continuing violation of his right to be presumed innocent (article 14, paragraph 2) and to be treated accordingly until proceedings, or failing that, disciplinary proceedings were concluded against him. These proceedings were apparently not initiated.[268]

In *Morael* v. *France*[269] the HRC had to consider the possibility of the application of the presumption in a civil context. M had been subjected to penalties for breach of his duties as a director of a company towards its creditors.[270] Notwithstanding the severe penalties imposed the HRC expressed the view that the presumption of innocence in article 14(2) was not applicable and therefore there was no violation.[271]

Article 14(3)(a): 'To be informed promptly and in detail in a language which he understands of the nature and cause of the charge against him'

10.33 In *Antonaccio* v. *Uruguay*[272] A was tried in July 1980 and sentenced to thirty years' imprisonment plus fifteen years of special security measures. The HRC simply expressed the view that article 14(3)(*a*) had been violated. Similarly, in *Mbenge* v. *Zaïre*[273] M, while living in Belgium, was twice tried and sentenced to capital punishment by Zaïrian tribunals. He learned about these trials through the press. In its views the HRC gave some indication of the obligation on a State party to contact and inform an accused:

The Committee acknowledges that there must be certain limits to the efforts which can duly be expected of the responsible authorities of establishing contact with the accused. With regard to the present communication, however, those limits need not be specified. The State party has not challenged the author's contention that he had known of the trials only through press reports after they had taken place. It is true that both judgements state explicitly that summonses to appear had been issued by the clerk of the court. However, no indication is given of any steps actually taken by the State party in order to transmit the summonses to the author, whose address in Belgium is correctly reproduced in the judgement of 17 August 1977 and was therefore known to the judicial authorities. The fact that, according to the judgement in the second trial of March 1978, the summons had been issued only three days before the beginnings of the hearings before the court, confirms the Committee in its conclusion that the State party failed to make sufficient efforts with a view to informing the author about the impending court proceedings, thus enabling him to prepare his defence.[274]

Thus, if there is prima-facie evidence of a failure to comply with article 14(3)(*a*) there is a burden on the State party to show the steps it has actually taken and those steps must amount to a 'sufficient effort' to inform the alleged victim. The failure to comply with article 14(3)(*a*) may then result in other violations of article 14(3) as happened in the *Mbenge* case.[275]

Article 14(3)(*b*): 'To have adequate time and facilities for the preparation of his defence and to communicate with counsel of his own choosing'.

10.34 The matter of access to counsel is clearly covered by both article 14(3)(*b*) and (*d*) at least. In *Perdomo and de Lanza* v. *Uruguay*[276] the HRC expressed the view that there was a violation of article 14(3) on the ground, *inter alia*, that P and de L had no effective access to legal assistance. In *Antonaccio* v. *Uruguay*[277] it was alleged that A was denied the rights of defence as he had never been able to contact the lawyer assigned to him and although A's relatives had appointed M.C. to be A's lawyer, M.C. was twice denied the right to examine A's dossier and to visit him. The HRC expressed the view that article 14(3)(*b*) was violated because he was unable either to choose his own counsel or communicate with appointed counsel and was, therefore, unable to prepare his defence.[278] The HRC made no comment on the question of the right of access to the court file.[279] In *O.F.* v. *Norway*[280] O.F. alleged, *inter alia*, that he had been denied adequate access to and copies of documents relevant to his case. The HRC noted that, 'The Covenant does not explicitly provide for a right of a charged person to be furnished with copies of all relevant documents in a criminal investigation . . . Even if all the allegations of the author were to be accepted as proven, there would be no ground for asserting that a violation of article 14, paragraph 3(b), occurred'.[281] It is submitted that 'whether a denial of access to relevant documents violates the Covenant will depend on whether in the particular case it unfairly deprives the accused of adequate facilities to prepare his defence. Denial of access to certain documents may be permissible under national laws relating to public interests, privilege, and confidentiality.[282] As noted, in its General Comment on article 14 the HRC stated that 'facilities', 'must include access to documents and other evidence which the accused requires to prepare his case'.[283]

10.35 Allegations have been made in communications to the HRC of the harassment of defence lawyers in Uruguay and Zaïre but most of the allegations have concerned situations prior to the entry into force of the OP in the State party concerned.[284] We have already noted the clear statements of the HRC on the importance of unhindered access to it for individuals[285] and of States not taking exception to anyone acting as legal counsel for alleged victims.[286] In *Scarrone* v. *Uruguay*[287] S did not have counsel of his own choice, but a court appointed lawyer, who did not visit him nor inform him of developments in the case.[288] The HRC expressed the view that article 14(3)(*b*) had been violated because S did not have adequate legal assistance for the preparation of his defence.[289]

10.35.1 In *Estrella* v. *Uruguay*[290] E's choice was limited to one of two officially appointed defence lawyers. E saw him only four times in over two years. The HRC expressed the view that there had been a breach of article 14(3)(*b*) but it did not make any express comment on the inadequacy of E's opportunity to communicate with his lawyer. A more helpful finding is that in *Marais* v. *Madagascar*[291] where the HRC expressed the view that M was 'denied adequate opportunity to communicate with counsel'.[292] This finding clearly suggests that the opportunity afforded to communicate with counsel must be adequate enough to allow for the preparaton of his defence.[293]

10.35.2 In *Vasilskis* v. *Uruguay*[294] the court had appointed V a defence counsel who was not a lawyer. The HRC expressed the view that there had been a violation of article 14(3)(*b*) and (*d*) because V did not have adequate legal assistance for the preparation of her defence.[295]

10.35.3 The decision in *Caldas* v. *Uruguay*[296] is important because it highlights the difficulty of securing the rights in article 14(3)(*b*) when the accused person is detained incommunicado. The HRC stated that in formulating its views it had taken account of the following consideration,

The Committee observes that the holding of a detainee incommunicado for six weeks after his arrest is not only incompatible with the standard of humane treatment required by article 10(1) of the Covenant, but it also deprives him, at a critical stage, of the possibility of communicating with counsel of his own choosing as required by article 14(3)(b) and, therefore, of one of the most important facilities for the preparation of his defence.[297]

In *Machado* v. *Uruguay*[298] M was held incommunicado from November 1980 to May 1981. The HRC expressed the view that there had been a violation of article 14(3)(*b*) because the conditions of detention during this period effectively barred M from access to legal assistance.

Not surprisingly, the HRC expressed the view that there is a breach of article 14(3)(*b*) when trial proceedings take place without the alleged victim's knowledge[299] or without notification to his counsel.[300]

Article 14(3)(*c*): The right to be tried without undue delay.

10.36 The HRC has expressed the view that article 14(3)(*c*) has been violated in a number of communications mostly concerning the operation of military tribunals in Uruguay. It is unfortunate that despite a number of opportunities to do so the HRC has neither clearly spelt out the precise time period covered by article 14(3)(*c*) nor indicated how it relates to the period covered by article 9(3) of the ICCPR.[301] For example, in *de Casariego* v. *Uruguay*[302] C was arrested in Brazil in November 1978 by Uruguayan agents with the connivance of two Brazilian police officials. He was forcibly abducted to Uruguay where his arrest was publicly confirmed in the same month. In March 1979 C was charged. On 29 July 1981 the HRC expressed the view that there had been a violation of article 14(3)(c) because C had not been tried without undue delay. The HRC did not express the view that article 9(3) had been violated. If the period up to a trial at first instance is covered by article 14(3)(c) then what is the scope of article 9(3)? Most of the HRC's other views give no clue to the relative scope of the two provisions because the HRC has almost invariably been of the view that the facts as found constitute violations of both provisions.[303] Another case where the HRC has expressed the view that article 14(3)(c) alone had been violated was in *Pinkey* v. *Canada*[304] where P's appeal against conviction could not be heard for thirty-four months because the transcript of the original trial was not made available. This decision would suggest that article 14(3)(c) would cover the period up to the final appeal judgment. This view seems to be confirmed in the HRC's General Comment.[305]

10.37 In *Pinkey* P alleged that the delay in the hearing was a deliberate attempt by the State party to block the exercise of his right of appeal.[306] The State party rejected this allegation and any allegation of wrong doing, negligence, or carelessness on the part of the Ministry of the Attorney-General.[307] It acknowledged that the delay was due to 'administrative mishaps in the Official Reporter's Office', but submitted that responsibility must nevertheless rest with P in that he failed to seek an order from the Court of Appeal requiring production of the transcripts as he was entitled to do under the Criminal Code and the Rules of the British Colombia Supreme Court.[308]

In reply it was submitted on P's behalf that the government of British Colombia must be held responsible for the delay resulting from mishaps in producing the trial transcripts and that the Court of Appeal itself, being aware of the delay, should of its own motion have taken steps to expedite their production.[309]

The HRC considered that 'the authorities of British Colombia must be considered *objectively responsible*. Even in the particular circumstances this delay appears excessive and might have been prejudicial to the effectiveness of the right of appeal. At the same time, however, the Committee has to take note of the position of the Government that the Supreme Court of Canada would have been competent to examine the complaints. This remedy, nevertheless, does not seem likely to have been effective for the purpose of avoiding delay.'[310]

Matters of organization and administration will generally be the responsibility of the State.[311] However, the meaning of the expression 'objective responsibility' is not spelt out.[312] It could indicate that there must have been some fault and that the State authorities were responsible because they should have taken the initiative to obtain the transcripts. Alternatively, it could indicate that the State is to be held liable on a no-fault based system simply because the delay was excessive. It is submitted that the first of these is the better view. It is also interesting to contrast the view of the HRC with the approach under the ECHR which takes a much more subjective approach to the examination of the responsibility of the relevant authorities, courts, or individuals involved at the various stages.[313] On the facts of the case, however, the result may well have been the same under either approach. An approach based on objective responsibility in the no-fault sense might make it difficult to accommodate the various legal systems of States parties and unduly limit the margin of appreciation for States in this respect.[314] The decision on the need for the alleged domestic remedy to be effective accords with the general approach of the HRC to the matter of domestic remedies.[315]

10.38 Many of the HRC's decisions have concerned time periods spanning the date of the entry into force of the ICCPR and the OP for the State concerned.[316] For example, in *Sequeira* v. *Uruguay*[317] S was arrested in September 1975 and detained until he escaped custody on 4 June 1976. The OP entered into force in Uruguay on 23 March 1976. The HRC expressed the view that the facts, in so far as they occurred or had effects which themselves constituted a violation after that date disclosed violations of, *inter alia*, article 14(3) because he was not brought to trial without undue delay. The decision also represents the shortest period of time held by the HRC to violate article 14(3)(*c*). S was in detention for nine months in total and for less than three months after the OP entered into force.[318]

10.39 There has been little attempt by any State party to date to justify any alleged delay in holding a trial.[319] Exceptionally, in *Vasilskis* v. *Uruguay*[320] the submission of the State party under article 4(2) OP referred to 'the extraordinary load placed on the Uruguayan judicial system by the numerous proceedings during the period of high seditious activity'.[321] Unfortunately the HRC made no comment on this point and simply expressed the view that article 14(3)(*c*) had been violated. Presumably this approach was taken because the State party had not supplied any specific or detailed information to substantiate its claim.[322] To date no view of the HRC has indicated the responsibility of the State for delays attributable to the structural or administrative problems in legal systems. The EUCT has taken a strict approach to such factors.[323] Similarly the HRC have made no comment on the responsibility of individuals for delays.[324] The HRC has not yet developed criteria for the determination of what is 'undue delay' in a particular case.[325]

In a number of communications concerning Uruguay the HRC has concluded by way of default that article 14(3)(*c*) has been violated because Uruguay had simply failed to supply any information or documentation as to the outcome of criminal proceedings.[326]

10.39.1 In *Bolanos* v. *Ecuador*[327] the HRC noted that the State party had not explained why it was necessary to keep B under detention for five years prior to his indictment for murder. The HRC expressed the view that there had been violations of articles 9(3) and 14(3)(*c*) because B was not tried within a reasonable time and was denied a fair hearing without undue delay.[328]

Article 14(3)(*d*): Trial in own presence, counsel of own choosing, right to legal assistance

10.40 It is instructive to begin with the HRC's views in a case in which the HRC stressed the vital importance of the safeguards in article 14(3) of the Covenant. In *Mbenge* v. *Zaïre*[329] M, a Zaïrian citizen and former Governor of the province of Shaba, had left Zaïre in 1974 and was living in Belgium. He was twice tried and sentenced to capital punishment by Zaïrian tribunals. M learned of the trials through the newspapers. He had received no summons to appear before the tribunals. The HRC observed that,

According to article 14(3) of the Covenant, everyone is entitled to be tried in his presence and to defend himself in person or through legal assistance. This provision and other requirements of due process enshrined in article 14 cannot be construed as invariably rendering proceedings *in absentia* inadmissible irrespective of the reasons for the accused person's absence. Indeed, proceedings *in absentia* are in some circumstances (for instance, when the accused person, although informed of the proceedings sufficiently in advance, declines to exercise his right to be present) permissible in the interest of the proper administration of justice. Nevertheless, the effective exercise of the rights under article 14 presupposes that the necessary steps should be taken to inform the accused beforehand about the proceedings against him (art.14(3)(a)). Judgement *in absentia* requires that, notwithstanding the absence of the accused, all due notification has been made to inform him of the date and place of his trial and to request his attendance. Otherwise, the accused, in particular, is not given adequate time and facilities for the preparation of his defence (art.14(3)(*b*)), cannot defend himself through legal assistance of his own choosing (art.14(3)(d)) nor does he have the opportunity to examine, or have examined, the witnesses against him and to obtain the attendance and examination of witnesses on his behalf (art.14(3)(e)).[330]

On the facts the HRC expressed the view that Zaïre had violated article 14(3)(*a*), (*b*), (*c*), (*d*), and (*e*) because M was charged, tried, and convicted in circumstances in which he could not effectively enjoy the safeguards of due process enshrined in those provisions.[331]

10.41 Most of the allegations in the communications submitted to the HRC have concerned the same pattern of violations in the operation and practice of military tribunals in Uruguay: closed trials, no choice of counsel or a limited choice, no access or no effective access to legal assistance, neither the alleged victim, his counsel or close relatives allowed the right to be present at the trial.[332] Many of those communications raise the problem of conflicting submissions by the author and the State party.[333]

In *Burgos* v. *Uruguay*[334] B was arrested, allegedly tortured, and after a delay of fourteen months his trial began. He was sentenced in March 1979 but the sentence was reduced on appeal. It was alleged, *inter alia*, that B was denied the right to have legal defence counsel of his own choice and that a military '*ex officio*' counsel, Colonel M.R., was appointed by the authorities. Four witnesses asserted that B and others were forced under threat to refrain from seeking any legal counsel other than Colonel M.R.

In its reply the State party submitted that B had legal assistance at all times and that he had lodged an appeal. The State party also rejected the allegation that B was denied the right to have defence counsel of his own choosing asserting that he was not prevented from having one and that accused persons themselves and not the authorities choose from the list of court-appointed lawyers.[335] In reply the author indicated that, 'since accused persons can only choose their lawyers from a list of military lawyers drawn up by the Uruguayan Government', her husband (B) had no access to a civilian lawyer, unconnected with the government, who might have provided a 'genuine and impartial defence' and that he did not enjoy the proper safe-guards of a fair trial.[336]

In its expression of views the HRC indicated that it had taken account of the fact that although the State party had stated that B was not prevented from choosing his own counsel, 'It has not, however, refuted witness testimony indicating that Lopez Burgos and others arrested with him, including M.S. and I.Q., whose parents are attorneys, were forced to agree to *ex officio* legal counsel'.[337]

The HRC expressed the view that article 14(3)(*d*) had been violated because B was forced to accept Colonel M.R. as legal counsel.[338] It is unfortunate that the HRC did not take this opportunity to spell out the extent of the obligation of a State party to permit the free choice of counsel, for example, whether it is permissible for a State party to preclude the possible choice of a civilian counsel.[339]

10.41.1 In *Pratt and Morgan* v. *Jamaica*[340] the HRC had to consider the qualitative aspect of an assigned counsel. The HRC expressed the view that, 'Although persons availing themselves of legal representation provided by the State may often feel they would have been better represented by a counsel of their own choosing, this is not a matter that constitutes a violation of article 14, paragraph 3 (d), by the State party. Nor is the Committee in a position to ascertain whether the failure of Mr. Pratt's lawyer to insist upon calling the alibi witness before the case was closed was a matter of professional judgement or of negligence'.[341] There might, however, be exceptional cases where the requirements of an effective defence would require a court or tribunal to intervene and replace an assigned counsel who was clearly incapable of effectively representing a defendant.[342]

10.41.2 In *Robinson* v. *Jamaica*[343] the HRC had to consider the question, whether a State party is under an obligation itself to make provision for effective representation by counsel in a case concerning a capital offence, should the counsel selected by the author for whatever reason decline to appear. The Committee, noting that article 14(3)(d) stipulates that everyone shall have 'legal assistance assigned to him, in any case where the interests of justice so require', believes that it is axiomatic that legal assistance be available in capital cases. This is so even if the unavailability of private counsel is to some degree attributable to the author himself, and even if the provision of legal assistance would entail an adjournment of proceedings. This requirement is not rendered unnecessary by efforts that might otherwise be made by the trial judge to assist the author in handling his defence in the absence of counsel. In the view of the Committee, the absence of counsel constituted unfair trial.[344]

10.42 Some of the difficulties in securing the rights of defence when a person is detained incommunicado have already been noted.[345] In a number of cases the HRC has had to consider the effect of detention on the right to have access to legal assistance. For example, in *Carballal* v. *Uruguay*[346] the allegations included more than five months' incommunicado detention, much of the time tied and blindfolded, and subjection to an extremely harsh regime of detention. The HRC expressed the view that there had been a violation of article 14(3) because 'the conditions of his detention effectively barred him from access to legal assistance'.[347] It would be more helpful if the HRC in its views indicated which of the alleged conditions, or perhaps all of them, 'effectively barred' C from access to legal assistance.

10.43 As noted there have been allegations of harassment of defence lawyers in cases before military tribunals in Uruguay but the HRC has not yet expressed any views on these allegations.[348] A case where the harassment of defence lawyers was more directly considered by the HRC was the decision in *Marais* v. *Madagascar*.[349] M, a South African national, was a passenger on a chartered aircraft which, en route to Mauritius, made an emergency landing in Madagascar. M was tried and sentenced for overflying the country without authority and thereby endangering the national security of the country. The HRC's statement of facts outlines the difficulties faced by M's lawyer.

Dave Marais' first attorney, Jean-Jaques Natai, left Madagascar; he was subsequently refused re-entry into Madagascar. Later Maitre Eric Hamel became the defence attorney for Dave Marais. Although Maitre Hamel obtained a permit from the examining Magistrate to see his client, he was repeatedly prevented from doing so. From December 1979 to May 1981, Dave Marais was unable to communicate with Maitre Hamel and to prepare his defence, except for two days during the trial itself. On 11 February 1982, Malagasy political police authorities arrested Maitre Hamel, detained him in the basement of the Ambohibao political police prison and, subsequently, expelled him from Madagascar, thereby further impairing his ability effectively to represent Dave Marais.[350]

In an interim decision the HRC requested information and clarification on, *inter alia*, 'the means of communication between the alleged victim, his

family and legal counsel, in particular his access to Maitre Eric Hamel'.[351] In
the light of the failure of the State party to provide the information and
clarification requested the HRC noted that the failure had hampered its
consideration of the communication and it 'requested the State party, should
there hitherto have been any obstacles barring Maitre Eric Hamel from
access to ensure that the lawyer and his client had the proper facilities for
effective access to each other. The State party should inform this Committee
of the steps taken by it in this connection.'[352] These requests and subsequent
ones went unheeded except for a copy of a letter purportedly written by M
requesting a remission of sentence.[353] The HRC expressed the view that the
facts as found disclosed violations of article 14(3)(*b*) and *(d)* because M had
been denied adequate opportunity to communicate with his counsel, Maitre
Hamel, and because his right to the assistance of his counsel to represent him
and prepare his defence has been interfered with by the Malagasy authorities.[354] The decision is important in finding a violation of M's rights to
effective legal assistance, representation, and preparation in the inter-
ferences of the Malagasy authorities. The freedom of lawyers to defend without interference, intimidation, or harassment is a most important principle of
the rule of law and often a precondition to securing the rights in article 14.[355]

10.44 It has already been noted above how the experience of the HRC
under the OP can assist its deliberations under the article 40 reporting
procedure.[356] Another example of this process in operation can be seen in
respect of the matter of pre-trial access to counsel. This matter was raised in a
number of communications concerning Uruguay. For example, in *Sequeira*
v. *Uruguay*[357] it was alleged that S had no right to legal assistance while kept
in detention because the right to defence is not recognized by the authorities
until a prosecution has been initiated. S had been brought before a military
judge on three occasions but no steps had been taken to commit him for trial.
The HRC expressed the view that article 14(3) had been violated because he
had no access to legal assistance.[358] During the consideration of the State
report of Uruguay members of the HRC took the opportunity to raise with
the State representative a number of relevant matters including pre-trial
access to and communication with counsel.[359]

10.45 No decision on the merits has been concerned with the legal aid
aspect of article 14(3)(*d*). In *J.S.* v. *Canada*[360] the HRC took the view that,
notwithstanding the existence of a domestic dispute as to the appropriate
remuneration authority in respect of a legal aid award to a defendant, where
the defendant had in fact been represented by legal counsel of her own
choosing and one of the legal aid authorities had offered to pay the counsel
chosen by her, there were no grounds substantiating an alleged violation of
article 14(3)(*d*).[361]

In *O.F.* v. *Norway*[362] O.F. was prosecuted for two minor offences (non-
compliance with a duty to fill in a form and exceeding the speed limit). Both

charges were trivial and could in practice only lead to a small fine.[363] His request for counsel to be appointed at the expense of the State was refused. The HRC expressed the view that the author had failed to show that in this particular case the 'interests of justice' would have required the assignment of a lawyer at the expense of the State party.[364]

Article 14(3)(*e*): 'To examine, or have examined, the witnesses against him and to obtain the attendance and examination of witnesses on his behalf under the same conditions as witnesses against him'

10.46 The HRC has expressed the view that article 14(3)(*e*) has been violated in a small number of cases. In *Antonaccio* v. *Uruguay*[365] A was not allowed to present witnesses in support of his case before a military tribunal. In *Mbenge* v. *Zaïre*[366] the HRC observed that trial *in absentia* without due notification to the accused deprived him, *inter alia*, of the rights in article 14(3)(*e*). In *Pratt and Morgan* v. *Jamaica*[367] the HRC expressed the view that, where counsel had failed to call a witness at the trial stage, there was no violation of article 14(3)(*e*) where the Court of Appeal did not itself insist upon the calling of the witness.[368]

Article 14(3)(*f*): 'To have the free assistance of an interpreter if he cannot understand or speak the language used in court'[369]

10.47 In *Guesdon* v. *France* the HRC expressed the view that there was no violation of article 14(1), or (3)(e) or (f) where the Defendant (G) and the witnesses in the case were obliged to give evidence in French, provided they could express themselves adequately, rather than in Breton as they wished to do.

Article 14(3)(*g*): 'Not to be compelled to testify against himself or to confess guilt'

10.48 The HRC has expressed the view that article 14(3)(*g*) has been violated in a small number of cases. It is unfortunate that in each of these cases the State party concerned, Uruguay, made no reply to the allegations and the decisions are in effect decisions by default based simply on the allegations of the victim. For example, in *Burgos* v. *Uruguay*[370] it was asserted by four witnesses that B and several others were forced under threats to sign false statements which were subsequently used in the legal proceedings against them. Considering that the State party had not refuted these allegations the HRC expressed the view that article 14(3)(*g*) had been violated.[371] Presumably, in order to refute such allegations a State party would need to provide a transcript of the trial or the judgment of the court or tribunal to show either that the allegation was considered and rejected or that it had not been raised at all. In *Burgos* Uruguay had ignored the HRC's requests for copies of any court orders or decisions of relevance.

Both physical and psychological compulsion would seem to be covered. In *Estrella* v. *Uruguay*[372] E, a concert pianist, was allegedly subject to severe physical and psychological torture, including the threat that his hands would be cut off by an electric saw, in an effort to force him to admit subversive activities. Again the State party made no reply. On the basis of these allegations the HRC expressed the view that article 14(3)(*g*) had been violated because of the attempts made to compel him to testify against himself and to confess guilt.[373]

In *Conteris* v. *Uruguay*[374] the HRC expressed the view that there had been a violation of article 14(3)(*g*) as C was forced by means of torture to confess guilt. This is interesting because the HRC's view on article 7 refers only to C's severe ill-treatment rather than to torture.[375]

Article 14(4): 'In the case of juvenile persons, the procedure shall be such as will take account of their age and the desirability of promoting their rehabilitation'

10.49 To date, no views have concerned this provision.[376]

Article 14(5): 'Everyone convicted of a crime shall have the right to his conviction and sentence being reviewed by a higher tribunal according to law'

10.50 In *de Montejo* v. *Colombia*[377] M was tried and sentenced to one year of imprisonment by a military tribunal on 7 November 1979 for the offence of having sold a gun contrary to article 10 of Decree No. 1923 of 6 September 1978, also called the Statute of Security. This instrument did not make this particular type of offence (*contravención*) subject to review by a higher court. M alleged that the application of the Decree violated, *inter alia*, article 14(5). The State party contested this allegation:

It argued that in that provision, the phrase 'according to the law' leaves it to national law to determine in which cases and circumstances application may be made to a court of higher instance and that if the meaning of this provision should be differently interpreted, it must be borne in mind that Colombia is experiencing a situation of disturbed public order, within the meaning of article 4(1) of the Covenant, and that consequently the Government may take the measures referred to.

 ... article 14(5) establishes the general principle of review by a higher tribunal without making such a review mandatory in all possible cases involving a criminal offence since the phrase 'according to law' leaves it to national law to determine in which cases and circumstances application may be made to a higher court. It explained that under the legal regime in force in Colombia, criminal offences are divided into two categories, namely *delitos* and *contravenciones* and that convictions for all *delitos* and for almost all *contravenciones* are subject to review by a higher court.[378]

In her additional information and observations the author argued,

that article 14(5) of the Covenant provides for dual jurisdiction for judgements in criminal cases and, therefore, the Government of Colombia cannot restrict that guarantee, particularly not by emergency provisions such as the 'Security Statute'.[379]

With respect to article 4 the HRC expressed the view that in the specific context of the communication there was no information to show that article 14(5) was derogated from in accordance with article 4 of the Covenant.[380] With regard to the argument advanced by the State party on the application of article 14(5),

The Committee considers that the expression 'according to law' in article 14(5) of the Covenant is not intended to leave the very existence of the right to review to the discretion of the States parties, since the rights are those recognized by the Covenant, and not merely those recognized by domestic law. Rather, what is to be determined 'according to law', is the modalities by which the review by a higher tribunal is to be carried out. It is true that the Spanish text of article 14(5), which provides for the right to review, refers only to '*un delito*', while the English text refers to 'crime' and the French text refers to '*une infraction*'. Nevertheless the Committee is of the view that the sentence of imprisonment imposed on Mrs. Consuelo Salgar de Montejo, even though for an offence defined as '*contravención*' in domestic law, is serious enough, in all the circumstances, to require a review by a higher tribunal as provided for in article 14(5) of the Covenant.[381]

The decision seems somewhat ambiguous. If the phrase 'according to law' refers simply to the domestic modalities of the right to review, the question of how serious the sentence imposed is in all the circumstances should be irrelevant. If the offence is a criminal one then there must be a right to review. However, the approach indicated by this decision of looking to the seriousness of the offence in all the circumstances suggests perhaps that the HRC may take the view that the exclusion of a right of review for minor offences may not be a violation of article 14(5). This approach would obviously raise difficult problems as to when an offence would be 'serious enough' to require review.[382] The decision in *de Montejo* might be taken to indicate that where a conviction results in a sentence of imprisonment a review would be required, but would a heavy fine be sufficient, or a restriction on civil and political rights? What if the conviction had resulted in the convicted person losing his or her employment? We have already noted that in its General Comment the HRC stated that, 'The guarantee is not confined only to the most serious offences'.[383] That comment could be read to support the above view that minor offences might not necessarily require a right of review or that the guarantee applies in all cases and not just the 'most serious'.

The General Comment also suggests that 'domestic modalities' would include such matters as the procedures of appeal, access to and the powers of reviewing tribunals, requirements for appeals, and the way in which the procedure before review tribunals takes account of the fair and public hearing requirements of paragraph 1 of article 14.[384]

It is also interesting to note that having expressed its view that article 14(5) had been violated the HRC expressed the view that the State party was not only under an obligation to provide effective remedies for the violation but also that it should adjust its laws in order to give effect to the right set forth in article 14(5) of the Covenant.[385]

10.51 In *Pinkey* v. *Canada*[386] there had been a two and a half year delay in the production of the transcripts of the trial for the purpose of P's appeal. The HRC observed that,

the right under Article 14(3)(c) to be tried without undue delay should be applied in conjunction with the right under Article 14(5) to review by a higher tribunal, and that consequently there was in this case a violation of both these provisions taken together.[387]

The HRC could simply have taken the approach, stated in its General Comment, that the right to be tried without undue delay extends to cover the period up to the end of a final appeal.[388] This is the approach taken by the EUCT under article 6(1) of the ECHR.[389] Such an approach would obviate the holding of a violation of article 14(5) which would perhaps be more realistic since in this case P did in fact have his conviction and sentence reviewed by a higher tribunal.

10.51.1 In *Pratt and Morgan* v. *Jamaica*[390] there was a delay of forty-five months in the delivery of the Court of Appeal's written judgment. The HRC expressed the view that,

the responsibility for the delay ... lies solely with the authorities of Jamaica. This responsibility is neither dependent on a request for production by the accused in a trial nor is non-fulfilment of this responsibility excused by the absence of a request from the accused.[391]

The HRC followed the view in *Pinkey* v. *Canada*[392] and found a violation of article 14(3)(*c*) in conjunction with article 14(5).

10.52 Some interesting points concerning article 14(5) arose in *Fanali* v. *Italy*.[393] F, a retired Air Force General, was convicted and sentenced in a criminal suit based on charges of corruption and abuse of public office in connection with the purchase by the Italian government of military planes of the type Hercules C130 from the United States of America company, Lockheed. The suit also involved members of the government for whom the 'Constitutional Court' was the only competent tribunal. Article 134 of the Italian Constitution provided that no appeal is allowed against decisions of the Constitutional Court in as far as they concern the President of the Republic and the Ministers. An 'ordinary' law No. 20 of 25 January 1962 extended the constitutional provisions of 'no appeal' to 'other individuals' sentenced by the Constitutional Court for crimes related to those committed by the President of the Republic or Ministers. F claimed that this aspect of the Italian juridical system violated article 14(5) of the Covenant.

The State party objected to the admissibility of the communication on two grounds; (*a*) under article 5(2)(*a*) of the OP,[394] and (*b*) by invoking the reservation to article 14(5) made upon ratification. The reservation reads as follows,

Article 14, paragraph 5, shall be without prejudice to the application of existing Italian provisions which, in accordance with the Constitution of the Italian Republic, govern the conduct, at one level only, of proceedings instituted before the Constitutional Court in respect of charges brought against the President of the Republic and its Ministers.[395]

F contested the applicability of the reservation to his case. He raised objections as to its constitutional validity and argued further that he could not be classed under either of the two categories referred to in the reservation.[396] The State party rejected both of these objections. It referred to a decision of the Constitutional Court of 2 July 1977 upholding the Constitutionality of the law of 25 January 1962.

The HRC expressed the view that there was no doubt about the international validity of the reservation despite its alleged irregularity at the domestic level,[397] and that it was 'outside its competence to pronounce itself on the constitutionality of domestic law'.[398] On the scope of the reservation the HRC continued

... its applicability to the present case depends on the wording of the reservation in its context, where regard must be had to its object and purpose. Since the two parties read it differently, it is for the Committee to decide this dispute.[399]

This approach is clearly important as it gives the Committee jurisdiction to determine the applicability of a reservation and excludes any idea of a State party reserving to itself the determination of the scope of international supervision.[400]

The Committee then proceeded to consider the question of the applicability of the reservation and accepted the view of the State party as the correct reading because a narrow construction would have been contrary to both its wording and its purpose.[401]

F had also argued that his right of appeal was not only confirmed by the inapplicability of the Italian reservation to him, but also by the provisions of article 2(3) of the Covenant to which no reservation had been made. He argued that he could not be deprived of the right to appeal provided for in article 2(3) of the Covenant even if the Italian reservation to article 14(5) were applicable.[402] The HRC rejected this argument:

The Committee is unable to share this view which seems to overlook the nature of the provisions concerned. It is true that article 2(3) provides generally that persons whose rights and freedoms, as recognized in the Covenant, are violated 'shall have an effective remedy'. But this general right to a remedy is an accessory one, and cannot be invoked when the purported right to which it is linked is excluded by a reservation, as in the present case. Even had this not been so, the purported right, in the case of article 14(5), consists itself of a remedy (appeal). Thus it is a form of *lex specialis* besides which it would have no meaning to apply the general right in article 2(3).[403]

It is submitted that this decision is correct but there are two separate arguments here which need to be distinguished. First, the HRC describes the right in article 2(3) as an accessory one. This might be taken to suggest that the HRC would not hold that this article can be the subject of a violation independent of a violation of another substantive right in the Covenant. However, the HRC has found article 2(3) to be violated independently.[404] This approach follows that of the EUCT to article 13 ECHR.[405] The second argument in terms of article 14(5) being a *lex specialis* is logically sensible and the same view would probably be taken of other provisions, for example, article 9(5) ICCPR (right to compensation for unlawful arrest or detention). Again the approach of the HRC mirrors the jurisprudence under the ECHR.[406]

Article 14(6): Compensation for miscarriage of justice

10.53 In *Muhonen* v. *Finland*[407] a Military Service Examining Board rejected M's application to do alternative service subject to civil authorities (instead of armed or unarmed service in the armed forces) on the ground that he had not proved that serious moral considerations based on ethical conviction prevented him from doing armed or unarmed military service.[408] That decision was confirmed twice on appeal by the Ministry of Justice. M refused to perform military service when called up. He was convicted for this refusal and sentenced to eleven months' imprisonment. That verdict was confirmed by a higher court. While serving that sentence M applied for a new hearing before the Examining Board. The Board acceded to this request and found in favour of M. Subsequently a presidential pardon was requested and granted and M was released. The second decision of the Examining Board was considered by the HRC to have dealt with M's allegation of a violation of article 18(1) (freedom of thought, conscience, and religion). *Ex officio* the HRC observed that the facts of the case might raise an issue under article 14(6) which should be considered. The State party made submissions on this question but M did not.[409]

The HRC expressed the view that,

Such a right to compensation may arise in relation to criminal proceedings if either the conviction of a person has been reversed or if he or she 'has been pardoned on the ground that a new or newly discovered fact shows conclusively that there has been a miscarriage of justice'.[410]

On the facts of the case the HRC took the view that M's conviction had never been set aside by a later judicial decision and that his pardon had been motivated by considerations of equity rather than that it had been established that his conviction rested on a miscarriage of justice.[411] Accordingly, there had been no violation of article 14(6) because M had no right to compensation. The HRC's view makes it clear that the requirement of a miscarriage of justice is a strict one. It is not sufficient that the decision affecting the alleged victim is altered.

Article 14(7): 'No one shall be liable to be tried or punished again for an offence for which he has already been finally convicted or acquitted in accordance with the law and penal procedure of each country'

10.54 In *Schweizer* v. *Uruguay*[412] S alleged that article 14(7) had been violated because he had been charged anew before the competent military tribunal for the same acts which had already been investigated by an ordinary judge between 1971 and 1974 with the addition of one new charge. The new indictment against S was issued in March 1980 and sentence was pronounced in September 1980. The HRC expressed the view that,

based on the authors' submission, the criminal proceedings initiated against David Campora (S) in 1971 were not formally concluded at first instance until the military tribunal pronounced its judgement on 10 September 1980. Article 14(7), however, is only violated if a person is tried again for an offence for which he has already been finally convicted or acquitted. This does not appear to have been so in the present case. Nevertheless, the fact that the Uruguayan authorities took almost a decade until the judgement at first instance was handed down indicates a serious malfunctioning of the judicial system contrary to article 14(3)(c) of the Covenant.[413]

Thus for a State party to reject an alleged violation of article 14(7) on the ground that the original proceedings are still continuing may, in the circumstances, amount to an admission that those original proceedings have not been conducted without undue delay.

10.55 In *Nieto* v. *Uruguay*[414] N had been tried in 1972 and sentenced to ten years of imprisonment by the civil judiciary (as distinct from the military judiciary) for a series of offences. In December 1980, shortly before he was due for release, new criminal proceedings were started against N allegedly based on the same facts as those for which he had been tried and sentenced by the civil judiciary.[415] The State party rejected this allegation on the ground that, 'The proceedings concerned were brought because of the emergence of fresh evidence regarding the commission of offences' of 'robbery' and 'assault on the safety of transport'.[416] The State party's submission added that, 'The fact that these offences had been investigated by the police authorities in no way signified that there was any repetition of proceedings; no proceedings had been instituted on that account, since the authorities did not possess the evidence now available'.[417]

As of 25 July 1983, the date of its final views under article 5(4) OP, the HRC had received no information as to the outcome of those proceedings or that they had been concluded. In its views the HRC observed that,

the State party has not specified what the new evidence was which prompted the Uruguayan authorities to initiate new proceedings. In the absence of information as to the outcome of those proceedings, the Committee makes no finding on the question of a violation of article 14(7), but is of the view that the facts indicate a failure to comply with the requirements of article 14(3)(c) of the Covenant that an accused person should be tried 'without undue delay'.[418]

The HRC's view implies that if a State party concludes proceedings against an accused person which allegedly violate article 14(7) of the Covenant it will be obliged to specify the new evidence which constituted the basis of those proceedings. The initiation of proceedings by a State party a considerable period after the alleged events (in the case of *Nieto* some eight to nine years after) might well be thought to raise some acute difficulties in the securing of a fair hearing for the accused person, assuming that there is a residual aspect to the requirement of a 'fair hearing' beyond the specific guarantees in article 14.[419] It is interesting to consider whether the HRC could raise such a point *ex officio* and then express a view upon it, and whether they would be willing to examine the evidential problems that would inevitably be involved. The HRC might take the view that they could only examine this matter in respect of a trial that has in fact taken place.

10.56 In *Cabreira* v. *Uruguay*[420] it was alleged on C's behalf that a judgment of 15 February 1977 contained grave technical defects including acts for which he was allegedly punished twice. The State party informed the HRC that the Supreme Military Tribunal had sentenced C to twelve years of imprisonment and in addition to one to three years of 'security measures' basically for the same offences with aggravating circumstances. In reply it was alleged that the imposition of precautionary detention measures (*medidas de seguridad eliminatives*) was illegal and that such measures merely served the purpose of preventing any proceedings aimed at obtaining release on parole. The submission added that military justice had often imposed such measures when dealing with political offences. No further information was received from the State party on this point. In its statement of considerations taken into account the HRC observed that,

As to the alleged technical defects in the judgement at second instance, the Committee considers that due to lack of specific information provided by the author it cannot make a finding on the alleged violations of articles 2(3) and 14 of the Covenant.[421]

This view is consistent with the HRC's general approach in requiring specific information with respect to alleged violations. It might be suggested that the HRC could inform the alleged victim that unless more specific information is forthcoming in respect of any particular provision of the Covenant they will be obliged to refrain from making any finding with regard to that particular provision.

10.57 In *A.P.* v. *Italy*[422] A.P. alleged that article 14(7) had been violated because he was prosecuted in Italy for the same currency offence for which he had already been convicted and sentenced in Switzerland. The State party rejected A.P.'s contention that, 'article 14, paragraph 7, of the Covenant protects the principle of "international *ne bis in idem*". In the opinion of the State party, article 14, paragraph 7, must be understood as referring exclusively to the relationships between judicial decisions of a single State and not between those of different States'.[423] The HRC accepted the view of Italy and declared the communication inadmissible: 'The Committee observes that this provision prohibits double jeopardy only with regard to an offence adjudicated in a given State.'[424] The HRC's decision seems to be in accordance with the literal wording in article 14(7).

APPRAISAL

10.58 The consideration under the reporting process of the complex of rights in article 14 cries out for a consistent and systematic approach. The range and depth of the Committee's considerations of article 14 has undoubtedly been impressive. Members have adopted a very positive approach and subjected national reports to searching dissection and analysis. The extensive repertoire of questions and comments has facilitated the building up of a substantial body of information on the relevant laws and practices of States parties. Having collected most of the basic information the HRC's analysis increasingly focuses on particular problem areas, difficulties of implementation, and new developments in the State concerned. During its consideration of second periodic reports the HRC has already had occasion to observe that laws and practices identified as contrary to article 14 during the consideration of initial or supplementary reports have not been repealed or removed.[425]

The HRC's considerations of article 14 again suggest that part of the usefulness of the article 40 procedure lies in its flexibility. Members can put to State representatives appropriate matters from the standard repertoire of questions and comments detailed above, look closely at particular features of the different legal regimes that come before them, for example, the operation of military or revolutionary tribunals,[426] and the denial of, or restricted access to, counsel. Members can also draw on the difficulties or inadequacies of implementation revealed through the examination of individual communications under the Optional Protocol which can indicate both general and specific defects in the operation of civil and criminal justice systems. Inevitably the two aspects of the HRC's work interrelate. Moreover, the experience of other human rights institutions can be put to the same use. For example, the practice under the ECHR may well have inspired a number of questions and comments put to State representatives.[427]

10.59 The HRC's General Comment on article 14 has been analysed and, while some criticisms of it have been made, it represents a useful addition to the HRC's jurisprudence. Apart from reflecting the HRC's experience to date it states its interpretation of some of the key elements of article 14 and a response to the interpretations advanced by States parties.[428] The General Comment also now has an important input back into the reporting process. It is now common for the 'list of issues' sent to State representatives prior to the consideration of second and third periodic reports, or the additional questions put to State representatives, to request a response to the General Comment on article 14 or to comment on any observations it has already made under article 40(5) of the ICCPR.[429] To the extent that State representatives respond so the dialogue between the HRC and the States parties is strengthened and developed.[430] This survey of the HRC's considerations of article 14 has revealed some impressive work. A solid foundation has been established on which further work and development can be based. If States parties respond in a positive and constructive manner, as most have done to date, the dialogue between them and the HRC can play a constructive role in securing the implementation of the rights in article 14.

10.60 Obviously the Optional Protocol is in its early stages of development but already the HRC has dealt with a number of important aspects of article 14 and made some important pronouncements on the scope and meaning of some of its terms.[431] The HRC's views are more explicitly interpretational than the questions and comments put under the reporting process and, therefore, provide a clearer guide to the content of article 14. That jurisprudence is complemented by the practice of the HRC under the article 40 process, including its general comments, which we have examined above. As noted the two aspects of the HRC's work interrelate.[432] Similarly comparisons have been made to the more highly developed jurisprudence under the ECHR which can provide valuable and instructive comparisons for the HRC. The accommodation of various legal systems of civil and criminal justice inevitably poses a challenge to the consistent implementation and application of the ICCPR.[433] The practice under article 6 of the ECHR would suggest that a great many key issues may potentially be raised under article 14 including the margin of discretion that will be afforded to States who rely on the limitations in article 14(1) to limit public hearings or public judgments, whether article 14 guarantees any right of access to courts or tribunals,[434] the relationship between article 14 and article 9 on the liberty and security of the person.[435] Although it will take longer for a clear picture to emerge it seems fair to comment that at the general level the HRC seems to have adopted a similar approach to the EUCT in looking for the practical and 'effective' implementation of the rights in article 14.[436] It has certainly not been content simply to note applicable laws and regulations. Similarly its approach of spelling out what States parties in violation of article 14 must do to remedy the situation, for example, affording the victim a fair trial or granting compensation, is to be commended.

10.61 Whether the views of the HRC have actually produced any practical results is more problematic. No State has actually informed the HRC that its views under article 14 have been followed as a direct consequence thereof. When the individuals concerned have been released this does not necessarily seem to have been a result of the HRC's views although they may have been a limited factor.[437] One must also bear in mind the limited number of States parties to the Optional Protocol and that the majority of communications have concerned Uruguay during a period when the Uruguayan authorities were not co-operating with the HRC. The result is that much of the HRC's jurisprudence under article 14, as under other articles, is largely developed by default. This situation is rapidly changing as more decisions and views are given after States parties have co-operated with the HRC and argued for particular interpretations of the terms of article 14.

NOTES

1 For similar provisions see arts. 10, 11 UDHR; art. 6 ECHR; art. XXVI ADRD; arts. 8, 10 AMR; arts. 7, 26 AFR. For the drafting history of article 14 see Docs. A/2929 pp. 42–4; A/4299 pp. 9–17 (1959); and Bossuyt, *Guide*, pp. 277–319. See H. A. Noor Muhammed, 'Due Process of Law for Persons Accused of Crime', in L. Henkin (ed.), *The International Bill of Rights—The ICCPR*, pp. 138–65 (1981); H. A. Noor Muhammed, 'Guarantees for Accused Persons under the U.N. Human Rights Covenant', 20 Ind. JIL (1980) p. 177 at pp. 198–211; R. Lillich, 'Civil Rights', in T. Meron (ed.), *Human Rights in International Law—Legal and Policy Issues*, p. 115 at pp. 139–45 (1984); F. Newman, 'Natural Justice, Due Process and the New International Covenants on Human Rights: Prospectus', [1967] Public Law pp. 274–313; P. Sieghart, *The International Law of Human Rights*, pp. 268–85, 291–307 (1983); P. Van Dijk, *The Right of an Accused to a Fair Trial under International Law* (1983); *UN Action in the Field of Human Rights*, pp. 212–17 (1988).

For further material and recent studies in this area see D. J. Harris, 'The Right to a Fair Trial in Criminal Proceedings as a Human Right', 16 ICLQ (1967) pp. 352–78; J. A. Andrews (ed.), *Human Rights in Criminal Procedure—A Comparative Study* (1982); S. Hertzberg and C. Zammuto, *The Protection of Human Rights in the Criminal Process under International Instruments and National Constitutions* (1981); I. D. Duchacek, *Rights and Liberties in the World*

Today, ch. 4 (1973). See also the following U.N. studies: M. A. Rannat, 'Study of Equality in the Administration of Justice', Doc. E/CN.4/Sub. 2/296/Rev. 1 (1972); L. Joinet, 'Amnesty Laws and their Role in the Safeguard and Promotion of Human Rights', Doc. E/CN.4/Sub. 2/296/Rev. 1 (1985); L. M. Singvi, 'Independence and Impartiality of the Judiciary, Jurors and Assessors and the Independence of Lawyers', Doc. E/CN.4/Sub. 2/1985/18 and Add. 1–6; A. S. Chowdhurry, 'Study on Discriminatory Treatment of Members of Racial, Ethnic, Religious or Linguistic Groups at the Various Levels in the Administration of Criminal Justice, such as Police, Military, Administrative and Judicial Investigations, Arrest, Detention, Trial and Execution of Sentences, Including the Ideologies or Beliefs which Contribute or Lead to Racism in the Administration of Criminal Justice', Docs. E/CN.4/Sub. 2/L.766, introduction and ch. 1 and E/CN.4/Sub. 2/1982/7.

2 On Derogation see ch. 7 above. It has been argued that at least some parts of article 14 should be non-derogable, see International Commission of Jurists, *Study of States of Emergency* (1983), p. 426 where it is suggested that, 'Some progress in this direction has already been made by international law'.

3 General Comment 13/21, Doc. A/39/40, pp. 143–7 (adopted on 12 April 1984 (SR 516) and 23 July 1984 (SR 537)). Also in Doc. CCPR/C/21/Add. 3.

4 Article 9 covers the right to liberty and security of the person.

5 GC 13/21, n. 3 above, pr. 1.

6 The ICJ Study, n. 2 above, identifies 20 distinct rights within article 14, pp. 424–6.

7 See e.g. SR 366 pr. 12 (Tomuschat on Iran).

8 GC 13/21, n. 3 above, pr. 1. It is important to note that information relevant to article 14 is also often contained in the general introductions to and in the sections on article 2 of States parties reports. On article 2 see ch. 6 above.

9 See e.g. SR 67 pr. 19 (Tarnopolsky on GDR).

10 See e.g. SR 65 pr. 34 (Graefrath on Czechoslovakia); SR 188 pr. 24 (Dieye on Sweden) concerning the requirement for a deposit *cautio judicatum solvi*. Reply at SR 188 pr. 31. See also paragraph 2 of the General Comment of the HRC on 'The position of aliens under the Covenant', GC 15(27), Doc. A/41/40, pp. 117–19 (1986).

11 See e.g. SR 51 pr. 63 (Tomuschat on Libya); SR 293 pr. 32 (Lallah on Portugal).

12 See e.g. SR 116 pr. 24 (Mora-Rojas on Belorussian SSR); SR 213 pr. 94 (Sadi on Senegal).

13 See e.g. Doc. A/41/40, pr. 330 (on Czechoslovakia).

14 SR 392 pr. 6 (Graefrath on Iceland). For Iceland's report see Doc. CCPR/C/10/ Add. 4 (1981). Similarly see SR 117 pr. 50 (Graefrath on Belorussian SSR), SR 221 pr. 31 (Vincent-Evans on Colombia).

15 SR 187 pr. 26 (Tomuschat on Poland). See also ibid., pr. 50 (Tarnopolsky on Poland).

16 See the decision of the EUCT in the *Delcourt Case*, EUCT, Series A, Vol. 11 (1970).

17 GC 13/21, n. 3 above, pr. 3.

18 Cf. the comments of Graefrath in text to n. 50 below. For a recent UK perspective see C. R. Munro, *Constitutional Law*, ch. 9 (1987).

19 During the consideration of the report of the FRG Mr Opsahl referred to the *Konig Case*, EUCT, Series A, Vol. 27 (1978), and asked whether labour, finance, and social courts would be covered by article 14, SR 92 pr. 37. See n. 20 below.

20 As regards the expression 'civil rights and obligations' the EUCT has declined to give an abstract definition but has established a set of applicable principles. Members of the EUCT still differ, however, on the application of those principles, see e.g. *Bentham* v. *Netherlands*, EUCT, Series A, Vol. 97 (1985): article 6 ECHR held applicable by 11 votes to 6. Recently the EUCT has considered for the first time the applicability of article 6(1) ECHR to social security matters. It has reaffirmed the principles established in its case law and decided the cases by determining whether the private or public law elements involved predominated. See *Feldbrugge* v. *Netherlands*, EUCT, Series A, Vol. 99 (1986): *Deumeland* v. *FRG*, EUCT, Series A, Vol. 100 (1986). The EUCT is similarly divided on the expression 'criminal charge', see e.g. *Campbell and Fell* v. *UK*, EUCT Series A, Vol. 80 (1984): article 6 held applicable by 4 votes to 3. Generally on the scope of article 6 ECHR see Fawcett, pp. 133–47; Van Dijk and Van Hoof, pp. 238–47; D. J. Harris, 'The Application of Article 6(1) of the ECHR to Administrative Law' (1974) 47 BYIL pp. 157–200; A. W. Bradley, 'The ECHR and Administrative Law—First Impressions', 21 Osgoode Hall LJ (1983) pp. 609–35; C. J. F. Kidd, 'Disciplinary Proceedings and the Right to a Fair Criminal Trial under the European Convention on Human Rights', 36 ICLQ (1987) pp. 856–72.

21 See *Y.L.* v. *Canada*, pr. 10.26 below.

22 GC 13/21, n. 3 above, pr. 2.

23 See e.g. SR 282 pr. 50 (Tomuschat on Tanzania), SR 366 pr. 13 (Tomuschat on Iran). If in a given situation, that crucial freedom was interfered with, the entire judicial system became warped', SR 431 pr. 72 (Aguilar on Peru).

24 SR 132 pr. 53 (Tomuschat on Bulgaria). 'It was his understanding that President Aquino had increased by decree the penalty imposed on anyone who prevented the accused from contacting a lawyer to up to six years of imprisonment. Even so there had been communications concerning violations of that right, and also threats and attacks, and even the killing of lawyers. He looked forward to hearing the Philippine delegation's comments on the matter', SR 884 pr. 14 (Cooray on the Philippines).

25 See the decision of the EUCT in *Airey* v. *Ireland*, Series A, Vol. 32 (1980). See also A.8158/78, 21 D. & R. p. 95; A.11714/85 v. UK (refusal of legal aid concerning minor charges). *Granger* v. *UK*, EUCT Series A, Vol. 174 (1990).

26 SR 439 pr. 44. The French report is Doc. CCPR/C/22/Add. 2 (1982). Similar questions were put to UK representatives.

27 See pr. 10.12 below.

28 See Doc. A/40/40, pr. 396.

29 Although the ICCPR does not use the term 'court' in the second sentence of article 14 members have generally used the term in preference to 'tribunals'.

30 See e.g. SR 77 pr. 29 (Hanga on Norway). See n. 18 above.

31 See e.g. SR 51 pr. 63 (Tomuschat on Libya); SR 328 pr. 36 (Tomuschat on Morocco).

32 This concern has also been noted in the consideration of article 2 in ch. 6 above.

33 See e.g. SR 89 pr. 17 (Vincent-Evans on Iran); SR 199 pr. 25 (Bouziri on Iraq); SR 475 pr. 19 (Opsahl on Guinea). Many of the communications under the Optional Protocol have concerned the operation of military tribunals.

34 See e.g. SR 221 pr. 30 (Vincent-Evans on Colombia).

35 See e.g. SR 84 pr. 28 (Vincent-Evans on Madagascar).

36 See e.g. SR 90 pr. 13 (Tarnopolsky on Iran).

37 See e.g. SR 98 prs. 51–2 (Vincent-Evans on Yugoslavia).

38 See e.g. SR 155 pr. 15 (Tomuschat on Ukrainian SSR).

39 See e.g. SR 200 pr. 8 (Graefrath on Iraq).

40 See e.g. SR 283 pr. 22 (Opsahl on Mali).

41 See e.g. SR 291 pr. 44 (Vincent-Evans on Jamaica).

42 This information was contained in a Government Declaration of 1 May 1980 which was circulated to members of the HRC.

43 SR 224 pr. 15 (Mr Tarnopolsky). The replies of the State representative are in SR 227. He did not reply specifically to the point raised by Mr Tarnopolsky but he did inform the HRC that, 'On 14 June 1980 the Military Council had transferred to the jurisdiction of the civilian judicial authorities all persons in its custody', ibid., pr. 2. Note the comments of Professor Lillich, 'Whether such independence and impartiality can be assured when a State resorts to ad hoc or special tribunals, as frequently occurs after revolutions or in national emergencies, is a doubtful proposition: for this reason, it is disappointing that article 10 [of UDHR] does not speak directly to this point. In contrast, article 14(1) of the Political Covenant and article 8(1) of the American Convention add the requirement that the tribunal be 'competent', a word which, according to the travaux préparatoires of the former, "was tended to ensure that all persons should be tried in courts whose jurisdiction had been previously established by law, and arbitrary action so avoided". Article 8(1) of the American Convention goes one step further, specifically stating that a trial must be conducted by a tribunal 'previously established by law', Lillich, n. 1 above, p. 141 (footnotes omitted). See also Sieghart, ibid., pp. 283–4; ICJ Study, n. 2 above, p. 459, recommendation 8.

44 GC 13/21, n. 3 above, pr. 4. See n. 40 above.

45 See the decision in *Mbenge* v. *Zaire*, ch. 8, pr. 8.25 above and 10.40 below.

46 See SR 537 prs. 61–4. See R. B. Elbert, *N.A.T.O. Fair Trial Safeguards* (1963).

47 See e.g. SR 199 pr. 40 (Prado-Vallejo on Iraq); SR 391 pr. 10 (Opsahl on Denmark); SR 475 pr. 38 (Aguilar on Guinea).

48 SR 422 pr. 33. Reply at SR 428 pr. 32. The Nicaraguan Report is Docs. CCPR/C/14/Add. 2 and 3 (1982–3).

49 SR 98 pr. 51. See also SR 67 pr. 46 (Prado-Vallejo on GDR).

50 See e.g. SR 214 pr. 57 (on Senegal). Similarly at SR 142 pr. 107 (on Spain), SR 155 pr. 54 (on Ukrainian SSR). Mr Graefrath was an expert from the GDR.

51 See e.g. SR 131 pr. 19 (Tarnopolsky on Bulgaria).

52 See e.g. SR 109 pr. 71 (Hanga on USSR). See C. T. Reid, 'The Ombudsman's Cousin: The Procuracy in Socialist States', [1986] PL pp. 311–26. H. Oda, 'The Soviet Procuracy under Gorbachev', in R. Rideout and J. Jowell (eds.), CLP 1988 pp. 213–35.

53 See e.g. SR 142 pr. 67 (Hanga on Spain).
54 See e.g. SR 346 pr. 22 (Prado-Vallejo on Rwanda); SR 431 pr. 71 (Aguilar on Peru).
55 See e.g. SR 132 pr. 58 (Dieye on Bulgaria).
56 See e.g. SR 421 pr. 58 (Errera on Nicaragua).
57 See e.g. SR 131 pr. 32 (Bouziri on Bulgaria).
58 See e.g. SR 142 pr. 12 (Tarnopolsky on Spain).
59 Ibid.
60 Ibid.
61 See e.g. SR 11 pr. 22 (Esperson on Mauritius).
62 See e.g. SR 109 pr. 38 (Hanga on USSR).
63 See e.g. SR 99 pr. 8 (Opsahl on Yugoslavia); SR 365 pr. 14 (Tarnopolsky on Iran).
64 See e.g. SR 98 pr. 35 (Mora-Rojas on Yugoslavia); SR 132 pr. 24 (Hanga on Bulgaria); SR 137 pr. 23 (Dieye on Romania); SR 154 pr. 49 (Tarnopolsky on Ukrainian SSR).
65 See e.g. SR 32 pr. 37 (Tomuschat on Hungary). Hungary subsequently supplied additional information, Doc. CCPR/C/1/Add. 44, parts II and V (1979).
66 See e.g. SR 89 pr. 40 (Esperson on Iran).
67 See e.g. SR 69 pr. 24 and SR 148 pr. 58 (Graefrath on UK); SR 92 pr. 54 (Graefrath on FRG).
68 See e.g. SR 156 pr. 15 (Dieye on Ukrainian SSR).
69 See e.g. SR 154 pr. 26 (Bouziri on Ukranian SSR); SR 67 pr. 46 (Prado-Vallejo on GDR), reply at SR 68 pr. 5.
70 See e.g. SR 354 pr. 34 (Dieye on Guyana).
71 SR 421 pr. 61, reply at SR 422 pr. 37. For the Nicaraguan report see n. 48 above.
72 GC 13/21, n. 3 above, pr. 3.
73 See GC 13/21, n. 3 above, pr. 15. In the *Piersack Case* the EUCT stated that, 'Whilst impartiality normally denotes absence of prejudice or bias, its existence or otherwise can, notably under article 6 of the Convention, be tested in various ways. A distinction can be drawn in this context between a subjective approach, that is endeavouring to ascertain the personal conviction of a given judge in a given case, and an objective approach, that is determining whether he offered guarantees sufficient to exclude any legitimate doubt in this respect. . . . it is not possible to confine oneself to a purely subjective test. In this area, even appearances may be of a certain importance', EUCT, Series A, Vol. 53 (1982), prs. 30–1. See also *Campbell and Fell* v. *UK*, EUCT, Series A, Vol. 80 (1984); *Sramek* v. *Austria*, EUCT, Series A, Vol. 84 (1984); *De Cubber* v. *Belgium*, EUCT, Series A, Vol. 86 (1984); *Langborger* v. *Sweden*, EUCT, Series A, Vol. 155 (1989) *Hauschildt* v. *Denmark*, EUCT, Series A, Vol. 154 (1989).
74 See e.g. SR 475 pr. 31 (Vincent-Evans on Guinea). When the representatives from Rwanda appeared before the HRC he stated that his country was poor and had limited resources for the training of judges. He suggested that a training grant from the HRC would assist Rwanda in training its judges and would concretize the HRC's desire to apply the Covenant, SR 348 pr. 32. On the approach under the ECHR to structural problems see *Buchholz* v. *Germany*, EUCT, Series A, Vol. 42 (1981); *Zimmerman and Steiner* v. *Switzerland*, EUCT, Series A, Vol. 66

(1984); *Guincho* v. *Portugal*, EUCT, Series A, Vol. 81 (1983); *Marijnissen* v. *Netherlands*, EUCM (12 March 1984); *Dores and Silviera* v. *Portugal*, EUCM (6 July 1986); *Union Alimentaria Sanders SA* v. *Spain*, EUCT, Series A, Vol. 157 (1989).

75 See e.g. SR 392 pr. 69 (Tomuschat on Iceland); SR 430 pr. 47 (Tomuschat on Peru). See also the Australian position on article 14(3)(*c*) noted in pr. 10.15 below.

76 SR 469 pr. 3. For El Salvador's report see Doc. CCPR/C/14/Add. 5 (1983). For a more recent view see Doc. E/CN.4/1990/26.

77 See the decision of the EUCT in *Airey* v. *Ireland*, n. 25 above, in which the EUCT rejected Ireland's view that the ECHR should not be interpreted in a way that would impose financial obligations on the contracting parties. See also ch. 4, prs. 4.55–4.58 above concerning views under the Optional Protocol with significant financial implications.

78 Cf. *Le Compte, Van Leuven and De Meyere* v. *Belgium*, EUCT, Vol. 43 (1981); *H.* v. *Belgium*, EUCT, Series A, Vol. 127 (1987); *Ekbatani* v. *Sweden*, EUCT, Series A, Vol. 134 (1988).

79 A similar comment with respect to the terms 'criminal charge' and 'rights and obligations in a suit at law' has been made above, pr. 10.4. For an isolated example on the 'public order' limitation see the comment of Tomuschat at SR 109 pr. 59 (on USSR).

80 See n. 3 above.

81 See e.g. SR 64 pr. 44 (Tarnopolsky on Czechoslovakia); SR 116 pr. 34 (Prado-Vallejo on Belorussian SSR).

82 See e.g. SR 64 pr. 60 (Tarnopolsky on Czechoslvakia); SR 98 pr. 68 (Tomuschat on Yugoslavia); SR 258 pr. 61 (Bouziri on Italy).

83 SR 69 pr. 56 (Hanga), referring to the Official Secrets Act 1920. See the Official Secrets Act 1989.

84 SR 109 pr. 46 (Prado-Vallejo). Reply at SR 112 pr. 27. The USSR report is Doc. CCPR/C/1/Add. 22 (1978).

85 SR 65 pr. 26 (Opsahl). Reply in SR 66 pr. 16.

86 SR 135 pr. 41 (Bouziri). In reply the State representative explained that the expression meant 'acts contrary to public policy', SR 141 pr. 10. Similarly on 'Socialist Justice' see SR 155 pr. 15 (Tomuschat on Ukranian SSR).

87 SR 189 pr. 4 (Opsahl). The State representative replied that it was difficult to gather accurate information on the application of such proceedings, SR 189 pr. 7.

88 See e.g. Doc. A/39/40, pr. 509 (on GDR). Cf. A.11552/85, 11553/85, and 11658/85 v. UK on reporting restrictions under the Contempt of Court Act 1981.

89 See e.g. SR 136 pr. 47 (Tarnopolsky on Romania).

90 See e.g. SR 132 pr. 64 (Dieye on Bulgaria). See also on the question of publicity for trials SR 154 pr. 50 (Tarnopolsky on Ukrainian SSR); SR 187 pr. 49 (Tarnopolsky on Poland).

91 SR 357 pr. 11. The State representative replied, *inter alia*, that, 'it was untrue that prisoners had been convicted without any written judgement and no evidence could be produced in support of that allegation', SR 373 pr. 22. In March 1989 the Uruguayan representative commented before the HRC that, 'it should be borne

in mind that Uruguayan court proceedings were conducted in writing . . . There was a draft of an amended penal code, as in the case of the Civil Code, for which the oral approach was adopted, but there was very strong conservative resistance on the part of judges and lawyers', SR 878 pr. 43.

92 GC 13/21, n. 3 above, pr. 6.

93 See e.g. A.10038/82, *Harman* v. *UK*, 7 EHRR 146; A.10243/83, *Times Newspapers and Others* v. *UK*, 8 EHRR 54; A.11552/85, 11553, and 11658/85 v. UK.

94 Note that article 14 of the Covenant requires that the judgment 'shall be made public', whereas article 6 ECHR requires that the 'judgement shall be pronounced publicly'. See the decisions of the EUCT in *Pretto* v. *Italy*, EUCT, Series A, Vol. 71 (1983); *Axen* v. *FRG*, EUCT, Series A, Vol. 72 (1983); *Albert and Le Compte* v. *Belgium*, EUCT, Series A, Vol. 58 (1983); *Sutter* v. *Switzerland*, EUCT, Series A, Vol. 74 (1984); *Campbell and Fell* v. *UK*, EUCT, Series A, Vol. 80 (1984).

95 GC 13/21, n. 3 above, pr. 15.

96 Note also article 10(2)(*a*) ICCPR which provides that, 'Accused persons shall, save in exceptional circumstances, be segregated from convicted persons and shall be subject to separate treatment appropriate to their status as unconvicted persons'. In its General Comment on article 10 the HRC noted the presumption of innocence in the context of the segregation of accused prisoners from convicted ones, GC 9(16), Doc. A/37/40, pp. 96–7, pr. 8.

97 See e.g. SR 64 pr. 44 (Tarnopolsky on Czechoslovakia); SR 897 pr. 19 (Dimitrijevic on Bolivia).

98 See e.g. Doc. A/41/40, pr. 392 (on Hungary); Doc. A/42/40, pr. 658 (on Afghanistan), reply at pr. 663.

99 See e.g. Doc. A/39/40, pr. 344 (on Gambia); reply at pr. 353.

100 See e.g. SR 402 pr. 21 (Prado-Vallejo on Australia), reply at SR 407 pr. 52. The operation of statutory exceptions is controversial in the UK, see P. Healy, 'Proof and Policy: No Golden Threads', [1987] CLR pp. 355–66; D. J. Birch, 'Hunting the Snark: The Elusive Statutory Exception', [1988] CLR 221 and reply by P. Mirfield at p. 233, all commenting on *R.* v. *Hunt* [1987] 2 AC 352. See also J. C. Smith, *Justification and Excuse in the Criminal Law* (1989). See *Salabiaku* v. *France*, EUCT, Series A, Vol. 141 A (1988).

101 See e.g. A/39/40, pr. 151 (on Guinea).

102 See e.g. SR 65 pr. 26 (Opsahl on Czechoslovakia); SR 386 pr. 18 (Prado-Vallejo) and 35 (Graefrath on Mexico); SR 402 pr. 46 (Hanga on Australia); SR 473 pr. 23 (Tomuschat on Sri Lanka), reply at SR 477 pr. 44.

103 GC 13/21, n. 3 above, pr. 7. See n. 100 above.

104 SR 205 pr. 30. A number of these points would clearly seem to be inspired by experience under the ECHR. See also SR 110 pr. 24 (Opsahl on Mauritius).

105 See n. 96 above.

106 SR 198 pr. 5 (on Mongolia).

107 SR 357 pr. 12 (on Uruguay). A number of decisions under the Optional Protocol concerning article 19 have related to prosecutions for 'subversive activities', see ch. 11 below. See also SR 475 pr. 51 (Tomuschat on Guinea) concerning the use

of confessions and SR 413 pr. 29 (Tomuschat on Austria) on the possibility of arrest on the ground that an individual might repeat the offence.

108 GC 13/21, n. 3 above, pr. 7. Cf. Fawcett, pp. 179–83.

109 Ibid.

110 See *Minelli* v. *Switzerland*, EUCT, Series A, Vol. 62 (1983); *Adolf* v. *Austria*, ibid., Vol. 49 (1984); *Lutz* v. *FRG*, *Nolkenbockoff* v. *FRG*, EUCT, Series A, Vol. 123 (1987); *Salabiaku* v. *France*, EUCT, Series A, Vol. 141A (1988).

111 See e.g. SR 187 pr. 50 (Tarnopolsky on Poland).

112 GC 13/21, n. 3 above, pr. 5.

113 See Fawcett, p. 148; *Nielson* v. *Austria*, EUCM, 4 YBECHR p. 518 at 548–50.

114 GC 13/21, n. 3 above, pr. 15.

115 See pr. 10.5 above.

116 See e.g. SR 475 pr. 31 (Vincent-Evans on Guinea).

117 GC 13/21, n. 3 above, pr. 8.

118 See Fawcett pp. 145–7, 184; Van Dijk and Van Hoof, pp. 307–10.

119 See Fawcett pp. 186–8.

120 See e.g. SR 51 pr. 35 (Vincent-Evans on Libya); SR 92 pr. 39 (Opsahl on FRG).

121 SR 186 pr. 47. The Polish report is Doc. CCPR/C/4/Add. 2 (1979). See also SR 327 pr. 49 (Tarnopolsky on Morocco). Cf. *R.* v. *Samuel*, [1988] 2 WLR 920.

122 See e.g. SR 357 pr. 14 (Tomuschat on Uruguay).

123 See e.g. SR 93 pr. 40 (Tarnopolsky on FRG).

124 Doc. CCPR/C/1/Add. 33, p. 18 (1978).

125 See SR 135 pr. 43 (Bouziri), pr. 59 (Vincent-Evans), SR 136 pr. 22 (Opsahl). Reply at SR 140 pr. 60. Cf. Police and Criminal Evidence Act 1984, s. 58.

126 See *Caldas* v. *Uruguay*, pr. 10.35 below.

127 Doc. CCPR/C/14/Add. 1 prs. 256–7 referring to the decision of the United States Supreme Court in *Bounds* v. *Smith* (1977) 97 S. Ct. 1491.

128 GC 13/21, n. 3 above, pr. 8.

129 See Fawcett p. 188. See also *Kamasinski* v. *Austria*, EUCT, Series A, Vol. 168 (1990).

130 See pr. 10.14 below.

131 See e.g. Doc. A/41/40, pr. 292 (on Finland); Doc. A/42/40, pr. 79 (on Poland).

132 SR 92 pr. 40 (Opsahl on FRG). The question of delay was also raised during consideration of the second periodic report of the FRG, see Doc. A/41/40, pr. 292; reply at pr. 294. See the decision of the EUCT in the *Wemhoff* v. *FRG*, EUCT, Series A, Vol. 7 pp. 11–15 (1968), on the simplification of proceedings.

133 See e.g. SR 293 pr. 34 (Lallah on Portugal); SR 439 pr. 44 (Vincent-Evans on France); SR 413 pr. 33 (Tomuschat on Austria).

134 See Doc. CCPR/C/14/Add. 1, pr. 263 (1981) and Doc. CCPR/C/42/Add. 2, p. 78 (1987).

135 See 'States Parties to the ICCPR', p. xlv above.

136 GC 13/21, n. 3 above, pr. 10.

137 See pr. 10.13 above.

138 So too under the ECHR, see *Wemhoff* v. *FRG*, EUCT, Seies A, Vol. 7, pr. 18 (1968); Fawcett, pp. 164–70; Van Dijk and Van Hoof, pp. 328–35.

139 For recent examples see *Baggetti* v. *Italy*, *Milasi* v. *Italy*, EUCT, Series A, Vol. 119 (1987).

140 Particularly so in the case of serious offences, see e.g. SR 271 pr. 29 (Tarnopolsky on Kenya). See also the decision in *Mbenge* v. *Zaïre*, pr. 10.40 below.

141 See e.g. SR 93 pr. 40 (Tarnopolsky on FRG); SR 84 pr. 28 (Vincent-Evans on Madagascar).

142 See e.g. SR 357 pr. 16 (Tomuschat on Uruguay); SR 78 pr. 14 (Tomuschat on Norway). See also the *Mbenge Case*, pr. 10.40 below; *Colozza* v. *Italy*, EUCT, Series A, Vol. 89 (1985).

143 SR 222 pr. 53 (Koulishev on Colombia).

144 See e.g. SR 64 pr. 20 (Esperson on Czechoslovakia).

145 See e.g. SR 108 pr. 53 (Vincent-Evans on USSR); SR 67 pr. 40 (Epserson on GDR). See Fawcett, pp. 190–1.

146 See e.g. SR 250 pr. 24 (Graefrath on Denmark); SR 475 pr. 19 (Opsahl on Guinea).

147 See e.g. SR 250 pr. 35 (Tomuschat on Denmark).

148 See e.g. SR 69 pr. 36 (Tarnopolsky on UK).

149 See e.g. SR 31 pr. 42 (Tarnopolsky on Ecuador).

150 See e.g. SR 99 pr. 12 (Lallah on Yugoslavia). This question is also important with respect to article 14(3)(*b*), see e.g. SR 132 pr. 9 (Janca on Bulgaria).

151 SR 475 pr. 50. The Guinean report is Doc. CCPR/C/6/Add. 5 (1980).

152 See e.g. SR 92 pr. 41 (Opsahl on FRG).

153 See e.g. SR 92 pr. 54 (Graefrath on FRG). For the applicable provisions of the law of the FRG see its report, Doc. CCPR/C/1/Add. 18, p. 19 (1977). Shortly after the consideration of the initial report of the FRG the EUCT found the applicable practice in the FRG violated article 6(3)(*e*) ECHR, see *Leudicke, Belkacem and Koc* v. *FRG*, EUCT, Series A, Vol. 29 (1978).

154 Subsequently withdrawn, see *Human Rights—Status of International Instruments*, pp. 86–7 (1987).

155 GC 13/21, n. 3 above, pr. 11.

156 See also GC 13(21), ibid., pr. 8 cited in pr. 10.14.1 above.

157 See e.g. SR 135 pr. 59 (Vincent-Evans on Romania); SR 440 pr. 29 (Herdocia-Ortega on France).

158 See e.g. SR 440 pr. 29 (Herdocia-Ortega on France).

159 SR 357 pr. 17. See also SR 327 pr. 49 (Tarnopolsky on Morocco); SR 387 pr. 36 (Vincent-Evans on Mexico), reply at SR 404 pr. 62.

160 See e.g. SR 89 pr. 40 (Esperson on Iran). See also the decision in *Sutter* v. *Switzerland*, EUCT, Series A, Vol. 74 (1984).

161 See A.768/60 Recueil, i (1962), cited by Fawcett, pp. 196–7; *Pfunders* v. *Austria*, A.788/60, 6 YBECHR 490. See also A.11454/84 *v.* Netherlands, EUCM, 10 EHRR 145.

162 GC 13/21, n. 3 above, pr. 12. Cf. *Bonisch* v. *Austria*, EUCT, Series A, Vol. 92 (1985); *Artico* v. *Italy*, EUCT, Series A, Vol. 37 (1980); *Goddi* v. *Italy*, EUCT, Series A, Vol. 76 (1984); A.11170/84, *B.* v. *Austria*, EUCM, admiss. decn. (14 July 1987).

163 Cf. *Kostovski* v. *Netherlands*, EUCT, Series A, Vol. 166 (1989).

164 See the decisions of the EUCT in *Luedicke, Belkacem and Koc* v. *FRG*, Series A, Vol. 23 (1978), prs. 40–2; *Ozturk* v. *FRG*, ibid., Vol. 73 (1984).

165 See e.g. SR 92 pr. 41 (Opsahl on FRG); SR 186 pr. 37 (Opsahl on Poland); SR 320 pr. 20 (Tomuschat on Japan). See also the Icelandic State representative at SR 251 pr. 10.

166 Doc. CCPR/C/1/Add. 11, p. 5 (1977).

167 SR 228 pr. 4.

168 Ibid., pr. 18.

169 GC 13/21, n. 3 above, pr. 13.

170 See e.g. SR 142 pr. 13 (Tarnopolsky on Spain); SR 187 pr. 26 (Tomuschat on Poland). See A.1083/61, Recueil i (1962), cited in Fawcett, p. 197.

171 SR 441 pr. 13 (on France). For limited provision in this area in the UK see the Interception of Communications Act 1985 enacted to meet the decision in *Malone* v. *UK*, EUCT, Series A, Vol. 82 (1984).

172 GC 13/21, n. 3 above, pr. 14.

173 See ch. 9, pr. 9.6 above.

174 Other provisions of the ICCPR that specifically concern juveniles or children are articles 6(5), 10(2)(*b*) and (3), 14(1), 18(4), 23(4) and 24.

175 See e.g. SR 132 pr. 4 (Graefrath on Bulgaria); SR 482 pr. 5 (Cooray on New Zealand); SR 249 pr. 5 (Hanga on Venezuela); SR 319 pr. 58 (Hanga on Japan).

176 Cf. K. Tomasevski, *Children in Adult Prisons: An International Perspective* (1986). On the UK law affecting juveniles under the Police and Criminal Evidence Act 1984 see J. O'Driscoll, [1986] JSWL pp. 32–41, 65–76.

177 GC 13/21, n. 3 above, pr. 16.

178 The right is also now provided for in the Seventh Protocol to the ECHR, article 2. Under the ECHR a Contracting party is not compelled to set up courts of appeal or cassation but if it does then article 6 applies to such proceedings, see the *Delcourt Case*, EUCT, Series A, Vol. 11, pr. 25 (1970).

179 See e.g. Doc. A/40/40, pr. 56 (on Chile).

180 See e.g. SR 356 pr. 13 (Tarnopolsky on Uruguay).

181 See e.g. SR 223 pr. 9 (Vincent-Evans on Colombia); SR 328 pr. 13 (Dieye on Morocco). See the decision in *Monnell and Morris* v. *UK*, EUCT, Series A, Vol. 115 (1987).

182 See e.g. SR 89 pr. 18 (Vincent-Evans on Iran); SR 319 pr. 20 (Graefrath on Japan); SR 355 pr. 20 (Prado-Vallejo on Uruguay). The report of Costa Rica acknowledged that, 'Unfortunately the Costa Rican Code of Criminal Procedure establishes some sentences against which there is no appeal, that is to say, cases which are heard in the sole instance. In this connexion, legislative reforms are called for', Doc. CCPR/C/1/Add. 46, p. 11 (1979). For some comments see SR 235 pr. 12 (Prado-Vallejo), SR 236 pr. 27 (Hanga), pr. 52 (Janca); reply at SR 240 pr. 23.

183 For Iraq's report see Doc. CCPR/C/1/Add. 45 (1979). See also GC 13/21, n. 3 above, pr. 4.

184 SR 203 pr. 29.

185 SR 203 pr. 30.

186 SR 203 pr. 31.

187 SR 204 pr. 7. Noor Muhammed in Henkin (ed.), n. 1 above, comments, 'Review "by a higher tribunal according to law" suggests that the form of the review might differ from State to State. It suggests also that the review must be "according to law" both in procedure and substance, not merely by the will or whim of an official', pp. 155–6. The importance of the right of review has been highlighted in recent years by allegations before the U.N. Human Rights Commission of summary executions in certain States including Iraq, see Reports of the Special Rapporteur, ch. 8, notes 7, 35, above.

188 Doc. CCPR/C/37/Add. 3. See Doc. A/42/40, prs. 373, 374. It appears that the situation has not been altered.

189 SR 413 pr. 10. The Austrian reservation provided that Article 14 would be applied provided that 'paragraph 5 is not in conflict with legal regulations which stipulate that after an aquittal or a lighter sentence passed by a court of first instance, a higher tribunal may pronounce conviction or a heavier sentence for the same offence, while they exclude the convicted person's right to have such conviction of heavier sentence reviewed by a still higher tribunal', *Human Rights—Status*, n. 154 above, pp. 29–31.

190 GC 13/21, n. 3 above, pr. 17. See also the decision in *Fanali* v. *Italy*, pr. 10.52 below

191 See n. 178 above on the situation under the ECHR.

192 This provision complements article 9(5) ICCPR which provides for an enforceable right to compensation for victims of unlawful arrest or detention. It is interesting to note that article 9(5) provides for an 'enforceable right to compensation', whereas article 14(6) provides only that the sufferer 'shall be compensated'. This wording was preferred to the former because the majority of the HRCion felt that each State should be left to choose between an administrative or judicial remedy according to its own preference. See also now article 3 of the Seventh Protocol to the ECHR which provides for compensation according to the law 'or practice of the State concerned'. See G. Ganz, [1983] Public Law p. 517.

193 See e.g. SR 111 pr. 25 (Esperson on Mauritius); SR 291 pr. 27 (Bouziri on Jamaica).

194 See e.g. SR 213 pr. 21 (Tarnopolsky on Senegal).

195 It is interesting to note that Australia made a reservation to article 14(6) that compensation 'may be by administrative procedures rather than pursuant to specific legal provision', *Human Rights—Status*, n. 154 above, p. 28. The Australian report stated that, 'this is considered to be as satisfactory as making specific legislative provision', Doc. CCPR/C/14/Add. 1, pr. 302 (1981). Despite withdrawing most of its reservations this reservation has been maintained, see Australia's second periodic report Doc. CCPR/C/42/Add. 2, p. 84 (May 1987).

196 See e.g. SR 327 pr. 51 (Tarnopolsky on Morocco).

197 See e.g. SR 482 pr. 12 (Hanga on New Zealand); reply at SR 487 pr. 43 (as corrected). For an interesting provision on the publicity to be given to a judgment or decision establishing innocence see Article 621 of the Moroccon Code of Criminal Procedure, Doc. CCPR/C/10/Add. 2, p. 25.

198 SR 69 pr. 24 (Graefrath), pr. 36 (Tarnopolsky), pr. 92 (Tomuschat) and SR 596

pr. 38, 597 pr. 15 (Tomuschat); replies at SR 596 pr. 51, 597 pr. 20. For the UK reports see Doc. CCPR/C/1/Add. 17 (1977), Add. 35 (1978). It is interesting to note that New Zealand expressly reserved 'the right not to apply article 14(6) to the extent that it is not satisfied by the existing system for *ex gratia* payments to persons who suffer as a result of a miscarriage of justice', *Human Rights—Status*, n. 154 above, p. 43.

199 SR 148 pr. 73 (Mr Cairncross).

200 See 'Miscarriages of Justice', Sixth Report of the Home Affairs Committee, Session 1980–1, HC 421. For the government's reply see Cmnd. 8856 (1983). See also two reports by JUSTICE, 'Home Office Reviews of Criminal Convictions' (1968), 'Compensation for Wrongful Imprisonment' (1982); A. T. H. Smith, 'The Prerogative of Mercy, the Power of Pardon and Criminal Justice', Public Law [1983] p. 398 at pp. 436–9.

201 See s. 133 Criminal Justice Act 1988.

202 GC 13/21, n. 3 above, pr. 18.

203 Cf. ECHR, Protocol 7, article 4.

204 See e.g. SR 207 pr. 13 (Movchan on Canada).

205 See Doc. A/39/40, pr. 299.

206 See Doc. CCPR/C/10/Add. 3.

207 See *A.P.* v. *Italy*, pr. 10.57 below.

208 See Doc. A/38/40, prs. 148, 169. See also ch. 9, n. 36 above.

209 For the texts of these reservations see *Human Rights—Status*, n. 154 above.

210 See Doc. A/4299, n. 1 above, prs. 46–63 (1959).

211 See e.g, SR 30 pr. 13 (Graefrath on Finland).

212 GC 13/21, n. 3 above, pr. 19.

213 See prs. 10.1–10.23 above.

214 The French text reads 'droits et obligations de caractère civil'. The identical French expression appears in article 6 ECHR. Until the day before the ECHR was signed in 1950 the two draft English texts had used the terms 'rights and obligations in a suit at law'. The English text was then altered to 'civil rights and obligations' to make it conform more closely to the French text. See Newman, n. 1 above; *ECHR—Travaux préparatoires*, Vol. iv, pp. 1007–19. On article 6 ECHR see n. 20 above.

215 Doc. A/41/40, p. 145.

216 Ibid., pr. 4.

217 Ibid., pr. 5.

218 Ibid. Further questions related to domestic remedies.

219 Recent decisions under the ECHR have taken the approach of examining the public and private law aspects of a particular situation. See the *Feldbrugge* and *Deumeland* cases, n. 20 above.

220 Doc. A/41/40, p. 145, prs. 9.1–9.3. In *Van Meurs* v. *Netherlands*, V.M. alleged a violation of article 14(1) as regards proceedings that led to the dissolution of his labour contract. The HRC, 'observed that the proceedings at issue related to the rights and obligations of the parties in a suit at law', Doc. A/45/40, Apx., pr. 5.2.

221 Ibid., pr. 9.5. Cf. *Le Compte, Van Leuven and De Meyere* v. *Belgium*, EUCT, Series A, Vol. 43, pp. 22–3 (1981).

222 Doc. A/41/40, p. 150.
223 See the important decision of the EUCM in the *Kaplan Case*, 21 D. & R. (1981) p. 5, concerning the application of article 6 to executive decisions, 'An interpretation of article 6(1) under which it was held to provide a full right of appeal on the merits of every administrative decision affecting private rights would therefore lead to a result which was inconsistent with the existing, and long-standing, legal position in most of the Contracting States', p. 32. Article 6 did, however, guarantee a right to judicial review of executive decisions before a body complying with its terms. Recent decisions of the EUCT have con cerned the degree of supervision necessary to comply with the requirements of article 6, see e.g. *W.* v. *UK*, EUCT, Series A, Vol. 121, prs. 80–3 (1987).
224 Doc A/38/40, p. 237.
225 Ibid., pr. 12.
226 On waiver under the ECHR see *De Weer* v. *Belgium*, EUCT, Series A, Vol. 35 (1980); *H.* v. *Belgium*, EUCT, Series A, Vol. 127, pr. 54 (1987); *Colozza* v. *Italy*, n. 142 above; *Håkansson and Sturesson* v. *Sweden*, EUCT, Series A, Vol. 171 (1990); A. 1197/61, 5 YBECHR p. 88; Merrills, pp. 160–6. On ignorance of domestic remedies see *Y.L.* v. *Canada*, pr. 10.26, including the individual opinion thereto, pr. 10.26.1 above.
227 Doc. A/38/40, p. 237, pr. 6.
228 Doc. A/37/40, p. 101; SD p. 12.
229 SD p. 12, prs. 12–13.
230 Ibid., pr. 14. The allegations concerning deportations were held inadmissible on the ground of non-exhaustion of domestic remedies, ibid., prs. 12–14. Cf. A.2991 and 2992/66, *Alam, Khan and Singh* v. *UK*, 10 YBECHR (1967) p. 478 at pp. 500–4. For recent EUCM decisions that decisions on expulsion and deportation do not normally involve the determination of civil rights and obligations see A.8244/78, *Uppal and Others* v. *UK*, 3 EHRR 319; A.12122/86, *Lukka* v. *UK*, 9 EHRR 512.
231 Doc. A/43/40, p. 258.
232 Ibid., pr. 5.2,
233 Ibid., pr. 6.3.
234 Doc. A/37/40, p. 101, pr. 21; SD p. 12.
235 Doc. A/44/40, p. 200. "While article 14 of the Covenant guarantees the right to a fair trial, it is for the appellate courts of States parties to the Covenant to evaluate facts and evidence in a particular case. It is not in principle for the Committee to review specific instructions to the jury by the judge in a trial by jury, unless it can be ascertained that the instructions to the jury were clearly arbitrary or amounted to a denial of justice", *D.F.* v. *Jamaica*, Doc. A/45/40, Apx. ". . . the judge's instructions to the jury must meet particularly high standards as to their thoroughness and impartiality in cases in which a capital sentence may be pronounced on the accused; this applies, *a fortiori*, to cases in which the accused pleads legitimate self-defence", *Pinto* v. *Trinidad and Tobago*, Doc. A/45/40, Apx., pr. 12.3.
236 Ibid., pr. 11.1. In an individual opinion to this view three members of the HRC

further commented that, 'The principles of a fair hearing, known in some systems as the rules of natural justice, as agreed in article 14, paragraph 1 of the Covenant, include the concept of *audi alteram partem*. Those principles were violated because it would appear that the author was deprived of a hearing both by the administrative authorities . . . and by the Supreme Court', ibid., appendix I, pr. 3. Cf. *Bricmont* v. *Belgium*, EUCT, Series A, Vol. 158 (1989).

237 Doc. A/44/40, p. 210.
238 Ibid., pr. 9.3.
239 Doc. A/40/40, p. 196.
240 Ibid., pr. 9. Cf. A.911/60, EUCM, 4 YBECHR p. 198 at p. 222.
241 In *Mpandanjilla and Others* v. *Zaïre*, Doc. A/41/40, p. 121, the trial was not held in public; no summonses were served on two of the accused; and in three cases the accused were not heard at the pre-trial stage. The HRC expressed the view, *inter alia*, that article 14(1) was violated because they were denied a fair and public hearing. The position adopted under the ECHR is that no abstract definition of criteria for a fair hearing can be given and that in each individual case the course of the proceedings as a whole has to be assessed, see the *Nielsen Case*, A.343/57, 4 YBECHR (1961) p. 494 at pp. 548–50.
242 Doc. A/43/40, p. 184.
243 Ibid., pr. 10.
244 See pr. 10.7 above. For ECHR cases on military tribunals see *Engel and Others* v. *Netherlands*, EUCT, Series A, Vol. 22 (1976); *Sutter* v. *Switzerland*, EUCT, Series A, Vol. 74 (1984).
245 Doc. A/44/40, p. 286.
246 Ibid., pr. 6.4.
247 Doc. A/44/40, p. 241.
248 Ibid., pr. 10.4.
249 Doc. A/44/40, p. 196.
250 Ibid., prs. 10.1–11.
251 The duty to hold public hearings is not dependent on any request by interested parties. Courts must make information on time and venue of oral hearings available to the public and provide for adequate facilities for the attendance of interested members of the public within reasonable limits: see *van Meurs* v. *Netherlands*, Doc. A/45/40, Apx., prs. 6.1–2. Cf. the decisions under the ECHR cited in notes 78 and 94 above.
252 See e.g. *Conteris* v. *Uruguay*, Doc. A/40/40, p. 196; *Weinberger* v. *Uruguay*, Doc. A/36/40, p. 114; *Pietraroia* v. *Uruguay*, Doc. A/36/40, p. 153.
253 Doc. A/36/40, p. 120.
254 Ibid., pr. 5. In *Gilboa* v. *Uruguay*, Doc. A/41/40, p. 128, the author alleged that, pursuant to a decree of June 1973 the publication of any judgment of military courts was expressly prohibited. The HRC made no findings on alleged article 14 violations because the trial had not been completed, ibid., pr. 7.2.
255 In *Gilboa* v. *Uruguay*, ibid., the author alleged that, 'The entire procedure before the military courts is in violation of article 14'. The HRC made no response to this allegation, pr. 7.2. Cf. the finding of a practice of inhuman treatment at Libertad prison in Uruguay, ch. 9, prs. 9.18–9.18.1 above.

256 Doc. A/36/40, p. 120.

257 Ibid., pr. 11.

258 The State representative promised that his government would in future co-operate with the HRC, see SR 355–7, 359, and 373.

259 Doc. A/38/40, p. 150.

260 Ibid., pr. 10.

261 Doc. A/44/40, p. 300.

262 Ibid., pr. 6.4.

263 *Ambrosini, de Massera and Massera* v. *Uruguay*, Doc. A/34/40, p. 124; *Perdoma and De Lanza* v. *Uruguay*, Doc. A/35/40, p. 111.

264 See the *Nielsen Case*, 2 YBECHR p. 412 at pp. 446–8, admiss. decn. Under the ECHR no inquiry is made as to a possible violation of article 6(2) when a violation of the fair trial requirement in article 6(1) has already been found, see *De Weer* v. *Belgium*, n. 226 above. See also the decision of the German Federal Court noted in 1 HRLJ (1980) p. 339.

265 See e.g. *Sequeira* v. *Uruguay*, Doc. A/35/40, p. 127.

266 See pr. 10.11 above.

267 Doc. A/44/40, p. 200. See pr. 10.29 above.

268 Doc. A/44/40, p. 200, Appendix I, pr. 2(*c*).

269 Doc. A/44/40, p. 210.

270 Ibid., prs. 1.1–1.6.

271 Ibid., pr. 9.5.

272 Doc. A/37/40, p. 114.

273 Doc. A/38/40, p. 134. Cf. *Brozicek* v. *Italy*, EUCT, Series A, Vol. 167 (1990).

274 Ibid., pr. 14.2.

275 See pr. 10.40 below. Cf. Resolution (75)11 of the Committee of Ministers of the Council of Europe, 'On the criteria governing proceedings held in the absence of the accused', Resolutions Adopted by the Committee of Ministers Relating to Crime Problems, Vol. iii (1977).

276 Doc. A/35/40, p. 111.

277 Doc. A/37/40, p. 114.

278 Ibid., pr. 20. Similarly, in *Simones* v. *Uruguay*, Doc. A/37/40, p. 174. That case is also interesting on the failure of a court-appointed counsel to invoke alleged domestic remedies. See ch. 4, pr. 4.108, n. 706.

279 Under the equivalent provision of the ECHR (art.6(3)(b)) the EUCM has held that the facilities granted to an accused person do not include an absolute right of access to the court file, although it may be implied that in certain circumstances he or his lawyer must have reasonable access to it, *X* v. *Austria*, A.7138/75, 9, D. & R. p. 50. See also *X* v. *UK*, A.5282/71, CD 42, p. 99; *Hendriks* v. *Netherlands*, 5 EHRR 223, prs. 140–4. *Kamasinski* v. *Austria*, EUCT, Series A, Vol. 168 (1990).

280 Doc. A/40/40, p. 204.

281 Ibid., pr. 5.5.

282 For a recent UK case see *Taylor* v. *Anderton*, *The Times*, 21 October 1986, Scott J.

283 See pr. 10.4.1 above.

284 See e.g. *Izquierdo* v. *Uruguay*, Doc. A/37/40, p. 179. See, however, *Marais* v. *Madagascar*, pr. 10.43 below.
285 See ch. 4, pr. 4.11 above.
286 Ibid.
287 Doc. A/39/40, p. 154.
288 Ibid., prs. 5.1, 9.2.
289 Ibid., pr. 11.
290 Doc. A/38/40, p. 150.
291 Doc. A/38/40, p. 141.
292 Ibid., pr. 19. For the facts of the case see pr. 10.43 below.
293 In *De Voituret* v. *Uruguay*, Doc. A/39/40, p. 164, the author alleged that her daughter, the alleged victim, could expect very little assistance from her defence lawyer because, 'She is prevented from consulting him freely. The conversations have to take place by telephone while the defence lawyer and her daughter are separated by a glass wall and continuously watched by guards standing at their side', pr. 2.8. The HRC expressed no view on the alleged article 14 violations. In *Reid* v. *Jamaica* the HRC found a violation of article 14(3)(b) because the court had failed to grant counsel sufficient minimum time to prepare his examination of witnesses, Doc. A/45/40, Apx., pr. 11.3.
294 Doc. A/38/40, p. 173.
295 Ibid., pr. 11.
296 Doc. A/38/40, p. 192.
297 Ibid., pr. 13.3.
298 Doc. A/39/40, p. 148.
299 See *Mbenge* v. *Zaire*, pr. 10.33 above.
300 See *Nieto* v. *Uruguay*, Doc. A/38/40, p. 201. In *Goddi* v. *Italy*, the EUCT held that the failure of the Italian Court of Appeal to notify the lawyer acting for Goddi, 'was instrumental in depriving the applicant of a "practical and effective" defence', EUCT, Series A, Vol. 76 (1984).
301 See pr. 10.15 above, text to n. 136.
302 Doc. A/36/40, p. 185.
303 For the practice under the ECHR see Van Dijk and Van Hoof, pp. 274–81 and 328–35.
304 Doc. A/37/40, p. 101.
305 See pr. 10.15 above, text to n. 136. See also *Acosta* v. *Uruguay*, Doc. A/39/40, p. 169; *Lluberas* v. *Uruguay*, Doc. A/39/40, p. 175.
306 Doc. A/37/40, p. 101.
307 Ibid. The government of British Colombia described the delay as 'unusual and unsatisfactory', ibid., pr. 10.
308 Ibid., pr. 15.
309 Ibid., pr. 17.
310 Ibid., pr. 22 (my emphasis).
311 See I. Brownlie, *Systems of the Law of Nations—State Reponsibility*, pp. 72–3, 144.
312 Ibid., pp. 38–40. See the *Caire Claim*, 5 RIAA, p. 516 at pp. 529–31 (1929).
313 Cf. the EUCT approach in the cases cited in n. 318 below.

314 See e.g. the majority and dissenting opinions in *Wemhoff* v. *FRG*, EUCT, Series A, Vol. 7 (1968).

315 See ch. 4, prs. 4.103–4.104 above.

316 Ibid., prs. 4.49–4.52 above

317 Doc. A/35/40, p. 127. See also *Machado* v. *Uruguay*, Doc. A/39/40, p. 148.

318 See the approach of the EUCT in the *Baggetti* and *Milasi* cases, n. 139 above.

319 See e.g. *G. Barbato* v. *Uruguay*, Doc. A/38/40, p. 124, pr. 9.5.

320 Doc. A/38/40, p. 173.

321 Ibid., pr. 7.1.

322 See ch. 4, prs. 4.27–4.36 on the general approach of the HRC.

323 See the decisions of the EUCT in n. 74 above.

324 For the approach of the EUCT see e.g. *Eckle* v. *FRG*, Series A, Vol. 51 (1982).

325 Cf. Fawcett, pp. 164–70 (though note that the text is misprinted in parts). The established criteria used by the EUCT are the complexity of the factual or legal issues raised by the case; the applicants own conduct and the manner in which the competent national authorities have dealt with the case, see *Buchholz* v. *FRG*, EUCT, Series A, Vol. 42, pr. 49 (1981); *Zimmerman and Steiner* v. *Switzerland*, EUCT, Series A, Vol. 66, pr. 24 (1983). For a more recent application of the criteria see *Erkner and Hofauer* v. *Austria*, EUCT, Series A, Vol. 117 (1987).

326 See e.g. *Caldas* v. *Uruguay*, Doc. A/38/40, p. 192; *Nieto* v. *Uruguay*, Doc. A/38/40, p. 201.

327 Doc. A/44/40, p. 246.

328 Ibid., prs. 8.3–8.4.

329 Doc. A/38/40, p. 134.

330 Ibid., pr. 14.1.

331 Ibid., pr. 21. It is interesting to note the use of the term 'due process' which does not appear in the Covenant. The decision in *Mbenge* is also considered in ch. 8, pr. 8.25 above. See also *Goddi* v. *Italy*, EUCT, Series A, Vol. 76 (1984).

332 See the cases cited in pr. 10.30 above.

333 For the approach of the HRC to these problems see ch. 4, prs. 4.27–4.36 above.

334 Doc. A/36/40, p. 176.

335 Ibid., prs. 7.1, 7.4.

336 Ibid., pr. 8.

337 Ibid., pr. 11.5.

338 Ibid., pr. 13.

339 In *Machado* v. *Uruguay*, the State party argued that *ex officio* defence counsels, 'Are independent lawyers who are not subject to the military hierarchy in the performance of their technical functions. These were in strict conformity with the principles that should regulate any counsel of a technical and legal nature', Doc. A/39/40, p. 148, pr. 8.

340 Doc. A/44/40, p. 222.

341 Ibid., pr. 13.2.

342 See pr. 10.41.2 below. '... the State party should have accepted the author's arrangements for another attorney to represent him for the purposes of the appeal, even if this would have entailed an adjournment of the proceedings ...

legal assistance to the accused in a capital case must be provided in ways that adequately and effectively ensure justice', *Pinto* v. *Trinidad and Tobago*, Doc. A/45/40, Apx., pr. 12.5. See also *Reid* v. *Jamaica*, Doc. A/45/40, Apx., pr. 11.4.

343 Doc. A/44/40, p. 241.
344 Ibid., pr. 10.3. R's petition to the Privy Council has been dismissed in a 3:2 majority decision, [1985] 2 All ER 594. The HRC also stated that the obligation of the State party to take effective measures to remedy the violations suffered by R involved his release, ibid., pr. 12.
345 See pr. 10.34.3 above.
346 Doc. A/36/40, p. 125.
347 Ibid., pr. 13. Similarly in *Machado* v. *Uruguay*, Doc. A/39/40, p. 148, pr. 13.
348 See pr. 10.35 above.
349 Doc. A/38/40, p. 141.
350 Ibid., pr. 17.3. Maitre Hamel subsequently brought a communication to the HRC in his own right, see ch. 4, pr. 4.11 above.
351 Doc. A/38/40, p. 141, pr. 5.1.
352 Ibid., pr. 7 at (*b*).
353 Ibid., prs. 15.1–15.2.
354 Ibid., pr. 19.
355 See prs. 10.34–10.35.3 above. The 'IACM has expressed the view that fundamental human rights are violated in a State where lawyers who assume responsibility for defending individuals detained for political reasons are subjected to threats and acts of intimidation, including such measures as withholding their licences to practice; a fortiori where they are killed, detained, maltreated or "disappear"', Sieghart, n. 1 above, citing 3 Paraguay pp. 86–7 and Argentina p. 233. See also *Valasquez Rodriguez* v. *Honduras*, IACT, Judgment of 29 July 1988, 9 HRLJ (1988) pp. 212–49.
356 See pr. 10.30 above.
357 Doc. A/35/40, p. 127. See also *Weinberger* v. *Uruguay*, Doc. A/36/40, p. 114.
358 Doc. A/35/40, p. 127, pr. 16.
359 See the summary in Doc. A/37/40, prs. 274–5.
360 Doc. A/38/40, p. 243.
361 Ibid., pr. 6.
362 Doc. A/40/40, p. 204.
363 Ibid., pr. 3.4.
364 Ibid., pr. 5.6. See pr. 10.5 above.
365 Doc. A/37/40, p. 114.
366 Doc. A/38/40, p. 134. See pr. 10.40 above.
367 Doc. A/44/40, p. 222. See pr. 10.41.1 above.
368 Doc. A/44/40, p. 222, pr. 13.2. See also *Guesdon* v. *France*, pr. 10.47 below.
369 Cf. Fawcett, pp. 198–9 on ECHR practice.
370 Doc. A/36/40, p. 176.
371 Ibid., pr. 13.
372 Doc. A/38/40, p. 150.
373 Ibid., pr. 10.
374 Doc. A/40/40, p. 196.

375 Ibid., pr. 10. Cf. Italy's reservations to article 9(5) Covenant, *Human Rights—Status*, n. 154 above, p. 38. For the HRC's most recent view on article 14(3)(*g*) see *Cariboni* v. *Uruguay*, Doc. A/43/40, p. 184.

376 Cf. on permissible restrictions on the right of access to court see the decisions of the EUCT in *Golder* v. *UK*, Series A, Vol. 18, p. 19 (1975); *Winterwerp* v. *Netherlands*, Series A, Vol. 33, p. 29 (1980).

377 Doc. A/37/40, p. 168.

378 Ibid., prs. 3.2, 7.1.

379 Ibid., pr. 8.1.

380 Ibid., pr. 10.3. See ch. 7 above on article 4.

381 Doc. A/37/40, p. 168, pr. 10.4.

382 Under the ECHR the EUCT has taken the view that the expression 'criminal charge' is an autonomous concept, see *Engel and Others* v. *Netherlands*, EUCT, Series A, Vol. 22 (1976) and n. 20 above.

383 See pr. 10.21 above, text to n. 190.

384 See GC 13/21, pr. 17, cited in pr. 10.21, above text to n. 190.

385 Doc. A/37/40, p. 168, pr. 12.

386 Doc. A/37/40, p. 101. See also pr. 10.37 above.

387 Doc. A/37/40, p. 101, pr. 22.

388 See pr. 10.15, text to n. 136.

389 Note that the ECHR does not itself guarantee a right of appeal, see the *Delcourt Case*, n. 178 above.

390 Doc. A/44/40, p. 222.

391 Ibid., pr. 13.4.

392 See pr. 10.51 above.

393 Doc. A/38/40, p. 160.

394 On article 5(2)(*a*) OP see ch. 4, prs. 4.87–4.99. For the decision of the EUCM see A.8630/79, 8722/79, 8723/79, 8729/79, *Crociani et al.* v. *Italy*, decn. of 18 Dec. 1980, 22 D. & R. p. 147 (1981).

395 Doc. A/38/40, p. 160, pr. 11.4.

396 Ibid., prs. 9.2, 9.3.

397 Ibid., pr. 11.6.

398 Ibid., pr. 11.8.

399 Ibid., pr. 11.6.

400 If this submission is correct it would reject a view that States had some power of autointerpretation. Cf. the individual opinion of Judge Lauterpacht in the *Norwegian Loans Case*, *France* v. *Norway*, ICJ Reports, (1957) p. 9; J. S. Watson, 'Autointerpretation, Competence and the Continuing Validity of Article 2(7) of the United Nations Charter', 71 AJIL (1977) pp. 60–83.

401 Doc. A/38/40, p. 160, pr. 11.8.

402 Ibid., pr. 6.3.

403 Ibid., pr. 13. See also ch. 6, pr. 6.35 above.

404 See *Ex-Philibert* v. *Zaïre*, Doc. A/38/40, p. 197. See ch. 6, pr. 6.33 above and the HRC's view in *Lubicon Lake Band* v. *Canada* (1990).

405 On article 13 ECHR see Fawcett pp. 289–94; Van Dijk and Van Hoof, pp. 520–32.

406 See n. 405 above.
407 Doc. A/40/40, p. 164.
408 Ibid., prs. 1–2.1.
409 Ibid., prs. 3–9.
410 Ibid., pr. 11.2.
411 Ibid., prs. 11.2–11.3.
412 Doc. A/38/40, p. 117.
413 Ibid., pr. 18.2.
414 Ibid., Doc. A/38/40, p. 201.
415 It has been alleged in communications to the HRC that the institution of new proceedings towards the end of a term of imprisonment is common practice in Uruguay, see e.g. *Nieto*, ibid., pr. 6.
416 Ibid., pr. 7.
417 Ibid.
418 Ibid., pr. 10.5.
419 See text to and n. 241 above. The recent trials of war criminals raises this problem in an acute form.
420 Doc. A/38/40, p. 209.
421 Ibid., pr. 10.3.
422 Doc. A/43/40, p. 242.
423 Ibid. pr. 5.3. The State party also argued that A.P. was tried for two different offences in Switzerland and Italy, ibid., pr. 5.1.
424 Ibid., pr. 7.3.
425 See e.g. pr. 10.21 above (on Iraq).
426 See pr. 10.7 above.
427 See e.g. pr. 10.15 above (on FRG).
428 See e.g. pr. 10.23 above (on article 14(7)).
429 See e.g. Doc. A/41/40, prs. 67 (Luxembourg); 129 (Sweden).
430 See e.g. the replies in Doc. A/40/40 pr. 492 (representative of Spain); ibid., pr. 562 (UK representative).
431 See e.g. the important decision in *Y.L.* v. *Canada*, pr. 10.26–10.26.1 above.
432 See pr. 10.58 above.
433 Obviously this process of accommodation is easier, though still difficult, under the ECHR in the more homogenous Council of Europe. See also G. Bettocchi, 'Human Rights and Inquisitorial Procedures in Latin America', 42 Rev. ICJ (1989) pp. 57–66.
434 See *Golder* v. *UK*, EUCT, Series A, Vol. 18 (1975); *Kaplan Case*, EUCM, n. 223 above.
435 Cf. Clovis C. Morrisson, *The Dynamics of Development in the European Human Rights Convention System*, ch. 6 (1981).
436 See the views cited in notes 251 and 342 above. Cf. the decisions of the EUCT in *Artico* v. *Italy*, Series A, Vol. 37 (1980); *H* v. *Belgium*, Series A, Vol. 147 (1987). See Merrills, ch. 5.
437 See generally ch. 4, prs. 4.127–4.133 above.

Article 19[1]

1. Everyone shall have the right to hold opinions without interference.

2. Everyone shall have the right to freedom of expression; this right shall include freedom to seek, receive and impart information and ideas of all kinds, regardless of frontiers, either orally, in writing or in print, in the form of art, or through any other media of his choice.

3. The exercise of the right provided for in paragraph 2 of this Article carries with it special duties and responsibilities. It may therefore be subject to certain restrictions, but these shall only be such as are provided by law and are necessary:

(a) For respect of the rights or reputations of others;

(b) For the protection of national security or of public order (ordre public), or of public health or morals.

Introduction

11.2 Freedom of opinion and expression have been important concerns at the United Nations since its inception.[2] In 1948 the UN convened a Conference on Freedom of Expression which prepared, *inter alia*, a draft Convention on Freedom of Expression.[3] However, despite the consistent attention given to freedom of expression at the UN it is an area where the UN has achieved very little.[4] In recent years, and principally through the work of the United Nations Educational, Scientific and Cultural Organization (UNESCO), the focus of the United Nations' work on freedom of expression has shifted to the demands for a new world information and communication order (NWICO).[5] The demands for a NWICO have principally come from the Third World States and are related to the more general demands for a new international economic order (NIEO).[6] The initiatives from UNESCO have provoked a strong reaction from Western States which have viewed it as an attempt to justify increased State controls and censorship on the press and other information media.[7] The United Nations has also established a new Committee on Information.[8] Within the context of the United Nations' work on freedom of expression, the work of the HRC was going to provide a useful guide to the possibilities of further progress in respect for this right.

A. ARTICLE 19 UNDER THE REPORTING PROCESS

11.3 Article 19 is not covered by the non-derogation provision in article 4(2).[9] It has been the subject of a General Comment under article 40(4).[10] In the consideration of State reports its relationship to articles 18,[11] 20,[12] 21,[13] and 25[14] has been noted.

Article 19(1)

11.4 Members of the HRC have noted the clear difference between paragraphs 1 and 2 of article 19, the former being absolute, the latter being open to limited restrictions. The preparatory work on the Covenant supports the view that freedom of opinion and expression are separate freedoms.[15] Apart from this, however, the HRC has had very little of substance to say on paragraph 1. The Chairman of the HRC pointed to the obvious reason for this during discussion of the draft General Comment on article 19,

It should however be pointed out that absolute protection for holding opinions ended when they were aired or manifested. At that point restrictions might start. In normal circumstances, the phraseology in paragraph 1 meant very little. Holding an opinion could not be interfered with if no one knew about it. Some phrase should perhaps be added to make clear what was being protected. Perhaps it was the right freely to form opinions without their being imposed either directly or indirectly, publicly or in private.[16]

Partsch has commented that,

During the discussions of this article, it was suggested that paragraph 1 should bar interference only 'by a public authority'. That suggestion was rejected. An individual has the right to freedom of opinion without interference by private parties as well, and the State is obliged to ensure that freedom. Thus, the danger that the State might encourage such interference from private or so-called private sources is eliminated. It is doubtful, however, whether the complex problem of protecting a person's opinion against interference by other individuals can be solved in this global and absolute manner.[17]

In its General Comment on article 19 the HRC stated that, 'Paragraph 1 requires protection of "the right to hold opinions without interference". This is a right to which the Covenant permits no exception or restriction. The Committee would welcome information from States parties concerning paragraph 1'.[18] The comment is not helpful to States parties. There is no indication of the kind of information it would welcome from States parties. Allegations of mind control techniques and brainwashing and re-education centres in certain parts of the world suggest obvious areas of potential concern on which the HRC could seek specific information.[19]

Article 19(2), (3)

11.5 Almost all of the HRC's attention has been focused on paragraphs 2 and 3 of article 19. The starting point has again been the detailed consideration of the constitutional and legal bases of the right to freedom of expression and the limitations and restrictions thereon. The approach of members has been very practically orientated, their comments rarely being abstract or theoretical. Equally members have consistently indicated their views on the central importance of freedom of expression and how it should operate in practice.[20] It is interesting to note, however, that the following proposed sentence was not included in the General Comment on article 19: 'This is a right the effective enjoyment of which is essential to enable individuals to ensure for themselves the enjoyment of other rights protected in the Covenant'.[21] The sentence was opposed by the Eastern European members on the basis that it purported to establish a hierarchy of rights which was not to be found in the Covenant,[22] introduced a philosophical aspect, and was too 'one-sided' in that it ignored the problem of 'economic power'.[23] The views expressed within the HRC during discussion of the General Comment were reminiscent of the debates during the drafting of the Covenant.[24] The conclusion to be drawn from the failure to include the proposed sentence is perhaps that the approach of the HRC is that although freedom of expression is regarded as important, it is not accorded the pre-eminence given to it under American constitutional law.[25]

11.6 The general approach of members has been to examine, comment, and request clarification in respect of the different aspects of freedom of expression revealed in the State reports. This has involved, for example, matters such as general and specific banning or censorship,[26] registration or notification requirements,[27] governmental control and direction in its various forms,[28] limitations applicable to particular groups, for example, armed forces, civil servants,[29] prior restraints[30] or subsequent penal responsibility for publications,[31] rights of reply or correction,[32] the applicable limitations embodied in the criminal law or penal codes for offences[33] such as blasphemy or blasphemous libel,[34] sedition,[35] subversive propaganda,[36] anti-State or anti-ideological propaganda, and the effective remedies demanded by article 2(3) to an individual who claims that his rights under article 19 have been violated.[37]

11.6.1 Varied domestic provisions have attracted the attentions and criticisms of HRC members. The Yugoslavian State representative stated before the HRC that,

The freedom of the press and other media of information and public expression is known, at least normatively, as a more or less universal political right in contemporary constitutions. In the Constitution of the S.F.R.Y. it is dealt with separately and enriched with some new elements which, in the aggregate, enable the integration and the supercession of the classical freedom of the press in its numerous aspects by a new right of the citizen and the working man to be informed.[38]

Members of the HRC expressed concern about such a specifically ideological conception of freedom of expression.[39] This concern with specific ideological conceptions of freedom of expression has been a feature of the HRC's practice. Similar questions and comments to those made to the Yugoslavian State representative were made, for example, to representatives from the USSR,[40] Romania,[41] Hungary,[42] Syria.[43] The following comments of Mr Tomuschat concerning the Ukrainian SSR are typical of the emphasis on this issue, particularly by the Western members of the HRC:

In his view, freedom of opinion and speech could be conceived in very simple terms. It gave the individual the right to say what he thought was the truth. He would not agree, therefore, that freedom of expression should be subject to the inherent limitation as having to contribute to strengthening any general State philosophy, so that views other than socialist ones would *ab initio* be outside the scope of article 19. How could the prohibition of political discrimination be respected if specific substantive opinion was discriminated against. More clarification seemed required on the scope of the provisions of the Penal Code which made anti-Soviet agitation and propaganda a punishable offence. What was meant by that formula and how was it interpreted and applied?[44]

The Iranian representative (pre-revolution) was questioned on the prohibition of discussion of the Constitution, the imperial Monarchy, and the Revolution of the Shah and the people.[45] During consideration of the report of Sweden concern was expressed in respect of the system for registration on account of political opinion.[46] The representatives from Czechoslovakia were questioned about the 'Charter 77' document.[47] During consideration of the report of the Federal Republic of Germany Mr Movchan raised the question of the application of *Berufsverbot* (occupational bans).[48]

11.7 Where domestic legal provisions have declared the right to freedom of expression without any express ideological restriction the HRC members have closely examined and requested definition, clarification, and explanation of the applicable grounds of limitation.[49] Such limitations have been described as 'the defence of the national interests and social service' (Ecuador),[49a] 'offensive to public feelings and interests of the community as a whole' (United Kingdom),[50] 'the security of the realm, the economic well-being of people' (Sweden),[51] 'the national economy' (Nicaragua).[52]

11.8 A common example taken by HRC members as a guide to the practical application of article 19 has concerned the possibility of criticizing the existing governmental regime at all, or only in an institutionalized manner, for example, through the 'Party' in a one-party State.[53] Many members of the HRC have stressed the importance of allowing peaceful dissent.[54] For example, Sir Vincent-Evans commented during consideration of the report of the USSR,

Article 19 of the Covenant guaranteed the right to hold opinions without interference and the right to freedom of expression, and laid down that they should be subject to only such restrictions as were 'necessary'. Those freedoms which were clearly inherent in the dignity and worth of the human being and were essential to the full development of his personality, were among the most important rights in a democratic society, applying across the whole range of human experience and not least in the political field. No regime was perfect but, in any healthy society, the individual should be free to express his views, offer his criticism and canvas his ideas for change and improvement, provided he did not seek to propagate his ideas by violent means. Yet it was well known that there had been cases in the Soviet Union in which severe measures had been taken against persons who sought to express their views, propagate their ideas and promote their rights by peaceful means. The cases had given rise to much publicity in many countries and people did not see how they could be reconciled with the Covenant.

He understood that the limitations on the freedoms guaranteed under article 50 of the Soviet Constitution were expressed in the Soviet Criminal Code in terms of anti-Soviet agitation and propaganda and defamation of the State and socialist system. Laws couched in such terms could be so interpreted and applied as to produce a seemingly low threshold, by comparison with other countries, in determining what was permissible by way of political comment and propagation of political ideas. He asked whether such limitations could really be said to be necessary for the protection of national security and public order in a great and powerful State such as the Soviet Union. Was the State not being unduly sensitive to criticism and suggestions for change?[55]

Members of the HRC have attached great significance to how legal restrictions and limitations operate in practice. How and by whom were they interpreted and enforced?[56] How was their discriminatory application avoided?[57] State representatives are often requested to provide statistical information on the availability and circulation of books, newspapers, magazines, and other publications.[58] Other information commonly sought concerns the operation of licensing regimes,[59] direct or indirect support or control or authorization of the press,[60] the languages of publications, the variety of cultural performances,[61] the possibility of subscribing to foreign newspapers and periodicals,[62] restrictions on the activities of foreign correspondents or dispatches from foreign press agencies.[63] During consideration of the report of Guyana Professor Tomuschat raised the question of indirect practical limitations on freedom of expression as a result of difficulties in obtaining newsprint.[64] Such information provides invaluable indications of the practical state of freedom of expression in a given country.

11.9 The HRC's General Comment on article 19 merely restated most of paragraph 2 and added,

Not all States parties have provided information concerning all aspects of the freedom of expression. For instance, little attention has so far been given to the fact that, because of the development of modern mass media, effective measures are necessary to prevent such control of the media as would interfere with the right of everyone to freedom of expression in a way that is not provided for in paragraph 3.

Many State reports confine themselves to mentioning that freedom of expression is guaranteed under the Constitution or the law. However, in order to know the precise regime of freedom of expression, in law and in practice, the Committee needs in addition pertinent information about the rules which either define the scope of freedom of expression or which set forth certain restrictions, as well as any other conditions which in practice affect the exercise of this right. It is the interplay between the principle of freedom of expression and such limitations and restrictions which determines the actual scope of the individual's right.[65]

11.10 The only specific example in the General Comment of an aspect of freedom of expression, 'the development of modern mass media', reflected an interesting discussion in the HRC.[66] That discussion concerned the question of the different forms of monopoly control and economic power problems involved and a recognition that 'the situation of the media had evolved since the Covenant was drafted in 1966'[67] and that 'the comments should take into account new developments and new dangers'.[68]

11.11 The HRC's General Comment simply restates paragraph 3 of article 19 and notes that,

certain restrictions on the right are permitted which may relate either to the interests of other persons or of the community as a whole. However, when a State party imposes certain restrictions on the exercise of freedom of expression, these may not put in jeopardy the right itself . . .[69]

11.12 The General Comment points to the extreme limits of permissible restrictions in stating that they must not jeopardize the right itself. However, there is no indication of the nature of the 'special duties and responsibilities' which exercise of the right to freedom of expression carries.[70] Similarly, no content is given to requirements that restrictions be 'provided by law'[71] and 'necessary'.[72] There is no comment on the scope of the specified grounds of restriction in sub-paragraphs (*a*) and (*b*) of paragraph 3.[73] Finally, there is no reference to any doctrine of a margin of appreciation even though this has been raised during the reporting procedure[74] and featured in an important view under the OP.[75]

11.13 It remains to note that there is no reference in the General Comment on article 19 on the relationship between article 19 and article 20 (concerning war and racial propaganda).[76] Article 20 is dealt with in the next chapter and the General Comment on article 20 does deal with this relationship.[77] The relationship between the two articles raises important questions concerning permissible restrictions of freedom of expression.[78]

B. ARTICLE 19 UNDER THE OPTIONAL PROTOCOL

11.14 Article 19 has been invoked in a number of communications under the Optional Protocol. The majority of them have concerned Uruguay. Uruguay has offered very little co-operation to the HRC and therefore many of the views are effectively views by default.

11.15 The views of the HRC clearly establish that punishment for the expression of views violates article 19 unless justified by reference to article 19(3). In *Perdoma and De Lanza* v. *Uruguay*[79] P was detained on a charge of 'subversive association' apparently on no other basis than his political views and connections, while L was detained on a charge of 'assisting a subversive association', apparently on similar grounds to those in the case of P.[80] After noting the terms of article 19(2) and (3) the HRC expressed the view that,

The Government of Uruguay has submitted no evidence regarding the nature of the political activities in which (L) and (P) were alleged to have been engaged and which led to their arrest, detention and trial. Information that they were charged with subversive association is not in itself sufficient. The Committee is therefore unable to conclude on the information before it that the arrest, detention and trial of (L) and (P) were justified on any of the grounds mentioned in article 19(3).[81]

Clearly then freedom of opinion and expression extends to political views. Restrictions on the expression of political views could be covered by article 19(3)(*a*) or (*b*) but general allegations of 'subversive associations' are not sufficient to justify limitation.

11.16 The HRC has been more specific as to the information required from States parties in similar cases. In *Grille Motta* v. *Uruguay*[82] the HRC noted that Uruguay had submitted no evidence regarding the nature of the political activities in which GM was alleged to have been engaged.[83] It then commented that, 'Bare information that he was charged with subversive association and an attempt to undermine the morale of the armed forces is not in itself sufficient, without details of the alleged charges and copies of the court proceedings'.[84] In other cases the HRC has referred to the absence of any explanation by Uruguay of the scope and meaning of 'subversive activities',[85] the absence of any explanation by Uruguay of the concrete factual bases of the alleged offences,[86] and the duty on Uruguay to provide specific information if it wanted to refute allegations that an author had been persecuted because of his involvement in trade union activities.[87]

In *Weinberger Weisz* v. *Uruguay*[88] the HRC commented that,

The concrete factual basis of this offence has not been explained by the Government, although the author of the communication claims that the true reasons were that WW had contributed information on trade union activities to a newspaper opposed to the government and his membership in a political party which had lawfully existed while the membership lasted.[89]

The HRC expressed the view that there had been a violation of article 19(2) because WW was detained for having disseminated information relating to trade union activities.[90] The HRC also stated that, 'It was aware that under the legislation of many countries criminal offenders could be deprived of certain political rights. In no case, however, may a person be subjected to such sanctions (deprivation of political rights) *solely* because of his or her political opinions (articles 2(1) and 26)'.[91] It seems clear that sanctions may be imposed in accordance with limitations on the expression of political opinion which are in accordance with article 19(3), but the limitations must not operate in a discriminatory manner contrary to articles 2(1) and 26.

11.17 In only one case has there been a finding of a violation of article 19 in conjunction with a related article. In *Lopez Burgos* v. *Uruguay*[92] the HRC expressed the view that there had been a violation of article 22(1) (freedom of association including the right to form and join trade unions) in conjunction with articles 19(1) and (2) because LB had suffered persecution for his trade union activities.[93] There is no accompanying explanation of why article 22 is considered to have been violated in this case but not in other similar factual cases. There is no explanation of what distinguished LB's case sufficiently to constitute 'persecution' but this founded the only violation to date of the right to hold opinions without interference (article 19(1)). Similar views have only referred to article 19(2).[94]

11.18 In *Waksman* v. *Uruguay*[95] W argued, *inter alia*, that by refusing to renew his passport the Uruguayan authorities had restricted his ability to cross frontiers in the course of seeking, receiving, and imparting information and ideas, in violation of article 19 of the Covenant. Unfortunately, the HRC did not have an opportunity to consider this aspect of article 19 because the communication was discontinued when W's passport was renewed.[96]

11.19 Arguably the most important view of the HRC concerning article 19 is that in *Hertzberg and Others* v. *Finland*.[97] In *Hertzberg* the authors alleged that the Finnish authorities, including the State-controlled Finnish Broadcasting Company (FBC), had interfered with their right to freedom of expression and information by imposing sanctions against participants in, or censoring, radio and television programmes dealing with homosexuality. Finland argued, *inter alia*, that the purpose of the relevant prohibition in its Penal Code on the public encouragement of indecent behaviour between members of the same sex was to reflect the prevailing moral conceptions in Finland as interpreted by Parliament and by large groups of the population.[98] Finland further argued that the decisions of the FBC concerning the programmes referred to did not involve the application of censorship but were based on 'general considerations of programme policy in accordance with the internal rules of the Company'.[99]

In its final views the HRC accepted the contention of two of the authors that their rights under article 19(2) had been restricted on the basis of two censored programmes. The HRC continued,

While not every individual can be deemed to hold a right to express himself through a medium like TV, whose available time is limited, the situation may be different when a programme has been produced for transmission within the framework of a broadcasting organization with the general approval of the responsible authorities.[100]

This approach to a right of access to media accords with common sense and is similar to that under article 10 ECHR.[101] The State party had argued that the authors were appearing to give article 19 a different content to that normally used by maintaining that it would restrict the right of the owner of a means of communication to decide what material would be published.[102] The HRC's view suggests that there might be some restriction on the owners of means of communication where the material has been prepared within the framework of a broadcasting organization with the general approval of the responsible authorities.[103] After noting the terms of article 19(2) the HRC continued, 'In the context of the present communication the Finnish Government has specifically invoked public morals as justifying the actions complained of'.[104] Although the HRC had considered requesting the parties to submit the full text of the censored programmes so that the HRC could assess the 'necessity' of the actions complained of[105] it decided that the information before it was sufficient for it to formulate its views as follows:

It has to be noted, first, that public morals differ widely. There is no universally applicable common standard. Consequently, in this respect, a certain margin of discretion must be accorded to the responsible national authorities.

The Committee finds that it cannot question the decisions of the responsible organs of the Finnish Broadcasting Company that radio and TV are not appropriate forums to discuss issues related to homosexuality, as far as a programme could be judged as encouraging homosexual behaviour. According to article 19(3), the exercise of the rights provided for in article 19(2) carries with it special duties and responsibilities for those organs. As far as radio and TV programmes are concerned, the audience cannot be controlled. In particular, harmful effects on minors cannot be excluded.[106]

Accordingly the HRC expressed the view that there had been no violation of the rights of the authors under article 19(2).[107]

11.19.1 The introduction of the 'margin of discretion' is fundamental to the development of the HRC's jurisprudence. Though it has not been without its critics it has assumed great importance in the jurisprudence under the ECHR.[108] Only subsequent cases will determine how wide or narrow the margin of discretion (or appreciation) will be and whether it will vary from restriction to restriction and from context to context. The approach taken determines the balance struck between national and international implementation. It is no doubt true that there is 'no universally applicable moral standard' but the HRC's approach does little to suggest that it will attempt to establish some standards of international morality.[109] However, on the facts of this case the margin of discretion accorded to the responsible national authorities appears to be very wide. There was not even the most cursory consideration of the 'necessity' of the restrictions imposed and the HRC felt that, 'it could not question the decisions of the responsible organs of the FBC'. On the alleged facts the restrictions on the presentation of any information concerning homosexuality appeared to be very wide indeed.[110] Moreover, potentially wide-ranging restrictions might be considered acceptable to the HRC under article 19(3) on the bases that a programme could *per se* 'be judged as encouraging homosexual behaviour',[111] that the audience for radio and TV programmes cannot be controlled, and that, 'in particular, harmful effects on minors cannot be excluded'.[112]

11.19.2 An interesting individual opinion was appended to the HRC's view by Mr Opsahl and two other members of the HRC associated themselves with it.[113] While agreeing with the conclusion of the HRC, the opinion raised a number of important points. First, it was stated that,

In my view the conception and contents of 'public morals' referred to in article 19(3) are relative and changing. State-imposed restrictions on freedom of expression must allow for this fact and should not be applied so as to perpetuate prejudice or promote intolerance. It is of special importance to protect freedom of expression as regards minority views, including those that offend, shock or disturb the majority. Therefore, even if such laws as paragraph 9(2) of chapter 20 of the Finnish Penal Code may reflect prevailing moral conceptions, this is not in itself sufficient to justify it under article 19(3). It must also be shown that the application of the restriction is 'necessary'.[114]

The reference to the expression of minority views clearly echoes the case law under the ECHR.[115] The reference to prevailing moral conceptions raises difficult and important questions concerning the relationship between the will of the majority and respect for minority rights which again have arisen under the ECHR.[116] As to the question of necessity it has already been commented that the HRC's view is open to criticism for not really considering this key requirement.[117]

After noting that the communication raised the questions of whether the authors had been 'indirectly affected' by the laws in question in a way which interfered with their freedom of expression, and if so, whether the grounds of interference were justifiable, the individual opinion addressed the point concerning access to the media:

It is clear that nobody—and in particular no State—has any duty under the Covenant to promote publicity for information and ideas of all kinds. Access to the media operated by others is always and necessarily more limited than the general freedom of expression. It follows that such access may be controlled on grounds which do not have to be justified under article 19(3).

It is true that self-imposed restrictions on publishing, or the internal programme policy of the media may threaten the spirit of freedom of expression. Nevertheless, it is a matter of common sense that such decisions either entirely escape control or must be accepted to a larger extent than externally imposed restrictions such as enforcement of criminal law or official censorship, neither of which took place in the present case. Not even media controlled by the State can under the Covenant be under an obligation to publish all that may be published. It is not possible to apply the criteria of article 19(3) to self-imposed restrictions. Quite apart from the 'public morals' issue, one cannot require that they shall be only such as are 'provided by law and are necessary' for the particular purpose. Therefore I prefer not to express any opinion on the possible reasons for the decisions complained of in the present case.

The role of mass media in public debate depends on the relationship between journalists and their superiors who decide what to publish. I agree with the authors of the communication that the freedom of journalists is important, but the issues here can only be partly examined under article 19 of the Covenant.[118]

It is submitted that while purely self-imposed restrictions might well be outside article 19(3), on the facts of this case the restrictions were clearly imposed to comply with the provisions of the Penal Code. It would be a serious gap in the protection of article 19 if such restrictions could not found a violation of freedom of expression in the absence of the enforcement of the criminal law or official censorship. The approach of the majority that denial of access to the media in the context of a programme produced within the framework of a broadcasting organization with the general approval of the responsible authorities must be justified by reference to article 19(3) is to be commended, although it is not absolutely clear that the individual opinion advocates a different view.

11.20 Some indication of the limit of the positive obligations on States under article 19 can be taken from *R.T.* v. *France*[119] in which the HRC observed that the author could not invoke a violation of his right to freedom of expression under article 19, paragraph 2, of the Covenant, on grounds of having been denied tenure as a teacher of the Breton language.

11.20.1 Finally, the relationship between article 19 and article 20 (prohibition on propaganda for war and advocacy of national, racial, or religious hatred) was raised in the case of *J.R.T. and W.G. Party* v. *Canada* which is considered in ch. 12 below.[120]

APPRAISAL

11.21 The practice of the HRC in respect to article 19 has again illustrated the close, detailed, and critical analysis undertaken by members under the reporting process. The dialogue between the HRC and the States parties, in so far as it has developed, has been both direct and constructive. HRC members have in a diplomatic but forthright way criticized or expressed strong doubts concerning the compatability with article 19 of specific ideological conceptions of and wide restrictions on freedom of expression.[121] They have built up a consistent repertoire of practice concerning the press and other media. The discussions leading to the adoption of the General Comment on article 19 revealed some important differences within the HRC concerning article 19. It is interesting to note that many of the differences duplicate arguments during the drafting of article 19.[122] In decisions under the OP the HRC have stressed that punishment for violation of views can only be justified by reference to the terms of article 19(3),[123] and specifically introduced the concept of a 'margin of discretion'.[124] If the experience under the ECHR provided a reliable guide that concept was likely to play a fundamental role in the jurisprudence of the HRC.[125] However, there has been no subsequent reference to it in any decision or view.

11.22 In a number of respects, however, the HRC's practice concerning article 19 is perhaps the most disappointing of the articles examined in this work. The right to hold opinions has been little dealt with.[126] The considerations of the HRC and the General Comment on article 19, apart from the brief reference to the 'development of modern mass media',[127] have been confined to rather narrow aspects of the right to freedom of expression. Very little attention has focused on its more positive and progressive aspects,[128] although one of the newer HRC members, Mr Mommersteeg, appears to take a particular interest in this area.[129] The 'freedom to seek, receive and impart information and ideas of all kinds' is open to a much more dynamic approach in terms of the openness of local and national government, the accessibility of the various forms of media to political, ideological, and social groups,[130] access to official records and other public documents,[131] developments concerning vital commercial information,[132] the increasing use of computers and the consequent demand for personal data protection.[133] More generally the expression raises fundamental questions in terms of the relationship between the State and individual privacy (which is protected by article 17 of the Covenant). Members of the HRC appear to have been more interested in this relationship since the adoption of a General Comment on the right to privacy (article 17) in 1988.[134]

11.23 Similarly the expression 'regardless of frontiers' could well be usefully amplified by the HRC particularly when they are considering a report from a State party which is also a signatory to the Helsinki Final Act,[135] parts of which are clearly relevant to freedom of expression and the international free flow of information.[136]

11.24 Despite a decade of analysis and consideration of the approaches and methods adopted by States parties all over the world to give effect to article 19 the HRC's General Comment makes no specific references to the positive or negative aspects of those approaches or to methods used which could provide instructive parallels for other States parties. Members have not sought to assist States parties by giving content to the 'special rights and duties' and the key definitional components of 'prescribed by law' and 'necessary' and the criteria of permissible restriction in paragraph 3(*a*) and (*b*).[137]

11.25 The opportunity to formulate general comments is an extremely valuable and important one. The comments should represent the HRC's accumulated experience of years of consideration of a particular article. On that basis they have the potential to be profoundly influential. Although the predominant purpose of the General Comments to date appears to have been to provide clear guidelines for the States parties on information required by the HRC, they also perform a key function of giving some substantive content to the articles concerned. It is critical then that the comments are purposeful, positive, and progressive. Unfortunately the General Comment on article 19 was both weak and disappointing, being little more than a reiteration of article 19. Perhaps the comment was not considered for a long enough time, the HRC's characteristic caution was being displayed to abundance, or the limitations inherent in consensus were being evidenced.[138] It is interesting to note the following comment of Mr Aguilar during the discussions on the draft General Comment. He

agreed that it was important to reach a common understanding of the article. He was somewhat concerned, however, and shared Mr. Opsahl's surprise, that there was no reference to problems affecting freedom of expression seen everyday throughout the world, such as the fact that in some countries control of the mass media and means of communication by monopoly financial groups not merely restricted freedom of expression but resulted in its manipulation, while in other countries similar restrictions were imposed by the Government or the ruling party. The fact that such things were not mentioned in the general comment might be interpreted as a lack of awareness on the part of the Committee or a guilty silence. The general comment was not an attempt to advocate a philosophical or political position but to contribute to implementation of the Covenant which had, after all, been ratified by countries having very varied ideologies. He was afraid that the Committee was avoiding the issue. It asked States parties to tell of their difficulties in implementing the Covenant, but was skirting round its own difficulties.[139]

That the HRC seems to be avoiding the difficulties of article 19 might suggest that there are fundamental divisions within it on the implementation of article 19. The fundamental norms within article 19 remain undefined and largely undeveloped. It appears unlikely that the work of the HRC will redress the disappointing record of the United Nations concerning freedom of expression.[140]

NOTES

1 For similar provisions see art. 19 UDHR, art. 10 ECHR, art. IV ADRD, art. 13 AMR, art. 9 AFR. The annotated drafting history of article 19 can be found in Docs. A/2929, ch. 6, prs. 119-138 (1954); A/5000, prs. 5-35 (1961); Bossuyt, *Guide*, pp. 373-402. See generally, *U.N. Action in the Field of Human Rights*, pp. 222-30 (1988); K. J. Partsch, 'Freedom of Conscience and Expression, and Political Freedoms', in L. Henkin (ed.), *The International Bill of Rights—The ICCPR* (1981), p. 210 at pp. 216-26; P. Sieghart, *The International Law of Human Rights*, pp. 327-37 (1983); L. J. MacFarlane, *The Theory and Practice of Human Rights*, ch. 4 (1985); E. Barendt, *Freedom of Speech* (1985); J. P. Humphrey, 'Political and Related Rights', in T. Meron (ed.), *Human Rights in International Law—Legal and Policy Issues*, p. 170 at pp. 181-8 (1984); G. Malinverni, 'Freedom of Information in the European Convention on Human Rights and in the International Covenant on Civil and Political Rights', 4 HRLJ (1983) pp. 443-60; Report of the VIth International Colloquy on the European Convention on Human Rights, Council of Europe Doc. H/Coll (85) 1-17. On limitation provisions see A. Kiss, 'Permissible Limitations on Rights', in Henkin (ed.), above, pp. 229-310; O. Garibaldi, 'General Limitations on Human Rights: The Principle of Legality', 17 Harv. ILJ. (1976) pp. 503-57; E. I. A. Daes, *The Individual's Duties to the Community and the Limitations on Human Rights and Freedoms under Article 29 of the UDHR*, Doc. E/CN.4/ Sub. 2/432/Rev. 2, chs. 2 and 3 (1983, republished 1990); Siracusa Principles, ch. 7, n. 1 above.

2 See *U.N. Action*, n. 1 above; J. F. Green, *The United Nations and Human Rights*, pp. 76-88 (1956). See GA Resn. 59(1), (14 Dec. 1946).

3 UN Conference on Freedom of Information, Final Act, Doc. E/Conf. 6/79 (1948). See Humphrey, ch. 1, n. 1 above (1984), pp. 50-3; The Conference adopted a draft text which became the Convention on the International Right of Correction (1952), 453 UNTS 191.

4 See Green, n. 2 above, p. 77.

5 See L. R. Sussman, 'Freedom of the Press: Problems in Restructuring the Flow of International News', in R. D. Gastil, *Freedom in the World: Political Rights and Civil Liberties*, pp. 53-98 (1980); *Many Voices, One World—Towards a New, More Just and More Efficient World Information and Communication Order*, Report of the International Commission for the Study of Communication Problems, MacBride (Chairman), UNESCO (1980); K. Venkata Raman, 'Towards a New World Information and Communication Order: Problems of Access and Cultural Development', in R. St. J. MacDonald and D. M. Johnston (eds.), ch. 1, n. 7 above, pp. 1027-68; K. Nordenstreng, *The Mass Media Declaration of UNESCO* (1984).

6 For literature on the NIEO see ch. 5, pr. 5.4, n. 10 above.

7 Demands within UNESCO for a NWICO were partly responsible for the withdrawal from UNESCO of the US and the UK.

8 See GA Resns. 33/115C, 34/182, 37/94B and UN Doc. A/33/45 (1978). While

recognizing the central role of UNESCO the Committee was assigned a degree of primacy within the UN system.

9 On derogation see ch. 7 above. See SR 356 pr. 18 (Tarnopolsky on Uruguay).

10 GC 10(19), adopted by the HRC at its 461st meeting on 27 July 1983, Doc. A/38/40, p. 109. Also in Doc. CCPR/C/21/Add. 2. For the HRC's discussion see SR 449, 457, and 461.

11 Concerning the right to freedom of thought, conscience, and religion. See e.g. SR 742 pr. 68 (Aguilar on Romania) concerning the alleged destruction and poor distribution of religious books.

12 Concerning war propaganda and the advocacy of national, racial, or religious hatred. Article 20 is dealt with in ch. 12 below. Partsch, n. 1 above, comments that article 20, 'is practically a fourth paragraph to Article 19', p. 227.

13 Concerning the right to peaceful assembly.

14 Concerning the political freedoms of citizens to take part in the conduct of public affairs, to vote, to be elected, and to have access to the public service.

15 See Doc. A/2929, n. 1 above, ch. 6, pr. 120.

16 SR 449 pr. 45. For the HRC's discussion see n. 10 above. Cf. Barendt, n. 1 above, on the right to silence as an aspect of freedom of speech, pp. 63–7. The judgments of the EUCT in *Glasenapp* and *Kosiek*, n. 48 below, could have been considered in this context as requiring a positive expression of a particular opinion.

17 Partsch, n. 1 above, pp. 217–18 (footnotes omitted). In fact the expression without interference 'by governmental action' was not voted upon, see Bossuyt, n. 1 above, pp. 378–9.

18 GC 10(19), n. 10 above, pr. 1. See also SR 457 pr. 21 (Tarnopolsky).

19 See K. Glasser and S. T. Possony, *Victims of Politics* (1978).

20 'Article 19 of the Covenant had a central function in terms of the realization of a whole range of other rights, the development of individual countries, and the successful pursuit of international relations', SR 784 pr. 38 (Mommersteeg on Rwanda). Cf. the EUCT has repeatedly stated the fundamental importance in a democratic society of freedom of expression, *Handyside Case* v. *UK*, EUCT, Series A, Vol. 24 (1976); *Sunday Times* v. *UK*, EUCT, Series A, Vol. 30 (1979); *Muller and Others* v. *Switzerland*, n. 73 below; *Lingens* v. *Austria*, EUCT, Series A, Vol. 103 (1986). For a comment on the last of these between the opinion of the EUCM and the judgment of the EUCT see D. Elder, 'Freedom of Expression and the Approach to Defamation: The American Approach to the Problems Raised by the Lingens Case', 35 ICLQ (1986) pp. 891–924. See also *Barfod* v. *Denmark*, EUCT, Series A, Vol. 149 (1989).

21 SR 457 pr. 24 (proposed by Sir Vincent-Evans). Cf. the famous comment of Justice Cardoza in *Palko* v. *Connecticut*, describing freedom of speech as '. . . the matrix, the indispensable condition of nearly every other form of freedom', 302 US 319, 327 (1927).

22 Cf. the HRC's stress on the importance of self-determination in its general comment on article 1 (self-determination), in ch. 5, pr. 5.3 above.

23 See the discussion in SR 457 prs. 24–8 and SR 461 prs. 41–9.

24 See n. 1 above.

25 See Barendt, n. 1 above. See also B. Markesinis, 'The Right to Freedom of Speech Versus the Right to be Let Alone', [1986] PL pp. 67–82.
26 See SR 26 pr. 10 (Vincent-Evans on Syria); SR 715 pr. 22 (Mommersteeg on Tunisia). For a recent ECHR application concerning censorship see A.12381/86 *v*. UK, 10 EHRR (1988).
27 See SR 715 pr. 27 (Higgins on Tunisia).
28 SR 89 pr. 41 (Esperson on Iran).
29 SR 321 pr. 27 (Movchan on Netherlands). Cf. *Glasenapp* and *Kosiek* cases on West German civil servants, n. 48 below.
30 Cf. article 13(2) AMR prohibits prior censorship.
31 SR 54 pr. 36 (Tarnopolsky on Denmark); SR 84 pr. 15 (Opsahl on Madagascar).
32 See the Convention noted in n. 3 above. See Doc. A/2929, pr. 138.
33 'Concerning article 19, ... it appeared that many Czechoslovak citizens had been prosecuted and imprisoned simply for having exercised or attempted to exercise their right to freedom of speech, and had been convicted under articles 98, 100, 102, 103 and 112 of the Penal Code, relating to subversion, instigation to violence, violation of the laws of the Republic and anti-State activities. In her opinion, those articles of the Penal Code defined freedom of expression too restrictively and were therefore not compatible with the provisions of the Covenant. Thus she doubted that persons could be said not to have been arrested for having expressed their opinions but for having broken the law; that type of argument lost all validity if according to the law any criticism of the state or the Government was an offence', SR 683 pr. 3 (Higgins on Czechoslovakia). Reply, ibid., pr. 13.
34 See e.g. SR 161 pr. 23 (Bouziri on Belize, then a UK Dependency); SR 890 pr. 29 (Dimitrijevic on New Zealand). Cf. A.8710/79, *Gay News Ltd. and Lemon* v. *UK*, 5 EHRR 123.
35 See e.g. SR 402 pr. 6 (Tarnopolsky on Australia).
36 See e.g. SR 222 pr. 32 (Tomuschat on Colombia).
37 On article 2 see ch. 6 above.
38 Doc. CCPR/C/1/Add. 23, p. 28 (1978) citing article 168 of the Constitution of the SFRY.
39 See the comments at SR 98 pr. 41 (Mora-Rojas), 59 (Vincent-Evans), 62, 71 (Tomuschat), SR 99 pr. 25 (Tarnopolsky). Reply at SR 102 prs. 45–6.
40 See SR 108 pr. 39 (Prado-Vallejo), prs. 56–8 (Vincent-Evans), SR 109 pr. 24 (Opsahl), 63 (Tomuschat). Reply at SR 112 prs. 34, 37.
41 See SR 136 pr. 2 (Bouziri), 53 (Tarnopolsky), SR 137 pr. 14 (Tomuschat). Reply at SR 140 pr. 28. SR 742 prs. 63–4 (Mommersteeg).
42 See SR 32 pr. 45 (Vincent-Evans); reply at SR 32 pr. 67. SR 687 pr. 35 (N'Diaye); reply at ibid., pr. 41.
43 See SR 26 pr. 10 (Vincent-Evans). See art. 38 of Constitution cited in Doc. CCPR/C/1/Rev. 1, pr. 13. See Partsch, n. 1 above, pp. 222–6.
44 SR 155 pr. 19. The Ukranian SSR Report is Doc. CCPR/C/1/Add. 34.
45 SR 89 pr. 26 (Opsahl).
46 SR 52 pr. 59 (Vincent-Evans). Doc. CCPR/C/1/Add. 9, p. 26 (1977). See also the additional replies in Doc. CCPR/C/1/Add. 42, pp. 24–6 (1979). Cf. *Leander* v. *Sweden*, EUCT, Series A, Vol. 116 (1987).

47 SR 65 pr. 27 (Esperson), 47 (Tarnopolsky).

48 'He wondered whether the application of Berufsverbot for the expression of one's views was consistent with liberal democracy. He also wanted to know what kinds of convictions—socialist, communist, Nazi—were used to justify Berufsverbot and what kinds of posts and professions it covered', SR 94 pr. 6, reply at SR 96 prs. 14–16. See Anon., 'ILO Inquiry's Findings on Discrimination in Public Employment in FRG', 38 Rev. ICJ (1987) pp. 26–30; *Glasenapp* v. *FRG*, EUCT, Series A, Vol. 104 (1986); *Kosiek* v. *FRG*, EUCT, Series A, Vol. 105 (1986).

49 '. . . any restriction on freedom of opinion required convincing proof that a clear and present danger could not otherwise be overcome. It was reasonable to ban any incitement to use violent means of overthrowing the Government, but how could peaceful criticism of Government policies or the objective exposure of governmental deficiencies amount to a threat which could justify repressive sanctions?', SR 128 pr. 21 (Tomuschat on Chile).

49a SR 31 pr. 25 (Mora-Rojas), 36 (Esperson).

50 SR 69 pr. 39 (Tarnopolsky on UK). Key developments in this area since the consideration of the second UK periodic report have been the Public Order Act 1986, the Education Act No. 2 (1986), s. 28 of the Local Government Act 1988 and the Official Secrets Act 1989. See also *R.* v. *Home Secretary ex. p. Brind and Others*, 1990 1 All ER 469 (CA), which unsuccessfully challenged reporting restrictions concerning the terrorist problem in Northern Ireland.

51 SR 52 pr. 9 (Tarnopolsky), 43 (Tomuschat), 58–9 (Vincent-Evans). Cf. *Leander* v. *Sweden*, EUCT, n. 46 above.

52 SR 421 pr. 63 (Bouziri), reply at SR 429 prs. 44–53.

53 See e.g. SR 116 pr. 49 (Opsahl on Belorussian SSR). SR 272 pr. 30 (Dieye on Kenya). See generally, International Commission of Jurists, *Human Rights in a One Party State* (1978).

54 See e.g. SR 784 pr. 40 (Mommersteeg on Rwanda).

55 SR 108 prs. 56–7. Reply at SR 112 pr. 34. See also SR 98 pr. 62 (Tomuschat on Yugoslavia); SR 272 pr. 16 (Lallah on Kenya).

56 See SR 28 pr. 51 (Tarnopolsky on Tunisia), SR 724 pr. 7 (Dimitrijevic on Senegal).

57 See SR 200 pr. 8 (Tomuschat on Iran), and text to n. 44 above (Tomuschat).

58 See SR 353 pr. 27 (Tomuschat on Guyana).

59 SR 772 pr. 40. Note that there is no express reference to licensing in the Covenant. See Doc. A/2929, ch 6, prs. 126, 132, which note that, 'during the debate the term "public order" was interpreted as covering the rights of a State to license media of information and to regulate the importation of material'; Doc. A/5000, pr. 23. Cf. article 10 ECHR. Before the HRC the Danish representative stated that the ECHR could not be understood as excluding in any way a public television monopoly as such and that, in his opinion, that interpretation also applied to the Covenant, SR 780 prs. 34–5. For the leading ECHR applications see A.6452/74, *Saachi* v. *Italy*, 5 D. & R. p. 43; A.9297/81, *X. Association* v. *Sweden*, 28 D. & R. p. 204; *Autronic AG* v. *Switzerland*, EUCT, Series A, Vol. 178 (1990); *Groppera Radio AG and Others* v. *Switzerland*, EUCT, Series A, Vol. 173 (1990) in which the EUCT considered article 19 of the ICCPR.

60 See e.g. SR 89 pr. 41 (Esperson on Iran), SR 282 pr. 51 (Tomuschat on Tanzania). Cf. the 5th Advisory Opinion of the IACT, No. OC-5/85, on *Compulsory Membership in an Association Prescribed by Law for the Practice of Journalism*, 7 HRLJ (1986) pp. 74–106.

61 See generally I. Szabo, *Cultural Rights* (1974).

62 See e.g. SR 65 pr. 9 (Tomuschat on Czechoslovakia). It is interesting to note the comments of the State representative from Zambia, 'There was no ban on the receipt or purchase of foreign newspapers and magazines, though economic constraints had made it difficult for booksellers and newsagents to procure them and, even when available, their prices were beyond the means of most Zambians', SR 776 pr. 40.

63 SR 65 pr. 55 (Prado-Vallejo on Czechoslovakia), SR 784 pr. 43 (Ando on Rwanda). Cf. 'Protection of journalists', Report to Sub-Cion by Mr Sadi, UN Doc. E/CN.4/Sub. 2/1990/17.

64 SR 353 pr. 27.

65 GC 10(19), n. 10 above, prs. 2 and 3.

66 See the UNESCO Mass Media Declaration, n. 1 above, on which see Nordenstreng, n. 5 above. The problems raised by private financial interests and monopoly control of information media were discussed during the drafting of the Covenant, see Doc. A/2929, ch. 6, pr. 137; Doc. A/5000, pr. 24.

67 SR 449 pr. 48 (Bouziri).

68 SR 449 pr. 50 (Dimitrijevic). A number of members voiced the concerns and complaints of Third World States of 'politically oriented, unbalanced and biased' reporting, SR 449 pr. 48 (Bouziri).

69 GC 10(19), n. 10 above, pr. 4 in part. Meron, ch. 6 n. 1 above, comments that, 'It is doubtful whether that interpretation will limit the many restrictions on freedom of expression which may be permissible under the vague terms of Art. 19(3)', p. 116.

70 'Presumably they include the duty to present information and views truthfully, accurately and impartially', Partsch, n. 1 above. See also E. I. Daes, n. 1 above, pp. 53–60.

71 Cf. Van Dijk and Van Hoof, pp. 573–8; *Kruslin* v. *France*, EUCT, Series A, Vol. 176-A (1990); *Groppera Radio AG and Others* v. *Switzerland*, ibid., Vol. 173 (1990). 5th IACT Advisory Opinion, n. 60 above; Daes, n. 1 above, pp. 112–15.

72 Cf. Van Dijk and Van Hoof, pp. 583–606. See in particular *Handyside* v. *UK*, EUCT, Series A, Vol. 24 (1976).

73 For limitations suggested during the drafting see Bossuyt, n. 1 above, pp. 387–94. For the ECHR practice see Van Dijk and Van Hoof, ibid. See *Muller and Others* v. *Switzerland*, EUCT, Series A, Vol. 133 (1988), concerning the applicants' fine and conviction for obscene publications and the subsequent confiscation of those paintings. HRC members effectively offer interpretations when they often make it clear in their comments that they do not consider that the requirements of article 19(3) have been observed, for example, 'admittedly, the Covenant provided that the exercise of freedom of information could be subject to certain restrictions which might be necessary for respect of the rights or reputations of

others, but he did not believe that "others" could be taken to mean a legal entity or government body, or even the State itself', SR 715 pr. 18 (Mommersteeg on Tunisia).

74 'In relation to article 19 of the Covenant . . . he wished clarification concerning the margin of discretion used by the State in prohibiting the expression of opinions which it considered detrimental to its own welfare. The situation under the Covenant was rather complex. Although a margin of discretion was admissible, it must be kept within strict limits', SR 610 pr. 49 (Tomuschat on Ukrainian SSR).

75 See *Hertzberg* v. *Finland*, pr. 11.18 below.

76 See Doc. A/5000, n. 1 above, pr. 30.

77 See ch. 12, pr. 12.17 below.

78 Ibid.

79 Doc. A/35/40, p. 111.

80 Ibid., pr. 14.

81 Ibid., pr. 16.

82 Doc. A/35/40, p. 132.

83 Ibid., pr. 17.

84 Ibid.

85 'To date, the State party has never explained the scope and meaning of "subversive activities", which constitute a criminal offence under the relevant legislation. Such an explanation is particularly necessary in the present case, since the author of the communication contends that he has been prosecuted solely for his opinions', *Carballal* v. *Uruguay*, Doc. A/36/40, p. 125.

86 *Pietraroia* v. *Uruguay*, Doc. A/36/40, p. 153, pr. 13.2: violation of article 19(2) because P arrested, detained, and tried for his political and trade union activities.

87 *Lopez Burgos* v. *Uruguay*, Doc. A/36/40, p. 176, pr. 11.5. Cf. in *V.R.M.B.* v. *Canada*, Doc. A/43/40, p. 258, the HRC expressed the view that the 'Deportation of an alien on security grounds does not constitute an interference with the rights guaranteed by articles 18 and 19 of the Covenant', pr. 6.3.

88 Doc. A/36/40, p. 114.

89 Ibid., pr. 12.

90 Ibid., pr. 16. See also *Pietraroia* v. *Uruguay*, n. 86 above.

91 Ibid., pr. 15 (my emphasis).

92 Doc. A/36/40, p. 176.

93 Ibid., pr. 13.

94 See e.g. *Pietraroia* v. *Uruguay*, n. 86 above.

95 Doc. A/35/40, p. 120.

96 Ibid.

97 Doc. A/37/40, p. 161.

98 Ibid., pr. 6.1. On the relevance of public support for a particular law see *Tyrer* v. *UK*, EUCT, Series A, Vol. 26, pr. 31 (1978); *Dudgeon* v. *UK*, EUCT, Series A, Vol. 45, prs. 57–8 (1981). See also *Bowers* v. *Hardwick*, 106 S. Ct. 2841 (1986), on which see J. K. Sullens, 'Thus Far and No Further: The Supreme Court Draws the Outer Boundary of the Right to Privacy', 61 Tulane LR (1987) pp. 907–29.

99 Doc. A/37/40, p. 161, pr. 6.4.

100 Ibid., pr. 10.2.

101 See A.4515/70, *X and Association of Y* v. *UK*, 18 D. & R. (1980) p. 66 at p. 76; 38 CD (1972), p. 86 at p. 88.

102 Doc. A/37/40, p. 161, pr. 4.

103 On recent UK controversies with respect to broadcasting decisions see A. E. Boyle, 'Political Broadcasting, Fairness and Administrative Law', [1986] PL pp. 562–96; A. W. Bradley, 'Parliamentary Privilege, Zircon and National Security', [1987] PL pp. 488–95.

104 Doc. A/37/40, p. 161, pr. 10.2.

105 Ibid. On the interpretation of 'necessity' under the ECHR see the material cited in nn. 20, 72 above.

106 Ibid., prs. 10.3–10.4.

107 Ibid., pr. 11.

108 See the literature cited in ch. 4, pr. 4.48, n. 383 above.

109 See the decision of the EUCT in *Muller and Others* v. *Switzerland*, n. 20 above, in which the EUCT took a similar a view on the interpretation of public morals.

110 See Doc. A/37/40, p. 161, pr. 7.

111 Ibid., pr. 10.4.

112 Ibid.

113 Ibid., pp. 166–7. The two members were Mr Lallah and Mr Tarnopolsky.

114 Ibid.

115 See the references in notes 20, 72 above.

116 See e.g. *Tyrer* v. *UK*, n. 98 above; *Dudgeon* v. *UK*, n. 98 above, *Rees* v. *UK*, EUCT, Series A, Vol. 106 (1986); Merrills, pp. 130–4.

117 See pr. 11.19.1 above.

118 See n. 113 above.

119 Doc. A/44/40, p. 277. France had argued that, '"Freedom of expression" within the meaning of article 19 cannot be construed as including a right to exercise a specific teaching activity', pr. 5.5. In *M.K.* v. *France*, France argued that freedom of expression cannot be deemed to encompass the freedom of French citizens to use whatever language or dialect they choose before French administrative tribunals, Doc. A/45/40, Apx., pr. 6.4. The communication was declared inadmissible on different grounds. See also *Delgado Paez* v. *Colombia*, Doc. A/45/40, Apx., pr. 5.8, on the requirement that an advocate of 'liberation theology' teach the Catholic religion in its traditional form.

120 Doc. A/38/40, p. 231. See ch. 12, prs. 12.27–12.31 below.

121 See pr. 11.6.1 above.

122 See e.g. notes 24, 66 above.

123 See prs. 11.15–11.16 above.

124 See prs. 11.19–11.19.2 above.

125 See n. 108 above.

126 See pr. 11.4 above.

127 See pr. 11.9 above.

128 For a rare example see SR 170 pr. 34 (Opsahl on Finland); SR 392 pr. 7 (Graefrath on Iceland).

129 See e.g. his comments at SR 767 pr. 7 (on Trinidad and Tobago) concerning access of political parties to television.

130 This matter has occasionally been raised, see e.g. SR 142 pr. 70 (Hanga on Spain); SR 319 pr. 62 (Hanga on Japan).

131 See SR 780 pr. 38 (Ando on Denmark). See N. S. Marsh (ed.), *Public Access to Government Held Information* (1987). In *Gaskin* v. *UK*, EUCT, Series A, Vol. 160, pr. 52 (1989), the EUCT unanimously held that article 10 ECHR did not embody an obligation on the government to impart the information in question (G's child care records) to an individual.

132 See *X. and Church of Scientology* v. *Sweden*, 16 D. & R. p. 68 (1979); *Barthold* v. *FRG*, EUCT, Series A, Vol. 90 (1985); A. Lester and D. Pannick, 'Advertising and Freedom of Expression in Europe', [1985] PL pp. 349–52.

133 See the Council of Europe Convention for the Protection of Individuals with Regard to Automatic Processing of Personal Data (1981), ETS 108; N. Savage and C. Edwards, *A Guide to the Data Protection Act* (2nd, 1985); I. N. Walden and N. Savage, 'Data Protection and Privacy Laws: Should Organisations be Protected?' 37 ICLQ (1988) pp. 337–47.

134 In its General Comment on article 17 the HRC stated that, 'The gathering and holding of personal information on computers, databanks and other devices, whether by public authorities or private individuals or bodies, must be regulated by law. Effective measures have to be taken by States to ensure that information concerning a person's private life does not reach the hands of persons who are not authorized to receive, process and use it, and it is never used for purposes incompatible with the Covenant. In order to have the most effective protection of his private life, every individual should have the right to ascertain in an intelligible form, whether, and if so, what personal data is stored in automatic data files, and for what purposes. Every individual should also be able to ascertain which public authorities or private individuals or bodies control or may control their files. If such files contain incorrect personal data or have been collected or processed contrary to the provisions of the law, every individual should have the right to request rectification or elimination', GC 16(32), Doc. A/43/40, pp. 181–3, adopted by the HRC at its 791st meeting (March 1988), also in Doc. CCPR/C/21/Add. 6. For recent examples of questioning see SR 878 pr. 59 (Mommersteeg on Uruguay), SR 890 pr. 35 (Wennergren on New Zealand).

135 See ch. 1, pr. 1.38, n. 256 above.

136 See V. Leary, 'The Implementation of the Human Rights Provisions of the Helsinki Final Act: A Preliminary Assessment', in T. Buergenthal (ed.), *Human Rights, International Law, and the Helsinki Final Accords*, pp. 140–8 (1977).

137 See the literature on limitation provisions in n. 1 above.

138 See ch. 2, pr. 2.7 above.

139 SR 461 pr. 46.

140 See pr. 11.2 above. In its Resn. 1990/35 the ECOSOC endorsed the decision of the HRCion in its Resn. 1990/32 to prepare a study on the right to freedom of opinion and expression, the current problems of its realization, and on measures necessary for its strengthening and promotion. See Doc. E/CN.4/Sub.2/1990/11 for the first report.

Article 20[1]

1. Any propaganda for war shall be prohibited by law.
2. Any advocacy of national, racial or religious hatred that constitutes incitement to discrimination, hostility or violence shall be prohibited by law.

Introduction

12.2 The inclusion of article 20 in the Covenant was controversial. Its opponents argued that the prohibition might lead to abuse and would be detrimental to freedom of opinion and expression (article 19), might encourage the establishment of governmental censorship, that the expressions used were vague and subjective, that the article did not establish any particular right or freedom, and that such prohibitions would not be effective.

Those in favour of the article argued that such prohibitions could not be considered as a threat to freedom of opinion and expression, that the general limitation provisions in article 19(3) were not adequate, legislative provision was necessary because of the strong influence of modern propaganda,[2] a specific prohibition on war propaganda would put an end to the cold war and promote peaceful co-existence, and that the question of propaganda had been dealt with in national laws and constitutions as well as in international instruments and documents.[3] However, substantial opposition to the article remained when it was adopted by the Third Committee of the General Assembly in 1961.[4] Article 20 is notable in that it is the only provision of the Covenant that specifically requires that certain conduct 'shall be prohibited by law'.[5]

A. ARTICLE 20 UNDER THE REPORTING PROCESS

12.3 Article 20 is not covered by the non-derogation provision in article 4(2).[6] It has been the subject of a General Comment under article 40(4)[7] and reference was also made to article 20 in the first of the General Comments on article 6 (right to life).[8] In the consideration of State reports article 20 has generally been considered separately but members have often commented on the terms of its relationship with article 19 (freedom of opinion and expression)[9] and this question again arose during the drafting of the General Comment on article 20.[10]

Article 20(1)

12.4 In its General Comment the HRC stated that,

Not all reports submitted by States parties have provided sufficient information as to the implementation of article 20 of the Covenant. *In view of the nature of article 20, States parties are obliged to adopt the necessary legislative measures prohibiting the actions referred to therein.* However, the reports have shown that in some States such actions are neither prohibited by law nor are appropriate efforts intended or made to prohibit them. Furthermore, many reports failed to give sufficient information concerning the relevant national legislation and practice.[11]

12.5 Such deficiencies in the information supplied to the HRC has led members to point out to State representatives the general and specific ends of the prohibition in article 20 and how the measures reported to the HRC by the States parties fail to satisfy article 20 by reason of inadequacy, inapplicability, ineffectiveness, or imprecision.[12] The HRC's considerations of article 20 have shown it to be a provision the implementation of which raises particularly acute problems of interpretation and conflict. Neither 'war'[13] nor 'propaganda' are defined—the latter term is capable of a very expansive meaning.[14] The absence of definition caused some difficulty during the drafting of the General Comment on article 20 which a number of members hoped would clarify the meaning of 'war propaganda'.[15]

12.6 Partly because of the lack of definition to article 20 there have been a number of reservations and interpretative declarations to it.[16] A number of these have attracted criticism from HRC members. An instructive example of the approach of members is that taken as regards Finland. In its initial report Finland explained its reservations to article 20:

When this provision was dealt with in the General Assembly of the United Nations, Finland voted against its adoption for the following reasons.

First of all, this provision may come into conflict with article 19, paragraph 2, of the Covenant, recognizing the right of everyone to freedom of expression. Since the concept of war propaganda is somewhat vague, it would be difficult to draw a definitive line between lawful expression of opinion and ideas, on the one hand, and forbidden propaganda on the other.

Secondly, a prohibition by law, in order to be effective should be sanctioned by penalizing the breach against it. This would cause difficulties since, according to the principles recognized in the criminal law, the characteristics of a punishable crime or offence must be accurately defined. The provision contained in article 20, paragraph 1, of the Covenant does not fulfil this requirement.

Consequently, the reservation will be maintained for the present.[17]

Mr Graefrath commented that, 'Finland's reservation ... would have the effect of removing the need to implement an entire [provision] of the Covenant. He was not sure that that was acceptable.'[18] Presumably the reference to acceptability is in terms of the legality of the reservation. Mr Koulishev regretted the reservation and said that,

He understood the difficulties involved but felt that they were not insurmountable, especially as propaganda for war had been condemned in the Declaration on Principles of International Law Concerning Friendly Relations and Co-Operation Among States in accordance with the Charter of the United Nations (G.A. Resn. 2625 (XXV)) and the Final Act of the Helsinki Conference.[19]

Mr Opsahl

asked why Finland had found it necessary to enter a reservation to article 20, paragraph 1, which embodied an obligation imposed on States, and yet made no reservation to paragraph 2 of that article which imposed a similar obligation and was equally difficult to define and punish.[20]

Mr Movchan stated quite simply that he could accept neither of Finland's arguments.[21]

12.7 It seems clear then that members consider themselves competent to comment on and assess the legal validity of reservations or interpretative declarations even though the HRC has not adopted any formal decision concerning its jurisdiction as regards reservations or interpretative declarations.[22] Most of the members have at least understood, though not always been convinced by the difficulties and objections proffered by States parties, and accordingly their comments and criticisms have generally been temperate.

12.8 During consideration of the report of the Netherlands Mr Tomuschat made an important observation on the difficulties occasioned by article 20:

Noting the Netherlands' comments on article 20, he said that the concept of 'propaganda for war' had never been adequately defined. Obviously, the drafters of the provisions had in mind only a war of aggression and not a war of defence or liberation, but opinions as to what constituted a war of defence or liberation differed. Again, he wondered whether the provision covered only written propaganda or could also be held to extend, for example, to public military parades involving the display of tanks or rockets. The Committee should attempt to clarify the meaning of 'propaganda for war', for as long as the expression remained ill-defined, the States would, perhaps rightly, remain reluctant to accept such a far-reaching obligation.[23]

As noted above a number of the reservations by States have been based on the lack of definition in article 20.[24] Mr Tomuschat's comment was a portent of the difficulties encountered by the HRC in drafting a General Comment on article 20, which is dealt with below.[25]

12.9 The comments in the report of Canada on article 20(1) raised the important question of the extent of the responsibility of a State party[26] under article 20(1):

There is no law prohibiting propaganda in favour of war. An individual or organization may, therefore, legally disseminate such propaganda. The Government cannot do so, however, without breaking the commitments it made by signing the Covenant.[27]

During consideration of Canada's report Mr Graefrath noted that, 'this was not in conformity with the Covenant which made it quite clear that it was the responsibility of the State to prohibit propaganda for war within its area of jurisdiction'.[28] It is submitted that Mr Graefrath's view must be correct.

Article 20(2)

12.10 The HRC's considerations of article 20(2) have extended to the existence of racist and fascist type organizations.[29] In reply to such questioning Mr Cairncross, a United Kingdom State representative, commented that,

For Government or Parliament to proscribe an organization because of its racist character would appear to confer on the authorities of the country a power that could be abused and that might be incompatible with the right of freedom of information. Proscription of any organization in ordinary times would be a very serious step for his country to contemplate.[30]

Note though that article 20 proscribes certain propaganda rather than the organizations engaging in such propaganda.[31]

12.11 Members of the HRC have not refrained from direct questions and comments on some of the potentially sensitive matters covered by article 20(2). For example during consideration of the report of the USSR[32] Mr Opsahl asked, 'Was it true, as it was sometimes alleged, that Soviet authorities had in recent years authorised what would seem to constitute anti-Semitic propaganda'.[33] The State representative did not reply to this specific point.[34]

Similarly Mr Movchan commented during consideration of the report of the FRG,[35]

The report also stated that the acts described in article 20, paragraph 2, were punishable under the penal provisions relating to demagogy, incitement to racial hatred and disturbance of religious peace. Article 20 of the Covenant was not, however, covered by Federal German Legislation, for paragraph 2 of that article stated that any advocacy of national, racial or religious hatred that constitutes incitement to discrimination, hostility or violence should be prohibited by law, and the report indicated no suppression of racial hatred and mentioned no legislation prohibiting the advocacy of national hatred. Propaganda fomenting national hatred and the organization of fifth columns had paved the way for German imperialism in the Second World War and the suppression of national hatred, including the prohibition of Nazi propaganda and SS-type organizations, was therefore extremely important. He wondered how the activities of Radio Free Europe in Munich could be reconciled with the . . . provision of the Basic Law regarding acts tending to and undertaken with intent to disturb peaceful relations between nations.[36]

Again, however, there was no reply from the State representative.[37]

12.12 The HRC's considerations of article 20 have been of more limited scope than the other articles examined in this thesis. However, the drafting of the General Comment on article 20 occasioned strong divisions within the HRC and threatened to break the practice of consensus decision making which has operated since the HRC's inception.[38]

The General Comment on Article 20

12.13 The Working Group on General Comments[39] undertook consideration of article 20 at the HRC's thirteenth session (July 1981) and produced a working document drafted by Mr Bouziri. Subsequently texts were introduced by Mr Movchan (fifteenth session, March–April 1982), Mr Opsahl (1982), and a joint text by Mr Tomuschat and Mr Graefrath (eighteenth session, 1983). The latter text was introduced to the HRC at its eighteenth session.[40] After substantial discussion and some important amendments the General Comment on article 20 was adopted on 25 July 1983, some three years after its initial consideration.

12.14 The text introduced at the eighteenth session included the following:

The obligation in article 20 is of a peremptory nature. States parties have the duty to adopt appropriate legislative acts prohibiting the acts referred to in article 20.[41]

A number of objections were raised to the use of the term 'peremptory'. It was argued that the term was used in a very different sense in the Vienna Convention on the Law of Treaties, namely in the sense that a norm was 'jus cogens' and could not be challenged by a treaty.[42] It was suggested that the term should be replaced by 'mandatory' but it was objected that the meaning of that term was almost identical.[43] Some members thought that the whole sentence should be deleted because it was 'superfluous',[44] 'meaningless',[45] and 'those interpreting that comment might reach the conclusion that certain articles of the Covenant were not mandatory'.[46]

12.15 Those in favour of retaining the sentence argued that while all of the articles were mandatory some were more so than others,[47] article 20 was the only one which stipulated the adoption of domestic legislation,[48] the term 'peremptory' corresponded to a concept of law,[49] the authors had stressed the mandatory nature of article 20,[50] and that the sentence met a real need because many countries believed that they were not obliged to promulgate an act in accordance with article 20.[51]

12.16 Ultimately the solution adopted was to delete the second sentence and combine the essential point of the immediacy of the obligation under article 20 with the necessity for States to take appropriate measures:

In view of the nature of article 20, States parties are obliged to adopt the necessary legislative measures prohibiting the actions referred to therein.[52]

12.17 After stating the terms of the prohibition in article 20 the draft comment continued:

In the opinion of the Committee these prohibitions (constitute a necessary corollary to article 19)[53] {cannot be considered as being in contradiction with article 19}.[54]

Some difficulty was occasioned by this reference to article 19. There was some debate on the correct relationship between articles 19 and 20 in terms of whether article 20 was a restriction or limitation on article 19[55] on the bases of 'respect for the rights or reputations of others' and the 'protection of national security',[56] part of the 'special duties and responsibilities' which the exercise of the rights in article 19(2) carries with it, or not a case of the application of article 19 at all: '... propaganda for war had no more relation to freedom of expression than crime or theft to freedom of action'.[57] Above all members were anxious to meet some of the declarations and reservations of States parties concerning the relationship between articles 19 and 20 and assure them of the consistency of the two provisions.[58] The formula finally adopted clearly states this element of consistency:

In the opinion of the Committee, these required prohibitions are fully compatible with the right of freedom of expression as contained in article 19 the exercise of which carries with it special duties and responsibilities.[59]

It is submitted that this must be correct. If possible a treaty must be interpreted in a way that its provisions are consistent with one another.

12.18 The draft text continued:

The prohibition under paragraph 1 extends to all forms of propaganda made with a view to, or resulting in, a breach of peace or act of aggression, while paragraph 2 is directed against advocacy of national, racial or religious hatred that constitutes incitement to discrimination, hostility or violence, in particular when such propaganda aims at destabilizing another country.[60]

Various doubts, suggestions, and amendments were raised to this sentence.[61] 'Destabilizing' was a broad term with no precise legal meaning;[62]

'propaganda' at the end of the sentence should be replaced with 'advocacy' so as to maintain the subtle distinction made by the drafters.[63] One member wanted an express reference to propaganda by States and governments as distinct from individuals and organizations and to forms other than the written or spoken word, for example, threatening demonstrations of armed force.[64] Another member was 'not happy with the phrase "in particular when such propaganda aims at destabilizing another country" which introduced an element aimed more at inter-State relations'.[65] There was some debate on the attempted definition of the propaganda covered by paragraph 1, which extended to the need to take account of all forms of propaganda and all forms of war,[66] the desirability of a reference to the threat or use of force in a manner inconsistent with the Charter of the United Nations, (reference was made to article 2(4) and 39 of the Charter,[67] the Friendly Relations Declaration 1970,[68] and the United Nations Resolution on the Definition of Aggression),[69] and the concerns of small countries sensitive to threats or acts of aggression, undeclared wars and the use of force.[70] Finally the HRC reached a consensus on the following text:

The prohibition under paragraph 1 extends to all forms of propaganda threatening or resulting in an act of aggression or breach of the peace contrary to the Charter of the United Nations, while paragraph 2 is directed against advocacy of national, racial or religious hatred that constitutes incitement to discrimination, hostility or violence, whether such propaganda or advocacy has aims which are internal or external to the State concerned.[71]

12.19 The most divisive of the difficulties encountered by the HRC was perhaps that which arose in respect of the following draft sentence: 'The provisions of article 20 do not form an obstacle to self-defence [or to the struggle of peoples for self-determination and independence].'[72] Mr Ermacora thought that the provision should be amended, 'because the provisions of article 20 did not form an obstacle to self-defence or the struggle of peoples for self-determination in themselves but could form an obstacle to propaganda for such actions'.[73] Strong opposition emerged to the last phrase of the sentence, 'or to the struggle of peoples for self-determination and independence'. The independent expert from the United Kingdom, Sir Vincent-Evans, led this opposition:

He knew that that was a generally accepted phrase in United Nations parlance and understood the reasons for it in the earlier history of the decolonization process. However, at a time when very few countries were under colonial domination, such a wording might be taken as an invitation to minorities to use armed force and civil war to attain self-determination and independence. Such an approach should not be encouraged by the Human Rights Committee. Any form of war was a threat to the lives of individuals and peaceful means of achieving the same ends should be sought.[74]

Professor Tomuschat commented that,

It was his conviction that disputes and struggles for independence should be settled by peaceful means although he admitted that there might be recourse to violence in extreme circumstances, but the Committee must not appear to be urging the Kurds, Armenians or the people of the Sahara, for example, to take up arms. The Committee's text must be consistent with the philosophy of the United Nations as set out in article 2(4) of the Charter.[75]

12.20 Consultations with members of the working group led to a proposal to replace the words 'do not form an obstacle to self-defence or to the struggle of peoples for' with 'do not prohibit advocacy of the sovereign right of self-defence or the right of peoples to' (self-determination and independence).[76] Again this proposal attracted strong opposition, from Sir Vincent-Evans in particular:

That wording meant that a people had the right not only to resort to propaganda but also to advocate national and racial hatred in order to achieve self-determination and independence. That was a monstrous idea and contrary to everything the Covenant was intended to achieve.[77]

12.21 It was suggested by Professor Ermacora that the insertion of the word 'peaceful' might solve the difficulties encountered by a small minority of the members.[78] However, this suggestion itself encountered fierce opposition, which revealed some interesting perspectives on the view of members of the relationship between articles 20 and 1 (self-determination):[79]

It was desirable that the exercise of the right to self-determination should be peaceful and not violent. Unfortunately, that was not always possible so the word, 'peaceful' should not be included.[80]

He could not believe that someone who defended the right of peoples to self-determination was thereby promoting violence or national, racial or religious hatred. The right of peoples to self-determination was enshrined in the Charter and the Covenant but the way in which the right was exercised depended upon the conditions in which a particular people found itself.[81]

To include the word 'peaceful' . . . would be beyond the Committee's competence, since it was for peoples themselves to decide how to conduct their struggle for self-determination, using violence if necessary. It was equally essential to retain the word 'independence' since some independent States were fighting for their survival.[82]

Professor Tomuschat explained the problem lucidly:

Nobody was challenging the right to self-determination. Nevertheless, a distinction had to be made between the recognition of the right and its enforcement. The question was whether the prohibition contained in article 20 of the Covenant was to be attenuated when the attainment of certain ends was being sought. Did the Committee wish to affirm that propaganda for war was permissible with a view to obtaining independence and that, for the same purpose, the advocacy of national, racial or religious hatred was also lawful and legitimate? Some members of the Committee were afraid that those were the logical implications of including a reference to the right of self-determination and independence in the context of article 20.

The sentence as it stood was extremely ambiguous. Mr. Al Douri had apparently drawn the conclusion that it legitimized the armed struggle for independence. However, article 20 of the Covenant referred to 'any propaganda for war'. What kind of propaganda for war was meant? Had the General Assembly created a rule of customary law whereby it was permissible to resort to armed struggle in order to attain independence? Everything depended on how the Committee interpreted the sentence before it.[83]

12.22 Professor Tarnopolsky argued that the objectors had missed the point of the draft paragraph 2. After referring to articles 55 and 56 of the UN Charter and article 1 of the Covenant[84] he continued,

In the text before it the Committee was stating that, if States were asked to provide for laws prohibiting propaganda for war and the advocacy of national, racial and religious hatred, such laws were not interpreted as meaning that someone who advocated the sovereign right of self-defence or the right to self-determination and independence was thereby advocating national, racial or religious hatred. Surely that was acceptable to all members of the Committee?

He personally would go further. In his opinion a right to self-determination which was not granted would lead to a right to take up arms. That was not, however, what the sentence under consideration meant. He preferred the words 'The provisions of article 20 do not prohibit advocacy of . . .' to the words 'The provisions of article 20 do not in any way prejudice the sovereign right . . .'. What was at issue was the interpretation to be given to the laws which the Committee claimed were necessary. In his opinion, someone who immediately advocated the taking up of arms or national, racial or religious hatred did not fall within the exemption provided for in the sentence now under discussion, which meant only that persons advocating self-defence and self-determination and independence should not be considered to be advocating war or national, racial or religious hatred. The original wording should therefore be retained.[85]

12.23 Professor Tomuschat suggested amending the sentence to read,

Advocacy of the sovereign right of self-defence or of the right of all peoples to self-determination cannot as such be interpreted as being prohibited by the provisions of article 20.[86]

However, it was objected that the wording was 'unacceptable and illogical because it was obvious that the authors of the Covenant had not drafted an article which would be incompatible with others'.[87] Mr Bouziri suggested that the words 'paragraph 1' should be inserted after the words 'article 20' so as to avoid any misunderstanding.[88] Sir Vincent-Evans argued that the proposal only solved half of the difficulties because the continued reference to article 20, paragraph 1, still rendered the sentence unacceptable.[89] It is important to note, however, that the text finally adopted does refer only to article 20, paragraph 1.[90]

12.24 In the light of the protracted discussions over the proposed draft sentence it was suggested that the final solution might have to be recourse to a footnote in which the minority could express its position or a summary of the Committee's discussions.[91] However, the members continued to search for a text which would command a consensus because resort to a footnote would represent a 'confus[ing]'[92] and 'unfortunate'[93] precedent and

would put the Committee in a difficult position, since it implied, *a contrario*, that the sentence to which it referred endorsed violence and terrorism. If it was published as it stood, it would have to be accompanied by a counter-reservation, which would be ridiculous.[94]

Ultimately an acceptable text was achieved by adopting the suggestion of the Chairman that,

the latter half of the sentence was qualified by adding, at the end of the sentence, the time-honoured phrase 'in accordance with the Charter of the United Nations', the Charter of the United Nations being the primary document in international law, which had been universally accepted. That still left the phrase in the United Nations Charter open to interpretation, but would keep the Committee's comments within the language of the United Nations.[95]

12.25 The text finally adopted then reads,

The provisions of article 20, paragraph 1, do not prohibit advocacy of the sovereign right to self-defence or the right of peoples to self-determination and independence in accordance with the Charter of the United Nations.[96]

We have already noted in chapter five that there is disagreement between States on the permissibility of using force to assist in the attaining of self-determination.[97]

12.26 The General Comment on article 20 concludes by joining two draft sentences, slightly amended:

For article 20 to become fully effective there ought to be a law making it clear that propaganda and advocacy as described therein are contrary to public policy and providing for an appropriate sanction in case of violation. The Committee therefore believes that States parties which have not yet done so should take the measures necessary to fulfil the obligations contained in article 20, (and should themselves refrain from any such propaganda or advocacy).[98]

The Committee's discussion of the first sentence above raised one point of interest. Mr Ermacora objected to the reference to 'sanctions' because the Committee was exceeding its powers and was not authorized by the Covenant to appeal to States as it was doing.[99] He commented that the question of something declared unlawful being free from sanction, 'raised the whole position of the Covenant in domestic law. The draft comment represented merely an intellectual exercise undertaken by the Committee and, in his country's case at any rate, a government was entirely free to adopt it or not do so'.[100] Mr Opsahl had agreed that the choice of sanctions was at the discretion of the State party but he posited the role of the Committee in more positive terms:

Even an imperfect law would be in accordance with the Covenant. The Committee was, however, fully entitled to express its opinion that for 'effective' implementation of the article some kind of sanctions were necessary. There were other types of sanction in addition to those Mr. Errera mentioned,[101] such as censorship or prohibition of the publication of certain newspapers. He was not himself advocating such methods, but indicating that they were possible. The Committee should not specify the type of sanctions in its text but should state that countries' reports should indicate that some did exist.[102]

The final text adopted retained the reference to 'an appropriate sanction'. The final phrase of the last sentence, in parenthesis above, was added to the draft text introduced at the eighteenth session and adopted without any discussion in the plenary Committee.

B. ARTICLE 20 UNDER THE OPTIONAL PROTOCOL

12.27 Article 20 has only been dealt with in one admissibility decision, *J.R.T. and W.G. Party* v. *Canada*.[103] Mr T and the Party had used tape-recorded messages linked to the Bell Telephone system in Toronto to attract membership and promote the Party's policies. A member of the public could listen to the messages by dialling the relevant telephone number. The basic content of the recorded messages was to warn 'of the dangers of international finance and international Jewry leading the world into wars, unemployment and inflation and the collapse of world values and principles'.[104]

12.28 By application of sections 3 and 13(1) of the Canadian Human Rights Act 1978 the telephone service of the Party and Mr T were severely curtailed. The Party and Mr T claimed to be victims of the right to hold and maintain their opinions without interference in violation of article 19(1) of the Covenant, and the right to freedom of expression and of the right to seek, receive and impart information and ideas of all kinds through the media of their choice, in violation of article 19(2) of the Covenant.[105]

12.29 Pursuant to section 7 of the Post Office Act (Canada), which forbids the transmission of 'scurrilous material', Mr T has also, since May 1965, been proscribed from receiving or sending any mail in Canada. Mr T claimed that this violated article 19.[106] The State party submitted, *inter alia*, that the impugned provisions did not contravene the Covenant but in fact gave effect to article 20(2).[107]

12.30 In respect of the alleged violations of article 19(1) and (2) by application of the Canadian Human Rights Act the HRC was of the opinion that,

The opinions which Mr. T seeks to disseminate through the telephone system clearly constitute the advocacy of racial or religious hatred which Canada has an obligation under article 20 (2) of the Covenant to prohibit. In the Committee's opinion, therefore, the communication is, in respect of this claim, incompatible with the provisions of the Covenant, within the meaning of article 3 of the Optional Protocol.[108]

The HRC's decision appears to be a logical one. As submitted above articles 19 and 20 must be interpreted consistently with each other.[109] A prohibition established in accordance with the terms of article 20 cannot found a violation of article 19.

12.31 In respect of the possible violations of article 17 and 19 by application of the Post Office Act (Canada) the HRC accepted that, 'The broad scope of the prohibitory order, extending as it does to all mail, whether sent or received, raises a question of compatibility with articles 17 and 19 of the Covenant'.[110] However, this claim was held inadmissible for failure to comply with domestic remedies (article 5(2)(*b*) OP).[111]

APPRAISAL

12.32 This examination of the HRC's work under article 20, in particular on its General Comment, has revealed a number of interesting aspects of the workings of the HRC. The drawing up of General Comments under article 40(4) of the ICCPR represents important opportunities for the HRC to consider the general and specific principles applicable in respect of each of the articles of the ICCPR, the problems and difficulties that have arisen during the consideration of State reports, and the relationship between the different rights in the ICCPR. The General Comments produced form an important reference point both during the consideration of State reports under article 40[112] and the consideration of communications under the Optional Protocol.[113]

12.33 The General Comment under article 20 took over three years of discussion to produce. Relatively little of that discussion took place in the plenary Committee in public. Publication of the summary records of the Working Group meetings and the various draft texts could usefully aid the understanding of how the final version developed and is to be interpreted. The discussion in the HRC displayed interesting and often conflicting perspectives on article 20. The HRC also exhibited a strong desire to maintain the practice of consensus decision making.[114] Members have recognized the importance of the General Comments being clear, purposive, and of assistance to States parties in implementing the ICCPR. The standard by which General Comments must be judged has thus been established by the HRC and an assessment is possible of whether consensus has served to increase or diminish the usefulness of the General Comment on article 20.

12.34 The General Comment on article 20 does contain a number of positive and noteworthy aspects including the stress on the immediacy of the obligation,[115] the compatibility of articles 19 and 20,[116] the reference to 'all forms of propaganda',[117] the 'internal' and 'external' application of article 20,[118] and the need for an 'appropriate sanction' before article 20 can become 'fully effective'.[119] However, a number of difficulties remain. The meaning of 'war' and 'propaganda' remain ambiguous and uncertain and it may well be that article 20 will eventually need some added definition.[120] The difficulties raised concerning the relationship between propaganda, the use of violence or force, and self-determination and independence were ultimately avoided only by an ambiguous reference to the United Nations Charter.[121] Members anticipated that their subsequent consideration of a General Comment on article 1 (self-determination) would resurrect some of these problems. In fact, as we have seen, the General Comment on article 1 was adopted with relatively little difficulty.[122]

NOTES

1 On the drafting of article 20 see in particular Doc. A/2929, ch. 6, prs. 189–94; A/5000, prs. 36–50; M. Bossuyt, *Guide*, pp. 403–11. See B. S. Murty, *The International Law of Propaganda* (1989); L. John Martin, *International Propaganda—Its Legal and Diplomatic Control* (1958); K. Nordenstreng, ch. 11, n. 5 above, at ch. 6; J. B. Whitton, 'The United Nations Conference on Freedom of Information and the Movement Against International Propaganda', 43 AJIL (1949) pp. 73–87; 'Symposium on the International Control of Propaganda', 31 L. & C.P. pp. 437–634 (1966). See also the following international instruments: Declaration on the Inadmissibility of Intervention in the Domestic Affairs of States and the Protection of Independence and Sovereignty, pr. 2, GA Resn. 2131(XX) (1965); Declaration on Principles of International Law Concerning Friendly Relations and Cooperation among States in Accordance with the Charter of the United Nations, pr. 3 of first principle, GA Resn. 2625 (XXV); Declaration on the Enhancement of the Effectiveness of the Principle of Refraining from the Threat or Use of Force in International Relations, pr. 9; GA Resn. 42/22 (1988), 27 ILM (1988) pp. 167–9; International Convention Concerning the Use of Broadcasting in the Cause of Peace (1936), 186 LNTS 301 (1938), 140 BFSP 262.

2 See John Martin, n. 1 above, chs. 1, 3.

3 See, in particular, John Martin, n. 1 above, chs. 5–7. Reference was made to the 1936 Convention noted in n. 1 above. Propaganda is still a major concern for

States, see article II (10) of the Bilateral Agreement between Afghanistan and Pakistan on Principles of Mutual Relations, 27 ILM (1988) p. 578.

4 Article 20 was adopted by 52 votes to 19 with 12 abstentions, Doc. A/5000, n. 1 above, pr. 49.

5 'The words "shall be prohibited by the law of the State" were chosen in preference to the words "constitutes a crime and shall be punished under the law of the State". It was feared by some that the words "shall be prohibited by the law of the State" might encourage the establishment of governmental censorship. Another opinion was that the article could not be interpreted as suggesting that States should impose censorship. The view was expressed that States parties would be free to enact whatever legislation they deemed appropriate to put the article into effect', Doc. A/2929, n. 1 above, pr. 194. On the general obligation to implement the Covenant see ch. 6 above on article 2.

6 See ch. 7 above.

7 GC 11(19), adopted by the HRC at its 457th meeting (nineteenth session) on 25 July 1983, Doc. A/38/40, pp. 109–10; also in Doc. CCPR/C/21/Add. 2. For the HRC's discussion see SR 429, 447, 448, 450, 451, 454, and 457.

8 GC 6(16), Doc. A/37/40, pp. 93–4, cited in ch. 8, pr. 8.11 above.

9 See ch. 11 above.

10 See pr. 12.17 below.

11 GC 11(19), n. 7 above, pr. 1 (my emphasis). Members of the HRC have consistently stressed the immediacy of the obligation under article 20. The reference to the 'nature' of article 20 would seem to be referring to the specific obligation in article 20 to '[prohibit] by law', see n. 5 above.

12 See e.g. SR 69 pr. 48 (Prado-Vallejo on UK); SR 214 pr. 31 (Koulishev on Senegal); SR 257 pr. 33 (Graefrath on Italy); '. . . he did not fully understand how propaganda for war could be punished under international law. Accession to "international instruments" . . . was insufficient on its own; specific provisions had to be included in the Penal Code', SR 897 pr. 23 (Dimitrijevic on Bolivia). See also the comments of Tarnopolsky at SR 213 pr. 24 concerning 'regionalist propaganda' (on Senegal).

13 'The drafting groups [of the HRC] had been working for two years on the definition of war. At its thirteenth session, he had proposed the following definition: "The term 'war' is not understood in a restrictive sense; it includes not only open conflicts between two or more countries but also any direct or indirect armed intervention in another country for any reason". The present Working Group had in the end preferred not to provide a definition of war because, unless it simply referred the reader to the definition given by the United Nations itself, that task would take the Working Group too far afield', SR 429 pr. 57 (Bouziri). The UN Charter uses the terms 'threat or use of force' rather than 'war'. France has declared that 'the term "war" appearing in article 20, paragraph 1, is to be understood to mean war in contravention of international law and considers, in any case, that French legislation in this matter is adequate', *Human Rights—Status of International Instruments*, p. 35 (1987).

14 See John Martin, n. 1 above, ch. 2.

15 See prs. 12.8 (Tomuschat), and 12.18 below.

16 See n. 13 above (on France) and *Human Rights—Status*, n. 13 above, pp. 28–49. The States concerned are Australia, Belgium, Denmark, Finland, France, Iceland, Luxembourg, Netherlands, New Zealand, Norway, Sweden, UK (and for the Dependent Territories).

17 Doc. CCPR/C/1/Add. 10, p. 4 (1977). See SR 30.

18 SR 30 pr. 14. (I have corrected 'position' to 'provision').

19 SR 30 pr. 17. Note, however, that both of these international documents are only concerned with State obligations rather than individual action.

20 SR 30 pr. 27. The State representative replied that Finland had been able to accept article 20(2) because it had adopted provisions in its Penal Code to comply with the terms of the ICERD and the Convention on the Prevention and Punishment of the Crime of Genocide.

21 SR 30 pr. 39.

22 See ch. 6, pr. 6.3 text to n. 8 above, in particular Shelton at n. 8. See now the decisions of the HRC in *T.K.* v. *France*, Doc. A/45/40, Apx., *M.K.* v. *France*, Doc. A/45/40, Apx. See e.g. the comments of Movchan at SR 30 pr. 38. Cf. the recent decision of the EUCT in *Belilos* v. *Switzerland*, EUCT, Series A, Vol. 132 (1988).

23 SR 322 pr. 73. See also SR 322 pr. 64 (Al Douri). See also the strong criticism of the Australian reservation to article 20(1) at SR 402 pr. 23 (Prado-Vallejo). See Triggs, ch. 6, pr. 6.3, n. 8 above, at p. 298.

24 See n. 16 above.

25 See prs. 12.13–12.26 below.

26 See A. Larson, 'The Present Status of Propaganda in International Law', in Symposium, n. 1 above, pp. 437–51.

27 Doc. CCPR/C/1/Add. 43, Vol. i, pp. 86–7, dealing with the position in Federal Law.

28 SR 206 pr. 32. It is interesting to note that only occasionally have the matters of conscientious objection and pacifist propaganda been raised by HRC members, see e.g. SR 320 pr. 4 (Ermacora on Japan).

29 'During a session of the Committee on the Elimination of Racial Discrimination the existence of a Fascist party in the Netherlands had been found to constitute a violation of the International Convention on the Elimination of Racial Discrimination. Did not a violation of that Convention automatically mean a violation of the Covenant?', SR 321 pr. 26 (Movchan). See also SR 148 pr. 46 (Hanga), 60 (Graefrath on UK). Article 4 ICERD condemns propaganda and organizations based on racial superiority or which attempt to justify or promote racial hatred and discrimination in any form. See T. Meron, *Human Rights Law-Making in the United Nations*, pp. 23–35 (1986).

30 SR 148 pr. 75. The UK has reserved the right not to introduce any further legislation, see *Human Rights—Status*, n. 13 above, p. 48, Cf. the proscription by the UK of organizations under the Prevention of Terrorism (Temporary Provisions) Act 1989. See also the UK's stated understanding of article 4 ICERD, n. 29 above, in *Human Rights—Status*, ibid., pp. 116–17.

31 Cf. Article 4 ICERD, n. 29 above.

32 Doc. CCPR/C/1/Add. 22.

33 SR 109 pr. 25. Recent reports suggest that such propaganda continues.

34 See SR 112 pr. 34.

35 Doc. CCPR/C/1/Add. 18.

36 SR 94 pr. 4. The 'provision' referred to is article 26 of the Basic Law of the FRG.

37 SR 96.

38 See ch. 2, pr. 2.7 above.

39 See ch. 2, pr. 2.6, n. 145 above, and ch. 3, pr. 3.34 above.

40 See SR 429 pr. 36.

41 SR 429 pr. 36, draft pr. 3.

42 SR 447 pr. 3 (Opsahl). The relevant provision is article 53 VCLT (1969).

43 SR 447 pr. 3 (Opsahl), and pr. 13 (Cooray).

44 SR 448 pr. 19 (Ermacora).

45 Ibid., pr. 10 (Vincent-Evans).

46 Ibid., pr. 19 (Dimitrijevic).

47 Ibid., pr. 22 (Prado-Vallejo).

48 Ibid. See pr. 12.2, text to n. 5 above, and pr. 12.4 above.

49 SR 448 pr. 17 (Hanga).

50 Ibid., pr. 24 (Graefrath).

51 Ibid., pr. 25 (Bouziri).

52 GC 11(19), n. 7 above, pr. 1. See pr. 12.4 above for the full text.

53 SR 429 pr. 36, draft pr. 2.

54 SR 447 pr. 2, draft pr. 2. This second draft text is produced here to facilitate understanding of the HRC's discussions.

55 SR 429 pr. 49 (Errera); SR 321 pr. 50 (Errera). Partsch, ch. 11 n. 1 above, suggests that, 'a State may do under article 20 only what is strictly required by that article and is also compatible with article 19(3)', p. 230.

56 SR 448 pr. 52 (Cooray).

57 SR 450 pr. 10 (Bouziri).

58 See pr. 12.6 above (on Finland), pr. 12.10 above (on UK) and n. 16 above.

59 GC 11(19), n. 7 above, pr. 2.

60 SR 429 pr. 36, draft pr. 2.

61 The HRC had accepted the view of Mr Tarnopolsky that both articles 20(1) and 20(2) were intended to cover domestic and international cases, see SR 429 pr. 41, SR 447 pr. 42, SR 447 pr. 49.

62 SR 447 pr. 9 (Dimitrijevic).

63 Ibid., pr. 14 (Cooray).

64 Ibid., pr. 21 (Vincent-Evans).

65 Ibid., pr. 34 (Tomuschat).

66 SR 450 pr. 38 (Movchan); and see SR 447 pr. 49 (Tarnopolsky).

67 SR 447 pr. 16 (Mavrommatis).

68 See n. 1 above. The 1970 Declaration states that, 'A war of aggression constitutes a crime against the peace for which there is responsibility under international law' (paragraph 2 of principle 1). A similar provision appears in the UN Definition of Aggression, n. 69 below.

69 GA Resn. 3314 (XXIX) of 14 Nov. 1974.

70 SR 450 prs. 37, 40 (Bouziri), 41 (Dimitrijevic).

71 GC 11(19), n. 7 above, pr. 2. Just before this sentence was adopted Mr Tomuschat, 'observed that the concept of breach of the peace had never been defined in the United Nations system. In so far, however, as it was to be understood as the result of an act of aggression, he could endorse the proposed text, but it should not extend to all forms of interference covered by the non-intervention provisions', SR 450 pr. 57. Note also pr. 2 of the Declaration on the Inadmissibility of Intervention, n. 1 above, and article 23(2) AFR. The 1988 GA Resolution, n. 1 above, states that, 'In accordance with the purposes and principles of the United Nations, States have the duty to refrain from propaganda for wars of aggression', pr. 9.

72 SR 429 pr. 36, draft pr. 2.

73 SR 447 pr. 5.

74 Ibid., pr. 20. Mr Errera also expressly agreed with Sir Vincent-Evans, ibid., pr. 41.

75 Ibid., pr. 35. See also *Military and Paramilitary Activities in and Against Nicaragua (Nicaragua v. United States)*, Merits, ICJ Reports, 1986, p. 14 at pr. 290.

76 SR 448 prs. 8–9 (Tarnopolsky).

77 SR 450 pr. 59. Sir Vincent-Evans referred to the situation in the Lebanon to 'show that a people could not be encouraged to resort to violence and engage in terrorist activities in order to exercise its right to self-determination and independence'.

78 SR 451 pr. 2.

79 On self-determination under article 1 of the Covenant see ch. 5 above.

80 SR 451 pr. 5 (Prado-Vallejo).

81 Ibid., pr. 21 (Prado-Vallejo).

82 Ibid., pr. 20 (Al Douri).

83 Ibid., prs. 11–12.

84 See ch. 5 above.

85 SR 451, prs. 17–18. Mr Tomsuchat was prepared to accept this interpretation of the text, ibid., pr. 22, but Sir Vincent-Evans, 'could not share the view that the sentence should be adopted on the basis of an interpretation of its meaning expressed in the course of the meeting. General Comments were formulated for the benefit of those who were not members of the Committee and it was therefore essential to clarify the text', ibid., pr. 25.

86 Ibid., pr. 36.

87 Ibid., pr. 39 (Aguilar).

88 SR 454 pr. 12.

89 Ibid., pr. 17.

90 See pr. 12.25 below.

91 See SR 451 pr. 46 (Vincent-Evans), SR 454 prs. 38 (Vincent-Evans), 39 (Bouziri).

92 SR 451 pr. 49 (Hanga).

93 Ibid., pr. 52 (Bouziri).

94 SR 454 pr. 43 (Aguilar). See also SR 454 pr. 58 (Movchan).

95 SR 457 pr. 1. Both the 1970 Declaration and the 1974 Resolution on Aggression, n. 1 above, also confirm the supremacy of the UN Charter.

96 GC 11(19), n. 7 above, pr. 2. See also the last two paragraphs of the 1988 GA Resolution in n. 1 above.

97 See ch. 5, pr. 5.19 above.

98 Ibid.

99 SR 451 prs. 70, 76.

100 Ibid., pr. 85.

101 'Mr. Errera pointed out that in most countries if conduct was prohibited by law those engaging in such conduct were normally liable to sanctions. The latter might take the form of a fine or the obligation to recompense the victim', SR 451 pr. 65.

102 SR 451 pr. 71. On imperfect laws see *Albert* v. *Lavin* [1982] AC 546 (HL).

103 Doc. A/38/40, p. 231.

104 Ibid., pr. 2.1.

105 Ibid., pr. 1.

106 In its objections to the admissibility of the communication the State party noted the possible relevance of article 17 of the Covenant, ibid., pr. 6.3. See the General Comment on article 17, Doc. A/43/40, p. 181, pr. 8; also in Doc. CCPR/C/21/Add. 6.

107 Doc. A/38/40, p. 231, pr. 6.2.

108 Ibid., pr. 8 at (*b*). On article 3 of the OP see ch. 4, prs. 4.44–4.86 above. On the subsequent proceedings in Canada see *Re Taylor et al. and Canadian Human Rights Commission et al.* 37 DLR (4th) 577 (1987): s. 13(1) of the Canadian Human Rights Act a reasonable limit on the freedom of expression guaranteed in section 2(*b*) of the Canadian Charter of Human Rights and Freedoms.

109 See pr. 12.17 above. See also pr. 12.9 above on war propaganda (Canada).

110 Doc. A/38/40, p. 231, pr. 8 at (*c*).

111 Ibid.

112 See ch. 3 above.

113 See ch. 4 above.

114 See ch. 2, pr. 2.7 above.

115 See pr. 12.4 above.

116 See pr. 12.17 above. That compatibility is also evident in the HRC's only decision on article 20 under the OP, see prs. 12.27–12.31 above.

117 See pr. 12.18 above.

118 Ibid.

119 See pr. 12.26 above.

120 See prs. 12.5, 12.8, and 12.18 above.

121 See prs. 12.19–12.25 above.

122 See ch. 5 above.

13

Appraisal and Prospectus

13.1 Thirteen years is too short a period in which to fully evaluate the activities of the HRC under the Covenant. It is long enough, however, to permit an interim evaluation of the effectiveness of the HRC's work. On the basis of that evaluation it is possible to offer some general observations and assess the prospects for the work of the HRC. This assessment must be read in conjunction with the comments and appraisals contained in the foregoing chapters.

13.2 In chapter 1 we traced the development of the International Bill of Rights from the vision of its role in a new post-war world order through the reality of the confrontations of the Cold War.[1] The long gestation period permitted a more universal input in the international Covenants as the community of States expanded in the era of decolonization. In appraising the significance of the Covenant it was submitted that the signally important feature of the Covenant is that it is a universal instrument which contains binding legal obligations for the States parties to it.[2] Further significant features of the Covenant to which attention was drawn are that it clearly protects aliens and stateless persons as well as nationals;[3] that some of its provisions may reflect, or contribute significantly to the development of, customary international law;[4] the use of the Covenant in domestic law;[5] its adoption as a basic standard of international human rights by international, regional, and national institutions; and its role as a stimulus or model for new international instruments.[6] In the long term this last feature may prove to be the most enduring achievement and the Covenant (together with the Covenant on economic, social, and cultural rights) may come to replace the Universal Declaration of Human Rights as *the* 'common standard of achievement for all peoples and all nations'.[7]

13.3 The Human Rights Committee had survived the drafting process to become the central international implementation body for the Covenant.[8] In chapter 2 we examined its basic institutional characteristics. It was submitted that its independent nature was of fundamental importance and that in practice members of the HRC have appeared to operate as independent experts.[9] Working relations between members are as good, if not better, in 1990, as they have ever been. The HRC has managed to establish itself as an impartial and highly respected human rights organ, despite a dearth of publicity, and developed a constructive consensus practice.[10] Attention was also drawn to the increasingly important role of the Secretariat in the work of the HRC,[11] and the strong administrative and financial links between the HRC and the United Nations.[12] It was further submitted that the nature of the HRC alters in accordance with its exercise of the various functions and roles it performs or could perform.[13]

13.4 Chapter 3 examined the practices and procedures under the reporting system. Attention was drawn to its limitations and the difficulties encountered. These included inadequate guidelines for the preparation of reports;[14] inadequate and incomplete reports which do not deal with the realities of the human rights situation in the States concerned;[15] the absence of procedures to determine the adequacy of the reports submitted; delays in the submission of State reports;[16] the absence of agreement on procedures for requesting reports under article 40(1)(*b*) 'whenever the Committee so requests';[17] the absence of any formal role for specialized agencies or non-governmental organizations in the reporting procedure;[18] the duplication of questions and the pressures placed on State representatives;[19] the absence of any clear 'Committee view' of the human rights performance in a particular State, although this has improved with the emergence of the 'general observations' by members at the end of the consideration of State reports as a more distinct aspect of the procedure;[20] the disagreement within the HRC on the interpretation of the HRC's jurisdiction under article 40 which has resulted in no country specific reports or country specific general comments;[21] and the limited roles played by ECOSOC,[22] and the General Assembly.[23]

13.5 However, it was also possible to point to some successes. These include the establishment of a procedure applicable to 92 States (as of 27 July 1990) from all geographical regions of the world, the 'constructive dialogue' with each State party with regard to the practical and effective implementation of the Covenant,[24] the maintaining of consensus in the application of those procedures,[25] the establishment of a realistic five-year reporting period,[26] the establishment of a possible precedent for action on article 40(1)(*b*) in the request for specific information from El Salvador,[27] the establishment of a series of gradual responses aimed at securing the submission of reports,[28] that most of the State reports are eventually submitted,[29] the consistent use by initially a substantial number and eventually all members of the HRC of information outside that contained in the State reports,[30] that the HRC has eventually obtained the presence of a State representative (and usually a small number of high quality) from every State party,[31] the development of a more rationalized and efficient procedure for the consideration of second periodic reports and sensible procedures for the consideration of third periodic reports beginning in October 1989,[32] and the adoption of nineteen general comments (as of 27 July 1990) of varying quality and usefulness.[33] On balance it was submitted that, 'the reporting procedure has

been developed into a much more useful procedure of international implementation (in the broad sense) than could confidently have been predicted
when the Covenant was adopted in 1966'.[34] That appraisal is given further
support in chapters 5–12 which examined the approach of the HRC to
selected articles of the Covenant.[35]

13.6 Overall, despite its acknowledged limitations, the reporting system
presents a serious and formidable challenge to States parties and many of
them have responded positively. No State or geographical region has been
excepted from a detailed critique and appraisal and it is evident from the
summary records that all States have been found wanting in various degrees.
In effect the procedure obliges States systematically and periodically to
appraise and explain their human rights performance. Such appraisal and
examination can only be healthy even for States with an acknowledged
record of respect for human rights. Greater involvement of national and
international non-governmental organizations is needed along with
increased publicity for the content of the periodic reports and of their
consideration by the HRC.

13.7 Chapter 4 examined the practices and procedures of the HRC under
the Optional Protocol. It was submitted that the OP represents another
important advance in terms of the status of the individual in international law,
particularly in the light of the ratification of the OP by an Eastern bloc State
(Hungary in 1988).[36] Attention was drawn to some of the advantageous
characteristics of the OP procedure. These include the independent nature of
the HRC, the secure treaty basis of the OP, the defined legal norms
established by the Covenant, the avoidance of 'pre-judging' resolutions,
political selectivity, and alleged double standards.[37] Other sections analysed
the practices and procedures developed by the HRC and many aspects of its
work were commented upon favourably.[38] The most critical internal
problem for the OP procedure is that the system of consensus is under great
strain. A number of the more recent views and decisions have occasioned
substantial splits within the HRC even though this is not evident from the
form in which the views appear. Recent procedural amendments should
enable the HRC to keep pace with the increase in communications submitted
to it. It was noted that compliance with the HRC's views has been disappointing although some States have shown both a willingness to co-operate with
the HRC and give effect to its views.[39] The most disappointing feature of the
practice under the OP had perhaps been the limited number of communications but there has been a substantial increase in recent years.[40] None the less,
although other procedures of international investigation and settlement
undoubtedly siphon off a substantial number of potential communications
the Optional Protocol procedure is not widely known to national lawyers and
advisers in the States parties. There is clearly still a need for much better and
wider publicity for the Optional Protocol procedure.

13.8 In the appraisal it was submitted that the HRC have fashioned a practicable and functional procedure that has the potential to develop into an effective counterpart on the universal level to the established regional systems.[41] It was also submitted that a long term view must be taken and in that perspective it is important to keep the Protocol alive and functioning.[42]

13.9 Chapters 5–12 reviewed the work of the HRC by examining its approach to selected rights under the reporting and individual communications systems respectively. Each of those chapters contains specific comments and criticisms on the various approaches taken and issues dealt with by the HRC and concludes with a general appraisal. However, it is useful to highlight some of the key features noted and some of the principal submissions made.

13.10 Chapter 5 (article 1—Self-Determination): although the inclusion of article 1 in the Covenant was controversial[43] the HRC recognized that self-determination is an 'essential condition for the effective guarantee and observance of individual rights and for the promotion and strengthening of those rights'.[44] In their questions and comments HRC members have been very direct and forceful even in the context of national sensitivities, e.g. over secession,[45] or major current international disputes.[46] However, the General Comment on article 1 was criticized as being vague and uninformative.[47]

13.11 Chapter 6 (article 2—General Obligation): the HRC clearly established that it was for each State party to determine exactly how it implemented the terms of the Covenant,[48] that the primary focus of its attention was on the 'national implementation' of the provisions of the Covenant,[49] and that the obligation to implement was essentially an immediate one although the HRC has taken a realistic approach and been sympathetic to States with genuine difficulties in implementing the provisions of the Covenant.[50] The General Comments on article 2 and on non-discrimination clearly state that the Covenant places positive obligations on States parties that call for 'specific activities' and 'affirmative action'.[51] The statement of positive obligations is also repeated in a number of the General Comments adopted by the HRC.[52] The HRC also stressed the fundamental importance of 'effective remedies' for alleged victims of violations of the Covenant,[53] a theme echoed in the subsequent chapters,[54] and the importance of publicizing the terms of the Covenant.[55]

13.12 Chapter 7 (article 4—Derogation Provision): it was observed that the HRC has refused simply to accept the sovereign determinations of States parties in the context of public emergencies and has assumed some degree of international supervision over compliance with the requirements of article 4 with the onus of proof being placed heavily on the derogating State.[56] The importance attached by the HRC to the notification requirements in article 4(3) eventually drew more response from the States parties concerned.[57] Chapter 7 was also used to present a review of the workings of the reporting procedure through a country specific analysis on the United Kingdom.[58] The absence of a decision by the HRC on its jurisdiction under article 40(1)(*b*) to request a report is particularly acute in the derogation context.[59]

13.13 Chapter 8 (article 6—The Right to Life): the HRC stated that the right to life is the 'supreme right'.[60] A much wider interpretation has been given to the right to life than might have been expected including such matters as infant mortality, malnutrition, and public health schemes.[61] The importance attached by the HRC to the right to life is also attested to by the fact that it has been the subject of two general comments. The second of those aroused controversy with its statement that, 'the production, testing, possession, deployment and use of nuclear weapons should be prohibited as crimes against humanity'.[62] Chapter 8 also served as an excellent example of the way in which decisions and views under the Optional Protocol can offer authoritative interpretations of the terms of the Covenant.[63]

13.14 Chapter 9 (article 7 and 10(1)—Ill Treatment, Deprivation of Liberty): The HRC stated that it was of vital importance to establishing some 'domestic machinery of control' through procedural safeguards and stressed the need for effective remedies.[64] The chapter also served to illustrate the deficiencies in the presentation of the decisions and views of the HRC under the Optional Protocol.[65] For the future it will be interesting to watch the development of the relationship between the work of the HRC in this area and that of the institutions established under the new regional and universal conventions on torture and other ill-treatment, in particular the work of the new United Nations Committee against Torture.[66]

13.15 Chapter 10 (article 14—Fair Trial): the extensive coverage of article 14 attracted a great deal of attention from HRC members and a lengthy General Comment. Again that chapter serves as an excellent illustration of the searching dissection and analysis under the reporting procedure of the laws and practices of States parties and how the reporting and communications procedures can interact and feed off each other.[67] Similarly, it illustrates how key interpretations in views under the OP, for example, on the expression 'suit at law', will inevitably have implications for the reporting procedure.[68]

13.16 Chapter 11 (article 19—Freedom of Opinion and Expression): we noted the concern expressed at specific ideological conceptions of freedom of expression,[69] and the introduction, and subsequent disappearance, of the doctrine of the 'margin of discretion' which has played an important role in the jurisprudence under the European Convention on Human Rights.[70] It was submitted that the HRC's General Comment on article 19 was somewhat disappointing.[71]

13.17 Chapter 12 (article 20—War Propaganda, Advocacy of National, Racial, or Religious Hatred): it was observed that the inclusion of article 20 was controversial and it has been the subject of a number of reservations.[72] The statement of the HRC on the compatibility of articles 19 and 20 may go someway to relieving the fears of the States making such reservations.[73] In chapter 12 we also took the opportunity to examine the development of a General Comment. This served to demonstrate the importance attached by the HRC to its General Comments and the compromises and accommodations necessary to reach a consensus text.[74] The General Comment produced was accorded a mixed reception.[75]

13.18 Having evaluated and appraised the work of the HRC it is appropriate to make some general recommendations for its future work. First and foremost, more States should ratify or accede to the Covenant and the Protocol. The rate of new States parties has substantially declined. In particular strong pressure should be exerted on the United States and China to become parties.[76] States parties should improve the publicity given to the Covenant and the Protocol and their national reports under the Covenant. They should also provide a full account of the examination of their reports by the HRC.[77] When States reports are being considered the presence of ministers or senior representatives from the key domestic departments concerned would substantially assist the proper examination of State reports and practice. Similarly national and international non-governmental organizations, education institutions, and specific interest bodies have an important role to play in publicizing the terms and procedures of the Covenant and the Protocol.[78] The General Comments adopted by the HRC have contained some useful elements. The HRC must continue to develop them so as to produce comments that are practically relevant and comprehensible to national administrators, executives, and other authorities. Recent work by non-governmental bodies has produced excellent texts on various aspects of the HRC's work, for example, the Siracusa Principles.[79] Those texts provide a precedent for how the General Comments could be developed.

13.19 Discussion of General Comments inevitably raises the controversy over whether the HRC has jurisdiction under article 40(4) to issue General Comments addressed to specific countries and, in turn, specific reports on the human rights performance of States parties. It is undoubtedly the case that such country specific comments and reports would be more potent weapons in securing the implementation of the Covenant. However, there is a strong argument that the HRC was sensible in its early years to move cautiously and develop and refine its procedures. Such an approach has allowed it to gain the confidence and respect of States parties. Country specific comments and reports which alienated the States parties, divided the HRC and politicized its proceedings would have achieved little in the long term. So, for the present, the balance of the case is probably in favour of the approach taken to date but it must be accompanied by increased publicity and far greater non-governmental involvement at the national and international level. It should also be borne in mind that the HRC have not closed the door on country specific comments and reports.[80] Such a development could prove possible if the HRC ultimately found that even with continued development and refinement its present procedures and General Comments were not proving effective.[81] More generally there is a strong case for rationalization of the international reporting obligations of States.[82] In any such rationalization the positive achievements of the HRC's work should not be undermined,[83] provision should be made for more substantial remuneration for the HRC members,[84] and the United Nations Human Rights Secretariat must be properly funded to provide an effective and more wide-ranging support service.[85]

13.20 It is very difficult to provide positive evidence that the existence of the Covenant and the work of the HRC is having any concrete and positive effect on the human rights position in the States parties. However, many of the State representatives that have appeared before the HRC have stated that the Covenant and the work of the HRC have played an important role at the national level. It would be immensely helpful if the HRC could catalogue and reproduce those claims together with any more specific evidence of whole-sale or partial national reviews of the implementation of the Covenant and of account being taken of the Covenant and the HRC, for example, in legislative assemblies, executive decision making, judicial or administrative decisions.[86]

13.21 In the words of Louis Henkin, 'Human rights is the idea of our time'.[87] From a different perspective Richard Ulman has commented that, 'No time is ever really good for human rights . . . But some times are worse than others'.[88] Human rights are being subjected to increasingly sophisticated analysis from various disciplines including lawyers,[89] philosophers,[90] political scientists and international relations experts,[91] and social scientists concerned with evaluating human rights performance.[92] The function of the HRC has been much less esoteric but of no less importance. The HRC was charged with giving life to the structures and mechanisms of the Covenant and the Protocol and meaning to its language. The primary purposes of this work have been to determine and evaluate the nature of the HRC and assess its contribution to the development of the 'idea of our time' and to bringing closer a time of improved respect for human rights.[93] It is submitted that, on the basis of the evidence presented in the foregoing chapters, its contribution has been substantial, positive, and constructive.[94] The improved climate of international relations in the light of the political revolutions in Eastern Europe in 1989–90, and the more general return of democratically elected governments in the 1980's, will hopefully permit that contribution to be sustained and enhanced.[95]

NOTES

1 See ch. 1, prs. 1.1–1.15 above.
2 Ibid., pr. 1.34.
3 Ibid., pr. 1.35.
4 Ibid., pr. 1.36.
5 Ibid., pr. 1.37.
6 Ibid., pr. 1.38. See also OP2 in Apx. IV below.
7 Preamble to the Universal Declaration of Human Rights (1948).
8 See ch. 1, pr. 1.12.
9 See ch. 2, prs. 2.2–2.4, 2.18–2.19 above.
10 See ch. 2, prs. 2.7–2.8 and ch. 3, pr. 3.40 above. It was also noted that the HRC has provided a model for the new United Nations Committee on Economic, Social, and Cultural Rights on which see ch. 2, n. 38 above.
11 See ch. 2, prs. 2.16–2.17 above.
12 Ibid., prs. 2.18–2.19.
13 Ibid., pr. 2.22.
14 Ibid.
15 See ch. 3, prs. 3.4, 3.11 above.
16 See ch. 3, prs. 3.7, 3.9, 3.10.
17 See ch. 3, prs. 3.8, 3.8.1 above.
18 See ch. 3, prs. 3.12–3.18.
19 See ch. 3, pr. 3.23 above.
20 Ibid., pr. 3.24. See the discussion in SR 950.
21 Ibid., prs. 3.29–38 above. See the discussion in SR 950.
22 Ibid., pr. 3.39.
23 Ibid., pr. 3.40.
24 See ch. 3, prs. 3.3, 3.19–3.21 above.
25 See ch. 2, pr. 2.7 on consensus and ch. 3, pr. 3.5 on the HRC's 'Consensus Statement'.
26 See ch. 3, prs. 3.6, 3.46 above.
27 See ch. 3, prs. 3.8.1, 3.47 above.
28 See ch. 3, prs. 3.9, 3.10 above.
29 Ibid.
30 See ch. 3, prs. 3.17–3.18 above.
31 See ch. 3, prs. 3.19, 3.22.
32 Ibid., prs. 3.25–3.28 above.
33 Ibid., pr. 3.35. The specific terms of most of the general comments are analysed in chs. 3–12 above.
34 Ch. 3, pr. 3.52 above.
35 See also prs. 13.9–13.17 below.
36 See ch. 4, pr. 4.37 above.
37 Ibid., pr. 4.120.
38 Ibid., prs. 4.9–4.118.
39 Ibid., prs. 4.127–4.133. The appointment of a Special Rapporteur for 'Follow-Up

on Views' in July 1990 will hopefully improve compliance with the HRC's views.

40 See ch. 4, pr. 4.8. 50 States parties (as of 27 July 1990) is a substantial number of participating states.

41 Ibid., pr. 4.126.

42 Ibid., pr. 4.133.

43 See ch. 1, prs. 1.22–1.24 and ch. 5, pr. 5.2 above.

44 See ch. 5, prs. 5.3, 5.5 above.

45 Ibid., prs. 5.6–5.7 above.

46 Ibid., pr. 5.15 above.

47 Ibid., pr. 5.24 above.

48 See ch. 6, pr. 6.3 above.

49 Ibid., pr. 6.9 above.

50 Ibid., pr. 6.11 above.

51 Ibid., pr. 6.12 above.

52 See e.g. ch. 8, prs. 8.3–8.4 above on article 6.

53 See ch. 6, prs. 6.21–6.22 above.

54 See e.g. text to n. 65 below (on article 7).

55 See ch. 6, pr. 6.23 above.

56 See in particular ch. 7, prs. 7.35–7.43 above.

57 Ibid., prs. 7.19–7.22 above.

58 Ibid., prs. 7.23–7.34 above.

59 See ch. 3, prs. 3.8–3.8.1 and ch. 7, pr. 7.48 above.

60 See ch. 8, pr. 8.2 above.

61 Ibid., prs. 8.3–8.4, 8.27–8.28 above.

62 Ibid., pr. 8.12 above.

63 Ibid., prs. 8.14–8.26 above.

64 See ch. 9, prs. 9.4–9.4.1 above.

65 Ibid., prs. 9.12–9.12.3 above.

66 Ibid., prs. 9.30–9.31 above. For the first decisions of the CAT on individual communications see *O.R., M.M. and M.S.* v. *Argentina*, CAT/C/3/D/1, 2, and 3/1988.

67 See ch. 10, prs. 10.58–10.60 above.

68 Ibid., prs. 10.26–10.26.1 above.

69 See ch. 11, pr. 11.6.1 above.

70 Ibid., prs. 11.19–11.19.2 above.

71 Ibid., pr. 11.22 above.

72 See ch. 12, prs. 12.2, 12.6 above.

73 Ibid., prs. 12.6–12.8 above.

74 Ibid., prs. 12.13–12.26 above.

75 Ibid., prs. 12.33–12.34 above.

76 On the US position see ch. 1, pr. 1.25 above. It is understood that the question of ratification of the Covenant has the lowest level of priority in the United States. It is known that Chinese representatives have observed the work of the HRC. See Chan and Lau, ch. 1 n. 257 above.

77 See Tomuschat, ch. 6, n. 1 above (1984–5), p. 60.

78 When the reports of Sri Lanka were being considered by the HRC a collection of artwork by Sri Lankan schoolchildren on the theme of human rights was displayed outside the HRC's meeting room. A number of HRC members commended such educational initiatives by States.

79 See ch. 7, n. 1 above (1985).

80 See ch. 3, prs. 3.29–3.38 above.

81 Cf. the fascinating development of the procedures by the Human Rights Commission for considering complaints of human rights violations, see H. Tolley, *UN Commission on Human Rights*, chs. 2–4 (1987). The HRCion continues to evolve as an institution, see 44 Rev. ICJ (1990) pp. 16–31.

82 See the conclusions and recommendations in 'Reporting Obligations of States Parties to the U.N. Human Rights Instruments—Note by the Secretary-General', Doc. A/44/98 (3 Feb. 1989). See also Doc. A/44/668.

83 See generally L. Sohn, 'Human Rights: Their Implementation and Supervision by the United Nations', in T. Meron (ed.), *Human Rights in International Law—Legal and Policy Issues*, pp. 369–70 (1984).

84 See ch. 2, pr. 2.2 above.

85 On the HRC and the Secretariat see ch. 2, prs. 2.16–2.17 above. The failure of the UN to renew the contract of Mr Van Boven as Director of the then Human Rights Division and the cancellation of sessions of human rights organs suggests that human rights are still not accorded the necessary priority within the United Nations system. The commitment of the individual members of the Secretariat is evident to any observer but resources are not made available to match that commitment. The Secretariat for the reporting procedure is only the Secretary of the Committee with limited secretarial assistance. The Secretariat for the OP procedure is permanently understaffed. The UN Secretariat faces substantial staffing cuts unless the financial position of the UN improves. Less than 1% of the UN's regular budget is spent on its human rights programmes.

86 For example the Iraqi State representative stated that the Covenant was taken into account in rejecting a draft bill and that numerous cases could be noted where provisions of Covenant had been invoked before Iraqi courts, SR 744 pr. 37. In his concluding comments the UK state representative stated that, 'he had noted the suggestion that his Government might attempt a detailed analysis of the Covenant and how the various articles were being implemented in law and practice in the United Kingdom. Such a study had in fact been undertaken at the time the Covenant had been signed. Since then circumstances had changed, as also had ideas regarding the interpretation of the Covenant itself. The time might therefore have arrived to make a further study', SR 598 pr. 35.

87 L. Henkin, 'Introduction', to L. Henkin (ed.), *The International Bill of Rights—The Covenant on Civil and Political Rights*, p. 1 (1981).

88 R. H. Ulman, 'Introduction: Human Rights—Toward International Action', in J. Dominguez *et al.*, *Enhancing Global Human Rights*, p. 1 (1979).

89 See P. Sieghart, *The International Law of Human Rights* (1983); M. McDougal, H. Lasswell, and L. C. Chen, *Human Rights and World Public Order* (1980).

90 For recent contributions see J. Donnelly, *The Concept of Human Rights* (1985); J. W. Nickel, *Making Sense of Human Rights* (1987).

91 For notable recent contributions see H. Shue, *Basic Rights: Subsistence, Affluence and United States Foreign Policy* (1980); R. J. Vincent, *Human Rights and International Relations* (1987).

92 See J. Dominguez *et al.*, n. 88 above; McDougal, Lasswell, and Chen, n. 89 above; Symposium, 'Statistical Issues in the Field of Human Rights', 8 HRQ (1986) pp. 551–699; J. Donnelly and R. E. Howard (eds.), *International Handbook of Human Rights* (1987); D. L. Cingranelli (ed.), *Human Rights: Measurement and Theory* (1988).

93 See notes 87–8 above.

94 For similarly positive assessments of the HRC see Brar, ch. 3, n. 1 above, 229–32; Ahmed, ch. 4, n. 1 above, pp. 204–8; Fischer, ch. 3, n. 1 above (1982), p. 153; Nowak, ch. 3, n. 1 above (1980), pp. 169–70; Jhabvala, ch. 3, n. 1 above (1984), pp. 104–6.

95 See the discussion in SR 1003. Cf. D. McGoldrick, 'Human Rights Developments in the Helsinki Process', 39 ICLQ (1990) pp. 923–40.

Appendix I
The International Covenant on Civil and Political Rights

Preamble

THE STATES PARTIES TO THE PRESENT COVENANT,

Considering that, in accordance with the principles proclaimed in the Charter of the United Nations, recognition of the inherent dignity and of the equal and inalienable rights of all members of the human family is the foundation of freedom, justice and peace in the world,

Recognizing that these rights derive from the inherent dignity of the human person,

Recognizing that, in accordance with the Universal Declaration of Human Rights, the ideal of free human beings enjoying civil and political freedom and freedom from fear and want can only be achieved if conditions are created whereby everyone may enjoy his civil and political rights, as well as his economic, social and cultural rights,

Considering the obligation of States under the Charter of the United Nations to promote universal respect for, and observance of, human rights and freedoms,

Realizing that the individual, having duties to other individuals and to the community to which he belongs, is under a responsibility to strive for the promotion and observance of the rights recognized in the present Covenant,

Agree upon the following articles:

PART I.

Article 1.

1. All peoples have the right of self-determination. By virtue of that right they freely determine their political status and freely pursue their economic, social and cultural development.

2. All peoples may, for their own ends, freely dispose of their natural wealth and resources without prejudice to any obligations arising out of international economic co-operation, based upon the principle of mutual benefit, and international law. In no case may a people be deprived of its own means of subsistence.

3. The States Parties to the present Covenant, including those having responsibility for the administration of Non-Self-Governing and Trust Territories, shall promote the realization of the right of self-determination, and shall respect that right, in conformity with the provisions of the Charter of the United Nations.

PART II.

Article 2.

1. Each State Party to the present Covenant undertakes to respect and to ensure to all individuals within its territory and subject to its jurisdiction the rights recognized in the present Covenant, without distinction of any kind, such as race, colour, sex, language, religion, political or other opinion, national or social origin, property, birth or other status.

2. Where not already provided for by existing legislative or other measures, each State party to the present Covenant undertakes to take the necessary steps, in accordance with its constitutional processes and with the provisions of the present Covenant, to adopt such legislative or other measures as may be necessary to give effect to the rights recognized in the present Covenant.

3. Each State party to the present Covenant undertakes:

(a) To ensure that any person whose rights or freedoms as herein recognized are violated shall have an effective remedy, notwithstanding that the violation has been committed by persons acting in an official capacity;

(b) To ensure that any person claiming such a remedy shall have his right thereto determined by competent judicial, administrative or legislative authorities, or by any other competent authority provided for by the legal system of the State, and to develop the possibilities of judicial remedy;

(c) To ensure that the competent authorities shall enforce such remedies when granted.

Article 3.

The States Parties to the present Covenant undertake to ensure the equal right of men and women to the enjoyment of all civil and political rights set forth in the present Covenant.

Article 4.

1. In time of public emergency which threatens the life of the nation and the existence of which is officially proclaimed, the States Parties to the present Covenant may take measures derogating from their obligations under the present Covenant to the extent strictly required by the exigencies of the situation, provided that such measures are not inconsistent with their other obligations under international law and do not involve discrimination solely on the ground of race, colour, sex, language, religion or social origin.

2. No derogation from articles 6, 7, 8 (paragraphs 1 and 2), 11, 15, 16 and 18 may be made under this provision.

3. Any State Party to the present Covenant availing itself of the right to derogation shall immediately inform the other States Parties to the present Covenant, through the intermediary of the Secretary-General of the United Nations, of the provisions from which it has derogated and of the reasons by which it was actuated. A further communication shall be made, through the same intermediary, on the date on which it terminates such derogation.

Article 5.

1. Nothing in the present Covenant may be interpreted as implying for any State, group or person any right to engage in any activity or perform any act aimed at the destruction of any of the rights and freedoms recognized herein or at their limitation to a greater extent than is provided for in the present Covenant.

2. There shall be no restriction upon or derogation from any of the fundamental rights recognized or existing in any State Party to the present Covenant pursuant to law, conventions, regulations or custom on the pretext that the present Covenant does not recognize such rights or that it recognizes them to a lesser extent.

PART III.

Article 6.

1. Every human being has the inherent right to life. This right shall be protected by law. No one shall be arbitrarily deprived of his life.

2. In countries which have not abolished the death penalty, sentence of death may only be imposed for the most serious crimes in accordance with the law in force at the time of the commission of the crime and not contrary to the provisions of the present Covenant and to the Convention on the Prevention and Punishment of the Crime of Genocide. This penalty can only be carried out pursuant to a final judgement rendered by a competent court.

3. When deprivation of life constitutes the crime of genocide, it is understood that nothing in this article shall authorize any State Party to the present Covenant to derogate in any way from any obligation assumed under the provisions of the Convention on the Prevention and Punishment of the Crime of Genocide.

4. Anyone sentenced to death shall have the right to seek pardon or commutation of the sentence. Amnesty, pardon or commutation of the sentence of death may be granted in all cases.

5. Sentence of death shall not be imposed for crimes committed by persons below eighteen years of age and shall not be carried out on pregnant women.

6. Nothing in this article shall be invoked to delay or to prevent the abolition of capital punishment by any State Party to the present Covenant.

Article 7.

No one shall be subjected to torture or to cruel, inhuman or degrading treatment or punishment. In particular, no one shall be subjected without his free consent to medical or scientific experimentation.

Article 8.

1. No one shall be held in slavery; slavery and the slave trade in all their forms shall be prohibited.

2. No one shall be held in servitude.

3. (a) No one shall be required to perform forced or compulsory labour;

(b) Paragraph 3 (a) shall not be held to preclude, in countries where imprisonment with hard labour may be imposed as a punishment for a crime, the performance of hard labour in pursuance of a sentence to such punishment by a competent court;

(c) For the purpose of this paragraph the term 'forced or compulsory labour' shall not include:

(i) Any work or service, not referred to in sub-paragraph (b), normally required of a person who is under detention in consequence of a lawful order of a court, or of a person during conditional release from such detention;

(ii) Any service of a military character and, in countries where conscientious objection is recognized, any national service required by law of conscientious objectors;

(iii) Any service exacted in cases of emergency or calamity threatening the life or well-being of the community;

(iv) Any work or service which forms part of normal civic obligations.

Article 9.

1. Everyone has the right to liberty and security of person. No one shall be subjected to arbitrary arrest or detention. No one shall be deprived of his liberty except on such grounds and in accordance with such procedure as are established by law.

2. Anyone who is arrested shall be informed, at the time of arrest, of the reasons for his arrest and shall be promptly informed of any charges against him.

3. Anyone arrested or detained on a criminal charge shall be brought promptly before a judge or other officer authorized by law to exercise judicial power and shall be entitled to trial within a reasonable time or to release. It shall not be the general rule that persons awaiting trial shall be detained in custody, but release may be subject to guarantees to appear for trial, at any other stage of the judicial proceedings, and, should occasion arise, for execution of the judgement.

4. Anyone who is deprived of his liberty by arrest or detention shall be entitled to take proceedings before a court, in order that that court may decide without delay on the lawfulness of his detention and order his release if the detention is not lawful.

5. Anyone who has been the victim of unlawful arrest or detention shall have an enforceable right to compensation.

Article 10.

1. All persons deprived of their liberty shall be treated with humanity and with respect for the inherent dignity of the human person.

2. (a) Accused persons shall, save in exceptional circumstances, be segregated from convicted persons and shall be subject to separate treatment appropriate to their status as unconvicted persons;

(b) Accused juvenile persons shall be separated from adults and brought as speedily as possible for adjudication.

3. The penitentiary system shall comprise treatment of prisoners the essential aim of which shall be their reformation and social rehabilitation. Juvenile offenders shall be segregated from adults and be accorded treatment appropriate to their age and legal status.

Article 11.

No one shall be imprisoned merely on the ground of inability to fulfil a contractual obligation.

Article 12.

1. Everyone lawfully within the territory of a State shall, within that territory, have the right to liberty of movement and freedom to choose his residence.

2. Everyone shall be free to leave any country, including his own.

3. The above-mentioned rights shall not be subject to any restrictions except those which are provided by law, are necessary to protect national security, public order (*ordre public*), public health or morals or the rights and freedoms of others, and are consistent with the other rights recognized in the present Covenant.

4. No one shall be arbitrarily deprived of the right to enter his own country.

Article 13.

An alien lawfully in the territory of a State Party to the present Covenant may be expelled therefrom only in pursuance of a decision reached in accordance with law and shall, except where compelling reasons of national security otherwise require, be allowed to submit the reasons against his expulsion and to have his case reviewed by, and be represented for the purpose before, the competent authority or a person or persons especially designated by the competent authority.

Article 14.

1. All persons shall be equal before the courts and tribunals. In the determination of any criminal charge against him, or of his rights and obligations in a suit at law, everyone shall be entitled to a fair and public hearing by a competent, independent and impartial tribunal established by law. The press and the public may be excluded from all or part of a trial for reasons of morals, public order (*ordre public*) or national security in a democratic society, or when the interest of the private lives of the parties so requires, or to the extent strictly necessary in the opinion of the court in special circumstances where publicity would prejudice the interests of justice; but any judgement rendered in a criminal case or in a suit at law shall be made public except where the interest of juvenile persons otherwise requires or the proceedings concern matrimonial disputes or the guardianship of children.

2. Everyone charged with a criminal offence shall have the right to be presumed innocent until proved guilty according to law.

3. In the determination of any criminal charge against him, everyone shall be entitled to the following minimum guarantees, in full equality:

    (a) To be informed promptly and in detail in a language which he understands of the nature and cause of the charge against him;

    (b) To have adequate time and facilities for the preparation of his defence and to communicate with counsel of his own choosing;

    (c) To be tried without undue delay;

    (d) To be tried in his presence, and to defend himself in person or through legal assistance of his own choosing; to be informed, if he does not have legal assistance, of this right; and to have legal assistance assigned to him, in any case where the interests of justice so require, and without payment by him in any such case if he does not have sufficient means to pay for it;

    (e) To examine, or have examined, the witnesses against him and to obtain the attendance and examination of witnesses on his behalf under the same conditions as witnesses against him;

(f) To have the free assistance of an interpreter if he cannot understand or speak the language used in court;

(g) Not to be compelled to testify against himself or to confess guilt.

4. In the case of juvenile persons, the procedure shall be such as will take account of their age and the desirability of promoting their rehabilitation.

5. Everyone convicted of a crime shall have the right to his conviction and sentence being reviewed by a higher tribunal according to law.

6. When a person has by a final decision been convicted of a criminal offence and when subsequently his conviction has been reversed or he has been pardoned on the ground that a new or newly discovered fact shows conclusively that there has been a miscarriage of justice, the person who has suffered punishment as a result of such conviction shall be compensated according to law, unless it is proved that the non-disclosure of the unknown fact in time is wholly or partly attributable to him.

7. No one shall be liable to be tried or punished again for an offence for which he has already been finally convicted or acquitted in accordance with the law and penal procedure of each country.

Article 15.

1. No one shall be held guilty of any criminal offence on account of any act or omission which did not constitute a criminal offence, under national or international law, at the time when it was committed. Nor shall a heavier penalty be imposed than the one that was applicable at the time when the criminal offence was committed. If, subsequent to the commission of the offence, provision is made by law for the imposition of a lighter penalty, the offender shall benefit thereby.

2. Nothing in this article shall prejudice the trial and punishment of any person for any act or omission which, at the time when it was committed, was criminal according to the general principles of law recognized by the community of nations.

Article 16.

Everyone shall have the right to recognition everywhere as a person before the law.

Article 17.

1. No one shall be subjected to arbitrary or unlawful interference with his privacy, family, home or correspondence, nor to unlawful attacks on his honour and reputation.

2. Everyone has the right to the protection of the law against such interference or attacks.

Article 18.

1. Everyone shall have the right to freedom of thought, conscience and religion. This right shall include freedom to have or to adopt a religion or belief of his choice, and freedom, either individually or in community with others and in public or private, to manifest his religion or belief in worship, observance, practice and teaching.

2. No one shall be subject to coercion which would impair his freedom to have or to adopt a religion or belief of his choice.

3. Freedom to manifest one's religion or beliefs may be subject only to such limitations as are prescribed by law and are necessary to protect public safety, order, health, or morals or the fundamental rights and freedoms of others.

4. The States Parties to the present Covenant undertake to have respect for the liberty of parents and, when applicable, legal guardians to ensure the religious and moral education of their children in conformity with their own convictions.

Article 19.

1. Everyone shall have the right to hold opinions without interference.

2. Everyone shall have the right to freedom of expression; this right shall include freedom to seek, receive and impart information and ideas of all kinds, regardless of frontiers, either orally, in writing or in print, in the form of art, or through any other media of his choice.

3. The exercise of the rights provided for in paragraph 2 of this article carries with it special duties and responsibilities. It may therefore be subject to certain restrictions, but these shall only be such as are provided by law and are necessary:

(a) For respect of the rights or reputations of others;

(b) For the protection of national security or of public order (*ordre public*), or of public health or morals.

Article 20.

1. Any propaganda for war shall be prohibited by law.

2. Any advocacy of national, racial or religious hatred that constitutes incitement to discrimination, hostility or violence shall be prohibited by law.

Article 21.

The right of peaceful assembly shall be recognized. No restrictions may be placed on the exercise of this right other than those imposed in conformity with the law and which are necessary in a democratic society in the interests of national security or public safety, public order (*ordre public*), the protection of health or morals or the protection of the rights and freedoms of others.

Article 22.

1. Everyone shall have the right to freedom of association with others, including the right to form and join trade unions for the protection of his interests.

2. No restrictions may be placed on the exercise of this right other than those which are prescribed by law and which are necessary in a democratic society in the interests of national security or public safety, public order (*ordre public*), the protection of public health or morals or the protection of the rights and freedoms of others. This article shall not prevent the imposition of lawful restrictions on members of the armed forces and of the police in their exercise of this right.

3. Nothing in this article shall authorize States Parties to the International Labour Organisation Convention of 1948 concerning Freedom of Association and Protection of the Right to Organise to take legislative measures which would prejudice, or apply the law in such a manner as to prejudice, the guarantees provided for in that Convention.

Article 23.

1. The family is the natural and fundamental group unit of society and is entitled to protection by society and the State.
2. The right of men and women of marriageable age to marry and to found a family shall be recognized.
3. No marriage shall be entered into without the free and full consent of the intending spouses.
4. States Parties to the present Covenant shall take appropriate steps to ensure equality of rights and responsibilities of spouses as to marriage, during marriage and at its dissolution. In the case of dissolution, provision shall be made for the necessary protection of any children.

Article 24.

1. Every child shall have, without any discrimination as to race, colour, sex, language, religion, national or social origin, property or birth, the right to such measures of protection as are required by his status as a minor, on the part of his family, society and the State.
2. Every child shall be registered immediately after birth and shall have a name.
3. Every child has the right to acquire a nationality.

Article 25.

Every citizen shall have the right and the opportunity, without any of the distinctions mentioned in article 2 and without unreasonable restrictions:

(a) To take part in the conduct of public affairs, directly or through freely chosen representatives;

(b) To vote and to be elected at genuine periodic elections which shall be by universal and equal suffrage and shall be held by secret ballot, guaranteeing the free expression of the will of the electors;

(c) To have access, on general terms of equality, to public service in his country.

Article 26.

All persons are equal before the law and are entitled without any discrimination to the equal protection of the law. In this respect, the law shall prohibit any discrimination and guarantee to all persons equal and effective protection against discrimination on any ground such as race, colour, sex, language, religion, political or other opinion, national or social origin, property, birth or other status.

Article 27.

In those States in which ethnic, religious or linguistic minorities exist, persons belonging to such minorities shall not be denied the right, in community with the other members of their group, to enjoy their own culture, to profess and practice their own religion, or to use their own language.

PART IV.

Article 28.

1. There shall be established a Human Rights Committee (hereinafter referred to in the present Covenant as the Committee). It shall consist of eighteen members and shall carry out the functions hereinafter provided.
2. The Committee shall be composed of nationals of the States Parties to the present Covenant who shall be persons of high moral character and recognized competence in the field of human rights, consideration being given to the usefulness of the participation of some persons having legal experience.
3. The members of the Committee shall be elected and shall serve in their personal capacity.

Article 29.

1. The members of the Committee shall be elected by secret ballot from a list of persons possessing the qualifications prescribed in article 28 and nominated for the purpose by the States Parties to the present Covenant.
2. Each State Party to the present Covenant may nominate not more than two persons. These persons shall be nationals of the nominating State.
3. A person shall be eligible for renomination.

Article 30.

1. The initial election shall be held no later than six months after the date of the entry into force of the present Covenant.
2. At least four months before the date of each election to the Committee, other than an election to fill a vacancy declared in accordance with article 34, the Secretary-General of the United Nations shall address a written invitation to the States Parties to the present Covenant to submit their nominations for membership of the Committee within three months.
3. The Secretary-General of the United Nations shall prepare a list in alphabetical order of all the persons thus nominated, with an indication of the States Parties which have nominated them, and shall submit it to the States Parties to the present Covenant no later than one month before the date of each election.
4. Elections of the members of the Committee shall be held at a meeting of the States Parties to the present Covenant convened by the Secretary-General of the United Nations at the Headquarters of the United Nations. At that meeting, for which two thirds of the States Parties to the present Covenant shall constitute a quorum, the persons elected to the Committee shall be those nominees who obtain the largest number of votes and an absolute majority of the votes of the representatives of States Parties present and voting.

Article 31.

1. The Committee may not include more than one national of the same State.
2. In the election of the Committee, consideration shall be given to equitable geographical distribution of membership and to the representation of the different forms of civilization and of the principal legal systems.

Article 32.

1. The members of the Committee shall be elected for a term of four years. They shall be eligible for re-election if renominated. However, the terms of nine of the members elected at the first election shall expire at the end of two years; immediately after the first election, the names of these nine members shall be chosen by lot by the Chairman of the meeting referred to in article 30, paragraph 4.

2. Elections at the expiry of office shall be held in accordance with the preceding articles of this part of the present Covenant.

Article 33.

1. If, in the unanimous opinion of the other members, a member of the Committee has ceased to carry out his functions for any cause other than absence of a temporary character, the Chairman of the Committee shall notify the Secretary-General of the United Nations, who shall then declare the seat of that member to be vacant.

2. In the event of the death or the resignation of a member of the Committee, the Chairman shall immediately notify the Secretary-General of the United Nations, who shall declare the seat vacant from the date of the death or the date on which the resignation takes effect.

Article 34.

1. When a vacancy is declared in accordance with article 33 and if the term of office of the member to be replaced does not expire within six months of the declaration of the vacancy, the Secretary-General of the United Nations shall notify each of the States Parties to the present Covenant, which may within two months submit nominations in accordance with article 29 for the purpose of filling the vacancy.

2. The Secretary-General of the United Nations shall prepare a list in alphabetical order of the persons thus nominated and shall submit it to the States Parties to the present Covenant. The election to fill the vacancy shall then take place in accordance with the relevant provisions of this part of the present Covenant.

3. A member of the Committee elected to fill a vacancy declared in accordance with article 33 shall hold office for the remainder of the term of the member who vacated the seat on the Committee under the provisions of that article.

Article 35.

The members of the Committee shall, with the approval of the General Assembly of the United Nations, receive emoluments from United Nations resources on such terms and conditions as the General Assembly may decide, having regard to the importance of the Committee's responsibilities.

Article 36.

The Secretary-General of the United Nations shall provide the necessary staff and facilities for the effective performance of the functions of the Committee under the present Covenant.

Article 37.

1. The Secretary-General of the United Nations shall convene the initial meeting of the Committee at the Headquarters of the United Nations.
2. After its initial meeting, the Committee shall meet at such times as shall be provided in its rules of procedure.
3. The Committee shall normally meet at the Headquarters of the United Nations or at the United Nations Office at Geneva.

Article 38.

Every member of the Committee shall, before taking up his duties, make a solemn declaration in open committee that he will perform his functions impartially and conscientiously.

Article 39.

1. The Committee shall elect its officers for a term of two years. They may be re-elected.
2. The Committee shall establish its own rules of procedure, but these rules shall provide, *inter alia*, that:
   (a) Twelve members shall constitute a quorum;
   (b) Decisions of the Committee shall be made by a majority vote of the members present.

Article 40.

1. The States Parties to the present Covenant undertake to submit reports on the measures they have adopted which give effect on the rights recognized herein and on the progress made in the enjoyment of those rights:
   (a) Within one year of the entry into force of the present Covenant for the States Parties concerned;
   (b) Thereafter whenever the Committee so requests.
2. All reports shall be submitted to the Secretary-General of the United Nations, who shall transmit them to the Committee for consideration. Reports shall indicate the factors and difficulties, if any, affecting the implementation of the present Covenant.
3. The Secretary-General of the United Nations may, after consultation with the Committee, transmit to the specialized agencies concerned copies of such parts of the reports as may fall within their field of competence.
4. The Committee shall study the reports submitted by the States Parties to the present Covenant. It shall transmit its reports, and such general comments as it may consider appropriate, to the States Parties. The Committee may also transmit to the Economic and Social Council these comments along with the copies of the reports it has received from States Parties to the present Covenant.
5. The States Parties to the present Covenant may submit to the Committee observations on any comments that may be made in accordance with paragraph 4 of this article.

Article 41.

1. A State Party to the present Covenant may at any time declare under this article that it recognizes the competence of the Committee to receive and consider communications

to the effect that a State Party claims that another State Party is not fulfilling its obligations under the present Covenant. Communications under this article may be received and considered only if submitted by a State Party which has made a declaration recognizing in regard to itself the competence of the Committee. No communication shall be received by the Committee if it concerns a State Party which has not made such a declaration. Communications received under this article shall be dealt with in accordance to the following procedure:

(a) If a State Party to the present Covenant considers that another State Party is not giving effect to the provisions of the present Covenant, it may, by written communication, bring the matter to the attention of that State Party. Within three months after the receipt of the communication the receiving State shall afford the State which sent the communication an explanation, or any other statement in writing clarifying the matter which should include, to the extent possible and pertinent, reference to domestic procedures and remedies taken, pending, or available in the matter.

(b) If the matter is not adjusted to the satisfaction of both States Parties concerned within six months after the receipt by the receiving State of the initial communication, either State shall have the right to refer the matter to the Committee, by notice given to the Committee and to the other State.

(c) The Committee shall deal with a matter referred to it only after it has ascertained that all available domestic remedies have been invoked and exhausted in the matter, in conformity with the generally recognized principles of international law. This shall not be the rule where the application of the remedies is unreasonably prolonged.

(d) The Committee shall hold closed meetings when examining communications under this article.

(e) Subject to the provisions of sub-paragraph (c), the Committee shall make available its good offices to the States Parties concerned with a view to a friendly solution of the matter on the basis of respect for human rights and fundamental freedoms as recognized in the present Covenant.

(f) In any matter referred to it, the Committee may call upon the States Parties concerned, referred to in sub-paragraph (b), to supply any relevant information.

(g) The States Parties concerned, referred to in sub-paragraph (b), shall have the right to be represented when the matter is being considered in the Committee and to make submissions orally and/or in writing.

(h) The Committee shall, within twelve months after the date of receipt of notice under sub-paragraph (b), submit a report:

(i) If a solution within the terms of sub-paragraph (e) is reached, the Committee shall confine its report to a brief statment of the facts and of the solution reached;

(ii) If a solution within the terms of sub-paragraph (e) is not reached, the Committee shall confine its reports to a brief statement of the facts; the written submissions and record of the oral submissions made by the States Parties concerned shall be attached to the report.

In every matter, the report shall be communicated to the States Parties concerned.

2. The provisions of this article shall come into force when ten States Parties to the present Covenant have made declarations under paragraph 1 of this article. Such declarations shall be deposited by the States Parties with the Secretary-General of the

United Nations, who shall transmit copies thereof to the other States Parties. A declaration may be withdrawn at any time by notification to the Secretary-General. Such a withdrawal shall not prejudice the consideration of any matter which is the subject of a communication already transmitted under this article; no further communication by any State party shall be received after the notification of withdrawal of the declaration has been received by the Secretary-General, unless the State Party concerned has made a new declaration.

Article 42.

1. (a) If a matter referred to the Committee in accordance with article 41 is not resolved to the satisfaction of the States Parties concerned, the Committee may, with the prior consent of the States Parties concerned, appoint an *ad hoc* Conciliation Commission (hereinafter referred to as the Commission). The good offices of the Commission shall be made available to the States Parties concerned with a view to an amicable solution of the matter on the basis of respect for the present Covenant;

(b) The Commission shall consist of five persons acceptable to the States Parties concerned. If the States Parties concerned fail to reach agreement within three months on all or part of the composition of the Commission, the members of the Commission concerning whom no agreement has been reached shall be elected by secret ballot by a two-thirds majority vote of the Committee from among its members.

2. The members of the Commission shall serve in their personal capacity. They shall not be nationals of the States Parties concerned, or of a State not party to the present Covenant, or of a State Party which has not made a declaration under article 41.

3. The Commission shall elect its own Chairman and adopt its own rules of procedure.

4. The meetings of the Commission shall normally be held at the Headquarters of the United Nations or at the United Nations Office at Geneva. However, they may be held at such other convenient places as the Commission may determine in consultation with the Secretary-General of the United Nations and the States Parties concerned.

5. The Secretariat provided in accordance with article 36 shall also service the commissions appointed under this article.

6. The information received and collated by the Committee shall be made available to the Commission and the Commission may call upon the States Parties concerned to supply any other relevant information.

7. When the Commission has fully considered the matter, but in any event not later than twelve months after having been seized of the matter, it shall submit to the Chairman of the Committee a report for communication to the States Parties concerned:

(a) If the Commission is unable to complete its consideration of the matter within twelve months, it shall confine its report to a brief statement of the status of its consideration of the matter.

(b) If an amicable solution to the matter on the basis of respect for human rights as recognized in the present Covenant is reached, the Commission shall confine its report to a brief statement of the facts and of the solution reached;

(c) If a solution within the terms of sub-paragraph (b) is not reached, the Commission's report shall embody its findings on all questions of fact relevant to the issues between the States Parties concerned, and its views on the possibilities of an amicable solution of the matter. This report shall also contain the written submissions and a record of the oral submissions made by the States Parties concerned;

(d) If the Commission's report is submitted under sub-paragraph (c), the States Parties concerned shall, within three months of the receipt of the report, notify the Chairman of the Committee whether or not they accept the contents of the report of the Commission.

8. The provisions of this article are without prejudice to the responsibilities of the Committee under article 41.

9. The States Parties concerned shall share equally all the expenses of the members of the Commission in accordance with estimates to be provided by the Secretary-General of the United Nations.

10. The Secretary-General of the United Nations shall be empowered to pay the expenses of the members of the Commission, if necessary, before reimbursement by the States Parties concerned, in accordance with paragraph 9 of this article.

Article 43.

The members of the Committee, and of the *ad hoc* conciliation commissions which may be appointed under article 42, shall be entitled to the facilities, privileges and immunities of experts on mission for the United Nations as laid down in the relevant sections of the Convention on the Privileges and Immunities of the United Nations.

Article 44.

The provisions for the implementation of the present Covenant shall apply without prejudice to the procedures prescribed in the field of human rights by or under the constituent instruments and the conventions of the United Nations and of the specialized agencies and shall not prevent the States Parties to the present Covenant from having recourse to other procedures for settling a dispute in accordance with general or special international agreements in force between them.

Article 45.

The Committee shall submit to the General Assembly of the United Nations, through the Economic and Social Council, an annual report on its activities.

PART V.

Article 46.

Nothing in the present Covenant shall be interpreted as impairing the provisions of the Charter of the United Nations and of the constitutions of the specialized agencies which define with respective responsibilities of the various organs of the United Nations and of the specialized agencies in regard to the matters dealt with in the present Covenant.

Article 47.

Nothing in the present Covenant shall be interpreted as impairing the inherent right of all peoples to enjoy and utilize fully and freely their natural wealth and resources.

PART VI.

Article 48.

1. The present Covenant is open for signature by any State Member of the United Nations or member of any of its specialized agencies, by any State Party to the Statute of the International Court of Justice, and by any other State which has been invited by the General Assembly of the United Nations to become a party to the present Covenant.

2. The present Covenant is subject to ratification. Instruments of ratification shall be deposited with the Secretary-General of the United Nations.

3. The present Covenant shall be open to accession by any State referred to in paragraph 1 of this article.

4. Accession shall be effected by the deposit of an instrument of accession with the Secretary-General of the United Nations.

5. The Secretary-General of the United Nations shall inform all States which have signed this Covenant or acceded to it of the deposit of each instrument or ratification or accession.

Article 49.

1. The present Covenant shall enter into force three months after the date of the deposit with the Secretary-General of the United Nations of the thirty-fifth instrument of ratification or instrument of accession.

2. For each State ratifying the present Covenant or acceding to it after the deposit of the thirty-fifth instrument of ratification or instrument of accession, the present Covenant shall enter into force three months after the date of the deposit of its own instrument of ratification or instrument of accession.

Article 50.

The provisions of the present Covenant shall extend to all parts of federal States without any limitations or exceptions.

Article 51.

1. Any State Party to the present Covenant may propose an amendment and file it with the Secretary-General of the United Nations. The Secretary-General of the United Nations shall thereupon communicate any proposed amendments to the State Parties to the present Covenant with a request that they notify him whether they favour a conference of States Parties for the purpose of considering and voting upon the proposals. In the event that at least one third of the States Parties favours such a conference, the Secretary-General shall convene the conference under the auspices of the United Nations. Any amendment adopted by a majority of the States Parties present and voting at the conference shall be submitted to the General Assembly of the United Nations for approval.

2. Amendments shall come into force when they have been approved by the General Assembly of the United Nations and accepted by a two-thirds majority of the States Parties to the present Covenant in accordance with their respective constitutional processes.

3. When amendments come into force, they shall be binding on those States Parties which have accepted them, other States Parties still being bound by the provisions of the present Covenant and any earlier amendment which they have accepted.

Article 52.

Irrespective of the notifications made under article 48, paragraph 5, the Secretary-General of the United Nations shall inform all States referred to in paragraph 1 of the same article of the following particulars:

    (a) Signatures, ratifications and accessions under article 48;

    (b) The date of the entry into force of the present Covenant under article 49 and the date of the entry into force of any amendments under article 51.

Article 53.

1. The present Covenant, of which the Chinese, English, French, Russian and Spanish texts are equally authentic, shall be deposited in the archives of the United Nations.

2. The Secretary-General of the United Nations shall transmit certified copies of the present Covenant to all States referred to in article 48.

Appendix II
The Optional Protocol to the International Covenant on Civil and Political Rights

The States Parties to the present Protocol,

Considering that in order further to achieve the purposes of the Covenant on Civil and Political Rights (hereinafter referred to as the Covenant) and the implementation of its provisions it would be appropriate to enable the Human Rights Committee set up in part IV of the Covenant (hereinafter referred to as the Committee) to receive and consider, as provided in the present Protocol, communications from individuals claiming to be victims of violations of any of the rights set forth in the Covenant.

Have agreed as follows:

Article 1.

A State Party to the Covenant that becomes a party to the present Protocol recognizes the competence of the Committee to receive and consider communications from individuals subject to its jurisdiction who claim to be victims of a violation by that State Party of any of the rights set forth in the Covenant. No communication shall be received by the Committee if it concerns a State Party to the Covenant which is not a party to the present Protocol.

Article 2.

Subject to the provisions of article 1, individuals who claim that any of their rights enumerated in the Covenant have been violated and who have exhausted all available domestic remedies may submit a written communication to the Committee for consideration.

Article 3.

The Committee shall consider inadmissible any communication under the present Protocol which is anonymous, or which it considers to be an abuse of the right of submission of such communications or to be incompatible with the provisions of the Covenant.

Article 4.

1. Subject to the provisions of article 3, the Committee shall bring any communications submitted to it under the present Protocol to the attention of the State Party to the present Protocol alleged to be violating any provision of the Covenant.
2. Within six months, the receiving State shall submit to the Committee written explanations or statements clarifying the matter and the remedy, if any, that may have been taken by that State.

Article 5.

1. The Committee shall consider communications received under the present Protocol in the light of all written information made available to it by the individual and by the State Party concerned.

2. The Committee shall not consider any communication from an individual unless it has acertained that:

(a) The same matter is not being examined under another procedure of international investigation or settlement;

(b) The individual has exhausted all available domestic remedies. This shall not be the rule where the application of the remedies is unreasonably prolonged.

3. The Committee shall hold closed meetings when examining communications under the present Protocol.

4. The Committee shall forward its views to the State Party concerned and to the individual.

Article 6.

The Committee shall include in its annual report under article 45 of the Covenant a summary of its activities under the present Protocol.

Article 7.

Pending the achievement of the objectives of resolution 1514(XV) adopted by the General Assembly of the United Nations on 14 December 1960 concerning the Declaration on the Granting of Independence to Colonial Countries and Peoples, the provisions of the present Protocol shall in no way limit the right of petition granted to these peoples by the Charter of the United Nations and other international conventions and instruments under the United Nations and its specialized agencies.

Article 8.

1. The present Protocol is open for signature by any State which has signed the Covenant.

2. The present Protocol is subject to ratification by any State which has ratified or acceded to the Covenant. Instruments of ratification shall be deposited with the Secretary-General of the United Nations.

3. The present Protocol shall be open to accession by any State which has ratified or acceded to the Covenant.

4. Accession shall be affected by the deposit of an instrument of accessions with the Secretary-General of the United Nations.

5. The Secretary-General of the United Nations shall inform all States which have signed the present Protocol or acceded to it of the deposit of each instrument of ratification or accession.

Article 9.

1. Subject to the entry into force of the Covenant, the present Protocol shall enter into force three months after the date of the deposit with the Secretary-General of the United Nations of the tenth instrument of ratification or instrument of accession.

2. For each State ratifying the present Protocol or acceding to it after the deposit of the tenth instrument of ratification or instrument or accession, the present Protocol shall enter into force three months after the date of the deposit of its own instrument of ratification or instrument of accession.

Article 10.

The provisions of the present Protocol shall extend to all parts of federal States without any limitations or exceptions.

Article 11.

1. Any State Party to the present Protocol may propose an amendment and file it with the Secretary-General of the United Nations. The Secretary-General shall thereupon communicate any proposed amendments to the States Parties to the present Protocol with a request that they notify him whether they favour a conference of States Parties for the purpose of considering and voting upon the proposal. In the event that at least one third of the States Parties favours such a conference, the Secretary-General shall convene the conference under the auspices of the United Nations. Any amendment adopted by a majority of the States Parties present and voting at the conference shall be submitted to the General Assembly of the United Nations for approval.

2. Amendments shall come into force when they have been approved by the General Assembly of the United Nations and accepted by a two-thirds majority of the States Parties to the present Protocol in accordance with their respective constitutional processes.

3. When amendments come into force, they shall be binding on those States Parties which have accepted them, other States Parties still being bound by the provisions of the present Protocol and any earlier amendment which they have accepted.

Article 12.

1. Any State Party may denounce the present Protocol at any time by written notification addressed to the Secretary-General of the United Nations. Denunciation shall take effect three months after the date of receipt of the notification by the Secretary-General.

2. Denunciation shall be without prejudice to the continued application of the provisions of the present Protocol to any communication submitted under article 2 before the effective date of denunciation.

Article 13.

Irrespective of the notifications made under article 8, paragraph 5, of the present Protocol, the Secretary-General of the United Nations shall inform all States referred to in Article 48, paragraph 1, of the Covenant of the following particulars:

    (a) Signatures, ratifications and accessions under article 8;

    (b) The date of the entry into force of the present Protocol under article 9 and the date of the entry into force of any amendments under article 11;

    (c) Denunciations under article 12.

Article 14.

1. The present Protocol, of which the Chinese, English, French, Russian and Spanish texts are equally authentic, shall be deposited in the archives of the United Nations.
2. The Secretary-General of the United Nations shall transmit certified copies of the present Protocol to all States referred to in article 48 of the Covenant.

Appendix III
Model Communication under the Optional Protocol

Communication to:
The Human Rights Committee   Date:
c/o Centre for Human Rights
United Nations Office,
Geneva (Switzerland).
    Submitted for consideration under the Optional Protocol to the International
Covenant on Civil and Political Rights.

I. Information Concerning the Author of the Communication.

Name   First Name(s)
Nationality   Profession
Date and place of birth
Present Address
Address for exchange of confidential correspondence (if
other than present address):
Submitting the communication as:
(a) victim of the violation or violations set
forth below   —[1]
(b) representative of the alleged victim(s)   —
(c) other   —

If the author is submitting the communication as a representative of the alleged
                            victim(s) he should clearly indicate in
                            what capacity he is doing so:

If the author is neither the victim nor his/their representative, he should clearly
                            indicate:

(a) his reasons for acting on behalf of the alleged victim(s)
(b) his reasons for believing that the victim(s) is (are) unable to submit a
                            communication himself (themselves):
(c) his reason for believing that the victim(s) would approve the author's acting on
                            his (their) behalf:

II. Information Concerning the Alleged Victim(s). (If other than Author).[2]

Name   First Name(s)
Nationality   Profession.
Date and place of birth
Present address or whereabouts
Name   First Name(s)
Nationality   Profession.
Date and place of birth
Present address or whereabouts
Name   First Name(s)
Nationality   Profession.
Date and place of birth
Present address or whereabouts
Name   First Name(s)
Nationality   Profession.
Date and place of birth
Present address or whereabouts

III. State Concerned/Articles Violated/Domestic Remedies/Other International Procedures.

Name of the State party (country) to the International Covenant and the Optional Protocol against which the communication is directed:

Articles of the International Covenant on Civil and Political Rights allegedly violated:

Steps taken by or on behalf of the alleged victim(s) to exhaust domestic remedies (recourse to the courts or other public authorities, when and with what results—if possible, enclose copies of all relevant judicial and administrative decisions:

If domestic remedies have not been exhausted, explain why:

Has the same matter been submitted for examination under another procedure of international investigation or settlement? If so, when and with what results?

IV. Facts of the Claim.

Detailed description of the facts of the alleged violation or violations (including relevant dates).[3]

NOTES

1 Mark the appropriate box or boxes.
2 List each victim individually and add as many pages as necessary to complete the list of victims.
3 Add as many pages as needed for this description.

Appendix IV
The Second Optional Protocol to the International Covenant on Civil and Political Rights

General Assembly Resolution 44/128.

Elaboration of a second optional protocol to the International Covenant on Civil and Political Rights, aiming at the abolition of the death penalty

Date: 15 December 1989   Meeting: 82
Vote: 59-26-48 (recorded)   Report: A/44/824

The General Assembly,

Recalling article 3 of the Universal Declaration of Human Rights adopted in its resolution 217 A (III) of 10 December 1948,

Recalling also article 6 of the International Covenant on Civil and Political Rights adopted in its resolution 2200 A (XXI) of 16 December 1966,

Mindful of its decision 35/437 of 15 December 1980, reaffirmed in its resolution 36/59 of 25 November 1981, to consider the idea of elaborating a draft of a second optional protocol to the International Covenant on Civil and Political Rights, aiming at the abolition of the death penalty,

Mindful also of its resolution 37/192 of 18 December 1982, in which it requested the Commission on Human Rights to consider this idea and its resolution 39/137 of 14 December 1984, in which it requested the Commission and the Sub-Commission on Prevention of Discrimination and Protection of Minorities to consider further the idea of elaborating a draft of a second optional protocol,

Taking note of the comparative analysis prepared by the Special Rapporteur of the Sub-Commission on Prevention of Discrimination and Protection of Minorities,[1]

Taking note also of the views expressed by Governments in favour of and against the death penalty and of their comments and observations regarding such a second optional protocol, as reproduced in the relevant reports of the Secretary-General,[2]

Referring to its decision 42/421 of 7 December 1987, Commission on Human Rights resolution 1989/25 of 6 March 1989 and Economic and Social Council decision 1989/139 of 24 May 1989,[3] by which the comparative analysis and the draft second optional protocol were transmitted to the General Assembly for suitable action,

Wishing to give States parties to the International Covenant on Civil and Political Rights that choose to do so the opportunity to become parties to a second optional protocol to that convention,

Having considered the draft second optional protocol to the International

Covenant on Civil and Political Rights, aiming at the abolition of the death penalty, which was prepared by the Special Rapporteur,

1. *Expresses its appreciation* for the work achieved by the Commission on Human Rights and the Sub-Commission on Prevention of Discrimination and Protection of Minorities;

2. *Adopts* and opens for signature, ratification and accession the Second Optional Protocol to the International Covenant on Civil and Political Rights, aiming at the abolition of the death penalty, contained in the annex to the present resolution;

3. *Calls upon* all Governments in a position to do so to consider signing and ratifying or acceding to the Second Optional Protocol.

ANNEX

Second Optional Protocol to the International Covenant on Civil and Political Rights, aiming at the abolition of the death penalty

The States Parties to the present Protocol,

Believing that abolition of the death penalty contributes to enhancement of human dignity and progressive development of human rights,

Recalling article 3 of the Universal Declaration of Human Rights[4] adopted on 10 December 1948 and article 6 of the International Covenant on Civil and Political Rights[5] adopted on 16 December 1966,

Noting that article 6 of the International Covenant on Civil and Political Rights refers to abolition of the death penalty in terms that strongly suggest that abolition is desirable,

Convinced that all measures of abolition of the death penalty should be considered as progress in the enjoyment of the right to life,

Desirous to undertake hereby an international commitment to abolish the death penalty,

Have agreed as follows:

Article 1.

1. No one within the jurisdiction of a State Party to the present Optional Protocol shall be executed.

2. Each State Party shall take all necessary measures to abolish the death penalty within its jurisdiction.

Article 2.

1. No reservation is admissible to the present Protocol, except for a reservation made at the time of ratification or accession that provides for the application of the death penalty in time of war pursuant to a conviction for a most serious crime of a military nature committed during wartime.

2. The State Party making such a reservation shall at the time of ratification or accession communicate to the Secretary-General of the United Nations the relevant provisions of its national legislation applicable during wartime.

3. The State Party having made such a reservation shall notify the Secretary-General of the United Nations of any beginning or ending of a state of war applicable to its territory.

Article 3.

The States Parties to the present Protocol shall include in the reports they submit to the Human Rights Committee, in accordance with article 40 of the Covenant, information on the measures that they have adopted to give effect to the present Protocol.

Article 4.

With respect to the States Parties to the Covenant that have made a declaration under article 41, the competence of the Human Rights Committee to receive and consider communications when a State Party claims that another State Party is not fulfilling its obligations shall extend to the provisions of the present Protocol, unless the State Party concerned has made a statement to the contrary at the moment of ratification or accession.

Article 5.

With respect to the States Parties to the (First) Optional Protocol to the International Covenant on Civil and Political Rights adopted on 16 December 1966, the competence of the Human Rights Committee to receive and consider communications from individuals subject to its jurisdiction shall extend to the provision of the present Protocol, unless the State Party concerned has made a statement to the contrary at the moment of ratification or accession.

Article 6.

1. The provisions of the present Protocol shall apply as additional provisions to the Covenant.
2. Without prejudice to the possibility of a reservation under article 2 of the present Protocol, the right guaranteed in article 1, paragraph 1, of the present Protocol shall not be subject to any derogation under article 4 of the Covenant.

Article 7.

1. The present Protocol is open for signature by any State that has signed the Covenant.
2. The present Protocol is subject to ratification by any State that has ratified the Covenant or acceded to it. Instruments of ratification shall be deposited with the Secretary-General of the United Nations.
3. The present Protocol shall be open to accession by any State that has ratified the Covenant or acceded to it.
4. Accession shall be effected by the deposit of an instrument of accession with the Secretary-General of the United Nations.
5. The Secretary-General of the United Nations shall inform all States that have signed the present Protocol or acceded to it of the deposit of each instrument of ratification or accession.

Article 8.

1. The present Protocol shall enter into force three months after the date of the deposit with the Secretary-General of the United Nations of the tenth instrument of ratification or accession.

2. For each State ratifying the present Protocol or acceding to it after the deposit of the tenth instrument of ratification or accession, the present Protocol shall enter into force three months after the date of the deposit of its own instrument of ratification or accession.

Article 9.

The provisions of the present Protocol shall extend to all parts of federal States without any limitations or exceptions.

Article 10.

The Secretary-General of the United Nations shall inform all States referred to in article 48, paragraph 1, of the Covenant of the following particulars:

(a) Reservations, communications and notifications under article 2 of the present Protocol;

(b) Statements made under its articles 4 or 5;

(c) Signatures, ratifications and accessions under its article 7;

(d) The date of the entry into force of the present Protocol under its article 8.

Article 11.

1. The present Protocol, of which the Arabic, Chinese, English, French, Russian and Spanish texts are equally authentic, shall be deposited in the archives of the United Nations.

2. The Secretary-General of the United Nations shall transmit certified copies of the present Protocol to all States referred to in article 48 of the Covenant.

RECORDED VOTE ON RESOLUTION 44/128:

In favour: Argentina, Australia, Austria, Belgium, Bolivia, Brazil, Bulgaria, Byelorussia, Canada, Cape Verde, Colombia, Costa Rica, Cyprus, Czechoslovakia, Democratic Kampuchea, Denmark, Dominican Republic, Ecuador, El Salvador, Finland, France, German Democratic Republic, Federal Republic of Germany, Greece, Grenada, Guatemala, Haiti, Honduras, Hungary, Iceland, Ireland, Italy, Luxembourg, Malta, Mexico, Mongolia, Nepal, Netherlands, New Zealand, Norway, Panama, Paraguay, Peru, Philippines, Poland, Portugal, Saint Kitts and Nevis, Saint Lucia, Saint Vincent and the Grenadines*, Samoa, Spain, Sweden, Togo, Ukraine, USSR, United Kingdom, Uruguay, Venezuela, Yugoslavia.

Against: Afghanistan, Bahrain, Bangladesh, Cameroon, China, Djibouti, Egypt, Indonesia, Iran, Iraq, Japan, Jordan, Kuwait, Maldives, Morocco, Nigeria, Oman, Pakistan, Qatar, Saudi Arabia, Sierra Leone, Somalia, Syria, United Republic of Tanzania, United States, Yemen.

Abstaining: Algeria, Antigua and Barbuda, Bahamas, Barbados, Bhutan, Botswana, Brunei Darussalam, Burkina Faso, Burundi, Chile, Congo, Cote d'Ivoire, Cuba, Democratic Yemen, Dominica, Ethiopia, Fiji, Gambia, Ghana, Guinea, Guyana, India, Israel, Jamaica, Kenya, Lebanon, Lesotho, Liberia, Libya, Madagascar, Malawi, Mali, Mauritius, Mozambique, Myanmar, Romania, Rwanda, Senegal, Singapore, Solomon Islands, Sri Lanka, Suriname, Trinidad and Tobago, Turkey, Uganda, Vanuatu, Zambia, Zimbabwe.

Absent: Albania, Angola, Belize, Benin, Central African Republic, Chad, Comoros, Equatorial Guinea, Gabon, Guinea-Bissau, Lao People's Democratic Republic, Malaysia**, Mauritania, Nicaragua***, Niger, Papua New Guinea, Sao Tome and Principe, Seychelles, Sudan**, Swaziland, Thailand, Tunisia, United Arab Emirates, Viet Nam, Zaïre.

* Later advised the Secretariat that it had intended to abstain.
** Later advised the Secretariat that it had intended to vote against.
*** Later advised the Secretariat that it had intended to vote in favour.

1 E/CN.4/Sub. 2/1987/20.
2 A/36/441 and Add. 1 and 2, A/37/407 and Add. 1, A/44/592 and Add. 1.
3 See *Official Records of the Economic and Social Council, 1989, Supplement No. 2* (E/1989/20), chap. II, sect. A.
4 Resolution 217 A (III).
5 See resolution 2200 A (XXI), annex.

Bibliography

Books, Theses, Studies

AGARWAL, H. O., *Implementation of Human Rights Covenants with Special Reference to India* (Kitab Mahal, Allahabad, 1983).

AHMED, A. K., 'Analysis of the Decisions of the Committee on Human Rights' (LL.M. thesis, Univ. of London, LSE, c. 1982).

AKEHURST, M., *A Modern Introducton to International Law* (6th, Allen & Unwin, London, 1987).

ALEXANDER, Y., and FRIEDLANDER, R., eds., *Self-Determination: National, Regional and Global Dimensions* (Boulder, Westview Press, 1980).

ALSTON, P., and TOMASEVSKI, K., eds., *The Right to Food* (Nijhoff, Dordrecht/Boston/Lancaster, 1984).

AMERSINGHE, C. F., *Local Remedies in International Law* (Grotius, Cambridge, 1990).

AMNESTY INTERNATIONAL DANISH MEDICAL GROUP Report, *Evidence of Torture* (AI, London, 1977).

AMNESTY INTERNATIONAL Report, *The Death Penalty* (AI, London, 1979).

—— Report, *Political Killings by Governments* (AI, London, 1983).

—— Report, *Torture in the 1980s* (AI, London, 1984).

—— Annual Reports (AI, London, latest report 1989).

ANDREWS, J. A., ed., *Human Rights in Criminal Procedure—A Comparative Study* (Nijhoff, The Hague/Boston, 1982).

ARANGIO-RUIZ, G., *The United Nations Declaration on Friendly Relations and the System of the Sources of International Law* (Sijthoff and Noordhoff, Alphen aan den Rijn/Maryland, 1979).

Article 19, Information, Freedom and Censorship (Longman, London, 1988).

ASMAL, K. (Chairman), *Shoot to Kill—International Lawyers' Inquiry* (Mercier Press, Irish Books Media, Eire, 1985).

BAILEY, S., ed., *Human Rights and Responsibilities in Britain and Ireland* (Macmillan, London, 1988).

BAILEY, S. H., HARRIS, D. J., and JONES, B., *Civil Liberties—Cases and Materials* (2nd, Butterworths, London, 1985).

BARENDT, E., *Freedom of Speech* (Clarendon Press, Oxford, 1985).

BARUAH, S. K., (Rapporteur), *The Right to Development and its Implications for Development Strategy*, Human Rights and Development Working Papers, No. 3 (Anti-Slavery Society, London, 1979).

BECK, P., *The Falkland Islands as an International Problem* (Routledge, London, 1988).

BEDDARD, R., *Human Rights and Europe* (2nd, Sweet and Maxwell, London, 1980).

BISHOP, W., *Cases and Materials on International Law* (3rd, Little & Brown, Boston/Toronto, 1971).

BLAUSTEIN, A. P., and FLANZ, G. H., *Constitutions of the Countries of the World* (Oceana, New York, 1971–   ).

BLOCH, S., and REDDAWAY, P., *Soviet Psychiatric Abuse* (Gollancz, London, 1984).

BONNER, D., *Emergency Powers in Peacetime* (Sweet and Maxwell, London, 1985).

BOSSUYT, M. J., *Guide to the 'Travaux Préparatoires' of the International Covenant on Civil and Political Rights* (Nijhoff, Dordrecht, 1987).

BOYLE, K., and HADDEN, T., *Ireland—A Positive Proposal* (Penguin, Harmondsworth, 1985).

BRAR, P. S., 'International Law and the Protection of Civil and Political Rights: A Critique of the United Nations' Human Rights Committee's Nature, Legal Status, Practices, Procedures and Prospects' (MALD, thesis, The Fletcher School of Law and Diplomacy, USA, 1984).

BROWN, P. G., and MACLEAN, D., eds., *Human Rights and U.S. Foreign Policy* (Lexington Books, Lexington, 1979).

BROWNLIE, I., *Principles of Public International Law* (4th, Clarendon Press, Oxford, 1990).

—— *Basic Documents in International Law* (3rd, Clarendon Press, Oxford, 1983).

—— *Systems of the Laws of Nations—State Responsibility*, Part I (Clarendon Press, Oxford, 1983).

BUCHHEIT, L. C., *Secession: The Legitimacy of Self-Determination* (Yale Univ. Press, New Haven, Conn., 1978).

BUERGENTHAL, T., ed., *Human Rights, International Law and the Helsinki Accords* (Allanheld Osmun, Montclair, NJ, 1977).

—— ed., *Contemporary Issues in International Law—Essays in Honour of Louis B. Sohn* (Engel, Kehl/Strasbourg/Arlington, 1984).

—— NORRIS, R., and SHELTON, D., *Protecting Human Rights in the Americas* (2nd, International Institute of Human Rights, Strasbourg, 1986).

BULAJIC, M., *Principles of International Development Law* (Nijhoff, Dordrecht, 1986).

BULL, H., ed., *Intervention in World Politics* (OUP, Oxford, 1984).

BURGERS. J. H., and DANELIUS, H., The United Nations Convention Against Torture (Nijhoff, Dordrecht/Boston/London, 1988).

BUZAN, B., *People, States and Fear—The National Security Problem in International Relations* (Wheatsheaf Books, Brighton, Sussex, 1983).

CAMPBELL, T., *et al.*, eds., *Human Rights—From Rhetoric to Reality* (Blackwell, Oxford, 1986).

CAPOTORTI, F., *Study on the Rights of Persons Belonging to Ethnic, Religious and Linguistic Minorities*, UN Doc. E/CN.4/Sub. 2/384 Rev. 1 (UN, New York, 1979).

CAREY, J., *U.N. Protection of Civil and Political Rights* (Syracuse Univ. Press, Syracuse, 1970).

CASSESE, A., ed., *UN Law/Fundamental Rights—Two Topics in International Law* (Sijthoff, Alphen aan den Rijn, 1979).

—— *International Law in a Divided World* (OUP, Oxford, 1986).

—— ed., *The Current Legal Regulation of the Use of Force* (Nijhoff, Dordrecht/Boston/Lancaster, 1986).

CHAKRAVARTI, R., *Human Rights and the United Nations* (Calcutta, 1958).

CHANDRA, S., *Civil and Political Rights of the Aliens: A Study of National and International Laws* (Deep and Deep Publications, New Delhi, 1982).

CHOMSKY, N. and HERMAN, E. S., *The Washington Connection and Third World Fascism*, Vol. 1 (Spokesman, Nottingham; South End Press, Boston, 1979).

CHOWDHURRY, S. R., *The Rule of Law in a State of Emergency—The Paris Minimum Standards of Human Rights Norms in a State of Emergency* (St Martin's Press, New York, 1988).

CINGRANELLI, D. L., ed., *Human Rights: Measurement and Theory* (Macmillan, London, 1988).

CLARK, R. S., *A United Nations Commissioner for Human Rights* (Nijhoff, The Hague, 1972).

CLAUDE, R. P., and WESTON, B. H., *Human Rights in the World Community—Issues and Action* (Univ. of Penn. Press, Philadelphia, 1989).

COHEN, E. R., *Human Rights in Israeli-Occupied Territories 1967–1982* (Manchester Univ. Press, Manchester/New Hampshire, 1985).

COLL, A. R., and ARENDT, A. C., *The Falklands War—Lessons for Strategy, Diplomacy and International Law* (Allen and Unwin, London/Boston, 1985).

CRAWFORD, J., *The Creation of States in International Law* (Clarendon Press, Oxford, 1979).

—— ed., *The Rights of Peoples* (Clarendon Press, Oxford, 1988).

CRISTESCU, A., *The Right to Self-Determination: Historical and Current Development on the Basis of United Nations Instruments*, UN Doc. E/CN.4/Sub. 2/404/Rev. 1 (UN, New York, 1981).

CROSS, R., and TAPPER, C., *Cross on Evidence* (6th, Butterworths, London, 1985).

DAES, E. I. A., *The Individual's Duties to the Community and the Limitations on Human Rights and Freedoms under Article 29 of the Universal Declaration of Human Rights: A Contribution to Freedom of the Individual Under Law*, UN Doc. E/CN. 4/Sub. 2/432/Rev. 2 (UN, New York, 1983). Reprinted as Human Rights Study Series No. 3 (New York, 1990).

DE AZCARATE, P., *League of Nations and National Minorities—An Experiment* (Carnegie Endowment for International Peace, Washington, DC, 1945).

DEL RUSSO, A. L., *International Protection of Human Rights* (Lerner Law Books, Washington, DC, 1971).

DESMOND, C., *Persecution East and West: Human Rights, Political Prisoners and Amnesty* (Penguin, Harmondsworth, 1983).

DIXON, M., ed., *On Trial: Reagan's War Against Nicaragua* (Zed Books, London, 1985).

DOMINGUEZ, J., RODLEY, N. S., WOOD, B., and FALK, R., *Enhancing Global Human Rights* (McGraw-Hill, New York, 1979).

DONNELLY, J., *The Concept of Human Rights* (Croom Helm, London, 1985).

—— and HOWARD, R. E., *International Handbook of Human Rights* (Greenwood, Westport, Conn., 1987).

DOWRICK, F. E., *Human Rights—Problems, Perspectives, Texts* (Saxon House, Farnborough, Hants, 1979).

DROST, P. N., *Human Rights as Legal Rights—The Realization of Human Rights in Positive International Law* (Sijthoff, Leiden, 1951; New York, 1965).

DRZEMCZEWSKI, A., *European Human Rights Convention in Domestic Law* (OUP, Oxford, 1983).

DUCHACEK, I. D., *Rights and Liberties in the World Today* (Clio Press, Santa Barbera/Oxford, 1973).

DUPUY, R. J., ed., *The Right to Health as a Human Right: Workshop, 1978* (Sijthoff and Noordhoff, Alphen aan den Rijn, 1979).

EIDE, A., and SCHOU, A., eds., *International Protection of Human Rights, Proceedings of the Seventh Nobel Symposium* (Interscience Publishers, Sweden/New York, 1968).

ELIAN, G., *The Principle of Sovereignty over Natural Resources* (Sijthoff, Leiden, 1979).

ELKIND, J. B., *Non-Appearance before the International Court of Justice: A Functional and Comparative Analysis* (Nijhoff, Dordrecht, 1984).

—— and SHAW, A., *A Standard for Justice—A Critical Commentary on the Proposed Bill of Rights for New Zealand* (OUP, Oxford/Auckland/New York, 1986).

ELLERT, R. B., *N.A.T.O. Fair Trial Safeguards* (Nijhoff, The Hague, 1963).

EMPELL, H. M., *Die Kompetenzen Des UN—Menschenrechtsausschusses Im Staatenberichtsverfahren* (Peter Lang, Frankfurt/Bern/New York/Paris, 1987).

EZEJIOFOR, G., *Protection of Human Rights under the Law* (Butterworths, London, 1964).

FALK, R., *Human Rights and State Sovereignty* (Holmes and Meier, New York, 1981).

—— et al., eds., *International Law: A Contemporary Perspective* (Westview Press, Boulder/London 1985).

FAREED, N. J., *The UN Commission on Human Rights and Its Work for Human Rights and Fundamental Freedoms* (University Microfilms, Ann Arbor, Michigan/London, 1979).

FAWCETT, J. E. S., *The Application of the European Convention on Human Rights* (2nd, Clarendon Press, Oxford, 1987).

FRANCK, T., *Nation Against Nation: What Happened to the UN Dream and What the U.S. Can Do About It* (OUP, New York/Oxford, 1985).

GANJI, M., *International Protection of Human Rights* (Droz, Geneva/Paris, 1962).

GASTIL, R. D., ed., *Freedom in the World: Political Rights and Civil Liberties* (Random House, New York, 1980).

GIFFORD, T., *Supergrasses—The Use of Accomplice Evidence in Northern Ireland* (Cobden Trust, London, 1984).

GLASSER, K., and POSSONY, S. T., *Victims of Politics: The State of Human Rights* (Columbia Univ. Press, New York, 1979).

GOODRICH, L. M., HAMBRO, E., and SIMONS, P., *Charter of the United Nations: Commentary and Documents* (Columbia Univ. Press, New York, 1969).

GORMLEY, W. P., 'The Implementation of United Nations Human Rights Covenants: Contemporary Legal Precedent and Future Procedural Remedies' (3 Vols., Ph.D. thesis, University of Manchester, 1972).

GOTLIEB, A., ed., *Human Rights, Federalism and Minorities* (Canadian Institute of International Affairs, Canada, 1970).

GREEN, J. F., *The United Nations and Human Rights* (Brookings Institute, Washington, DC, 1956).

GREER, S. C., and WHITE, A., *Abolishing the Diplock Courts—The Case for Restoring Jury Trial to Scheduled Offences in Northern Ireland* (Cobden Trust, London, 1986).

GROS-ESPIELL, H., *The Right to Self-Determination: Implementation of United Nations Resolutions* (UN, New York, 1980).

GRZYBOWSKI, K., *Soviet Public International Law* (Sijthoff, Leyden, 1970).

GUSTAFSON, L., *The Sovereignty Dispute over the Falkland (Malvinas) Islands* (OUP, Oxford/New York, 1988).

HADDEN, T., and BOYLE, K., The Anglo–Irish Agreement (Sweet and Maxwell, London, 1989).

HAKSAR, U., *Minority Protection and the International Bill of Rights* (Allied Publishers, Bombay, 1974).

HANNUM, H., *The Right to Leave and Return in International Law and Practice* (Nijhoff, Dordrecht/Boston/Lancaster, 1987).

—— ed., *Guide to International Human Rights Practice* (Macmillan, London, 1984).

—— *Autonomy, Sovereignty and Self-Determination* (Univ. of Penn. Press, Philadelphia, 1990).

HARRIS, D. J., *Cases and Materials on International Law* (3rd, Sweet & Maxwell, London, 1983).

—— *The European Social Charter* (Univ. of Virginia Press, Charlottesville, V., 1984).

HENKIN, A. H., *Human Dignity: The Internationalization of Human Rights* (Oceana, New York, 1979).

HENKIN, L., *How Nations Behave: Law and Foreign Policy* (2nd, Columbia Univ. Press, New York, 1979).

—— *The International Bill of Rights: The Covenant on Civil and Political Rights* (Colombia Univ. Press, New York, 1981).

—— PUGH, R. C., SCHACHTER, O., and SMIT, H., *International Law—Cases and Materials* (2nd, West, St Paul's, Minn., 1987).

HERTZBERG, S., and ZAMMUTO, C., *The Protection of Human Rights in the Criminal Process under International Instruments and National Constitutions* (Association International De Droit Pénal, 1981).

HEVENER, N., ed., *The Dynamics of Human Rights in US Foreign Policy* (Transaction Books, New Brunswick, NJ, 1981).

HIGGINS, R., *The Development of International Law Through the Political Organs of the United Nations* (OUP, Oxford, 1963).

HILL, D. M., ed., *Human Rights and Foreign Policy: Principle and Practice* (Macmillan, London, 1989).

HOSSAIN, K., ed., *Legal Aspects of the New International Economic Order* (Frances Pinter, London, 1980).

—— and CHOWDHURRY, S. R., *Permanent Sovereignty over Natural Resources in International Law—Principle and Practice* (Frances Pinter, London, 1984).

HUMANA, C., *World Human Rights Guide* (2nd, *The Economist*, London, 1986).

HUMPHREY, J. P., *Human Rights and the United Nations: A Great Adventure* (Transnational, Dobbs Ferry, New York, 1984).

HUSSAIN, I., *Dissenting and Separate Opinions in the World Court* (Nijhoff, Dordrecht, 1984).

INTERNATIONAL COMMISSION OF JURISTS, *Human Rights in a One Party State* (Search Press, London, 1978).
—— *Human Rights in Islam* (ICJ, Geneva, 1982).
—— *States of Emergency—Their Impact on Human Rights* (ICJ, Geneva, 1983).
—— AND THE SWISS COMMITTEE AGAINST TORTURE, *Torture: How to Make an International Convention Effective* (2nd, ICJ, Geneva, 1981).
JACOBS, F. G., *The European Convention on Human Rights* (Clarendon Press, Oxford, 1975).
JENNINGS, A., ed., *Justice under Fire: The Abuse of Civil Liberties in Northern Ireland* (Pluto, London, 1988).
JONES, G. J., *The United Nations and the Domestic Jurisdiction of States* (Univ. of Wales Press, Cardiff, 1979).
KAMENKA, E., ed., *Ideas and Ideologies: Human Rights* (Edward Arnold, London, 1978).
KELSEN, H., *The Law of the United Nations* (Stevens, London, 1950).
LANDY, E. A., *The Effectiveness of International Supervision—30 Years of ILO Experience* (Stevens, London, 1966).
LAUTERPACHT, H., *An International Bill of the Rights of Man* (Colombia Univ. Press, New York, 1945).
—— *International Law and Human Rights* (Praeger, New York, 1950).
—— *International Law—Collected Papers*, Lauterpacht, E., ed., Vol. iii, *The Law of Peace* (Cambridge Univ. Press, Cambridge, 1977).
—— *The Development of International Law by the International Court* (Stevens, London, 1958; reprinted Grotius, Cambridge, 1982).
LEE, R., and MORGAN, D., eds., *Birthrights—Law and Ethics at the Beginning of Life* (Routledge, London, 1989).
LERNER, N., *The United Nations Convention on the Elimination of Racial Discrimination* (2nd, Sijthoff and Noordhoff, Alphen aan den Rijn/Rockville, Md., 1980).
LILLICH, R. B., ed., *U.S. Ratification of Human Rights Treaties: With or Without Reservations?* (Univ. Press of Virginia, Charlottesville, 1981).
—— *International Human Rights Instruments* (Hein, Buffalo, New York, 1983).
—— *The Human Rights of Aliens in Contemporary International Law* (Manchester Univ. Press, Manchester/New Hampshire, 1984).
—— and NEWMAN, F., *International Human Rights—Problems of Law and Policy* (Little & Brown, Boston, 1979).
LUARD, E., ed., *The International Protection of Human Rights* (Thames and Hudson, London, 1967).
—— *A History of the United Nations*, Vol. i, *The Years of Western Domination* (Macmillan, London, 1982); Vol. ii, *The Age of Decolonization* (1989).
MACBRIDE, S. (Chairman), *Many Voices, One World—Toward a New, More Just and More Efficient World Information and Communication Order*, Report of the Commission for the Study of Communication Problems (UNESCO, Kogan Page, London, 1980).
MACDONALD, R. ST. J., and HUMPHREY, J. P., eds., *The Practice of Freedom* (Butterworths, London, 1979).

MacDonald, R. St. J., and Johnston, D., eds., *The Structure and Process of International Law* (Nijhoff, Dordrecht/Boston/Lancaster, 1983).

McDougal, M., Lasswell, H., and Chen, L. C., *Human Rights and World Public Order* (Yale Univ. Press, New Haven/London, 1980).

Macfarlane, L. J., *The Theory and Practice of Human Rights* (Maurice Temple Smith, London, 1985).

McKean, W., *Equality and Discrimination under International Law* (Clarendon Press, Oxford, 1983).

McNair, A., *The Law of Treaties* (Clarendon Press, Oxford, 1961).

Maier, I., ed., *Protection of Human Rights in Europe—Limits and Effects* (Muller, Heidelberg, 1982).

Martin, L. John, *International Propaganda—Its Legal and Diplomatic Control* (Univ. of Minnesota Press, Minneapolis, 1958).

Marsh, N., ed., *Public Access to Government Held Information* (Stevens, London, 1987).

Mason, J. K., and McCall-Smith, R. A., *Law and Medical Ethics* (2nd, Butterworths, London, 1987).

Mélanges offerts à Polys Modinos (Pedone, Paris, 1968).

Meron, T., ed., *Human Rights in International Law—Legal and Policy Issues*, 2 Vols. (Clarendon Press, Oxford, 1984; issued as a single volume 1985).

—— *Human Rights Law-Making in the United Nations—A Critique of Instruments and Process* (Clarendon Press, Oxford, 1986).

—— *Human Rights in Internal Strife: Their International Protection* (Grotius, Cambridge, 1987).

—— *Human Rights and Humanitarian Norms as Customary International Law* (OUP, Oxford, 1989).

Merrills, J. G., *The Development of International Law by the European Court of Human Rights* (Manchester Univ. Press, Manchester, 1988).

Mikaelson, L., *European Protection of Human Rights* (Sijthoff and Noordhoff, Alphen aan den Rijn, Netherlands/Germantown, Md. 1980).

Morrisson, C. C., *The Dynamics of Development in the European Human Rights Convention System* (Nijhoff, The Hague/Boston, London, 1981).

Moscowitz, M., *Human Rights and World Order—The Struggle for Human Rights* (Oceana, New York, 1958).

—— *The Politics and Dynamics of Human Rights* (Oceana, Dobbs Ferry, New York, 1968).

—— *International Concern with Human Rights* (Oceana, Sijthoff-Leiden, 1974).

Movchan, A., *Human Rights and International Relations* (Progress, Moscow, 1988).

Mower, A. J. G., Jr., *The United States, the United Nations and Human Rights—The Eleanor Roosevelt and Jimmy Carter Eras* (Greenwood Press, Westport, Conn., 1979).

Munro, C. R., *Constitutional Law* (Butterworths, London, 1987).

Murty, B. S., *The International Law of Propaganda* (New Haven Press, New Haven; Nijhoff, Dordrecht/Boston/Lancaster, 1989).

Nickel, J. W., *Making Sense of Human Rights* (Univ. of California Press, Berkeley/Los Angeles/London, 1987).

NORDENSTRENG, K., *The Mass Media Declaration of Unesco* (Ablex, Norwood, NJ, 1984).

NOVAK, M., *CCPR-Kommentar* Kommentar zum UNO-Pakt über bürgerliche und politische Rechte und dem Fakultativprotokoll (Engel Verlag, Kiehl am Rhein/ Strasbourg/Arlington, 1989). An english version of this important work is being prepared.

OPPENHEIM, L., *International Law: A Treatise*, Lauterpacht, H., ed. (8th, Longmans, London, 1955).

PANNICK, D., *Judicial Review of the Death Penalty* (Duckworth, London, 1982).

PETERS, E., *Torture* (Blackwell, Oxford, 1985).

POGANY, I., ed., *Nuclear Weapons and International Law* (Avebury, Aldershot, 1987).

POMERANCE, M., *Self-Determination in Law and Practice: The New Doctrine in the United Nations* (Nijhoff, Dordrecht/Boston/Lancaster, 1982).

QUIESTIAUX, N., *Study of the Implications for Human Rights of Recent Developments Concerning Situations Known as States of Siege or Emergency*, UN Doc. E/CN. 4/ Sub. 2/1982/15 (July 1982).

QUIROGA, C. M., *The Battle of Human Rights* (Nijhoff, Dordrecht/Boston/Lancaster, 1988).

RAMCHARAN, B. G., ed., *Human Rights—Thirty Years After the Universal Declaration* (Nijhoff, The Hague, 1979).

—— ed., *International Law and Fact-Finding in the Field of Human Rights* (Nijhoff, Dordrecht/Boston/Lancaster, 1982).

—— *Humanitarian Good Offices in International Law* (Nijhoff, Dordrecht/Boston/ Lancaster, 1983).

—— *The Concept and Present Status of the International Protection of Human Rights* (Nijhoff, Dordrecht/Boston/Lancaster, 1989).

—— ed., *The Right to Life in International Law* (Nijhoff, Dordrecht/Boston/ Lancaster, 1985).

Recueil d'études de droit international en hommage à Paul Guggenheim (Geneva, 1968).

REISMAN M. W. and WESTON, B. H., eds., *Towards World Order and Human Dignity*, pp. 262–90 (The Free Press, London/New York, 1976).

REMBE, N. S., *Africa and Regional Protection of Human Rights* (Leoni, Rome, 1985).

RIGO-SUREDA, A., *The Evolution of the Right to Self-Determination: A Study of United Nations Practice* (Sijthoff, Leiden, 1973).

ROBERTS, A., and GUELFF, R., *Documents of the Law of War* (2nd, Clarendon Press, Oxford, 1989).

ROBERTSON, A. H., *Human Rights in Europe* (2nd, Manchester Univ. Press, Manchester, 1977).

—— and MERRILLS, J. G., *Human Rights in the World* (3rd, Manchester Univ. Press, Manchester/New Hampshire, 1989).

RODLEY, N. S., *The Treatment of Prisoners under International Law* (OUP, Oxford, 1987).

RONZITTI, N., *Rescuing Nationals Abroad through Military Coercion and Intervention on Grounds of Humanity* (Nijhoff, Dordrecht, 1985).

ROTUNDA R. D., NOWAK, J. E., and YOUNG, J. N., *A Treatise on Constitutional Law: Substance and Procedure* (West, St Paul, Minn., 1986).

SANDIFER, D., *Evidence before International Tribunals* (revised edn., Univ. of Virginia Press, Charlottesville, 1975).

SAVAGE, N., and EDWARDS, C., *A Guide to the Data Protection Act* (2nd, Financial Training, London, 1985).

SCHOULTZ, L., *Human Rights and U.S. Policy Towards Latin America* (Princeton Univ. Press, Princeton, NJ, 1981).

SCHWARZENBERGER, G., *International Law—International Courts*, Vol. iv (Stevens, London, 1986).

SCOBLE, H. M., and WIESBERG, L., *Access to Justice—The Struggle for Human Rights in South East Asia* (Zed Books, London, 1985).

SELASSIE, B. K., ed., *Consensus and Peace* (UNESCO, UNIPUB, 1980).

SHAW, M., *Title to Territory in Africa: International Legal Issues* (Clarendon Press, Oxford, 1986).

SHUE, H., *Basic Rights: Subsistence, Affluence and U.S. Foreign Policy* (Univ. of Princeton Press, Princeton, NJ, 1980).

SIEGHART, P., *The International Law of Human Rights* (OUP, Oxford, 1983, 1984).

—— *The Lawful Rights of Mankind* (OPUS, Oxford, 1985).

—— ed., *Human Rights in the United Kingdom* (Pinter, London, 1988).

—— *Aids and Human Rights* (British Medical Association, London, 1989).

SINCLAIR, I., *The Vienna Convention on the Law of Treaties* (2nd, Manchester Univ. Press, Manchester, 1984).

SINGH, N., *Enforcement of Human Rights in Peace and War and the Future of Humanity* (Nijhoff, Dordrecht, 1986).

SMITH, J. C., *Justification and Excuse in the Criminal Law* (Stevens, London, 1989).

SNYDER, F., and SLINN, P., *International Law of Development: Comparative Perspectives* (Professional Books, Abingdon, 1987).

SOHN, L., and BUERGENTHAL, T., *International Protection of Human Rights* (Bobbs-Merrill, Indianapolis, 1973).

SZABO, I., *Cultural Rights* (Sijthoff, Alphen aan den Rijn/Germantown, Md., 1974).

TARDU, M., *Human Rights—The International Petition System* (Oceana, Dobbs Ferry, NY, 1979–).

TESON, F. R., *Humanitarian Intervention: An Inquiry into Law and Morality* (Transnational Publishers, Dobbs Ferry, New York, 1989).

THIRLWAY, H. W. A., *Non-Appearance before the International Court of Justice* (Cambridge Univ. Press, Cambridge, 1985).

THOOLEN, H., and VERSTAPPEN, B., *Human Rights Missions* (Nijhoff, Dordrecht/Boston/Lancaster, 1986).

TOLLEY, H., JR., *The UN Commission on Human Rights* (Westview Press, Boulder/London, 1987).

TOMASEVSKI, K., ed., *Children in Adult Prisons—An International Perspective* (Frances Pinter, London, 1986).

—— *The Right to Food: Guide Through Applicable International Law* (Nijhoff, Dordrecht/Boston/Lancaster, 1987).

—— and ALSTON, P., eds., *The Right to Food* (Nijhoff, Dordrecht/Boston/Lancaster, 1984).

TORNUDD, K., *Finland and the International Norms of Human Rights* (Nijhoff, Dordrecht/Boston/Lancaster, 1986).

TRINDADE, A. A. C., *The Application of the Rule of Exhaustion of Local Remedies in International Law* (Cambridge Univ. Press, Cambridge, 1983).

TUNKIN, G., *Theory of International Law*, trans. Butler, W. (Harvard Univ. Press, Cambridge, Mass., 1974).

TUTTLE, J. C., ed., *International Human Rights Law and Practice* (American Bar Association, 1978).

UMOZURIKE, U. O., *Self-Determination in International Law* (Archon Books, Hamden, Conn., 1972).

United Nations Action in the Field of Human Rights (UN, New York, 1983).

United Nations Action in the Field of Human Rights (UN, New York, 1988).

UNITED NATIONS, *Human Rights—A Compilation of International Instruments* (UN, New York, 1988).

VALTICOS, N., *The International Labour Organization* (Kluwer, Deventer, 1979).

VAN DIJK, P., *The Right of an Accused to a Fair Trial Under International Law* (Studie En Informatiencentram Mensrechten, Utrecht, 1983).

—— and VAN HOOF, G. J. H., *Theory and Practice of the European Convention on Human Rights* (Deventer, Kluwer, 1984).

VAN DYKE, V., *Human Rights, the United States and the World Community* (OUP, Oxford, New York, 1970).

VASAK, K., ed., ALSTON, P. (English ed.), *The International Dimensions of Human Rights* (UNESCO, Greenwood Press, Westport, Conn., 1982).

VERZIJL, J. H. W., *International Law in Historical Perspective*, Vol. v (Sijthoff, Leiden, 1972).

VIERDAG, E. W., *The Concept of Discrimination in International Law* (Nijhoff, The Hague, 1973).

VINCENT, R. J., ed., *Foreign Policy and Human Rights: Issues and Responses* (Cambridge Univ. Press, Cambridge, 1986).

—— *Human Rights and International Relations* (Cambridge Univ. Press, Cambridge, 1987).

WALKER, C., *The Prevention of Terrorism in British Law* (Manchester Univ. Press, Manchester, 1986).

WALLACE, R., *International Law* (Sweet and Maxwell, London, 1986).

WALSH, D. J. P., *The Use and Abuse of Emergency Legislation* (Cobden Trust, London, 1983).

WHITTON, J. B., and LARSON, A., *Propaganda towards Disarmament in the War of Words* (Oceana, New York, 1958).

WILLIAMS, P., ed., *The International Bill of Human Rights* (Entwhistle Books, Glenn Ellen, Calif., 1981).

WILSON, H., *International Law and the Use of Force by National Liberation Movements* (OUP, Oxford, 1988).

WHITEMAN, M., *Digest of International Law*, Vols. v, xiii (US Gov. Printing Office, Washington, DC).

ZIMAN, J., SIEGHART, P., and HUMPHREY, J. P., *The World of Science and the Rule of Law* (OUP, Oxford, 1986).

ZUIDJWICK, T. J. M., *Petitioning the United Nations—A Study in Human Rights* (Gower, Aldershot, 1982).

Articles

ACKERMAN, S., 'Torture and Other Forms of Cruel and Unusual Punishment in International Law', 11 Vand. J. Trans. L. (1978) pp. 653–707.

ADDO, M. K., 'The Justiciability of Economic, Social and Cultural Rights', 14 CLB (1989) pp. 1425–32.

AKEHURST, M., 'Humanitarian Intervention', in Bull, H., ed., above (1984), pp. 93–118.

ALEXANDER, G. J., 'The Illusory Protection of Human Rights by National Courts During Periods of Public Emergency', 5 HRLJ (1984) pp. 1–65.

ALSTON, P., 'The United Nations' Specialized Agencies and Implementation of the International Covenant on Economic, Social and Cultural Rights', 10 Col. J. Trans. L. (1979) pp. 79–118.

—— 'The Universal Declaration at 35: Western and Passé or Alive and Universal', 31 Rev. ICJ (1983) pp. 60–70.

—— 'Conjuring up New Human Rights: Proposals for Quality Control', 78 AJIL (1984) pp. 607–21.

—— 'Out of the Abyss: The Challenges Confronting the New U.N. Committee on Economic, Social and Cultural Rights', 9 HRQ (1987) pp. 332–81.

—— 'Making Space for New Human Rights', 1 Harv. HRY (1988) pp. 3–40.

—— and QUINN, G., 'The Nature and Scope of States Parties' Obligations under the International Covenant on Economic, Social and Cultural Rights', 9 HRQ (1987) pp. 156–229.

—— and SIMMA, B., 'First Session of the U.N. Committee on Economic, Social and Cultural Rights', 81 AJIL (1987) pp. 747–56.

—— —— 'Second Session of the U.N. Committee on Economic, Social and Cultural Rights', 82 AJIL (1988) pp. 603–15.

ANON., 'Individual Petition: Special Study', 5 Rev. ICJ (1970) pp. 23–7.

—— 'The New Human Rights Committee', 19 Rev. ICJ (1977) pp. 19–22.

—— 'Torture: Prosecution and Compensation in Colombia', 35 Rev. ICJ (1985) pp. 5–6.

—— 'ILO Inquiry's Findings on Discrimination in Public Employment in FRG' 38 Rev. ICJ (1987) pp. 26–30.

—— 'UN Committee on Economic, Social and Cultural Rights', 42 Rev. ICJ (1989) pp. 33–9.

—— 'UN Commission on Human Rights', 44 Rev. ICJ (1990) pp. 16–31.

ARCHER, P., 'Action by Unofficial Organizations on Human Rights', in Luard, E., ed., above (1967), pp. 160–82.

ARMSTRONG, J. D., 'Non-Governmental Organizations', in Vincent, R. J., ed., above (1986), pp. 243–60.

ARTZ, D. E., 'The Application of International Human Rights Law in Islamic States', 12 HRQ (1990) pp. 202–30.

BARSH R. L., 'Indigenous Peoples: An Emerging Object of International Law', 80 AJIL (1986) pp. 369–85.

BASSIOUNI, C., 'Self-Determination and the Palestinians', ASIL Proc. (1971) pp. 31–40.

—— and DERBY, D., 'An Appraisal of Torture in International Law and Practice: The Need for an International Convention for the Suppression and Prevention of Torture', 48 RIDP (1977) pp. 17–114.

BAYEFSKY, A. F., 'The Human Rights Committee and the Case of Sandra Lovelace', 20 Can. YIL (1982) pp. 244–66.

BELLO, E. G., 'The African Charter on Human and Peoples Rights—A Legal Analysis', 194 Rec. des cours (1985-V) pp. 21–268.

BENNETT, W. H., Jr., 'A Critique of the Emerging Convention on the Rights of the Child', 20 Corn. ILJ (1987) pp. 1–64.

BERENSTEIN, A., 'Economic and Social Rights: Their Inclusion in the ECHR—Problems of Formulation and Interpretation', 2 HRLJ (1981) pp. 257–80.

BERGESON, H. O., 'Human Rights—The Property of the Nation State or a Concern for the International Community?', 14 Cooperation and Conflict (1979) pp. 239–54.

BERNHARDT, R., 'Domestic Jurisdiction of States and International Human Rights Organs', 7 HRLJ (1986) pp. 205–16.

BETTOCCHI, G., 'Human Rights and Inquisitorial Procedures in Japan', 42 Rev. ICJ (1989) pp. 57–66.

BHAGWATI, Justice, 'Human Rights as Evolved by the Jurisprudence of the Supreme Court of India' (Part I), 13 Comm. LB (1987) pp. 236–45.

BILDER, R. B., 'Rethinking International Human Rights: Some Basic Questions', 1969 Wisc. LR pp. 171–217.

BIRCH, D. J., 'Hunting the Snark: The Elusive Statutory Exception', [1988] CLR pp. 221–32.

BLAY, K. W., 'Self-Determination Versus Territorial Integrity in Decolonization Revisited', 25 Ind. JIL (1985) pp. 386–410.

BLAY, S. K. N., 'The ICCPR and the Recognition of Customary Law Practices of Indigenous Peoples: The Case of Australian Aborigines', 19 CILSA (1986) pp. 199–219.

BOKOR-SZEGO, H., 'The Attitude of Socialist States towards the International Regulation of the Use of Force', in Cassese, A., ed., above (1986), pp. 448–50.

BOSSUYT, M. J., 'La distinction juridique entre les droits civils et politiques et les droits économiques, sociaux et culturels', 8 RDH/HRJ (1975) pp. 783–820.

—— 'The United Nations and Civil and Political Rights in Chile', 27 ICLQ (1978) pp. 462–71.

—— 'Le Règlement intérieur du Comité Des Droits De L'homme', 14 Revue belge de droit international (1978–9) pp. 104–56.

—— 'The Development of Special Procedures of the United Nations Commission on Human Rights', 6 HRLJ (1985) pp. 179–210.

—— 'Human Rights and Non-Intervention in Domestic Matters', 35 Rev. ICJ (1985) pp. 45–52.

—— 'International Protocols Aimed at the Abolition of the Death Penalty', 48 RIDP (1987) pp. 371–85.

Boyle, A., 'Administrative Justice, Judicial Review and the Right to a Fair Hearing under the European Convention on Human Rights', [1984] PL pp. 89–111.

—— 'Political Broadcasting, Fairness and Administrative Law', [1986] PL pp. 562–96.

Boyle, K., 'The Concept of Arbitrary Deprivation of Life', in Ramcharan, B. G., ed., above (1985), pp. 221–44.

—— and Hannum, H., 'Individual Applications under the ECHR and the Concept of an Administrative Practice: The Donnelly Case', 68 AJIL (1974) pp. 440–53.

—— —— 'The Donnelly Case, Administrative Practice and Domestic Remedies under the European Convention: One Step Forward and Two Steps Back', 71 AJIL (1977) pp. 316–21.

Bradley, A. W., 'The ECHR and Administrative Law—First Impressions', 21 Osgoode Hall LJ (1983) pp. 609–35.

—— 'Parliamentary Privilege, Zircon and National Security', [1987] PL pp. 488–95.

Brar, P. S., 'The Practice and Procedures of the Human Rights Committee under the Optional Protocol of the International Covenant on Civil and Political Rights', 26 Ind. JIL (1986) pp. 506–43.

Brudner, A., 'The Domestic Enforcement of International Covenants on Human Rights: A Theoretical Framework', 35 Univ. Tor. LJ (1985) pp. 219–54.

Buergenthal, T., 'Implementing the Racial Convention', 12 Tex. ILJ (1977) pp. 187–221.

—— 'International and Regional Human Rights Law and Institutions: Some Examples of Their Interaction', 12 Tex. ILJ (1977) pp. 321–30.

—— 'To Respect and to Ensure: State Obligation and Permissible Derogations', in Henkin, L., ed., above (1981), pp. 72–91.

—— 'The Inter-American System for the Protection of Human Rights', in Meron, T., ed., above (1984), pp. 439–93.

—— 'The Advisory Jurisdiction of the Inter-American Court of Human Rights', in Buergenthal, T., ed., above (1984), pp. 127–47.

—— 'The United States and International Human Rights', 9 HRLJ (1988) pp. 141–62.

Burmeister, H., 'Federal Clauses: An Australian Perspective', 34 ICLQ (1985) pp. 522–37.

Byrnes, A., 'The "Other" Human Rights Treaty Body: The Work of the Committee on the Elimination of Discrimination Against Women', 14 Yale JIL (1989) pp. 1–67.

Bystricky, R., 'The Universality of Human Rights in A World of Conflicting Ideologies', in Eide, A., and Schou, A., eds., above (1968) pp. 83–93.

Capotorti, F., 'The International Measures of Implementation Included in the Covenants on Human Rights', in Eide, A., and Schou, A., eds., above (1968) pp. 131–48.

—— 'Human Rights—The Hard Road towards Universality', in MacDonald, R. St. J., and Johnston, D., eds., above (1983), pp. 977–1000.

Carey, J., 'Human Rights—The Soviet View', 53 Kentucky LR (1964) pp. 115–34.

Carty, A., 'Human Rights in a State of Exception: The I.L.A. Approach and the Third World', in Campbell, T., et al., eds., above (1986), pp. 60–79.

Cassese, A., 'The Helsinki Declaration and Self-Determination', in Buergenthal, T., ed., above (1977), pp. 83–110.

—— 'Political Self-Determination—Old Concepts and New Developments', in Cassesse, A., ed., above (1979), pp. 137–165.

—— 'The Self-Determination of Peoples', in Henkin, L., ed., above (1981), pp. 92–113.

—— 'The New Approach to Human Rights: The European Convention for the Prevention of Torture', 83 AJIL (1989) pp. 128–53.

CHEBABI, H. E., 'Self-Determination, Territorial Integrity and the Falkland Islands', 100 PSQ (1985) pp. 215–25.

CHEE, C. I., 'Alien Registration Law of Japan and the International Covenant for Civil and Political Rights', 10 Korea and World Affairs (1986) pp. 649–86.

CHEN, L. C., 'Self-Determination as a Human Right', in Reisman, M. W., and Weston, B. H., eds., above (1976), pp. 198–261.

CHIRLA, G., 'Signifiance of the Ratification by Romania of the International Covenants on Human Rights', 1 Revue d'études internationales (1975) pp. 57–62.

CLARK, R., 'Legal Representation', in Ramcharan, B. G., ed., above (1982), pp. 104–36.

CLAUDE, R. P., 'The Western Tradition of Human Rights in Comparative Perspective', 14 Comparative Judicial Review (1977) pp. 3–66.

CLAYDON, J., 'The Application of International Human Rights by Canadian Courts', 30 Buffalo LR (1981) pp. 727–52.

COHEN, M. and BAYEFSKY, A. F., 'The Canadian Charter of Rights and Freedoms and Public International Law', 61 Can. Bar. Rev. (1983) pp. 265–313.

COHEN, R., 'International Covenant on Civil and Political Rights', 6 Int. Problems (1968) pp. 38–49.

COHN, H., 'International Fact-Finding Processes', 18 Rev. ICJ (1977) pp 40–8.

COTE, M. J., 'Le Recours au Comité Des Droits De L'Homme de l'ONU—Une illusion?' 1985 Cahier de droit (Quebec), pp. 531–47.

COTE-HARPER, G., 'Le Comité Des Droits De L'Homme des Nations Unies', 28 Cahiers de droit (Quebec), (1987) pp. 533–46.

COUSSIRAT-COUSTERE, V., 'L'Adhésion de la France au Protocole Facultatif se rapportant au Pacte International Relatif aux Droits Civils et Politiques', 29 AFDI (1983) pp. 510–32.

CRAIG, M. D., 'The ICCPR and U.S. Law: Department of State Proposals for Preserving the Status Quo', 19 Harv. ILJ (1978) pp. 845–86.

D'AMATO, A., 'The Concept of Human Rights in International Law', 82 Col. LR (1982) pp. 1110–59.

DAS, K., 'United Nations Institutions and Procedures Founded on Conventions on Human Rights and Fundamental Freedoms', in Vasak, K./Alston, P., eds., above (1982), pp. 303–62.

DEAN, R. N., 'Beyond Helsinki: The Soviet View on Human Rights in International Law', 21 Virg. JIL (1980) pp. 55–95.

DECAUX, E., 'La Mise en vigeur du Pacte International Relatifs aux Droits Civils et Politiques', 84 Revue générale de droit international publique (1980) pp. 487–534.

DE WAART, P. J. M., 'The Inter-Relationship between the Right to Life and the Right to Development', in Ramcharan, B. G., above (1985), pp. 84–96.

DE ZAYAS, A., and MOLLER, J. TH., 'Optional Protocol Cases Concerning the Nordic

States before the United Nations Human Rights Committee', 4 Nordic JIL (1986) pp. 384–400.

—— —— and OPSAHL, T., 'Application of the International Covenant on Civil and Political Rights under the Optional Protocol by the Human Rights Committee' 28 GYIL (1985) pp. 9–64.

—— —— —— 'Application of the International Covenant on Civil and Political Rights under the Optional Protocol by the Human Rights Committee', 26 Comparative Juridical Review (1989) pp. 3–52.

DIEYE, A., 'Hearings', in Ramcharan, B. G., ed., above (1982), ch. 5.

DINSTEIN, Y., 'Collective Rights of Peoples and Minorities', 25 ICLQ (1976) pp. 102–20.

—— 'The Right to Life, Physical Integrity and Liberty', in Henkin, L. ed., above (1981), pp. 114–37.

DOMINGUEZ, J., 'Assessing Human Rights Conditions', in Dominguez, J., et al., above (1979), pp. 21–116.

DONNELLY, J., 'The Emerging International Regime Against Torture', 33 NILR (1986) pp. 1–23.

—— 'Cultural Relativism and the Consequences for Human Rights', 6 HRQ (1984) pp. 400–19.

—— 'International Human Rights: A Regime Analysis', 40 Int. Org. (1986) pp. 599–642.

—— and Howard, R., 'Assessing National Human Rights Performance', 10 HRQ (1988) pp. 214–48.

DORE, I. I., 'Self-Determination of Namibia—Paradigm of a Paradox', 27 Harv. ILJ (1986) pp. 159–91.

DUFFY, P. J., 'Article 3 of the European Convention on Human Rights', 32 ICLQ (1983) pp. 316–46.

DUGARD, J., 'The Nuclear Tests Cases and the South West Africa Cases: Some Realism about the International Judicial Decision', 16 Virg. JIL (1975–6) pp. 463–504.

DUNNETT, D., 'Self-Determination and the Falklands', 59 Int. Affairs (1983) pp. 415–28.

EISSEN, A., 'The European Convention on Human Rights and the ICCPR: Problems of Co-existence', 22 Buff. LR (1972) pp. 181–216.

ELDER, D., 'Freedom of Expression and the Approach to Defamation: The American Approach to the Problems Raised by the Lingens Case', 35 ICLQ (1986) pp. 891–924.

ELKIND, J. B., 'Application of the International Covenant on Civil and Political Rights in New Zealand', 75 AJIL (1981) pp. 169–72.

ELDRIDGE, J. T., 'Domestic Human Rights Advocacy: Strategies for Influencing Government Policy', in Hannum, H., ed., above (1984), pp. 270–9.

ERMACORA, F., 'Human Rights and Domestic Jurisdiction', 124 Rec. des cours (1968-II) pp. 371–415.

—— 'International Enquiry Commissions in the Field of Human Rights', 1 RDH/HRJ (1968) pp. 180–218.

—— 'United Nations and Human Rights in Chile', 1 HR Rev. (1976) pp. 145–56.

—— 'The Protection of Minorities before the United Nations', 182 Rec. des cours (1983-IV) pp. 251–370.

FALK, R., 'Comparative Protection of Human Rights in Capitalist and Socialist Third World Countries', 1 Univ. HR (1979) pp. 3–29.

—— 'Responding to Severe Violations', in Dominguez, J., *et al.*, above (1979), pp. 207–57.

—— 'Intervention and National Liberation Claims', in Bull, H., ed., above (1984), pp. 119–34.

FARER, T. J., 'The United Nations and Human Rights: More than a Whimper Less than a Roar', 9 HRQ (1987) pp. 550–85.

FAWCETT, J., 'Human Rights and Domestic Jurisdiction', in Luard, E., ed., above (1967), pp. 286–303.

—— 'The Role of the United Nations in the Protection of Human Rights—Is it Misconceived?', in Eide, A., and Schou, A., eds., above (1968), pp. 95–101.

FEINGOLD, C., 'The Little Red Schoolbook and the European Convention on Human Rights', 3 HR Rev. (1978) pp. 263–86.

FERGUSON, C. C., JR., 'The UN Human Rights Covenants: Problems of Ratification and Implementation', 62 ASIL Proc. (1968) pp. 83–96.

FISHER, D., 'Reporting under the Covenant on Civil and Political Rights: The First Five years of the Human Rights Committee', 76 AJIL (1982) pp. 142–53.

—— 'International Reporting Procedures', in Hannum, H., ed., above (1984) pp. 165–85.

FISCHER, H., 'The Human Rights Covenants and Canadian Law', 15 Can YIL (1977) pp. 42–83.

FITZMAURICE, G., 'The Problem of the Non-Appearing Defendant Government', 51 BYIL 1981 (1982) pp. 89–122.

FLETCHER, G. P., 'The Right to Life', 13 Georgia LR (1979) pp. 1371–94.

FOREST, R., 'Quelques aspects de la mise en oeuvre au Canada des pactes de L'O.N.U. relatifs aux droits de l'homme', 36 Revue juridique et politique, indépendance et coopération (1982) pp. 376–94.

FORSYTHE, D. P., 'Political Prisoners: The Law and Politics of Protection', 9 Vand. J. Trans. L. (1976) pp. 295–322.

—— 'The United Nations and Human Rights', 100 PSQ (1985) pp. 249–69.

FRANCK, T., 'The Stealing of the Sahara', 70 AJIL (1976) pp. 694–721.

—— and FAIRLEY, H. S., 'Procedural Due Process in Human Rights Fact Finding by International Agencies', 74 AJIL (1980) pp. 308–45.

—— and HOFFMAN, P., 'The Right of Self-Determination in Very Small Places', 8 NYUJILP (1975–6) pp. 331–86.

FROWEIN, J., 'The Interrelationship between the Helsinki Final Act, the International Covenants and the European Convention on Human Rights', in Buergenthal, T., ed., above (1977), pp. 71–82.

GALEY, M., 'International Enforcement of Womens Rights', 6 HRQ (1984) pp. 463–90.

GARIBALDI, O., 'General Limitations on Human Rights—The Principle of Legality', 17 Harv. ILJ (1976) pp. 503–57.

—— 'On the Ideological Content of Human Rights Instruments: The Clause: "In a Democratic Society"', in Buergenthal, T., ed., above (1984), pp. 23–68.

GARRETT, S., 'Foreign Policy and the American Constitution: The Bricker Amendment in Contemporary Perspective', 16 Int. SQ (1972) pp. 187–220.

GASSER, J. P., 'Internationalized Non-International Armed Conflicts: Case Studies of Afghanistan, Kampuchea and Lebanon', 33 Am. ULR (1983) p. 145–61.

GHANDI, P. R., 'The Human Rights Committee and the Right of Individual Communication', 57 BYIL 1986 (1987) pp. 201–51.

—— 'The Human Rights Committee and Derogation in Public Emergencies', 32 GYIL (1990) pp. 321–61.

GITTLEMAN, R., 'The African Charter on Human and Peoples' Rights: A Legal Analysis', 22 Virg. JIL (1982) pp. 667–714.

GOLSONG, H., 'Implementation of International Protection of Human Rights', 110 Rec. des cours (1963) pp. 1–115.

GOMEZ DEL PRADO, J. L., 'United Nations Conventions on Human Rights: The Practice of the Human Rights Committee and the Committee on the Elimination of Racial Discrimination in Dealing with the Reporting Obligations of States parties', 7 HRQ (1985) pp. 492–513.

GONZALEZ, T. D., 'The Political Sources of Procedural Debates in the United Nations: Structural Impediments to the Implementation of Human Rights', 13 NYUJILP (1981) pp. 427–72.

GORMLEY, W. P., 'The Right to Life and the Rule of Non-Derogability: Peremptory Norms of Jus Cogens', in Ramcharan, B. G., ed., above (1985), pp. 120–59.

GOSIGER, M. C., 'Strategies for Disinvestment from United States Companies and Financial Institutions Doing Business in South Africa', 8 HRQ (1986) pp. 517–39.

GRAEFRATH, B., 'Trends Emerging in the Practice of the Human Rights Committee', 3 Bull. GDR Committee for Human Rights (1980) pp. 3–32.

—— 'How Different Countries Implement International Standards on Human Rights', (1984–5) CHRYB pp. 3–30.

—— 'Human Rights and International Cooperation—Ten years in the Human Rights Committee', 14 Bull. GDR Committee for Human Rights (1988) pp. 5–55.

GREEN, J. F., 'Protection of Minorities in the League of Nations and the United Nations', in Gotlieb, A., ed., above (1970), pp. 180–210.

—— 'Changing Approaches to Human Rights: The U.N. 1954 and 1974', 12 Texas ILJ (1977) pp. 223–38.

GREEN, L. C., 'Self-Determination and the Settlement of the Arab-Israeli Conflict', ASIL Proc. (1971) pp. 40–8.

—— 'Derogations of Human Rights in Emergency Situations', 16 Can. YIL (1978) pp. 92–115.

GREENBERG, J., 'Race, Sex and Religious Discrimination in International Law', in Meron, T., ed., above (1984), pp. 307–43.

GREENWOOD, C., 'The International Tin Council Litigation', All ER Rev 1989 pp. 240–6.

GREER, S. C., 'Supergrasses and the Legal System in Britain and Northern Ireland', 102 LQR (1986) pp. 198–249.

—— 'The Rise and Fall of the Northern Ireland Supergrass System', 1987 Crim. L. R. pp. 663–70.

GRIEF, N. J., 'The International Protection of Human Rights: Standard Setting and

Enforcement by the United Nations and the Council of Europe', (1983) Bracton LJ pp. 41–65.

—— 'Nuclear Tests and International Law', in Pogany, I., ed., above (1987), pp. 217–44.

GROS-ESPIELL, H., 'Self-Determination and Jus Cogens', in Cassese, A., ed., above (1979) pp. 167–73.

GUELKE, A., 'International Legitimacy, Self-Determination and Northern Ireland', 11 Rev. Int. St. (1985) pp. 37–52.

GUTTAL, G. H., 'Human Rights: The Indian Law', 26 Ind. JIL (1986) pp. 53–71.

HAIGHT, G. W., 'Human Rights Covenants', 62 ASIL Proc. (1968) pp. 96–103.

HAKSAR, U., 'The International Human Rights Treaties: Some Problems of Policy and Interpretation', 126 U. Pa. LR (1978) pp. 886–929.

HALPERIN, D., 'Human Rights and Natural Resources', 9 Will. & Mary LR (1968) pp. 770–87.

HARRIS, D. J., 'The Right to a Fair Trial in Criminal Proceedings as a Human Right', 16 ICLQ (1967) pp. 352–78.

—— 'The Application of article 6(1) of the European Convention on Human Rights to Administrative Law', 47 BYIL (1973–4) pp. 157–200.

HARTMAN, J. F., 'Derogations from Human Rights Treaties in Public Emergencies', 22 Harv. ILJ (1981) pp. 1–52.

—— 'Working Paper for the Committee of Experts on Article 4', 7 HRQ (1985) pp. 89–131.

HASSAN, P., 'International Covenants on Human Rights: An Approach to Interpretation', 19 Buff. LR (1969) pp. 35–50.

—— 'International Covenant on Civil and Political Rights: Background and Perspective on Article 9(1)', 3 Denver JILP (1973) pp. 153–83.

HEALY, P., 'Proof and Policy: No Golden Threads', 1987 CLR pp. 355–66.

HENKIN, L., 'Introduction', in Henkin, L., ed., above (1981), pp. 1–31.

—— 'Human Rights and Domestic Jurisdiction', in Buergenthal, T., ed., above (1977), pp. 21–40.

HEVENER, N. K., 'Drafting the Human Rights Covenants', 148 World Affairs (1986) pp. 233–44.

—— and MOSHER, S. A., 'General Principles of Law and the United Nations Covenant on Civil and Political Rights', 27 ICLQ (1978) pp. 596–613.

HIGGINS, R., 'Derogations under Human Rights Treaties', 48 BYIL (1976–7) pp. 281–320.

—— 'Some Recent Developments in Respect of the Right to Leave and Return in International Law', in Cheng, B., and Brown, E. D., eds., *Contemporary Problems of International Law* (Stevens, London, 1988).

—— 'Human Rights: Some Questions of Integrity', 52 MLR (1989) pp. 1–21.

—— 'Conceptual Thinking about the Individual in International Law', 4 Brit. JIS (1978) pp. 1–19.

—— 'Reality and Hope in International Human Rights Law', 9 Hofstra LR (1981) pp. 1485–99.

—— 'The European Convention on Human Rights', in Meron, T., ed., above (1984), pp. 497–549.

—— 'Some thoughts on the implementation of human rights', 89/1, Bull. of Human Rights pp. 60–66.

HOARE, S., 'The UN Commission on Human Rights', in Luard, E., ed., above (1967), pp. 59–98.

HOWARD, R., 'Is There an African Concept of Human Rights?', in Vincent, R. J., ed., above (1986), pp. 11–32.

HUMPHREY, J. P., 'The United Nations Charter and the Universal Declaration of Human Rights', in Luard, E., ed., above (1967), pp. 39–58.

—— 'International Bill of Rights—Scope and Implementation', 17 Will. & Mary LR (1976) pp. 527–41.

—— 'The World Revolution and Human Rights', in Gotlieb, A., ed., above (1970), pp. 147–79.

—— 'The Implementation of International Human Rights Law', 24 NYLSLR (1978) pp. 31–62.

——'Political and Related Rights', in Meron, T., ed., above (1984), pp. 171–203.

—— 'The Just Requirements of Morality, Public Order and the General Welfare in a Democratic Society', in MacDonald, R., and Humphrey, J., eds., above (1979), pp. 146–56.

HUSTON, J., 'Human Rights Enforcement Issues at the United Nations Conference on International Organization', 53 Iowa LR (1967) pp. 272–90.

HYDE, J. N., 'Permanent Sovereignty over Natural Wealth and Resources', 50 AJIL (1956) pp. 854–67.

HYNDMAN, P., 'Human Rights, The Rule of Law and the Situation in Sri Lanka', 8 Univ. NSWLJ (1985) pp. 337–61.

IMBERT, P. H., 'Reservations and Human Rights Conventions', 3 HR Rev. (1981) pp. 28–60.

—— 'Reservations to the European Convention on Human Rights before the Strasbourg Commission: The Temeltasch Case', 33 ICLQ (1984) pp. 558–95.

IINTERNATIONAL LAW ASSOCIATION, 'Human Rights in a State of Emergency: Proclamation of Emergency, Martial Law, States of Siege', ILA Report, 59th Conference (Belgrade, 1980), pp. 89–100.

—— 'Regional Problems in the Implementation of Human Rights: Minimum Standards in a State of Exception', ILA Report, 60th Conference (Montreal, 1982), pp. 88–100.

—— 'Minimum Standards in a State of Exception', ILA Report, 61st Conference (Paris, 1984), pp. 56–96.

—— 'Enforcement of Human Rights', ILA Report (Seoul, 1986), pp. 108–97.

ISLAM, M. R., 'Use of Force in Self-Determination Claims', 25 Ind. JIL (1985) pp. 424–47.

IVY, A. C., 'The History and Ethics of the Use of Human Subjects in Medical Experiments', 108 Science (1948) pp. 1–5.

IWASAWA, Y., 'Legal Treatment of Koreans in Japan: The Impact of International Human Rights Law on Japanese Law', 8 HRQ pp. 131–79.

JENKS, C. W., 'The United Nations Covenants on Human Rights Come to Life', in *Recueil d'études de droits international en hommage à Paul Guggenheim*, above (1968), pp. 805–13.

JHABVALA, F., 'The Practice of the Covenant's Human Rights Committee, 1976–82: Review of State Party Reports', 6 HRQ (1984) pp. 81–106.

—— 'On Human Rights and the Socio-Economic Context', 31 NILR (1984) pp. 149–82.

—— 'Domestic Implementation of the Covenant on Civil and Political Rights', 32 NILR (1985) pp. 461–86.

—— 'The Soviet Bloc's View of the Implementation of the Human Rights Accords', 7 HRQ (1985) pp. 461–91.

—— 'The ICCPR as a Vehicle for the Global Promotion and Protection of Human Rights', 15 Isr. YHR (1985) pp. 184–203.

JOHNSON, M. G., 'The Contributions of Eleanor and Franklin Roosevelt to the Development of International Protection of Human Rights', 9 HRQ (1987) pp. 19–48.

JOINET, L., 'Amnesty Laws', 35 Rev. ICJ (1985) pp. 27–30.

JONES, C., 'Note' [The Quinteros Case], 25 Harv. ILJ (1984) pp. 440–77.

KABAALIOGLU, H. A., 'The Obligations to "Respect" and to "Ensure" the Right to Life', in Ramcharan, B. G., ed., above (1985), pp. 160–81.

KAMMINGA, M., 'The Thematic Procedures of the United Nations Commission on Human Rights', 34 NILR (1987) pp. 299–323.

—— and RODLEY, N. S., 'Direct Intervention at the United Nations: N.G.O. Participation in the Commission on Human Rights and its Sub-Commission', in Hannum, H., ed., above (1984), pp. 186–99.

KARTASHKIN, V. A., 'Human Rights and Peaceful Coexistence', 9 RDH/HRJ (1976) pp. 5–19.

—— 'Covenants on Human Rights and Soviet Legislation', 10 RDH/HRJ (1977) pp. 97–115.

—— 'The Socialist Countries and Human Rights', in Vasak, K./Alston, P., eds., above (1982), pp. 631–50.

KAUFMAN, E., and WEISS FAGEN, P., 'Extrajudicial Executions: An Insight into the Global Dimensions of a Human Rights Violation', 3(4) HRQ (1981) pp. 81–100.

KAUFMAN, N. H., and WHITEMAN, D., 'Opposition to Human Rights Treaties in the United States Senate: The Legacy of the Bricker Amendment', 10 HRQ (1988) pp. 309–37.

KAWASHIMA, Y., 'The International Covenants on Human Rights and the Japanese Legal System', 22 Jap. Ann. IL (1978) pp. 54–74.

KENNEDY, R. L., 'McClesky v. Kemp: Race, Capital Punishment and the Supreme Court', 101 Harv. LR (1988) pp. 1388–443.

KIDD, C. F., 'Disciplinary Proceedings and the Right to a Fair Criminal Trial under the European Convention on Human Rights', 36 ICLQ (1987) pp. 856–72.

KISS, A., 'Permissible Limitations on Rights', in Henkin, L., ed., above (1981), pp. 290–310.

—— 'The Peoples' Right to Self-Determination', 7 HRLJ (1986) pp. 165–75.

KLAYMAN, B. H., 'The Definition of Torture in International Law', 51 Temple LQ (1978) pp. 449–515.

KLERK, Y., 'Working Paper on Article 2(2) and Article 3 of the International Covenant on Economic, Social and Cultural Rights', 9 HRQ (1987) pp. 250–73.

KNOPPERS, B. M., 'Modern Birth Technology and Human Rights', 33 Am. J. Comp. L. (1985) pp. 1–31.

KOREY, W., 'The Key to Human Rights—Implementation', 570 Int. Conc. (Nov. 1968) pp. 5–70.

KORYAGIN, A., 'Involuntary Patients in Soviet Psychiatric Hospitals', 26 Rev. ICJ (1981) pp. 49–56.

KRAMER, D., and WEISSBRODT, D., 'The 1980 U.N. Commission on Human Rights and the Disappeared', 3 HRQ (1981) pp. 18–33.

KRUGER, H. C., 'Visits on the Spot—The Experience of the European Commission on Human Rights', in Ramcharan, B. G., ed., above (1982), pp. 151–9.

KUPER, L., 'Genocide and Mass Killings: Illusion and Reality', in Ramcharan, B. G., ed., above (1985), pp. 114–19.

LAING, Y. L., 'Colonial and Federal Clauses in U.N. Multilateral Instruments', 45 AJIL (1951) pp. 108–28.

LANDERER, L. E., 'Capital Punishment as a Human Rights Issue before the United Nations', 4 RDH/HRJ (1971) pp. 511–34.

LANE, E., 'Demanding Human Rights: A Change in the World Legal Order', 6 Hofstra LR (1978) pp. 269–95.

—— 'Mass Killings by Governments: Lawful in the World Legal Order?', 12 NYUJILP (1979) pp. 239–80.

LARSON, A., 'The Present Status of Propaganda in International Law', in Symposium (1966), below, pp. 439–51.

LAUTERPACHT, H., 'The International Protection of the Individual', in Lauterpacht, H., *International Law—Collected Papers*, Lauterpacht, E., ed., Vol. iii, above (1977), pp. 407–30.

LEARY, V., 'A New Role for N.G.O.'s in Human Rights—A Case Study of N.G.O. Participation in the Development of International Norms of Torture', in Cassese, A., ed., above (1979), pp. 197–210.

LECKIE, S., 'The Inter-State Complaint Procedure in International Human Rights Law: Hopeful Prospects or Wishful Thinking?' 10 HRQ (1988) pp. 249–303.

LERNER, N., 'The Golan Heights Case and the U.N. Committee on Racial Discrimination', 3 Isr. YHR (1973) pp. 118–35.

LESTER, A., and PANNICK, D., 'Advertising and Freedom of Expression in Europe', [1985] PL pp. 349–52.

LILLICH, R. B., 'Forcible Self-Help to Protect Human Rights', 53 Iowa LR (1967) pp. 325–51.

—— 'The Enforcement of International Human Rights Norms in Domestic Courts', in Tuttle, J. C., ed., above (1978) pp. 105–31.

—— 'Civil Rights', in Meron, T., ed., above (1984), pp. 115–70.

—— 'The Role of Domestic Courts in Enforcing International Human Rights Law', in Hannum, H., ed., above (1984), pp. 224–47.

—— 'Duties of States Regarding the Civil Rights of Aliens', 161 Rec. des cours (1978-III) pp. 333–443.

—— 'Invoking International Human Rights in Domestic Courts', 54 Univ. Cincinnati LR (1985) pp. 367–415.

LIPPMAN, M., 'Human Rights Revisited: The Protection of Human Rights under the International Covenant on Civil and Political Rights', 26 NILR (1979) pp. 221–77; also in 5 South African YIL (1979) pp. 82–137; 10 Calif. WILJ (1980) pp. 450–513.

LUTTWAK, E. N., 'Intervention and Access to Natural Resources', in Bull, H., ed., above (1984), pp. 79–94.

LYSAGHT, C., 'The Scope of Protocol II and its Relation to Common Article 3 of the Geneva Conventions of 1949 and other Human Rights Instruments', 33 Am. ULR (1983) pp. 9–27.

MACCHESNEY, A., 'Promoting the General Welfare in a Democratic Society: Balancing Human Rights and Development', 27 NILR (1980) pp. 283–334.

MACCHESNEY, B., 'Should the U.S. Ratify the Covenants? A Question of Merits, Not of Constitutional Law', 62 AJIL (1968) pp. 912–17.

MACDONALD, R. ST. J., 'The United Nations Charter: Constitution or Contract', in MacDonald, R. St. J., and Johnston, D., eds., above (1983), pp. 889–912.

MCDOUGAL, M. S., and BEBR, G., 'Human Rights in the United Nations', 58 AJIL (1964) pp. 603–41.

MCGOLDRICK, D., 'Human Rights Developments in the Helsinki Process', 39 ICLQ (1990) pp. 923–40.

MCRAE, D., 'The Legal Effect of Interpretative Declarations', 49 BYIL 1978 (1979) pp. 155–73.

MAHONEY, P., 'Development in the Procedure of the European Court of Human Rights: The Revised Rules of Procedure', 3 YEL (1983) pp. 127–67.

MALIK, M. I., 'The Concept of Human Rights in Islamic Jurisprudence', 3 HRQ (1981) pp. 56–67.

MALINVERNI, G., 'Freedom of Information in the European Convention and in the International Covenant on Civil and Political Rights', 4 HRLJ (1983), pp. 443–60.

MANGAN, B., 'Protecting Human Rights in National Emergencies: Shortcomings in the European System and a Proposal for Reform', 10 HRQ (1988) pp. 372–94.

MANKE, H. I., 'The Exhaustion of Domestic Remedies in the U.N. Sub-Commission on the Prevention of Discrimination and the Protection of Minorities', 24 Buff. LR (1968) pp. 643–81.

MARCOUX, L., Jr., 'Protection from Arbitrary Arrest and Detention under International Law', 5 Bost. Coll. ICLR (1982) pp. 345–76.

MARKESINIS, B., 'The Right to Freedom of Speech Versus the Right to be Let Alone', [1986] PL pp. 67–82.

MARKOVIC, M., 'Implementation of Human Rights and the Domestic Jurisdiction of States', in Eide, A., and Schou, A., eds., above (1968) pp. 47–68.

MARKS, S., 'The Complaint Procedure of UNESCO', in Hannum, H., ed., above (1984), pp. 94–107.

—— 'Emerging Human Rights: A New Generation for the 1980s?', in Falk, R., *et al.*, eds., above (1985), pp. 501–13.

—— 'Reservations unhinged: the *Belilos* Case before the EUCT', 39 ICLQ (1990) pp. 300–27.

MARSTON, G., 'United Kingdom Materials in International Law', 56 BYIL 1985 (1986) pp. 426–31.

—— 'United Kingdom Materials in International Law', 59 BYIL 1988 (1989) pp. 457–71.

MENGHISTU, F., 'The Satisfaction of Survival Requirements', in Ramcharan, B. G., ed., above (1985), pp. 63–83.

MERON, T., 'The International Convention on the Elimination of All Forms of Racial Discrimination and the Golan Heights', 8 Isr. YHR (1978) pp. 222–39.

—— 'Applicability of Multilateral Conventions to Occupied Territories', 72 AJIL (1978) pp. 542–57.

—— 'The Meaning and Reach of the International Convention on the Elimination of All Forms of Racial Discrimination', 79 AJIL (1985) pp. 283–318.

MILLER, W., 'United Nations Fact-Finding Missions in the Field of Human Rights' (1970–3) Australian YIL pp. 40–50.

MONTEALEGRE, H., 'The Compatibility of State Party's Derogations under Human Rights Instruments with its Obligations under Protocol II and Common Article 3', 33 Am. ULR (1983) pp. 41–51.

MORRISSON, C., 'Margin of Appreciation in European Human Rights Law', 6 RDH/HRJ (1973) pp. 263–86.

MORPHET, S., 'The Development of Article 1 of the Human Rights Covenants', Paper presented to Conference on Foreign Policy and Human Rights, Centre for Policy Studies, University of Southampton, March 1987, in Hill, D. M., above, pp. 67–88.

—— 'The Palestinians and their Right to Self-Determination', in Vincent, R. J., ed., above (1986), pp. 85–103.

—— 'Economic, Social and Cultural Rights: The Development of Governments' Views', Paper presented to the Human Rights Group Workshop, Centre for Policy Studies, University of Southampton, March 1988.

MOSCOWITZ, M., 'Whither the UN Human Rights Program?', 6 Isr. YHR (1976) pp. 81–90.

MOSE, E., and OPSAHL, T., 'The Optional Protocol to the International Covenant on Civil and Political Rights', 21 Santa Clara LR (1981) pp. 271–331.

MOURGEON, J., 'Les Pactes Internationaux relatifs aux droits de l'homme', 12 AFDI (1967) pp. 326–63.

—— 'L'entrée en vigueur des pactes internationaux relatifs aux droits de l'homme', 22 AFDI (1976) pp. 290–304.

MOVCHAN, A. P., 'The Human Rights Problem in Present Day International Law', in Tunkin, G., ed., *Contemporary International Law*, pp. 233–50 (Progress Publishers, Moscow, 1969).

MOWER, A. G., 'Human Rights in Black Africa: A Double Standard?' 9 RDH/HRJ (1976) pp. 39–70.

—— 'The Implementation of the UN Covenant on Civil and Political Rights', 10 RDH/HRJ (1977) pp. 271–95.

—— 'Organizing to Implement the UN Civil/Political Rights Covenant: 1st Steps by the Committee', 3 HR Rev. (1978) pp. 122–31.

MUCHLINSKI, P. T., 'The Status of the Individual under the European Convention on Human Rights and Contemporary International Law', 34 ICLQ (1985) pp. 376–82.

MURPHY, C. F., 'Objections to Western Conceptions of Human Rights', 9 Hofstra LR (1981) pp. 433–74.

NALDI, G. J., 'The Statehood of the Saharan Arab Democratic Republic', 25 Ind. JIL (1985) pp. 448–81.

—— 'Case Concerning the Frontier Dispute Between Burkina Faso and Mali: Provisional Measures of Protection', 35 ICLQ (1986) pp. 970–5.

NASH, M. L., 'Contemporary Practice of the United States Relating to International Law', 72 AJIL (1978) pp. 620–31.

NAYAR, K. M. G., 'Human Rights: The UN and US Foreign Policy', 19 Harv. ILJ (1978) pp. 813–43.

—— 'Human Rights and Economic Development: The Legal Foundations', 2 Univ. HR (1980) pp. 55–81.

NEAL, M., 'The United Nations and Human Rights', 489 Int. Conciliation (March 1953), pp. 111–74.

NEWMAN, F., 'The International Bill of Rights: Does it Exist?', in Cassese, A., ed., *Current Problems of International Law*, pp. 107–16 (Guiffre, Milan, 1975).

—— 'Natural Justice, Due Process and the New International Covenants on Human Rights: Prospectus', [1967] Public Law pp. 274–313.

NOBLE, A., 'The Covenant on Civil and Political Rights as the Law of the Land', 25 Vill. LR (1979) pp. 119–40.

NOOR MUHAMMED, H., 'Due Process of Law for Persons Accused of a Crime', in Henkin, L., ed., above (1981), pp. 138–65.

—— 'Guarantees for Accused Persons under the United Nations Human Rights Covenant', 20 Ind. JIL (1980) pp. 177–215.

NOORANI, A. G., 'Afghanistan and the Rule of Law', 24 Rev. ICJ (1980) pp. 37–52.

NORRIS, R., 'The Suspension of Guarantees', 30 Am. ULR (1980) pp. 189–223.

—— 'Observations *In Loco*—Practice and Procedure of the Inter-American Commission on Human Rights', 15 Tex. ILJ (1980) pp. 46–95.

NOWAK, M., 'The Effectiveness of the ICCPR—Stocktaking after the First 11 Sessions of the UN Human Rights Committee', 1 HRLJ (1980) pp. 136–70.

—— 'UN Human Rights Committee: Survey of Decisions', 2 HRLJ (1981) pp. 168–72.

—— 'UN Human Rights Committee: Survey of Decisions', 3 HRLJ (1982) pp. 207–20.

—— 'UN Human Rights Committee: Survey of Decisions', 5 HRLJ (1984) pp. 199–219.

—— 'UN Human Rights Committee: Survey of Decisions, 7 HRLJ (1986) pp. 287–307.

O'DONNELL, D., 'States of Exception', 21 Rev. ICJ (1978) pp. 52–60.

O'DONNELL, T., 'The Margin of Appreciation Doctrine: Standards in the Jurisprudence of the European Court of Human Rights', 4 HRQ (1982) pp. 474–96.

OKERE, B. O., 'The Protection of Human Rights in Africa and the African Charter of Human Rights and People's Rights: A Comparative Analysis with the European and American Systems', 6 HRQ (1984) pp. 141–59.

OPSAHL, T., 'Human Rights Today: International Obligations and National Implementation', 23 Scandinavian Studies in Law (1979) pp. 149–76.

—— 'Instruments of Implementation of Human Rights', 10 HRLJ (1989) pp. 13–34.

—— and DE ZAYAS, A., 'The Uncertain Scope of Article 15(1) of the International Covenant on Civil and Political Rights', (1983) CHRYB pp. 237–54.

ORUCU, E., 'The Core of Rights and Freedoms: The Limits of Limits', in Campbell, T., *et al.*, eds., above (1986), pp. 37–59.

OWERS, A., 'Immigration', in Sieghart, P., ed., above (1988), pp. 18–28.

PARSON, D. P., 'The Individual Right of Petition: A Study of Methods Used by International Organizations to Utilize the Individual as a Source of Information on the Violation of Human Rights', 13 Wayne LR (1967) pp. 678–705.

PARTSCH, K. J., 'Freedom of Conscience and Expression, and Political Freedoms', in Henkin, L., ed., above (1981), pp. 209–45.

—— 'Fundamental Principles of Human Rights: Self-Determination, Equality and Non-Discrimination', in Vasak, K./Alston, P., eds., above (1982), pp. 61–86.

PATHAK, R. S., 'The Protection of Human Rights', 18 Ind. JIL (1978) pp. 265–73.

PECHOTA, V., 'The Development of the Covenant on Civil and Political Rights', in Henkin, L., ed., above (1981), pp. 32–71.

PIZA, R., 'Coordination of the Mechanisms for the Protection of Human Rights in the American Convention with those Established by the United Nations', 30 Am. ULR (1981) pp. 167–87.

POGANY, I., 'Humanitarian Intervention in International Law: The French Intervention in Syria Re-examined', 35 ICLQ (1986) pp. 182–90.

PRICE, N., 'Human Rights, "Death-Row", and Administrative Remedies', 34 ICLQ (1985) pp. 162–7.

PROUNIS, O. A., 'The Human Rights Committee: Towards Resolving the Paradox of Human Rights Law', 17 Col. HRLR (1985) pp. 103–19.

PRZETACZNIK, F., 'The Right to Life as a Basic Human Right', 9 RDH/HRJ (1976) pp. 585–609.

RAMCHARAN, B. G., 'Implementation of the International Covenant on Economic, Social and Cultural Rights', 23 NILR (1976) pp. 151–62.

—— 'A Critique of Third World Responses to Violations of Human Rights', in Cassese, A., ed., above (1979), pp. 249–58.

—— 'Implementing the International Covenants on Human Rights', in Ramcharan, B. G., ed., above (1979), pp. 159–95.

—— 'The Emerging Jurisprudence of the Human Rights Committee', 6 Dalhousie LJ (1980) pp. 7–40.

—— 'Equality and Non-Discrimination', in Henkin, L., ed., above (1981), pp. 246–69.

—— 'The Right to Life', 30 NILR (1983) pp. 297–329.

—— 'Evidence', in Ramcharan, B. G., ed., above (1982), pp. 64–82.

REDELBACH, A., 'Protection of the Right to Life by Law and Other Means', in Ramcharan, B. G., ed., above (1985), pp. 182–220.

REES, A., 'The Soviet Union', in Vincent, R. J., ed., above (1986), pp. 61–83.

REID, C. T., 'The Ombudsman's Cousin: The Procuracy in Socialist States', [1986] PL pp. 311–16.

REID, Lord, 'The Judge as Law Maker', (1972) 12 JSPTL (NS) pp. 22–9.

RENTELN, A. D., 'The Unanswered Challenge of Relativism and the Consequences for Human Rights', 7 HRQ (1985) pp. 514–40.

RITTERSPACH, T., 'Abortion Law in Italy', 5 HRLJ (1984) pp. 383–8.

ROBERTSON, A. H., 'The UNCCPR and the European Convention on Human Rights', 43 BYIL (1968–9) pp. 21–48.

—— 'The Implementation System', in Henkin, L., ed., above (1981), pp. 332–69.

ROBERTSON, B., 'Exhaustion of local remedies in international human rights litigation—the burden of proof reconsidered', 39 ICLQ (1990) pp. 191–6.

RODLEY, N. S., 'Monitoring Human Rights Violations in the 1980's', in Dominguez, J., et al., above (1979), pp. 117–51.

—— 'U.N. Action against "Disappearances", Summary or Arbitrary Executions and Torture', 8 HRQ (1986) pp. 700–30.

—— 'Human Rights and Humanitarian Intervention: The Case Law of the World Court', 38 ICLQ (1989) pp. 321–33.

RUBINO, P., 'Colonialism and the Use of Force by States', in Cassese, A., ed., above (1986), pp. 133–45.

RUSK, D., 'A Personal Reflection on International Covenants on Human Rights', 9 Hofstra LR (1981) pp. 515–22.

RYAN, H. R. S., 'Seeking Relief under the UN ICCPR', 6 Queens LJ (1981) pp. 389–407.

SABA, H., 'Les Droits de l'homme et de l'expérimentation biomédicale sur l'homme', in *Mélanges offerts à Polys Modinos*, above (1968), pp. 260–6.

SAITO, Y., 'Japan and Human Rights Covenants', 2 HRLJ (1981) pp. 79–107.

SALZBERG, J., 'Monitoring Human Rights Violations—How Good is the Information?', in Brown, P., and MacLean, D., eds., above (1979), pp. 173–82.

SAPIENZA, R., 'International Legal Standards on Capital Punishment', in Ramcharan, B. G., ed., above (1985), pp. 284–96.

SASKENA, K. P., 'International Covenants on Human Rights', 15–16 Ind. YIA (1970) pp. 596–613.

SCHACHTER, O., 'The Obligation to Implement the Covenant in Domestic Law', in Henkin, L., ed., above (1981), pp. 311–31.

—— 'The Obligation of Parties to Give Effect to the Covenant on Civil and Political Rights', 73 AJIL (1979) pp. 462–5.

SCHECTER, L. F., 'The Views of "Charterists" and "Skeptics" on Human Rights in the World Legal Order—Two Wrongs Don't Make a Right', 9 Hofstra LR (1981) pp. 357–98.

SCHINDLER, D., 'Human Rights and Humanitarian Law', 31 Am. ULR (1982) pp. 935–77.

SCHMIDT, M., 'The OP to the ICCPR', 4 Interights Bull. (1989) pp. 27–30.

SCHWELB, E., 'The International Convention on the Elimination of Racial Discrimination', 15 ICLQ (1966) pp. 996–1068.

—— 'Notes on the Early Legislative History of the Measures of Implementation of the Human Rights Covenant', in *Melanges offerts à Polys Modinos*, above (1968), pp. 270–89.

—— 'Some Aspects of the International Covenants on Human Rights of December 1966', in Eide, A., and Schou, A., eds., above (1968) pp. 103–29.

—— 'The Nature of the Obligation of the States Parties to the ICCPR', in *René Cassin Amicorum Discipulorumque Liber*, pp. 301–24 (Pedone, Paris, 1969).

—— 'The United Kingdom Signs the Covenants on Human Rights', 18 ICLQ (1969) pp. 457–68.

—— 'The International Court of Justice and the Human Rights Clauses of the Charter', 66 AJIL (1972) pp. 337–51.

—— 'Entry into Force of the International Covenants on Human Rights and the Optional Protocol', 70 AJIL (1976) pp. 511–19.

—— 'The Law of Treaties and Human Rights', in Reisman, M. W., and Weston, B. H., eds., above (1976), pp. 262–90.

SCHWELB, E., 'Civil and Political Rights—The International Measures of Implementation', 62 AJIL (1968) pp. 828–68 (revised in 12 Tex. ILJ (1977) pp. 141–86).

SCOTT, C., 'The Interdependence and Permeability of Human Rights Norms: Towards a partial fusion of the International Covenants on Human Rights', 27 Osg.HLJ (1989) pp. 769–878.

SHAW, M., 'The Western Sahara Case', 49 BYIL 1978 (1979) pp. 118–54.

SHELTON, D., 'Abortion and the Right to Life in the Inter-American System: The Case of the "Baby Boy"', 2 HRLJ (1981) pp. 309–18.

—— 'State Practice on Reservations to Human Rights Treaties', CHRYB (1983) pp. 204–34.

—— 'Individual Complaint Machinery under the United Nations 1503 Procedure and the Optional Protocol to the International Covenant on Civil and Political Rights', in Hannum, H., ed., above (1984), pp. 59–73.

SHESTACK, J., 'Sisyphus Endures: The International Human Rights N.G.O.', 24 NY Sch. LR (1978) pp. 89–123.

—— 'The Jurisprudence of Human Rights', in Meron, T., ed., above (1984), pp. 69–113.

SINGHVI, A. M., 'The State of Emergency and the Law of Nations', 25 Ind. JIL (1985) pp. 554–75.

SKELTON, J., Jr., 'The U.S. Approach to Ratification of the International Covenants on Human Rights', 1 Hous. JIL (1979) pp. 103–25.

SKOLER, D. L., 'World Implementation of the U.N. Standard Minimum Rules for the Treatment of Prisoners', 10 J. Int. L. & Econ. (1975) pp. 453–82.

SMITH, A. T. H., 'The Prerogative of Mercy, the Power of Pardon and Criminal Justice', [1983] PL pp. 398–439.

SOHN, L. B., 'A Short History of United Nations Documents on Human Rights', in *The United Nations and Human Rights—Eighteenth Report of the Commission to Study the Organization of Peace*, pp. 39–186 (Oceana, Dobbs Ferry, New York, 1968).

—— 'The Human Rights Law of the Charter', 12 Tex. ILJ (1977) pp. 129–40.

—— 'The Rights of Minorities', in Henkin, L., ed., above (1981), pp. 270–89.

—— 'The International Law of Human Rights: A Reply to Recent Criticism', 9 Hofstra LR (1981) pp. 347–56.

—— 'The New International Law: Protection of the Rights of Individuals Rather Than States', 32 Am. ULR (1982) pp. 1–64.

—— 'Human Rights: Their Implementation and Supervision by the United Nations', in Meron, T., ed., above (1984), pp. 369–401.

—— 'Improving the Image of the United States in International Human Rights', 82 AJIL (1988) pp. 319–20.

SORENSON, M., 'Federal States and the International Protection of Human Rights', 46 AJIL (1952) pp. 195–218.

—— 'Report Concerning Obligations of a State Party to a Treaty as Regards its Municipal Law', in Robertson, A. H., ed., *Human Rights in National and International Law*, pp. 11–46 (Manchester Univ. Press, Manchester; Oceana, Dobbs Ferry, NY, 1968).

SPJUT, R., 'The "Official" Use of Deadly Force by the Security Services Against Suspected Terrorists: Some Lessons from Northern Ireland', [1986] PL pp. 38–64.

STARR, R., 'International Protection of Human Rights and the United Nations Covenants', 1967 Wisc. LR (1967) pp. 841–90.

STEIN, P., 'Derogations from Guarantees Laid Down in Human Rights Instruments', in Maier, I., ed., above (1982), pp. 123–33.

STEINER, H. J., 'Political Participation as a Human Right', 1 Harv. HRY (1988) pp. 77–134.

SULLENS, J. K., 'Thus Far and No Further: The Supreme Court Draws the Outer Boundary of the Right to Privacy', 61 Tulane LR (1987) pp. 907–29.

SUSSMAN, L. R., 'Freedom of the Press: Problems in Restructuring the Flow of International News', in Gastil, R. D., ed., *Freedom in the World: Political Rights and Civil Liberties*, above (1980), pp. 53–98.

SUZUKI, E., 'Self-Determination and World Public Order', 16 Virg. JIL (1976) pp. 781–862.

SZABO, I., 'Historical Foundations of Human Rights and Subsequent Developments', in Vasak, K./Alston, P., eds., above (1982), pp. 11–40.

SZAWLOWSKI, R., 'The International Protection of Human Rights—A Polish and a Soviet View', 28 ICLQ (1979) pp. 775–81.

TARDU, M., 'The Protocol to the United Nations Covenant on Civil and Political Rights and the Inter-American System: A Study of Coexisting Petition Procedures', 70 AJIL (1976) pp. 778–800.

—— 'The Convention against Torture and Other Cruel, Inhuman or Degrading Treatment or Punishment', 4 Nordic JIL (1987) pp. 303–21.

TARNOPOLSKY, W. S., 'A Comparison between the Canadian Charter of Rights and Freedoms and the International Covenant on Civil and Political Rights', 8 Queens LJ (1982–3) pp. 211–31.

—— 'The Canadian Experience with the ICCPR as seen from the Perspective of a Former Member of the HRC', 20 Akron LR (1987) pp. 611–28.

TESON, F. R., 'International Human Rights and Cultural Relativism', 25 Virg. JIL (1985) pp. 869–98.

TIKHONOV, A. A., 'The Inter-Relationship between the Right to Life and the Right to Peace', in Ramcharan, B. G., ed., above (1985), pp. 97–113.

TOLLEY, H., 'The Concealed Crack in the Citadel: The United Nations Commission on Human Rights' Response to Confidential Communications', 6 HRQ (1984) pp. 420–62.

TOMAN, J., 'Quasi-Legal Standards and Guidelines for Protecting the Rights of Detained Persons', in Hannum, H., ed., above (1984), pp. 200–19.

TOMUSCHAT, C., 'Evolving Procedural Rules: The U.N. Human Rights Committee's First Two Years of Dealing with Individual Communications', 1 HRLJ (1980) pp. 249–57.

—— 'Is Universality of Human Rights an Outdated Concept, in *Das Europa Der Zweiten Generation—Gedachtnisschrift Für Christophe Sasse*, Vol. ii, pp. 585–609 (Kehl/Rhine, Strasburg, 1981).

—— 'Equality and Non-Discrimination under the International Covenant on Civil and Political Rights', in von Ingo von Munch, ed., *Staatsrecht—Volkerrecht—Europarecht, Festschrift Für Hans-Jürgen Schlochauer*, pp. 691–716 (Berlin/New York, 1981).

TOMUSCHAT, C. 'Human Rights in a World-Wide Framework, Some Current Issues', 45 ZaoRV (1985) pp. 547–84.

—— 'Protection of Minorities under Article 27 of the International Covenant on Civil and Political Rights', in Bernhardt, R., *et al.* (eds.), *Volkerrecht Als Rechtordnung, Internationale Gerichtsbarkeit, Mensrechten: Festschrift für Hermann Mosler*, pp. 949–79 (Berlin/Heidelberg/New York, 1983).

—— 'National Implementation of International Standards on Human Rights', (1984–5) CHRYB pp. 31–61.

TOWNSHEND, C., 'Northern Ireland', in Vincent, R. J. ed., above (1986), pp. 119–40.

TRIGGS, G., 'Australia's Ratification of the ICCPR: Endorsement or Repudiation?', 31 ICLQ (1982) pp. 278–306.

—— 'Australia's Ratification of the ICCPR: Its Domestic Application to Prisoners Rights', 3 HRLJ (1982) pp. 65–102.

TRINDADE, A. A. C., 'The Burden of Proof with Regard to the Exhaustion of Local Remedies in International Law', 9 RDH/HRJ (1976) pp. 81–121.

—— 'Exhaustion of Local Remedies in International Law and the Role of National Courts', Archiv des Volkerrechts (1977–8), pp. 333–70.

—— 'The Time Factor in the Application of the Rule of Exhaustion of Local Remedies in International Law', 61 Rivista di diritto internazionale (1978) pp. 232–57.

—— 'Exhaustion of Local Remedies in the Inter-American System', 18 Ind. JIL (1978) pp. 345–51.

—— 'Exhaustion of Local Remedies under the U.N. Covenant on Civil and Political Rights and its Optional Protocol', 28 ICLQ (1979) pp. 734–65.

—— 'Exhaustion of Local Remedies under the International Convention on the Elimination of Racial Discrimination', 22 Germ. YIL (1979) pp. 374–83.

—— 'Co-existence and Co-ordination of Mechanisms of International Protection of Human Rights (at global and regional levels)', 202 Rec. des cours (1987–II).

TRUBEK, D., 'Economic, Social and Cultural Rights in the Third World—Human Rights Law and Human Needs Programmes', in Meron, T., ed., above (1984), pp. 205–71.

TUDIN, K., 'The Development of Soviet Attitudes towards Implementing Human Rights under the United Nations Charter', 5 RDH/HRJ (1972) pp. 399–418.

TYAGI, Y., 'Cooperation between the Human Rights Committee and Non-Governmental Organizations', 18 Tex. ILJ (1983) pp. 273–90.

UMOZURIKE, U. O., 'The African Charter on Human and Peoples' Rights', 77 AJIL (1983) pp. 902–12.

VAN BOVEN, TH. C., 'Fact-Finding in the Field of Human Rights', 3 Isr. Y.H.R. (1973) pp. 93–117.

—— 'Distinguishing Criteria of Human Rights', in Vasak, K./Alston, P., eds., above (1982), pp. 43–59.

VAN DIJK, P., 'International Law and the Promotion and Protection of Human Rights', 24 Wayne LR (1978) pp. 1529–53.

VAN HOOF, G. J. H., 'The Legal Nature of Economic, Social and Cultural Rights: A Rebuttal of some Traditional Views', in Alston, P., and Tomasevski, K., eds., above (1984), pp. 97–110.

VARGAS CARRENO, E., 'Visits on the Spot—The Experience of the Inter-American Commission of Human Rights', in Ramcharan, B. G., ed., above (1982), pp. 137–50.

VENKATA RAMAN, K., 'Towards a New World Information and Communication Order—Problems of Access and Cultural Development', in MacDonald, R., and Johnston, D., eds., above (1983), pp. 1027–68.

VIERDAG, E. W., 'The Legal Nature of the Rights Granted in the ICESCR', 9 NYIL (1979) pp. 69–105.

VIJAPUR, A. P., 'The U.N. Mechanisms and Procedures for the Promotion and Implementation of Human Rights', 25 Ind. JIL (1985) pp. 576–611.

VINCENT-EVANS, Sir, 'The International Covenant on Civil and Political Rights and the Human Rights Committee Established Under It', 4 Topical Law (1982) pp. 1–7.

VOLIO, F., 'Legal Personality, Privacy, and the Family', in Henkin, L., ed., above (1981), pp. 185–208.

VON POTOBSKY, G., 'Visits on the Spot—The Experience of the I.L.O.', in Ramcharan, B. G., ed., above (1982), pp. 160–75.

WALDEN, I., and SAVAGE, N., 'Data Protection and Privacy Laws: Should Organizations be Protected?', ICLQ (1988) pp. 337–47.

WALKATE, J. A., 'The Human Rights Committee and Public Emergencies', in Symposium, 9 Yale JWPO (1982), below, pp. 133–47.

WARBRICK, C., 'The Protection of Human Rights in National Emergencies', in Dowrick, F. E., ed., above (1979), pp. 89–106.

WATSON, J. S., 'Autointerpretation, Competence and the Continuing Validity of Article 2(7) of the United Nations Charter', 71 AJIL (1977) pp. 60–83.

—— 'Legal Theory, Efficacy and Validity in the Development of Human Rights Norms in International Law', Univ. Ill. LF pp. 609–41 (1979).

—— 'The Limited Utility of International Law in the Protection of Human Rights', ASIL. Proc. (1980) pp. 1–6.

WEERMANTRY, C. G., 'The Right to Development, 25 Ind. JIL (1985) pp. 482–505.

WEIS, P., 'The Denunciation of Human Rights Treaties', 8 RDH/HRJ (1975) pp. 3–7.

WEISSBRODT, D., 'U.S. Ratification of the Human Rights Covenants', 63 Minn. LR (1978) pp. 35–78.

—— 'The Role of International N.G.O.'s in the Implementation of Human Rights', 12 Tex. ILJ (1977) pp. 293–320.

—— 'The 1980 U.N. Commission on Human Rights and the Disappeared', 3 HRQ (1981) pp. 18–33.

—— 'Fact-Finding by N.G.O.'s, in Ramcharan, B. G., ed., above (1982), pp. 186–230.

—— 'The Contribution of Non Governmental Organizations to the Protection of Human Rights', in Meron, T., ed., above (1984), pp. 403–38.

—— 'Protecting the Right to Life: International Measures against Arbitrary or Summary Killings by Governments', in Ramcharan, B. G., ed., above (1985), pp. 297–314.

—— and ANDRUS, R., 'The Right to Life during Armed Conflict: Disabled Peoples International v. United States', 29 Harv. ILJ (1988) pp. 59–83.

WESTON, B. H., 'Human Rights', 6 HRQ (1984) pp. 257–83.

—— Lukes, R. A., and HNATT, K. M., 'Regional Human Rights Regimes: A Comparison and Appraisal', 20 Vanderbilt J. Trans. Law (1987) pp. 585–637.

WHITE, R., 'Self-Determination: A Time for Re-assessment', 28 NILR (1981) pp. 147–70.

WHITTON, J. B., 'The United Nations Conference on Freedom of Information and the Movement against International Propaganda', 43 AJIL (1949) pp. 73–87.

WIDDOWS, K., 'The Application of a Treaty to Nationals of a Party Outside its Territory', 35 ICLQ (1986) pp. 724–30.

WOLF, F., 'Human Rights and the International Labour Organization', in Meron, T., ed., above (1984), pp. 273–305.

YEO, C., 'Psychiatry, the Law and Dissent in the Soviet Union', 14 Rev. ICJ (1975) pp. 34–41.

YOUROW, H. C., 'The Margin of Appreciation in the Dynamics of European Human Rights Jurisprudence', 3 Connecticut JIL (1987) pp. 111–59.

ZEMANEK, K., 'Majority Rule and Consensus Technique in Law-Making Diplomacy', in MacDonald, R. St. J., and Johnston, D., eds., above (1983), pp. 857–87.

ZOGLIN, K., 'U.N. Action against Slavery', 8 HRQ (1986) pp. 306–39.

ZUIDJWICK, TON M. 'The Right to Petition the United Nations because of Alleged Violations of Human Rights', 59 Can. Bar. Rev. (1981) pp. 103–23.

Miscellaneous

Developing Human Rights Jurisprudence: The Domestic Application of International Human Rights Norms, Judicial Colloquium in Bangalore (Commonwealth Secretariat, London, 1988).

—— Vol. 2, Judicial Colloquium in Harare (1990).

DIMITRIJEVIC, V., *The Roles of the Human Rights Committee* ('Europa Institut', Univ. of Saarland, 1986).

European Convention on Human Rights—Collected Texts (Nijhoff, Dordrecht/Boston/Lancaster, 1987).

HIGGINS, R., *Human Rights and Foreign Policy*, Report for Colloquy: 'Democracy and Human Rights', Thessalonika (Greece), 24–6 Sept. 1987, Council of Europe Doc. H/Coll (87) 6.

Human Rights—Status of International Instruments (UN New York, 1987).

JUSTICE, *Home Office Reviews of Criminal Convictions* (JUSTICE, London, 1968).

JUSTICE, *Compensation for Wrongful Imprisonment* (JUSTICE, London, 1982).

United Nations Yearbook on Human Rights 1977–78 (UN, New York, 1982).

'U.S. Senate Hearings on Human Rights Treaties', S Exec. Doc. C, D, E, and F. 95th Congress, 2nd Sess. (1978).

'Perspectives on Enforcement of Human Rights', ASIL Proc. (1980) pp. 1–30.

SIEGHART, P., 'An Introduction to the International Covenants on Human Rights', Paper prepared for the Commonwealth Secretariat, London, 1988.

Symposium, 'International Control of Propaganda', 31 L & CP (1966) pp. 437–634.

Symposium, 'Human Rights and U.S. Foreign Policy', 14 Virg. JIL (1973–4) pp. 591–701.

Symposium, 'Limitation and Derogation Provisions in the ICCPR', 7 HRQ (1985), part I.

Symposium, 'Statistical Issues in the Field of Human Rights', 8 HRQ (1986) pp. 551–699.

Symposium, 'Security of the Person and Security of the State: Human Rights and Claims of National Security', 9 Yale JWPO (1982), part I.

'Selected Bibliography relating to the ICCPR' (Centre for Human Rights, Geneva).

Subject Index

Optional Protocol (*cont.*)
  interim measures 4.128
  legal aid, provision of 4.12
  opposition to proposals 4.2
  possibility of, discussion on 4.3
  prison sentence, consequences of 4.51,
    4.52
  prisoners, treatment of 9.11–9.25
  provisions of 1.11
  public emergency derogations 7.35–7.43
  ratifications 4.7
  review of 4.133
  right to life under 8.14–8.26
  rules of procedure 4.13
  self-determination, issue of 5.20–5.23
  Special Rapporteur 4.14
  States parties, co-operation of 4.131
  status of 4.6
  structure of 4.4, 4.5
  terms of 4.4, 4.5
  text of App. II
  torture under 9.11–9.25
  Uruguay, co-operation of 4.129

periodic reporting:
  Annual Report 3.40
  appraisal of 3.41–3.53
  consideration, process of: initial and
    supplementary reports: criticisms of
    3.23, 3.24, first round 3.20, general rule
    3.19, second round 3.21–3.24, State
    representatives, questions to 3.24;
    periodic reports: Consensus Statement
    3.25; effective procedures for 3.28,
    second 3.25–3.28, third 3.28.1
  co-operation of States 3.44
  ECOSOC, role of 3.39
  general comments: comment and
    observations on 3.36; consideration of
    3.34; criticisms of 3.37; jurisprudence,
    developing 3.38; number of 3.35;
    purpose of 3.34; subject matter of 3.35
  guidelines 3.43
  HRC, jurisdiction of: consideration and
    study of reports 3.29; consensus on
    3.33, 3.34; liberal approach to 3.31;
    reports 3.30; restrictive approach to
    3.32; schools of thought 3.31, 3.32
  implementation technique, as 3.1
  information, sources of: co-operation 3.13,
    3.14; ILO 3.16; importance of 3.12;
    non-governmental organizations 3.17,
    3.18; specialized agencies 3.13–3.16
  national reports: additional 3.4;
    consideration of, *see* consideration,
    process of, *above*; initial 3.3, 3.43;
    periodic 3.5; periodicity 3.6–3.8;

request for by HRC 3.8; Supplementary
  3.4; types of 3.2
non-governmental organizations, role of
  3.17, 3.18, 3.48
obligation 3.1
periodicity 3.6–3.8, 3.46, 3.47
specialized agencies, role of 3.13–3.16,
  3.48
submission of reports: initial 3.9–3.11;
  patience and flexibility of HRC 3.42;
  quality of 3.11; record on 3.9; second
  and third 3.10
pollution, protection of natural resources
  against 5.10
prison sentence, consequences of 4.51, 4.52
prisoners, humane treatment of:
  Article 10: conditions of detention
    violating 9.17–9.20; Optional Protocol,
    under 9.11–9.25; text of 9.1
  cruel and inhuman punishment, meaning
    9.21
  HRC, views of: allegations categorized as
    torture 9.13, 9.14; appraisal of 9.26–
    9.31, 13.14; evidential and procedural
    matters, decisions on 9.11;
    unsatisfactory nature of 9.12; Uruguay,
    concerning 9.12, 9.29; violations,
    finding 9.24
  judicial proceedings, delays in 9.23.1
  mail, restriction and censorship of 9.19
  relatives as victims 9.23
  reporting procedure, effectiveness of 9.27
  unconvicted prisoner 9.25
public emergency:
  Article 4: approach of members to 7.5;
    France, approach of 7.12;
    implementation, approach to 7.50;
    information on 7.4; Optional Protocol,
    under 7.35–7.43, 7.49; reporting
    process, under, 7.3–7.22; reservations to
    7.17; State not relying on, application
    where 7.36; text of 7.1
  Colombia, in 7.42, 7.43
  declaration of, application of criteria to
    7.14
  derogation in: *ad hoc* reports 7.48;
    discrimination, not involving 7.11;
    extent of 7.2; HRC, practice of 7.2,
    7.13–7.15, 7.45–7.50, 13.12; non-
    derogable articles 7.18; notifications
    7.19–7.22, 7.44; obligations, consistent
    with 7.10
  legal effects 7.7
  legal regime and requirements of
    Covenant 7.8
  notification of 7.3
  official proclamation of 7.6

Printed in the United Kingdom
by Lightning Source UK Ltd.
113